Expedited International Arbitration

Expedited International Arbitration

Policies, Rules and Procedures

Edited by

Alan M. Anderson
Herman Verbist

Foreword by Anna Joubin-Bret

Wolters Kluwer

Published by:
Kluwer Law International B.V.
PO Box 316
2400 AH Alphen aan den Rijn
The Netherlands
E-mail: lrs-sales@wolterskluwer.com
Website: www.wolterskluwer.com/en/solutions/kluwerlawinternational

Sold and distributed by:
Wolters Kluwer Legal & Regulatory U.S.
920 Links Avenue
Landisville, PA 17538
United States of America
E-mail: customer.service@wolterskluwer.com

ISBN 978-94-035-2587-7

e-Book: ISBN 978-94-035-2597-6
web-PDF: ISBN 978-94-035-2607-2

Editors

Alan M. Anderson, PhD, FCIArb, specializes in dispute resolution, particularly international arbitration, both as counsel and as an arbitrator. He received his Master of Business Administration and Doctor of Law (*magna cum laude*) from Cornell University, the United States. He received a Master of Laws, with distinction, specializing in international dispute resolution, from the University of London, England. He earned his PhD in War Studies from King's College London, England. Dr Anderson is a Fellow of the Chartered Institute of Arbitrators, a Fellow of the Australian Centre for International Commercial Arbitration, a Fellow of the Asian Institute of Alternative Dispute Resolution and an accredited international mediator. A frequent presenter and writer, Dr Anderson is the secretary and a director of the Forum for International Conciliation and Arbitration (FICA), an international think-tank. He has participated in the work of UNCITRAL's Working Groups II and III since 2015. Alan co-edited *The Investor-State Dispute Settlement System: Reform, Replace or Status Quo?*, published in 2020 by Kluwer Law International. He is the president of Alan Anderson Law Firm LLC based in Minneapolis, Minnesota, USA and an associate tenant with Littleton Chambers in London, where he is a member of its international arbitration practice group.

Herman Verbist, PhD, FCIArb, is an attorney at the Ghent and Brussels Bar in Belgium with Everest Attorneys, focusing primarily on arbitration and alternative dispute resolution. He received his Master of Law from the University of Leuven, Belgium and his Doctor of Law from the University of Ghent, Belgium. He is a Fellow of the Chartered Institute of Arbitrators and is a member of numerous international arbitration associations and is registered on the list of arbitrators of several arbitration institutions worldwide, including CAS, WIPO, NAI, CAfA, VIAC, ICDR, HKIAC, SIAC, THAC, AIAC, KCAB. He is also an accredited mediator (Belgian Federal Mediation Commission) and is registered on the ICSID Panel of Conciliators. He worked as counsel at the Secretariat of the International Court of Arbitration of the International Chamber of Commerce in Paris and has taught a course on international commercial arbitration at the University of Ghent, Belgium. Since 2020, he has taught the course 'Case Study Investment Mediation' at the Europa-Institut of Saarland University,

Saarbrücken, Germany. Since 2022, he is co-chair of the Forum for International Conciliation and Arbitration (FICA), an international think-tank. He has participated in the work of UNCITRAL's Working Groups II and III since 2009.

Contributors

Venetia Argyropoulou, PhD, is a Law Lecturer at the Hellenic International University, Greece and a researcher at the University of Cyprus, Cyprus. She received her Master's from the University of Oslo, Norway and her PhD from the University of Tilburg, the Netherlands. She is educated in both civil and common laws and has been actively practising law in Greece and Cyprus. She has worked as a researcher for Oxford University, England; University Nanterre, France; the European University of Cyprus, Cyprus and as a lecturer for the University of West London, England and the University of South Wales, the United Kingdom. She is the General Counsel of Kap Technologies PLC, a listed company on the London Stock Exchange. Her field of expertise is international investment law. She teaches the subject at the University of Cyprus, Cyprus. She additionally has several publications on this subject. She has received various awards for her research and is recognized as an expert in Financial Law by the European Court of Auditors.

James Clanchy, FCIArb, is a full-time arbitrator in independent practice and an associate member of Six Pump Court chambers in London. He is an aspiring full member of the London Maritime Arbitrators Association (LMAA) and served as the association's Honorary Secretary from September 2021 until September 2022. As an arbitrator, he has taken appointments in ad hoc and institutional arbitrations, seated in London, Dubai, Singapore, and Copenhagen, as a sole arbitrator and as a member of two- and three-member tribunals. He is a solicitor in England & Wales (admitted 1990, non-practising since 2019) and was an avocat at the Paris bar from 1994 to 2008. He spent twenty years as a commercial disputes lawyer in London and Paris, with Withers, Holman Fenwick Willan, and Stephenson Harwood, specializing in shipping, energy, and international trade. He was Registrar and Deputy Director General of the London Court of International Arbitration (LCIA) for four years (2008-2012) and is a co-author of *A Commentary on the LCIA Arbitration Rules 2014* (Sweet & Maxwell, 2015). Since July 2022, James has been co-editor (arbitration) of Lloyd's Maritime Law Newsletter, writing and editing anonymized summaries of London maritime arbitration awards.

Erin Cronjé is a South African attorney (akin to a solicitor) with over nine years of diverse arbitration and litigation experience in major law firms in South Africa and the Netherlands. Erin is currently a senior associate at De Brauw Blackstone Westbroek (Amsterdam), practising in the field of international arbitration and litigation (investor-state and commercial disputes). She has acted as counsel in multiple arbitration proceedings under the Rules of the ICC, ICSID, VIAC, NAI, AFSA and UNCITRAL, and in the South African courts and alternative fora. Erin is also a CEDR-accredited mediator for the United Kingdom and Southern Africa. Erin holds an Advanced LLM in Public International Law from Leiden University, the Netherlands (cum laude, 2017) and an LLM in Environmental Law (2014) and LLB (cum laude, 2010) from the University of the Witwatersrand in Johannesburg, South Africa. Since 2019 Erin has co-authored annual contributions to the Global Arbitration Review Know-How Series, on Challenging and Enforcing Arbitral Awards in the Netherlands, and Investment Treaty Arbitration in the Netherlands. Erin is the Europe representative of the African Arbitration Association (AfAA) Young Members Committee and Director of Africa in the Moot.

Ylli Dautaj, PhD, currently teaches as a lecturer in commercial law at Brunel University, London. Meanwhile, he teaches as an adjunct professor at Penn State Law, Pennsylvania. Ylli graduated with a PhD from the University of Edinburgh, UK as a stipendiary scholar of the Scottish Graduate School for Arts & Humanities. Ylli practises out of Stockholm, Sweden. He represents clients in planning, drafting, negotiating, and disputing commercial agreements – in both litigation and arbitration, domestic and international. He represents individuals, private enterprises, State-owned enterprises, and States in various litigation matters and international arbitrations, including matters incidental or ancillary to arbitration. Ylli has represented clients in investor-State arbitration matters, shareholders' and joint-venture disputes, jurisdictional objections (investment and commercial arbitration), post-award proceedings (set-aside and enforcement/execution), oil and gas matters. Ylli has published extensively with various leading law journals, books, and authored book chapters, as well as book reviews in ICSID Review and other publications.

Yasaschandra Devarakonda is a dispute resolution attorney based in India. He is a member of the Bar Council of India and practises before the Supreme Court of India and the High Court of Delhi. His practice primarily focuses on commercial and construction arbitrations and insolvency matters. He has published widely in the field of international commercial arbitration. He holds a Bachelor's in Law from the National Law University Odisha, Cuttack, India.

Can Eken, PhD, currently serves as an assistant professor at Durham Law School, England, a Central Asian Legal Research Fellow at the Tashkent State University of Law, Uzbekistan, and independent arbitration consultant. He is admitted to practise law as an attorney in California, Turkey, and as a solicitor in England and Wales. He is also a Fellow of the Chartered Institute of Arbitrators. He was a visiting scholar at Stanford University, California and the Max Planck Institute, Luxembourg for Procedural Law. He has authored numerous publications on international commercial arbitration, investment law, third-party funding, and online dispute resolution. He is the recipient of the 2021 Postgraduate Research Output Award from the Chinese University of Hong Kong. Prior to joining the faculty at Durham, Dr Eken was a practising lawyer in Turkey following a brief stint as a research assistant. He completed a PhD at the Faculty of Law at the Chinese University of Hong Kong, China. He also completed two LLM degrees, one from the London School of Economics and Political Science, England and another from Dokuz Eylul University, Turkey, where he also obtained a Bachelor's in Law with high honours.

Yuan Fang is currently a JSD Candidate at Washington University in St Louis School of Law, the United States. Prior to joining WashU Law, he earned his LLM from the University of California, Berkeley School of Law in 2019. Mr Fang has been a researcher at the Asia-Pacific Interest Group (APIG) of the American Society of International Law (ASIL) since 2020. He formerly served as the Associate Editor of *Berkeley Technology Law Journal* (BTLJ) between 2018 and 2019 and served as a Member of the International Advisory Board of the *Washington University Global Studies Law Review* from 2019 to 2020. Mr Fang's research interests encompass international law, technology law, and dispute resolution. His doctoral project focuses on the intersections of public international law and cybersecurity, examining how to make contemporary international law a better fit for the cyber context through the dynamics between human rights and state sovereignty. His recent scholarly works, including a co-edited book, two book chapters, three journal articles, and several blog posts, have appeared or are forthcoming in China, the United States, Singapore, and the Netherlands.

Peter Ferrer is co-head of Harneys' Global Litigation, Insolvency and Restructuring team. Peter acts on behalf of institutions, companies, corporate entities and high-net-worth individuals. His experience includes shareholder actions, fraud claims, hedge fund disputes, insolvency and restructuring matters. He has extensive experience in enforcement proceedings, including tracing actions in multiple jurisdictions. He is an experienced trial advocate who regularly appears in the British Virgin Islands Commercial Court Division, the ECSC Court of Appeal and international arbitration. Prior to joining Harneys, he practised as a barrister in England, where he appeared at every court level, including the Court of Appeal and the United Kingdom Supreme Court. Peter has been ranked in Chambers and Partners for the last four years for his BVI Dispute Resolution expertise. *Legal 500* ranked him as a 'leading individual' and described him as 'an elegant, cerebral partner with exceptional management client skills'. He sits on the BVI Commercial Court Users Committee, the BVI Civil Procedure Rules Steering Committee and acts as the CIArb BVI Chapter Vice Chair.

Guillermo García-Perrote is an executive counsel in Herbert Smith Freehills' Sydney office, specializing in international arbitration and restructuring, turnaround and insolvency. He holds degrees from the Universidad Carlos III de Madrid, Spain and the University of Sydney, Australia and has been admitted to practise in the Spanish courts, the High Court of England and Wales, the Supreme Court of New South Wales and the High Court of Australia.

Carlos Eduardo Torres Giraldez is a Venezuelan and Spanish professional with a law degree from the Central University of Venezuela, Venezuela and a Master's in Digital and Artificial Intelligence Law from the University of La Coruña, Spain. He specializes in providing legal consultancy services in the field of artificial intelligence, focusing on regulatory compliance, risk assessment, data governance, and cybersecurity. Additionally, he has experience in alternative dispute resolution, particularly in arbitration and mediation, offering a holistic perspective on the intersections of law, technology, and ADR.

Juan Pablo Gómez is an independent expert consultant with experience in more than thirty-five complex cases. He advises national and international clients on global disputes, from investment to commercial arbitrations. He also serves as a legal adviser to international organizations and public agencies, offering insights into various aspects of international law, including human rights, trade, and investment policy. Juan Pablo is a lecturer at Universidad de los Andes and Universidad El Bosque, Colombia, teaching courses like Global Legal Issues, Contracts, International Economic Law, and Constitutional Law at undergraduate and postgraduate levels. He has published over fifty works and has been invited as a guest speaker at conferences in more than ten countries. His current research interests include local communities, environmental debates, and disruptive technologies.

Jonas C. Hinrichsen is admitted to the Dutch bar and works as a senior associate in the International Dispute Resolution and Arbitration Department of De Brauw Blackstone Westbroek N.V. Jonas specializes in international disputes, including international commercial and investment arbitration and cross-border litigation. He has acted as counsel and advised on large-scale, highly political and sensitive international energy and intellectual property disputes in arbitration proceedings under the ICC, LCIA, NAI and UNCITRAL rules and under a variety of applicable laws. He also regularly engages in enforcement and setting-aside proceedings before Dutch courts. Jonas' years of experience in the oil and gas industry include in-house experience gathered during a one-year secondment to Shell's global litigation department in Hamburg (Germany) and the Hague (the Netherlands) offices. He is a DAA, DIS40, ICC YAAF and NAI member, as well as part of the selected Dutch-German Arbitration Group, an initiative of the Dutch Arbitration Association, the German Arbitration Institute (DIS) and the Netherlands Arbitration Institution (NAI), aiming to improve mutual knowledge of Dutch and German arbitration practice and to promote personal exchange among arbitration practitioners, in-house counsels as well as users.

Anna Joubin-Bret is the Secretary of the United Nations Commission on International Trade Law (UNCITRAL) and the Director of the International Trade Law Division in the Office of Legal Affairs of the United Nations. Prior to her appointment, Ms Joubin-Bret practised law in Paris, specializing in International Investment Law and Investment Dispute Resolution. She focused on serving as counsel, arbitrator, mediator and conciliator in international investment disputes. Prior to 2011, she was the Senior Legal Adviser for the United Nations Conference on Trade and Development (UNCTAD). She edited and authored seminal research and publications on international investment law, notably the Sequels to UNCTAD IIA Series and co-edited with Jean Kalicki a book on the Reform of Investor-State Dispute Settlement in 2015. Anna holds a DEA in Private International Law from the University of Paris I, Panthéon-Sorbonne, France; a Master's in International Economic Law from the University of Paris I, France and in Political Science from Institut d'Etudes Politiques, France. She was Legal Counsel in the legal department of the Schneider Group, General Counsel of the KIS Group and Director-Export of Pomagalski S.A. She was appointed judge at the Commercial Court in Grenoble (France) and was elected Regional Counsellor of the Rhône-Alpes Region in 1998.

Rahul Kr. Kanoujia is a graduate of Gujarat National Law University, Gandhinagar, India. Currently he is a professional in the field of arbitration, insolvency and restructuring. His areas of interest include insolvency and bankruptcy, arbitration, civil litigation and issues pertaining to the Prevention of Money Laundering Act.

Tariq Mahmood, PhD, is an offshore litigation barrister with multi-jurisdictional experience, specializing in international commercial dispute resolution (litigation, arbitration and mediation), restructuring, insolvency litigation, contentious trust litigation, funds litigation, and insurance litigation. He has represented clients in a wide variety of commercial disputes in London, Asia and the Middle East. He is an Honorary Lecturer at the University of Keele. Dr Mahmood has experience with all of the major arbitration rules and seats and appears as a barrister in arbitration hearings regularly. He speaks and publishes regularly on topics relating to international arbitration, mediation and issues of diversity in the legal profession. He is on the Approved Faculty List with the Chartered Institute of Arbitrators and provides training in International Arbitration, Domestic Arbitration and Mediation. Dr Mahmood sits as an arbitrator and mediator on a regular basis.

Marcia McFarlane is a partner in Harneys' Litigation, Insolvency and Restructuring team. She provides legal advice to office holders, institutions and high-net-worth individuals in relation to fraud claims, cross-border insolvency and restructuring claims and shareholder disputes. She appears as counsel and advocate in the British Virgin Islands (BVI) Commercial Court and Court of Appeal. Marcia sits on the BVI Commercial Court Users Committee, Insol Offshore Technical Committee and currently serves as President of the BVI Bar Association. As a member of the BVI Commercial Court Users Committee and BVI Bar Association, she has worked to secure the passing of legislation to improve legal services in the BVI. As a member of Insol's Offshore Technical Committee, Marcia coordinated the launch of the Insol Future Leaders Programme for the BVI in February 2023. She has completed certification courses in international arbitration and tribunal secretary training offered respectively by the Chartered Institute of International Arbitration, BVI Chapter and the Caribbean ADR Initiative in collaboration with the BVI International Arbitration Centre.

Juan Felipe Merizalde is a highly experienced civil and common law lawyer specializing in international arbitration, with over sixteen years of practice. He has acted as counsel and arbitrator in over eighty cases, representing States, State-owned entities, and private parties before major arbitral institutions such as ICSID, UNCITRAL, ICC, ICDR, and CIAM, securing many landmark victories for his clients. Currently, he acts as counsel and arbitrator in commercial and investment cases involving over ten jurisdictions, representing Latin American parties in disputes. Juan Felipe is Adjunct Lecturer of International Contracts at Universidad de los Andes, Colombia and Universidad del Rosario, Colombia and is consistently recognized by Who's Who Legal, Global Arbitration Review, the Legal 500, Chambers Latin America, Leaders League, and Latin Lawyer. He holds a dual degree in Law from the University Panthéon Assas, Paris, France, and Colegio Mayor de Nuestra Señora del Rosario, Bogotá, Colombia, a Master's in General Private Law from the former institution and a Master's in International Business and International Arbitration from New York University, the United States.

Daniel O'Neil is a solicitor practising in Sydney, New South Wales, Australia. He holds degrees from the University of Sydney, the University of Oxford, and the University of Melbourne, and has been admitted to practise in the Supreme Court of New South Wales and the High Court of Australia.

Srilal M. Perera, PhD, is currently Adjunct Professor of Law at the University of Miami, School of Law, Florida, the United States. He retired as Adjunct Professor of Law at the Washington College of Law of the American University in Washington DC, in 2018, after teaching international investment law for nearly twenty years. Prof. Perera was also Chief Counsel of Operations in the Multilateral Investment Guarantee Agency (MIGA) of the World Bank Group until his retirement in June 2010. He served from 1986 to 1989 as Legal Counsel at the Iran-United States Claims Tribunal in the Hague, the Netherlands. He has an LLB from the Faculty of Law, University of Sri Lanka, Sri Lanka; JD equivalence from the Sri Lanka Law College, Sri Lanka; an MA from the School of Advanced International Studies (SAIS) Johns Hopkins University, the United States; and a PhD in International Law and International Relations from Georgetown University, the United States. He is in the Panel of Arbitrators and Conciliators of the International Centre for the Settlement of Investment Disputes (ICSID); a member of the Distinguished Panel of Arbitrators of the Thailand Arbitration Center (THAC) and a member of the Panel of Arbitrators of the China International Economic and Trade Arbitration Commission (CIETAC).

James Petkovic is a counsel in the Dispute Resolution team of Harneys, Westwood & Riegels LP based in Road Town, Tortola. He works on court litigation and arbitration proceedings, as well as providing general legal advice on a range of commercial topics. He formerly practised as a barrister at One Essex Court, London, where he retains a tenancy. He has been involved in a number of arbitrations conducted under the LCIA and other rules, including multi-billion-dollar arbitration proceedings administered by the Permanent Court of Arbitration in the Hague and, separately, acting on behalf of the UK Government in ad hoc proceedings in England. He has also acted (as sole Counsel) on behalf of a bank in LCIA proceedings resulting in an award in excess of USD 20 million.

Parnika Rai is a penultimate-year student pursuing Law from the Faculty of Law, Banaras Hindu University. A National Moot Court and drafting competition winner, Parnika is an empathetic orator and wants to make a difference in the areas of commercial, civil and criminal litigation. She has pursued internships with eminent litigation firms in the domain of dispute resolution.

Yassine Sangaré, PhD, is a bilingual legal consultant, lecturer in Law and International Business, and also an aspiring solicitor in England & Wales. She graduated in Business Law from Nice Sophia Antipolis, France and holds a Master of Laws in International Business Law from Coventry University, UK. In November 2022, she successfully completed her PhD in International Arbitration. Her research focused on the enforcement of arbitral awards in both developing and developed countries, with a focus on the UK and the OHADA Regime. With a diverse educational background, she has also acquired certifications in various disciplines, including business administration & management and professional consulting which brings a multidisciplinary approach to her work. Dr Sangaré is a member of the Chartered Institute of Arbitrators (MCIArb), Associate Fellow of the Advance Higher Education (Advance HE UK), and a lecturer at King Stage Business School London. She has gained practical experience working as a paralegal for prestigious law firms such as Hogan Lovells. She has co-authored articles on topics including French and OHADA arbitration, anti-suit injunctions, among others. She also possesses expertise as a freelance translator.

Hugo Luz dos Santos, PhD, received his PhD in Mediation. He teaches Mediation, Arbitration, Gaming Law, Criminal Procedure and Criminal Law to master degree students at the Faculty of Law of the University of Macau, China. In addition, Hugo teaches Mediation and Gaming Law to bachelor's degree students at the City University of Macau, China. Hugo has published 30 books and over hundred peer-reviewed papers. He has a high reading proficiency in six languages (Portuguese, Spanish, French, Italian, English, and German). Hugo also has a basic grasp of Chinese (Mandarin). He has delivered speeches in fifteen countries and three continents. Hugo is a Fellow of the Royal Society of Arts of the United Kingdom 'for outstanding contributions to the field of justice, rule of law and policy worldwide'. He is also a Fellow of the Forum for International Conciliation and Arbitration (FICA). Hugo Luz dos Santos is the author of the book *Towards a Four-Tiered Model of Mediation: Against the Background of a Narrative of Social Sub-systems in Everlasting Cross-Fertilization* (New York/Singapore/Beijing/Berlin, Springer, 2023), which has received praise worldwide for its unique and multidisciplinary approach to mediation.

Rose Maria Sebi is currently working as an associate in the Dispute Resolution team of a law firm. She graduated from National Law University Odisha, Cuttack, India, in 2022 with BBA and LLB degrees. In her role as an associate, she is part of a team representing clients in arbitral proceedings pertaining to commercial disputes, specifically in the infrastructure sector. In addition to arbitration, she has also worked on several insolvency and restructuring mandates. While in law school, she participated in several Moot Court Competitions and authored articles published by renowned publishers, including Kluwer Law International. Her areas of interest include domestic and international arbitration, commercial litigation, and insolvency and restructuring.

Reza Shahrokhi is an international arbitration paralegal at De Brauw Blackstone Westbroek, specializing in international disputes such as international commercial and investment arbitration. Reza has been involved in arbitration proceedings under the ICC, ICSID, SIAC, VIAC, and UNCITRAL rules. He also served as an intern at the Singapore International Arbitration Centre and as junior legal counsel at the National Iranian Gas Company. He holds an LLM. in International Civil and Commercial Law from Leiden University, the Netherlands and an LLM in International Commercial Arbitration Law from Stockholm University, Sweden along with an LLB from Shahid Beheshti University of Tehran, Iran.

Joshua B. Simmons, FCIArb, is a partner at Wiley Rein LLP and an Adjunct Professor at the University of Virginia School of Law, the United States. He has extensive experience in treaty and commercial arbitration proceedings around the world. He has represented foreign sovereigns and international investors across a broad range of industries, including energy, natural resources, technology, and financial services. He also advises companies on national security law, public international law, and transnational litigation in US courts. Prior to joining Wiley, Josh practised international arbitration at Covington & Burling and Three Crowns. He also served as an attorney-adviser and as senior adviser in the Office of the Legal Adviser at the US Department of State.

Natalia Szlarb is an associate in the Global Disputes group of Wiley Rein LLP. She represents and advises private companies in a variety of complex litigation matters and international disputes in state and federal courts, as well as before arbitral tribunals. She has experience in disputes in a wide range of industries, including energy, real estate, manufacturing, and technology. Before starting in private practice, Natalia worked at leading international arbitration institutions, advising and managing international cases.

Esra Yildiz Üstün, PhD, graduated from Kocaeli University School of Law, Turkey in 2010 with honours before receiving a full scholarship for graduate studies from the Turkish Ministry of National Education to undertake postgraduate study from 2012 to 2018. She received her LLM in International Investment Arbitration from Queen Mary University of London, England (2013). She holds a PhD from the University of Exeter, England (2018), for which she researched the enforcement of international investment arbitral awards. Currently, she is an assistant professor at Ataturk University School of Law, Turkey. She is also a registered lawyer in the Istanbul Bar Association (2011) and holds professional memberships in the fields of international investment arbitration and commercial arbitration. Esra also provides legal consultancy to law firms in particular in international commercial arbitration, foreign direct investment, and all aspects of private international law.

Ella Wisniewski is a senior associate in the International Arbitration team at Herbert Smith Freehills LLP, based in Singapore. She represents clients in international commercial and investor-State arbitration proceedings and specializes in the resolution of cross-border disputes in the construction and energy sectors. Qualified in Western Australia, Ella also holds a Master of Laws in International Dispute Resolution from Humboldt University, Berlin. Ella was recognized as 'One to Watch' for International Arbitration by Best Lawyers (2022).

Shahrizal M. Zin, PhD, FCIArb, FAIADR, FMIArb, is a legal academic and alternative dispute resolution (ADR) practitioner. As a Public Service Department scholarship recipient, he read Law at the University of Malaya. He graduated with LLM from the University of Malaya, Malaysia and held a PhD from Monash University, Australia. He has been awarded a diploma in International Commercial Arbitration (DipICArb) from the Chartered Institute of Arbitrators (CIArb) UK and was admitted as a fellow in 2016. He is also a fellow of the Asian Institute of Alternative Dispute Resolution (AIADR) and the Malaysian Institute of Arbitrators (MIARB), Malaysia. He regularly sits as an arbitrator and adjudicator concerning construction claims under the Arbitration Act (2005) and the Construction Industry Payment and Adjudication Act (CIPAA) 2012. He is the author of several publications, among others, *Common Issues in Malaysian Adjudication: Guide to CIPAA 2012, Cases and Materials* (LexisNexis, 2020), and 'Reappraising Access to Justice: A Critical Review on State Recourse to Counterclaim' in Alan Anderson and Ben Beaumont, *The Investor-State Dispute Settlement System: Reform, Replace or Status Quo?* (Kluwer, 2020). He is currently a senior lecturer at the Faculty of Law, University Technology MARA (UiTM), Malaysia.

Summary of Contents

Table of Contents

Foreword

In 2021, the United Nations Commission on International Trade Law (UNCITRAL) adopted the Expedited Arbitration Rules as an appendix to the UNCITRAL Arbitral Rules to respond to the growing demand for more efficient and cost-effective resolution of international disputes. These rules are designed to streamline the arbitration process and expedite the resolution of disputes while upholding the core standards of due process and fairness of the proceedings and ultimately the enforceability of arbitral awards. During the annual session in 2018, UNCITRAL had mandated its Working Group II to take up issues relating to expedited arbitration, based on the recognition by its Member States of the value of expedited arbitration and its increased usage, including the adoption of expedited procedures by several leading arbitration institutions. The Expedited Arbitration Rules are accompanied by an Explanatory Note, which provides an article-by-article guidance.

This book, *Expedited International Arbitration: Policies, Rules and Procedures*, is therefore very timely and topical also from a UNCITRAL perspective, as it illustrates the continued trajectory towards enhancing efficiency and effectiveness of dispute resolution processes, which responds to the needs of disputing parties. It provides a comprehensive analysis of the case for expedited arbitration and the principles underpinning expedited arbitration. It also reviews the approaches in various geographical regions. It is the result of an open call for contributions launched in September 2022, and consequently, this book represents diverse and rich perspectives.

Each chapter offers a unique perspective, showcasing the multifaceted nature of expedited arbitration and its impact on the broader practice of international dispute resolution, particularly with respect to the UNCITRAL Arbitration Rules. The first chapters look at the context and the content of the rules and altogether offer a comprehensive analysis of expedited arbitration, starting with the advantages of the arbitral process and reiterating the qualities that make arbitration an invaluable tool for resolving international disputes. Interestingly, these chapters commonly refer to the findings of the annual Queen Mary International Arbitration Survey to make the case for expedited proceedings. The following chapters describe and analyse when and how expedited arbitration rules are applied. Thereafter, several chapters delve into the nuances of expedited arbitration and how these rules can strike the necessary balance between efficiency and due process. Chapter 6 analyses the UNCITRAL Expedited Arbitration Rules in more detail, and Chapter 11 contrasts them with the 2022 ICSID Arbitration Rules and discusses the suitability of expedited proceedings for investment disputes. The approaches of international arbitration institutions in various regions to expedited arbitration give the readers a complete picture of the uptake of expedited arbitration, particularly in China, including the Special Administrative Region of Macao, the offshore jurisdictions of the British Virgin Islands, Bermuda and the Cayman Islands, the Middle East and North Africa region and the United Kingdom.

We commend the editors for this thought-provoking compilation of articles and contributions by academics and practitioners in international law and international arbitration. These contributions remind the readers of the continued role of party autonomy and of the parties' expectations in international arbitration – effectiveness and efficiency – and how dispute resolution services need to respond to these expectations without losing sight of the fundamental principles to ensure certainty and enforceability.

Anna Joubin-Bret
Secretary
United Nations Commission on International Trade Law

Acknowledgements

This book arose out of the editors' participation as representatives of the Forum for International Conciliation and Arbitration at the sessions of UNCITRAL Working Group II in New York City and Vienna between 2018 and 2021, when the Working Group took up the topic of expedited arbitration. We were struck by the intensity and diversity of the debates surrounding the issues arising out of the need in the international commercial arbitration community for model rules for expedited arbitration that could be applied in the many ad hoc international arbitration proceedings that occur.

The two of us agreed that a monograph that presents a variety of views on expedited arbitration, the issues that arise out of it, and the various approaches by arbitral institutions to the concept would be a welcome and useful contribution to the literature. Although the effects of the COVID-19 pandemic somewhat delayed this project, the editors at Kluwer Law International welcomed our suggestion and readily accepted our proposal. We were gratified by the number and quality of the proposals received from potential contributors, which made the final selections difficult. We were able to choose contributions addressing most of the key topics regarding expedited international arbitration, from authors located literally around the world, and representing diverse points of view drawn from academia, practitioners, and those focused on special interest topics.

All of the contributors have worked hard to meet the demands we have placed on them. It has been a pleasure working with them, and we thank them for their efforts. The quality and significance of this book are due to their contributions. We must also extend special thanks to the wise and thoughtful guidance provided by our editors at Kluwer Law International. They have been a pleasure to work with from start to finish. Great thanks and appreciation must also be extended to Anna Joubin-Bret, the secretary of the United Nations Commission on International Trade Law, who graciously and immediately agreed to write a Foreword to this book.

This has truly been a team effort by each of us as editors, and we had good and constructive cooperation throughout the process. Neither of us could have done this alone. Finally, we accept responsibility for any errors or omissions that may inadvertently exist in this book.

Alan M. Anderson
Herman Verbist
December 2023

Introduction

Alan M. Anderson & Herman Verbist

The raison d'être for commercial arbitration, from its inception, was that the 'official system was too slow; the dispute could not always wait for the justiciar to arrive on circuit, or for the lord to return from the wars. It was too expensive; ... and a formalized legal system invariably breeds professional lawyers', who consistently spend too much time and money to resolve a dispute.[1] The purposes of commercial arbitration, therefore, were 'to eliminate the expense of litigation, to save delays in legal proceedings, to improve business relations ..., and to substitute the decisions of practical men for those of inexperienced juries'.[2]

However, today, international commercial arbitration is ill. To a great extent, it no longer fulfils its mission of providing an efficient and cost-effective means of resolving a dispute. It suffers from a disease that has been slowly developing and spreading for decades, if not centuries, since it was first developed.[3] It has become unduly professionalized. Arbitration now more resembles the judicial process it was intended to replace.[4] Instead of being a 'fast-track' method of resolving disputes, it has become 'slow-track'.[5] The international arbitration community has recognized the need to treat this illness for a long time. As long ago as 1437, the government of the then-Republic of Venice adopted legislation to address the undue length of the

1. Michael John Mustill, 'Arbitration: History and Background', 6 *J. Int'l Arb.* 43 (1989), 43 DOI: 10.54648/joia1989017.
2. Sabra A. Jones, 'Historical Development of Commercial Arbitration in the United States', 12 *Minn. L. Rev.* 240 (1928), 240.
3. While some have argued that its origin 'is lost in obscurity', commercial arbitration has been in existence for hundreds of years. *See, e.g.*, Frank D. Emerson, 'History of Arbitration Practice and Law', 19 *Cleveland St. L. Rev.* 155 (1970), 155-156 (dating international arbitration to at least 600 BCE); Earl S. Wolaver, 'The Historical Background of Commercial Arbitration', 83 *U. Penn. L. Rev.* 132 (1934), 132 DOI: 10.2307/3308189.
4. *See* Alan Redfern, 'The Changing World of International Arbitration', in David D. Caron, Stephan W. Schill, Abby Cohen Smutny and Epaminontas E. Triantafilou (eds), *Practising Virtue: Inside International Arbitration* (Oxford U. Press, 2015), 45-51.
5. Michael J. Mustill, 'Comments on Fast-Track Arbitration', 10 *J. Int'l Arb.* 121 (1993), 122 DOI: 10.54648/joia1993034.

arbitration process.[6] As early as 1955, the International Chamber of Commerce (ICC) Rules of Arbitration introduced a requirement that the arbitrator 'within as short a period as possible, ascertains the facts relating to the case'.[7] Under the 1955 ICC Rules, the arbitrator was required to 'make the award within sixty days from the date on which he signed' the Terms of Reference.[8]

Despite these efforts, the disease has persisted and gotten worse. The first Queen Mary International Arbitration Survey in 2006 cited the 'need for a mechanism to reduce arbitration costs' as a major issue for the future of international arbitration.[9] The 2010 Survey revealed that respondents believed the main causes of delay were the parties themselves, although arbitrators and arbitral institutions were best positioned to address this issue. 'Control of proceedings' was considered 'by many to be key to questions of cost and delay'.[10] By 2015, the Queen Mary Survey report dedicated 10 pages to the topic of reducing time and costs in international arbitration.[11] 'Cost and lack of speed were both ranked by respondents as amongst the worst characteristics of international arbitration.'[12]

At first, international arbitral institutions generally left it to the parties to address the disease. As recently as 2014, many of the leading arbitration-administering institutions did not have integral rules specific to expedited arbitration. Instead, the institutions left it to the parties to agree to a shortened schedule or procedures for accelerated dispute resolution.[13] Institutions suggested that the parties could address the time and cost issues in their arbitration clause.[14] In 2007, the ICC first published a short report suggesting various guidelines to parties for speeding up the arbitration process and thereby reducing costs.[15] However, parties proved themselves incapable of seriously tackling the problem, as the 2015 Queen Mary Survey report revealed.

---

6. *See* Giacomo Marchisio, 'Recent Solutions to Old Problems: A Look at the Expedited Procedure under the Newly Revised ICC Rules of Arbitration', *ICC Dispute Resolution Bulletin*, No. 1 (2017), 76 DOI: 10.2139/ssrn.3092128.
7. International Chamber of Commerce, 'ICC Rules of Arbitration' (1955), Article 20.
8. *Ibid.*, Article 23. *See also ibid.*, Article 19 ('Arbitrator's terms of reference').
9. Queen Mary University of London, School of International Arbitration, 'International Arbitration: Corporate Attitudes and Practices 2006' (2006), 22.
10. Queen Mary University of London, School of International Arbitration, '2010 International Arbitration Survey: Choices in International Arbitration' (2010), 32.
11. Queen Mary University of London, School of International Arbitration, '2015 International Arbitration Survey: Improvements and Innovations in International Arbitration' (2015), 24-33.
12. *Ibid.*, 24.
13. Gary Born, *International Commercial Arbitration*, 2nd ed. (Kluwer Law International, 2014), 2306.
14. Giacomo Marchisio, 'Recent Solutions to Old Problems: A Look at the Expedited Procedure under the Newly Revised ICC Rules of Arbitration', *ICC Dispute Resolution Bulletin*, No. 1 (2017), 76. Article 32 of the ICC Rules (now Article 39), provided that the parties could shorten the time limits in the Rules, with the ICC Court of Arbitration still having the power to extend them. *See* International Chamber of Commerce, 'ICC Rules of Arbitration 1998' (1998), Article 32. For a discussion of the ICC's experience with expedited arbitration through 1993, *see* Benjamin G. Davis, Odette Lagacé and Michael Volkovitsch, 'When Doctrines Meet – Fast – Track Arbitration and the ICC Experience', 10:4 *J. Int'l Arb.* 69 (1993), 69-96 DOI: 10.54648/joia1993032.
15. *See* ICC Commission on Arbitration Report, 'Techniques for Controlling Time and Costs in Arbitration', 2nd ed. (2012), 6-16.

Recognizing the need for treatment, if not a cure, for the illness, international arbitral institutions responded by adopting rules for expedited arbitration. Today, virtually every major – and most minor – arbitration institution has some form of rules or procedures to expedite the arbitral process. The approaches are varied, from imposing expedition on parties where the dispute falls within some monetary limit, to ensuring party autonomy by focusing on whether the parties agree to an expedited process.

Against this background, this book endeavours to contribute to the ongoing efforts to realign international commercial arbitration more closely to its foundational principles. This book provides a wide-ranging discussion of the policies, procedures and rules of expedited international arbitration. In doing so, it intends to encourage continuing discussion and debate and hopefully engender further refinements, amendments and use of expedited arbitration in and by the international arbitral community.[16] Major efforts to develop and utilize rules for expedited international arbitration have occurred for over 20 years. The fact that arbitral institutions continue to amend and modify their expedited arbitration rules – including the recent (2021) adoption of expedited arbitral rules by the United Nations Commission on International Trade Law (UNCITRAL) for use in ad hoc arbitrations and the even more recent adoption by the International Centre for Settlement of Investment Disputes (ICSID) of rules for expedited resolution of those often exceptionally lengthy arbitration proceedings[17] – confirms the need for and usefulness of a volume such as this book.

This book brings together 31 exceptional contributors drawn from around the world – Asia, Australia, Europe, the Middle East and the Americas – who have authored 19 chapters. They include distinguished practitioners, academics and experts in international arbitration. Their insights, opinions and suggestions should prove useful to all who read or even just peruse this book. Their points of view are varied, as well as their approaches to analysing expedited arbitration rules and the attendant issues. The majority of the chapters take a comparative approach, either explicitly or implicitly. A comparative approach focuses on the search for the 'best' 'cure' for the disease afflicting international arbitration. More than one way to address the present deficiencies may exist. This book illuminates different methods of providing an expeditious and cost-effective means for dispute resolution, as well as the risks inherent in expedition. Principles of due process and party autonomy are often in conflict with speed.

This book is divided roughly into five sections. The first five chapters consider overarching issues pertinent to expedited arbitration generally and efforts to cure or at least ameliorate the disease. Chapters 6 through 10 provide in-depth looks at the expedited arbitration rules of leading institutions and the recently adopted UNCITRAL

16. For one recent discussion of possible changes to international arbitral rules generally, including a brief consideration of expedited arbitration procedures, *see* Marcin Aslanowicz, 'Do the Rules of Europe's Leading Institutional Arbitration Courts and the UNCITRAL Arbitration Rules Need to Be Revised? Assessment from the Perspective of 2023', 53:2 *Rev. European and Comp. L.* 169 (2023), 169-188 DOI: 10.31743/recl.15823.
17. *See* ICSID Arbitration Rules, Chapter XII (2022).

Expedited Arbitration Rules. The next three chapters compare the expedited procedures of leading institutions, including, among others, the ICC, ICSID, German Arbitration Institute (DIS) and the Swiss arbitral rules. Chapters 14 and 15 look at a too-frequently overlooked method of expeditiously resolving disputes: mediation. The final four chapters return to a comparative approach, albeit on a regional basis. Chapters 16 through 19 look at expedited arbitration rules in various geographic regions, including China, South Asia, the Caribbean, and the Middle East.

Ylli Dautaj leads the book off with an analysis of the traditional underpinnings for international commercial arbitration. He reviews the path traditional arbitration has followed to bring it to its current 'judicialized' state. He argues that expedited arbitration is simply returning the process to its traditional methods and advantages, mainly efficiency in terms of speed and cost. Three solicitors from the Netherlands next address the extent to which expedited arbitration procedures have created their own questions regarding their overall effectiveness. Messrs Hinrichsen and Shahrokhi and Ms Cronjé provide a critical statistical data study to identify possible gains to be achieved under certain expedited rules and procedures. Their chapter uses statistics they obtained – some never before published – from leading arbitral institutions such as the ICC, Hong Kong International Arbitration Centre (HKIAC), the Swiss Arbitration Centre (SAC) and the Japan Commercial Arbitration Association (JCAA) to determine whether expedited arbitration in fact achieves increased efficiency. Their research leads to the conclusion that expedited arbitration rules have in fact increased efficiency and are associated with lower costs compared with regular proceedings. Parties also play a crucial role in upholding time limits by actively cooperating with tribunals, establishing reasonable and concise procedural timetables, showing restraint in requesting extensions, and holding their counsel accountable for adhering to time limits.

Practitioners Joshua B. Simmons and Natalia Szlarb then provide an important analysis of an often-ignored facet of international arbitral practice that leads to excessive time and delays: the inherent prolixity and verbosity of lawyers. They argue that greater use of limitations on submissions through page- or word-count limitations, which are well-established in judicial systems, would reduce costs and delay. Dr Shahrizal Zin's chapter addresses the critical issue of enforcement of arbitral awards arising out of expedited proceedings. He concludes that a thoughtful balancing of party autonomy and due process is required in expedited procedures by the arbitral tribunal, to relieve the inevitable strain that exists between efficiency and due process.

Attorney Yasaschandra Devarakonda ends the first section of the book by providing a remarkable – and necessary – contribution. Lest the international arbitration community become seduced by the siren call of expedited arbitration, Mr Devarakonda presents a clear and forceful argument questioning expedited arbitration in light of the impact on a party's opportunity to fully present its case. He argues that this impact, as well as other potential adverse consequences, including strict scrutiny in the national courts of jurisdictions where public policy may give primacy to the mutual consent of parties, may lead parties to eschew expedited procedures and thereby leave expedited arbitration 'very much at risk of remaining as a mere on-paper procedural mechanism'.

The editors' kick-off chapters focused on particular expedited rules by reviewing UNCITRAL's new expedited arbitration rules, intended for use in ad hoc arbitrations. UNCITRAL's expedited arbitration rules are premised on party autonomy. Chapter 6 also reveals UNCITRAL's very recent efforts to speed arbitration up even more through a proposed provision for 'highly expedited arbitration'. Arbitrator James Clanchy then discusses the rules of the London Maritime Arbitrators Association. He cogently argues that its arbitral rules could be a model for expedited arbitration and should have been considered by UNCITRAL in adopting its new expedited arbitration rules.

Juan Felipe Merizalde and Juan Pablo Gómez then explore the ICC's Expedited Procedure Provisions, examining its policy reasons and implementation. While the ICC's expedited arbitral provisions offer a cost-effective and efficient dispute resolution process, they conclude that parties should carefully consider the suitability of the procedures and specifically include reference to the expedited provisions in their arbitration clauses because this procedure may otherwise not be automatically applicable. Three experienced Australian practitioners, Guillermo García-Perrote, Ella Wisniewski and Daniel O'Neil, next examine the Australian Centre for International Commercial Arbitration's 2021 expedited rules. They optimistically conclude that these rules offer a balanced approach to a mode of commercial dispute resolution that is efficient, cost-effective and credible.

The next two chapters focus on the very important topic of investor-State dispute settlement (ISDS), the subject of continuing discussions in UNCITRAL's Working Group III, focused on the reform of the ISDS system.[18] In Chapter 10, Prof. Venetia Argyropoulou from the University of Cyprus looks at ICSID's expedited arbitration provisions. She discusses the deficiencies in the traditional ICSID arbitration rules that led to the new expedited rules. She examines the reasoning behind the choices made in the new rules and assesses them critically from an investor's view. She concludes that the main characteristics of the new rules raise questions regarding whether they will achieve the goal of increased efficiency. Carlos Torres Giraldez then transitions to the next section of the book by providing a comparative analysis of the ICSID expedited arbitration procedures and UNCITRAL's expedited rules. He sheds light on their distinctive features and implications.

Dr Yassine Sangaré next assesses reforms under the ICC and Swiss arbitration rules, using France and Switzerland as a backdrop. Her chapter addresses the question of whether these two institutions' rules have succeeded in 'preserving the delicate balance between efficiency and the principle of party autonomy in the arbitration process'. The ICC and Swiss rules prioritize efficiency over party autonomy and as a result, she also concludes that parties should carefully weigh the advantages and disadvantages of expedited arbitration procedures in each jurisdiction to determine whether they best suit their dispute resolution needs.

Prof. Esra Üstün next provides a comparative analysis of the expedited arbitration rules of the ICC, DIS and the Istanbul Arbitration Centre (ISTAC). The ICC and ISTAC

18. *See generally* Alan M. Anderson and Ben Beaumont (eds), *The Investor-State Dispute Settlement System: Reform, Replace or Status Quo?* (Kluwer Law International, 2020).

limit the application of expedited arbitration rules based on the amount of money in dispute, while DIS requires the consent of the parties rather than a certain amount in dispute. While there are differences and similarities between the rules, she concludes that despite their shortcomings, the ISTAC expedited rules offer a preferred option for expedited arbitration, particularly for low-value claims.

Chapters 14 and 15 offer insightful analyses on the use of mediation as a means to quickly and efficiently resolve disputes. Arbitrator and counsel Srilal Perera reviews the important and new ICSID rules on mediation of ISDS disputes. He concludes that these new mediation rules, if used by the parties to ISDS disputes, 'can be an extremely practical ADR mechanism to resolve investor-State or commercial international arbitration disputes in an expeditious and cost-effective manner, perhaps even more so than expedited arbitration alone'. Professor Hugo Luz dos Santos follows with a scholarly and erudite discussion of expedited arbitration and arbitration-mediation (Arb-Med) in the Far East, focusing on Macau. His thorough analysis of the different cultural backgrounds involved in Arb-Med and expedited arbitration should prove incredibly beneficial to practitioners and parties involved in disputes in the Far East.

The final section of this book returns to a comparative approach, focusing on regional analyses. Researcher and scholar Yuan Fang examines the approaches to expedited arbitration in all major Chinese arbitration institutions. He presents a path forward for the best practices for Chinese expedited arbitration, including a recommendation to remove requirements based on the amount in dispute to incentivize more parties to participate in expedited arbitration and to expand the application of expedited rules. Three practitioners from the Caribbean, Peter Ferrer, Marcia McFarlane and James Petkovic, follow with a careful comparative analysis of the expedited arbitration rules in the British Virgin Islands, Bermuda and the Cayman Islands. They conclude that the more detailed rules of the British Virgin Islands, and to a lesser extent those of Bermuda, are preferable to the approach adopted by the Cayman Islands.

Rose Maria Sebi, Rahul Kr. Kanoujia, and Parnika Rai next compare and contrast leading arbitral institutions' expedited procedures in South Asia, including the rules of SIAC, HKIAC and the emerging institutions of the Mumbai Centre of International Arbitration and the Delhi International Arbitration Centre. They conclude that there is a trend towards homogenization and standardization of expedited international arbitration rules, which should lead towards greater use of expedited procedures in international dispute resolution. Finally, scholars and arbitration specialists Can Eken and Tariq Mahmood conclude the book with a comparison of expedited arbitration rules in the all-important Middle East and North Africa (MENA) region. Their chapter provides a comparative analysis of the expedited arbitration rules in Bahrain, Saudi Arabia, the United Arab Emirates, Turkey, Qatar, Egypt, Morocco and Lebanon. They conclude that because not all arbitral institutions in the MENA region have expedited arbitration provisions, room for improvement exists. Expedited arbitration has a great potential to offer a viable and efficient dispute resolution process in the region, especially in light of the number of lower-value disputes in the MENA area.

Together, these 19 chapters provide a broad overview and analysis of expedited arbitration and the rules, policies, procedures and issues arising from them. The chapters provide a cross-institutional and regional consideration of various expedited arbitration procedures and focus on the delicate balance between due process and party autonomy and the need to increase efficiency and decrease costs in international dispute resolution. The often-ignored use of mediation to quickly resolve disputes is also raised for increased consideration. Readers of this book should gain a greater understanding of many of the issues, options, and consequences that may result from expedited arbitration. They will learn of the various approaches of different institutions and rules for ad hoc arbitrations that may well influence decisions in drafting arbitration clauses and deciding whether expedited arbitration is the best approach because which rules apply certainly will matter. These insights can only benefit international commercial arbitration as its stakeholders seek to cure or at least ameliorate its present condition and problems and seek to return international commercial arbitration to its foundational underpinnings: a prompt, efficacious and cost-effective means of resolving commercial disputes.

CHAPTER 1

Expedited International Arbitration: (Re)discovering Traditional Advantages of the Arbitral Process

Ylli Dautaj

The textbook advantages of international commercial arbitration (ICA) suggest that the procedure is both faster and cheaper than litigation. Practitioners understand that this is not necessarily the case. For some types of parties and for some types of disputes, there is an obvious and perhaps damaging dissonance between what the users expect and what they get. It may even be questioned whether ICA has moved too far from its equilibrium state. If so, what are the possible solutions to bring it back on track? Expedited arbitration is the innovative product of the arbitration community utilizing another of its traditional advantages—flexibility—in order to design a more cost- and speed-efficient alternative to the status quo. This chapter suggests improving ICA through rediscovering the traditional advantages of the process in the expedited version. It highlights the fundamental elements of ICA, analyzes the fragmentation of the process, discusses the process becoming more "judicialized," and finally explains what expedited arbitration is, how it works, when it should be used (and conversely, not used), and why it came about.

§1.01 INTRODUCTION

This chapter underscores the traditional ("schoolbook") advantages of international commercial arbitration (ICA). Such an exercise lends itself to a more contemporary analysis and scrutiny of the institution's current operation and performance. Having identified some reasons for moderate concern, the policies underlying one possible improvement will be highlighted, i.e., expedited arbitration. Somewhat ironically, the practical appeal of—and the normative justification for—expedited arbitration rests on the same perceived advantages as ICA. Put differently, expedited arbitration is in fact schoolbook ICA.[1] Consequently, it is ICA as it operates today that has moved from its equilibrium state. In this light, there is no need to reinvent the wheel to improve the institution's current performance for some parties and for some types of disputes. Instead, the task is much, much simpler. Practitioners should merely rediscover the advantages of the arbitral process in its equilibrium state and implement and apply them faithfully. Less is more.

Expedited arbitration is intended to achieve the purported goal of offering a more streamlined, efficient procedure while not undercutting the quality of the adjudicatory process. The appetite for expedited arbitration has grown in taste. Today, expedited rules even constitute the default route at some of the leading arbitral institutions ("opt-out"), and other leading institutions offer the expedited route as an alternative ("opt-in"). Meanwhile, and even though faster and cheaper arbitration is reentering the global scene of dispute resolution, the policy architects relying on the underlying philosophy of ICA understand that the market and its participants have changed. The customers of today's arbitration landscape cannot be treated in the same manner as those continental Europeans who once started outsourcing disputes to a more informal panel of inquisitorial scholars. While rediscovering the utility in a simpler, more straightforward arbitration process, we must take into account situations where the expedited rules may be either inapplicable or impractical. Put differently, when and why should the arbitration process proceed pursuant to the "ordinary" rules? Asking the question in that manner treats expedited arbitration as the default and "ordinary" arbitration as the exception. That is an important point. In short, this chapter will explain *what* expedited arbitration is, *how* it works, *when* it should be used (and conversely, not used), and *why* it came about. But before that, and to put things in perspective, this chapter will highlight the fundamental elements of ICA, analyze the fragmentation of the process, and discuss judicialization.

The current ICA procedure has been described as an "arbitral trial"; that is, an arbitral legal order that has shaken off many of its old ideals and instead cloaked itself in many features and characteristics traditionally belonging exclusively to ordinary, adversarial, court litigation.[2] The traditional ICA process has become judicialized in "three manifestations," that is, "procedural judicialization," "court judicialization," and "institutional judicialization."[3] In other words, the evolution of ICA started off from a relatively informal, flexible alternative to litigation and moved to a more formal, judicial-like institution. This evolution is not entirely bad, nor is the current trajectory, but critics have urged the arbitration community to assess the regime's current functioning in scope, degree, and nuance. Having undertaken such analysis, one may spot both positive and negative aspects of judicialization in each of its three manifestations. For example, the more "judicialized" version of ICA may be suited to deal with certain complex subject-matter disputes in a fragmented, specialized world of dispute

1. *See e.g.*, Michael Mustill, *Comments on Fast-Track Arbitration*, 10 J. INT'L ARB. 121, 122 (1993) DOI: 10.54648/joia1993034.
2. *See generally* Ylli Dautaj, *Fragmentation and Judicialization of International Commercial Arbitration: Expedited Arbitration and the "Arbitral Trial"*, 13 PENN. STATE L. ARB. L. REV. (2021).
3. *Ibid.*

resolution, while other types of disputes (e.g., low-value and purely contractual disputes) may benefit from rediscovering the traditional hallmarks and benefits of arbitration.

This chapter addresses questions such as: What is ICA and how does it operate? What are the policies underlying the process and why is it the preferred venue for settling transborder commercial disputes? What are its advantages and disadvantages? While answering these questions, we must continue our forensic exercise by asking: Is ICA operating in a manner true to its objectives and purported goals? What concerns exist? Can we improve ICA? How? Furthermore, is expedited arbitration a plausible way, or alternative, forward? If yes, are we discovering something new or merely *re*discovering the arbitral wheel? To answer these questions, this chapter will first underscore ICA and its fundamental elements. It will then discuss and analyze the specialization of transborder commerce, trade, and investment, and in that light, dispute resolution. Finally, this chapter will observe the "judicialization" of ICA and discuss its "de-judicialization" through expedited arbitration.

§1.02 ICA AND ITS FUNDAMENTAL ELEMENT

International arbitration is an alternative dispute resolution method whereby the parties can settle a dispute outside of court, with appointed experts, pursuant to their own procedural directions, and yet with an outcome that is as binding (perhaps more so) as a court judgment. The process has key characteristics that makes it unique and resonate well with its users, for example, party autonomy, expertise, neutrality, flexibility, finality, and enforceability.[4] International arbitration moves commercial justice from the realm of cumbersome court procedures (sometimes idiosyncratic and parochial) and places it in the hands of the parties' own procedure. Predominantly, however, its success comes from the effective multilateral enforcement conventions in place (i.e., the International Centre for Settlement of Investment Disputes Convention, known as the "ICSID Convention," and the New York Convention). For parties, the ends justify the means. An arbitral award is generally binding, directly recognizable and enforceable. For these reasons, international arbitration is the preferred venue of dispute resolution for cross-border disputes.[5] As authors have noted, "informal and speedy procedure" is probably the most often mentioned characteristics of ICA.[6] They

4. *See* Stephen B. Goldberg, et al., *Dispute Resolution, Negotiation, Mediation, and Other Processes* 234 (1999). White & Case and Queen Mary School of International Arbitration, 2018 International Arbitration Survey: the Evolution of International Arbitration, available at: https://www.whitecase.com/publications/insight/2018-international-arbitration-survey-evolution-international-arbitration (last accessed March 23, 2023).
5. White & Case and Queen Mary School of International Arbitration, 2018 International Arbitration Survey: the Evolution of International Arbitration, available at: https://www.whitecase.com/publications/insight/2018-international-arbitration-survey-evolution-international-arbitration (last accessed March 23, 2023).
6. Tibor Várady et al., *International Commercial Arbitration—A Transnational Perspective* 669 (7th ed. 2019).

further note that when ICA "emerged as an alternative to litigation, its hallmarks were, indeed, speed, informality, low cost, simplicity."[7] These traditional, schoolbook advantages of ICA represented the key characteristics of arbitration and were indeed its fundamental elements.

ICA is unquestionably the preferred method of dispute resolution for commercial entities in a transborder context.[8] The proof of the pudding is in the eating as they say. The main advantages as ICA is practiced today are perceived to be enforceability, avoidance of specific legal systems and national courts, flexibility, and the ability of parties to select their arbitrators (expert adjudicators).[9] Notwithstanding these advantages, 21st century ICA is tainted with a few shortcomings. In contrast to the schoolbook advantages of the procedure being cost- and speed-effective, the procedure is actually perceived to be too costly and too slow.[10] These two disadvantages have been said to be a result of ICA becoming "judicialized" (or, as some refer to it, "Americanized"[11]). Some even argue that ICA has become merely "a new litigation venue."[12]

Today, ICA is practiced in a way, shape, and form much different from what the procedure looked like when it was initially developed in continental Europe in the early 20th century.[13] As a result, one may argue that ICA is "functioning in a manner untrue to its original character [and therefore] finds itself entrapped by the error of practices that it was meant to rectify."[14]

---

7. *Ibid.*
8. White & Case and Queen Mary School of International Arbitration, *2018 International Arbitration Survey: the Evolution of International Arbitration* at 2, https://www.whitecase.com/sites/whitecase/files/files/download/publications/qmul-international-arbitration-survey-2018-19.pdf (last accessed March 23, 2023).
9. *Ibid.* I would add here that its utility is also a manifestation of globalization and liberal capitalism. I usually refer to this development as a "post World-War II virtue." *See also,* Thomas E. Carbonneau, *Carbonneau on International Arbitration: Collected Essays* 7-8 (2010) ("In its contemporary embodiment, ICA emerged soon after the Second World War—more than likely, as part of Western efforts to export the virtues of capitalism and to maintain the unity and develop the prosperity of the free world alliance.").
10. *Ibid.*
11. *See* Carbonneau, *supra* n. 9, at 137 ("In their uniquely adaptive manner, the American common law and the American common law lawyer have adapted to the emergence of arbitration.").
12. *See, e.g.*, Thomas J. Stipanowich, *Arbitration: The "New Litigation"*, 1 U. Ill. L. Rev. 1, 4 (2010) and Irina Tymczyszyn, *Using Fast Track Arbitration for Resolving Commercial Dispute*, 6 Corp. and Com. Disp. Rev. 1, 25 (2018). *See also* Jan Paulsson, *Fast-Track Arbitration in Europe (With Special Reference to the WIPO Expedited Arbitration Rules)*, 18 Hastings Int'l & Comp. L. Rev. 713, 713 (1995).
13. *See e.g.*, Mustill, *supra* n. 1, at 122 and Javier Tarjuelo, *Fast Track Procedures: A New Trend in Institutional Arbitration*, 11 Pérez-Llorca L.J. 105, 105 (2017). White & Case and Queen Mary School of International Arbitration, 2018 International Arbitration Survey: the Evolution of International Arbitration, available at: https://www.whitecase.com/publications/insight/2018-international-arbitration-survey-evolution-international-arbitration (last accessed March 23, 2023) (underscoring that cost continues to be seen as arbitration's worst feature, and the lack of speed is closely following such, both of which used to be advantages of arbitration).
14. Carbonneau, *supra* n. 9, at 127.

Since the "advent"[15] of ICA in continental Europe, as practiced by its "grand old men," judicial cultures have melded and harmonized as a result of globalization, economic interaction and integration. Additionally, the subject-matter arbitrability has continuously widened and the arbitration has increasingly been used to solve high-stakes and complex transborder disputes. To solve these disputes effectively, the emphasis on "quality" trumped the focus on "speed" and "cost-efficiency," which led practitioners to adopt more rigorous trial techniques. Arbitrators increasingly approved such practices or at least became hesitant to refuse them.[16] As a result, "formalization" or "judicialization" has occurred. Judicialization was approved and facilitated through arbitral institutions' rules and other soft rules, e.g., the International Bar Association (IBA) rules on the taking of evidence. These rules helped craft a decentralized arbitral legal order by generating workable templates based on best practices that furthers formality, i.e., a judicial norm.[17]

The negative aspects of judicialization of ICA have caused the arbitral procedure to become too lengthy and costly. Thus, a gap exists between commercial entities' expectations and their experiences with ICA.[18] Users are now demanding a more cost- and speed-efficient solution to both litigation and ICA.[19] This chapter makes the categorical and unequivocal point that expedited arbitration meets that demand.[20]

Why has this evolution occurred and why did parties allow it to proceed in the given direction and at an unstoppable speed? Surely, the judicialization came as a result of improving the quality of the procedure and therefore redressing the perceived deficit of due process protection. Incidentally, or ancillary perhaps, it was also a result of securing enforceable awards. In large part, it was also due to wider participation—both in terms of broader jurisdictional appeal and due to an increase in service providers (law firms and arbitral institutions). Today, think tanks, NGOs, and equivalent entities participate as stakeholders to shape the arbitral process.

With years of improving the ICA regime, users have learned to live with it and act by routine in its improvement and development. Put simply, users learned to live with the trial-like ICA process. The question that arose with urgency was: do users

15. Arbitration in its purest form has been around since ancient times, as reflected in various religious teachings. The commercial arbitration practice as we know it, i.e., as evolved in continental Europe is not really the "advent" of arbitration.
16. For a discussion on the difficulty between balancing speed, cost, and quality, *see, e.g.*, Jennifer Kirby, *Efficiency in International Arbitration: Whose Duty Is It?*, J. INT. ARB. 689 (2015) DOI: 10.54648/joia2015032.
17. The "formalization" has also been a source of critique. *See, e.g.*, Leon Trakman & Hugh Montgomery, *The Judicialization of International Commercial Arbitration: Pitfall or Virtue*, 30 LJIL 405, 405 (2017) DOI: 10.1017/s0922156517000024. *See, e.g.*, AAA-ICDR, SCC, ICC, IBA, and UNCITRAL.
18. Thomas J. Stipanowich, *Arbitration and Choice: Taking Charge of the "New Litigation"*, 7 DEPAUL BUS. & COM. L. J. 400 (2009). *See also* Thomas J. Stipanowich, *ADR and the "Vanishing Trial": The Growth and Impact of "Alternative Dispute Resolution"*, 1 J. EMPIRICAL LEGAL STUD. 843, 895 (2004) and Stipanowich, *supra* n. 12, at 4 and Peter Morton, *Can a World Exist Where Expedited Arbitration Becomes the Default Procedure?*, 26:1 ARB. INT'L., 104 (2010).
19. *See, e.g.*, Morton, *supra* n. 18, at 104.
20. *See, e.g.*, Michael Mcllwrath and Roland Schroeder, *The View from an International Arbitration Customer: In Dire Need of Early Resolution*, 74 ARB. 3 (2008).

appreciate it? Should participants merely accept status quo? Perhaps, participants should draw a "relative" red line in the sand of dispute resolution, i.e., delineating where current ICA is welcomed and where it is not? But is it even possible in today's dispute resolution climate to once more argue that the litigation-like emphasis on ultimate procedural and substantive due process and the tools necessary to achieve that alleged or purported goal can (or even should) surrender for a more "reasonable" or "relative" (due) process? Is the quality in such a more downsized arbitration enough and acceptable? Do users even dare to challenge "Big Law" and their costly yet undeniably high-quality services (and practices)? Do participants once again dare to think differently by questioning the mental representation of full-fledged arbitration-litigation lawyers? Is it "offensive" to suggest that the utility of dispute resolution does not depend on the lawyers' timetable but rather on the users' need for speed and cost-savings?[21] Arbitration-litigation lawyers' price models and means of achieving the highest possible quality may be outdated or not needed—at least not for all parties and all types of disputes.

The arbitral community is both courageous and ready to question the status quo arbitral-trial practices and instead offer an alternative procedure for some (not all) disputes and for some (not all) parties. This is exactly what expedited arbitration achieves. This argument can be advanced and defended despite the presumption that increased judicialization leads to improved overall quality. Increased quality (whatever that may be) is not always desirable and should at times surrender for "reasonable" or "sufficient" quality.

The negative aspects of judicialization can be redressed through increased use of expedited arbitration.[22] Furthermore, treating expedited arbitration as the default mechanism for certain low-value and less-complex disputes would further entrench the currency and standing of ICA, in particular, making it a more accessible and practical utility for small and medium enterprises (SMEs).[23] Put simply, expedited arbitration is a compelling alternative to the arbitral trial. These are not arguments directly against "ordinary" arbitration. Expedited arbitration is not a competitor to ordinary arbitration—it is not. Expedited arbitration is best treated as either a supplement or additional offering to the current ICA practice.

Ultimately, what kind of arbitral procedure is suitable for a particular dispute at any given time will depend on the case at hand with its particular facts and evidence,

---

21. In many conferences, the reason expedited arbitration often does not work is suggested to be because lawyers' timetables do not permit an expedited procedure. This is quite frankly an incomprehensible—and even unethical—"concern." Lawyers are not entitled to casework. The increased trend of boutique, specialized law firms will help redress this issue. Again, less is more.
22. This is not to be confused with "fast-track arbitration," which is merely an accelerated form of arbitration with tighter scheduling and perhaps less maneuvering when it comes to requests for extension. *See, e.g.*, *See generally* Mustill, *supra* n. 1.
23. *See, e.g.*, Haflidi Kristjan Larusson, *Expedited Arbitration—Meeting the Needs of SMEs*, 63 Scandinavian Stud. 169, 176 (2017).

even if expedited arbitration enters the transnational scene as an exceptional development in the world of transnational dispute resolution.[24] The important caveat that expedited arbitration is not suitable for all types of complex and high-stakes disputes must be presented with equal force. As various stakeholders to the arbitral process engage in reform work, they can wear an "academic" and "practical" hat simultaneously. Stakeholders to the arbitral legal order are constantly engaging in the almost impossible task of balancing cost, speed, and quality (known as the "iron triangle") from a theoretical as well as practical level.[25] This is a daunting and cumbersome task. Whether to proceed with expedited arbitration or the arbitral trial underscores and illustrates the dilemma of how much quality one would, should, or even can (due to mandatory law) sacrifice for the advantages of speed and cost reduction. When should a client be instructed to proceed with expedited arbitration, and when is it not suitable? If the expedited process is treated as the default procedure, when and why should arbitrators or the institutions step in and say that the expedited rules are not suitable? There is no easy or uniform answer. The ICA process as practiced today includes litigation-like elements that were inevitable as the consumers of arbitration increased and the nature of the disputes changed. Thus, the "arbitral trial" is still the best dispute resolution venue for redressing most high-value and complex commercial disputes with a transborder component to it.

[A] Fragmentation of International Arbitration

The traditional advantages of ICA emerged not only as a result of the inherent characteristics of arbitration but also as a result of the types of cases typically submitted to arbitration.[26] The cases submitted to arbitration tended to be mostly commercial and of less value. However, today, the subject matter varies from complex intellectual property matters to contract law disputes implicating statutory provisions (including antitrust), all the way to public international law. As ICA has grown for various kinds of disputes, the arbitral process has been tailored and customized with the various kinds of specific subject-matter issues that may arise in mind. Fragmentation in international arbitration can be seen in the thickened subject-matter arbitrability. Various kinds of arbitrations have developed to facilitate growing complexity (even as exclusively dealing with certain types of disputes),[27] and law firms have focused on ICA in an increasingly niche manner (e.g., focusing on energy, construction, IT, and joint ventures).

In other words, over time, ICA as a dispute resolution venue was asked to handle not only commercial disputes between commercial parties but also financial services

24. To some degree, this is new wine in old bottles. But whether it is a novel development or a revisiting of ICA's gravamen is too important to touch upon in brief and merits a discussion in its own. *See, e.g.*, Mustill, *supra* n. 1, at 122.
25. *See generally* Kirby, *supra* n. 16.
26. Várady et al., *supra* n. 6, at 669.
27. *See, e.g.*, Meng Chen, *Emerging Internal Control in Institutional Arbitration*, 18 Cardozo J. Conflict Resol. 295, 305 (2017).

disputes, labor disputes, consumer disputes, investment disputes, intellectual property disputes, disputes implicating fraud and corruption claims, antitrust, insolvency matters, and other complex subject matters or else in-built adhesiveness.[28] To meet these demands at the highest level, institutional rules had to be formed with the subject-matter complexity or context in mind. The default procedure grew into an arbitral trial with all the necessary litigation tools available for a proper Anglo-Saxon-like adversarial procedure. This was merely adaptation to meet the new reality of arbitrating complex and high-stake matters in a transborder context.

Thus, the thickened subject-matter arbitrability and increased demand for enhanced due process (primarily as a call from academicians, other noncore practitioners, and Big Law) have pushed the procedure to embrace litigation-like features not necessarily necessary for all commercial matters but needed for more complex, context-specific, and/or high-value disputes. This led to a more tightly regulated arbitral procedure as well as tightening of the back-end court scrutiny of arbitral awards. This debate on procedural "fairness" and "justice" in ICA also invited scholars and policymakers from not purely commercial fields to "think" about (or rather level an attack on) ICA. The critics, for example, of consumer arbitration, labor arbitration, investment arbitration, and commercial matters implicating antitrust, corruption, non-core bankruptcy matters, etc., transplanted their arguments from such contexts right into the ICA debate. Therefore, critiques that sometimes make sense in other contexts have spilled over to ICA *sensu stricto*. This harms the institution's legitimacy unnecessarily. Especially, the critique leads to further judicialization. This also harms commercial parties that have—relatively speaking—pure commercial disputes, sometimes of lower value.

With the thickening of the subject matter to be arbitrated, one of the advantages of arbitration, *expertise*, became instrumental. More and more parties wanted "expert procedures." Other desired advantages were confidentiality and privacy. In fact, appointing an expert should actually speed up the procedure and make it cheaper. This is because compared to court litigation the arbitrator should be on "familiar ground" on the subject matter at hand. This appears to not be the case, however, given that ICA has become more costly and more time-consuming. The fact that parties can appoint experts and the procedure is typically confidential and private should be features more suited to an expedited process.

In light of the current operations and practice of ICA, the process is indeed tailored with the subject matter and complexity in mind while always preserving—i.e., never undercutting—the fundamental elements of the procedure. Thus, ICA should be divided into two broader categories: (1) "ordinary" arbitration (i.e., the arbitral trial as mostly practiced today) and (2) expedited arbitration. Within these broader categories, subcategories can develop to meet the specialization even further. As has been noted:

> [T]he value of ICA ought to transcend a single and determinative pathway, such as streamlined, quick, and timely awards, or even the converse of exhaustive case analyses, voluminous written proceedings, and meticulously reasoned awards.

28. For a discussion on "specialization" in ICA, *see* Trakman & Montgomery, *supra* n. 17, at 428-429.

> The nature of arbitration should, rather, be contextually determined, taking account of the dispute, jurisdiction, applicable law, and reasonable expectations of the parties. In this way "best international practice" can provide a more *situational* way of looking at ICA, rather than trying to promote the "one-size-fits-all" model of the "ideal" arbitration often promoted in the narrative of "judicialization."[29]

[B] Judicialization of International Arbitration

Judicialization is the process by which a nonjudicial, alternative dispute resolution mechanism (e.g., mediation or arbitration) comes to be dominated by quasi-judicial (i.e., "legalistic") rules and procedures.[30] In the early 1900s, ICA was used primarily by commercial parties from continental Europe.[31] English and American lawyers were not arbitration-friendly at the time. Even as late as early post-World War II, arbitration in the United States existed mostly in two forms: (i) as a procedure for small monetary value disputes and (ii) as a procedure to solve labor grievances.[32]

This changed dramatically over the years, and ICA is now vividly used by American and English commercial entities and therefore practiced by its lawyerly community. As a result, ICA has undergone a radical change. Particularly due to U.S. involvement in ICA, the process has become "judicialized" or as some would say, "Americanized."[33] Eric Bergsten rightly noted that:

> American lawyers participating in international commercial arbitration brought and used American litigation skills. The Americans utilized a more aggressive form of advocacy than the continental Europeans were used to in international commercial arbitration. The European arbitrators tended to be the "Grand Old Men" of the European legal community. While this is a broad generalization, it is accurate. The American attorneys tended to be fact-oriented while European attorneys tended to be law-oriented and wanted to hear more about the appropriate legal theories relevant to the dispute.[34]

The European (civil law-based) model of arbitration was based on the active role of the arbitrator in constituting the record and in applying the law (i.e., inquisitorial and law-oriented approach).[35] The common law model, however, is adversarial and fact-oriented. Thus, a "battle" between adjudicatory methodologies had to answer

29. *Ibid.*, at 406.
30. C. Neal Tate, *Why the Expansion of Judicial Power?*, THE GLOBAL EXPANSION OF JUDICIAL POWER 27, 28; C. Neal Tate & Torbjörn Vallinder (eds.), *The Global Expansion of Judicial Power* 28 (1995).
31. Eric Bergsten, *Americanization of International Arbitration*, 18 PACE INT'L L. REV. 289, 292 (2006) DOI: 10.58948/2331-3536.1081.
32. *Ibid.*, at 290.
33. *See* Roger P. Alford, *The American Influence on International Arbitration*, 19 OHIO ST. J. ON DISP. RESOL. 69 (2003); Elena V. Helmer, *International Commercial Arbitration: Americanized, "Civilized," or Harmonized?*, 19(2) OHIO ST. J. ON DISP. RESOL. 35, 35 (2003); Steven Seidenberg, *International Arbitration Loses Its Grip: Are U.S. Lawyers to Blame?*, 96 A.B.A. J. 50 (2010); and George M. von Mehrem & Alana C. Jochum, *Is International Arbitration Becoming Too American?*, 2 GLOBAL BUS. L. REV. 47, 49 (2011).
34. Bergsten, *supra* n. 31, at 294. *See also* Helmer, *supra* n. 33, at 36; Mehrem & Jochum, *supra* n. 33, at 47.
35. Carbonneau, *supra* n. 9, at 153.

questions such as: "What fact-finding techniques should apply? Who bears responsibility for and has the final authority in fact-finding? How much discovery should take place? What probative value should be given to variegated factual elements?"[36] Carbonneau described the Anglo-American influence and the common law-civil law divide as follows:

> The influence of the Anglo-American legal profession extended to the structure of arbitral proceedings, which began to mirror the basic characteristics of a United States common law trial. In effect, the coexistence of two influential centers of legal doctrine on arbitration instituted a struggle between the European civil law and the Anglo-American common law for dominance in the conduct of arbitral proceedings. This tension continues to be present in contemporary arbitral practice.[37]

This "judicialization," then, leads to the inevitable surrendering of certain key features of arbitration as traditionally understood and practiced, such as cost-reduction and speedy outcomes, in favor of increased "quality" as allegedly approximated through supposed predictability, reliability, and equity advanced by adversarial and fact-oriented approaches to law and legal procedure.[38] The American participation moved the traditional continental European informality and simplicity of arbitral proceedings to a more formal litigation-kind venue "that includes expert opinions and witnesses, cross-examination, extensive discovery, lengthy interrogatories and depositions, and all of the other ingredients of the American-style adversarial trial."[39] Put differently, the influence of the common law trial techniques allegedly improved the quality of the ICA procedure, but at the expense of cost and speed. But is such a trade-off always meritorious? Most likely, it is not. Rediscovering the utility of speedy and cost-efficient arbitral procedures would be beneficial. Participants in ICA should once more elevate the currency and standing of relative and reasonable due process.

[1] *The Arbitral Procedure, Arbitral Institutions, and Soft Rules*

Much of the criticism of judicialization in ICA "stems from standard arbitration procedures [having] taken on the trappings of litigation," that is, U.S.-style litigation and with it "extensive discovery and motion practice, highly contentious advocacy, long cycle time and high cost."[40] Within contentious advocacy through adversarial procedures, the two most prevalent features would be the American style of document submission and examination of witnesses.[41] However, not all aspects of U.S. litigation have grown into integral parts of ICA; e.g., interrogatories and depositions are rarely used.

36. *Ibid.*, at 166.
37. *Ibid.*, at 13.
38. *See* Helmer, *supra* n. 33, at 36.
39. Carbonneau, *supra* n. 9, at 137.
40. Stipanowich, *supra* n. 18, at 384. *See also* Helmer, *supra* n. 33, at 50.
41. *See, e.g.*, Irene Welser & Christian Klausegger, *Fast Track Arbitration: Just Fast or Something Different*, AUSTRIAN YEARBOOK ON INT'L ARB. 259, 260 (2009).

Many of the reasons behind the procedural judicialization of ICA have been a result of the thickening subject-matter arbitrability.[42] As a result, and in order to "grapple more effectively with a range of business disputes, including many large, complex cases, arbitration procedures," ICA took longer and became more detailed.[43] Put simply, adversarial lawyers had to utilize trial techniques to ultimately do what counsel are supposed to do: win. Fact-finding through discovery, advocacy through cross-examination, and extensive hearings to present one's case with full due process are important features of litigation and should be maintained for certain high-stake ICA matters.

The "Common Law-Civil Law Divide" may be slightly exaggerated.[44] Some American trial techniques are here to stay. Notwithstanding this, an alternative to the arbitral trial should exist. The critique of ICA being "judicialized" is not a critique of the procedure lacking sufficient quality as "entrapped" by U.S. litigation-like practices. It is actually closer to the opposite. The critique is rather focused on where to draw the line and when to instead elevate the importance of lower costs and increased speed. Put simply: where does the buck of quality-search stop, and who bears the responsibility for lengthy and costly procedures? Again, no reason exists against rediscovering traditional advantages of ICA by streamlining the process through expedited arbitration rules.

Moreover, as ICA has matured as a household dispute resolution forum, it has developed its own institutional personality and status. Rules on arbitral procedure have developed an established content, and arbitral institutions have provided the necessary physical and digital infrastructure for the proceedings to proceed smoothly.[45] As has been rightly observed:

> Except for judicial review, arbitration institutions also play important roles in controlling international arbitration process. Arbitration rules and regulations established by numerous arbitration institutions take on major responsibility to regulate arbitration process in the modern age. Because arbitration institutions are at the leading positions that can make sensitive and timely responses to their clients' needs and have sophisticated legislative experience, institutional arbitration rules and regulations are tailored as practice-oriented and have effective enforcement. In addition, arbitration institutions can interpret and execute their own arbitration rules in a more consistent and certain manner. Furthermore, defects discovered in arbitration rules are easier and faster to get revised or repaired in practice.[46]

Arbitral institutions supplement the institutional vacuum resulting from the arbitration's "ad hoc" nature. In offering institutionalization, these arbitral institutions

42. *See generally* Dautaj, *supra* n. 2.
43. Stipanowich, *supra* n. 12, at 11.
44. *See, e.g.*, Siegfried H. Elsing & John M. Townsend, *Bridging the Common Law-Civil Law Divide in International Arbitration*, 18 Arb. Int'l 59 (2002) DOI: 10.1023/a:1014200908066. Cf. Carbonneau, *supra* n. 9, at 153.
45. *See* Carbonneau, *supra* n. 9, at 71.
46. *Ibid.*, at 308.

improve ICA's legitimacy, authority, reliability, and effectiveness.[47] This does not mean that "ad hoc" arbitration is bad or worse. Rather, some level of judicialization may be good. In fact, the use of UNCITRAL Arbitration Rules (including soft rules) achieves that aim also for ad hoc arbitration. However, such institutionalization inevitably demands legalistic rules and procedures. Both institutional rules and soft rules (developed by, e.g., the International Bar Association) establish formal arbitral authority. These rules are agreed and therefore also an expression of party autonomy. But how detailed should the rules and procedures be?

Again, much of the institutional arbitration development has been positive. It is a form of harmonization of the arbitral legal order, which has been accomplished, *inter alia*, through arbitral institutional rules (e.g., International Chamber of Commerce (ICC), Stockholm Chamber of Commerce (SCC), AAA International Dispute Resolution Procedure (AAA-ICDR), and London Court of International Arbitration (LCIA)), UNCITRAL Arbitration Rules (often used for ad hoc arbitrations and sometimes administered by institutions, e.g., the Permanent Court of Arbitration), and soft rules (e.g., IBA rules on the taking of evidence and ethics).[48] The UNCITRAL Arbitration Rules and procedural soft rules institutionalize ad hoc arbitration, not only purely institutional arbitration. It gives the process a predictable judicial order and formality. Notwithstanding this, arbitral institutions have also realized that the development may have gone too far. Institutions have, therefore, sought alternative procedures for achieving a speedy and cost-effective procedure. That being so, arbitral institutions must continuously ask themselves what more they can do to increase speed and reduce costs. The introduction of expedited arbitration is a step in the right direction. The mission and objective for arbitral institutions should be "to bring to the attention of counsel and the parties the possibilities of adopting an expedited process."[49] Making expedited arbitration the default procedure for low-value and less-complex matters is an important step in the right direction.

[C] Expedited Arbitration

Expedited arbitration has the potential to bring the regime of ICA back to its roots by increasing the speed and reducing costs. Expedited arbitration is not a competitor to ICA as practiced today but rather an alternative for some disputes or a supplement to ICA. Expedited arbitration constitutes an important tool to fend off some of the negative aspects of judicialization.[50] Expedited arbitration is an alternative approach to both litigation and the arbitral trial (i.e., contemporary ICA). It is "designed for parties

47. *See* Chen, *supra* n. 27, at 310.
48. *See, e.g.*, Helmer, *supra* n. 33, at 55-63.
49. Morton, *supra* n. 18, at 111.
50. *See, e.g.*, Giacomo Marchisio, *Recent Solutions to Old Problems, A Look at the Expedited Procedure under the Revised ICC rules of Arbitration*, ICC DISPUTE RESOLUTION BULLETIN, 76, 80 (2017) DOI: 10.2139/ssrn.3092128.

who consider time to be of the essence, and who are willing to accept the marginal reduction in legal security for greater speed and lower costs."[51]

In 2010, Peter Morton asked whether a "world can exist where expedited arbitration becomes the default procedure."[52] Thus, the trend of rediscovering the traditional advantages of ICA started relatively recently and has already seen leading arbitral institutions create templates for expedited or streamlined arbitration. Fast-forward to today, expedited arbitration has become the default procedure at certain arbitral institutions.[53]

Stipanowich listed some reasons why businesses' expectations do not necessarily resonate with experience.[54] He lists, *inter alia*: (i) difficulties of designing an appropriate system prospectively, (ii) inexperience of transactional counsel, and (iii) limited guidance.[55] "Unless a client is entering into a significant commercial relationship or preparing a contract template that will be used multiple times, it is unrealistic to expect counsel to spend considerable time planning and drafting arbitration agreements."[56] For that reason, it is important that: (a) expedited arbitration rules are increasingly part of the arbitral offering, (b) expedited arbitration rules are being treated as the default rules applicable to certain disputes, and (c) transactional lawyers start drafting expedited arbitration escalation clauses.

[1] What *Is Expedited Arbitration?*

Expedited arbitration holds the traditional advantages of arbitration, i.e., the procedure is: (a) flexible; (b) confidential; and the awards are (c) final, binding, and directly enforceable.[57] In addition, the procedure is, as it once was, (d) speedier and (e) cheaper. These last two elements came as a response to the criticism of international arbitration having become too costly, lengthy, and complex.[58] Thus, the underlying intention behind expedited arbitration is to predefine a cost- and speed-effective procedure that is proportional to the value or complexity of the dispute.[59] Mostly, expedited arbitration is used for small-value claims and for the benefit of SMEs.

---

51. Paulsson, *supra* n. 12, at 715.
52. Morton, *supra* n. 18.
53. For example, the International Chamber of Commerce (ICC) automatically directs certain arbitration matters into the expedited route per default. The ICC makes expedited arbitration applicable by default to a dispute that does not exceed USD 3 million. The parties can of course "opt-out" of using the expedited rules. *See* Int'l Chamber of Commerce, *Expedited Procedure Provisions*, ICCWBO.ORG, https://iccwbo.org/dispute-resolution-services/arbitration/expedited-procedure-provisions/ (last visited March 18, 2023).
54. Stipanowich, *supra* n. 18, at 388-390.
55. *Ibid.*
56. *Ibid.*
57. *See, e.g.*, https://sccinstitute.com/our-services/expedited-arbitration/.
58. *See* Piotr Wójtowicz & Franco Gevaerd, *How UNCITRAL's Working Group II on Arbitration Is Analyzing the Field to Help Expedited Processes*, 37(6) INTERNATIONAL ADR 90 (2019) DOI: 10.1002/alt.21794. For a good discussion on the "judicialization" of arbitration (in the negative and positive, respectively), *see* Alec Stone Sweet & Florian Grisel, *The Evolution of International Arbitration: Judicialization, Governance, Legitimacy* (Oxford University Press 2017).
59. Marchisio, *supra* n. 50, at 77.

[2] What *Role Does Expedited Arbitration Play for SMEs?*

The "corporate retreat from litigation was fueled by concerns about cost."[60] Traditional, full-scale arbitration (i.e., the so-called arbitral trial) is in some cases too expensive to pass the optimal cost-benefit test, particularly for SMEs.[61] For SMEs, such a full-scale procedure decreases liquidity and deflects focus from growth initiatives. The risk for losing or costs of arbitrating being split or not awarded in whole are also considerations taken into account.

Having a reliable and effective dispute resolution venue for SMEs operating in a transborder context is of major importance and an important objective. SMEs contribute about 50% to the economic output in both U.S. and EU and enter cross-border contracts daily.[62] Today's world is globalized. It is not only multinational corporations (MNCs) that enter into commercial agreements across borders. Moreover, not all commercial transactions are valued in the millions or billions of dollars. "Therefore, it is of particular importance that SMEs can have access to timely and cost-effective arbitration options in the context of their cross-border contracts."[63]

[3] When *Is Expedited Arbitration (Im)practical?*

Expedited arbitration is practical when the clients' goals and priorities are met by a less judicial procedure for dispute resolution. If costs and time can be reduced while not significantly undercutting the ability to present a case once or not losing trust in the institution (e.g., if the value is very high and the process is too speedy), the expeditious format is apt for the task at hand. For these procedures, extensive adversarial procedures with U.S. litigation-style fact-finding and evidence gathering and presentation are not the name of the game.

Conversely, then, expedited arbitration is not suitable for complex matters or matters with a high value in dispute.[64] Moreover, expedited arbitration is likely not suitable for multiparty disputes.[65] The rules of expedited arbitration "were intended to satisfy the demand for a simplified and more cost-effective means of arbitration in cases of less complexity and monetary value."[66] Some guidance for when expedited arbitration rules are not practical can be found in the recent UNCITRAL Working Group II's "Draft provision 3" (sub-paragraph 3):

60. Stipanowich, *supra* n. 12, at 24.
61. Larusson, *supra* n. 23, at 170-172.
62. *Ibid.*, at 171.
63. *Ibid.*
64. It is important to point out here that value is not the single decider of complexity. Complex cases can have a low value or no determined value (e.g., when a claim for specific performance of declaratory statement has been put forth). *See, e.g.*, Tymczyszyn, *supra* n. 12, at 27.
65. *Ibid.*, at 27.
66. Robin Oldenstam et al., *Mannheimer Swartling's Concise Guide to Arbitration in Sweden* 66-67 (2019).

Elements to be taken into account when making the determination

3. In making the determination pursuant to paragraph 2, the arbitral tribunal shall invite the parties to express their views and take into account, among others, the following:

(a) The urgency and time-sensitivity of resolving the dispute;
(b) At which stage of the proceedings the request is made;
(c) The legal and factual complexity of the dispute, for example, the anticipated volume of documentary evidence and the number of witnesses;
(d) The anticipated amount in dispute (the sum of claims made in the notice of arbitration, any counterclaim made in the response thereto as well as any amendment or supplement) and its proportionality to the expected cost of arbitration;
(e) The terms of the parties' agreement referring their dispute to arbitration under the Expedited Arbitration Provisions and whether the exceptional circumstance could have been foreseeable at the time of agreement; and
(f) The consequences of the determination on the proceedings, including on the procedural fairness.[67]

The final applicability of the UNCITRAL expedited rules is less detailed and excludes sub-paragraph 3. The final rules are contained in an Annex to the generic UNCITRAL Arbitration Rules. Article 2 states:

1. At any time during the proceedings, the parties may agree that the Expedited Rules shall no longer apply to the arbitration.
2. At the request of a party, the arbitral tribunal may, in exceptional circumstances and after inviting the parties to express their views, determine that the Expedited Rules shall no longer apply to the arbitration. The arbitral tribunal shall state the reasons upon which that determination is based.
3. When the Expedited Rules no longer apply to the arbitration pursuant to paragraph 1 or 2, the arbitral tribunal shall remain in place and conduct the arbitration in accordance with the UNCITRAL Arbitration Rules.[68]

Even so, future arbitrators—sitting in ad hoc arbitrations pursuant to the new UNCITRAL Expedited Arbitration rules or sitting in an institutional arbitration under any institutional rules—could nevertheless be guided by the working group's initial Draft Provision 3 with respect to the "[e]lements to be taken into account when making the determination" on whether the expedited rules should be applicable or not.

In order to solve the situation of when the expedited rules should not be applicable, either counsel diligence or a more holistic institutional reform is necessary. Institutions can determine that the expedited rules should not apply where the amount in dispute is above a prespecified figure and/or could give arbitrators the discretion to determine suitability.[69] For example, the ICC holds that the court can determine "that

67. A/CN.9/WG.II/WP.214, https://documents-dds-ny.un.org/doc/UNDOC/LTD/V20/039/81/PDF/V2003981.pdf?OpenElement (last visited October 16, 2023).
68. https://uncitral.un.org/sites/uncitral.un.org/files/media-documents/uncitral/en/21-07996_expedited-arbitration-e-ebook.pdf.
69. Int'l Chamber of Commerce, *Expedited Procedure Provisions*, ICCWBO.ORG, https://iccwbo.org/dispute-resolution-services/arbitration/expedited-procedure-provisions/ (last visited 18 March 2023).

it is inappropriate in the circumstances to apply the expedited procedure provisions."[70] Counsel, too, can redress this issue by drafting effective arbitration clauses in similar manners.[71] The following two clauses could be drafted in any commercial agreement:

> Clause 1
>
> The Rules for Expedited Arbitration shall apply to any dispute, controversy, or claim arising out of or in connection with this agreement, or the breach termination or invalidity hereof, unless the SCC or the Sole Arbitrator in its discretion determines, taking into account the complexity of the case, the amount in dispute, and other such circumstances, that the SCC Arbitration Rules shall apply. If so, the SCC shall also decide whether the Tribunal shall be composed of a Sole Arbitrator or three Arbitrators. The seat of arbitration shall be Stockholm, Sweden. The language shall be English.
>
> Clause 2
>
> The Rules for Expedited Arbitration shall apply to any dispute, controversy, or claim arising out of or in connection with this agreement, or the breach termination or invalidity hereof, for any dispute below USD 3 000 000, unless the SCC or the Sole Arbitrator in its discretion determines, taking into account the complexity of the case and other such circumstances, that the SCC Arbitration Rules shall apply. For any dispute above USD 3 000 000, the SCC Arbitration Rules shall apply. The seat of arbitration shall be Stockholm, Sweden. The language shall be English.

Expedited arbitration is not practical for all disputes. If a matter is not suitable for expedited arbitration, the institution or sole arbitrator should be able to decide whether and when to proceed with the ordinary rules instead.[72] Arbitral institutions and counsel can make life easier in this respect, which has largely been the case. Even if neither the arbitration agreement nor the arbitration rules provide for such guidance of switching rules, arbitrators should have the mandate to make that determination against due process considerations and should be guided by the UNCITRAL working group's Draft Provision 3, which was eventually not included in the final UNCITRAL Expedited Arbitration Rules.[73] Arbitrators doing so would not exceed their mandate, nor would it be an infringement on party autonomy. A problematic situation could appear where both parties insist on expedited rules, but the arbitrator makes the determination that the rules would undercut due process guarantees. Even in such a situation, the arbitrator should have the mandate to proceed with the ordinary rules due to mandatory law.

[4] Why *Should Expedited Rules Be the Default Option?*

ICA in its current form has rightly been criticized for often being too costly, too lengthy, and unnecessarily complex.[74] The truth of the matter is that the current arbitral-trial

70. Article 30(3)(c), 2017 ICC Rules.
71. *See generally* Ylli Dautaj & Per Magnusson, *An SCC Perspective: What Happens when the Expedited Arbitration Provisions No Longer Remain Practical?* Juridisk Tidskrift (2022/23).
72. *See ibid.*
73. *Ibid.*
74. *See* Wójtowicz & Gevaerd, *supra* n. 58, at 90 (pt. 1).

practice may simply be inefficient for *some* types of disputes and for *some* kinds of parties. These "some" parties are now demanding a viable alternative but, meanwhile, one that preserves the fundamental elements of ICA. The good news is that the international arbitration community has been observant and already implemented countermeasures to uncontrolled judicialization, including primarily by drafting expedited arbitration rules and other tailored rules/institutions.[75] The ICA landscape is now seriously opening its doors for offering a compelling alternative to the arbitral trial, i.e., the expedited arbitration route. Expedited arbitration has been, and must continue to be, welcomed as something that increases the versatility of institutional arbitration.[76]

Paying more than lip service to the demands of the market, some institutional providers have even treated the new expedited rules as the default procedure for low-value and less-complex disputes. Thus, expedited arbitration can now be found either as an automatic offering (i.e., the default procedure) or as an elective choice (i.e., in an arbitration clause or in a submissions clause).[77] A third evolution merits attention and reinforces the market demand and the versatility of the arbitration market to tailor its services to the customers, that is, the UNCITRAL Expedited Arbitration Rules.[78] Thus, parties can even opt for organized ad hoc expedited arbitration. The differences between institutional arbitration (e.g., ICC, AAA-ICDR, and SCC) and ad hoc arbitration, which is often conducted under the UNCITRAL Arbitration Rules, should also be clarified. The new UNCITRAL Expedited Arbitration Rules mean that parties can agree to expedited arbitration also in an ad hoc arbitration clause referring to the UNCITRAL rules framework.

Because parties generally tend to be less agreeable in limiting the arbitral width when the dispute has ensued, there is a need for tackling this problem through institutional reform, i.e., by institutions adopting special rules for expedited procedures and even going as far as to make the rules applicable per default under certain circumstances:

> Clients and counsel tend to have neither the time nor the expertise to craft their own process templates, and usually need straightforward, dependable guidance from those that develop and administer the procedures upon which they rely. Provider institutions are awakening to the need to promote real choices in arbitration, but much remains to be done.[79]

The ICC is one of the leading institutions that has made expedited arbitration the default procedure for certain types of disputes. Another is the American Arbitration Association (AAA). The ICC rules from 2017 were, among other things, aimed at

75. *Ibid.*; Morton, *supra* n. 18, at 104; Paulsson, *supra* n. 12, at 713; and Thomas E. Carbonneau, *Building the Civilization of Arbitration—Introduction*, 113(4) PENN ST. L. R. 983 (2009).
76. Tarjuelo, *supra* n. 13, at 116.
77. *Ibid.*, at 108.
78. *See* UNCITRAL Expedited Arbitration Rules: https://uncitral.un.org/en/content/expedited-arbitration-rules (last accessed February 1, 2023).
79. Stipanowich, *supra* n. 18, at 386.

enhancing the time-and cost-efficiency of the arbitral procedure. The ICC made expedited arbitration the default rule for disputes of amounts less than USD 2 million (and USD 3 million if the arbitration agreement was concluded after January 1, 2021).[80] Thus, unless the parties expressly opt out from the expedited rules, any request for arbitration based on an arbitration clause that refers to ICC arbitration signed after March 1, 2017 proceeds as an expedited arbitration, provided it stays within the threshold amount and the process is not otherwise made inapplicable pursuant to the rules. The expedited rules provide for a six-month time frame for rendering the award following the date of the case management conference, with a possible extension at the discretion of the court.[81] For the AAA-ICDR, the expedited procedures apply unless the overall value of the claim (including counterclaim) is USD 500 000.[82] Furthermore, such procedures can apply to cases of any size with party agreement and presume cases up to USD 100,000 should be decided on documents only.

[5] Why *Could* Digital *Expedited Procedures Become the Default Procedure?*

Arbitral institutions are increasingly incorporating rules that specifically empower arbitrators to decide whether to conduct the hearing digitally. For example, on January 1, 2021, the ICC introduced new procedures by updating key provisions in its arbitration rules. The new Article 26 provides:

> A hearing shall be held if any of the parties so requests or, failing such a request, if the arbitral tribunal on its own motion decides to hear the parties. When a hearing is to be held, the arbitral tribunal, giving reasonable notice, shall summon the parties to appear before it on the day and at the place fixed by it. The arbitral tribunal may decide, after consulting the parties, and on the basis of the relevant facts and circumstances of the case, that any hearing will be conducted by physical attendance or remotely by videoconference, telephone or other appropriate means of communication.[83]

The 2017 ICC rules had not expressly accounted for the option to pursue remote/digital arbitration hearings. This addition in 2021 has been a natural development of the experiences gathered during the COVID-19 arbitral landscape. More arbitral institutions may follow suit. A world where digital expedited arbitration is the default procedure may become the norm. It is within the arbitral tribunal's discretion to proceed with a digital hearing if it is deemed suitable, even despite the protest of one

80. Parties may agree to the use of expedited arbitration also for disputes above the threshold amount. However, the ICC may at its own discretion determine that the procedure is not suitable for expedited arbitration. Moreover, the complexity of the case can give rise to a challenge on the lack of due process.
81. ICC Rules 2021, Article 30 with reference to appendix VI, Article 1(4).
82. *See* AAA-ICDR Rules: https://www.adr.org/sites/default/files/ICDR_Rules_1.pdf (last accessed January 20, 2023).
83. ICC Rules 2021, Article 26.

of the parties.[84] Without clear rules or law providing sufficient authority for such discretion, one can disagree with this position, but that is the minority view.[85]

Even though one may disagree with the legal position in nuance, scope, and degree, that does not equal a disagreement with digital hearings or that such procedures have important utility and functions. It may even be advocated that digital hearings should be used as the default hearing-mode for expedited hearings.[86] One may even go as far as to consider—and promote—a world where *digital* (i.e., remote) expedited arbitration becomes the default mechanism for certain low-value and less-complex disputes. Such an evolution—as well as documents only arbitration for certain disputes—would further facilitate demands of increased speed and cost reduction in ICA.

[6] Why *Should Parties Draft Expedited Arbitration Clauses and* How?

The judicialized ICA version as largely practiced today came to present serious obstacles for many users. Expedited arbitration procedures present a response to such perceived negative development and instead offer a compelling alternative that is both cost- and speed-efficient. In this light, both counsel and service providers (arbitral institutions) are waking up to their task and offering their customers a solution—i.e., a product that they want.

Six reasons have been expressed why business expectations do not resonate well with the actual experience of arbitration: (1) failure to plan with specific business goals in mind; (2) difficulty of designing an appropriate system prospectively before disputes arise; (3) inexperience of transaction counsel when negotiating and crafting contracts with dispute resolution clauses; (4) realities of the negotiating process with parties' different goals and priorities; (5) limited guidance; and (6) post-dispute realities ("the arbitration spiral").[87] Couple this with the relative unsatisfaction with the ICA today. For example, in 2004, a corporate general counsel explained that "arbitration is as expensive [as litigation] ... less predictable, and not appealable. Arbitration is often unsatisfactory because litigators ... run it exactly like a piece of litigation."[88] Of course, the bigger solution to this issue may be (as discussed above) arbitral institutions elaborating expedited rules and treating those as applicable by default. But counsel, particularly transactional lawyers, should not feel absolved from their responsibility until we live in that world. Lawyers must be informed about expedited arbitration and

---

84. *See* International Council for Commercial Arbitration, *Does a Right to a Physical Hearing Exist in International Arbitration?* (2021-2022), available at: https://www.arbitration-icca.org/right-to-a-physical-hearing-international-arbitration (last accessed February 14, 2023).
85. *See* Ylli Dautaj & Bruno Gustafsson, *Covid-19 and Arbitral Practice: Lessons Learned and Challenges Ahead*, 54:4 Creighton Law Review (2020-2021) and Ylli Dautaj, *Det glömda (eller gömda) partsperspektivet i rätten till ett fysiskt skiljeförfarande—förväntningar, perceptioner och högre (rätts)värden* Juridisk Tidskrift (2021/2022).
86. Ylli Dautaj & Sarah van der Stad, *Digital Expedited Arbitration: Can a World Exist Where Digital Expedited Arbitration Becomes the Default Procedure?* in Savola et al., *Digital Hearings—Civil Procedure and Arbitration* (2022).
87. Stipanowich, *supra* n. 18, at 388.
88. *See ibid.*, at 895 and Stipanowich, *supra* n. 12, at 9.

learn about its function and why and how to draft expedited arbitration escalation clauses. An expedited arbitration escalation clause is essentially a reference to expedited arbitration, and if, for example, the amount in dispute exceeds a set value or the matter is too complex, the matter can be "escalated" to an "ordinary" arbitration.

If effective alternatives to the time-consuming and costly arbitration trial are not actively elaborated, the procedure of ICA may slowly diminish into the hands of other, less-effective alternative dispute settlement regimes, e.g., mediation, fact-finding, conciliation or even litigation.[89] Such systems are not as effective as ICA in facilitating commerce, trade, and investments and do not result in a product that is final, binding, and directly enforceable in most jurisdictions around the world. Lest we forget the reason for dispensing with litigation to begin with, i.e., largely due to formality, on the one hand, and expense and delay, on the other.[90] The same negative litigation-like evolution is now manifesting for ICA. The same adversarial, excessively fact-oriented approach is practiced even where it may not be needed.

Notwithstanding this negative depiction, and in contrast to litigation, arbitration still holds as one of its traditional advantages the fundamental element of *flexibility* and *party autonomy*, which makes it possible to amend the procedure to reflect the needs of the business community without undercutting reasonable due process. That is exactly what expedited arbitration achieves as an alternative to litigation. Expedited arbitration has reasonable judicial qualities and still renders a product that is superior in the transborder dispute resolution context.

§1.03 CONCLUSION

ICA's initial success as an informal, speedy, and cost-efficient transborder dispute resolution mechanism is undeniable. ICA's continued success as a dispute resolution venue for transborder commerce, trade, and investment is still undeniable. However, the procedure today has largely become judicialized, both good and bad. As adversarial, fact-oriented Anglo-Saxon law firms and U.S. corporate culture entered the ICA market, litigation features increasingly became an integral part of international arbitration. Users wanted to win and wanted aggressively skillful lawyers on their side. The subject-matter *in*arbitrability doctrine became less and less relevant; arbitrators aided by skillful lawyers could handle increasingly more complex and even statutory matters. Thus, ICA suddenly "passed from the state of nature to life in a civilized society, and in the process ha[d] acquired many of the trappings of the dysfunctional judicial trial—an omen perhaps of its ultimate fate."[91]

However, even if contemporary ICA is "better" than expedited arbitration from a quality standpoint, it may still be disproportionally so for *some* types of disputes and for *some* categories of commercial parties. For some parties—in particular SMEs—

89. *See* Carbonneau, *supra* n. 9, at 15.
90. *See* Stipanowich, *supra* n. 18, at 387. Institution for the Advancement of the American Legal System, *Final Report on the Joint Project of the American College of Trial Lawyers Task Force on Discovery and the Institute for the Advancement of the American Legal System* at 3 (2009).
91. Carbonneau, *supra* n. 9, at 127.

expedited arbitration will be the only sensible alternative from a cost and speed standpoint. Litigation in court does not always do the trick, especially in a transborder context.

Rediscovering the traditional advantages of ICA—mainly efficiency in terms of speed and cost—by offering expedited arbitration as an alternative to "ordinary" ICA or even as the default route will improve the arbitral experience and increase the institution's global standing. While trust in the institution increases, so does its legitimacy in all corners of the world. If disputes are settled in a civil manner and the currency of the award is strong, goods will cross borders and soldiers will not. If individuals and SMEs can rely on effective dispute resolution when exploring opportunities in a transborder context, "foreigners" will interact, competition will flourish, and interdependence will remain an integral part of the global world order. As a result, traditional barriers and obstacles to transborder communication and collaboration will be less prevalent. No longer will culture, religion, politics, language, domestic law and procedure, and history place obstacles on the road. Self-positioning in the global market, as facilitated, promoted, and protected through pragmatic rules and effective dispute resolution, cuts sharply through regressive ideas and fear. Instead, such procedural safety elevates risk-taking and liberal and pragmatic values. Rediscovering the values endorsed and embraced in a post-World War II era goes hand in hand with appreciating the role that arbitration has played in our globalized world. International arbitration has strengthened the global rule of law and provided a workable rules-based transnational legal order. It still works. The task is instead limited to rendering international arbitration readily available to more parties as well as making it cheaper and quicker.

Conclusively, no "one" perfect dispute resolution process will ever be discovered, especially not in the transborder context. With different preferences stemming from legal, cultural, and political backgrounds, all possible demands and expectations cannot be met. Professor Carbonneau once wrote that the "work of intermediating between different concepts of the trial and justice and tailoring remedies to human needs remains unfinished."[92] The work of adjudicatory perfection—whatever that is—will likely remain an ongoing and unfinished project. However, ICA is as close to adjudicatory perfection as one can achieve because it effectively facilitates, promotes, and protects transborder commerce, trade, and investment. Thus, the point is simple: if ICA's traditional advantages are rediscovered and more frequently practiced through expedited arbitration, we would live in a slightly more perfect world. Less is more.

92. Carbonneau, *supra* n. 9, at 141 and William F. Fox, *International Commercial Agreements and Electronic Commerce* (2018) at 88.

CHAPTER 2

Expedited Arbitration in Action: Is the Practice Making Perfect?

Jonas C. Hinrichsen, Reza Shahrokhi & Erin Cronjé

Expedited arbitration proceedings arose to address certain long-standing critiques of traditional international commercial arbitration, namely the varying inefficiencies experienced by parties in terms of time and costs. While from one perspective expedited procedures have offered a tangible solution to closing some of the efficiency gaps of traditional arbitral proceedings, the growing practice of expedited arbitration rules and procedures has given rise to further critiques and questions regarding the overall effectiveness of such procedures and their interaction with other aspects of arbitral proceedings and enforcement. Now, in the nearly three decades since expedited process mechanisms were introduced and formalized through procedural rules of major arbitral institutions, and with a plethora of other institutions following suit, the efficacy of utilizing these mechanisms instead of traditional arbitration process can be assessed against existing data from practice.

§2.01 INTRODUCTION

Expedited arbitration proceedings arose to address certain long-standing critiques of traditional international commercial arbitration, namely the varying inefficiencies experienced by parties in terms of time and costs.[1] While from one perspective expedited procedures have offered a tangible solution to some of the efficiency gaps of traditional arbitral proceedings, the growing practice of expedited arbitration rules and procedures has given rise to further critiques and questions regarding the overall

1. According to the International Arbitration Survey conducted by White & Case, the School of International Arbitration of the Queen Mary University of London, "cost" and "lack of speed" are seen as some of arbitration's worst features. *2018 International Arbitration Survey: The Evolution of International Arbitration*, Queen Mary University of London, https://arbitration.qmul.ac.uk/research/2018/.

effectiveness of such procedures and their interaction with other aspects of arbitral proceedings.

While the rules of arbitral institutions may differ slightly, the common aim of all of these institutions is to increase procedural efficiency and complete proceedings within a shorter time frame, thereby resulting in reduced costs. Typically, waiting for the arbitral award to be rendered caused the greatest delay.[2] There are, however, multiple phases or elements of arbitral proceedings which can be optimized and thus expedited. This chapter seeks to identify, among other things, where the gains for the arbitration user occur under certain existing expedited rules and procedures.

This chapter first identifies the main objectives of expedited arbitration procedures as envisaged in the existing policies and rules and the scope and meaning of "expedited arbitration" to determine which phase(s) of the proceedings—from commencement of proceedings to rendering of an award—are intended to benefit from an expedited process. Thereafter, drawing on available statistical data and authorities regarding expedited proceedings conducted under current institutional rules,[3] this chapter assesses whether these objectives are being met in practice and to what extent. In particular, this chapter explores whether expedited proceedings result in overall lower costs and reduced duration of the proceedings—as compared to traditional arbitration proceedings of a similar type and monetary value—and at what stage of the proceedings such gains may have taken place. For each institution, this analysis is premised on core research questions. First, since the introduction of the expedited procedure rules, how many expedited arbitration proceedings have taken place and what is the ratio as compared to traditional proceedings? Second, has there been an increase in expedited arbitration proceedings compared to traditional arbitration proceedings of a similar type and monetary value? Third, do expedited proceedings result in overall lower costs and reduced duration of the proceedings? Finally, within what time frames have tribunals rendered the final award?

Finally, this chapter explores the interaction between these expedited rules and procedure, the mandate and discretion of a tribunal under such proceedings, and the possible consequences for the enforceability of an award. In particular, this chapter considers possible frictions between the expedited rules and procedures and other entrenched principles of international arbitration. While the various institutional rules governing expedited processes envisage greater time- and cost-efficiency for the parties and many examples exist where this efficiency has successfully been observed, ultimately, the process is heavily influenced by the behavior of the disputing parties, including their cooperation with arbitral tribunals.

2. Nigel Blackaby, Constantine Partasides QC, Alan Redfern & Martin Hunter, *Redfern and Hunter on International Arbitration*, 6.27 (Oxford University Press 6th ed. 2015).
3. Using available data from the International Chamber of Commerce (ICC), the Arbitration Institute of the Stockholm Chamber of Commerce (SCC), the Swiss Arbitration Centre (SAC), the Japan Commercial Arbitration Association (JCAA) and the Hong Kong International Arbitration Centre (HKIAC), this chapter will analyze and seek to answer these questions. For the German Institution of Arbitration (DIS) and the Singapore International Arbitration Centre (SIAC) no verified data was available at the date of this publication.

§2.02 OVERVIEW AND OBJECTIVES OF EXPEDITED PROCEDURES

The expedited arbitration process is designed to achieve a prompt and cost-effective resolution, which is accomplished by expediting and simplifying key aspects of the proceedings. Various strategies may be implemented to enhance efficiency and hasten the arbitral process, such as imposing strict time limits or rules with regard to the overall duration of the proceedings.[4] By now expedited proceedings have become a familiar procedural mechanism under different arbitral institutions and their respective rules. Numerous Western arbitral institutions' expedited procedures are now well known and anchored in their existing institutional rules, having gained popularity in the past three decades. SCC introduced rules for expedited proceedings in as early as 1995. The current version entered into force on January 1, 2023.[5] DIS presented new supplementary rules to facilitate expedited proceedings in April 2008 and an entire separate Annex 4 in 2018.[6] SAC included an option of expedited proceedings in 2004, which now appears in Article 42 of the current Swiss Rules.[7]

Turning to arbitration practice in the Eastern hemisphere, JCAA introduced a mechanism for expedited proceedings relatively early, in 1997.[8] The relevant provisions can currently be found under Articles 83-90 JCAA Rules.[9] HKIAC adopted expedited proceedings in its rules in 2008,[10] which can be currently found under Article 42.[11] SIAC followed suit soon afterward, providing for an expedited procedure in Article 5 of its arbitration rules in 2010.[12] Most recently, ICC introduced an expedited procedure in its arbitration rules in March 2017, found in Article 30 and Appendix VI.[13]

---

4. Yas Banifatemi, *Expedited Proceedings in International Arbitration*, 13 (Laurent Lévy and Michael Polkinghorne eds. (ICC) 2017).
5. Rules For Expedited Arbitrations of the SCC Arbitration Institute (January 1, 2023), https://sccarbitrationinstitute.se/sites/default/files/2022-12/scc_expedited_arbitration_2023_english.pdf (SCC Rules).
6. Annex to the DIS Arbitration Rules 1998—Supplementary Rules for Expedited Proceedings 2008 (April 25, 2008), https://www.trans-lex.org/750110; Arbitration Rules of the DIS Arbitration Institute: Annex 4 (March 1, 2018), https://www.disarb.org/fileadmin/user_upload/Werkzeuge_und_Tools/2018_DIS-Arbitration-Rules.pdf (DIS Rules).
7. Swiss Rules of International Arbitration: Section V (July 1, 2004), https://www.swissarbitration.org/wp-content/uploads/2021/07/2004-SRIA-SwissRules_-2004_English_ok.pdf; Swiss Rules of International Arbitration: Article 42 (June 1, 2021), https://www.swissarbitration.org/wp-content/uploads/2022/07/Swiss-Rules-2021-EN.pdf (Swiss Rules).
8. Masato Dogauchi, Shinji Ogawa and Jieying Peng, *Amendment of JCAA Rules and Promulgation of Appoint Authority Rules*, Japan Commercial Arbitration Journal, vol. 3 (2022).
9. Arbitration Rules of the JCAA Arbitration Institute: Part 2 (July 1, 2021), https://www.jcaa.or.jp/en/common/pdf/arbitration/Commercial_Arbitration_Rules2021_en.pdf?211223 (JCAA Rules).
10. Expedited HKIAC Arbitration, HKIAC, https://hkiac.org/arbitration/process/expedited-hkiac-arbitration.
11. 2018 Administered Arbitration Rules: Article 42 (November 1, 2018), https://hkiac.org/sites/default/files/ck_filebrowser/PDF/arbitration/2018%20Rules%20book/2018%20AA%20Rules_English.pdf (HKIAC Rules).
12. Arbitration Rules of the SIAC Arbitration Institute: Rule 5 (August 1, 2016), https://siac.org.sg/wp-content/uploads/2022/06/SIAC-Rules-2016-English_28-Feb-2017.pdf (SIAC Rules).
13. Arbitration Rules of the ICC Arbitration Institute: Article 30 and Appendix VI ICC Rules (January 1, 2021), https://cdn.iccwbo.org/content/uploads/sites/3/2020/12/icc-2021-arbitration-rules-2014-mediation-rules-english-version.pdf (ICC Rules).

[A] Unpacking the Arbitral Process: Expedited Procedure in Parts

There are several core elements or phases of arbitration proceedings which can be expedited within the overall process. These phases include the commencement stage, the suitability of the matter for an expedited process, constitution of the tribunal, the number of written submissions to be exchanged, including expert reports or witness statements, and the conduct of an oral hearing and the time period for rendering an award.

[1] Suitability of Disputes for Resolution by Expedited Process

Subject to minor exceptions, disputes are typically eligible for expedited process if they meet a monetary threshold or if the parties consent to following an expedited process. Under the ICC Rules, the expedited procedure rules apply if either the amount does not exceed a certain value[14] or the parties to the dispute agree to the application of the ICC Rules.[15] The expedited procedure provisions do not apply if: (i) the arbitration agreement under the Rules was concluded before the date on which the expedited procedure provisions came into force; (ii) the parties have agreed to opt out of the expedited procedure provisions; or (iii) the International Court of Arbitration (ICC Court), upon the request of a party before the constitution of the tribunal or on its own motion, determines that it is inappropriate to apply the expedited procedure provisions.[16]

Under the SIAC Rules, a party may file its application for the expedited procedure if: (i) the amount does not exceed a certain value;[17] (ii) the parties agree to the expedited procedure;[18] or (iii) in cases of exceptional urgency.[19] Alternatively, a separate application for expedited procedure may be filed subsequent to filing a notice of arbitration.[20] The President of the SIAC Court of Arbitration will determine whether the arbitration proceedings will be conducted in accordance with the expedited procedure (subject to SIAC's receipt of the requisite deposits).[21]

According to the HKIAC Rules, an expedited procedure applies if: (i) parties agree to expedited procedure or (ii) in cases of exceptional urgency or (iii) the amount in dispute does not exceed a certain value.[22] Under the JCAA Rules, an expedited procedure

14. Article 1.2 Appendix VI ICC Rules: (a) USD 2 million if the arbitration agreement under the Rules was concluded on or after March 1, 2017 and before January 1, 2021; or (b) USD 3 million if the arbitration agreement under the Rules was concluded on or after January 1, 2021.
15. Article 30(2) ICC Rules.
16. Article 30(3) ICC Rules.
17. Rule 5.1(a) SIAC Rules. SGD 6 million (approximately USD 4.47 million) capped total amount in dispute (representing the aggregate of the claim, counterclaim and defense of set-off).
18. Rule 5.1(b) SIAC Rules.
19. Rule 5.1(c) SIAC Rules.
20. *SIAC Expedited Procedure*, SIAC, https://siac.org.sg/expedited-procedure.
21. *Ibid.*
22. Article 42.1 HKIAC Rules. If the amount in dispute representing the aggregate of any claim and counterclaim (or any set-off defense) does not exceed USD 250,000 to HKD 25,000,000 (over USD 3 million). For an overview setting out the requirements for application of expedited proceedings with different arbitral institutions, *see* Table 2.1 as created by the author.

applies if the parties agree to expedited procedure or the amount in dispute does not exceed a certain value.[23] The expedited procedure provisions shall not apply if: (i) a party notifies the JCAA in writing of the agreement by the parties not to submit the dispute to expedited arbitration; or (ii) the JCAA, before the constitution of the tribunal, finds that the parties' agreement concerning the arbitral proceedings contains provisions that are contrary to the expedited procedure provisions or other circumstances exist that make it clearly inappropriate to apply the expedited procedure provisions.[24]

The SCC and DIS Rules provide that parties may agree on expedited proceedings from the outset by means of an arbitration clause.[25] The DIS Rules specifically provide that parties may also make an agreement during a case management conference, even after the dispute has arisen.[26] According to the Swiss Rules, an expedited procedure applies if: (i) the parties agree to expedited procedure or (ii) the amount in dispute does not exceed a certain value, unless the Arbitration Court of the Swiss Arbitration Centre (SAC Arbitration Court) decides otherwise, taking into account all relevant circumstances.[27]

Table 2.1 Requirements for Application of Expedited Proceedings

Institution	*In Case of Party Autonomy*	*In Case of Monetary Threshold*	*Other*
ICC	Yes	Yes	Certain exceptions apply
SIAC	Yes	Yes	In cases of exceptional urgency
HKIAC	Yes	Yes	In cases of exceptional urgency
JCAA	Yes	Yes	Certain exceptions apply
SCC	Yes	No	–
DIS	Yes	No	–
SAC	Yes	Yes	Discretion of the SAC Arbitration Court

23. Article 84.1 (a) and (b) JCAA Rules. In 2019, the applicable amount in dispute was increased from JPY 20 million (approximately USD 133,385) to JPY 50 million (approximately USD 333,462). Further in 2021, the applicable amount in dispute (the total amount of the claim, counterclaim and set-off defense, the amount of claims for interest and cost shall be excluded) was increased to JPY 300 million (in the case of a foreign currency, the applicable amount shall be converted into Japanese yen at the Telegraphic Transfer Midrate or any other reasonable exchange rate designated by JCAA as of the business day immediately preceding the date of filing of the Request for Arbitration) (approximately USD 2 million). Article 84.2 JCAA Rules: Where the JCAA determines that the economic value cannot be calculated, or its calculation is extremely difficult, the amount set forth in Article 84.1 (a) shall be deemed to exceed JPY 300 million. Even where the amount in dispute exceeds JPY 300 million due to amendment to claim after the notification set forth in Article 84.4 is given, the provisions of Part 2 JCAA shall continue to apply.
24. Article 84.3 JCAA Rules.
25. Article 6 SCC Rules. Article 5.2 DIS Rules.
26. Article 27.4 (ii) DIS Rules.
27. Article 42.1 Swiss Rules. The amount may not exceed CHF 1 million (approximately USD 1,120,580).

In summary, most assessed institutional rules provide an opt-out system (ICC Rules, SIAC Rules, HKIAC Rules, JCAA Rules and Swiss Rules). Expedited proceedings apply automatically if the aggregate value of the claims made in the arbitration falls under a specified monetary value. Parties that do not want expedited arbitration have to exclude it. Only the DIS Rules and the SCC Rules provide for an opt-in system; expedited proceedings only apply if the parties agree to their application.

[2] Composition of Tribunal and Time Limit for Formation

Despite some exceptional circumstances where a three-member tribunal is constituted, most of the reviewed institutional rules and procedures provide for a sole arbitrator in expedited cases. The ICC Rules provide that the arbitral tribunal shall consist of a sole arbitrator,[28] who the parties may nominate within the time limit to be fixed by the ICC Secretariat. In the absence of such nomination, the sole arbitrator shall be appointed by the ICC Court within as short a time as possible.[29]

According to the SIAC Rules, the tribunal shall consist of a sole arbitrator, unless the SIAC President decides otherwise.[30] If within 21 days after the date of commencement of the arbitration, or within the period otherwise agreed by the parties or set by the SIAC Registrar, the parties have not reached an agreement on the nomination of a sole arbitrator, or if at any time either party so requests, the SIAC President shall appoint the sole arbitrator.[31]

In a somewhat different approach, under the HKIAC Rules, the tribunal shall consist of a sole arbitrator, unless the arbitration agreement provides for more than one arbitrator.[32] In the latter case, the HKIAC shall invite the parties to agree to refer the case to a sole arbitrator. If the parties do not agree, the case shall be referred to three arbitrators.[33] With respect to the timing of the tribunal's constitution, the HKIAC Rules envisage different scenarios depending on whether one or three arbitrators are to be appointed and when parties agree on the number of arbitrators to be designated.[34] With regard to the default scenario of one arbitrator, where the parties have agreed *before* the arbitration commences that the dispute shall be referred to a sole arbitrator, they shall jointly designate that arbitrator within 30 days from the date the notice of arbitration was received by the respondent.[35] Where the parties have agreed on one arbitrator *after* the institution of proceedings, they shall designate the arbitrator within 15 days from the date of such agreement.[36] Where the parties have not agreed upon the number of arbitrators and HKIAC has decided that the dispute shall be referred to a sole arbitrator, the parties shall jointly designate the sole arbitrator within 15 days from the date

28. Article 2.1 Appendix VI ICC Rules.
29. Article 2.2 Appendix VI ICC Rules.
30. Article 5.2 b) SIAC Rules.
31. Article 10.2 SIAC Rules.
32. Article 42.2(a)-(b) HKIAC Rules.
33. Article 42.2(b) HKIAC Rules.
34. Articles 7-8 HKIAC Rules.
35. Article 7.1(a) HKIAC Rules.
36. Article 7.1(b) HKIAC Rules.

HKIAC's decision was received by the last of them.[37] In the absence of an agreement, the HKIAC will make the appointment.[38]

Similar to the HKIAC, the JCAA Rules provide that there shall be a sole arbitrator, unless the parties agree there shall be three. In the latter case, the JCAA may invite the parties to agree to refer the case to a sole arbitrator.[39] The JCAA Rules do not have a rule under which it can force parties to follow this invitation. The JCAA Rules consider different scenarios depending on whether one or three arbitrators are to be appointed and when the parties have agreed on the number of arbitrators to be designated.[40] For the default scenario with a sole arbitrator, parties shall agree on and appoint such an arbitrator and notify the JCAA of such appointment within two weeks from the respondent's receipt of the notice of the request for arbitration.[41]

Under the SCC Rules, the tribunal shall also consist of a sole arbitrator, who, unless agreed otherwise, shall be jointly appointed by the parties within a ten-day period set by the SCC.[42] If the parties fail to appoint the arbitrator within this time, the SCC Board of Directors shall make the appointment.[43]

According to the DIS Rules, the tribunal shall consist of one, three, or any other odd number of arbitrators.[44] If the parties do not agree upon an arbitrator within a time limit fixed by the DIS, the appointing committee of the DIS shall select and appoint the sole arbitrator.[45] If the tribunal is comprised of three arbitrators, each party shall nominate one co-arbitrator. If a party fails to nominate a co-arbitrator, such co-arbitrator shall be selected by the appointing committee of the DIS.[46]

Finally, under the Swiss Rules, the tribunal shall consist of a sole arbitrator, unless the arbitration agreement provides for more than one.[47] Similar to HKIAC Rules, the Secretariat of the SAC Arbitration Court (SAC Secretariat) shall in the latter case invite the parties to agree to a sole arbitrator.[48] The Swiss Rules do not contain a rule under which the SAC Arbitration Court can force parties to follow this invitation. In principle, SAC expedited proceedings can have three arbitrators. Where the parties have agreed to a single arbitrator, they shall jointly designate the sole arbitrator within 30 days from the date on which the notice of arbitration was received by the respondent, unless the parties' agreement provides otherwise. Where parties have not agreed upon the number of arbitrators and the SAC Arbitration Court decides that the dispute shall be referred to a sole arbitrator, the parties shall jointly designate the sole arbitrator within 30 days from the date of receipt of the SAC Arbitration Court's decision.[49]

37. Article 7.1(c) HKIAC Rules.
38. Article 7.2 HKIAC Rules.
39. Article 86 JCAA Rules.
40. Articles 27-28 JCAA Rules.
41. Article 27.1 JCAA Rules.
42. Article 17 SCC Rules.
43. Article 18.3 SCC Rules.
44. Article 10 DIS Rules.
45. Article 11 DIS Rules.
46. Article 12.1 DIS Rules.
47. Article 42.2(a) Swiss Rules.
48. Article 42.2(b) Swiss Rules.

Table 2.2 Comparative Summary of the Composition of and Time Frames for the Constitution of the Tribunal

Institution	*Composition of Tribunal*	*Time Frame Composition (Sole Arbitrator)*
ICC	Sole arbitrator	Within a time limit fixed by the ICC Secretariat
SIAC	Sole arbitrator unless SIAC President decides otherwise	Within 21 days after the date of commencement of the arbitration
HKIAC	Sole arbitrator (unless parties decide on three)	Within 30 days after the date of commencement of the arbitration/15 days after parties agreed on sole arbitrator/15 days after parties received HKIAC decision to refer to sole arbitrator
JCAA	Sole arbitrator (unless parties decide on three)	Within 14 days after the date of commencement of the arbitration
SCC	Sole arbitrator	To be agreed by parties
DIS	Sole or three or any other odd number of arbitrators	Within a time limit fixed by the DIS
SAC	Sole arbitrator (unless arbitration agreement provides for more)	Within 30 days after the date of commencement of the arbitration/within 30 days after parties received SAC Arbitration Court's decision to refer to sole arbitrator

[3] Rounds and Extent of Written Submissions

Under the ICC Rules, the tribunal has the discretion to adopt such procedural measures as it considers appropriate. In particular, the tribunal may, after consultation with the parties, decide not to allow requests for document production or to limit the number, length and scope of written submissions and written witness evidence (both fact witnesses and experts).[50] In contrast, the SIAC and JCAA Rules do not specify the number of submissions allowed. Following the request for arbitration and the answer, the SCC Rules provide for one written round, unless the tribunal finds compelling circumstances that call for further written submissions.[51] Similarly, the HKIAC, DIS

49. Articles 10.1 and 10.2 Swiss Rules. For an overview setting out a comparative summary of the composition of and time frames for the constitution of the tribunal with different arbitral institutions, *see* Table 2.2 as created by the author.
50. Article 3.4 Appendix VI ICC Rules.
51. Article 30 SCC Rules.

and Swiss Rules allow only one round of submissions following the request for arbitration and the answer. In case of a counterclaim, the claimant may, however, file its statement of defense.[52]

[4] *Hearing and Delivery of Final Award*

The ICC Rules provide that the arbitrator may, after consulting the parties, decide the dispute solely on the basis of the documents submitted, with no hearing and no examination of witnesses or experts.[53] The final award must be rendered six months from the date of the case management conference, but this may be extended by the ICC Court.[54] In 2021, the ICC released a note to parties and arbitral tribunals on the conduct of the arbitration under the ICC Rules.[55] In this note, the ICC states that in order to effectively comply with the six-month time limit, an arbitral tribunal acting under the expedited procedure provisions is expected to submit its draft award to the ICC Court within five months from the case management conference.[56] Pursuant to the note, the ICC Court may increase or decrease the arbitrators' fees based on how expeditiously the arbitrators draft the award.[57] Where the draft is submitted later than five months after the case management conference, the ICC Court may lower the fees, unless it is satisfied that the delay is attributable to factors beyond the arbitrators' control or to exceptional circumstances, and without prejudice to any other measures that it may take, such as replacing one or more of the arbitrators. For draft awards that are submitted up to seven months after the case management conference, fees are reduced by 5% to 10%. If the draft is submitted up to 10 months after the case management conference, fees are reduced by 10% to 20%. If the draft is submitted even later than 10 months, fees are reduced by 20% or more.[58] This policy serves as a tool to promote effective and efficient conduct of the arbitration proceedings and to incentivize arbitrators to expedite proceedings.[59]

Under the SIAC Rules, a hearing is not compulsory.[60] The tribunal may, in consultation with the parties, decide if the dispute is to be decided on the basis of

52. Article 42.2(d) HKIAC Rules Annex 4, Article 3 DIS Rules and Article 42.2(c) Swiss Rules.
53. Article 3.5 Appendix VI ICC Rules.
54. Article 31(2) ICC Rules and Article 4.1 Appendix VI ICC Rules.
55. Note to Parties and Arbitral Tribunals on the Conduct of the Arbitration under the ICC Rules of Arbitration (January 1, 2021) https://iccwbo.org/wp-content/uploads/sites/3/2020/12/icc-note-to-parties-and-arbitral-tribunals-on-the-conduct-of-arbitration-english-2021.pdf. The regular proceedings know a similar policy already since 2016. ICC Court announces new policies to foster transparency and ensure greater efficiency (January 5, 2016) https://iccwbo.org/news-publications/news/icc-court-announces-new-policies-to-foster-transparency-and-ensure-greater-efficiency/.
56. Note to Parties and Arbitral Tribunals on the Conduct of the Arbitration under the ICC Rules of Arbitration (January 1, 2021) https://iccwbo.org/wp-content/uploads/sites/3/2020/12/icc-note-to-parties-and-arbitral-tribunals-on-the-conduct-of-arbitration-english-2021.pdf, para. 159.
57. *Ibid.*, paras 160-161.
58. *Ibid.*, para. 161.
59. *Ibid.*, para. 158.
60. Rule 5.2 c) SIAC Rules.

documentary evidence only or if a hearing is required for the examination of any witness and expert witness as well as for any oral argument. A final award is to be rendered within six months of the constitution of the tribunal, unless the SIAC Registrar extends the time for making the final award.[61] There is no financial consequence if the six-month time limit to render the award is not met by the tribunal.[62]

Similarly, under the HKIAC Rules, a hearing is not compulsory.[63] The timing for the final award is six months from the date when HKIAC transmitted the file to the tribunal. In exceptional circumstances, HKIAC may extend this time limit.[64] Similar to the SIAC Rules, the HKIAC holds no power to impose financial consequences if the six-month time limit to render the award is not met.[65] However, the HKIAC has soft power in pushing arbitrators to render their awards timely because arbitrators look to institutions for repeat appointments in future cases.[66] The same logic applies to the other institutions that do not impose a reduction in fees (SIAC, JCAA and SAC Arbitration Court).

According to the JCAA Rules, a hearing is not compulsory.[67] The final award shall be rendered six months from the date when the tribunal was constituted.[68] If the amount in dispute is JPY 50 million or less, the tribunal shall make reasonable efforts to render an arbitral award within three months from the date when it is constituted.[69] In exceptional circumstances, the JCAA may extend the time limit for rendering the arbitral award.[70] The JCAA Rules do not contain a rule pursuant to which a tribunal faces financial consequences if the time limit to render the award is not met.

The SCC Rules also provide that a hearing shall be held only at the request of a party and if the arbitrator considers the reasons for the request to be compelling.[71] The final award must be delivered three months after the case was referred to the tribunal. The SCC Board of Directors may extend this time limit upon a reasoned request from the arbitrator or, if otherwise deemed necessary, having due regard to the expedited nature of the proceedings.[72] While the SCC Rules do not contain an explicit provision

61. Rule 5.2 d) SIAC Rules.
62. Liber Amicorum Pierre A. Karrer, *The Powers and Duties of an Arbitrator*, p. 292 (Patricia Louise Shaughnessy, Sherlin Tung eds., Kluwer Law International 2017).
63. Article 42.2(e) HKIAC Rules.
64. Article 42.2(f) HKIAC Rules. Pursuant to Article 42.2(g) HKIAC Rules, the arbitral tribunal shall state the reasons upon which the award is based in summary form, unless the parties have agreed that no reasons are to be given.
65. Liber Amicorum Pierre A. Karrer, *The Powers and Duties of an Arbitrator*, p. 292 (Patricia Louise Shaughnessy, Sherlin Tung eds., Kluwer Law International 2017).
66. Nathaniel Lai (Sidley Austin), *The Use of Time Limits in International Arbitration: Help or Hindrance?* (April 16, 2020), https://www.hkiac.org/content/time-limits-help-or-hindrance.
67. Article 87 JCAA Rules. The tribunal shall hold one hearing where it considers it necessary after consultation with the parties and if they all agree. The hearing shall be held via videoconference.
68. Article 88.1 JCAA Rules.
69. Article 88.2 JCAA Rules.
70. Article 89 JCAA Rules.
71. Article 33 SCC Rules.
72. Article 43 SCC Rules.

pursuant to which a noncompliant tribunal is penalized, the SCC Board of Directors retains the capacity to modify arbitrators' fees in exceptional situations.[73]

A hearing is under the DIS Rules not compulsory because it may be dispensed with if all parties agree.[74] The final award shall be rendered within six months after conclusion of the case management conference.[75] If the final award cannot be made within the time limit, the tribunal must inform parties and DIS in writing of the reasons.[76] Because the DIS Rules apply *mutatis mutandis* to the separate Annex 4 dealing with expedited proceedings,[77] the DIS Arbitration Council, in its discretion, may reduce the fee of one or more arbitrators based upon the time taken to issue its final award. In deciding whether to reduce the fee, the DIS Arbitration Council shall consult the arbitral tribunal and take into consideration the circumstances of the case.[78]

The Swiss Rules do not prescribe a mandatory oral hearing.[79] Instead, the final award must be made within six months from the date on which the tribunal received the file from the SAC Secretariat. In exceptional circumstances, the SAC Arbitration Court may extend this time limit.[80] The SAC Arbitration Court has no authority to impose financial consequences if the six-month time limit to render the award is not met by the arbitrator.[81]

Table 2.3 Comparative Summary of Hearing (If Any) and Timing of Final Award

Institution	*Hearing (If Any)*	*Delivery of Final Award*	*Discretion for Extension of Timing*
ICC	Not compulsory	Six months after the case management conference	ICC Court
SIAC	Not compulsory	Six months after the constitution of tribunal	SIAC Registrar
HKIAC	Not compulsory	Six months after the case was referred to the arbitrator	Institution

73. Article 2 Appendix IV of the SCC Rules.
74. Annex 4, Article 4 DIS Rules.
75. Annex 4, Article 1 DIS Rules.
76. Annex 4, Article 5 DIS Rules: If such time limit is exceeded, the arbitral tribunal shall not for that reason cease to have jurisdiction, and final award shall be made as soon as possible.
77. Article 1.4 DIS Rules.
78. Article 37 DIS Rules.
79. Article 42.2(d) Swiss Rules. Unless the dispute is decided on the basis of documentary evidence only, a single hearing shall be held for the examination of witnesses and experts or for oral argument.
80. Article 42.2(e) Swiss Rules. Article 42.2(f) Swiss Rules: The tribunal may state the reasons upon which the award is based in summary form.
81. Liber Amicorum Pierre A. Karrer, *The Powers and Duties of an Arbitrator*, p. 292 (Patricia Louise Shaughnessy, Sherlin Tung eds., Kluwer Law International 2017).

Institution	*Hearing (If Any)*	*Delivery of Final Award*	*Discretion for Extension of Timing*
JCAA	Not compulsory	Three to six months after the constitution of tribunal	Institution
SCC	Not compulsory	Three months after the case was referred to the arbitrator	SCC Board of Directors
DIS	Not compulsory	Six months after the case management conference	Tribunal
SAC	Not compulsory	Six months after the case was referred to tribunal	SAC Arbitration Court

§2.03 EXPEDITED PROCEEDINGS IN PRACTICE: USE OF EXPEDITED MECHANISMS IN DIFFERENT INSTITUTIONS

[A] ICC

Between the introduction of the ICC Rules in March 2017 and December 2021, 400 cases have been or are being conducted under those rules.[82] The rules applied automatically in 293 cases (i.e., cases not exceeding the monetary threshold and based on contracts concluded on or after entry in force of the expedited procedure rules).[83] There have been 340 requests to opt in to expedited proceedings, of which 107 were agreed by the other party(ies).[84] The number of cases falling under the expedited procedure rules constitutes approximately one-third of the overall number of ICC cases.[85]

Of the total 195 final awards rendered under the ICC Rules since 2017, 95 were delivered on or around the six-month time limit, comprising 48% of the caseload. Delays were apparently minimal.[86] The delay exceeded one month in 45 cases and, in

82. Email from International Chamber of Commerce to Jonas Hinrichsen dated January 20, 2023, subject ICC Expedited Arbitration proceedings (copy in author's possession).
83. *Ibid.*
84. *Ibid.*
85. *International Chamber of Commerce: Dispute Resolution Bulletin 2018*, Issue 2, Publication No. @18BUL2, p. 61 (2018); *International Chamber of Commerce: Dispute Resolution 2018 Statistics*, Publication No.: 898E, p. 13 (2019); *International Chamber of Commerce: Dispute Resolution 2019 Statistics*, Publication No.: DRS 901, p. 15 (2020); *International Chamber of Commerce: Dispute Resolution 2020 Statistics*, Publication No.: DRS895, p. 17 (2021).
86. Email from International Chamber of Commerce to Jonas Hinrichsen dated 20 January 2023, subject ICC Expedited Arbitration proceedings (copy in author's possession).

most cases, was due to justified circumstances.[87] In 15 cases, parties agreed to a new procedural timetable.[88] In 12 cases, the delay resulted in a fee reduction.[89]

[B] HKIAC

Since the implementation of expedited proceedings rules in 2008, HKIAC has received 153 requests for the administration of cases under the expedited procedures. Of these requests HKIAC has granted 120.[90] Since broadening the circumstances for allowing expedited proceedings in 2013, the HKIAC has seen more users opt for expedited proceedings.[91]

Table 2.4 Number of HKIAC Expedited Procedures (2017-2022) Compared to the Total Number of HKIAC Arbitrations

Year	*Number of Expedited Procedures*	*Total Number of Cases*	*Approximate Ratio to Total (%)*
2017	11	297	3
2018	13	265	4

87. *See also International Chamber of Commerce: Dispute Resolution 2019 Statistics*, Publication No.: DRS 901, p. 16 (2020); *International Chamber of Commerce: Dispute Resolution 2020 Statistics*, Publication No.: DRS895, p. 19 (2021). Decisions on fee reduction and assessments of what qualifies as a delay are made individually, considering the unique circumstances of each case. Examples of justified circumstances include but are not limited to complexity in terms of procedure and/or substance, conduct of the parties, etc. For awards rendered in 2020 and subsequently, delays due to the COVID-19 pandemic were also taken into consideration. Email from International Chamber of Commerce to Jonas Hinrichsen dated September 20, 2023, subject ICC Expedited Arbitration proceedings (copy in author's possession).
88. *International Chamber of Commerce: Dispute Resolution 2018 Statistics*, Publication No.: 898E p. 15 (2019); *International Chamber of Commerce: Dispute Resolution 2019 Statistics*, Publication No.: DRS 901, p. 16 (2020); *International Chamber of Commerce: Dispute Resolution 2020 Statistics*, Publication No.: DRS895, p. 19 (2021).
89. *International Chamber of Commerce: Dispute Resolution 2018 Statistics*, Publication No.: 898E, p. 14 (2019); *International Chamber of Commerce: Dispute Resolution 2019 Statistics*, Publication No.: DRS 901, p. 16 (2020); *International Chamber of Commerce: Dispute Resolution 2020 Statistics*, Publication No.: DRS895, p. 19 (2021) and Email from International Chamber of Commerce to Jonas Hinrichsen dated 20 January 2023, subject ICC Expedited Arbitration proceedings (copy in author's possession).
90. Status until December 31, 2022. As noted in Article 42.1 HKIAC Rules, expedited procedure is only available where the amount in dispute does not exceed the amount set by HKIAC (currently HKD 25 million, approximately worth USD 3.2 million), where the parties agree, or in cases of exceptional urgency. In several matters, HKIAC has declined to grant the expedited procedure when the above criteria have not been met. Even when one of the above criteria is met, HKIAC retains discretion not to grant an application for expedited procedure. This could be on the grounds that other factors in the arbitration militate against granting the expedited procedure (e.g., significant complexity of the case, need for significant witness/expert examination, or other external factors). The HKIAC does not have statistics on which grounds the HKIAC dismissed the 33 requests. Emails from Hong Kong International Arbitration Centre (Eric Ng, Deputy Secretary General) to Jonas Hinrichsen dated January 3 and September 19, 2023, subject HKIAC Expedited Arbitration proceedings (copy in author's possession).
91. HKIAC 2009-2022 statistics, https://www.hkiac.org/about-us/statistics.

Year	*Number of Expedited Procedures*	*Total Number of Cases*	*Approximate Ratio to Total (%)*
2019	16	308	5
2020	24	318	7
2021	20	277	7
2022	16	344	4

Available data from the HKIAC indicates that expedited proceedings are cost-efficient. This is demonstrated in the average costs over almost 10 years, between November 1, 2013 and April 30, 2023, where the average cost of expedited arbitrations was USD 55,932. In contrast, the average cost of HKIAC arbitration (expedited and non-expedited) during that period was USD 161,984. Accordingly, costs of expedited proceedings were 65.5% lower than normal costs.[92]

The HKIAC data also show that expedited proceedings succeed in reducing the duration of arbitral proceedings. Between November 1, 2013 and April 30, 2023, the average duration of expedited arbitration was 9.9 months. The average duration of all HKIAC arbitrations (expedited and non-expedited) during the same period was 17.7 months. Thus, the average duration of arbitrations under expedited procedure was 45% lower than traditional arbitrations.[93] Lastly, between November 1, 2013 and April 30, 2023, the average duration from the time the case file was transferred to the tribunal to the date of issuance of award was 6.1 months.[94]

[C] JCAA

From 2011 to 2022, JCAA data indicate that there were 33 cases where the expedited procedure rules applied. The annual number of expedited proceedings since 2017 shows that with the substantial increase of the upper monetary limit from JPY 50 million to JPY 300 million in 2021, the expedited procedure rules began to apply for a considerably higher number of cases.

92. Issues of comparability between non-expedited and expedited HKIAC arbitrations exist as the cases involved differ in reference values. Cases that are subject to expedited HKIAC arbitrations involve lower amounts in controversy or are not as complex. HKIAC Average Costs and Duration, https://www.hkiac.org/arbitration/costs-duration. Emails from Hong Kong International Arbitration Centre (Eric Ng, Deputy Secretary General) to Jonas Hinrichsen dated January 3, and September 19, 2023, subject HKIAC Expedited Arbitration proceedings (copy in author's possession).
93. Like with the point regarding costs, the authors acknowledge that in relation to duration, the same issues of comparability apply. Cases that are subject to expedited HKIAC arbitrations involve lower amounts in controversy or are not as complex. HKIAC Average Costs and Duration, https://www.hkiac.org/arbitration/costs-duration. Emails from Hong Kong International Arbitration Centre (Eric Ng, Deputy Secretary General) to Jonas Hinrichsen dated January 3 and September 19, 2023, subject HKIAC Expedited Arbitration proceedings (copy in author's possession).
94. HKIAC Average Costs and Duration, https://www.hkiac.org/arbitration/costs-duration.

Table 2.5 Number of JCAA Expedited Procedures Compared to the Total Number of JCAA Arbitrations in the Period 2017-2022

Year	*Number of Expedited Procedures*	*Total Number of Cases*	*Approximately Ratio to Total (%)*
2017	2	14	14
2018	4	13	30
In 2019, the applicable amount in dispute increased from JPY 20 million to JPY 50 million.			
2019	2	9	22
2020	3	18	16
In 2021, the applicable amount in dispute increased from JPY 50 million to JPY 300 million.			
2021	3	15	20
2022	8	19	40

The JCAA does not have conclusive data available for the applicable amount in dispute, and the calculation formula for the tribunal fees has been changed several times over the past few years. However, the JCAA confirmed that expedited proceedings have generally resulted overall in lower costs because parties usually agreed to refrain from having document production and that tribunals could decide the case based on documents only or at least have a hearing of only one day.[95]

According to the JCAA, expedited proceedings reduce the duration of arbitral proceedings. While from 2011 to 2020, the average duration of regular arbitral proceedings with an amount in dispute between JPY 50 million to JPY 300 million was 11.03 months, the average duration of disputes with a similar amount in dispute falling under the widened scope of expedited proceedings in 2021-2022 was 7.2 months.[96]

The timely resolution of expedited proceedings depends on the tribunal rendering a final award within the set time frame. Based on available data, overall, tribunals have successfully adhered to the rule that an award must be rendered six months from the date the tribunal was constituted.[97] Of all expedited proceedings since 2011, more than 70% were decided within the prescribed time frame. The remainder were extended either by party agreement or by the JCAA's decision, with none of the extensions exceeding three months.[98]

95. Emails from The Japan Commercial Arbitration Association (Takumi Ishizuka) to Jonas Hinrichsen dated March 17 and September 20, 2023, subject JCAA Expedited Arbitration proceedings (copy in author's possession).
96. *Ibid.*
97. Article 88.1 JCAA Rules. If the amount in dispute is JPY 50 million or less, the arbitral tribunal shall make reasonable efforts to render an arbitral award within three months from the date when it is constituted.
98. Emails from The Japan Commercial Arbitration Association (Takumi Ishizuka) to Jonas Hinrichsen dated March 17 and September 20, 2023, subject JCAA Expedited Arbitration proceedings (copy in author's possession).

[D] SCC

Since the introduction of the SCC expedited arbitration rules in 1995, the approximate average number of expedited cases amounted to roughly 30% of the SCC caseload.[99] The SCC Rules require a tribunal to render a final award within three months after the case was referred to the arbitrator. SCC statistics show that more than half of the awards rendered under the SCC Rules for expedited arbitration in 2017 were rendered within three months. A large portion of the remaining cases were resolved within six months.[100]

Table 2.6 Number of SCC Expedited Procedures (2017-2022) Compared to the Total Number of SCC Caseload

Year	*Number of Expedited Procedures*	*Total Number of Cases*	*Approximately Ratio to Total (%)*
2017	72	200	36
2018	52	152	34
2019	52	175	30
2020	67	213	31
2021	43	165	30
2022	44	143	31

99. SCC Arbitration Institute: SCC Statistics 2022, https://sccarbitrationinstitute.se/en/about-scc/scc-statistics#:~:text=In%202022%2C%20the%20SCC%20registered,all%20parties%20must%20be%20Swedish; SCC Arbitration Institute: SCC Statistics 2021, p. 2, https://sccarbitrationinstitute.se/sites/default/files/2023-02/scc-statistics-2021.pdf; SCC Arbitration Institute: SCC Statistics 2020, p. 2, https://sccarbitrationinstitute.se/sites/default/files/2022-11/statistics-scc-2020.pdf; SCC Arbitration Institute: SCC Statistics 2019, p. 2 https://sccarbitrationinstitute.se/sites/default/files/2022-11/statistics-2019.pdf; SCC Arbitration Institute: SCC Statistics 2018, p. 2, https://sccarbitrationinstitute.se/sites/default/files/2022-11/statistics-2018.pdf; and SCC Arbitration Institute: SCC Statistics 2017, p. 2, https://sccarbitrationinstitute.se/sites/default/files/2022-11/statistics-2017.pdf.

100. More than half of the awards rendered under the SCC Rules for expedited arbitration in 2017 were rendered within three months. The vast majority of awards were rendered within six months (SCC Arbitration Institute, SCC Statistics 2017, p. 6). In 2018, 61% of the awards rendered under the SCC Rules for expedited arbitration were delivered within three months after referral. Another 37% of the awards were rendered within three to six months, and all awards were rendered within nine months of referral (SCC Arbitration Institute, SCC Statistics 2018, p. 6). More than 50% of the awards rendered under the SCC Rules for expedited arbitration in 2019 were rendered within three months from referral. Another 45% of the awards were rendered within three to six months (SCC Arbitration Institute, SCC Statistics 2019, p. 4). In 2020, 40% of the awards rendered under the SCC Rules were rendered within six months from when the case was referred to the arbitrator or tribunal. Another 42% of the awards were rendered between 6 and 12 months from the date of referral (SCC Arbitration Institute, SCC Statistics 2020, p. 5). Sixty percent of the awards rendered under the SCC Rules for expedited arbitration in 2021 were rendered within three months from referral. Another 29% of the awards were rendered between three and six months from referral (SCC Arbitration Institute, SCC Statistics 2021, p. 4). In 2022, in 20% of the SCC expedited proceedings, an award was rendered within the first three months after referral. Another 64% were concluded within six months (SCC Arbitration Institute, SCC Statistics 2022).

[E] SAC

SAC confirmed that since the expedited procedure provisions were introduced in the Swiss Rules in 2004, 620 arbitrations were conducted under them.[101] This number constitutes 40% of the total caseload between 2004 and 2022. In the last couple of years, the number of expedited proceedings was slightly below average. While in 2019 the number still constituted 43% of the total caseload, in 2020 it was only 32%; in 2021, it was 35%; and in 2022, it was 35%.[102]

The application of expedited procedure provisions under the Swiss Rules does not per se result in lower fees. However, expedited procedure provides for several features which can lead to overall lower costs. For example, if the arbitration agreement provides for an arbitral tribunal composed of more than one arbitrator, the SAC Secretariat invites the parties to agree to a sole arbitrator.[103] After the submission of the answer to the notice of arbitration, the parties are in principle entitled to submit only one round of submissions.[104] The dispute should, in principle, be decided on documentary evidence only. Otherwise, only one hearing will be held for the examination of witnesses and experts or for oral argument.[105] The tribunal may state the reasons upon which the award is based in summary form.[106]

According to the SAC, expedited proceedings succeed in reducing the duration of arbitration. Although the tribunal may extend the time limit, in most of the cases, the award is rendered within six months from the submission of the file to the tribunal.[107]

In practice, institutions have noted mostly similar challenges. The application of the expedited procedure provisions requires an effort from the parties to timely file their submissions as well as from the arbitral tribunal to render the award within a short amount of time. Interferences, such as changes in party representation, requests for bifurcation of proceedings, or unforeseen developments in the arbitral procedure, may be difficult to reconcile with the application of the expedited procedure rules. However, most institutions provide that the expedited procedure rules may no longer apply on the motion of the tribunal or upon the request of a party. Thereafter, the arbitration would continue under the regular rules. In such cases, the same arbitral tribunal may remain in place.[108]

---

101. Email from the Swiss Arbitration Centre (Lukas Innerebner) to Jonas Hinrichsen dated January 18, 2023, subject ASA Expedited Arbitration proceedings (copy in author's possession).
102. Swiss Arbitration Centre, Statistics 2019, p. 1, https://www.swissarbitration.org/wp-content/uploads/2021/08/SCAI-Stats-2019_PDF_v20200609_for-publication.pdf and Swiss Arbitration Centre, Statistics 2020, p. 1, https://www.swissarbitration.org/wp-content/uploads/2021/10/SCAI-Stat-2020_for-publication-on-website-and-other-presentations-1.pdf.
103. Article 42(2)(b) Swiss Rules.
104. Article 42(2)(c) Swiss Rules.
105. Article 42(2)(d) Swiss Rules.
106. Article 42(2)(f) Swiss Rules.
107. Article 42(2)(e) Swiss Rules. Email from the Swiss Arbitration Centre (Lukas Innerebner, Legal Counsel) to Jonas Hinrichsen dated January 18, 2023, subject ASA Expedited Arbitration proceedings (copy in author's possession).
108. For example, Article 1.4 Appendix VI ICC Rules, Rule 5.4 SIAC Rules, Article 42.3 HKIAC Rules.

[F] Summary of Findings from Practice

In each institution, expedited procedure rules have been consistently used since their introduction. For the ICC, JCAA, SCC and SAC, expedited proceedings constituted approximately a third of the overall caseload. While most institutions did not experience a significant influx of expedited arbitration proceedings compared to traditional arbitration proceedings, the scope of most rules relating to expedited proceedings has widened over time, meaning more and more cases will likely by default fall under the expedited proceeding regimes.

While only the HKIAC could confirm with conclusive data that expedited proceedings result in lower costs,[109] institutions generally indicated that costs are lower than in regular proceedings. Parties usually refrain from further procedural phases that tend to be lengthier and thus contribute to higher costs to parties, for example, with second or third rounds of written submissions or document production. In most expedited cases, a sole arbitrator is appointed or the case is decided based only on documents.

All institutions confirmed that expedited proceedings reduce the duration of arbitral proceedings.[110] Most final awards have been rendered within a time frame of three to six months after the case management conference (under ICC and DIS Rules) or after the case was referred to the arbitrator (in the case of the SIAC, HKIAC, JCAA, SCC and Swiss Rules).

§2.04 NAVIGATING A POTENTIAL CLASH OF PRINCIPLES

The expedited arbitration process is designed to achieve a prompt and cost-effective resolution by expediting and simplifying key aspects of the proceedings. Various strategies may be implemented to enhance efficiency and hasten the arbitral process, such as imposing strict time limits for the arbitral tribunal by parties or rules with regard to the overall duration of the proceedings.[111] Most expedited arbitration rules have established a deadline for the issuance of the arbitral award by the tribunal. This deadline may range from 30 days to nine months, depending on the set of rules. The starting date may vary

109. Email from Hong Kong International Arbitration Centre (Eric Ng, Deputy Secretary General) to Jonas Hinrichsen dated January 3, 2023, subject HKIAC Expedited Arbitration proceedings (copy in author's possession).
110. Email from International Chamber of Commerce to Jonas Hinrichsen dated January 20, 2023, subject ICC Expedited Arbitration proceedings (copy in author's possession). Email from The Japan Commercial Arbitration Association (Takumi Ishizuka) to Jonas Hinrichsen dated March 17, 2023, subject JCAA Expedited Arbitration proceedings (copy in author's possession). Email from the SCC Arbitration Centre (Natalia Petrik, Deputy Secretary General) to Jonas Hinrichsen dated January 9, 2023, subject SCC Expedited Arbitration proceedings (copy in author's possession). Email from Hong Kong International Arbitration Centre (Eric Ng, Deputy Secretary General) to Jonas Hinrichsen dated January 3, 2023, subject HKIAC Expedited Arbitration proceedings (copy in author's possession). Email from the Swiss Arbitration Centre (Lukas Innerebner, Legal Counsel) to Jonas Hinrichsen dated January 18, 2023, subject ASA Expedited Arbitration proceedings (copy in author's possession).
111. Banifatemi, *supra* n. 4.

from the constitution of the arbitral tribunal to transmission of the case to the tribunal, case management conference, final written submission or hearing.

The use of shorter time frames is a distinctive hallmark of expedited arbitration proceedings. In order to promote the prompt resolution of disputes and align the expectations of the parties, expedited arbitration rules establish a deadline for the rendering of the final award. In addition, in certain situations, the parties may negotiate and agree upon mutually acceptable time limits for completion of the proceeding.[112]

However, the establishment of time limits raises questions concerning the enforceability of the final award in the event of noncompliance of the tribunal with the time limits.[113] The implementation of time limits for greater efficiency can sometimes result in restrictions on the arbitral tribunal's general authority to conduct proceedings as they see appropriate.[114] While expedited procedures often feature stricter timelines, the discretion of the arbitral tribunal in conducting the arbitration for the sake of flexibility should be preserved.[115] Limiting changes to time limits solely by the way of parties' agreement could hinder swift responses to changes during the proceeding by the tribunal.[116]

Differing views on the arbitral tribunal's power to modify procedural rules exist. Some argue that the arbitral tribunal has the inherent discretion to alter any time frame established by the expedited arbitration rules or the parties' agreement. Others believe that it may not be appropriate to allow the arbitral tribunal to modify the time limits set forth by the rules or the parties.[117]

Setting time limits in expedited arbitration can restore speed as an advantage while leading to challenges because of its potential conflicts with the procedural discretion of tribunal. This involves potential challenges that may arise out of the enforcement of awards.

[A] Consequences for Enforceability

Arbitration is rooted in the freedom of choice and autonomy of parties.[118] This autonomous nature sets arbitration apart from traditional court litigation and gives the

112. Meha Tandon & Aditya Singh, *Time-Bound Arbitrations: A Word of Caution*, Spain Arbitration Review | Revista del Club Español del Arbitraje, vol. 2029, 175 (2020).
113. *See X. AG v. Z.*, BGE/ATF 140 III 75, 4A 490/2013, January 28, 2014.
114. For example, Article 19, 22(2) ICC Rules, Article 15(1) Swiss Rules, Article 24.1 DIS Rules, Article 13.1 HKIAC Rules, Rule 16.1 SIAC Rules.
115. United Nations Commission on International Trade Law, *Report of Working Group II (Dispute Settlement) on the work of its seventieth session* (Vienna, September 23-27, 2019), at 12.
116. Karl-Heinz Böckstiegel, *Case Management by Arbitrators: Experiences and Suggestions* in Aksen/Böckstigel et al., International Law, Commerce and Dispute Resolution: Liber Amicorum in Honour of Robert Briner 120-121 (International Chamber of Commerce (ICC) 2005).
117. United Nations Commission on International Trade Law, *Report of Working Group II (Dispute Settlement) on the work of its sixty-ninth session* (New York, February 4-8, 2019), at 9; Daniel Girsberger & Nathalie Voser, International Arbitration: Comparative and Swiss Perspectives para. 963 (3rd ed., Schulthess Juristische Medien AG 2016); Klaus Sachs & Tom Christopher Pröstler, *Time Limits in International Arbitral Proceedings*, 280 (Patricia Louise Shaughnessy, Sherlin Tung eds., Kluwer Law International 2017).
118. Redfern & Hunter, *supra* n. 2, p. 605.

parties the ability to determine the procedural framework and the rules that govern the process. As a result, arbitration agreements are viewed as the primary means by which decision-making powers are granted to arbitrators.[119] Alongside its basis in freedom of choice and autonomy, arbitration tribunals do not exist or exercise their powers in a vacuum. They do possess reasonable inherent, implied, and/or discretionary powers to conduct the proceeding efficiently.[120]

Arbitration is also intended to reach a binding decision regarding the dispute that is enforceable to the extent possible.[121] In the case of expedited or fast-track proceedings, instances may exist where principles of arbitration may come into conflict, namely, extension of time limits by the tribunal. As a result, in the enforcement stage, national courts may closely scrutinize the proceedings to ensure that the fundamental principles have not been violated.[122] National courts typically apply the relevant regime governing the recognition and enforcement of foreign arbitral awards. The most prominent instrument is the New York Convention on the Recognition and Enforcement of Foreign Arbitral Awards (1958). This convention is widely considered as the primary instrument for recognition and enforcement of arbitral awards and approximately 75% of its signatories align their national laws with its principles.[123]

The provisions of Article 5 of the New York Convention hold significant relevance for the enforceability of arbitral awards. This article provides that the recognition or enforcement of an arbitral award may be denied on the following grounds: (i) lack of capacity of the parties to enter into an arbitration agreement; (ii) invalidity, expiration, or unenforceability of the arbitration agreement; (iii) the tribunal exceeds its mandate and/or rules *ultra petita*; (iv) improper composition of the tribunal or noncompliance of the proceedings with the arbitration agreement or applicable law; (v) nonfinality of the award or its suspension or setting aside at the place of arbitration; (vi) nonarbitrability of the dispute; or (vii) contradiction with public policy.[124]

In the time-framed arbitration process, the potential for refusal of recognition and enforcement of a final award can significantly be heightened when the time limits lapse without being legally and validly extended.[125] The New York Convention, as detailed in Article V(1)(a) and (d), provides grounds for refusing recognition and enforcement if the award was issued beyond the *ratione temporis* jurisdiction of the arbitral tribunal. This could signify either the expiration or absence of the arbitration agreement or a

---

119. Mohamed S. Abdel Wahab, *Expedited Institutional Arbitral Proceedings Between Autonomy and Regulation*, 135 (Laurent Lévy & Michael Polkinghorne eds., International Chamber of Commerce (ICC) 2017).
120. International Law Association (ILA), *ILA Report on Inherent and Implied Powers of International Arbitral Tribunals (2014)* and *ILA Resolution No.4/2016 on the Inherent and Implied Powers of International Arbitral Tribunals (2016)*.
121. Redfern & Hunter, *supra* n. 2, p. 605.
122. Abdel Wahab, *supra* n. 119, p. 136.
123. New York Convention: Contracting States available at: http://www.newyorkconvention.org/countries.
124. Article 5 the New York Convention on the Recognition and Enforcement of Foreign Arbitral Awards.
125. Gary Born, *International Commercial Arbitration vol. III* para. 25.04 (Kluwer Law International 2nd ed., 2014).

deviation of the tribunal from the parties' agreement and institutional rules in the conduct of the proceedings, namely noncompliance with time limits.[126] A delicate balance in the interplay between time limits and the procedural power of tribunal is necessary. Different expedited rules offer mechanisms to mitigate this risk.

[B] Expedited Arbitration Proceeding and Restraint of Tribunal Power: The Right Balance Between Speed and Flexibility

The relationship between the power of the arbitral tribunal and the need for expedited proceedings is complex and multifaceted. The principle of party autonomy is fundamental to the arbitration process. However, this principle often conflicts with the general power of the tribunal when it comes to the time-framed arbitration process.[127] At the same time, the power of the arbitral tribunal to conduct proceedings as it sees appropriate is a widely recognized principle and is endorsed by both national and international laws and institutions. This power is essential to the functioning of the arbitration process, as it allows the tribunal to adapt to the unique circumstances of each case and to make decisions that are in the best interests of the parties.[128]

The appropriate duration of arbitration is contingent upon several factors, such as the number and complexity of issues at hand, the necessity and intricacy of discovery or disclosure, the length of any hearing, and the availability of the parties, the tribunal, and counsels.[129] In addition, extensive evidence may need to be presented before the tribunal to determine the complexity of a dispute, resulting in time expended during the proceedings.[130] Accurately estimating the amount of time required for a proceeding can be challenging because it entails a number of factors that are not always easy to anticipate or measure. Therefore, time limits should maintain flexibility, allowing tribunals to make adjustments when they deem it necessary.

Imposing time limits in expedited proceedings is a response to the parties' desire for a more efficient and streamlined arbitration process. When the parties specify a time limit or which expedited rules are to be applied to their dispute, they are expressing their mutual will and intent regarding the conduct of the arbitration. The principle of party autonomy requires that this expressed intent be respected, subject only to exceptional circumstances. The New York Convention requires respect for the parties' choice of procedural provisions, and in cases where this choice is not respected, an arbitral award may be denied enforcement in the courts.[131]

The parties' express choice of time limits or deadlines specified in the expedited arbitration rules should take precedence over the general power of the tribunal. In such

126. Abdel Wahab, *supra* n. 119, p. 149; *see also* note 113.
127. Sachs, Pröstler, *supra* n. 117, pp. 281-282.
128. *Ibid.*
129. Born, *supra* n. 125, p. 2239.
130. Sanjeevi Seshadri, *Section 29A of the New Indian Arbitration Act—An Attempt at Slaying Hydra*, Kluwer Arb. Blog (February 2, 2016).
131. Born, *supra* n. 125, p. 375.

cases, it does not have any power to extend deadlines. Accordingly, disregarding the time limits could be characterized as a violation of the principle of party autonomy, and this could threaten the enforceability of the award.[132] This is particularly problematic in light of the tribunal's duty to determine the parties' common intent and give effect to that intent.[133]

However, lack of flexibility in procedural time limits presents a significant challenge in the administration of arbitrations, particularly in situations where modifications to such limits become necessary. Unlike other procedural rules that may be readily modified, time limits require greater flexibility due to the dynamic nature of disputes and the changing needs of parties.[134] If the tribunal lacks any power to amend the time limits and amendments are solely dependent on party agreement, the ability to respond quickly to changing circumstances will be hindered, and parties with an interest in stalling the arbitration process would be further empowered.[135] This undesirable consequence would be at odds with the primary objective of arbitration, which is to resolve disputes in an efficient and effective manner.

While parties typically have an expectation of a timely and expeditious resolution, it is generally not the intention of parties to prevent tribunals from modifying time limits.[136] Thus, in the absence of any explicit indication to the contrary, it can be inferred that parties, when agreeing upon time limits directly or application of a set of expedited rules, do not intend to preclude tribunals from subsequently modifying such time limits, as and when circumstances may necessitate. In other words, in the interest of ensuring effective resolution of disputes, tribunals should have the necessary power to modify time limits throughout the course of an arbitration, subject to any express agreement to the contrary.[137]

Thus, the issue of time limits in expedited arbitration is a multifaceted problem that requires a delicate balancing act. Tribunals possess general powers that must be respected to ensure a fair and just arbitration process. However, parties may desire expedited proceedings in order to achieve a timely resolution of their dispute and an enforceable award. Achieving this balance requires a nuanced understanding of the relationship between the two and the ability to reconcile conflicting demands. In order to analyze solutions adopted by expedited arbitration rules, institutional arbitration and ad hoc arbitration must be distinguished because institutions play a crucial role in supervising the procedure, ensuring the compliance of the tribunal with time limits and any extensions that may be necessary.

132. Borris/Hennecke, *Article V* in Wolff (ed.) paras. 232-233 (New York Convention: Commentary 2012).
133. Julian D.M. Lew et al., *Comparative International Commercial Arbitration*, 412 (Wolters Kluwer 2003).
134. Böckstiegel, *supra* n. 116.
135. *Ibid.*
136. Sachs, Pröstler, *supra* n. 117, p. 282.
137. Girsberger, Voser, *supra* n. 117.

[1] Institutional Arbitration

Most arbitral institutions have established rules and procedures for the extension of time limits and may also have the power to intervene in cases where time limits are not being met. For example, the ICC Rules expressly provide in Article 4.1, "The time limit within which the arbitral tribunal must render its final award is six months from the date of the case management conference. The ICC Court may extend the time limit pursuant to Article 31(2) of the ICC Rules."[138] Likewise, the HKIAC Rules expressly stipulate in Article 42.2(f):

> When HKIAC, after considering the views of the parties, grants an application made pursuant to Article 42.1, the arbitral proceedings shall be conducted in accordance with an Expedited Procedure based upon the foregoing provisions of these Rules, subject to the following changes:
>
> ...
>
> f. subject to any lien, the award shall be made within six months from the date when HKIAC transmitted the file to the arbitral tribunal. In exceptional circumstances, HKIAC may extend this time limit.[139]

The SIAC Rules expressly state in Article 5.2:

> Where a party has filed an application with the Registrar under Rule 5.1, and where the President determines, after considering the views of the parties, and having regard to the circumstances of the case, that the arbitral proceedings shall be conducted in accordance with the Expedited Procedure, the following procedure shall apply:
>
> ...
>
> d. the final Award shall be made within six months from the date when the tribunal is constituted unless, in exceptional circumstances, the Registrar extends the time for making such final Award.[140]

And, finally, the SCC Rules provide in Article 43:

> The final award shall be made no later than three months from the date the case was referred to the Arbitrator pursuant to Article 23. The Board may extend this time limit upon a reasoned request from the Arbitrator, or if otherwise deemed necessary, having due regard to the expedited nature of the proceedings.[141]

The time frame for delivering the final award in expedited proceedings typically falls between three and six months.[142] Nevertheless, procedural complexities or obstacles arising from ancillary disputes related to language, jurisdiction, arbitrator challenges, among others, may make it challenging to adhere to the three- to six-month time limit. Moreover, the low value of the disputed claim(s) in expedited proceedings

138. Article 4.15 Appendix VI ICC Rules.
139. Article 42.2(f) HKIAC Rules.
140. Rule 5.2 SIAC Rules.
141. Article 43 SCC Rules.
142. *See also* §3.03 above.

does not necessarily correlate with a higher likelihood of deciding the case in a shorter period of time. In some instances, low-value claims may be highly litigious and may even require the same or more time to resolve than high-value claims. Indeed, in certain cases, a three-month time limit, as stipulated by some institutions, may be deemed impracticable given the inherent intricacies and nuances of arbitration.

To mitigate the potential risk of unenforceability of awards, institutions provide a caveat that allows for time limits to be extended if warranted by the circumstances and a reasoned application is submitted. However, all extensions are assessed considering the expedited nature of the proceedings.[143] As a result, the regulations explicitly authorize the institutions' bodies and not the tribunal to extend time limits stipulated in their rules or any time limit agreed upon by the parties, except for the DIS rules, which empower the tribunal itself to extend the time limits.[144]

The effectiveness of not giving the tribunal the discretion to extend time limits in practice can be subject to scrutiny. In other words, in the event of noncompliance by an arbitral tribunal, institutions are presented with two options: reject or accept the extension request by the tribunal. While the former may be deemed effective due to its severity, it is likely to have a more significant impact on the parties, especially the successful one, than the dilatory tribunal. Additionally, rejecting the extension may undermine the parties' primary objective of resolving disputes via arbitration because the procedure will be concluded without an award. Thus, institutions, when making their decision, must consider the parties' interest in obtaining a binding resolution and weigh it against their interest in adhering to the relevant time limits. This is why, in most cases, institutions have found in favor of the former and have granted the extension.

At the same time, granting the extension request runs contrary to the nature and objectives of expedited proceedings because it permits tribunals to prolong the proceedings for days, weeks, or even months. Hence, even though the tribunal lacks the direction to extend the time limits, it may do so indirectly by requesting the institutions to grant an extension because the institutions do not have any alternative except to approve the request.

To incentivize the tribunal to adhere to time limits and complete proceedings within the designated time frame, several institutions have introduced two primary measures: (1) replacing arbitrators and (2) reducing tribunal fees. Some institution's rules allow for the replacement of arbitrators who cause undue delays or fail to fulfill their duties within specified time limits.[145] The rules differ in their wording, with some simply stating that arbitrators can be removed for "failing to act," while others are more explicit about "acting without undue delay" or fulfilling their "functions within prescribed time limits." Some arbitration rules, such as those of the ICC, Swiss, and SIAC, grant institutions an authority to remove dilatory arbitrators independently. In

143. Abdel Wahab, *supra* n. 119, p. 148.
144. Article 5 Annex 4 DIS Rules.
145. Article 15(2) ICC Rules, Article 12(1) Swiss Rules, Article 19.1 DIS Rules, Article 11.6 HKIAC Rules, Rule 14.2 SIAC Rules.

contrast, rules like the DIS and HKIAC require a party to initiate a challenge process against the dilatory arbitrator.

Nevertheless, when an arbitrator is replaced, certain procedural steps need to be repeated to allow the new arbitrator to form its own perspective on the case. This is especially relevant for oral hearings and witness examinations. Thus, replacing dilatory arbitrators can lead to significant delays and additional costs. However, it can be a practical choice in situations where no procedural steps need repetition (e.g., when only written submissions were exchanged) or when the expected future delay caused by the dilatory arbitrator would exceed the time required to redo the relevant procedural steps. Further, in some cases, repetition can be avoided by concluding the arbitration with a truncated tribunal.[146]

As an alternative sanction, there is a possibility to reduce the fees of delayed tribunals, but this hinges on having the right rules and mechanisms in place. In ICC arbitration, tribunal fees are determined at the end of proceedings by the ICC Court. This power has been traditionally used by the ICC Court to penalize tribunals that cause unnecessary delays.[147] Similarly, under the SCC Rules, the SCC Board of Directors will establish the fee of the tribunal, taking into account the dispute's monetary value, and it retains the capacity to modify arbitrators' fees in exceptional situations.[148]

However, most other institutions do not follow similar practices. In many cases, tribunal fees are determined at the outset, often based on the dispute's value or an hourly rate for arbitrators. Many arbitration rules leave the final determination of fees to the discretion of the tribunals.[149] Even if institutions are involved in determining tribunal fees, they rarely have the authority to reduce them. For example, under the SIAC Rules, the Registrar is able to increase the fees of tribunals under exceptional circumstances, but there is no authority for fee reduction.[150] Similarly, the HKIAC can increase tribunal fees under its rules but lacks the power to reduce them.[151] The Swiss Rules allow tribunals to increase their fees with the SAC Arbitration Court approval under certain conditions but do not provide for a fee reduction.[152]

[2] Ad Hoc Arbitration

In ad hoc arbitration, the responsibility to extend time limits typically falls upon the parties themselves, the arbitral tribunal, the appointing authority, or local authorities. An extension should be granted if the parties agree on the matter.[153] However, there is

146. Sachs, Pröstler, *supra* n. 117, p. 291.
147. Article 37(2) ICC Rules; Moss, Fry, Greenberg, Mazza, *The Secretariat's Guide to ICC Arbitration*, 3-1454-3-1457 (International Chamber of Commerce (ICC) 2012).
148. Article 2 Appendix IV the SCC Rules.
149. *See, e.g.*, Article 38(a) Swiss Rules, Article 40.2 DIS Rules.
150. Rule 32 SIAC Rules.
151. Article 10.3(c) HKIAC Rules.
152. Article 38(a) and section 2.3 Annex B the Swiss Rules.
153. United Nations Commission on International Trade Law, *Report of Working Group II (Dispute Settlement) on the work of its sixty-ninth session* (New York, February 4-8, 2019), at 9.

a level of uncertainty surrounding the arbitral tribunal's authority to extend time limits in the event of a failure to reach an agreement between the parties.

Article 16(1) of the UNCITRAL Expedited Arbitration Rules sets out a clear requirement that the tribunal must issue its award within six months from the date of its constitution. The parties may agree to a different time limit for the issuance of the award. However, under Article 16(2), the tribunal is permitted to extend the six-month time limit or other time limit agreed by parties but only in exceptional circumstances and after consulting with the parties. This extension must not exceed a total of nine months from the date of the tribunal's constitution.

In situations where the tribunal anticipates it may not be able to issue the award within nine months, Article 16(3) mandates that the tribunal must propose a final extended time limit to the parties, providing reasons for the extension sought. This extension can only be implemented with the consent of all parties. If no agreement is reached, Article 16(4) permits a party to request that the arbitration continues under the revised UNCITRAL Rules, thereby terminating the application of the expedited rules.[154]

This article aims to enhance procedural efficiency by motivating tribunals to expedite proceedings and prepare awards within an appropriate time frame. However, the efficacy of such time limits in achieving their intended purpose is not always straightforward, and two main points warrant consideration.

First, there is the discretion afforded to tribunals in determining what qualifies as "exceptional circumstances." This lack of clarity may result in inconsistent and subjective interpretations, which could potentially undermine the intended efficiency gains. Moreover, Article 16(2) does not impose an obligation on the tribunal to furnish reasons for extending the time limit set out in Article 16(1). The tribunal should generally indicate the reasons when extending time limits. This aims to grant the tribunal greater flexibility, especially in situations where a brief extension of time is deemed necessary.[155] Therefore, the absence of a requirement for tribunals to provide reasons for extending the time limit arguably enables decisions to be made without proper justification and puts less pressure on the tribunal compared to when the tribunal must provide reasons for the extension.

Second, there is the absence of direct remedies to enforce the time limits or impose sanctions on tribunals that fail to comply with them. An indirect remedy exists in the form of the arbitration cost review mechanism outlined in Article 41 of the UNCITRAL Arbitration Rules. According to this article, the arbitral tribunal determines its fees at the end of the proceeding.[156]

Subsequently, if the parties have chosen an appointing authority, they can request a review of the tribunal's determination of the costs by the appointing authority. If the parties have not designated an appointing authority or if the appointed authority does not take action within 45 days, the Secretary General of the Permanent

154. Byron Perez, *The UNCITRAL Expedited Arbitration Rules 2021*, Asian Dispute Review, 189 (2021).
155. Draft Explanatory Note to the UNCITRAL Expedited Arbitration Rules July 28, 2021, para. 85.
156. Article 41 UNCITRAL Arbitration Rules.

Court of Arbitration may step in to conduct the review. During this review, if the appointing authority or the Secretary General of the Permanent Court of Arbitration determines that the arbitral tribunal's assessment is inconsistent with its initial fee proposal or is unreasonably high, they have the authority to make necessary adjustments. These adjustments then become binding on the arbitral tribunal.[157]

Nonetheless, this mechanism primarily focuses on the review and adjustment of arbitration costs. While it can indirectly influence the behavior of tribunals by affecting their financial interests, it does not directly address the issue of time limits or delays in the arbitration process. It is primarily a financial remedy and may not effectively incentivize tribunals to speed up proceedings and respect time limits. Tribunals may be willing to accept cost adjustments as a consequence of delays, especially if they believe the delays are justified.

Therefore, while the psychological impact of deadlines as well as potential financial repercussions may motivate tribunals to expedite proceedings, the absence of effective punishment, such as replacement of arbitrators, means that there are no tangible consequences for failing to adhere to the rules. In some cases, this could lead to a scenario where the rules become aspirational guidelines rather than effective tools for enhancing efficiency. Thus, while time limits have been widely recognized as an effective means of streamlining arbitration proceedings, their effectiveness in practice can depend on a number of factors, including the degree of collaboration and good faith exhibited by all parties involved in the process.

§2.05 CONCLUSION

Expedited arbitration proceedings have emerged as a viable solution to address the inefficiencies inherent in traditional international arbitration, particularly with regard to time and costs. Empirical data from major arbitral institutions indicates that expedited proceedings have been consistently utilized since their introduction, with a substantial portion of cases falling under the expedited process regimes. Expedited proceedings apparently are associated with lower costs compared to regular proceedings and a reduction in the duration of arbitral proceedings, with most final awards rendered within a relatively short time frame.

Time limits play a crucial role in expediting the arbitration process. However, their effectiveness is contingent upon flexibility and adherence to certain principles. Flexibility in time limits is essential to account for the unique nature of each arbitration and the potential changes in parties' attitudes as the proceedings progress. Unamendable time limits may hinder the smooth progress of proceedings and may not adequately consider the nuances of a case. Moreover, time limits should strike a balance between allowing sufficient time for procedural steps and avoiding unnecessary delays caused by slack or proliferation.

157. Anne-Carole Cremades & Alexandre Mazuranic, *International Arbitration in Switzerland: A Handbook for Practitioners*, Chapter 9: Costs in Arbitration, 189-190 (Elliott Geisinger and Nathalie Voser eds., Kluwer Law International 2nd ed. 2013).

Arbitral institutions should continue to innovate and implement strategies to enhance the speed and efficiency of arbitrations, even if those strategies have been developed by others. In the context of ad hoc arbitration, tribunals should exercise their discretion to extend time limits, ensuring that such extensions are justified and not abused to unduly prolong the process.

Parties also play a crucial role in upholding time limits by actively cooperating with tribunals, establishing reasonable and concise procedural timetables, showing restraint in requesting extensions, and holding their counsel accountable for adhering to time limits. A collaborative approach between parties and tribunals, along with a commitment to efficient and timely proceedings, can significantly contribute to the success of expedited arbitration and enhance the overall effectiveness of the full arbitration process.

CHAPTER 3

Stopping the Arms Race: Page Limits in International Arbitration

Joshua B. Simmons & Natalia Szlarb

Expedited arbitration seeks to contain the costs and delays of proceedings. While most expedited arbitration rules establish ambitious time frames and deadlines, they often fail to implement adequate mechanisms to ensure efficiency. The most straightforward solution to the problem has proven elusive in practice: page limits on written submissions. After a dispute arises, parties and their counsel typically have misaligned incentives that prevent agreement on page limits, but a comparative study of judicial systems confirms the reasonableness of such limits. Arbitration rules should establish presumptions of page limits to make expedited arbitration a reality rather than an objective that remains out of reach.

§3.01 INTRODUCTION

In 2021, a leading international arbitration survey revealed a watershed development in the field. The survey asked hundreds of private practitioners, arbitrators, and party representatives which 'procedural options [they] would be willing to do without if this would make your arbitration faster or cheaper'? The answer was clear and decisive, as the responders chose only one option by majority: 'unlimited length of written submissions'.[1] Notably, a decade ago, the same survey reported that a majority of responders *opposed* or were unsure about imposing page limits.[2] Moreover, while 61%

1. 2021 International Arbitration Survey, Current Choices and Future Adaptations, White & Case LLP (2021), https://www.whitecase.com/publications/insight/2021-international-arbitration-survey/current-choices-future-adaptations.
2. 2012 International Arbitration Survey, White & Case LLP (2012) https://arbitration.qmul.ac.uk/media/arbitration/docs/2012_International_Arbitration_Survey.pdf.

of responders now support page limits, the next option for enhancing efficiency ('oral hearings on procedural issues') received a far lower percentage of votes at 38%. In other words, of all the ways to expedite arbitration, a significant majority of parties and counsel are willing to accept page limits but are not willing to give up any other procedural flexibility.

Despite that consensus, page limits remain the exception rather than the norm in international arbitration. Even most expedited arbitration rules fall short of the mark. For example, the UNCITRAL Expedited Arbitration Rules establish the aspirational goal that '[t]he award shall be made within six months from the date of the constitution of the arbitral tribunal unless otherwise agreed by the parties'.[3] However, the same Expedited Arbitration Rules, like most other arbitral rules, do not impose sufficient mechanisms to contain the parties' submissions and thus the proceedings. A diligent arbitral tribunal 'shall conduct the proceedings expeditiously',[4] but parties can derail such efforts with voluminous submissions. Thus, the goal of expedited (or even efficient) arbitration proceedings could ring hollow without adequate steps to ensure that the proceedings will be capable of resolution in a limited time frame.

The time has come for expedited arbitration rules – as potential trailblazers of efficiency – to put the emerging consensus on page limits into practice. After a dispute arises, the parties and their counsel typically have misaligned incentives that prevent agreement on page limits. Indeed, when the stakes are high, there is frequently an arms race of escalating submissions of hundreds of pages. Such lengthy tomes not only exacerbate delays and costs but may also undermine the legitimacy of arbitration because they fail to distil key issues and thus dilute the effectiveness of arbitrators' decision-making.

Page limits, of course, are not a novel idea. This chapter presents a comparative study of limits established in national and international judicial systems, which provide an important context for arbitral institutions. Based on those benchmarks, we propose that arbitration rules – and certainly expedited arbitration rules – should establish presumptions of page limits. Such presumptive limits are neutral between parties and would help ensure equality of arms and efficient proceedings. As with cost tables, arbitration rules can adopt scalable methods to accommodate the size and complexity of disputes, including unique considerations in investor-state arbitration.

Nothing in this proposal detracts from party autonomy in arbitration. Starting with a presumption of page limits would not prevent parties from agreeing on different limits, or no limits at all. However, unless limits are stipulated in advance, the arms race will likely continue and could even accelerate due to new artificial intelligence such as ChatGPT. The moment is ripe, from the field's consensus to the risks on the technological frontier, to implement page limits that will help make expedited, efficient arbitration a reality rather than a mere laudatory goal.

3. UNCITRAL Expedited Arbitration Rules (2021), Article 16(1).
4. *Ibid.*, Article 3(2).

§3.02 AN EMERGING CONSENSUS ON THE PROBLEM OF PROLIXITY AND THE PROMISE OF PAGE LIMITS

The beauty of arbitration is the flexibility and autonomy that it affords to parties. Rather than face artificial constraints on proceedings, the parties can typically agree to a wide range of procedural approaches that are suitable to their particular dispute.

However, when the stakes and intensity of arbitration rise, that beauty of arbitration can turn into a beast. As Toby Landau put it over a decade ago, written submissions can become 'huge, frightening written memorials'.[5] Others have described the 'sickening and depressing feeling' from an '800-page Statement of Case or a 350-page Rebuttal or an Opening submission of 500 pages, let alone a Closing submission of 300 pages'.[6] Another well-established arbitrator recalled receiving a post-hearing brief of 3,000 pages.[7] Constantine Partasides diagnosed the problem of prolixity as follows:

> Today we find ourselves in an arbitration world awash with redundancy and repetition .... [W]ritten submissions can be – and often [are] – hundreds of pages in length. As such they often confuse rather than clarify the key issues in dispute. They often lead counsel to lose the attention of the tribunal, and the tribunal to lose sight of the key points in dispute. They rarely have the effect of shortening the oral hearings (i.e. they do not lead to efficiencies elsewhere), but rather lengthen them. They represent a perfect example of our process taking on board the excesses of all the legal traditions from which it draws.[8]

Some have argued against page limits on the grounds that they undermine 'counsel's professional judgment about how best to present a party's case' and are 'inevitably arbitrary and (often) unprincipled'.[9] Such deference to professional judgment is admirable but, in many cases, will be misplaced when incentives go awry.[10] Counsel might have the misimpression that the longer the brief, the more persuasive it will be.[11] Brevity clashes with most lawyers' training to be thorough and

5. Landau, *Luncheon Address: Advocacy in International Arbitration*, 5 World Arb. & Med. Rev. 351 (2011) (criticizing 'huge, frightening written memorials').
6. Ina Popova, Restoring Efficiency to International Arbitration: Five Core Recommendations (2018) (quoting N. Kaplan, 'Winter of Discontent', 32 Kluwer L. Int'l, 3 (2017)).
7. Andrew Chin et al., Kick Off: HK Arbitration Week, Wolters Kluwer (30 October 2018), https://arbitrationblog.kluwerarbitration.com/2018/10/30/kick-off-hk-arbitration-week-2018/.
8. Constantine Partasides, *A Few Words on Prolixity in International Arbitration*, in International Arbitration Under Review: Essays in Honour of John Beechey, ICC, International Chamber of Commerce, 301 (2015).
9. Gary Born, International Commercial Arbitration (Kluwer Law International 2022).
10. *See* Charles T. Kotuby Jr and Luke A. Sobota, *Practical Suggestions to Promote the Legitimacy and Vitality of International Investment Arbitration*, 28 ICSID Review 454, 457 (2013) ('For various reasons, advocates may not change their practices on their own initiative. There may be institutional incentives for a State facing review of its sovereign acts to delay a final award. For example, the current administration may for political reasons be anxious to avoid resolution of the case during its tenure, and, to that end, instruct its counsel to brief any and all issues remotely related to the dispute. And with so much at stake, investors find it difficult to leave any argument unanswered.').
11. *See Coca Cola Bottling Co. v. Reeves*, 486 So.2d 374, 383-384 (Miss. 1986) ('A lawyer never uses one word when two or three will do just as well .... The legal mind finds magnetic attraction in redundancy and overkill.').

comprehensive, to include every possible claim, to chase down every footnote and caveat, and to advise on the full range of risks and scenarios.[12] A cynic could also point to counsels' financial incentives, as longer submissions typically require more time and produce more billable hours.

Page limits can effectively constrain such misaligned incentives and thereby: (i) improve efficiency, (ii) protect the equality of arms, and (iii) distil arbitral decision-making. Expedited arbitration rules, in particular, should focus on these benefits as bases for implementing page limits.

[A] Efficiency

Many commentators praise expedited arbitration rules for the important innovations that they bring to international arbitration.[13] The principal goals of such innovations are faster and cheaper proceedings, with greater predictability of schedules and legal fees.[14] Page limits further those goals directly. Shorter briefs can save time and money. Page limits mean fewer words that counsel will need to write and fewer pages for the arbitrators and opposing counsel to read. That certainly saves time and costs.[15] As the International Chamber of Commerce (ICC) has observed, setting a limit on the length and number of submissions may help cut fees and costs by 'help[ing] focus attention on the key issues to be addressed' and 'encourag[ing] the parties to present all key issues in their first submissions'.[16]

Of course, writing a more concise submission might require more time, as discussed further below. On the whole, however, page limits add predictability and control throughout the proceedings. Counsel can spend only so much time on a 20-page submission. And, such limited submissions make it far more likely that the parties will, in fact, complete proceedings within the target time frames set in most expedited arbitration rules.

---

12. *See* Louis Kaplow, *The Value of Accuracy in Adjudication: An Economic Analysis*, 23 J. Legal Stud. 307, 342, 384-386 (1994) (arguing that parties have incentives to present too much evidence during adjudication).
13. *See* Yas Banifatemi, Expedited Proceedings in International Arbitration, in Laurent Lévy and Michael Polkinghorne (eds), Expedited Procedures in International Arbitration, Dossiers of the ICC Institute of World Business Law, Vol. 16 (2017); *see also* Hamish Lal and Brendan Casey, *Ten Years Later: Why the 'Renaissance of Expedited Arbitration' Should Be the 'Emergency Arbitration' of 2020*, 37 J. Int'l Arb. 325 (2020).
14. *See* ICC Arbitration Commission, Report on 'Techniques for Controlling Time and Costs in Arbitration', 2007 (1st ed.), ¶ 6; Report on 'Controlling Time and Costs in Arbitration', 2012 (2nd ed.), ¶ 4 (encouraging parties to consider including fast-track arbitration procedures in their arbitration clauses).
15. ICC Commission Report, Controlling Time and Costs in Arbitration at 11-12 (March 2012), https://cdn.iccwbo.org/content/uploads/sites/3/2018/03/icc-arbitration-commission-report-on-techniques-for-controlling-time-and-costs-in-arbitration-english-version.pdf. According to the 2010 Queen Mary International Arbitration Survey, written submissions are one of the top three reasons for delaying arbitral proceedings: Paul Friedland & Loukas Mistelis, 2010 International Arbitration Survey: Choices in International Arbitration, The Sch. Int'l Arb. 32 (2010), https://arbitration.qmul.ac.uk/media/arbitration/docs/2010_InternationalArbitration SurveyReport.pdf.
16. ICC Commission Report, *supra*.

[B] Equality of Arms

Equality of arms is a fundamental principle of adjudication. As Thomas Wälde summarized it, equality of arms 'is, throughout comparative laws on civil or administrative procedure, international law in general and investment arbitration in particular, recognised as a key component of the principle of "procedural fairness", "integrity of process" or "good administration of justice" which tribunals have to apply'.[17]

The principle often arises in investor-state arbitration, but it is not limited to that field. In general, deep-pocketed parties, or those with major financial backing, can commit resources to arbitration that might overwhelm a party that lacks such resources. Some counsel teams comprise multiple partners and veritable armies of associates and support staff to prepare voluminous submissions accompanied by hundreds if not thousands of exhibits. Their opposing party, by contrast, might be represented by only a few lawyers without access to the latest technology and research databases. Needless to say, the fact that one party has more resources than another does not mean that the less-resourced party's case is weaker. On the contrary, in many cases, a party's lack of resources can result directly from another party's misconduct.

When a case presents such a disparity, one of the most common 'guns-blazing' tactics is the submission of extremely long and detailed pleadings that overwhelm the other side.[18] Limited pleadings would equalize the playing field, thereby enhancing and promoting international arbitration as a more accessible dispute resolution forum.

[C] Improved Decision-Making

In addition to reducing costs and levelling the playing field, page limits can frequently enhance arbitral decision-making. Many in the arbitration community have observed that parties tend to repeat their arguments and present too much duplicative material to the tribunal. As Charles Kotuby and Luke Sobota summarized the problem:

> Without the attorneys doing the hard work of synthesizing the case, arbitrators are largely left to figure it out for themselves. This is an abdication of the role of the advocate. Perhaps unsurprisingly, arbitrators – faced with multiple issues, hundreds of pages of memorials, documents that fill several bankers' boxes and numerous factual and expert witness statements – look for the narrowest grounds to dispose of the arbitration. The result, after years of toil and expense, can be

17. Thomas Wälde, Procedural Challenges in Investment Arbitration under the Shadow of the Dual Role of the State: Asymmetries and Tribunals' Duty to Ensure, Pro-actively, the Equality of Arms (2010).
18. *See, e.g.*, Fernando Dias Simões, *Clandestine Awards, Information Asymmetries, and Equality of Arms in Investment Arbitration*, J. Disp. Res. 317, 327 (2021) (discussing the 'power imbalance between parties who can afford to hire one of the magic circle law firms and those who lack the necessary financial resources'); *Bernhard von Pezold and Others v. Republic of Zimbabwe*, ICSID Case No. ARB/10/15, Award dated 28 July 2015, at ¶ 31 ('The voluminous nature of the Parties' pleadings and evidence cannot be overstated. The Parties have filed over 3,000 pages of pleadings alone.').

> awards decided on narrow grounds that do not advance the law and that are divorced from the real issues in dispute.[19]

Lucy Reed expounded on the underlying reasons for this problem in her 2012 Kaplan Lecture, where she noted that arbitrators often deploy cognitive shortcuts and survival tactics, intentionally or unintentionally, to navigate voluminous submissions. She explained that international arbitrators, like all humans, rely on intuition and heuristics to process complex and voluminous information quickly.[20]

These mental shortcuts permit people to solve problems, make judgments, and react to situations quickly and efficiently – which can be beneficial for life generally but inappropriate for arbitrators. Multiple cognitive risks can arise, such as anchoring or egocentric biases.[21] Anchoring is a strategy of latching upon prominent points through the mass of material: particular documents, facts, legal principles, or damages figures. Those points of reference or 'anchors' then become dispositive or overly influential in understanding the dispute.[22] In other words, the arbitrator might perceive all other factors through the lens of the anchor, as other significant details become lost in a tsunami of words and figures. Egocentric bias appears when an arbitrator relies on his or her own preconceptions and gives undue weight to or even seeks out evidence to support those preconceptions rather than being fully open to the parties' arguments.[23]

In light of such concerns, a significant benefit of distilled submissions is that they can improve the quality of decision-making. Ina Popova has summarized this well:

> [W]e should not lose sight of the ultimate purpose of written submissions: to persuade the decision maker. Brevity generally makes for better advocacy. The 'kitchen sink' approach to written pleadings is rarely effective. Page limits require prioritizing claims, distilling arguments to the essential questions that decide the case, and avoiding insignificant points that dilute the case theory – all techniques that make written submissions more persuasive.[24]

Page limits can also mitigate another procedural concern in arbitration: overreliance on tribunal secretaries. Most leading arbitrators use secretaries to provide support across their cases. But this arrangement presents temptations to outsource parsing through multi-hundred-page submissions to produce already synthesized distillations of the record, including summaries of arguments and key issues in disputes. The secretary's distillation helps prepare the arbitrator to address the parties' positions, follow and comprehend testimony during the hearing, and find a route through deliberations to an ultimate decision. However, such dependence means that tribunal secretaries could become a problematic filter between the arbitrator and the

19. Charles T. Kotuby Jr and Luke A. Sobota, *Practical Suggestions to Promote the Legitimacy and Vitality of International Investment Arbitration*, 28 ICSID Review 454, 457 (2013).
20. Lucy Reed, *Arbitral Decision-Making: Art, Science or Sport?, HKIAC Kaplan Lecture*, 30 J. Int'l Arb. 85 (2013) DOI: 10.54648/joia2013007.
21. *Ibid.*
22. Toby Thomas Landau, Dysfunctional Deliberations and Effective Advocacy, Dysfunctional Deliberations and Effective Advocacy, ICCA Congress Series No. 19 (Mauritius 2016).
23. Lucy Reed, *supra*.
24. Ina Popova, Restoring Efficiency to International Arbitration: Five Core Recommendations (2018).

record, potentially framing the arbitrator's understanding and conception of the entire case. If arbitrators had fewer pages to review, they could give each submission a greater share of their own personal attention.

[D] Other Innovations

In many fields, constraints have been proven to yield innovations. Imposition of page limits might similarly result in unanticipated collateral benefits. Brevity does not need to be unimaginative. For example, counsel will seek to be as persuasive as possible in the pages allotted to them. There could be innovations in pleading practices or new techniques for presenting arguments concisely and comprehensibly. Perhaps counsel would apply the wisdom of 'a picture is worth a thousand words' by presenting portions of their arguments through more demonstratives. Such measures could strengthen the impact of briefs or memoranda of points and authorities, as well as improve the quality of decisions.

Those innovations could prove particularly important with the rise of artificial intelligence text-generators such as ChatGPT. Commentators have already observed that 'ChatGPT's natural language understanding capabilities could automate the drafting of legal documents and agreements. . . .'[25] Such automated drafting may lead to efficiencies, but that is true only if both parties are utilizing artificial intelligence ("AI") text-generators – in which case the advocacy (and even the award drafting) could improperly fall outside human responsibility. The transition towards brevity might therefore be the best path forward for arbitration counsel to distinguish themselves from AI.

French philosopher Blaise Pascal famously wrote: 'I would have written a shorter letter, but I did not have the time.'[26] One could add: he also did not have sufficiently advanced AI. This sentiment reflects both the value and the challenge of page limits. On the one hand, page limits would force counsel to cut excess – to distil a message to its core. On the other hand, being accurate, clear, and concise requires rigorous synthesis and selection of the most important information. When it comes to persuasive written submissions, less is more, especially to the extent that counsel increasingly face competition from AI.

§3.03 PROGRESS ON PAGE LIMITS: A COMPARATIVE STUDY

The international arbitration community has much to learn from page limits established in many national courts. Yet, when a page limit is suggested in international arbitration, the 'right to be heard' argument inevitably rises in response, as arbitration

25. Leonardo F. Souza-McMurtrie, Arbitration Tech Toolbox: Will ChatGPT Change International Arbitration as We Know It?, Kluwer Arbitration Blog (26 February 2023).
26. Versions of this quotation can also be found in expressions of other renowned writers, such as John Locke and Benjamin Franklin.

practitioners expect a party to have the freedom to present its case fully and comprehensively. Tribunals and parties could therefore fear that imposing page limits might even be a ground for challenging an award. This is a common but flawed reason why arbitral institutions and arbitrators alike have long been disinclined to impose page limits. There is no basis under the New York Convention, for example, to challenge an award simply because the parties had to comply with reasonable page limits.[27] Such due process concerns should also be considered in light of the procedural rules of many national courts that have successfully utilized page limits without harming the parties' procedural rights.

Unlike arbitration, national judicial systems have long recognized and responded to the problem by imposing page limits on counsel's pleadings. Over the years, the trend towards achieving succinctness in legal submissions has found only stronger traction. This next section investigates the recent developments in this area and surveys page limits imposed by national courts across jurisdictions and, more recently, in international courts and tribunals.

[A] National Judicial Systems

Across the world, pleadings in domestic courts are frequently subject to page limits as a way to reconcile competing concepts of brevity and legal thoroughness. A survey of national court rules reveals that a majority of jurisdictions limit litigants to approximately 15 to 50 pages. It is also standard practice for courts to impose formatting requirements to prevent lawyers from fiddling with fonts and spacing to circumvent page limits.

United States. At the highest judicial level, the Supreme Court limits principal merits briefs to 15,000 words, with strict formatting requirements that result in a submission of approximately 50 pages. Other submissions to the Supreme Court – including petitions for a writ of certiorari and reply briefs on the merits – are even further limited to 9,000 and 6,000 words, respectively.[28] Those limits apply to cases of the greatest importance to public policy and complexity. As Chief Justice Roberts once said: 'I have yet to put down a brief and say, "I wish that had been longer."'

Of course, advocacy at the US Supreme Court rarely involves any question of fact. But even the fact-intensive US district courts control the length of briefs with limits on font size, spacing, and page lengths, often explicitly limiting submissions from 15 to 40 pages with precise formatting to prevent any bypass of the rules.[29] Alternatively, some

27. Charles T. Kotuby Jr and Luke A. Sobota, *Practical Suggestions to Promote the Legitimacy and Vitality of International Investment Arbitration*, 28 ICSID Review 454, 458-459 (2013) ('Arbitrators do not want to appear to be hindering the parties' arguments and, so it might seem, the fundamental right to be heard. But without deadlines or page limits, counsel may "labor in vain and give birth to confusion". And the strictures of due process do not prevent the imposition of reasonable requirements that facilitate prompt resolution of the case.').
28. 33 *Rules* and Guidance: Guidelines for the Submission of Documents to the *Supreme Court's* Electronic Filing System (Updated 1 January 2023).
29. US District Court Southern District of California Local Civil Rules, Rule 5.4(h); Local Rules of the US District Court for the District of Massachusetts, Rule 7.1(b)(4) ('Memoranda supporting or

US district courts impose word limitations.[30] The US Federal Rules of Appellate Procedure provide that appellate briefs are limited to 30 pages (13,000 words), with 15 pages (6,500 words) for reply.[31] Notably, those limitations are even shorter than prior appellate practice following amendments to the rules in 2016.[32] The majority of the federal courts of appeals have accepted the reduced word limits in the amended rules.[33]

In rare cases, when courts find that an adequate argument cannot be presented within the page limitations, extra pages are allowed by leave of court.[34] Because of judges' heavy workloads and desire for concise and refined briefs, these enlargements are granted only in truly exceptional circumstances. As the Seventh Circuit explained: 'Enforcing page limits and other restrictions on litigants is rather ordinary practice. This court has a page limit which is rather strictly, and cheerfully, enforced.'[35]

When attorneys violate page limits, consequences in US courts can range from a slap on the wrist to more serious sanctions, depending on the jurisdiction and the judge. Some courts will not accept briefs that exceed the page limit, while others will refuse to consider the portion that exceeds the limit.[36] Other courts impose monetary

---

opposing allowance of motions shall not, without leave of court, exceed 20 pages, double-spaced'); Local Civil and Criminal Rules of the US District Court for the District of New Jersey, Rule 7.2(b) ('Any brief ... shall not exceed 40 ordinary typed or printed pages'); US District Court District of Vermont Local Rules of Procedure, Rule 7(a)(4) ('a memorandum supporting or opposing a dispositive motion must not exceed 25 pages, excluding exhibits and attachments'); Local Rules of the US District Court Northern District of Illinois, Rule 7.1 ('Neither a brief in support of or in opposition to any motion nor objections to a report and recommendation or order of a magistrate judge or special master shall exceed 15 pages without prior approval of the court').

30. US District Court Central District of California Local Civil Rules, Rule 11-6.1 ('Except as otherwise provided in this rule or ordered by a judge, no memorandum of points and authorities, pretrial brief, trial brief, or posttrial brief may exceed 7,000 words'); US District Court Northern District of Florida, Rule 7.1(F) ('A memorandum must not exceed 8,000 words and must include a certificate stating the number of words in the memorandum'); US District Court for the District of Montana, Rule 7.1(d)(2)(A) ('Briefs in support of a motion and response briefs are limited to 6500 words'); US District Court Middle District of North Carolina, Rule 7.3(d)(1) ('Except with the Court's prior permission, briefs ... in support of motions and responsive briefs shall not exceed 6,250 words and reply briefs shall not exceed 3,125 words.').
31. Fed. R. App. P. 32.
32. Fed. R. App. P. 32, Committee Notes on Rules - 2016 Amendment.
33. The First, Third, Fourth, Fifth, Sixth, Eighth, Tenth, and Eleventh Circuits are all now operating within the newly reduced word limits. The Second, Seventh, Ninth, and the Federal Circuits, however, have amended their local rules in order to retain the longer pre-existing word limits. *See* 2nd Cir. R. 32.1(a)(4); 7th Cir. R. 28.1; 9th Cir. R. 28.1-1.
34. Practitioner's Handbook for Appeals to the United States Court of Appeals for the Seventh Circuit 49 (1994) ('Counsel should file a motion for leave to file an oversize brief long in advance of the due date. These motions are seldom granted and even then only for a specific number of additional pages. Producing an oversized brief before receiving permission can only result in needless delay and unnecessary production costs. The practice of tendering an oversized brief with a motion of leave to file has been unequivocally forbidden by this court.').
35. *Watts v. Thompson*, 116 F 3d 220, 224 (7th Cir. 1997); *see also* Charles T. Kotuby Jr and Luke A. Sobota, *Practical Suggestions to Promote the Legitimacy and Vitality of International Investment Arbitration*, 28 ICSID Review 454, 461 n. 47 (2013).
36. *See Cuevas v. Hartley*, 835 F.3d 892, 893 (2016) ('For my part, I don't feel bound to read beyond the 14,000 words allowed by our rules, so I won't read past page 66 of the state's brief.'); *Columbus-America Discovery Group v. Atlantic Mut. Ins. Co.*, 56 F.3d 556, 574 n. 23 (4th Cir. 1995) (refusing to consider pages exceeding limit).

sanctions.[37] Courts also rebuke counsel for their efforts to avoid page limits, as 'chicanery',[38] 'embarrassing', or 'manipulation'.[39]

United Kingdom. In the United Kingdom, a statement of case in English court proceedings should generally not exceed 25 pages and must not exceed 40 pages, unless the Court has given permission for a longer document, in which case it must not be longer than the increased length for which permission has been given.[40] English courts have commented on strict page limits, saying:

> Overlong pleadings and written submissions ... which are manufactured by parties and their lawyers have become the bane of commercial litigation in England and Wales. This prolixity only adds unnecessary costs; it does nothing to clarify and simplify the issues or to shorten proceedings, which aims should be the objectives of both pleadings and written submissions.[41]

Singapore. In Singapore, an appellant's submission is limited to 35 pages, and the core bundle of documents is limited to 55 pages.[42] Respondent's briefs are limited by the same constraints.[43] If a party does not comply with the imposed limits, it faces monetary sanctions.[44]

The Netherlands. Historically, Dutch courts did not impose page limits. In April 2021, however, courts of appeal in the Netherlands set page limits for civil matter legal briefs, constraining statements of appeal and defence to 25 pages and other briefs to 15 pages.[45] In complex cases, parties can request for more pages. Following a legal challenge, the matter was referred to the Supreme Court which held that judges are authorized to set page limits based on their general statutory power to take all decisions necessary for a proper conduct of the proceedings and on their statutory obligation to prevent undue delay of the proceedings.[46]

This survey could be supplemented by many other jurisdictions. The point is clear, however, that page limits are routine practice in national courts without causing due process concerns. Moreover, judges often become the most ardent endorsers of such limits. The international field has begun to take note and learn from such domestic procedures.

---

37. *See State v. Hudson*, 123 N.C. Ct. App. 336, 338, 473 S.E.2d 415, 417 (1996) (fining lawyer USD 500 for submitting 42-page brief where limit was 35 pages), rev'd on other grounds, 345 N.C. 729, 483 S.E.2d 436 (1997).
38. *Kelly v. Provident Life & Acc. Ins. Co.*, 2010 WL 5300807 *3 (D. Vt. 20 December 2010).
39. For example, *IMI Norgren Inc. v. D & D Tooling & Mfg., Inc.*, 2003 WL 40499 *1 (N.D. Ill. 6 January 2003).
40. The Business and Property Courts of England & Wales, The Commercial Court Guide (2022).
41. *Standard Bank Plc v. Via Mat International Ltd* (2013) EWCA Civ 490.
42. Supreme Court Practice Directions 2021 (last updated 13 February 2023).
43. *Ibid.*
44. *Ibid.*
45. Judgment of the Supreme Court, no. 21/02242, ECLI:NL:HR:2022:824.
46. *Ibid.*

[B] International Arbitration and Courts

[1] ICSID Expedited Arbitration Rules

In 2022, International Centre for Settlement of Investment Disputes (ICSID) amended its rules in response to concerns about, *inter alia*, the costs and efficiency of proceedings.[47] A key reform to reduce the length of the proceedings is the new option for expedited arbitration. To opt into expedited arbitration, both parties must consent and may choose to do so even if the proceedings were commenced under the normal ICSID rules.[48] For such expedited cases, ICSID introduced page limits on submissions. The new Rule 81 provides that statement of claim and statement of defence are limited to 200 pages each and the reply and rejoinder to 100 pages each.[49]

As explained in one working paper, these new Rules may be particularly useful in resolving 'low value claims' and reducing their cost.[50] These new provisions were intended to appeal to a broader pool of potential claimants, including to those who have more limited financial resources and who may be concerned about the time and cost of a long-running arbitration.

Undoubtedly, significant efforts have been made to address the criticisms of investor-State dispute settlement and make ICSID arbitration more streamlined. Although this is a welcome alternative for cases involving limited complexity, the expedited arbitration rules could have minimal impact in practice. First, disputing parties still need to opt in once the proceedings have commenced and can opt out at any time during the course of the proceedings.[51] The parties will rarely agree to such a limitation after a dispute has crystallized because they will then focus more on the risks of such an approach. Moreover, if there exists an 'inequality of arms', a party with greater resources might choose to weaponize unlimited submissions towards the other party.

Further, a one-size-fits-all 200-page limitation remains a rather high limit. If this is the limit for 'expedited proceedings', it only adds to the legitimacy of concerns about multi-hundred or multi-thousand-page submissions. The new rules are certainly an improvement, but if submissions in national courts can be limited to 20 or 30 pages with constrained formatting, lower limits – or at least limits scalable to the stakes, as proposed in Table 3.1 – could be implemented in investment arbitration.

[2] International Courts

Page limits have been established by several leading international tribunals and multinational courts. The European Court of Justice limits primary submissions to 50

47. ICISD, ICSID Rules and Regulations Amendment (21 July 2022), https://icsid.worldbank.org/resources/rules-amendments.
48. ICSID Rule 75. This contrasts with expedited arbitration under some institutional rules, where the expedited procedure is automatically triggered in a 'small claim', i.e., when the monetary value of the dispute falls below a certain threshold, e.g., ICC Arbitration Rules 2021, Article 30.
49. ICSID Rule 81.
50. ICSID, Working Paper 6.
51. ICSID Rule 86.

pages, with 25 pages for subsequent reply and rejoinder briefs.[52] Requests to the European Court of Human Rights should be only 10 pages. However, applications may supplement the request with the facts, alleged violations of the Convention and the relevant arguments, but such supplementary information shall not exceed 20 pages.[53] The International Criminal Court provides for 120 pages each for the pretrial brief, trial brief, and closing brief.[54]

Of course, page limits remain the exception in international jurisprudence. The International Court of Justice (ICJ) urges the parties 'to keep the written pleadings as concise as possible, in a manner compatible with the full presentation of their positions'.[55] In 2021, however, 'in view of an excessive tendency towards the proliferation and protraction of annexes to written pleadings', the ICJ imposed page limits on the annexes to written pleadings.[56] Moving forward, the parties are awarded a generous 750 pages in total for annexes attached by a party.

Other international adjudicative bodies do not impose any limits. For example, the World Trade Organization sets no limits despite recommendations to impose such limitations in order to improve the efficiency of the proceedings.[57]

In summary, the practice of national and international courts shows that prolixity does not have to be an inherent feature of legal pleadings, even in complex and high-stakes cases. Yet, the international legal field remains resistant despite the emerging consensus on the wisdom of page limits.

§3.04 PROPOSALS FOR EXPEDITED ARBITRATION

Despite the emerging consensus and many years of commentators encouraging parties to agree on – and arbitrators to impose – page limits, such efforts have largely proven futile due to the practical realities and incentives in international arbitration.[58] Expedited arbitration rules should lead the way by imposing presumptions of page limits.

These presumptions would, in effect, become the default rules that the parties accept when they agree upon the chosen arbitration rules. Scholars have long recognized that default rules can reduce the potential costs of legal uncertainty and

52. Practice Directions to Parties adopted by the General Court (Consolidated Version), https://curia.europa.eu/jcms/upload/docs/application/pdf/2009-07/en_instructions_pratiques_aux_parties.pdf.
53. Registry of the Court, Rules of Court, European Court of Human Rights (10 February 2023), https://www.echr.coe.int/Documents/Rules_Court_ENG.pdf.
54. International Criminal Court, Regulations of the Court, Reg. 38 (2018), https://www.icc-cpi.int/sites/default/files/Publications/Regulations-of-the-Court.pdf.
55. International Court of Justice, Practice Directions (2023), https://www.icj-cij.org/en/practice-directions.
56. *Ibid.*
57. World Trade Organization: Overview and Future Direction, Congressional Research Service (2 October 2019), https://crsreports.congress.gov/product/pdf/R/R45417/6; WTO Secretariat, Ongoing Efforts to Improve the WTO Dispute Settlement System, in A Handbook on the WTO Dispute Settlement System, 183-185 (Cambridge Univ. Press 2017).
58. Charles T. Kotuby Jr and Luke A. Sobota, *Practical Suggestions to Promote the Legitimacy and Vitality of International Investment Arbitration*, 28 ICSID Review 454, 458 (2013) ('[A]rbitrators can impose page limits on written submissions, as is done in many national appellate courts').

drafting to address gaps and silent issues.[59] Consistent with economic analyses in other areas, the parties are more likely to maximize their joint utility if they accept expedited rules incorporating page limit defaults *prior* to the conduct triggering a dispute rather than after the dispute arises. At the same time, the parties would retain the ability to draft their own bespoke rules for their particular circumstances.

Institutions can tout the many benefits of page limits, as outlined above, and they can point to the widespread practice of national and international courts that prove such limits work in practice. Such limits will present a comparative advantage to other institutional rules that lack such limits. For example, Article 3(4) of the ICC Expedited Procedure Rules provides:

> The arbitral tribunal shall have discretion to adopt such procedural measures as it considers appropriate. In particular, the arbitral tribunal may, after consultation with the parties, decide not to allow requests for document production or to limit the number, length and scope of written submissions and written witness evidence (both fact witnesses and experts).[60]

That is useful guidance, but it will often be inadequate for the reasons explained above. As with the latest expedited rules for ICSID, the ICC and other arbitral institutions should implement an explicit presumption of page limits. The task should be neither complicated nor controversial, as parties would remain free to opt out of such limits by agreement, even after a dispute arises.

Table 3.1 is an illustrative example that builds on the current ICC Scales of Administrative Expenses and Arbitrator's Fees for the Expedited Procedure and shows in the right column how page limits could be implemented.

Table 3.1 Scale of Administrative Expenses and Arbitrator's Fees and Page Limits for the Expedited Procedure[61]

Amount in Dispute (in US Dollars)				*Administrative Expenses(*)*	*Statements of Claim and Defence (Pages)*
up to			50,000	5,000	10
from	50,001	to	100,000	1.53%	15
from	100,001	to	200,000	2.72%	20
from	200,001	to	500,000	2.25%	30

59. *See* R.H. Coase, *The Problem of Social Cost*, 3 J. L. & Econ. 1, 15-19 (1960) (discussing the significance of transaction costs for legal rules); Ian Ayres and Robert Gertner, *Filling Gaps in Incomplete Contracts: An Economic Theory of Default Rules*, 99 Yale L. J. 87 (1989).
60. Article 3(4), Appendix VI, 2021 ICC Rules.
61. Consistent with the practice of international courts, the table utilizes page limits and could be accompanied by formatting restrictions. Alternatively, the rules could establish equivalent word-count limitations (e.g., 13,000 words rather than 30 pages). The rules could also specify page limits for subsequent submissions, such as a reply and rejoinder, that are proportionate to these limits.

Amount in Dispute (in US Dollars)				*Administrative Expenses(*)*	*Statements of Claim and Defence (Pages)*
from	500,001	to	1,000,000	1.62%	40
from	1,000,001	to	2,000,000	0.788%	50
from	2,000,001	to	5,000,000	0.46%	60
from	5,000,001	to	10,000,000	0.25%	70
from	10,000,001	to	30,000,000	0.10%	80
from	30,000,001	to	50,000,000	0.09%	90
from	50,000,001	to	80,000,000	0.01%	100
from	80,000,001	to	500,000,000	0.0123%	120
over	500,000,000			150,000	150

Arbitration practitioners could attempt to bypass such limits through lengthy witness statements or expert reports. Accordingly, a table such as Table 3.1 could either: (i) include limits on those supplemental materials or (ii) impose an overall limit that parties must stay within for all their submissions. Page limits could also be supported by corresponding restrictions on exhibits and other attachments. In any event, each institution can and should develop limits that best suit the parties that use it, even polling them for their own preferences as to appropriate default rules.

Of course, as in national courts, an overall page limit must be reasonably applied. The same limit should not be rigidly imposed in all cases. Some cases are inevitably more complex and require lengthier submissions than others. Arbitrators would retain discretion to increase the presumptive page limits depending on the needs of the case and the agreement of the parties.

Another approach would be to set a number of pages as guidance (rather than binding limits) that the tribunal can take into account when deciding whether and to what extent to award a party costs. Notably, comparison of costs for a potential cost award would be facilitated if counsel on both sides made equivalent submissions throughout the proceedings.

§3.05 CONCLUSION

The practice of national courts and international tribunals shows that prolixity need not be an inherent feature of legal pleadings, even in complex and high-stakes disputes. Unfettered by restrictions, however, international arbitration has witnessed the problem of unduly long submissions that thwart goals of efficiency and justice. There is a growing consensus in the field that the time has come to stop the arms race. Yet, when a dispute arises, the parties are often unable to agree on limits. The solution is to establish a presumption of limited written submissions, as many other courts and tribunals have successfully done. Expedited arbitration rules should lead the way by establishing such limits as a default rule to help bring the dream of fast and efficient arbitral proceedings into reality.

CHAPTER 4

The Strain Between Efficiency and Due Process in Expedited Arbitration: A Fertile Ground to Challenge the Award?

Shahrizal M. Zin

The inflated costs and time-consuming arbitration process have long been the cause for concern among its users. In response to this unhealthy trend of arbitration, various arbitral institutions have introduced expedited procedures to restore efficiency concerning the costs incurred and time spent on the arbitration proceedings. However, the question is whether the expedited features of the arbitration procedures have compromised party autonomy and due process. The perceived strain between efficiency and party autonomy is illustrated at the stage of the arbitrators' appointment, for example, when the composition of a sole arbitrator tribunal is inconsistent with a provision of the parties' arbitration agreement. Similarly, the expeditious manner of the procedures that accord arbitrator discretion to modulate the parties' right to a hearing may infringe the due process. Arguing that balancing efficiency and due process is the way forward, this chapter addresses the pressing issues concerning enforcement and the challenge of an award out of expedited arbitration.

§4.01 INTRODUCTION

The perceived need to restore 'efficiency' in international arbitration came about after arbitration was criticized for losing its appeal on speed and costs.[1] Among its users, arbitration is no longer a fast and inexpensive process that dilutes the element of

1. Friedland Paul and Mistelis Loukas, '2010 Queen Mary International Arbitration Survey: Choices in International Arbitration'. The authors on p. 32 identified the leading causes of delay and increased costs in arbitration as the disclosure of documents, the parties' written submissions, the constitution of the tribunal, and hearings.

efficiency that it once promised.[2] Therefore, simplified arbitration procedures have been introduced and preferred to address the issues of delay and increased costs.[3] In response to these developments, several arbitral institutions have taken the initiative to improve the arbitral process by emphasizing techniques to control time and costs with fast-track procedures as its primary concern. Accordingly, expedited arbitration has been introduced as a streamlined and simplified procedure with a shortened time frame, which makes it possible for the parties to reach a final resolution of the dispute in a cost- and time-effective manner.

The expedited rules should balance the efficiency of the arbitral proceedings and the need to respect due process and fair treatment. However, the pursuit of efficiency should maintain the legal quality of the award.[4] Therefore, the need for speed and cost reduction should preserve the quality of the adjudicatory service provided as an integral part of the efficiency goal. This is to safeguard the enforceability of the award by not jeopardizing due process and the right to fair treatment during the proceedings. In short, expedited procedures are specific procedures that are supposed to be faster and simplified. They are based on shorter time limits and fewer or less burdensome procedural steps. This is to ensure that the arbitral tribunal can render awards quicker, anticipating that a reduction of arbitration costs should flow naturally. In a simplified concept, the entire arbitration process is compressed into a shorter period for a quicker resolution of a dispute, technically involving an acceleration of the whole proceedings but which aims at disposing of the case on a summary basis.[5]

This chapter analyses the key approaches of some institutions in their expedited rules of arbitration. It discusses cases concerning the challenge of awards issued under the auspices of expedited procedure rules. As the way forward requires a balance between efficiency and due process, the role of the arbitral tribunal in providing a fair and impartial hearing is crucial to avoid a challenge of an award on the grounds of natural justice.

§4.02 GATEWAY PROVISIONS FOR EXPEDITED ARBITRATION

The gateway provisions of the respective arbitral institutions determine whether the referral of a dispute falls within the scope of its expedited arbitration rules.[6] In this respect, the expedited rules apply through either 'opt-in' or 'automatic application' to cases that meet the requirement of expedited arbitration. Often, the gateway provisions

---

2. Friedland Paul and Mistelis Loukas, 2015 International Arbitration Survey, 'Improvements and Innovations in International Arbitration', School of International Arbitration, Centre for Commercial Law Studies, Queen Mary University of London.
3. *Ibid.*, 3, 24, and 26. The survey reports that 92% of respondents are in favour of the adoption of simplified arbitration procedures in institutional rules.
4. *See* Christophe Seraglini and Patrick Beaten, *Expedited Rules and the Possibility of Immediate Measures Once a Tribunal Is Established* (Laurent Levy and Michael Polkinghorne eds, Dossier XVI of the ICC Institute of World Business Law, 2017), 40.
5. *See* Fouchard Gaillard Goldman, *International Commercial Arbitration* (Emmanuel Gaillard and John Savage eds, Kluwer Law International, 1999).
6. *See* Alexander Uff, *Expedited Arbitration, Autonomy and Due Process* (17 September 2021), http://expedited_arbitration_autonomy_and_due_process_-_au.pdf (quadrantchambers.com).

specify a certain financial threshold (on the value of dispute) where the expedited procedures apply automatically if the amount does not exceed the financial threshold set or in cases of exceptional urgency. Alternatively, the parties may opt in by an express agreement to resolve their disputes according to the expedited procedures.

According to Article 30 of the International Chamber of Commerce (ICC) Rules of Arbitration 2021, the expedited procedure provisions apply automatically where the amount in dispute is below a financial threshold of USD 3 million, subject to the ICC Court's determination or otherwise where the parties agree to an expedited procedure.[7] Article 5 of Singapore International Arbitration Centre (SIAC) Rules applies to a financial threshold of USD 6 million and includes cases of exceptional urgency.[8] Unlike the ICC Rules, a party must request expedited arbitration, and the request is subject to the decision of SIAC's president to apply the expedited procedure. The requirement of a financial threshold and a request for the expedited procedure are also illustrated under the AIAC Arbitration Rules 2021.[9]

In contrast, the Stockholm Chamber of Commerce (SCC) provides a freestanding set of Expedited Arbitration Rules, which require an express agreement by the parties.[10] The SCC offers a model arbitration clause in which the parties empower the

---

7. Pursuant to Article 30 of the Rules and Appendix VI (Expedited Procedure Provisions), by agreeing to arbitration under the Rules, the Expedited Procedure Provisions shall take precedence over any contrary terms of the arbitration agreement. The Expedited Procedure Provisions apply if: (a) the amount in dispute does not exceed USD 2,000,000 if the arbitration agreement was concluded on or after 1 March 2017 and before 1 January 2021; or (b) the amount in dispute does not exceed USD 3,000,000 if the arbitration agreement was concluded on or after 1 January 2021; and (c) the parties have not opted out of the Expedited Procedure Rules in the arbitration agreement or at any time thereafter.
8. Article 5 (Expedited Procedure) of SIAC Rules 2016 states as follows:

   > 5.1 Prior to the constitution of the tribunal, a party may file an application with the Registrar for the arbitral proceedings to be conducted in accordance with the Expedited Procedure under this Rule, provided that any of the following criteria are satisfied:
   >
   > a. The amount in dispute does not exceed the equivalent amount of $6,000,000 representing the aggregate of the claim and any defense or set-off;
   > b. The parties so agree; or
   > c. In cases of exceptional urgency.

   The parties applying for the arbitral proceedings to be conducted in accordance with the Expedited Procedure under this Rule 5.1 shall, at the same time as it flies an application for the proceedings to be conducted in accordance with the Expedited Procedure with the Registrar, send a copy of the application to the other party and shall notify the Registrar that it has done so, specifying the mode of service employed and the date of service.
9. A party may submit the request for fast-track procedure in three instances. First, the parties have agreed to adopt the fast-track procedure or any edition of the AIAC Fast Track Arbitration Rules under Rule 8(2)(a). Second, where the amount in dispute is less than USD 500,000.00 (international arbitration) or MYR 2,000,000 (domestic arbitration) under Rule 8(2)(b) and, finally, in the case of an exceptional urgency under Rule 8(2)(c). The AIAC's Director shall determine a fast-track request under Rule 8.3 by considering all relevant circumstances.
10. The preamble of the SCC Expedited Arbitration Rules 2023 states that 'under any arbitration agreement referring to the Rules for Expedited Arbitrations of the SCC Arbitration Institute or the Arbitration Institute of the Stockholm Chamber of Commerce, the parties shall be deemed to have agreed that the following rules, or such amendment, in force on the date of the commencement of the arbitration, or on the filing of an application for the appointment of an

SCC to decide whether to apply the expedited or standard arbitration rules. Similarly, the UNCITRAL Expedited Arbitration Rules will only apply by express agreement of the parties under Article 1.[11]

However, the London Court of International Arbitration (LCIA) Rules of Arbitration 2020 are silent on a gateway provision. Article 9A of the LCIA Rules of Arbitration 2020 retains the provision for expedited arbitration formation of an arbitral tribunal. Still, it does not provide a gateway provision, financial or otherwise, for the application of expedited procedures. Further, Article 14.5 allows the arbitral tribunal to exercise discretion in all cases to 'make any procedural order it considers appropriate with regard to the fair, efficient and expeditious conduct of the arbitration'. Finally, Article 14.6 includes a non-exhaustive list of procedural directions 'to expedite the procedure'. One should pay attention to the gateway provisions due to their profound impact on the parties' agreement, particularly on the issues of the arbitrator's appointment and due process of a hearing.[12]

§4.03 KEY FEATURES OF EXPEDITED ARBITRATION PROCEDURE

In the pursuit of efficiency, expedited arbitration procedures have adopted measures to accelerate certain specific milestones from the outset of the proceedings. As time is of the essence, an expedited arbitration procedure contains several key features that aim for a speedy dispute resolution from inception to completion. Therefore, the flashpoint of key features highlights the role of a sole arbitrator, shorter timelines, faster case management through timetabling, limitation of hearing by way of documents-only arbitration, and deadlines for issuing an award.[13]

[A] Referral of the Case to a Sole Arbitrator

Typically, the role of a sole arbitrator emerges once the cases satisfy the gateway provisions for the expedited procedure. The preference for a sole arbitrator is motivated by a desire to save time rather than spending more time to appoint a three-member arbitral tribunal. This preference also reduces the costs by paying a sole arbitrator's fee rather than a three-member arbitral tribunal. Accordingly, there are two approaches adopted by arbitral institutions when it comes to appointing a sole arbitrator, namely,

emergency arbitrator, shall be applied unless otherwise agreed by the parties'. Also *see* Article 11 (Agreement on the Application of the Arbitration Rules). Furthermore, it says, 'after receiving the answer, and prior to the appointment of the Arbitrator, the SCC may invite the parties to apply the Arbitration Rules with either a sole or three arbitrator(s), having regard to the complexity of the case, the amount in dispute and any other relevant circumstances'.

11. Article 1 of the UNCITRAL Arbitration Rules 2021 provides that 'express consent of the parties is required for the application of the Expedited Rules'.
12. The appointment of a sole arbitrator that is inconsistent with the parties' agreement would run the risk of setting aside an award or enforcement refused where the composition of the tribunal 'was not in accordance with the agreement of the parties' under Article 34(2)(a)(iv) of the UNCITRAL Model Law 2006 and Article V(1)(d) of the New York Convention 1958.
13. *See* Yas Banifatemi, *Expedited Proceedings in International Arbitration* (Laurent Levy and Michael Polkinghorne eds, Dossier XVI of the ICC Institute of World Business Law, 2017), 14.

a strict or a flexible approach. Institutions such as the ICC adopt stringent measures by appointing a sole arbitrator who overrides any contrary provision under the arbitration agreement.[14] Article 30.1 of the 2017 ICC Arbitration Rules makes clear that by submitting to arbitration under the Rules, the parties agree that any reference to three arbitrators in their arbitration agreement is subject to the court's discretion to appoint a sole arbitrator if the Expedited Procedure Provisions apply. Similarly, the SCC also mandates that a sole arbitrator shall decide the arbitration.[15]

In contrast, some institutions adopt a more flexible approach when appointing a sole arbitrator by vesting discretion to the president to exercise his determination. SIAC, for example, emphasizes the referral of the case to a sole arbitrator unless the president determines otherwise.[16] The UNCITRAL Expedited Arbitration Rules 2021 contain a default rule that an arbitral tribunal comprises a single arbitrator.[17] However, the parties can agree on more than one arbitrator in light of the particulars of the dispute and if collective decision-making is preferred. Hence, respect for party autonomy is preserved as the appointment of a sole arbitrator is not strictly mandated. Therefore, these approaches allow the parties to exercise the freedom to compose the arbitral tribunal with more than one arbitrator as they desire. Even if it involves a sole arbitrator, the parties are encouraged to agree on the sole arbitrator.[18] The AIAC Arbitration Rules 2021 has also adopted a flexible approach which indicates that a sole arbitrator shall hear the arbitration under the fast-track procedure. Nevertheless, the parties' choice on a number of arbitrators prevails if they prefer an arbitration with a three-member tribunal.[19]

Other institutions also adopt flexible measures on the composition of an arbitral tribunal member. For example, the China International Economic and Trade Arbitration Commission (CIETAC) allows the formation of a sole arbitrator tribunal but is subject to the parties' agreement.[20] If the parties disagree with the appointment of a sole arbitrator, the appointment must be made according to the parties' agreement. The Swiss Rules of International Arbitration 2021 illustrate another approach concerning

14. *See* Article 2.1 Appendix VI (Expedited Procedure Rules) of the ICC Rules of Arbitration 2020. It provides that the court may appoint a sole arbitrator, notwithstanding any contrary provision of the arbitration agreement. Moreover, Article 2.2 provides that the parties may nominate the sole arbitrator within a time limit to be fixed by the Secretariat. In the absence of such nomination, the sole arbitrator shall be appointed by the court within as short a time as possible.
15. Article 17 SCC Rules for Expedited Arbitrations 2023 – the arbitration shall be decided by a sole arbitrator. Also *see* Article 8.1 of the 2016 ACICA Expedited Arbitration Rules – there shall be one arbitrator.
16. Article 5.2(b) of the 2016 SIAC Arbitration Rules – the case shall be referred to a sole arbitrator unless the president determines otherwise.
17. *See* Article 7 of the UNCITRAL Expedited Arbitration Rules 2021. It says that 'unless otherwise agreed by the parties, there shall be one arbitrator'.
18. *See* Article 8 of the UNCITRAL Expedited Arbitration Rules 2021 stipulating that 'a sole arbitrator shall be appointed jointly by the parties'.
19. Article 8.5(a) of the AIAC Arbitration Rules 2021 provides that arbitration under the fast-track procedure shall be heard by a sole arbitrator to be appointed pursuant to Rule 9.4 or 9.7(a), unless otherwise agreed by the parties.
20. Article 58 of the 2015 CIETAC Arbitration Rules – unless otherwise agreed by the parties, a sole arbitrator tribunal shall be formed in accordance with Article 28 of the Rules to hear the case under a Summary Procedure.

the parties' agreement for international arbitration, which requires adherence to the number of arbitrators in the arbitration agreement.[21] Therefore, the case shall only be referred to a sole arbitrator if there is no provision to the contrary. Hence, these institutional rules are more flexible. A contrary agreement will be given effect based on the existing parties' agreement or if the parties agree to have three arbitrators instead of a sole arbitrator presiding over a dispute.

[B] Time

One of the key features found under various institutional rules is the requirement for an arbitral tribunal to provide faster case management. However, unlike standard arbitration rules, an arbitral tribunal under expedited arbitration is strictly required to promptly call for case management and establish a timetable within a specific deadline. For example, Article 29 of the SCC Rules for Expedited Arbitrations 2023 provides that the case management conference shall take place 'promptly', and the arbitrator and the parties shall seek to adopt procedures enhancing the efficiency and expeditiousness of the proceedings. Thus, the arbitrator shall seek to establish a timetable for the arbitration, including the date for making the award no later than seven days from the referral of the case to the arbitrator.[22]

The element of 'prompt' case management is also reflected under Article 9 of UNCITRAL Expedited Arbitration Rules 2021, which requires that 'promptly after and within 15 days of its constitution, the arbitral tribunal shall consult the parties, through a case management conference or otherwise, on the manner in which it shall conduct the arbitration'.[23] In addition, under the AIAC Arbitration Rules 2021, Rule 8.8(f) requires the arbitral tribunal to convene a case management meeting and deliver the first procedural order for the conduct of the arbitration within 10 days from the date when the AIAC notifies the parties of the constitution of the arbitral tribunal.

Despite the arbitral tribunal having the case management power, it does not stop an aggrieved party from seeking to set aside the award based on the grounds of breach of natural justice, depending on how the proceedings are managed. In *China Machine*

21. *See* Article 42.2(a) and (b) of the 2012 Swiss Rules for International Arbitration – the case shall be referred to a sole arbitrator unless the arbitration agreement provides for more than one arbitrator. However, where the agreement provides for more than one arbitrator, the Secretariat shall invite the parties to agree to refer the case to a sole arbitrator. If the parties do not agree, the case will be referred to the number of arbitrators provided for under the agreement.
22. Article 3.3 Appendix VI (Expedited Procedure Rules) of the 2017 ICC Arbitration Rules provides that case management shall take place no later than 15 days after the date on which the file is transmitted to the arbitral tribunal. Article 3.4 provides that the arbitral tribunal then has the discretion, after consultation with the parties, to adopt such procedural measures as it considers appropriate, namely limiting the number, length, and scope of written submissions and written evidence or not allowing document production.
23. *See* Article 9 (Consultation with the Parties) of the UNCITRAL Expedited Arbitration Rules 2021 – promptly after and within 15 days of its constitution, the arbitral tribunal shall consult the parties, through a case management conference or otherwise, on the manner in which it will conduct the arbitration.

New Energy Corp v. Jaguar Energy Guatemala LLC and another,[24] the appellant, China Machine New Energy Corporation (CMNC), sought to set aside an arbitral award because it was obtained in breach of natural justice. CMNC's argument was that the arbitral tribunal's mismanagement of the arbitral proceedings – particularly its procedural decisions relating to the document production process and the submission of expert evidence – resulted in its being denied a reasonable opportunity to present its case. The Singapore Court of Appeal rejected an application to set aside an award based on a tribunal case management under an agreement that provided for an expedited schedule, noting that this would be a context-specific enquiry and the tribunal's decisions should be afforded a margin of deference. Accordingly, the Court of Appeal dismissed CMNC's appeal and declined to set aside the award on the grounds of a breach of natural justice.

The Court of Appeal observed that the right to be heard – which refers to each party's right to present its case and respond to the case against it – was a fundamental rule of natural justice enshrined in Article 18 of the Model Law. However, the right to a 'full opportunity' of presenting one's case under Art. 18 was not unlimited and impliedly limited by considerations of reasonableness and fairness.[25] What constituted a 'full opportunity' was a contextual enquiry to be undertaken within the specific context of each case's particular facts and circumstances. The proper approach for the court was to ask itself if what the tribunal did (or decided not to do) fell within the range of what a reasonable and fair-minded tribunal in those circumstances might have done. In undertaking this exercise, the court must put itself in the shoes of the tribunal, and this meant that: (i) the tribunal's decisions could only be assessed by reference to what was known to and brought to the attention of the tribunal at the material time, and (ii) the court would accord a margin of deference to the tribunal in matters of procedure and would not intervene simply because it might have done things differently.[26]

In the final analysis, the Court of Appeal found that CMNC had not met its burden of showing that the tribunal's conduct of the proceedings fell outside the realm of what a reasonable and fair-minded tribunal might have done. Accordingly, CMNC was unable to prove that the award was made in breach of the rules of natural justice. Therefore, no basis existed to interfere with the judge's decision to dismiss the application to set aside.

---

24. *China Machine New Energy Corp v. Jaguar Energy Guatemala LLC and another*, [2020] SGCA 12.
25. In England, section 33 of the English Arbitration Act 1996 expresses the right to be heard as a requirement that parties be given a 'reasonable' opportunity of presenting their case. In *ASM Shipping Ltd of India v. TTMI Ltd of England* [2005] EWHC 2238 (Comm) ('*ASM Shipping*'), one of the bases on which the applicant sought to set aside the arbitral award was the tribunal's refusal of an adjournment of the proceedings requested after the requesting party's lead counsel had become unavailable for personal reasons. In refusing to set aside the award, the English High Court held that the test was whether the decision to refuse an adjournment was 'so far removed from what could reasonably be expected of the arbitral process that it must be rectified' (at [38]). The judge noted that although the choice between adjourning the case causing inconvenience and giving the applicant a chance to find another Queen's Counsel was not easy, he saw nothing wrong with the tribunal's decision to refuse adjournment (at [45]).
26. *China Machine New Energy Corp v. Jaguar Energy Guatemala LLC and another* [2020] SGCA 12, para. 104.

[C] Limitation of Hearing

The expeditious manner of the proceedings empowers the arbitral tribunal with discretion to modulate the parties' right to have a hearing. By exercising its power to assess the evidence based on documents only, the absence of a hearing may affect the due process of the proceedings. The concept of due process encompasses a basic guarantee of procedural fairness in legal proceedings.[27] It requires that each party be given, among other things, appropriate notice of the proceedings and the case it has to meet, as well as a fair opportunity to prepare and present its case before a neutral and unbiased decision-maker. These basic procedural safeguards are applied to ensure the fairness of the proceedings by which the parties' substantive rights are disposed of. In short, due process is concerned with ensuring a fair process. This is a matter of critical importance because the fairness of the process is integral to its legitimacy in the eyes of the parties who submit themselves to it.[28]

It is common to encounter provisions that demonstrate the arbitral tribunal's power to exclude a hearing while opting for an assessment of the evidence based only on documents. Among the notable examples is Article 3.5 of the ICC Expedited Procedure Provisions, which states that the arbitral tribunal may, after consulting the parties, decide the dispute solely based on the documents submitted by the parties, with no hearing and no examination of witnesses or experts. When a hearing is held, the arbitral tribunal may conduct it by videoconference, telephone, or similar means of communication.[29] Similarly, the requirement of 'consultation' with the parties also appears in Rule 5.2(c) of the 2016 SIAC Arbitration Rules, which says that the tribunal may, in consultation with the parties, decide if the dispute is to be decided on the basis of documentary evidence only, or if a hearing is required for the examination of any witness and expert witness as well as for any oral argument.[30] Rule 8.5(b) of the AIAC Arbitration Rules 2021 also contains the consultation requirement, although it is drafted to prioritize documents-only arbitration. It provides that arbitration under fast-track procedures shall proceed as a documents-only arbitration unless otherwise determined by the arbitral tribunal after consulting the parties. In other words, a consultation with the parties is a pre-requisite before the arbitral tribunal decides whether to hold a hearing.[31] Unsurprisingly, consultation is an essential procedural tool, particularly in expedited

27. As per the judgment of Sundaresh Menon, CJ, in *China Machine New Energy Corp v. Jaguar Energy Guatemala LLC and another* [2020] SGCA 12, 1.
28. *Ibid.*
29. *See* Article 3.4. The arbitral tribunal shall have the discretion to adopt such procedural measures as it considers appropriate. In particular, after consultation with the parties, the arbitral tribunal may decide not to allow requests for document production or to limit the number, length, and scope of written submissions and written witness evidence (fact witnesses and experts).
30. *See* Article 41.2 of 2013 HKIAC Administered Arbitration Rules – the arbitral tribunal shall decide the dispute on the basis of documentary evidence only unless it decides that it is appropriate to hold one or more hearings.
31. *See* Article 60 of 2015 CIETAC Arbitration Rules – the arbitral tribunal may examine the case as it considers appropriate. For example, the arbitral tribunal may decide whether to examine the case solely based on written materials and evidence submitted by the parties or to hold an oral hearing after hearing the parties of their opinions.

arbitration. Consultation between the arbitral tribunal and the parties at an early stage of the proceedings is the key to an efficient and fair organization of expedited arbitration. It thus conveys the expectation that the arbitral tribunal will engage actively with the parties rather than invite them to express their views.

While the arbitral tribunal can conduct the proceedings based on documents submitted (at the expense of a hearing), the discretion is not always absolute. A case in point is Article 11 of UNCITRAL Expedited Arbitration Rules 2021. It provides that the arbitral tribunal may, after inviting the parties to express their views and, in the absence of a request to hold hearings, decide that hearings shall not be held.[32] In this respect, the arbitral tribunal's determination on a hearing is subject to the parties' agreement. Thus, the discretionary power of the arbitral tribunal is limited by the request for a hearing. Article 11 allows the arbitral tribunal to conduct documents-based arbitration only in the absence of a request to hold a hearing. Therefore, if the parties agree to hold a hearing, the agreement is binding on the arbitral tribunal.[33] In this manner, the arbitral tribunal must safeguard the parties' autonomy by holding a hearing because its discretion to opt for documents-only arbitration is limited. In contrast, Article 33(1) of the SCC Rules for Expedited Arbitrations 2023 retains the arbitrator's discretionary power even if there is a request to hold a hearing. In this regard, a request of the parties to hold a hearing is subject to 'compelling reasons' based on the arbitrator's consideration.[34] Contrary to Article 11 of the UNCITRAL Expedited Arbitration Rules 2021, a mere request to hold a hearing is not automatically granted unless the arbitrator considers the reasons for the request to be compelling.

[D] Deadlines for the Issuance of an Award

Typically, institutional rules set a deadline for issuing an award. This ensures the efficiency of expedited arbitration with the promise of speed as its advantage. The standard deadline for issuing an award varies between three[35] and six[36] months from the starting point as specified by the institutional rules. Nevertheless, the rules allow an

32. Article 11 has to be read together with Article 17(3) of the UNCITRAL Arbitration Rules, which provides that: (1) the arbitral tribunal shall hold hearings if any party so requests at an appropriate stage of the proceedings; and (2) in the absence of such a request, the arbitral tribunal shall decide whether to hold hearings.
33. *See* Article 24.6 of ACICA Expedited Arbitration Rules 2021 – There shall be no hearing unless: (a) exceptional circumstances exist, as determined by the arbitrator; and (b) either the arbitrator or the parties require a hearing to take place. Also *see* Article 42.2(d) of the Swiss Rules of International Arbitration 2021 which provides unless the dispute is decided on the basis of documentary evidence only, a single hearing shall be held for the examination of witnesses and experts or for oral argument.
34. *See* Article 33 of the SCC Rules for Expedited Arbitrations 2023 – a hearing shall be held only at the request of a party and if the arbitrator considers the reasons for the request to be compelling.
35. *See* Article 43 of the SCC Rules for Expedited Arbitrations 2023 – three months from the referral of the case. Also *see* Article 62 of the CIETAC Arbitration Rules – three months from the date on which the tribunal was formed, Rule 8.8(n) of the AIAC Arbitration Rules 2021 – 90 days from the date when the proceedings were declared closed, and Article 4.1 of the 2016 ACICA Expedited Arbitration Rules – four months of the appointment of the arbitrator if there is no counterclaim or set-off.

extension of time for the arbitral tribunal to deliver its award under exceptional circumstances and subject to the parties' agreement.[37]

§4.04 SETTING ASIDE THE EXPEDITED ARBITRATION AWARD

The expedited arbitration pursuit of achieving efficiency is not free from legal challenges. For example, appointing a sole arbitrator and assessing evidence on documents causes considerable strain on party autonomy and due process. As a result, the aggrieved party may mount a challenge on the award, which constrains their choice on a number of arbitrators or the right to a hearing. Despite the clear objective of expedited procedures in providing expeditious and efficient proceedings, challenges may still arise in several areas. In practice, the parties may not necessarily comply with their chosen specific rules due to conduct undermining the application of the expedited procedure rules[38] or to the difficulties in implementing a mechanism ensuring expedited proceedings.[39] These challenges lingering on expedited rules may lead the parties to seek to set aside the award. The following cases illustrate how courts interpret the rules relating to the challenge of the award based on the facts of each case.

[A] The Strain on Party Autonomy

One might loosen the strain of a potential restriction on party autonomy by arguing that when the party chooses to submit its dispute to specific rules, they are deemed to implicitly accept the application of such rules within the scope of the arbitration agreement. In *Societe Guangzhou Ocean Shipping Co v. Societe Generale des Farines*,[40] the Paris Court of Appeal decided that the parties' reference to the arbitration centre for the dispute settlement (with no further details) is equivalent to the unconditional

36. *See* Article 4.1 Appendix VI of the 2017 ICC Arbitration Rules – six months from the case management conference unless the court extends the deadline. Also *see* Article 5.2(d) 2016 SIAC Arbitration Rules – six months from the date on which the tribunal was constituted and Article 16(1) of the UNCITRAL Expedited Arbitration Rules 2021 – the award shall be made within six months from the date of the constitution of the arbitral tribunal unless otherwise agreed by the parties.
37. *See* Article 42(d) Swiss Rules of International Arbitration 2021 – six months from the date the file was transmitted to the tribunal, except in 'exceptional circumstances'. Also *see* Article 16(2) of the UNCITRAL Expedited Arbitration Rules 2021 that the arbitral tribunal may, in 'exceptional circumstances' and after inviting the parties to express their views, extend the time established in accordance with paragraph 1. However, the extended time shall not exceed nine months from the date of the constitution of the arbitral tribunal.
38. For example, practical difficulty arises in determining whether a matter falls within the scope of the rules when procedural tactics include counterclaims to rise above the financial threshold.
39. When the institutional rules provide a sole arbitrator to hear the expedited proceedings, a question arises whether the aggrieved party may challenge the award based on the breach of the parties' agreement to constitute the tribunal with three arbitrators. Another example relates to the arbitrator's power that may compel the parties to present their case within certain constraints, i.e., limiting the time for a hearing that provides a setting aside ground on the lack of due process.
40. *Societe Guangzhou Ocean Shipping Co v. Societe Generale des Farines* CA Paris (1 Ch. suppl.) 17 January 1992, Rev. arb. 1992, p. 656.

adoption of the provisions. Therefore, when the parties decide to submit a dispute to specific rules, that includes the 'expedited rules' on a myriad of procedural matters, with the appointment of a sole arbitrator being one of them.

In *AQZ v. ARA*,[41] the respondent sought to set aside the arbitration award because a sole arbitrator was not in accordance with the parties' agreement because they had expressly agreed to arbitration before three arbitrators based on Article 34(2)(a)(iv) of the UNCITRAL Model Law. The court held that the SIAC Rules 2010 referred to by the parties contained expedited procedure provisions, and so it was consistent with party autonomy for the expedited procedure involving a sole arbitrator to override the parties' agreement on three arbitrators.

The Singapore court adopted a purposive interpretation of the arbitration agreement, which required recognition of the SIAC President's discretion under the chosen rules to appoint a sole arbitrator. The court observed that 'a commercially sensible approach to interpreting the parties' arbitration agreement would be to recognize that the SIAC President does have the discretion to appoint a sole arbitrator'.[42]

By applying a commercially sensible approach in interpreting the arbitration agreement, the court rightly reasoned that the reference to expedited procedures overrides the parties' agreement if the SIAC President had adequately exercised his discretion. However, the enforcement of this award by a Singaporean company against a Shanghai company encountered a hurdle when the Shanghai Court in *Noble Resources International v. Shanghai Good Credit*[43] dismissed an enforcement application due to the appointment of a sole arbitrator that disregarded the parties' express choice to have three arbitrators under the arbitration agreement. The issue before the court was whether the composition of the arbitral tribunal was consistent with the parties' agreement.

The Shanghai court's decision was premised on three grounds. First, because the President of SIAC was allowed to decide on the matter in question, the expedited procedure did not necessarily require the arbitration to be conducted before a sole arbitrator. Second, the 2013 SIAC Rules did not stipulate that a sole arbitrator tribunal would prevail and take precedence over the contrary agreement of the parties. Taking into account party autonomy, which is the bedrock of the arbitration process, the President of SIAC, when exercising his discretion in deciding on the composition of the tribunal under Article 5.2 of the SIAC 2013 Rules, should have taken into account the parties' express choice and agreement to have three arbitrators. Third, SIAC's appointment of a sole arbitrator contravened the parties' agreement and resulted in the award being unenforceable under Article 5(1)(d) of the New York Convention of 1958 (NYC 1958).

---

41. *AQZ v. ARA* [2015] SGHC 49.
42. *Ibid.*, para. 132. The court also reasoned in para. 131 that 'in *W Company v Dutch Company and Dutch Holding Company* [2012] 1 SAA 97, the parties had expressly chosen a version of the SIAC Rules that contained Expedited Procedure provision. Therefore, it was consistent with party autonomy for the Expedited Procedure provision to override their agreement for the arbitration before three arbitrators'.
43. *Noble Resources International v. Shanghai Good Credit* [2016] Shanghai No. 1 Intermediate People's Court (Hu 01 Xie Wai Ren No. 1).

In light of the foregoing, the Shanghai court concluded that SIAC's president had exercised his discretion by ignoring the parties' express choice of three arbitrators. By exercising discretion, SIAC's president should have considered appointing three arbitrators because the parties made an express choice regarding the composition of the arbitral tribunal. Moreover, the 2013 SIAC Rules did not restrict the appointment of a sole arbitrator such that they disallowed the appointment of three arbitrators. Therefore, a departure from the parties' express choice and agreement infringed on party autonomy. Consequently, the court refused the enforcement and recognition of the award under Article V(1)(d) of the NYC 1958 because 'the composition of the arbitral tribunal or the arbitral procedure was not in accordance with the agreement of the parties'.

While the Shanghai court recognized that the SIAC president has discretion under Article 5.2 on the composition of an arbitral tribunal, that is not absolute. Therefore, when exercising discretion, SIAC's president must fully consider the parties' express choice to have three arbitrators, failing which Article V(1)(d) of the NYC 1958 may deny the application for enforcement of the award. From the court's view, an appointment of a sole arbitrator amounts to a breach of the parties' agreement that requires a three-person arbitral tribunal.

The Shanghai court was cautious to safeguard the parties' autonomy by narrowly construing their express choice and specific agreement to effectuate the arbitral tribunal's constitution. In contrast, the parties' agreement is observed since the institution would apply its rules as the parties chose. Therefore, appointing a sole arbitrator as mandated by the chosen rules does not directly infringe Article V(1)(d) of the NYC 1958. While the Shanghai court's decision may be seen as challenging the expedited procedure, the context of Article 5.2 of SIAC 2013 Rules does not impose a prevailing effect on the parties' agreement.[44] Learning the lesson, SIAC amended its rules in 2016. The amended rules now expressly incorporate a provision that gives precedence to the rules over the parties' agreement to the contrary.[45]

A similar trend is also reflected in the language of some institutional rules due to the risk associated with enforcement applications being challenged on the parties' autonomy ground. Institutions such as Hong Kong International Arbitration Centre (HKIAC) and the Swiss Chamber of Commerce have adopted an approach aligned with party autonomy by providing a safety net for 'cases under the expedited procedural rules shall be referred to a sole arbitrator unless the arbitration agreement provides for more than one arbitrator'.[46] The cautious approach of prioritizing parties' express

---

44. *See* Mohamed S. Abdel Wahab, *Expedited Institutional Arbitral Proceedings Between Autonomy and Regulation: Procedural Efficiency and Enforcement Challenges* (Laurent Levy and Michael Polkinghorne eds, Dossier XVI of the ICC Institute of World Business Law, 2017), 143.
45. *See* Articles 5.3 of the SIAC 2016 Rules and 30.1 of the ICC Rules as amended in March 2017.
46. *See* Article 41.2 of the HKIAC Arbitration Rules:

> When HKIAC, after considering the views of the parties, grants an application made pursuant to Article 41.1 [the Expedited Procedure], the arbitral proceedings shall be conducted in accordance with an Expedited Procedure based upon the foregoing provisions of these Rules, subject to the following changes:

choice over the application of expedited rules is a laudable effort the institutions made to balance efficiency and party autonomy.

[B] The Strain on Due Process

A tendency to conduct proceedings based on documents-only arbitration[47] has caused a strain on due process, particularly the right to have a hearing.[48] Provisions relating to dispensing with a hearing are connected to a due process requirement. Accordingly, a breach of due process will trigger a setting aside of the award by the court of the seat under Article 34(2)(a)(ii) of UNCITRAL Model Law 'if a party is unable to present his case' or 'refusal of recognition and enforcement of the award by an enforcing court' under Article V(1)(b) of the NYC 1958.

> 1. The case shall be referred to a sole arbitrator unless the arbitration agreement provides for three arbitrators.
> 2. If the arbitration agreement provides for three arbitrators, HKIAC shall invite the parties to agree to refer the case to a sole arbitrator. If the parties do not agree, the case shall be referred to three arbitrators [...]

Swiss Chambers of Commerce Article 42.2 (a) states that the case shall be referred to a sole arbitrator unless the Arbitration Agreement provides for more than one arbitrator.

The Japan Commercial Arbitration Association (the JCAA) favours the parties' autonomy. Unlike HKIAC and the Swiss Chambers of Commerce, the JCAA expedited procedural rules would not apply if the parties agree on more than one arbitrator pursuant to Rule 75:

> 2. Expedited procedures shall be conducted where the amount or economic value of the claimant's claim(s) is not more than Yen 20,000,000; unless within two weeks from the respondent's receipt of the notice of the Request for Arbitration:
> [...]
> (2) a Party notifies the JCAA in writing of the agreement by the Parties that there will be more than one arbitrator [...]

47. *See* Article 5.2(c) SIAC Rules 2016 provides 'the tribunal may, in consultation with the parties, decide if the dispute is to be decided on the basis of documentary evidence only, or if a hearing is required for the examination of any witness and expert witness as well as for any oral argument'. Also *see* Article 5 of Appendix VI to the ICC Rules of Arbitration 2021, which takes a similar approach in providing that the tribunal may, after consulting the parties, 'decide the dispute solely based on documents submitted by the parties, with no hearing'. Article 33 of SCC Rules for Expedited Arbitrations 2023 provides a framework to dispense with a hearing that 'a hearing shall be held only at the request of a party and if the Arbitrator considers the reasons for the request to be compelling'. Article 11 UNCITRAL Expedited Arbitration Rules 2021 take a different approach providing that 'the arbitral tribunal may, after inviting the parties to express their views and in the absence of a request to hold hearings, decide that hearings shall not be held'. Finally, Article 14.6(v) of LCIA Rules of Arbitration 2020 includes a power of the tribunal to dispense with a hearing, subject always to Article 19, which provides that 'any party has the right to a hearing before the arbitral tribunal ...' (an LCIA arbitral tribunal, therefore, could only dispense with a hearing if the parties agree, although as with other arbitration rules, a tribunal has the power to refuse or limit the testimony of witnesses under Article 20 and thus control the content of the hearing).
48. *See* Article 17.3 UNCITRAL Rules 2012 provides that 'if at an appropriate stage of the proceedings any party so requests, the arbitral tribunal shall hold hearings for the presentation of evidence by witnesses ... or for oral argument'. Also *see* Article 26.1 of ICC Rules of Arbitration 2021 similarly requires that 'a hearing shall be held if any of the parties so request ... .'

The *Swiss Federal Tribunal* decision in *X v. Y*[49] arose from an arbitration governed by Swiss law under the auspices of the Geneva Chamber of Commerce and Industry (GCCI). The expedited procedures under the GCCI rules automatically applied since the amount in dispute was below CHF 1 million. The award was challenged on alleged violations of the respondent's right to be heard, both during the arbitral proceedings (including on alleged unequal time given to the parties) and in light of the arbitrator's alleged failure to provide any 'real reasoning' in support of the award. The Federal tribunal held that the right to be heard was violated when some manifest oversight led the arbitral tribunal to fail to consider some elements that one of the parties submitted to the tribunal. It further held that the right to be heard does not necessarily require an arbitral award to be reasoned. Instead, a brief statement of reasons (in a procedural order) may suffice when such an obligation applies.

The Svea Court of Appeal[50] addressed the issue involving a sole arbitrator's decision to dispense with a hearing conducted under the SCC Rules for expedited arbitration. The appellant challenged the award because the sole arbitrator had invalidly rejected its request to hold a hearing to hear the witnesses' testimony. The appellant argued that it had been prevented from presenting evidence to support its claim due to the sole arbitrator's decision not to hold a hearing. The Svea Court of Appeal dismissed the challenge, observing that under Article 27(1) of the SCC Rules for Expedited Arbitrations 2010, a hearing was to be held if requested by a party and deemed necessary by the arbitrator. In the court's view, the sole arbitrator had already decided, after considering the parties' submissions and witness statements, that it was unnecessary to hold a hearing. The court also noted that the sole arbitrator had correctly applied the applicable law, which was the law of the State of New York, which contained the parol evidence rule that excluded evidence beyond the parties' written agreement. Accordingly, the court ruled that when deciding to dispense with a hearing, the sole arbitrator had applied the arbitration rules and applicable law as agreed by the parties.[51]

The English High Court in *Travis Coal Restructured Holdings v. Essar Global Fund*[52] had to deal with an application to set aside an ex parte enforcement order relating to a New York arbitral award or to adjourn a decision on enforcement pending the outcome of a challenge to the award in the New York court. During the arbitration, Travis Coal had applied for summary judgment on fraud defences. Essar objected to the summary judgment application, arguing that adopting a summary procedure would violate its right to be heard on its defences. The tribunal held hearings and heard the oral testimony from a witness on both sides, including the one relevant to Essar's fraud defences. However, the tribunal held the hearings in a summary procedure that fell short of a full hearing on merits. The tribunal then issued a procedural order which

49. *X. v. Y.*, 4A_294/2008, ASA Bulletin, 2009, p. 144; Swiss International Arbitration Report, 2008, p. 495.
50. Judgment Svea Court of Appeal, Case No. T 6238-10, 24 February 2012. Swedish Arbitration Portal, accessible at http://www.arbitration.sccinstitute.com/Swedish-Arbitration-Portal.
51. Judgment Svea Court of Appeal, Case No. T 6238-10, 24 February 2012, para. 3, p. 9.
52. *Travis Coal Restructured Holdings LLC v. Essar Global Fund Ltd* [2014] EWHC 2510 (Comm) (24 July 2014).

ruled that Essar's fraud defences did not bar Travis Coal's claim based on certain waiver provisions in the agreement.[53]

The English High Court observed that the parties' arbitration agreement contained a clause empowering the tribunal to decide dispositive issues appropriately. Further, it also pointed to Article 22 of the applicable 2012 ICC Rules, which required the tribunal to conduct the arbitration expeditiously and cost-effectively and empowered the tribunal to adopt such procedural measures as it considered appropriate, provided that the measures were not contrary to the parties' agreement. Finally, the court observed that the tribunal's adoption of a summary procedure process did not necessarily amount to a denial of due process. In the court's view, whether the summary judgment process by arbitration necessarily amounts to a denial of due process is not a question that could be addressed in general terms. Instead, the facts of the particular case and the terms of the arbitration agreement must be taken into account to determine whether the measures adopted by the tribunal are within the scope of its powers and otherwise fair. Accordingly, the court finally found no 'realistic prospect' of resisting the award enforcement based on the arbitral tribunal's summary procedure.[54]

In *CBS v. CBP*,[55] the arbitration occurred under the Singapore Chamber of Maritime Arbitration[56] (SCMA Rules 2015). The buyer breached various timelines set by the arbitrator and needed to be more cooperative in the arbitral process. After a delayed filing of the buyer's defence, the arbitrator asked the parties to consider whether an oral hearing was necessary. The buyer requested a hearing for witnesses to give evidence on what transpired at a meeting, alleging that there was a subsequent meeting and an agreement to reduce the price of the coal. The arbitrator ruled that the buyer had to submit its proposed witness statements so that he could decide if they had substantive value before he would convene a hearing. The buyer refused to do so, insisting on its right to call witnesses without such a condition. The arbitrator then convened a hearing for oral submissions only. Accordingly, the arbitrator allowed the Bank's claim in the final award. The buyer challenged the award, claiming, among other things, that there had been a breach of natural justice. The High Court Judge agreed with the buyer and set aside the final award.

On appeal, the Singapore Court of Appeal found that an arbitral tribunal's refusal to hold an oral hearing on the request of a party was a breach of natural justice. The court attached weight to the fact that the applicable arbitration rules required the

53. *Travis Coal Restructured Holdings LLC v. Essar Global Limited (now Essar Global Fund Limited)* ICC Case No. 18724/VRO/AGF in paras 146-147 of the Final Award.

54. *Travis Coal Restructured Holdings v. Essar Global Fund* [2014] EWHC 2510 (Comm) (24 July 2014). Mr Justice Blair in para. 62 on p. 77 held that 'I have found that there is no realistic prospect of EFGL's establishing any of its grounds of challenge to the award. It follows that I consider that its application is at the bottom of the "sliding scale" in terms of prospects of success. I refer to the other considerations held in *IPCO* (*ibid.*) to be relevant to the question of adjournment. Whilst I do not accept the submission of Travis that the New York challenge is not brought in good faith, I do consider that the proceedings can properly be described as delaying tactics in the face of what is likely to be held to be an unimpeachable award.'

55. *CBS v. CBP* [2021] SGCA 4, Civil Appeal No. 30 of 2020.

56. *See* Singapore Chamber of Maritime Arbitration Rules, 3rd ed. (October 2015).

tribunal to hold a hearing at a party's request and also emphasized that case management powers did not override rules of natural justice.[57]

Following the precedent set by the Court of Appeal of Singapore in *China Machine New Energy Corp*,[58] the court found that there had been a breach of natural justice because the buyer did not have a 'full opportunity' to present its case. What is considered a 'full opportunity' is a fact-sensitive enquiry and the question is whether 'what the tribunal did (or decided not to do) falls within the range of what a reasonable and fair-minded tribunal in those circumstances might have done'. This is assessed by reference to what the tribunal knew at the time, and a court will generally accord a margin of deference to the tribunal in matters of procedure.[59]

The court further held that under Rule 28.1 of the SCMA Rules 2015, there are only two broad situations where a hearing need not be held: first, where the parties have agreed to a document-only arbitration without witness testimony, whether oral or written and, second, where the parties agree that no hearing would be held at all.[60] Accordingly, unless parties have agreed on a documents-only arbitration or that no hearing will be held at all, the arbitrator is obliged to hold a hearing to receive oral evidence from witnesses where a party requested it. Therefore, the arbitrator had no power to decide to convene a hearing only for oral submissions. Rule 28.1 of the SCMA did not give the tribunal the power to choose what type of hearing to hold in the absence of an agreement by the parties.[61] The court also observed that cases have stated that the broad procedural powers of an arbitral tribunal are subject to the fundamental rules of natural justice.[62]

57. *CBS v. CBP* [2021] SGCA 4, Civil Appeal No. 30 of 2020. In para. 79, the Court of Appeal of Singapore held that 'we therefore satisfied that the arbitrator's denial of the entirety of the witness evidence from the buyer constitute a breach of natural justice. Whilst it is correct that the courts would generally accord a margin of deference to the tribunal's decisions, especially on procedural matters, this is a clear case of a serious breach of the rules of natural justice and to decide otherwise would be to reduce the content of those rules to a vanishing point'.
58. *China Machine New Energy Corp v. Jaguar Energy Guatemala LLC and another* [2020] SGCA 12.
59. *CBS v. CBP* [2021] SGCA 4, Civil Appeal No. 30 of 2020 in paras 51 and 78.
60. *Ibid.*, in para. 56.
61. *Ibid.*, in paras 55-57. The court in paras 61 and 69 held that although tribunals can limit the oral examination of witnesses as part of their general case management powers, this cannot override the rules of natural justice. Indeed, the SCMA Rules do not explicitly confer a broad and unqualified power on the tribunal to gate witnesses, and Rule 25 expressly qualifies the 'widest discretion' conferred on arbitrators in the conduct of proceedings to be that 'allowed by' the International Arbitration Act (Cap 143A, 2002 Rev. ed.).
62. *See* the case of *Dalmia Dairy Industries v. National Bank of Pakistan* [1978] 2 Lloyd's Rep 233, involving an ICC arbitration which notably turned exclusively on legal issues. While arbitral tribunals have occasionally declined to hear witness evidence without a party agreement, this situation is likely a rarity. The Bank in the *CBS v. CBP* [2021] SGCA 4, Civil Appeal No. 30 of 2020, relies on *Dalmia* to argue that national courts have expressly recognized a tribunal's power to gate witnesses even where the arbitral rules, such as the ICC Rules, do not contain such an express provision. However, the exercise of the witness-gating power must be considered in the context of the facts in *Dalmia*. The issues were almost exclusively legal, and factual evidence from witnesses would not have assisted in arriving at or affecting the outcome. The one factual issue, the form, and content of *Dalmia*'s despatch instructions to the buyer to deliver cement, which formed part of the consideration under the sale and purchase agreement, though challenged before the arbitrator, was no longer pursued before the court during the enforcement proceedings. The court in para. 65 observed that 'the decision in *Dalmia* was, with respect,

In Malaysia, the AIAC introduced the Fast Track Arbitration Rules in 2018, designed for parties who wish to obtain an award quickly with minimal costs.[63] Incorporating the fast-track procedure for expedited arbitration under the recent version of the AIAC Arbitration Rules 2021 does away with the need for a stand-alone set of rules.[64] Since the fast-track procedure is relatively new in Malaysia, it is still underused for two reasons. First, the well-established use of standard arbitration has been associated with construction-related disputes that formed the majority of domestic disputes.[65] Second, the Construction Industry Payment and Adjudication Act 2012 (CIPAA 2012)[66] resembles the expedited procedures through statutory adjudication designed explicitly to resolve construction-related payment disputes. Whenever there is a need for a speedy dispute resolution, CIPAA 2012 is the first port of call due to its statutory nature that cuts across all contrary contractual provisions.[67] There is a paucity of reported cases under the Fast Track Arbitration Rules 2018 or the fast-track procedure under the AIAC Arbitration Rules 2021. In the following cases, the Malaysian courts analyse the application of CIPAA 2012 section 25(g), which provides that 'the adjudicator shall have the powers to conduct any hearing and limiting the hearing time'.

In *Permintex JSK Resources Sdn Bhd v. Follitile (M) Sdn Bhd and Another Case*,[68] the adjudicator had awarded the amount claimed to Follitile due to the failure of Permintex to file the necessary response to the claim on time. Permintex had requested an extension to file the response, but the adjudicator rejected it. Accordingly, Permintex applied to set aside the decision under section 15(b) based on a denial of natural justice. In addition, it argued there had been a breach of natural justice because the

correctly decided given the facts of the case and the issues before the arbitrator. It is not inconsistent with our explanation above that even *if* a witness-gating power can be implied from a tribunal's general case management powers, it is difficult to envision a scenario where they should not be weighed against the rules of natural justice'.

63. Rule 21 of the AIAC Fast Track Arbitration Rules 2018 provides that arbitration (with a substantive oral hearing) must be completed within a maximum of 160 days and tried before a sole arbitrator (unless parties prefer a larger panel).
64. Under the older version of the AIAC Arbitration Rules 2018, the standard arbitration rules exist independently of expedited arbitration governed by the AIAC Fast Track Arbitration Rules 2018. Rule 8 on the fast-track procedure under the recent AIAC Arbitration Rules 2021 applies to the expedited conduct of arbitral proceedings in an arbitration administered by the AIAC.
65. The arbitration law in Malaysia is governed by the Arbitration Act 2005 and the Arbitration (Amendment) (No. 2) Act 2018. In addition, the key institutional rules such as the AIAC Arbitration Rules 2023 apply to an administered arbitration.
66. Shahrizal M. Zin and Nik Hasbi Fathi, *Common Issues in Malaysian Adjudication: Guide to CIPAA 2012 (Cases and Materials)* (LexisNexis, 2020) at p. 47, which states that CIPAA 2012 aims to provide a speedy, economical, and temporary resolution mechanism for payment disputes under a construction contract. Through CIPAA 2012, adjudication is offered on a statutory framework attributed explicitly to the construction industry as an additional alternative to litigation and arbitration. Being statutory, CIPAA 2012 cut across any contrary provision under the construction contract.
67. The CIPAA 2012 provides a standard timeline of 90 days from start to finish for a dispute resolution pertaining to a payment claim under a construction contract. In addition, one of the key features of the CIPAA 2012 is a prohibition of conditional payment based on section 35, such as pay when paid or a back-to-back clause.
68. *Permintex JSK Resources Sdn Bhd v. Follitile (M) Sdn Bhd and Another Case* [2017] MLJU 377.

adjudicator had not invited parties for a meeting to clarify pending issues, to explain the procedure, the timelines, how he would be conducting the proceedings, and give guidance or directions or to extend any time limit imposed on the parties, all of which are powers conferred to an adjudicator under section 25.[69]

In dismissing the set-aside application, the Malaysian High Court held that CIPAA 2012 confers broad and vast powers on an adjudicator so that he may proceed with all speed and diligence in arriving at a decision within the tight time frame prescribed. In this case, the court noted that the adjudicator had issued four Orders for Directions to the parties. In the court's view, the rules of natural justice are satisfied even if parties are not heard in person. So long as the parties are allowed to be heard in writing, depending on the circumstances of the case, the court would not set aside an adjudication decision.[70]

A similar issuer cropped up in *Guangxi Dev & Cap v. Sycal Bhd and Another Case*,[71] in which the plaintiff argued that the refusal of the adjudicator to grant a hearing and allowing three witnesses to testify amounted to a denial of natural justice. The Malaysian High Court found that the adjudicator had considered the plaintiff's application and gave cogent reasons for rejecting the hearing of three expert witnesses. Accordingly, the court held that an adjudicator not holding a hearing did not amount to a breach of natural justice. No evidence existed that had the adjudicator heard the oral testimony of the witnesses, she would have arrived at a different conclusion.[72]

On appeal, the appellant complained that the adjudicator, in rejecting the application to call its three expert witnesses, had deprived him of an opportunity to present a complete defence against the respondent's claims.[73] The adjudicator believed no need existed for expert witnesses to give evidence for several reasons. First, she considered the time limit under CIPAA 2012 for the adjudicator to deliver the decision.[74] Second, she considered that the matter had already been referred to

69. *See* the judgment of Lee Swee Seng J in para. 62 on p. 10 based on the list of the adjudicator's powers under section 25(a) to (p) of the CIPAA 2012.
70. Lee Swee Seng J further observed in para. 66 on p. 11 that 'in fact, natural justice does not necessarily mean the decision maker has to meet the parties face to face'. Quoting the phrase from *R. (Morgan Grenfell & Co. Ltd.) v. Special Commissioner of Income Tax* [2001] EWCA Civ 329, the court emphasizes that 'natural justice does not generally demand orality'.
71. *Guangxi Dev & Cap v. Sycal Bhd and Another Case* [2017] MLJU 878.
72. *See* Mee Chun J in para. 19 on p. 4 held that 'here it cannot be said that there was a denial of natural justice on the assumption that had the witnesses been heard orally, the adjudicator would have come to a different conclusion in favour of Plaintiff. This would be tantamount to dwelling on the sufficiency of evidence and the weight to be attached to it'. The court went on further to say in para. 22 that 'the denial of natural justice (if there was one) would have to be decisive or considered of potential importance. Here this has not been demonstrated where there appears to be an assumption if witnesses had been allowed there would be a different decision'.
73. *See* the Court of Appeal's decision in *Guangxi Dev & Cap v. Sycal Bhd and Another Case* [2018] MLJU 1542.
74. According to section 12(2) of the CIPAA 2012, the adjudicator shall decide the dispute and deliver the adjudication decision within: (a) 45 working days from the service of the adjudication response or reply to the adjudication response, whichever is later; (b) 45 working days from the expiry of the period prescribed for the service of the adjudication response if no adjudication response if received; or (c) such further time as agreed to by the parties. The failure to comply with the period specified under section 12(2) will render the adjudicator's decision to be void.

arbitration and no prejudice would be caused because the witnesses could be called in the arbitration proceedings. Third, notwithstanding the earlier reasons, the defence of disputing the payment certificates was not raised in the response and, as such, could not be considered.[75]

The Malaysian Court of Appeal held that any application for an oral hearing must be considered on its merits, as that power is allowed in section 25.[76] In the court's view, a request for an oral hearing cannot be denied because time was limited, especially when the application has been made at the earliest opportunity. If all applications for an oral hearing were rejected on the timeline argument, then the power to order oral hearings under section 25(g) would be rendered illusory.[77] The court distinguished the *Guangxi* case from *Martego Sdn Bhd v. Arkitek Meor & Chew Sdn Bhd & Anor Case*,[78] where the request for an oral hearing was made six days before the deadline to deliver the adjudication decision. In *Guangxi*, the request for an oral hearing was made one day after the service of the adjudication reply.[79] Therefore, there was ample time to conduct the hearing. The adjudicator may still limit the hearing time as the case demands. Instead of holding an oral hearing, the adjudicator could also order the parties to submit written submissions with documents included, as was done in the *Martego* case.

In *Mammoth Empire Construction Sdn Bhd v. STAM Engineering Sdn Bhd and Another Case*,[80] the respondent applied to set aside the adjudication decision, arguing a breach of natural justice and excess of the adjudicator's jurisdiction when they dismissed the respondent's request for a hearing. As a result, the respondent could not submit some documents and evidence supporting its response.[81]

The court found that CIPAA 2012 does not allow the respondent to be orally heard at a hearing. Moreover, section 10(1) and (2) provide that the respondent shall serve a written response with any supporting documents within 10 days of receipt of the adjudication claim. Thus, the respondent should have availed itself of this right and served all documents it intended to rely on when the adjudication response was filed.

---

75. These are the grounds that the learned adjudicator has given in her adjudication decision to dismiss the Appellant's request to call for the expert witness to give evidence during the adjudication proceedings.
76. *See* section 25 of the CIPAA 2012, which contains the myriad of adjudicator's powers from paras (a) to (p).
77. *See* the reasoning given by the Court of Appeal in para. 24 on p. 6 of *Guangxi Dev & Cap v. Sycal Bhd and Another Case* [2018] MLJU 1542.
78. *Martego Sdn Bhd v. Arkitek Meor & Chew Sdn Bhd & Anor Case* [2016] MLJU 1051.
79. Since the Appellant has requested an oral hearing one day after the service of the adjudication reply, the Court of Appeal is of the view that there is ample time for the adjudicator to conduct the hearing. Moreover, under section 12(2)(b) of the CIPAA 2012, the adjudicator has 45 working days to prepare and deliver his adjudication decision, in which one can conduct an oral hearing within this period.
80. *Mammoth Empire Construction Sdn Bhd v. STAM Engineering Sdn Bhd and Another Case* [2019] 10 MLJU 58.
81. In para. 9(b) on p. 65, the respondent has laid down a ground to set aside the adjudication decision that 'the adjudicator had breached the rules of natural justice and/or acted in excess of jurisdiction when he dismissed the respondent's solicitor's request for hearing in order for the respondent to submit some documents and evidence in support of the adjudication response and also to call witnesses'.

The court noted that the adjudicator is empowered under section 25 to establish procedures for the conduct of the proceedings. Further, the respondent was given ample opportunity to present all the documentary evidence it sought to rely on and to be heard through a written submission. Instead, the respondent chose to refrain from complying with the statutory rights prescribed in CIPAA 2012 and to serve its documents in the manner and time prescribed. Having made that choice, the respondent had to live with it and could not now complain about a breach of natural justice or whether the adjudicator had acted in excess of jurisdiction.[82]

In the context of CIPAA 2012, section 12(1) provides that the adjudicator shall conduct the adjudication as the adjudicator considers appropriate within the powers provided in section 25. Thus, it is within the adjudicator's discretion to decide if they want to convene a hearing. The adjudicator is conferred with discretionary power to conduct the adjudication. It is not their duty or obligation to exercise all or any of the powers in section 25 nor to be dictated to by any of the parties to the adjudication.

The statutory adjudication under CIPAA 2012 offers a speedy, economical, and simple dispute resolution forum to alleviate the cash flow problem in the construction industry. Therefore, the expeditious elements of adjudication, such as limiting the hearing time and conducting documents-only proceedings when appropriately exercised by the adjudicator, may still bode well with the rule of natural justice. The adjudication cases apply to expedited arbitration due to its common goal of providing expeditious procedures without infringing on the rule of natural justice.

Whether arbitrators should or should not hear evidence and the parties in a hearing depends on the particular circumstances in every case. Therefore, arbitrators should judicially exercise their discretion. If the reference is such that the arbitrators cannot decide the dispute without hearing evidence, the refusal will amount to misconduct, warranting a court to set aside the award. However, if, in the exercise of prudent and wise discretion, the arbitrator declines to summon the witness, or where the evidence was unnecessary and would not have influenced their decision, the award will be upheld.[83] In other words, a party alleging a breach of natural justice must be able to demonstrate that the breach relied on is material and has a significant effect on the outcome of the arbitration. The materiality of the alleged breach has to be either decisive or of considerable importance to the outcome and not peripheral or irrelevant.

§4.05 CONCLUSION

Expedited arbitration rules seek to provide efficiency without compromising party autonomy and due process. The goal of efficiency includes rendering a quality award

82. *See* the Court of Appeal's reasoning in para. 13(I) on pp. 67-68. In the words of the court 'the fact is that the respondent was given ample opportunity to present all the documentary evidence that it seeks to rely on and be heard on it by way of written submissions. The respondent chose not to comply with the statutory rights prescribed in the CIPAA, and in particular section 10(1) and (2), and serve its documents in the manner and time prescribed. Having made that choice, the respondent will have to live with it, and cannot now be heard to complain about breach of natural justice and/or the adjudicator having acted in excess of jurisdiction'.
83. *CBS v. CBP* [2021] SGCA 4, Civil Appeal No. 30 of 2020 in para. 64.

from the decision-making process, respecting party autonomy and fair treatment. Therefore, the broad procedural powers of an arbitral tribunal are subject to the fundamental rules of natural justice. Various institutional rules stress that the arbitral tribunal shall make every effort to conduct the arbitration expeditiously and cost-effectively to meet the need for efficiency in expedited arbitration.[84] In doing so, striking a proper balance between efficiency and due process is the way forward. The arbitral tribunal must act fairly and impartially in the conduct of the proceedings by giving each party a reasonable opportunity to present its case. If this balancing act is satisfied, the strain on party autonomy and due process will be reduced, resulting in less fertile grounds to challenge the award. In short, the concerted efforts made by arbitral institutions to establish expedited rules will restore the lost grace of speedy measures and cost-saving measures that arbitration once promised. A reconfiguration of the arbitration system that currently takes place in the form of expedited procedure is the welcoming step to tackle concerns over time and costs in arbitral proceedings. With the advancement of technology and its integration into dispute resolution mechanisms, expedited arbitration proceedings will find their mark to govern low- and high-value claims with effective enforceability of the award. If the tribunal is mindful of safeguarding due process and party autonomy, expedited arbitration will relieve the potential strain between efficiency and due process.

84. Articles 2.1 and 23.2 of the SCC Rules for Expedited Arbitrations 2023 provide that 'throughout the proceedings, the SCC, the Arbitrator and the parties shall act in an efficient and expeditious manner' and 'in all cases, the Arbitral Tribunal shall conduct the arbitration in an impartial, efficient and expeditious manner, giving each party an equal and reasonable opportunity to present its case'. *See also* section 33(1)(a)-(b) of the English Arbitration Act 1996 incorporates parallel general duties of the arbitral tribunal to 'act fairly and impartially as between the parties giving each party a reasonable opportunity of putting his case …' while 'avoiding unnecessary delay or expense'.

CHAPTER 5
The Advent of Accelerated Arbitral Procedures: Public Policy Considerations in the Enforcement of Arbitral Awards

Yasaschandra Devarakonda

Traditional arbitration has become lengthier and procedurally more cumbersome, leading to the advent of accelerated, expedited arbitrations, which have, since inception, seen an exponential rise in demand by parties. Arbitral institutions allow parties to choose such arbitration procedures based on the type of dispute and the value of the arbitration. At the heart of this choice lies a crucial public policy consideration that is often overlooked. With the introduction of UNCITRAL Expedited Arbitral Rules in 2021, a relook at how institutional arbitration rules and national laws of various jurisdictions treat such accelerated procedures is in order. This treatment ultimately has a bearing on the enforcement of the arbitral awards arising out of such accelerated arbitral procedures. The chapter focuses on understanding the public policy considerations while examining the potential considerations that must be borne in mind by parties before choosing the procedure, based on the jurisprudence of the jurisdiction in which the award would be enforced, and the chosen arbitral rules.

§5.01 INTRODUCTION

Over time, the traditional method of alternative dispute resolution through arbitration has become a cumbersome and costly process.[1] The timelines of modern-day arbitrations far exceed the schedules within which the process was envisaged to resolve disputes between parties. In recognition of this limitation, there is an increasing

1. *See* International Arbitration Survey: The Evolution of International Arbitration, 2018. https://arbitration.qmul.ac.uk/media/arbitration/docs/2018-International-Arbitration-Survey--The-Evolution-of-International-Arbitration-(2).PDF.

demand for procedures that would reduce the timelines of an arbitral process and provide parties with relief on an ad-interim basis.

With the introduction of accelerated arbitral procedures by various arbitral institutions,[2] the tide appeared to have turned in favour of arbitration once again. Expedited arbitration as an alternative to the arbitral procedure reduces timelines by doing away with certain stages which may not have as much relevance to the dispute.[3] Depending on the applicable institutional rules, the parties either 'opt-in' or 'opt out' of such an expedited arbitral procedure. Protracted procedures, such as oral examination of fact and expert evidence by way of testimony and cross-examination and the scope of the pleadings/written submissions, are restricted. The timelines of the arbitral process thus are reduced.[4] The overall timeline within which the arbitral award is issued under such procedures is generally six months, as opposed to the ordinary period of one year.[5]

However, growing public policy concerns across various jurisdictions have led to difficulties in the enforcement of such awards. Accelerated arbitral procedures may not be as viable of an alternative to commercial parties. The procedures introduced by various arbitral institutions fall short of maintaining procedural efficacy, which may be the reason for difficulty in enforcing such arbitral awards in jurisdictions which have certain public policy considerations. This fact thus becomes a disincentivizing factor for commercial parties to adopt such procedures.

In 2021, the UNCITRAL Expedited Arbitration Rules were introduced as an appendix to the UNCITRAL Arbitration Rules. This introduction rekindled the debate over the need for consensus on the validity of such procedures from a public policy perspective. The UNCITRAL Expedited Arbitration Rules were framed by UNCITRAL Working Group II after having conducted extensive consultations with governments, intergovernmental, and international non-governmental organizations.[6] For this reason, the Expedited Arbitration Rules should take into consideration the public policy

2. Except for the London Court of International Arbitration, which introduced its expedited procedure or appointment of the arbitral tribunal in 1998, the Singapore International Arbitration Centre and the International Chamber of Commerce Arbitration introduced expedited arbitration procedures to their rules only in 2010 and 2017, respectively.
3. A fundamental difference exists between the two most popular forms of accelerated procedures: emergency arbitration and expedited arbitration. Emergency arbitration is intended to provide 'emergency' relief to the parties on an interim basis only. Such applications are made to the institution administering the arbitration before the constitution of the arbitral tribunal itself. The decision of emergency arbitrator has the same force of law as the decision of an arbitral tribunal. Major jurisdictions give recognition to emergency arbitrators by including the term 'emergency arbitrator' within the definition of arbitral tribunal in their national laws. *See*, for example, section 2(1) of the Arbitration Act, 2001 (Singapore). *See also Amazon.com Investment Holding LLC v. Future Retail Limited* (2022) 1 SCC 209. (Emergency Arbitrator awards are given effect to by the national courts at the place of enforcement.)
4. *See*, for example, Article 3(4) of Appendix VI of ICC Arbitration Rules.
5. *See*, for example, Article 4(1) of Appendix VI of ICC Arbitration Rules, Article 5.2(d) of SIAC Arbitration Rules, 2016. Expedited arbitration offers finality to the dispute within six months of reference, unlike emergency arbitrations where the only potential remedy for the parties is an ad-interim measure pending the final adjudication of the dispute.
6. *See* UNCITRAL, Responses to the UNCITRAL questionnaire on expedited arbitration (30 January 2020) https://uncitral.un.org/sites/uncitral.un.org/files/media-documents/uncitral/en/respons

considerations of various jurisdictions. The Rules should therefore trigger a much-needed overhaul in national legislation systems and/or institutional arbitration rules to give a much-needed boost to the newest forms of accelerated dispute resolution mechanisms.

This chapter examines the expedited arbitration practice of different arbitral institutions and their limitations concerning public policy concerns in various jurisdictions. It focuses on the UNCITRAL Expedited Arbitration Rules 2021. The UNCITRAL Rules emphasise the importance of consent between parties.[7] Consent is a public policy consideration of major national jurisdictions, which could lead to enforcement challenges. The UNCITRAL Expedited Rules brought to the fore a consent-based regime, as opposed to those arbitral institutions in which the accelerated procedure automatically applies if the amount in dispute is of a certain value. Expedited awards based on the value in dispute only may be subject to strict scrutiny in the national courts of jurisdictions where public policy may give primacy to the mutual consent of parties. The introduction of a consent-based regime, as an indication of the public policy consideration of various jurisdictions, may trigger a much-needed overhaul of the institutional rules.

§5.02 EXPEDITED ARBITRATION IN PRACTICE

Innovations in the field of arbitration to streamline the cumbersome process and make it more attractive for commercial parties have been at the fore since as early as 2010

es_to_questionnaire_30_january_2020.pdf; UNCITRAL, Submission from the Government of Hungary – Comments on Expedited Arbitration Provisions, https://uncitral.un.org/sites/uncitral.un.org/files/media-documents/uncitral/en/comments_of_hungary_on_expedited_arbitration_provisions.pdf; UNCITRAL, Submission from the Government of Turkey, https://uncitral.un.org/sites/uncitral.un.org/files/media-documents/uncitral/en/comments_on_uncitral_draft_mediation_rules_turkey.pdf; UNCITRAL, Submission from the International Centre for Settlement of Investment Disputes, https://uncitral.un.org/sites/uncitral.un.org/files/media-documents/uncitral/en/submission_by_icsid.pdf; UNCITRAL, Submission from the Belgian Centre for Arbitration and Mediation, https://uncitral.un.org/sites/uncitral.un.org/files/media-documents/uncitral/en/wp._216_cepani.pdf; UNCITRAL, Submission from the Miami International Arbitration Society, https://uncitral.un.org/sites/uncitral.un.org/files/media-documents/uncitral/mias_task_force_comments.pdf; UNCITRAL, Submission from Forum for Conciliation and Arbitration, https://uncitral.un.org/sites/uncitral.un.org/files/media-documents/uncitral/en/fica_task_force_report.pdf; UNCITRAL, Submission from the representative of Switzerland, https://uncitral.un.org/sites/uncitral.un.org/files/media-documents/uncitral/en/wp.214_submission_from_the_representative_of_switzerland_to_working_group_ii.pdf; UNCITRAL, Submission from the representative of Mexico, https://uncitral.un.org/sites/uncitral.un.org/files/media-documents/uncitral/en/submission_from_mexico_en.pdf; UNCITRAL, Submission from the Miami International Arbitration Society, https://uncitral.un.org/sites/uncitral.un.org/files/media-documents/uncitral/en/submission_from_mias.pdf; UNCITRAL, Submission from the Kingdom of Bahrain, https://uncitral.un.org/sites/uncitral.un.org/files/media-documents/uncitral/en/submission_from_bahrain.pdf.

7. The UNCITRAL Expedited Rules provide for the applicability of the procedure only if both parties consent to such procedure. This is contrary to the practice adopted by some arbitral institutions wherein the expedited arbitration procedure would apply depending on, in some cases, the value in dispute and/or 'exceptional urgency shown' by one party. These aspects shall be dealt with in later sections of the chapter.

when the Singapore International Arbitration Centre introduced the procedures for expedited arbitration. At the time, there was a need for innovation in the field of international arbitration to promote and protect the credibility of the arbitral mechanism. However, the lack of an express recognition in law, along with the absence of adequate discourse on the topic, were the mitigating factors against the rise of such accelerated procedures. Various arbitral institutions have amended their rules to provide for accelerated arbitral procedures, while parallelly, national jurisdictions have not amended their legislations analogously. This may be the reason for enforcement concerns due to varied judicial interpretations.

[A] Recognizing Expedited Arbitration: The Role of Arbitral Institutions and Courts

Arbitral institutions often play a key role in bringing about landmark shifts in the arbitral landscape of any jurisdiction. Because arbitral institutions are at the fore of administering arbitration between the commercial parties, these institutions benefit from direct interactions with the parties and their counsels, who are best equipped to pioneer innovation in the field as direct stakeholders. Likewise, arbitrators empanelled with these institutions play a key role in making advancements to the ways of resolving disputes through the rules of the arbitral institution.

Often, amendments to the rules of arbitral institutions fall prey to public policy concerns. This leads to difficulties at the stage of enforcement of award. This is due to the absence of competing public policy interests from legislators and bureaucracy, who could bring about synchronous amendments in their respective national legislations. While the introduction of expedited arbitration rules of different arbitral institutions was met with much jubilation, they fell short of meeting certain thresholds of public policy and comity in the arbitral process. This subsequently led to setting aside arbitral awards in various jurisdictions.

[1] Singapore International Arbitration Centre

In 2010, the institutional rules of the Singapore International Arbitration Centre introduced expedited arbitration in the form of Rule 5 to the Arbitration Rules (SIAC Rules). The current rules allow the parties to 'opt-in' to expedited arbitration by way of an application, if any of the following conditions are satisfied: (i) a maximum amount in dispute of SGD 6,000,000, including the claim, counterclaim and set-off; or (ii) the parties expressly agree; or (iii) if exceptional urgency is demonstrated by a party.[8] Rule 5.2 of the SIAC Rules envisages the rendering the final award within six months from the date of appointment of a sole arbitrator by potentially deciding the case on documentary evidence only.[9] At the time the SIAC Rules were introduced in 2010,

8. SIAC Rules, Rule 5.1 (2016). At the time of introduction in 2010, the threshold was SGD 5,000,000.
9. SIAC Rules, Rule 5.2 (2016).

Rules 5.3 and 5.4 were not present. Rule 5.3 provides that the limitations in Rule 5.2 override any contrary terms of reference in the arbitration agreement if the SIAC Rules have been chosen by the parties.[10] Rule 5.4 provides a 'way out' for the parties. The parties may apply to the arbitrator to not proceed with the procedure under expedited arbitrations.[11]

In this regard, the decision of Shanghai No. 1 Intermediate Court in 2016 in *Nobles Resources Pte. Ltd. v. Good Credit International Trade Co. Ltd.*[12] was a landmark. In this case, the 2013 SIAC Rules applied to a dispute arising out of a contract for the sale of iron ore. On the application for expedited arbitration by the seller, the buyer refused to consent to the expedited arbitration rules and had insisted on having a three-member arbitral tribunal constituted. In the absence of an agreement, the SIAC Court appointed a sole arbitrator, who rendered an award in favour of the seller. However, the Shanghai Court refused to enforce the award under Article V(1)(d) of the New York Convention, because the constitution of the arbitral tribunal was in contravention of the arbitration agreement between the parties.[13]

Consequently, SIAC amended its rules to include Rule 5.3. Rule 5.3 deems the consent of the parties to use of the SIAC Rules to override any express agreement which contravenes the SIAC Rules. Such a compromise on party autonomy, to give effect to the enforcement of an award rendered under the expedited procedure, could come at the cost of enforcement of arbitral awards in certain jurisdictions.

[2] International Arbitration and Mediation Centre, Hyderabad, India

One of the most recent arbitral institutions established in India,[14] the International Arbitration and Mediation Centre, Hyderabad, provide different sets of rules for domestic and international arbitrations (IAMC Rules and IAMC International Arbitration Rules). Under both sets of rules, IAMC allows parties to opt for accelerated arbitral procedures. Both sets of rules provide identical procedures. Expedited procedures apply to arbitrations administered by the IAMC Rules upon application by a party to the Registrar of IAMC who, in consultation with the Governing Council of IAMC, decides on the application for Expedited Procedure.[15] The Expedited Procedure is applicable in cases where the anticipated amount in dispute does not exceed INR 100 million (USD 1,200,000) or when there is an express agreement for Expedited Procedure between the

10. SIAC Rules, Rule 5.3 (2016).
11. SIAC Rules, Rule 5.4 (2016).
12. *Noble Resources International Pte. Ltd v. Shanghai Good Credit International Trade Co., Ltd.* (2016) Hu 01 Xie Wai Ren No. 1.
13. Article V(1)(d) provides that the composition of the arbitral authority must have been in accordance with the agreement of the parties, or in the absence of an agreement, the law of the country where the arbitration took place, failing which recognition and enforcement of the award may be refused.
14. The International Arbitration and Mediation Centre was inaugurated in Hyderabad, India, in December 2021.
15. Article 23.2 of the IAMC Arbitration Rules.

parties.[16] The IAMC Rules stipulate that a sole arbitrator will govern the Expedited Procedure notwithstanding any agreement to the contrary between the parties. However, the Governing Council of IAMC could determine otherwise.[17] An award must be rendered within six months based on documentary evidence only.[18]

Much like the SIAC Rules, the Expedited Procedure of IAMC provides the parties may 'opt-in' for expedited arbitration by way of an express agreement. However, the alternate basis to determine the applicability of Expedited Procedure, as is the case with the SIAC Rules, i.e., the financial threshold of the amount in dispute including an aggregate of claim, counterclaim and set-off, is not an objective threshold. Determination of the complexity of the arbitration will depend on the nature of the transaction and the nature of dispute between the parties. Therefore, the Registrar/Court of the IAMC must evaluate the applicability of Expedited Procedure on a case-to-case basis. Further, the financial threshold under both the IAMC Rules and the IAMC International Arbitration Rules (INR 100 million - about USD 1,200,000) is a small threshold cumulative value, especially in the context of international arbitration. With more arbitrations being administered by the IAMC and no other objective basis to determine the financial threshold, only statistical evidence could potentially lead to any increase in the threshold under the IAMC Rules.[19]

One significant obstacle to the applicability of the Expedited Procedure, and the subsequent enforcement of expedited awards in India, is the procedure for fast-track arbitrations under section 29B of the Arbitration and Conciliation Act, 1996.[20] Any clash between the two procedures has the potential to pose a significant threat to the enforcement of the institutional arbitral awards before the Indian courts. Section 29B of the Arbitration and Conciliation Act stipulates the application of the expedited procedures only upon express agreement 'in writing' between the parties either before or at the stage of appointment of the arbitral tribunal. Further, section 29B does not alter the composition of an arbitral tribunal in any manner. In contrast, the use of expedited procedures under the IAMC Rules is decided by the Registrar of IAMC upon application by one of the parties, with the case being referred to a sole arbitrator notwithstanding the agreement between the parties.[21] Such a compromise on the agreement between the parties could come at the cost of enforcement of such an arbitral award as in the case of *Nobles Resources*, discussed previously.

[3] London International Arbitration Centre

The London Court of International Arbitration Rules (LCIA Rules) envisage an entirely different format for parties seeking accelerated relief. Article 9A of the LCIA Rules

16. Article 23.1(a) of the IAMC Arbitration Rules.
17. Article 23.4(b) of the IAMC Arbitration Rules.
18. Article 23.4(d) of the IAMC Arbitration Rules.
19. For instance, as discussed above, SIAC increased the financial threshold for expedited arbitration from SGD 5,000,000 to SGD 6,000,000.
20. Section 29A of the Arbitration and Conciliation Act, 1996 (India) was introduced by way of an amendment in 2015.
21. Article 23.4(b) of the IAMC Arbitration Rules.

provides for an expedited formation of an arbitral tribunal by way of an application made to the LCIA Court justifying the urgency.[22] Such an application allows the parties to circumvent the detailed procedure laid down for the constitution of the arbitral tribunal by the LCIA Court and abridges the overall timeline for the arbitration. Expedited formation of the arbitral tribunal is often accompanied by an application seeking interim measures of protection under Article 25 of the LCIA Rules.[23] In addition to the procedure for expedited formation of the arbitral tribunal and emergency arbitrator, the LCIA Rules provide for expedited replacement of an arbitrator under Article 9C if doubts exist as to the suitability, independence or impartiality of the Arbitrator as may be determined by the LCIA Court under Article 11.[24]

Furthermore, Article 9B and Article 25 of the LCIA Rules permit the parties to seek intervention of the court under section 44 of the Arbitration Act, 1996.[25] However, the LCIA operates in a different ecosystem when it comes to accelerated arbitral procedures. It does not provide for any directions concerning accelerated arbitral procedures. It allows the arbitral tribunal the discretion to determine expedited procedures on a case-to-case basis. Most importantly, the LCIA rules do not provide for expedited arbitration procedures like the SIAC, which makes it simple for the parties to choose and adopt bespoke procedures. With the possibility of parties enforcing awards rendered by an emergency arbitrator on an ad-interim basis pending the constitution of an arbitral tribunal under the LCIA procedure for expedited formation, the commercial need of parties for accelerated relief is also met under the aegis of LCIA.

The LCIA Rules thus are the least prescriptive in terms of expedited procedures for the parties and arbitral tribunal to follow. There are no expedited rules for collecting evidence or timelines for rendering the arbitral award. The LCIA Rules give discretion to the arbitral tribunal to adopt a procedure that best suits the requirements of the case. This approach is unique amongst major arbitral institutions. More significantly, it does

22. Under Article 9A of the LCIA Rules 2020, the parties must, in their application, set out the specific grounds for exceptional urgency requiring expedited formation of the arbitral tribunal.
23. An application under Article 25 of the LCIA Rules 2020, alongside the application for the expedited formation of the arbitral tribunal under Article 9A of the LCIA Rules 2020, is the most unique approach to accelerated arbitral procedures, and allows the parties to obtain conservatory measures on an interim basis pending the final adjudication of the arbitral tribunal within timelines as may be abridged.

    In addition to the expedited formation of the arbitral tribunal under Article 9A of the LCIA Rules, an additional aid to parties seeking an interim measure is the emergency arbitrator procedure in Article 9B of the LCIA Rules. Any interim measure granted by an arbitral tribunal formed under Article 9B would be enforced as an order under Article 25, therefore limiting the 'expedited' nature of the arbitration to merely the constitution of the arbitral tribunal only. If the parties have entered into the arbitration agreement before 1 October 2014, i.e., the date of introduction of the emergency procedure in the LCIA Rules, the parties would have to agree to 'opt-in' to the emergency procedure under Article 9B of the LCIA Rules.
24. *See*, Article 9C of LCIA Rules. A party can apply for expedited formation of replacement arbitrator, and if the same is granted, for the purpose of expediting the appointment of the replacement arbitrator the LCIA Court may set or abridge any period of time in the Arbitration Agreement or any other agreement of the parties.
25. *See*, section 44 of the Arbitration Act, 1996: 'Unless otherwise agreed by the parties, the court has for the purposes of and in relation to arbitral proceedings the same power of making orders about the matters listed as it has for the purposes of and in relation to legal proceedings.'

not compromise party autonomy by overriding any express agreement between the parties. At the same time, the procedure to seek expedited formation of the arbitral tribunal, and thereafter seek an interim measure of protection, eliminates the need for parties to specifically apply for enforcement of an award which would otherwise have been rendered by an expedited arbitration tribunal.

[4] International Chamber of Commerce

The International Chamber of Commerce Rules of Arbitration (ICC Rules) define and regulate the management of cases received by the International Court of Arbitration. Undeniably, the ICC is one of the most sought-after arbitral institutions for the administration of arbitrations. It is one of the few institutions with no affiliation to any jurisdiction. It thereby is not bound by certain policy considerations of the State.

Three conditions must be satisfied for the application of the Expedited Procedure Provisions of the ICC Rules. First, the arbitration agreement must have been concluded after 1 March 2017. Second, the amount in dispute must not exceed USD 2,000,000 if the arbitration agreement was concluded between 1 March 2017 and 31 December 2020, and USD 3,000,000 if the arbitration agreement was concluded on or after 1 January 2021 respectively. Third, the parties must not have 'opted out' of the Expedited Procedures Rules in an arbitration agreement. In addition, the parties can choose to 'opt-in' for the Expedited Procedure Provisions by agreement at any time.[26] The Expedited Procedure Provisions take precedence over any contrary terms of arbitration agreement.[27] During the arbitration, the ICC Court of Arbitration, on application by a party, and in consultation with the arbitral tribunal, may decide that the Expedited Procedure Provisions no longer apply.[28]

Under the Expedited Procedures, the ICC Court may appoint a sole arbitrator or three arbitrators under appropriate circumstances. No requirement for terms of reference exists, and the arbitral tribunal may decide the dispute based on documents only. The arbitral tribunal may also limit the number, length and scope of written submissions and written witness evidence. The final award must be rendered within six months from the case management conference, which is to be convened within 15 days after the date on which the file was transmitted to the arbitral tribunal.[29]

---

26. Article 1(2) of Appendix VI to ICC Arbitration Rules.
27. Article 30 of the ICC Arbitration Rules read with Appendix VI.
28. Article 1(4) of Appendix VI to ICC Arbitration Rules.
29. Under Article 2 of Appendix VI to the ICC Arbitration Rules, the Court has the power to appoint a sole arbitrator notwithstanding the provisions of the arbitration agreement. Under appropriate circumstances, the court may appoint three arbitrators. However, in all circumstances, the court considers the views of the parties in writing and makes every effort to ensure the award will be enforceable. This is because recognition of an arbitral award can be refused on the ground that the composition of arbitral tribunal was in not accordance with the agreement between the parties under Article V(1)(d) of the United Nations Convention on the Recognition and Enforcement of Foreign Arbitral Awards (New York, 10 June 1958). *See* ICC, Expedited Procedure Provisions, https://iccwbo.org/dispute-resolution/dispute-resolution-services/arbitration/rules-procedure/expedited-procedure/.

On balance, the ICC Rules envisage leaving no stone unturned to ensure the efficacy of the arbitral process. Its rules expressly provide for a cost-effective and expeditious resolution of disputes in a manner that the award remains enforceable. Like most arbitral institutions, the ICC Expedited Procedure Rules are heavily dependent on the consent of the parties. The scope of the ICC Rules in case of lack of such consent is very restricted. The compromise on oral hearings/oral evidence,[30] in such cases could jeopardize the enforcement of such awards. Adding to the complexity of such situations are the public policy considerations of the jurisdictions where the award could be enforced. As an arbitral institution independent of any jurisdictional policy limitations, the public policy considerations of the place of enforcement, if not given adequate consideration, could lead to challenges to the award.[31]

[B] Recognition of Expedited Arbitration in National Legal Regimes

Irrespective of the institution administering the arbitration, expedited arbitration is dependent on the consent of the parties to a procedure with reduced timelines after the reference to arbitration. The likelihood of such an agreement is low, for the same reason that an agreement to arbitrate/submission agreement is far less likely over an arbitration agreement in the context of commercial arbitrations. In most cases, it trickles down to the decision of the court/registrar of the institution to determine the rules of procedure of an expedited arbitration, keeping in mind the public policy considerations of the jurisdiction where the parties would enforce the award.

[1] Singapore

SIAC introduced the expedited arbitration procedure in its 2010 rules. The International Arbitration Act, 1994 (Singapore Act), on the other hand, does not recognize expedited arbitration procedures. However, the Singapore Act recognizes emergency arbitrators within the definition of an arbitral tribunal,[32] thus giving an express legislative

30. Article 3(4) of Appendix VI of the ICC Arbitration Rules.
31. *See* Article 18 of the UNCITRAL Model Law on International Commercial Arbitration, section 33 of the English Arbitration Act, Article 1510 of the French Code of Civil Procedure. *See also*, *Trustees of Rotoaira Trust v. Attorney General* [1998] NZLR 452 [New Zealand High Court] at 463 ('The detailed demands of natural justice in a given case turn on a proper construction of the particular agreement to arbitrate, the nature of the dispute, and any inferences properly to be drawn from the appointment of arbitrators known to have special expertise.'); *CBS v. CBP* [2021] SGCA 4, Civil Appeal No. 30 of 2020 [Singapore Court of Appeal], para. 68 ('The fundamental nature of the rules of natural justice means that they must not be sacrificed in the name of efficacy and due weight must be afforded to those rules. It is self-evident that this balance is not amenable to prescriptive rules and each case will turn on its precise facts and circumstances.'). However, the lack of oral hearings is not a breach of due process. *See PT Asuransi Jasa Indonesia (Persero) v. Dexia Bank SA* [2006] SGCA 41. Due process does not entitle parties to unlimited rounds of oral submissions. *See, e.g.*, Decision of 1 August 2018 (Tokyo High Court), cited in F Ferrari et al. (eds), Due Process as a Limit to Discretion in International Commercial Arbitration, Kluwer Law International 2020, p. 21.
32. Section 2(1) of the International Arbitration Act, 1994 (Singapore).

mandate to emergency arbitrations as a form of an accelerated arbitration procedure under Singaporean law.

However, the Singapore Court recognized the expedited arbitration procedure in the case of *AQZ v. ARA*, in which the petitioner challenged an expedited arbitral award under the SIAC Rules.[33] The arbitration concerned a dispute over the sale of non-coking coal. The seller was a supplier incorporated in Singapore and the buyer was a Singaporean subsidy of an Indian conglomerate. The parties had entered a contract in December 2009 and subsequently entered certain negotiations in January 2010. The dispute arose over the seller's obligations under the subsequent negotiations. According to the buyer, the negotiations resulted in a second contract. In 2013, the seller commenced arbitration proceedings before SIAC under the 2010 rules. The buyer applied for expedited arbitration, to which the seller had objected. The SIAC Court allowed the application for expedited arbitration and appointed a sole arbitrator who issued a 'Ruling and Partial Award' in May 2014,[34] which affirmed the jurisdiction of the arbitrator[35] and found the seller liable for breach.

The seller challenged the award on two grounds. First, the arbitration agreement under the contract provided for a three-member arbitral tribunal and not a sole arbitrator. Second, as of the date of the contract, i.e., in 2009, the SIAC Rules did not contain the expedited procedure (which was introduced in 2010). Contrary to an express agreement between the parties in their arbitration agreement, the Singapore Court held that the SIAC Court had the power to override the intention of the parties to have three arbitrators in the event of conflict with the parties' choice of the SIAC Rules. Further, the Court held that the institution rules as on the commencement date of arbitration would apply to an arbitration, and not as on the contract date.[36] This decision suggests a strong approach to give priority to the commercial intention of the parties over strict interpretation of the legislative mandates/arbitral rules and the express terms of the arbitration agreement.

To avoid such challenges to expedited arbitral awards, various arbitral institutions have opted to determine the eligibility for the application of expedited arbitration other than by consent of both parties. Instead, they use a cut-off date, with only arbitration agreements entered into after the introduction of expedited procedure under the rules being impacted. Institutions have also created a legal fiction by deeming that the expedited procedure overrides any contrary agreement between the parties. This fiction flies directly in the face of party autonomy. The only apparent justification for creating such an overriding effect is that the parties have chosen the application of the arbitral rules which contain such a deeming provision. This legal fiction, to give primacy to the choice of arbitral rules over the express agreement between the parties, would only be justified if both parties consent to the application of the expedited procedure. In the absence of such consent, party autonomy must prevail to avoid any

33. *AQZ v. ARA* [2015] SGHC 49.
34. *Ibid.*, para. 24.
35. *Ibid.*, paras 131, 132.
36. *Ibid.*, para. 125.

challenges to arbitral awards rendered by an arbitral tribunal constituted as per the expedited procedure.

Singapore has gained the reputation of being a pro-arbitration jurisdiction. However, the lack of an express legislative mandate could still be a cause of concern for commercial parties to choose Singapore as the seat of arbitration or when Singapore would be the place of enforcement of an arbitral award. As in the case of India, an express legislative mandate, which could pose challenges, would be a more sensible approach to give recognition to the emerging ways of accelerated arbitral processes.

[2] India

The Arbitration and Conciliation Act, 1996 (Indian Act) was amended in 2015 to introduce a fast-track procedure under section 29B of the Indian Act.[37] Much like the expedited procedure, a dispute may be resolved by the fast-track procedure if the parties agree in writing at the time or before the appointment of the arbitral tribunal, while also agreeing that the dispute 'may' be resolved by a sole arbitrator. Under the fast-track procedure, the arbitral tribunal must resolve the dispute based on documentary evidence only. Oral hearings may be held upon the request of the parties, or if the arbitral tribunal deems it necessary to clarify certain issues. Fast-track awards are to be made within six months from the date of the constitution of the arbitral tribunal.[38]

Under section 29B of the Indian Act, the fast-track procedure is based on the mutual consent of both parties only. Unlike many arbitral rules, there is no financial threshold which determines the automatic applicability of the fast-track procedure. No provision stipulates that the expedited procedure overrides an arbitration agreement, thus preserving party autonomy as well. The parties only have the option to 'opt-in' for to the procedure, along with the option to reconsider the number of arbitrators.

Undoubtedly, there is a certain comfort with the legislature expressly recognizing such an accelerated arbitral procedure. Since its introduction in 2015, there has not been any challenge to an award rendered by an arbitral tribunal via a fast-track procedure. There have only been two instances in which section 29B of the Indian Act has been discussed by the Indian courts. The first is *Hamara Pump Mithoura HPCL Petrol Pump v. Chairman-Cum-Managing Director Hindustan Petroleum and Ors.*[39] In that case, the High Court of Allahabad dismissed an application for fast-track procedure on the basis that there was no consent between the parties. The second case is *Crayons Advertising Private Limited v. Bharat Sanchar Nigam Limited.*[40] In that case, the High Court of Delhi terminated the mandate of an arbitrator who failed to render an award

37. *See*, The Arbitration and Conciliation Act, 1996 [26 of 1996] as amended by The Arbitration and Conciliation (Amendment) Act, 2015 [3 of 2016] (India). Section 29B provides for a fast-track mode of arbitration procedure. As per section 29B, parties may mutually decide to adopt the fast-track mode of arbitration in which the Arbitrator has to decide and pass an award within six months of the date of reference.
38. *See* section 29B(3)(a)-(d) of the Arbitration and Conciliation Act, 1996 (India).
39. 2018 (1) ADJ 363.
40. 2018 (2) ArbLR 252 (Delhi).

within six months from the date of appointment under the fast-track procedure, and the parties could not consent to extend the timeline for rendering the award.

Thus, the genesis for a fast-track procedure as a function of the parties' express choice alone, while is a welcome move, comes with limitations. As one of the few jurisdictions recognizing expedited arbitrations, albeit with a different terminology – 'fast-track arbitration' – there is certainty with the enforcement of such awards. The difficulty, however, is with a potential clash between the expedited procedure under section 29B of the Indian Act and the procedure under the arbitral rules such as the IAMC. Certainly, the current form of the IAMC Rules is at odds, in certain aspects, with that of section 29B of the Indian Act. For example, the automatic application of the expedited procedure under the IAMC Rules based on the prescribed financial thresholds could contradict the principle of party autonomy if either of the parties prefers to not subscribe to the expedited procedure. At the same time, section 29B of the Indian Act provides that the parties 'may' agree that the arbitral tribunal shall consist of a sole arbitrator. This is, once again, contradictory to the IAMC Rules. The application of either procedure is a simple function of the choice of the parties. However, difficulties may arise at the time of enforcement of an award rendered by an arbitral tribunal under the expedited procedure of the IAMC Rules. Such an award could be challenged on at least two grounds. First, because the composition of the arbitral tribunal was not as agreed in the contract. Second, the award could be challenged because there was no reasonable opportunity to be heard. Such awards are at a greater risk of being set aside as being contrary to the Indian Act.

In *Amazon.com Investment Holding LLC v. Future Retail Limited*,[41] the Supreme Court of India, was asked to enforce an award made by an emergency arbitrator under the SIAC Rules in an Indian-seated arbitration. The Supreme Court questioned whether the Indian Act envisaged a procedure for 'emergency arbitrator'. The court held that despite the absence of an express provision in the Indian Act recognizing the emergency arbitration provision, the recommendations of the 246th Law Commission Report indicated the intention of the legislature to give effect to such a provision.[42] The court, therefore, has purposively read the legislative intent and given effect to emergency arbitrations in India.

This case law assists in understanding that the Indian judiciary places much reliance on the provisions of the Indian Act to understand the scope of the 'public policy', and whether an award which is challenged could be set aside on such grounds. In such a scenario, the judiciary could give primacy to section 29B of the Indian Act over the arbitral rules such as the IAMC, which provides for a different procedure. Nevertheless, arbitrations are not bound by the procedures under the Indian Act alone. There are various provisions under the Indian Act which allow for arbitral procedures to be determined by an 'institution'.[43] The lack of such a mandate under section 29B of

41. *Amazon.com Investment Holding LLC v. Future Retail Limited* (2022) 1 SCC 209.
42. Amendments to the Arbitration and Conciliation Act 1996, Report No. 246, August 2014, Law Commission of India, Government of India.
43. *See, e.g.*, section 6 of the Arbitration and Conciliation Act 1996 stipulates that parties may arrange for administrative assistance from a suitable institution to facilitate the conduct of the

the Indian Act may be a mitigating factor to allow arbitral institutions in India to prescribe different expedited arbitration procedures. Therefore, to the extent that there is no clash between section 29B and the expedited procedure of any arbitral institution in India, i.e., express consent by parties in all aspects of the expedited procedure, there likely will not be difficulty in the enforcement of such awards.

[3] United Kingdom

The LCIA Rules adopt an entirely different approach to expedited arbitration procedures. The expedited procedure under Article 9A of the LCIA Rules only allows for the speedy formation of the arbitral tribunal with the power to abridge the timelines of the arbitral process.[44] The LCIA Court appoints arbitrators after satisfying itself with the independence and impartiality of the arbitrator. Each arbitrator candidate must disclose to the LCIA Court the circumstances currently known to the candidate which are likely to give rise to any justifiable doubts regarding their independence and impartiality. A time period of 28 days from the date of the request for arbitration is prescribed for completing the appointment of the arbitral tribunal.

The procedure for the expedited formation of the arbitral tribunal under LCIA must be reconciled with the national law to understand the challenges, if any, at the time of enforcement of an award rendered by a tribunal constituted expediently. Under the Arbitration Act, 1996 (UK Act), the arbitrators are not per se required to disclose circumstances which could create justifiable doubts in the minds of the parties as to the independence and impartiality of the arbitrator. The UK Act merely imposes a general duty on the arbitrators to act fairly and impartially between the parties.[45] The parties have the power to apply to the Courts to remove an arbitrator on the ground that there are circumstances which give rise to justifiable doubts as to arbitrator's impartiality.[46] In common law, the standard for such 'justifiable doubts' is the test of 'apparent bias'/'reasonable apprehension of bias'.[47]

The debate over the independence and impartiality of the arbitrator and the disclosure obligations of arbitrators has been rekindled with a recent decision of the UK Supreme Court in the case of *Halliburton v. Chubb*.[48] The case arose out of the Deepwater Horizon incident and the claim by Halliburton (provider of offshore services) under the excess insurance liability policy that was rejected by the insurer. The English High Court appointed the presiding arbitrator in July 2015. The individual was proposed by Chubb but rejected by Halliburton on the ground that the policy was

---

arbitral proceedings. Section 11 of the Arbitration and Conciliation Act 1996 empowers an arbitral institution to appoint arbitrators as per the appointment procedure agreed upon by the parties.

44. Article 5 of the LCIA Rules 2020.
45. Section 33(1) of the Arbitration Act, 1996.
46. Section 24(1) of the Arbitration Act, 1996.
47. 'Whether the fair minded and informed observer, having considered the facts, would conclude that there was a real possibility that the tribunal was biased.' The principle was laid down in *Porter v. Magill* [2002] 1 All ER 465 at 507.
48. *Halliburton Company (Appellant) v. Chubb Bermuda Insurance Ltd* [2020] UKSC 48.

governed by New York law and the proposed arbitrator was an English Lawyer. After his appointment, the presiding arbitrator accepted appointments on behalf of Chubb in December 2015 in a similar arbitration arising out of the same insurance contract. In August 2016, the presiding arbitrator was appointed by one of those parties in its claim against a different insurer. The presiding arbitrator did not disclose his subsequent appointments in the arbitration between Halliburton and Chubb. Halliburton learned of the subsequent appointments in November 2016.[49] The UK Supreme Court held that the test to determine the independence and impartiality of an arbitrator was to assess whether there was a 'real possibility of bias' in each circumstance. It held that there is a continuing duty on an arbitrator to disclose circumstances which may impact their independence and impartiality.[50]

This understanding of arbitrators' duty to disclose and act independently and impartially is quintessential in the context of the expedited formation of the arbitral tribunal. An award rendered by an arbitral tribunal formed under Article 9A of the LCIA Rules would potentially jeopardize the arbitral process if there is not sufficient scrutiny in terms of LCIA Rule 5. Article 9A of the LCIA Rules does not prescribe any disclosure obligations of the arbitrator. Parties could also challenge the appointment of an arbitrator under Article 9A of the LCIA Rules when the other party applies to the LCIA Court for expedited formation of arbitral tribunal under Article 9.1.

§5.03 TACKLING ENFORCEMENT CONCERNS IN EXPEDITED ARBITRATIONS: THE FUTURE OF ACCELERATED ARBITRAL PROCEDURES

The introduction of accelerated procedures was necessitated by the growing needs of parties wanting to resolve their disputes in a speedy, yet practical manner. This, however, must not come at the cost of the ethos of the arbitration process as an out-of-court dispute resolution method. One of the key takeaways from the development of the accelerated arbitral procedures previously described is that there have been various concerns at the time of enforcement of such awards before national courts.

The United Nations Convention on the Recognition and Enforcement of Foreign Arbitral Awards, New York, 1958 (New York Convention) encouraged resort to international arbitration. The principles stated in it are of contemporary relevance because most States, even today, fall back on the provisions of the New York Convention as a guide to arrest potential irregularities in the arbitral process at the time of recognizing arbitral awards. Expedited arbitration procedures must conform with the principles stated in the New York Convention. For example, Article V(1)(b) and Article V(1)(d) directly fly in the face of certain aspects of expedited procedures, such as limits on pleadings/evidence (Article V(1)(b) (unable to present its case). and on the constitution of arbitral tribunal, as seen in the *AQZ* case).

49. *Ibid.*, para. 19.
50. *Ibid.*, para. 120.

One of the leading reasons for enforcement concerns about expedited arbitrations is the fact that the amendments to the rules of arbitral institutions are not in sync with changes in national legislation and the public policy considerations of the State. As a result, accelerated arbitral mechanisms are at the risk of different interpretation by the courts across various jurisdictions, thereby increasing further uncertainty in the context of international arbitrations. Crucially, there has been no consensus, until recently, on the circumstances which would trigger the application of accelerated arbitral procedures. There has been a lack of deliberations at a global level with stakeholders from across jurisdictions expressing their respective arbitral practices and national public policy considerations.

Since 2018, UNCITRAL Working Group II explored the development of expedited arbitration rules in the UNCITRAL Arbitration Rules to give effect to the modern forms of arbitration. Working Group II's deliberations culminated in 2021 with the introduction of UNCITRAL Expedited Arbitration Rules 2021 (Expedited Rules).[51] The Expedited Rules were the result of the combined efforts of all the participants of the Working Group, which included all the State members of all the commission, intergovernmental organizations and invited non-governmental organizations. Representations from various arbitral institutions also were included.

[A] When Diplomacy Meets Innovation: UNCITRAL Expedited Arbitration Rules 2021

Working Group II, after extensive deliberation on various aspects of the expedited arbitration procedure with State members, and views of all arbitral institutions introduced the Expedited Rules as an appendix to the UNCITRAL Arbitration Rules (the 'Arbitration Rules' as adopted in 2021).[52] The Working Group focused on due process and fairness while streamlining the arbitration procedure. It discussed when expedited arbitration would apply, the number of arbitrators, and the deadlines for written submissions and for the rendering of an award and the possibility to file counterclaims or additional claims.[53] The Working Group also considered including early dismissal by way of preliminary determination.[54] However, the Working Group later decided such a provision was counterproductive to expedited proceedings where the schedules are already trimmed. The Working Group felt that an additional procedure within the procedure would not simplify the arbitral process.[55] Additionally, consensus existed on

51. *See* United Nations General Assembly, A/Res/76/108, Resolution on Expedited Arbitration Rules of the United Nations Commission on International Trade Law.
52. Article 1, para. 5 of the UNCITRAL Arbitration Rules 2021.
53. *See*, A/CN.9/WG.II/WP.207 – Settlement of commercial disputes – Issues relating to expedited arbitration.
54. *See*, A/CN.9/1003 – Report of Working Group II (Dispute Settlement) on the work of its seventieth session.
55. *See*, A/CN.9/1010 – Report of Working Group II (Dispute Settlement) on the work of its seventy-first session.

the necessity to streamline written records considering 'due process paranoia',[56] while also underscoring the responsibility of an arbitrator to limit the scope of written pleadings and narrow the issues for determination.[57] There were also deliberations on the need to control duplicative evidence, reasonable limitations on the length of the pleadings and the number of witness statements, all of which could go a long way towards building in more efficiency.[58]

The Expedited Rules were added as an appendix to the regular UNCITRAL Arbitration Rules. The Expedited Rules provide for the parties to opt-in by way of an express agreement as the only determining factor for the application of Expedited Rules.[59] The Expedited Rules provide for consolidation of written pleadings. The notice of arbitration must accompany the statement of claim, which must be communicated to the arbitral tribunal as soon as it is constituted.[60] The Expedited Rules also provide for a sole arbitrator unless otherwise agreed by the parties.[61] They also allow the respondent to communicate the statement of defence along with counterclaim, if any, within 15 days.[62] The requirement for hearings has also been removed, unless otherwise requested by the parties, and the period for making the award has been restricted to six months.

[B] The Future of Expedited Arbitration Procedure

With the introduction of the UNCITRAL Expedited Arbitration Rules in 2021, which received the assent of the United Nations,[63] a pattern emerges regarding what would be an ideal procedure for expedited arbitration to ensure successful enforcement of such awards. At its heart lies a crucial aspect for consideration, for arbitral institutions, and legal counsel alike. Undoubtedly, expedited procedures are an efficacious method for parties seeking speedy resolution of their disputes. However, such a method comes with the risk of potentially jeopardizing a party's claim in the absence of a hearing or limited scope of written pleadings. Res judicata concerns for awards rendered by

---

56. Due process paranoia is the reluctance of the arbitrator to act decisively for fear of the award being challenged on the basis that the party has not had the chance to fully present its case. *See*, Sundaresh Menon, *Dispelling Due Process Paranoia: Fairness, Efficiency and the Rule of Law* 17 (1) AIAJ (2021) pp. 1-27 DOI: 10.54648/aiaj2021001.
57. *See*, A/CN.9/1043 – Report of Working Group II (Dispute Settlement) on the work of its seventy-second session.
58. *See*, A/CN.9/1049 – Report of Working Group II (Dispute Settlement) on the work of its seventy-third session. *See also*, A/CN.9/WG.II/WP.217 – Draft provisions on expedited arbitration – Compilation of comments on the application of the UNCITRAL Rules on Transparency in Treaty-based Investor-State Arbitration to expedited arbitration.
59. Article 1 of Appendix – UNCITRAL Expedited Arbitration Rules to UNCITRAL Arbitration Rules 2021.
60. Article 4 of Appendix – UNCITRAL Expedited Arbitration Rules to UNCITRAL Arbitration Rules 2021.
61. Article 7 of Appendix – UNCITRAL Expedited Arbitration Rules to UNCITRAL Arbitration Rules 2021.
62. Article 5 of Appendix – UNCITRAL Expedited Arbitration Rules to UNCITRAL Arbitration Rules 2021.
63. *See*, A/CN.9/1085 – Report of Working Group II (Dispute Settlement) on the work of its seventy-fourth session.

tribunals under expedited procedures are also grave, especially if the nature of the dispute/claim is continuous.[64] The essential point is that the alternative to shorten the timelines of the procedure in traditional arbitrations is to not restrict/limit the scope to merely written pleadings and/or documentary evidence. The compromise on such autonomy comes at the cost of an award that would be rendered only at the end of six months.

Thus, a major disincentivizing factor against a party's choice for expedited arbitration remains that the relief, albeit final, is not immediate, as opposed to the relief that may be obtained via an emergency arbitrator. With alternate procedures for seeking various ad-interim relief pending the final adjudication of the dispute including interim protection measures, there is little commercial sense for parties to forego the opportunity to fully present their case before the arbitral tribunal. The parties must be well-informed of the limitations of the procedure as well as available alternatives. For the same reasons, the parties should not be compelled into an expedited procedure.

§5.04 CONCLUSION

The emergence of accelerated arbitral procedures to incentivize parties to choose arbitration by offering solutions that quickly resolve disputes comes at the cost of procedural compromises. These compromises have the potential to discourage parties from entering arbitrations. Moreover, a party's compromise on the opportunity to fully present its case would only make sense if there is an overarching necessity to bring finality to a dispute within six months. Alternatively, procedures to obtain interim measures remain at the disposal of the parties. Therefore, expedited arbitration offers little.

Insofar as the deliberations of the UNCITRAL Working Group II to ensure that the arbitrators avoid duplicity of evidence/exhibits and pleadings is concerned, no reason exists for these guidance mechanisms to not apply in the case of regular arbitrations. Commercial parties could limit their pleadings and evidence, including the number of witnesses, on their own, without resort to expedited arbitration rules.

It therefore remains to be seen how the introduction of a United Nations instrument, adopted after deliberations with State members, will impact expedited arbitration and enforcement trends. However, in the absence of more appealing reasons for parties to choose expedited procedures, expedited arbitration is very much at risk of remaining as a mere on-paper procedural mechanism.

64. In some cases, the claims of the parties are not crystalized at the stage of filing of statement of claim and/or parties may have continuous claims which may attain finality at the stage of rendering the award.

CHAPTER 6

The UNCITRAL Expedited Arbitration Rules: A Critical Review

Herman Verbist & Alan M. Anderson

In February 2019, the United Nations Commission on International Trade Law's (UNCITRAL's) Working Group II began deliberations on issues relating to expedited arbitration. After more than two years of effort, Working Group II completed the UNCITRAL Expedited Arbitration (EA) Rules. The UNCITRAL Commission adopted these rules in July 2021, and they became effective on 19 September 2021. Parties may agree to the applicability of the EA Rules for ad hoc arbitration proceedings. Consisting of 16 articles, the Rules attempt to balance greater efficiency of arbitral proceedings and the need to preserve due process and fair treatment. This chapter reviews the UNCITRAL EA Rules and their critical provisions. It provides an analysis of their development, strengths and weaknesses. Finally, it discusses the very recent work of UNCITRAL Working Group II to develop a model clause for 'highly expedited arbitration'.

§6.01 INTRODUCTION

In February 2018, after completing its work on the Singapore Convention on International Settlement Agreements Resulting from Mediation,[1] the United Nations Commission on International Trade Law's (UNCITRAL's) Working Group II (WG II) considered

1. UNCITRAL adopted the Singapore Convention on 20 December 2018, and it was opened for signature on 7 August 2019. The Singapore Convention has been signed by 56 States, and 13 have ratified it as of 4 January 2024. *See* United Nations, 'Status: United Nations Convention on International Settlement Agreements Resulting from Mediation', available at: https://uncitral.un.org/en/texts/mediation/conventions/international_settlement_agreements/status. For a discussion of the development and provisions in the Singapore Convention, see generally Alan M. Anderson, Ben Beaumont and Herman Verbist, 'The United Nations Convention on International Settlement Agreements Resulting from Mediation: Its Genesis, Negotiation and Future', in *International Mediation*, Christian Campbell, ed. (Wolters Kluwer, 2020), 35-62.

possible future work. WG II considered three possible future topics: revision of the UNCITRAL Conciliation Rules and preparation of notes on mediation; expedited arbitration procedures and adjudication; and uniform principles on the quality and efficiency of arbitral proceedings.[2] General support existed within WG II for 'giving priority to work on expedited arbitration, which would maximize the benefits of arbitration'.[3] The Governments of Italy, Norway and Spain then submitted a broad proposal to the full UNCITRAL Commission that built on a joint proposal the Governments of Switzerland and the United States had made at the 68th Session of WG II in February 2018.[4] Recognizing the issues now faced by international arbitration, the proposal by Italy, Norway and Spain urged that WG II:

> should devote its expertise and capacity to the development of instruments that may contribute to the enhancement of arbitration as a method for settlement of international commercial disputes. Arbitration is increasingly under pressure and threatened to lose its role as a preferred means for dispute resolution for commercial disputes. Arbitration is under a double pressure: on the one hand, arbitral proceedings are getting increasingly complicated, and they expand both in terms of time frame and in terms of volume of documentation. This challenges one of the traditional advantages of arbitration as opposed to court litigation, namely efficiency.
>
> On the other hand, measures taken by arbitral tribunals or arbitral institutions are increasingly faced with court control. Possibly for the sake of preserving efficiency in a scenario where disputes get more complicated, steps may be taken that do not necessarily meet the quality criteria that arbitration is expected to meet. In order to render a valid arbitral award, and in order to obtain enforcement of the award, arbitration needs to comply with a series of fundamental principles, such as the principle of due process. The goal of ensuring efficient arbitration may lead to taking steps that compromise the quality of arbitration. This, in turn, may erode the trust in arbitration as a method for settlement of disputes, a trust that is the very foundation of the success of arbitration.[5]

This proposal was supported by the Government of Belgium.[6] At its 51st Session in June-July 2018, the UNCITRAL Commission gave a mandate to WG II to prepare a set of expedited arbitration rules.[7]

The decision that WG II undertake work on drafting expedited arbitration rules was logical and appropriate. Various arbitral institutions around the world had adopted expedited procedures years earlier.[8] The International Chamber of Commerce (ICC)

2. United Nations Commission on International Trade Law (UNCITRAL), 'Report of Working Group II (Dispute Settlement) on the work of its Sixty-eighth session (New York, 5-9 February 2018)', A/CN.9/934 (19 Feb. 2018), paras 149-156.
3. *Ibid.*, para. 160.
4. 'Possible future work: Proposal by the Governments of Italy, Norway and Spain: future work for Working Group II', A/CN.9.959 (30 April 2018), para. 3.
5. *Ibid.*, paras 5-6.
6. 'Possible future work: Proposal by the Government of Belgium: future work for Working Group II', A/CN.9.961 (20 June 2018), p. 2.
7. United Nations, 'Report of the United Nations Commission on International Trade Law, Fifty-first session (25 June-13 July 2018)', A/73/17 (31 July 2018), paras 244-245, 252.
8. For example, effective 1 July 1995, the Arbitration Institute of the Stockholm Chamber of Commerce adopted rules for expedited arbitration. *See* SCC Rules for Expedited Arbitration 1995

had adopted new expedited arbitration rules in 2017.[9] The results of a survey circulated by the Secretariat shortly after commencing work on the project revealed that of 24 arbitral institutions responding, 22 of them had a procedure or mechanism in place to expedite arbitral proceedings.[10] However, UNCITRAL, whose Arbitration Rules are widely preferred and used in ad hoc arbitration proceedings,[11] had not developed rules for expedited arbitration. In this regard, UNCITRAL was rather 'late to the game' in elaborating rules to speed up the arbitration process. However, that fact also gave WG II the ability to consider the various approaches to expedited arbitration already implemented, as well as the issues arising from those approaches. WG II's work, therefore, would benefit from the prior efforts of others to develop expedited arbitration rules. Presumably, the result of its work would be a virtual 'gold standard' of expedited arbitration rules for use in ad hoc international commercial arbitration.

Are the UNCITRAL Expedited Arbitration Rules (EA Rules) in fact the 'gold standard' for expedited arbitration proceedings? Do they adequately balance competing issues such as due process considerations, efficiency and issuance of a quality, acceptable award? This chapter seeks answers to these questions. It first considers the deliberations of WG II, focusing on those issues that provide the greatest insights into the foundational principles and underpinnings for the EA Rules. This chapter then reviews the key provisions in the EA Rules, analysing their efficacy, strengths and weaknesses as appropriate. It then briefly mentions the potential applicability of the EA Rules to investor-State disputes. Finally, this chapter considers the latest work of WG II to develop a model clause for 'highly expedited arbitration'.

(available at: https://www.acerislaw.com/scc-arbitration-rules/). The Swiss Rules of International Arbitration also were one of the first to contain provisions addressing expedited arbitration. *See* Matthais Scherer, 'New Rules of International Arbitration in Switzerland', 4 *Int'l Arb. Law. Rev.* (2004), 123-124 DOI: 10.54648/rba2011006. Other arbitral institutions followed suit soon thereafter. *See, e.g.*, Hong Kong International Arbitration Centre Administered Arbitration Rules, Article 41.1 (2013); Singapore International Arbitration Centre Arbitration Rules, Rule 5.1 (2016).

9. ICC Rules of Arbitration, Article 30 (2017). *See* Herman Verbist, 'Contribution of Benjamin Davis to Expedited Arbitration', 52 *U. Tol. L. Rev.*, 463-465 (2021).
10. UNCITRAL Secretariat, 'Note: Responses to UNCITRAL questionnaire on expedited arbitration' (January 2020), pp. 1-15. The two institutions that reported they did not have rules or procedures for expedited arbitration were the London Court of International Arbitration (LCIA) and the Milan Chamber of Arbitration. However, the Milan Chamber stated that it intended to revise its rules in 2019 to include provisions for expedited arbitration. *Ibid.*, pp. 4-5. Its 2003 arbitration rules include an annex that provides a 'simplified arbitration procedure' for claims less than EUR 250,000. Milan Chamber of Arbitration, 'Arbitration Rules' (1 March 2023), Annexe D. Perhaps unique among major institutional arbitral centres, the LCIA does not have any rules specific to expedited arbitration. The LCIA relies on Article 14.4 of its general rules, as providing the tribunal with the 'duty to adopt procedures suitable to the circumstances of the arbitration, avoiding unnecessary delay and expense, so as to provide a fair, efficient and expeditious means for final resolution of the parties' dispute'. UNCITRAL Secretariat, 'Note: Responses to UNCITRAL questionnaire on expedited arbitration' (January 2020), p. 5.

    For a review of the expedited arbitration rules of 59 institutions, *see* International Council for Commercial Arbitration, 'Overview of Selected Expedited Arbitration Provisions' (14 August 2019) (available at: https://uncitral.un.org/en/working_groups/2/arbitration).
11. The standard UNCITRAL Arbitration Rules are the most popular framework for ad hoc arbitration. Queen Mary University of London, School of International Arbitration, '2021 International Arbitration Survey: Adapting arbitration to a changing world' (2021), 9.

This chapter's review and analysis suggest that international arbitration may well be returning to its roots as a quick and efficient means of resolving commercial disputes, albeit in a rather painstaking manner.[12] In the final analysis, the UNCITRAL EA Rules represent a sound effort to balance the competing considerations inherent in returning international commercial arbitration to its historical foundation of an efficient and cost-effective means for resolving international commercial disputes.

§6.02 THE EA RULES: DELIBERATIONS AND FUNDAMENTAL PRINCIPLES

WG II began its deliberations on the preparation of the EA Rules in February 2019 and concluded its work in March 2021.[13] The UNCITRAL Commission adopted the EA Rules along with a new Article 1(5) to the standard UNCITRAL Arbitration Rules in July 2021.[14] At the same session, the Commission approved in principle the draft Explanatory Note to the EA Rules and asked WG II to finalize the text at its next session.[15] WG II finalized the Explanatory Note in September 2021.[16]

The deliberations of WG II generally were noncontentious and proceeded apace, particularly in light of the worldwide COVID-19 pandemic through which it laboured. However, several topics, which provide insights into the foundational principles underlying the EA Rules, deserve highlighting, especially due to the important and critical impact they had on the EA Rules and their direction.

From the beginning, WG II understood that 'expedited arbitration was a streamlined and simplified procedure with shortened time frame[s] that made it possible to reach a final resolution of the dispute in a cost- and time-effective manner'.[17] At the same time, WG II:

> stressed that the notions of due process and fairness were important elements of international arbitration that should not be overlooked in streamlining the arbitration procedure. The need to balance on the one hand, the efficiency of the arbitral proceedings and on the other, the rights of the parties to due process (including the right to present their case) and fair treatment was emphasized.[18]

12. *See* Michael Mustill, 'Comments on Fast-Track Arbitration', 10:4 *J. Int'l Arb.* (1993), 122 DOI: 10.54648/joia1993034.
13. *See* UNCITRAL, 'Report of Working Group II (Dispute Settlement) on the work of its Sixty-ninth session (New York, 4-8 February 2019)', A/CN.9/969 (18 February 2019); UNCITRAL, 'Report of Working Group II (Dispute Settlement) on the work of its Seventy-third session (New York (online), 22-26 March 2022)', A/CN.9/109 (31 March 2021).
14. United Nations, 'Report of the United Nations Commission on International Trade Law, Fifty-fourth session (28 June-16 July 2021)', A/76/17 (2021), para. 189.
15. *Ibid.*
16. UNCITRAL, 'Report of Working Group II (Dispute Settlement) on the work of its Seventy-fourth session (Vienna, 27 September-1 October 2021)', A/CN.9/1085 (5 October 2021), paras 12-48.
17. UNCITRAL, 'Report of Working Group II (Dispute Settlement) on the work of its Sixty-ninth session (New York, 4-8 February 2019)', A/CN.9/969 (18 February 2019), para. 14.
18. *Ibid.*, para. 23.

Thus, in drafting rules for expedited arbitration, one fundamental underlying principle was that the rules, while providing for a speedier and more cost-effective process, should not lose sight of the requirement of due process.

WG II initially faced the question of when, and under what circumstances, the EA Rules should apply. A survey conducted by the UNCITRAL Secretariat to obtain information regarding how they administered expedited arbitration (if at all) received responses from 24 arbitral institutions. Of the 22 arbitral institutions that administered expedited arbitration in one form or another, 14 – a clear majority – reported that they had monetary thresholds for the application of their expedited procedures.[19] Of those institutions reporting a monetary threshold, 11 were 'automatic'; i.e., the expedited arbitration procedures applied if the amount in controversy did not exceed a set sum.[20] The other three institutions provided maximum amounts that could not be exceeded for the expedited procedures to apply and required the arbitral institution to make a decision on applicability.[21] Thus, a key decision for WG II was whether the EA Rules would apply on an 'opt-in' or an 'opt-out' basis, the latter including a monetary value that would impose expedited procedures if it was not exceeded.[22]

At its first session considering expedited arbitration rules, most delegations expressed support that 'the parties' agreement should be the determining factor for the application of expedited arbitration'.[23] However, some delegates questioned the practicality of such an approach. Therefore, WG II proceeded to consider mechanisms for the application of expedited arbitration procedures 'without the explicit agreement of all parties'.[24] The discussion of whether to make the expedited procedures applicable only if the parties agreed or whether some means for application without the parties' consent should be developed continued at the next session of WG II.[25] By the next session, WG II had reached a consensus: the new EA rules would require 'the express agreement of the parties ... and that agreement would be the sole criterion for determining their application'.[26] On the scale between party autonomy and the approach used by most arbitral institutions with expedited procedures to impose their expedited rules on the parties based on some financial threshold, WG II came down

19. UNCITRAL Secretariat, 'Note: Responses to UNCITRAL questionnaire on expedited arbitration' (January 2020), pp. 24-33.
20. *Ibid. See, e.g.*, Bahrain Chamber for Dispute Resolution (BCDR-AAA) Rules, Article 6.1 (2017); CEPANI Arbitration Rules, Article 29 (2020); CIETAC Arbitration Rules, Article 56 (2015); Georgian International Arbitration Centre (GIAC), Arbitration Rules, Annex IV, Article 1 (2017).
21. UNCITRAL Secretariat, 'Note: Responses to UNCITRAL questionnaire on expedited arbitration' (January 2020), pp. 24-33. *See, e.g.*, HKIAC Administered Arbitration Rules, Article 42.1(A) (2018); SIAC Arbitration Rules, Rule 5 (2016).
22. UNCITRAL Secretariat, 'Note: Settlement of commercial disputes: Issues relating to expedited arbitration', A/CN.9/WG.II/WP.207 (16 November 2018), paras 23-27.
23. UNCITRAL, 'Report of Working Group II (Dispute Settlement) on the work of its Sixty-ninth session (New York, 4-8 February 2019)', A/CN.9/969 (18 February 2019), para. 95. *See generally ibid.*, paras 90-97.
24. *Ibid.*, para. 97.
25. UNCITRAL, 'Report of Working Group II (Dispute Settlement) on the work of its Seventieth session (Vienna, 23-17 September 2019)', A/CN.9/1003 (3 October 2019), paras 20-34.
26. UNCITRAL, 'Report of Working Group II (Dispute Settlement) on the work of its Seventy-first session (New York, 3-7 February 2020)', A/CN.9/1010 (12 February 2020), para. 27.

firmly on the side of party autonomy. Thus, party autonomy is another foundation upon which the EA Rules are built.

The decision to emphasize party autonomy also led WG II to decide that the parties could decide the expedited rules would not apply at any point in the process and essentially for any reason, so long as there was agreement.[27] The question of whether one party could ever withdraw from expedited arbitration then came to the fore. Delegates pointed out that allowing one party to unilaterally withdraw from the expedited procedures would 'run contrary to party autonomy'.[28] WG II stressed that any such effort by one party should be limited to exceptional circumstances, 'which would comfort parties entering into an agreement on expedited arbitration ... [but] would only allow parties to resort to non-expedited arbitration, if convincing and justified reasons were given in the request for withdrawal'.[29] Thus, while the clear foundation for the EA Rules is party autonomy, there is a small, restricted window for an 'out', that is limited. In essence, a party agreeing to application of the EA Rules should assume that they will not be able to avoid their application absent agreement by all parties to the dispute.

At the same time, WG II endowed the arbitral tribunal – a sole arbitrator unless otherwise agreed – with broad discretion to modify the time periods and procedures during the expedited process after asking the parties to express their views.[30] This broad discretion represents somewhat of a retreat from principles of party autonomy, although at the same time, the parties remain free to agree to modifications to the EA Rules in any respect.

Finally, a fair amount of discussion occurred regarding the time frame within which the tribunal would have to render the award. A discussion occurred between making the time period six months from constitution of the tribunal or nine months. Ultimately, WG II reached a consensus that six months should be the deadline 'as the expeditious nature of the proceedings would be emphasized'.[31] However, concerns were then expressed regarding whether the time period could be extended without the consent of the parties. Ultimately, WG II decided that the tribunal could extend the time period in exceptional circumstances after soliciting the views of the parties so as not to exceed nine months from the date of constitution of the tribunal absent agreement by all the parties.[32]

Thus, the fundamental principle underlying the EA Rules is party autonomy – with some limitations. At the same time, an agreement to expedited arbitration under

27. *Ibid.*, paras 29-33.
28. UNCITRAL, 'Report of Working Group II (Dispute Settlement) on the work of its Seventy-second session (Vienna, 21-25 September 2020)', A/CN.9/1043 (29 September 2020), para. 40.
29. *Ibid. See also ibid.*, paras 43-49 (factors to be considered by the tribunal when deciding a request by one party to withdraw from expedited procedures).
30. *See ibid.*, paras 89-92; UNCITRAL, 'Report of Working Group II (Dispute Settlement) on the work of its Seventy-third session (New York (online), 22-26 March 2021)', A/CN.9/1049 (31 March 2021), para. 34.
31. UNCITRAL, 'Report of Working Group II (Dispute Settlement) on the work of its Seventy-second session (Vienna, 21-25 September 2020)', A/CN.9/1043 (29 September 2020), para. 106.
32. UNCITRAL, 'Report of Working Group II (Dispute Settlement) on the work of its Seventy-third session (New York (online), 22-26 March 2021)', A/CN.9/1049 (31 March 2021), paras 56-57.

the EA Rules grants the arbitral tribunal considerable discretion in how the arbitration will proceed. The other underlying principle is due process. Regardless of how the EA Rules are applied, the tribunal must ensure that the parties have a fair opportunity to present their evidence.

§6.03 THE EA RULES: REVIEW AND ANALYSIS

The EA Rules endeavour to balance the efficiency of the arbitral proceedings and the need to preserve due process and fair treatment.[33] They provide a set of 16 articles to which the parties may agree for ad hoc arbitration proceedings.[34] The EA Rules and the standard UNCITRAL Arbitration Rules must be read in conjunction with each other. While some of the standard arbitration provisions do not apply to expedited arbitration, the parties maintain a large degree of flexibility under the EA Rules to tailor the arbitration according to their needs.[35] Specifically, absent agreement, Articles 3(4)(a) and (b); 6(2); 7; 8(1); the first sentence of Article 20(1); the first sentence of Article 21(1); Article 22; and the second sentence of Article 27(2) of the standard Arbitration Rules do not apply to expedited arbitration.[36]

An annex to the EA Rules contains a model clause for contracts and also a model statement of independence for arbitrators serving in expedited arbitration.[37] When considering whether to agree to the EA Rules in a dispute that has arisen or could arise in the future, the parties should take into account, among other factors, the urgency of resolving the dispute; the number of parties involved, including joinder or consolidation; the anticipated complexity of the dispute; the financial resources available to a party in proportion to the expected cost of the arbitration; and the likelihood of an award being rendered within the time frames provided in Article 16 EA Rules.[38]

[A] Applicability: Opt-In, but with an 'Out'

The touchstone of the EA Rules is party autonomy. The EA Rules apply only if the parties have expressly agreed.[39] Moreover, the agreement must be to specifically apply the EA Rules. An agreement to apply the standard 2021 UNCITRAL Arbitration Rules does not mean the EA Rules will apply.[40] Furthermore, the parties may modify the

33. UNCITRAL Arbitration Rules Appendix – UNCITRAL Expedited Arbitration Rules (2021), Explanatory Note, para. 1. *See also* Herman Verbist, 'UNCITRAL Expedited Arbitration Rules 2021', *b-Arbitra*, No. 2 (2022), 424-434.
34. *See generally* UNCITRAL Arbitration Rules Appendix – UNCITRAL Expedited Arbitration Rules (2021), Articles 1-16. All references hereinafter to the rules contained in the Appendix will be to 'EA Rules', followed by the appropriate article citation. The Explanatory Note is considerably longer than the EA Rules themselves, providing 24 pages of notes in 105 paragraphs. The EA Rules themselves comprise barely five pages of text.
35. *See* EA Rules, Article 1.
36. EA Rules, Article 1, note ***.
37. EA Rules, Annex to the UNCITRAL Expedited Arbitration Rules.
38. *See* EA Rules, Explanatory Note, para. 98.
39. UNCITRAL Arbitration Rules (2021), Article 1(5); EA Rules, Article 1.
40. UNCITRAL Arbitration Rules (2021), Article 1(5).

applicable provisions of the standard UNCITRAL Arbitration Rules as well as the EA Rules.[41]

Consistent with party autonomy, even if the parties had agreed to submit their dispute to expedited arbitration under the EA Rules, they may agree at any time that the EA Rules no longer apply.[42] However, inconsistent with the principle of party autonomy, one party may ask the tribunal to decide, 'in exceptional circumstances' and after receiving the views of the parties, that the EA Rules will no longer apply.[43] A possible 'out' from expedited arbitration therefore exists. 'Exceptional circumstances' means that 'the party requesting withdrawal should provide convincing and justified reasons for such request and that the arbitral tribunal should uphold the request only in certain circumstances. It introduces a high threshold for allowing a unilateral withdrawal from expedited arbitration'.[44]

The Explanatory Note provides guidance to the tribunal on various factors it may consider in deciding the request of a party to remove the dispute from expedited arbitration. These factors include, but are not limited to:

- the urgency of resolving the dispute;
- the stage of the proceedings at which the request is made;
- the complexity of the dispute (e.g., the anticipated volume of documentary evidence and the number of witnesses);
- the anticipated amount in dispute (the sum of claims made in the notice of arbitration, any counterclaim made in response thereto as well as any amendment or supplement);
- the terms of the parties' agreement to expedited arbitration and whether the current circumstances were foreseeable at the time of the agreement; and
- the consequences of the determination on the proceedings.[45]

The tribunal does not need to consider all of these factors in the non-exhaustive list.[46]

Moreover, the tribunal has the flexibility to decide that only certain provisions in the EA Rules will not apply, as opposed to removing the dispute from the EA Rules in their entirety.[47] Article 2 of the EA Rules thus empowers the tribunal to decide that the expedited arbitration rules will no longer apply – in whole or in part – despite the objection of a party. This is a decision the tribunal should not make lightly because it will result in a different type of dispute resolution procedure than the one to which the parties previously agreed. It may therefore have consequences for the ultimate enforceability of the final award.

41. EA Rules, Article 1.
42. EA Rules, Article 2(1).
43. EA Rules, Article 2(2).
44. EA Rules, Explanatory Note, para. 12.
45. EA Rules, Explanatory Note, para. 13.
46. EA Rules, Explanatory Note, para. 14.
47. EA Rules, Explanatory Note, para. 15.

If the parties or the tribunal decides the EA Rules no longer apply, then the proceedings will continue under the standard UNCITRAL Arbitration Rules. This does not mean that the arbitral tribunal, if already constituted, would have to be reconstituted in accordance with the standard rules. The arbitral tribunal remains in place.[48] However, the parties may agree to replace an arbitrator or reconstitute the tribunal. The arbitrator appointed under the EA Rules may resign, for example, if they determine they are not able to meet the commitments required for non-expedited arbitration.[49] Further, unless the arbitral tribunal decides otherwise, the non-expedited proceeding should resume at the stage they were at when the expedited proceedings ended. Decisions made during the expedited proceeding should remain applicable to the non-expedited proceedings, unless the arbitral tribunal decides to depart from its earlier decisions or from a decision made by the previous tribunal.[50]

[B] The Timetable: Overview

In general, the EA Rules admonish the parties and the arbitral tribunal to act expeditiously throughout the proceedings.[51] By agreeing to arbitrate under the EA rules, the parties 'are agreeing to cooperate in ensuring the efficiency of the proceeding as well as for a swift resolution of the dispute, particularly in an ad hoc setting where there is no administering institution to further expedite the process'.[52] The tribunal should take into account the fact the parties agreed to expedited arbitration and the time periods established in the EA Rules.[53] Therefore, arbitral tribunals in expedited arbitration have the same duty to conduct the proceedings to avoid unnecessary delay and expense and to provide a fair and efficient process to resolve the dispute as in standard arbitration. The arbitral tribunal should also comply with any due process requirements.[54]

The arbitral tribunal may utilize any technological means as it considers appropriate to conduct the proceedings, including to communicate with the parties and to hold consultations and hearings remotely.[55] The rule aims to assist the arbitral tribunal in streamlining the proceedings and to avoid unnecessary delay and expense, both of which are in line with the objectives of expedited arbitration. However, the use of technological means is subject to the overarching requirement in the standard Arbitration Rules to provide for a fair proceeding and to give each party a reasonable

48. EA Rules, Article 2(3).
49. EA Rules, Explanatory Note, para. 17.
50. EA Rules, Explanatory Note, para. 18.
51. EA Rules, Article 3(1), (2). *See generally* EA Rules, Explanatory Note, paras 19-33.
52. EA Rules, Explanatory Note, para. 20.
53. EA Rules, Article 3(2).
54. EA Rules, Explanatory Note, para. 21. To ensure that the arbitrator(s) understand their obligations under the EA Rules, the parties may add to the statement of independence of the arbitrator(s) a model statement highlighting the need to conduct the proceedings expeditiously and to render the award within the time frame established under the EA Rules. *Ibid.*, para. 22.
55. EA Rules, Article 3(3).

opportunity to present its case and that it should be mindful of any due process requirements.[56]

Table 6.1 summarizes the deadlines under the EA Rules and the relevant articles establishing those deadlines.

Table 6.1 Chart of Deadlines under EA Rules[57]

Time Frame	*Procedural Actions*	*Relevant Articles*
A	Notice of arbitration (including proposal for designation of appointing authority (A1) and the appointment of a sole arbitrator (A2)) to respondent	EA Rules 4(1)
A + 0 days	Statement of claim to respondent	EA Rules 4(2)
B A + 15 days	Response to notice of arbitration (including responses to A1 & A2) to claimant	EA Rules 5(1)
C 15 days after A1 or any proposal	If no agreement on appointing authority, any party may request Secretary-General of Permanent Court of Arbitration (PCA) to designate appointing authority or to serve as appointing authority	EA Rules 6(1)
D 15 days after A2 or any proposal	If no agreement on the arbitrator, any party may request appointing authority to appoint the sole arbitrator → Appointing authority to appoint as promptly as possible	EA Rules 8(2)
E	Constitution of arbitral tribunal	EA Rules 8; UNCITRAL Rules 8 & 9
E + 0 days	Claimant to communicate its notice of arbitration & statement of claim to arbitral tribunal (as soon as it is constituted)	EA Rules 4(3)
E + 15 days	Consultation with parties through case management conference or otherwise (promptly after and within 15 days)	EA Rules 9
	Establishment of provisional timetable (as soon as practicable)	UNCITRAL Rules 17(2)
F E + 15 days	Respondent to communicate statement of defence to claimant and arbitral tribunal (possible extension)	EA Rules 5(2); 10

56. EA Rules, Explanatory Note, para. 24.
57. EA Rules, Explanatory Note, para. 105.

Time Frame	*Procedural Actions*	*Relevant Articles*
F + 0 days	Counterclaim or claim for purposes of set-off included in statement of defence (permitted at a later date if arbitral tribunal agrees)	EA Rules 12
G E + 6 months	Issuance of the award	EA Rules 16(1)
E + 9 months	Possible extension of time for making the award (exceptional circumstances)	EA Rules 16(2)
E + 9 months + final extended time limit	Possible extension of time period for making the award (at risk of not rendering an award within nine months)	EA Rules 16(3)

The time periods for action under EA Rules generally are 15 days. Once the claimant files its notice of arbitration, proposed designation of the appointing authority, and proposed arbitrator, the respondent has 15 days to respond.[58] If there is no agreement on the appointing authority, then the Secretary-General of the PCA has 15 days to designate the appointing authority (which could be itself).[59] If there is no agreement on the arbitrator, then a party has 15 days to ask the appointing authority to appoint the sole arbitrator, which must be done as promptly as possible.[60]

While there are some opportunities for extensions, once the tribunal is constituted – and this date is critical because the deadline for completion of the arbitration runs from the date of constitution – the parties and the tribunal must hold a case management conference to set a provisional timetable within 15 days.[61] By the same deadline, the respondent has to serve its statement of defence and any counterclaim or set-off.[62] The tribunal must render the final award within six months from the date of constitution, which may, in exceptional circumstances, be extended with the agreement of the parties to nine months.[63] Thus, if the matter proceeds expeditiously in accordance with the established time frames, the tribunal should render the final award within approximately 8 months from the date the claimant files the notice of arbitration and within approximately 11 months if exceptional circumstances exist extending the deadline for rendering the final award.

[C] Appointing Authority

Although the keystone of the EA Rules is party autonomy, the designation of an appointing authority is critical in the case of subsequent disagreements or the inability

58. EA Rules, Article 5(1).
59. EA Rules, Article 6(1).
60. EA Rules, Article 8(2).
61. EA Rules, Article 9.
62. EA Rules, Articles 5(2), 10, 12.
63. EA Rules, Article 16.

of the parties to agree on various aspects of the expedited arbitration process. The appointing authority plays an important role in the expedited proceedings, particularly with regard to the constitution of the arbitral tribunal. Accordingly, the parties should agree on an appointing authority.[64] If the parties have not identified an appointing authority in their arbitration agreement or cannot agree within 15 days after a proposal for designation of an appointing authority is received by all the parties, then any party may request the PCA to designate an appointing authority or to serve as the appointing authority.[65] The 15-day time limit is shorter than under the standard UNCITRAL Model Rules. The EA Rules further accelerate the process because the PCA may be asked immediately to serve as appointing authority and not after a request has first been made to designate an appointing authority.[66] If a designated appointing authority fails or refuses to act within the set time limit, any party may immediately ask the PCA to act as appointing authority or to designate a substitute appointing authority.[67]

[D] Number of Arbitrators

The default presumption under the EA Rules is for a single arbitrator, unless the parties agree otherwise.[68] The parties should jointly appoint the sole arbitrator.[69] If the parties have not reached agreement on the appointment of a sole arbitrator within 15 days after a proposal has been received by all the parties, the appointing authority shall, at the request of a party, appoint a sole arbitrator in accordance with Article 8(2) of the standard UNCITRAL Arbitration Rules.[70] This time limit is shorter than the 30-day time limit in the standard arbitration rules. When making the appointment, the appointing authority should appoint an arbitrator who is ready and able to conduct the proceeding expeditiously and may consider factors that are likely to result in the appointment of an impartial arbitrator. The appointing authority may follow the list-procedure contained in Article 8(2) of the standard arbitration rules.[71]

Consistent with the EA Rules' emphasis on party autonomy, the parties may agree on a three-person tribunal. The time frames in Article 9 of the standard UNCITRAL Arbitration Rules then apply. The parties may shorten those time periods,

64. EA Rules, Explanatory Note, para. 40.
65. EA Rules, Article 6(1).
66. EA Rules, Article 6(2), (3); EA Rules, Explanatory Note, paras 40-45.
67. EA Rules, Explanatory Note, para. 44.
68. EA Rules, Article 7.
69. EA Rules, Article 8(1). The parties should consider requesting from the arbitrator, in addition to the statement pursuant to Article 11 of the standard UNCITRAL Arbitration Rules, a statement that they can devote the necessary time to conduct the arbitration expeditiously. UNCITRAL proposes the following model statement for confirmation by the proposed arbitrator in an expedited arbitration: 'I confirm, on the basis of the information presently available to me, that I can devote the time necessary to conduct this arbitration diligently, efficiently, expeditiously and in accordance with the time limits in the UNCITRAL Arbitration Rules and the UNCITRAL Expedited Arbitration Rules.' EA Rules, Annex to the UNCITRAL Expedited Arbitration Rules, p. 38.
70. EA Rules, Article 8(2).
71. EA Rules, Explanatory Note, paras 55-58.

however, to expedite the process.[72] If the parties agreed on a three-person tribunal but they cannot agree on the appointments for any reason, then the appointing authority may, upon request, appoint a sole arbitrator if it determines this is more appropriate in accordance with Article 7(2) of the UNCITRAL Arbitration Rules.[73]

[E] Case Management Conference

The EA Rules include a new provision specific to expedited arbitration. Article 9 of the EA Rules requires the tribunal, within 15 days of its constitution, to consult with the parties and hold a case management conference to determine the manner in which it will conduct the arbitration.[74] This consultation may occur before the respondent has submitted its statement of defence because the respondent has 15 days from the date the tribunal is constituted to submit it.[75] The case management conference process 'is particularly key to an efficient and fair organization of expedited arbitration'.[76] The expectation for the 'consultation' is that the tribunal will 'engage actively with the parties rather than simply invite them to express their views'.[77] Once the parties have expressed their agreement or objections to the way in which it intends to organize and conduct the arbitration, the tribunal may make a decision.[78]

Clearly, the timetable set must take into account the time frames in the EA Rules, particularly the deadline for rendering the award established in Article 16.[79] While the tribunal, after consulting with the parties, may decide to extend or shorten any of the deadlines under the standard UNCITRAL Arbitration Rules, the EA Rules, or as otherwise agreed by the parties, any such decision or agreement is subject to the overarching deadline in Article 16 of the EA Rules.[80] This ability to amend the timetable 'provides the tribunal with a robust mandate to act decisively without fearing that its award could be set aside for a breach of due process.'[81] At the same time, however, the tribunal must ensure compliance with due process.[82]

If a party fails to comply with the deadlines established either in the EA Rules or by the tribunal, Article 30 of the standard UNCITRAL Arbitration Rules applies.[83] The tribunal has the discretion to reject or disregard untimely submissions. However, the tribunal must exercise this discretion with care.[84]

72. EA Rules, Explanatory Note, para. 59.
73. EA Rules, Explanatory Note, para. 49. *See* UNCITRAL Arbitration Rules, Article 7(2).
74. EA Rules, Article 9.
75. EA Rules, Explanatory Note, para. 63.
76. EA Rules, Explanatory Note, para. 60.
77. *Ibid.*, para. 61.
78. *Ibid.*
79. *Ibid.*, para. 65.
80. EA Rules, Article 10.
81. EA Rules, Explanatory Note, para. 68.
82. *Ibid.*, para. 69.
83. *Ibid.*, para. 70.
84. *Ibid.*

[F] Procedure – Submissions

Consistent with the expedited nature of the proceedings, the submissions of the parties must be short, concise and to the point. A party filing a request for arbitration under the EA Rules must not only comply with the requirements of Article 3(3) and (4) of the standard UNCITRAL Arbitration Rules but also include the elements required by Article 4(1) of the EA Rules.[85] The additional elements required under the EA Rules are a proposal for the designation of an appointing authority, unless the parties have previously agreed to an appointing authority, and a proposal for the appointment of an arbitrator.[86] The proposal for the appointment of the arbitrator does not mean the claimant must then propose the name of an arbitrator. Rather, the claimant may propose a list of suitable candidates or a procedure to be used by the parties to agree on an arbitrator.[87]

The claimant must also submit its statement of claim at the same time and communicate it to the respondent.[88] Receipt of the notice and statement of claim by the respondent triggers the 15-day response deadline as well as the deadlines for designation of the appointing authority and appointment of the tribunal.[89]

The statement of claim should, as far as possible, be accompanied by all documents and other evidence relied upon by the claimant or contain references to them. It does not, however, mean that all evidence has to be communicated at this stage, which may be burdensome and counterproductive.[90] The claimant may decide to treat its notice of arbitration as its statement of claim as long as the notice of arbitration complies with all requirements. In that case, the claimant communicated a single document combining its notice of arbitration and statement of claim.[91]

The respondent has 15 days after receipt of the notice of arbitration to respond to the claimant's proposals regarding the appointment of an arbitrator and the designated appointing authority.[92] Once the arbitral tribunal is constituted, the respondent has 15 days to file its statement of defence.[93] The respondent may elect to treat its response to the notice of arbitration as its statement of defence, as long as the response complies with the requirement of Article 21(1) of the standard UNCITRAL Arbitration Rules.[94]

---

85. EA Rules, Article 4.
86. EA Rules, Article 4(1).
87. EA Rules, Explanatory Note, para. 27. In light of Article 7 of the EA Rules, which provides a default rule for a sole arbitrator, absent prior agreement by the parties to have a tribunal composed of more than one arbitrator, the claimant must suggest the constitution of an arbitral tribunal of more than one arbitrator in its notice. EA Rules, Explanatory Note, para. 30.
88. EA Rules, Article 4(2). This rule modifies Article 20(1) of the standard UNCITRAL Arbitration Rules, which provides that the statement of claim should be communicated within a period of time to be determined by the arbitral tribunal. EA Rules, Explanatory Note, para. 28.
89. EA Rules, Articles 5, 6, 8; EA Rules, Explanatory Note, para. 26.
90. EA Rules, Explanatory Note, para. 31.
91. EA Rules, Explanatory Note, para. 32.
92. EA Rules, Article 5(1); EA Rules, Explanatory Note, paras 36-37.
93. EA Rules, Article 5(2).
94. EA Rules, Explanatory Note, para. 39.

The respondent must file any counterclaim or claim of set-off with its statement of defence.[95] If it fails to do so, then the tribunal must decide whether to authorize a late assertion if deemed appropriate under the circumstances.[96] Similarly, a party may not amend or supplement its claim or defence during the course of the arbitration unless the tribunal considers it appropriate under the circumstances. A party may not make such an amendment or supplementation if the amendment or supplementation falls outside the jurisdiction of the tribunal.[97] If the counterclaim or amendments cause expedited arbitration no longer being the appropriate means for resolving the dispute, the parties may agree that the EA Rules no longer apply. Alternatively, one party may request the arbitral tribunal to decide that the expedited rules should not apply.[98]

The tribunal may, after consulting with the parties, decide whether to request any further written statement from either or both of them.[99] The arbitral tribunal thus may decide that the statement of claim and the statement of defence are sufficient.[100] The tribunal also has discretion to decide which documents, exhibits or other evidence the parties should produce.[101] Moreover, the tribunal has the discretion to refuse to allow one party to request the other to produce certain documents, unless both parties request such procedure.[102] All witness statements, whether from fact or expert witnesses, must be filed in writing and signed by the witness, again unless the tribunal decides otherwise.[103] The arbitral tribunal may decide which witnesses shall testify to the arbitral tribunal if hearings are held.[104]

[G] The Hearing

Under the EA Rules, the tribunal has broad discretion to decide, after consultation with the parties, not to hold any hearing in the absence of a request for a hearing.[105] 'The arbitral tribunal has broad discretion on how to conduct the hearings in a streamlined manner. Efforts should be made to limit the duration of the hearings, the number of witnesses as well as cross-examination and at the same time, to maintain due process.'[106] If no hearing is held, the tribunal will decide the dispute on the basis of documents and other materials, such as any witness statements.[107] Considering the short time frame of six months for rendering the award in expedited arbitration, the

95. EA Rules, Article 12(1).
96. EA Rules, Article 12(2).
97. EA Rues, Article 13.
98. EA Rules, Explanatory Note, para. 80.
99. EA Rules, Article 14.
100. EA Rules, Explanatory Note, para. 81.
101. EA Rules, Article 15(1).
102. *Ibid. See also* EA Rules, Explanatory Note, para. 82.
103. EA Rules, Article 15(2). This provision replaces the second sentence of Article 27(2) of the UNCITRAL Arbitration Rules. EA Rules, Explanatory Note, para. 83.
104. EA Rules, Article 15(3).
105. EA Rules, Article 11.
106. EA Rules, Explanatory Note, para. 76.
107. EA Rules, Explanatory Note, para. 75.

arbitral tribunal should decide at an early stage of the proceedings whether to hold a hearing.[108]

However, this provision in the EA Rules must be read and applied in conjunction with Article 17(3) of the UNCITRAL Arbitration Rules. If the parties agree on holding a hearing, or if one party timely requests a hearing, a hearing must be held.[109] A request to hold a hearing at a later stage may delay the proceedings and may have a negative impact on the tribunal complying with the time frame for completion of the arbitration.[110] The arbitral tribunal may utilize any technological means to hold hearings without the physical presence of the parties or witnesses, including remotely, in order to secure the speedy and timely resolution of the dispute.[111]

In light of UNCITRAL Arbitration Rule 17(1), the EA Rules inherently allow the tribunal to dismiss claims and defences that lack merit. They also allow the tribunal to consider any party's request to resolve any issues of law or fact without following every procedural step.[112] However, the tribunal must exercise care to ensure that it does not needlessly add another step in the proceedings or that it denies any party an appropriate opportunity to present its claim or defence.[113]

[H] Rendering the Award

The default presumption under the EA Rules is that the final award must be made within six months from the date the arbitral tribunal is constituted.[114] However, the parties may agree otherwise, consistent with the general primacy of party autonomy under the EA Rules. The parties thus may shorten or lengthen this time period according to their needs.[115]

The arbitral tribunal may extend the six-month time period only in exceptional circumstances after inviting the parties to express their views.[116] However, any extension may not exceed nine months from the date of constitution of the arbitral tribunal.[117] While the arbitral tribunal may indicate the exceptional circumstances that

108. EA Rules, Explanatory Note, para. 73.
109. EA Rules, Explanatory Note, paras 71, 74.
110. EA Rules, Explanatory Note, para. 73.
111. EA Rules, Article 3(3); EA Rules, Explanatory Note, para. 76.
112. *See* UNCITRAL Arbitration Rules, Article 17(1).
113. *See* EA Rules, Explanatory Note, para. 21.
114. EA Rules, Article 16(1). If an arbitrator has to be replaced, then the time period under Article 16 is suspended from the time the original arbitration ceased performing their duties until the date the new arbitrator resumes the proceedings. EA Rules, Article 15; EA Rules, Explanatory Note, para. 94. Similarly, if the tribunal suspends the proceedings for non-payment of the required deposits pursuant to Article 43(4) of the standard Arbitration Rules, the time period stops running until payment is made. EA Rules, Explanatory Note, para. 95.
115. EA Rules, Explanatory Note, para. 85. The power granted to the tribunal under Article 10 of the EA Rules to extend or abridge any period of time under the standard Arbitration Rules, the EA Rules, or agreed by the parties, is subject to Article 16 of the EA Rules.
116. EA Rules, Article 16(2).
117. *Ibid.*

justify an extension, the EA Rules do not require such a statement in order to provide flexibility to the arbitral tribunal, particularly when the extension is rather short.[118]

If the tribunal concludes it may not issue the final award within nine months from the date it was constituted, it may propose a final extended time limit, state the reasons for the proposal, and ask the parties to provide their views within a set time frame. The final extended time limit may be adopted only if all parties agree.[119] To obtain the parties' agreement, the extended time frame requested by the arbitral tribunal should be reasonable, taking into account any concerns of the parties, and still be sufficient for the arbitral tribunal to render the award.[120] If the parties do not agree to the tribunal's proposed final extended time limit, then any party may request that the EA Rules no longer apply to the arbitration. Again, after asking the parties to express their views, the tribunal may decide to continue the arbitration under the standard UNCITRAL Arbitration Rules.[121] If this occurs, the time limits for rendering the award, including any time limits agreed by the parties, will in effect be lifted.[122]

If the arbitral award is issued within the time limits set by Article 16, a later request to correct or interpret the award pursuant to Article 37 or 38 of the standard Arbitration Rules does not impact the timeliness of the award for purposes of Article 16.[123] Similarly, an additional award made in accordance with Article 39 of the standard UNCITRAL Arbitration Rules after the lapse of the time frame in Article 16 of the EA Rules does not affect the timeliness of the award.[124]

The parties and the tribunal must not forget the possible consequences if the absolute time limit of nine months from the date of constitution lapses without an award being rendered. Depending on the applicable law where a party seeks to enforce the award, this may result in the termination of the proceedings or the award rendered subsequently being the subject of possible annulment. In some jurisdictions such an award might also be refused enforcement.[125]

Finally, the parties may agree that the tribunal need not issue a reasoned award.[126] Absent such an agreement, the tribunal must issue a reasoned award.[127] The parties could agree that the award need not contain reasoning in order to reduce the time necessary for the arbitral tribunal to render the award. However, the absence of reasoning could impact any post-award actions by courts in enforcement or setting-aside proceedings regarding the arbitral award.[128]

118. EA Rules, Explanatory Note, para. 85.
119. EA Rules, Article 16(3).
120. EA Rules, Explanatory Note, para. 89.
121. EA Rules, Article 16(4). This mechanism is also stated in Article 2(2) of the EA Rules.
122. EA Rules, Explanatory Note, para. 92.
123. EA Rules, Explanatory Note, para. 93.
124. *Ibid.*
125. EA Rules, Explanatory Note, para. 88.
126. UNCITRAL Arbitration Rules, Article 34(3); EA Rules, Explanatory Note, para. 96.
127. EA Rules, Explanatory Note, para. 96.
128. *Ibid.*

§6.04 APPLICABILITY TO INVESTOR-STATE ARBITRATION

WG II also considered whether the EA Rules could or should apply to treaty-based investor-State arbitration.[129] This discussion arose in the context of application of the UNCITRAL Rules on Transparency to expedited arbitration.[130] WG II decided that the Explanatory Note to the EA Rules should advise parties to an investor-State dispute that they could agree to application of the EA Rules, as well as the Rules on Transparency.[131] The Explanatory Note to the EA Rules states:

> The suitability of the Expedited Rules for investment arbitration is a question left to the disputing parties, as express consent of the parties is required for the Expedited Rules to apply.... States could refer to and consent to the Expedited Rules in their respective investment treaty, based on which an investor claimant may consent to refer a dispute under the Expedited Rules. However, a reference to the [UNCITRAL Arbitration Rules] in investment treaties (regardless of whether the reference was included prior to or after the effective date of the Expedited Rules) should not be construed as express consent by the State Parties to the Expedited Rules as express consent is necessary for the application of the Expedited Rules.[132]

Thus, WG II and UNCITRAL wisely decided that expedited arbitration is beneficial not only to 'standard' international commercial arbitration but also potentially to treaty-based investor-State arbitration. In this regard, UNCITRAL presciently anticipated the action of ICSID in 2022, when ICSID adopted expedited arbitration rules for investor-State disputes subject to its procedures.[133] The possible use of the EA Rules in investor-State arbitration where the ICSID rules do not apply therefore should prove beneficial to making resolution of such disputes more efficient, cost-effective and in a reduced amount of time.

§6.05 FASTER, FASTER!: HIGHLY EXPEDITED ARBITRATION

In July 2022 and 2023, the UNCITRAL Commission asked WG II to consider the topics of technology-related dispute resolution and adjudication jointly, as well as ways to further accelerate the resolution of disputes, thereby building on the EA Rules.[134] The

129. UNCITRAL, 'Report of Working Group II (Dispute Settlement) on the work of its Seventy-third session (New York (online), 22-26 March 2021)', A/CN.9/1049 (31 March 2021), paras 63-65. *See* UNCITRAL, Note by the Secretariat, A/CN.9/WG.II/WP.216 (13 January 2021), paras 84-85.
130. UNCITRAL, 'Report of Working Group II (Dispute Settlement) on the work of its Seventy-third session (New York (online), 22-26 March 2021)', A/CN.9/1049 (31 March 2021), paras 63-64.
131. *Ibid.*, para. 64.
132. EA Rules, Explanatory Note, para. 99. The Explanatory Note also discusses various possible issues concerning application of the EA Rules and the Transparency Rules, including whether the investment treaty in issue was concluded before 1 April 2014. *See ibid.*, paras 100-104.
133. *See* ICSID Arbitration Rules, Chapter XII (2022).
134. UNCITRAL, 'Report of the United Nations Commission on International Trade Law, Fifty-fifth session (27 June-15 July 2022)', A/77/17 (2022), paras 217-229; UNCITRAL, 'Report of the United Nations Commission on International Trade Law, Fifty-sixth session (3-21 July 2023)', A/78/17 (2023), paras 143-145.

Commission agreed that model provisions, clauses, or other forms of legislative or non-legislative text could be prepared on matters such as shorter time frames, the appointment of experts and/or neutrals, confidentiality and the legal nature of the outcome of the proceedings. All of these topics would allow disputing parties to tailor the proceedings to their needs to further expedite the proceedings.[135]

WG II started its work on draft provisions for technology-related dispute resolution and adjudication in March 2022 in New York and has continued its discussions at its subsequent sessions.[136] The first three sessions considered such topics as early dismissal, preliminary determination, adjudication and technology-related dispute resolution methods.[137] During the discussion related to technology-related dispute resolution and adjudication in February 2023, WG II considered for the first time a draft model clause on 'highly expedited arbitration'.[138] In raising the topic of such a model clause, the UNCITRAL Secretariat stated:

> In response to increasing demand from business users and the arbitration community for a quicker dispute resolution mechanism, a number of arbitration institutions have developed expedited or fast-track proceedings, and their arbitration rules include either provisions to promote the expeditious resolution of disputes or a separate set of expedited arbitration rules. To achieve an accelerated time frame in expedited proceedings, the time frame for submission of pleadings is often condensed and the recommended time frame for rendering a final award ranges from one to four mouths. In some cases, financial incentives, for example an increased arbitration fee are provided to arbitrators for arbitral awards rendered within a certain period of time, e.g., within two to four months.[139]

In making this suggestion, the Secretariat noted the results of a questionnaire sent to experts and potential users. Just over half of the respondents (52.1%) indicated that

135. UNCITRAL, 'Report of the United Nations Commission on International Trade Law, Fifty-fifth session (27 June-15 July 2022)', A/77/17 (2022), para. 225.
136. *See generally* UNCITRAL, 'Report of the Colloquium on Possible Future Work on Dispute Settlement held during the Seventy-fifth session of Working Group II (New York, 28 March-1 April 2022)', A/CN.9/1091 (19 April 2022); UNCITRAL, 'Report of Working Group II (Dispute Settlement) on the work of its Seventy-sixth session (Vienna, 10-14 October 2022)', A/CN.0/1123 (17 October 2022); UNCITRAL, 'Report of Working Group II (Dispute Settlement) on the work of its Seventy-seventh session (New York, 6-10 February 2023)', A/CN.9/1129 (23 February 2023); UNCITRAL, 'Report of Working Group II (Dispute Settlement) on the work of its Seventy-eighth session (Vienna, 18-22 September 2023)', A/CN.9/1159 (27 September 2023); UNCITRAL, 'Report of Working Group II (Dispute Settlement) on the work of its Seventy-ninth session (New York, 12-16 February 2024)', A/CN.9/1166 (23 February 2024).
137. *See, e.g.*, UNCITRAL, 'Report of Working Group II (Dispute Settlement) on the work of its Seventy-sixth session (Vienna, 10-14 October 2022)', A/CN.0/1123 (17 October 2022), paras 10-92; UNCITRAL, 'Report of Working Group II (Dispute Settlement) on the work of its Seventy-seventh session (New York, 6-10 February 2023)', A/CN.9/1129 (23 February 2023), paras 10-101.
138. *See* UNCITRAL, 'Report of Working Group II (Dispute Settlement) on the work of its Seventy-seventh session (New York, 6-10 February 2023)', A/CN.9/1129 (23 February 2023); paras 43-55; UNCITRAL, 'Technology-related dispute resolution and adjudication: Model clauses and guidance text', A/CN.9/WG.II/WP.234 (7 July 2023), paras 7-18.
139. UNCITRAL, 'Technology-related dispute resolution and adjudication: Model clauses and guidance texts', A/CN.9/WG.II/WP.234 (7 July 2023), para. 8 (footnotes omitted).

the amount of time needed or preferred to resolve a dispute was 90 days to 6 months.[140] Thus, a majority of respondents revealed a desire to complete arbitration of disputes in no more than six months – a very quick process.

The draft model clause modifies Articles 8, 9 and 16 of the EA Rules.[141] When initially discussed, the model clause found 'general support'.[142] WG II delegates expressed the view that such a clause may be very useful to resolve high-tech disputes but also disputes in other industries.[143] However, delegates also asserted that such a model clause would not be suitable for complex cases and would not provide parties with sufficient time to present their case properly or discuss settlement options.[144] Some delegates also had 'principled concerns ... on the over-regulation of the arbitration process and due process. They suggested that instead of devising a model clause, speed could be achieved with good practices'.[145] Of course, parties, practitioners, arbitrators and arbitral institutions have by and large proven themselves incapable of consistently implementing and applying 'good practices'.

WG II concluded its discussions of the model highly expedited arbitration clause in February 2024.[146] The primary objective of the model clause is to ensure that the expeditious resolution of disputes is achieved through a fixed and non-negotiable time frame to prevent unnecessary delays, reduce costs, and provide parties with predictability.[147] However, delegates also asserted that while the goal was efficiency, a balance that allowed for a fair and just resolution while minimizing the risks that an arbitral tribunal could not render an enforceable award because a fixed deadline was too short was essential.[148] Some delegates also said that the requirement in Article 16(3) of the EA Rules for the parties to agree to any proposed extension could create a situation where parties felt compelled to consent. Parties might fear that rejecting an extension could be detrimental to their case or be perceived negatively by the arbitral tribunal. These delegates asserted that the model clause should therefore allow for the non-application of Article 16(3) of the EA Rules. However, Article 2(2) of the EA Rules allows the arbitral tribunal, at the request of a party, to reconsider and potentially revert to ordinary arbitration if it finds that the highly expedited procedure is not appropriate for the case. Delegates argued that if the model clause provided the possibility for the arbitral tribunal to move away from highly expedited arbitration to expedited arbitration or regular arbitration, the parties and the arbitral tribunal should keep in mind the initial desire for urgency when organizing the procedure.[149]

---

140. *Ibid.*, para. 8, n. 5.
141. *See ibid.*, paras 9-18.
142. UNCITRAL, 'Report of Working Group II (Dispute Settlement) on the work of its Seventy-eighth session (Vienna, 18-22 September 2023)', A/CN.9/1159 (27 September 2023), para. 15.
143. *Ibid.*
144. *Ibid.*, para. 17.
145. *Ibid.*, para. 16.
146. UNCITRAL, 'Report of Working Group II (Dispute Settlement) on the work of its Seventy-ninth session (New York, 12-16 February 2024)', A/CN.9/1166 (23 February 2024).
147. *Ibid.*, para. 23.
148. *Ibid.*
149. *Ibid.*, para. 24.

The model clause on highly expedited arbitration states:

> Any dispute, controversy, or claim arising out of or relating to this contract or the breach, termination or invalidity thereof, shall be settled by arbitration in accordance with the EA Rules, with the following modifications:
>
> (a) The arbitral tribunal's power pursuant to Article 2(2) of the EA Rules to determine that the EA Rules shall no longer apply to the arbitration also extends to the power to determine that the modifications to the EA Rules contained herein shall no longer apply;
> (b) The period of time for the parties to reach agreement on the appointment of a sole arbitrator pursuant to Article 8(2) of the EA Rules and after which the sole arbitrator shall, at the request of a party, be appointed by the appointing authority in accordance with Article 8(2) of the UNCITRAL Arbitration Rules shall be [7] days after a proposal has been received by all other parties;
> (c) The appointing authority shall be ... [name of institution or person];
> (d) The period of time within which the arbitral tribunal shall consult the parties pursuant to Article 9 of the EA Rules shall be [7] days;
> (e) The period of time within which the award shall be made pursuant to Article 16(1) of the EA Rules shall be [45] days;
> (f) [Option 1: The extended period of time referred to in Article 16(2) of the EA Rules shall not exceed a total of [90] days];
> [Option 2: The extended period of time referred to in Article 16(2) of the EA Rules shall not exceed a total of [90] days. The period of time within which the award is made shall not be further extended. Articles 16(3) – 16(4) of the EARs shall not apply.][150]

Together with the model clause, WG II prepared 'explanatory notes' which serve the purpose of explaining to the parties how the model clause can be utilized.[151]

The model clause on highly expedited arbitration will be presented to the full UNCITRAL Commission for approval in July 2024. This new model clause on highly expedited arbitration developed by UNCITRAL, which is believed to be the first such effort by any leading source of rules for international arbitration, shows the desire for international dispute resolution to proceed faster – faster!

§6.06 CONCLUSION

Although a number of arbitration institutions had adopted expedited arbitration rules during the last decade, rules for expedited international ad hoc arbitral proceedings did not exist as of early 2018. The EA Rules drafted by WG II and adopted by UNCITRAL fill this gap. UNCITRAL and WG II had the advantage of being able to consider the pros and cons of the expedited arbitration rules adopted by various institutions. Unlike the majority of arbitral institutions, WG II and the EA Rules eschew a monetary threshold for their application. The EA Rules are a pure 'opt-in' set of procedures that thus protect party autonomy to the utmost. At the same time, however, the EA Rules allow for a

150. UNCITRAL, 'Report of Working Group II (Dispute Settlement) on the work of its Seventy-ninth session (New York, 12-16 February 2024)', A/CN.9/1166 (23 February 2024), paras 25-29.
151. *Ibid.*, para. 30.

single party, or the arbitral tribunal, to decide after the fact that the EA Rules should not apply to the particular dispute. It will remain to be seen whether this 'out', as well as the ability to extend the deadline for issuance of the final award, undercut the desired benefits of expedited arbitration – speedy and efficient resolution of disputes. WG II also wisely determined that parties to an investor-State dispute should be able to adopt the EA Rules, similar to the expedited arbitration rules more recently adopted by ICSID. Finally, the fact that WG II has now also been working on a model clause for 'highly expedited' arbitration illustrates the demand to speed up the international dispute resolution process even more than under the EA Rules.

The fact that UNCITRAL and WG II have, in little more than three years, gone from drafting expedited arbitration rules to the preparation of a model highly expedited arbitration clause to speed up the arbitral process even more is telling. It shows the continuing interest in the international arbitral community in expedited arbitration. Perhaps more importantly, it illustrates the clear need to strive to return international arbitration to its roots and foundation – an efficient and cost-effective means of dispute resolution. While they may or may not become the 'gold standard' for expedited arbitration, the EA Rules offer a useful set of guidelines for parties wishing to conduct the dispute resolution process more rapidly than under the standard UNCITRAL Arbitration Rules. Overall, the EA Rules are well considered and should prove valuable to the international dispute resolution community, including those involved in investor-State disputes.

CHAPTER 7

A Neglected Blueprint: The LMAA's Small Claims Procedure

James Clanchy

The UNCITRAL Expedited Arbitration Rules are intended for ad hoc arbitration, but, ironically, their models came essentially from institutions. This chapter analyses how existing procedures in disintermediated arbitration can more efficiently provide the speed and cost-effectiveness which commercial parties look for. It examines, in particular, the Small Claims Procedure (SCP) of the London Maritime Arbitrators Association (LMAA), which has been used in thousands of ad hoc international commercial arbitrations since it was introduced in 1989. Features discussed include the speed of commencement, appointment of an experienced sole arbitrator, a fixed fee, a strict procedural timetable, and a cap on the recovery of costs.

§7.01 INTRODUCTION

Without an institution supervising and administering it, an ad hoc arbitration has the potential to be faster and more cost-effective. This chapter will first define ad hoc and institutional arbitration, briefly examining what distinguishes them. It will then discuss the background to UNCITRAL Working Group II's work on expedited arbitration and how it neglected existing rules for expedited procedures in ad hoc arbitration. The London Maritime Arbitrators Association (LMAA) Small Claims Procedure (SCP) is an exemplar. It will be placed in the context of the landscape of international commercial arbitration, the English Arbitration Act (AA) 1996, which supports ad hoc arbitration in London, and the main LMAA arbitration rules. This chapter will then review features of the SCP, including their informality, the quick appointment of an experienced arbitrator, a strict timetable with no meetings or hearings, and fixed and capped costs. It will conclude by suggesting that such features would fulfil UNCITRAL's priorities of speed and cost-effectiveness and are transferable to arbitrations in different sectors.

§7.02 DEFINITIONS: AD HOC AND INSTITUTIONAL ARBITRATION

Commercial arbitration has a long history. In Europe, it dates back more than two thousand years. Demosthenes mentions the submission of a shipping dispute to one or more arbitrators to be chosen from the merchants of the port of Piraeus.[1] The submission of a dispute to an intermediary who will supervise and administer the arbitration, registering it and collecting fees before putting it in the hands of a tribunal, is a modern invention. It has its origins in the dispute resolution services offered by trade associations in the 19th century.[2] The arbitration service of the Liverpool Cotton Brokers' Association (founded in 1841) has been described as the 'blueprint for the modern arbitral institution'.[3] According to the leading textbook on international commodity arbitration, it is 'never ad hoc' but always 'overseen by the secretariat of the relevant trade association'.[4]

The defining characteristics of institutional arbitration are supervision by the institution and administration by its secretariat. In contrast, ad hoc arbitration remains close to its ancient origins, requires no intermediaries, and is conducted by the parties and the arbitral tribunal without any supervision and without any administration.[5] Various organisations, notably associations of arbitrators, occasionally make appointments of arbitrators from their memberships, upon request, in the absence of party appointments. However, unless the association also takes on supervisory and administrative roles in such an arbitration, it will not become institutional.[6]

Certain significant business sectors favour ad hoc arbitration. Rules for arbitrations in these sectors are compiled and published by associations of arbitrators. Such professional associations should be distinguished from arbitration associations, such as the American Arbitration Association (AAA), whose purpose is to provide arbitration services and which therefore hold themselves out to be institutions.[7] The arbitrators' associations publish rules under which their members agree to conduct unadministered proceedings with all decisions and steps being taken by the parties and the tribunal alone without any role or function for the association. An example is

1. In Demosthenes, *Private Orations L-LVIII*, Loeb Classical Library, Harvard University Press, 1939, 204.
2. Mikaël Schinazi, *The Three Ages of International Commercial Arbitration*, Cambridge University Press, 2022, 59; Ross Cranston, *Making Commercial Law Through Practice, 1830-1970* (Cambridge University Press, 2021) 361-375.
3. Sundaresh Menon CJ, 'The Special Role and Responsibility of Arbitral Institutions in Charting the Future of International Arbitration', Keynote Address, SIAC Congress 2018 (17 May 2018) para. 7, https://www.judiciary.gov.sg/news-and-resources/news/news-details/chief-justice-sundaresh-menon-keynote-address-delivered-at-the-siac-congress-2018.
4. Derek Kirby Johnson, *International Commodity Arbitration* (Lloyd's of London Press, 1991) 7.
5. Gary Born, *International Commercial Arbitration*, 189-192 (Kluwer, 3rd ed., 2021) (Born contentiously refers to ad hoc arbitration as being conducted 'without the benefit of an appointing and administrative authority'); Rémy Gerbay, *The Functions of Arbitral Institutions*, 6 (Kluwer, 2016).
6. Gerbay, *supra* n. 5, at 7: 'The LMAA ... acts as appointing authority when needed ... LMAA arbitration would readily be recognized as a form of ad hoc arbitration because the LMAA does not provide any other services to parties engaged in arbitrations under the LMAA terms.'
7. According to its website, The International Centre for Dispute Resolution (ICDR) is 'the international division of the largest arbitral institution in the world, the American Arbitration Association (AAA)', https://www.icdr.org/about_icdr, accessed 7 October 2023.

ARIAS UK, the Insurance and Reinsurance Arbitration Society, a branch of the Association Internationale de Droit des Assurances (AIDA). The ad hoc nature of ARIAS arbitration is clearly stated in its Rules: 'ARIAS does not exercise any supervisory jurisdiction over the arbitral procedure nor does it provide advisory or administrative assistance to arbitrators. If such assistance is required, subject to Rule 20, application may be made to the Registrar of the London Court of International Arbitration (LCIA) … .'[8]

The LMAA dominates arbitration in shipping-related disputes worldwide.[9] The fact that LMAA arbitration is ad hoc is readily ascertainable from its website:

> The LMAA is an association of practising arbitrators. One of our main objects is: '*to advance and encourage the professional knowledge of London maritime arbitrators and, by recommendation and advice, to assist the expeditious procedure and disposal of disputes*'. Not being an institution, the LMAA does not administer arbitrations and so no administrative fees are charged. For a modest one-off fee, the LMAA can assist with the appointment of arbitrators where the parties so agree or cannot agree on a sole.[10]

A former president of the LMAA confirms, 'As its name tells us, the LMAA is purely an association of London maritime arbitrators. It does publish Terms to govern the conduct of arbitrations which are being run by its members, but it does not administer the arbitrations in any way.'[11]

Thomas Carbonneau describes the LMAA as 'a type of social club in the English or North American university sense of that term' and, after noting that members 'organize and conduct arbitrations on their own', concludes, 'Arbitrations done under LMAA terms are a pure form of *ad hoc* arbitration.'[12] Some authors have called the LMAA an institution but without providing reasons for doing so.[13] It has found itself erroneously included among institutions defined on the basis of their decision-making functions in arbitrations and on the basis that they provide a degree of administration.[14] The LMAA does not register, supervise or administer arbitrations in any way

8. ARIAS (UK) Arbitration Rules, Rule 1.6.
9. HFW, The Maritime Arbitration Universe in Numbers, September 2023: https://www.hfw.com/downloads/005239-HFW-Maritime-Arbitration-Universe-in-Numbers-Sep-23.pdf (accessed 6 October 2023). HFW note in their report that the LMAA's share of the maritime arbitration market 'highlights the continuing popularity of ad hoc arbitration'.
10. https://lmaa.london/about-lmaa/, accessed 6 October 2023.
11. Bruce Harris, *London Maritime Arbitration* (2011) 77 Arbitration 116, 121; *see also* Philip Clifford and Shai Wade, *A Commentary on the LCIA Arbitration Rules 2020*, 7 (I-009) (Sweet & Maxwell, 2022), comparing the LCIA to 'associations of arbitrators, such as the London Maritime Arbitrators Association (LMAA), which have rules but do not provide administration'.
12. Thomas E Carbonneau, *The Law and Practice of Arbitration*, 375-376, (Juris, 5th ed., 2014).
13. For example, Born, *supra* n. 5, at 93, has a table of caseloads of 'leading arbitral institutions' from 1993 to 2018. The LMAA is the only 'institution' in Born's table whose numbers are consistently in the thousands, but he says nothing in his book about the nature of the association or of its rules; Bertie Vigras, *The Role of Institutions in Arbitration* in *Handbook of Arbitral Practice* 461 (Ronald Bernstein & Derek Wood et al. eds., 2nd ed. 1993): Gerbay, *supra* n. 5, at 7, remarks, 'he seems to use the expression in a loose sense'.
14. Ulrich G. Schroeter, *Ad Hoc or Institutional Arbitration – A Clear-Cut Distinction? A Closer Look at Borderline Cases*, 10(2) Contemp. Asia Arb. J. 141, 163.

whatsoever and, aside from occasional appointments of members as arbitrators, makes no decisions of any kind in any arbitrations.[15]

The LMAA is not the only association of maritime arbitrators which publishes rules for use in ad hoc arbitration. Another important maritime centre is New York, where the Society of Maritime Arbitrators (SMA), founded in 1963, is a professional organisation which leaves the supervision of arbitrations to 'the discretion of the participating arbitrators' because it does not 'oversee or administer the arbitration proceeding'.[16] Similarly, the German Maritime Arbitration Association (GMAA) 'does not conduct any proceedings itself but merely provides the relevant regulations and procedural information'.[17] A few bodies are institutional in character or may be considered hybrid.[18] However, the predominance of ad hoc arbitration in the maritime sector led the author of a recent study of international maritime arbitration to say, 'Given the inherently international nature of the shipping industry and its preference for ad hoc arbitration, we will proceed on the basis of maritime arbitration being both international and ad hoc.'[19] Thus, while arbitral institutions may command more attention, the simple framework of ad hoc arbitration remains as it was in Demosthenes' day and is used in thousands of disputes around the world under many different sets of rules.

§7.03 BACKGROUND

[A] UNCITRAL Working Group II's Mission and Methodology

When UNCITRAL Working Group II (WGII) set about its work on expedited arbitration during its 69th session, it reminded itself that the UNCITRAL Arbitration Rules had been prepared mainly for ad hoc arbitration and therefore did not envisage an administering institution.[20] The words 'ad hoc' had not appeared in the report of WGII's previous session when proposals for examining expedited arbitration were initially discussed. The rationale for the proposals was explained in the report on that session:

> Expedited arbitration procedures had been a focus of many arbitral institutions in recent years, in part as a response to concerns among users about rising costs and lengthier timelines making arbitration more burdensome and similar to litigation.

---

15. In 2022, the president of the LMAA made 99 appointments from a total of 3,193 appointments reported to it by its members (3.1%): https://lmaa.london/wp-content/uploads/2023/03/Statistics-up-to-2022-for-website.pdf, accessed 8 October 2023.
16. SMA website: https://smany.org/about/, accessed 7 October 2023.
17. GMAA website: https://www.gmaa.de/en/, accessed 7 October 2023.
18. For example, the Chambre Arbitrale Maritime de Paris, UNUM (the Netherlands), Singapore Chamber of Maritime Arbitration (SCMA). The Hong Kong Maritime Arbitration Group (HKMAG) promotes ad hoc arbitration with rules based on the LMAA's but it allows parties to have their arbitrations administered if they need to apply to mainland courts for interim measures, in respect of which ad hoc tribunals are not recognised. *See* James Clanchy, *Ad hoc Arbitration and Its Enemies*, 86(4) Arbitration: The Int'l J. of Arb., Med. & Dispute Mgmt 536-538, 550 (2020).
19. Eva Litina, *Theory, Law and Practice of Maritime Arbitration* 123-126 (Kluwer, 2021).
20. UNCITRAL, *Report of Working Group II (Dispute Settlement) on the work of its sixty-ninth session* (New York, 4-8 February 2019), 6.

> The usefulness of having a common international expedited procedure framework was highlighted, as there was an increasing demand to resolve simple, low value cases by arbitration but there was a lack of international mechanisms to cope with such disputes.[21]

Concerns about the speed and cost of international commercial arbitration arose, WGII noted, in the context of institutional arbitration. No mention is made of expedited arbitration procedures in ad hoc arbitrations and of the experience of users of ad hoc arbitration, including users of the UNCITRAL Arbitration Rules in arbitral proceedings not administered by an institution. The omission is not surprising when the composition of WGII and of its corps of observers is considered. These overwhelmingly comprised representatives of states, arbitral institutions, and academic legal organisations.[22] Few associations of arbitrators, which promote arbitration conducted by their members and publish rules for use in ad hoc arbitrations, such as the London-based Chartered Institute of Arbitrators, were invited.[23]

The situation is comparable to the debates which led up to the UNCITRAL Model Law, as described to delegates at the Tenth International Congress of Maritime Arbitrators (ICMA) in Vancouver on 11 September 1991 by the distinguished English judge and arbitrator, The Rt Hon Lord Justice Mustill:

> It was both an honour and a pleasure to take part in these debates .... Nevertheless, it must be recognised that the distinguished people who took part, whether they were professors of law or senior officials in government departments or executives of national arbitration institutions, were in the main more acquainted with the theory than with the practice of arbitration. Again, the majority of those who did have direct personal experience of arbitration had acquired it in the field of large-scale, formal, heavily-documented and very expensive arbitrations of a kind quite different from those with which this present Congress is concerned. Thus, when we set out to explain that various more informal arbitral proceedings, of which maritime arbitration was typical, would not fit at all well into the earlier drafts of the Model Law, the reaction was not hostility but incomprehension. The delegates simply did not know what we were talking about.[24]

Lord Mustill called for maritime arbitration to 'step into public view, look around and assert itself'.[25] More than 30 years later, while the caseload of the LMAA stands at

21. *Ibid.*, 22.
22. *Ibid.*, 2. The section 'Organization of the session' lists state members, intergovernmental organisations and invited non-governmental organisations, most of which are arbitral institutions and academic law associations.
23. *Ibid.*, 2. The Chartered Institute of Arbitrators (CIArb) is a professional institute for arbitrators, many of whose members conduct arbitrations themselves without administration by an institution or other body. The CIArb publishes arbitration rules for use in ad hoc arbitrations. These rules do not provide for the CIArb to play any supervisory or administrative role in the arbitration. The institute is similar in these respects to the LMAA, SMA and ARIAS (UK) described in §7.02 *supra*.
24. Inaugural Cedric Barclay Lecture, 7, *The First Ten Cedric Barclay Lectures*, edited by Bruce Harris and Philip Yang, ICMA/Law Press 2017; *see also* an enlarged version, M Mustill, *Maritime Arbitration: The Call for a Wider Perspective*, 9(2) Journal of International Arbitration 5 (1992) DOI: 10.54648/joia1992013.
25. *Ibid.*

more than twice the size of the International Chamber of Commerce (ICC)'s, the voice of ad hoc maritime arbitration is still not being heard in international organisations and fora which propose reforms, including new rules and regulations.[26]

In considering recommendations for the regulation of third-party funding, the International Council for Commercial Arbitration (ICCA)-Queen Mary Task Force on Third-Party Funding in International Arbitration cited the White & Case Queen Mary International Arbitration Survey as a precedent for its decision to exclude ad hoc maritime arbitration, explaining that that survey did not 'generally take account of practices in *ad hoc* and trade association arbitration, most notably in the maritime industry, which account for a large number of arbitrations every year'.[27]

ICCA published a report on gender diversity in international arbitration in 2020 and an update in 2022.[28] The original report ignored ad hoc arbitration entirely. The updated version devoted 3 pages (out of 363) to ad hoc and had a curious and erroneous definition under which 'an institution assists with administering the arbitration in some way'.[29]

It was to ICCA that WGII turned for an overview of arbitral institutions that made provision for expedited arbitration. ICCA's memorandum was made available to WGII before its 70th session in Vienna on 23-27 September 2019.[30] The overview covered expedited arbitration provisions of 59 arbitral 'institutions'. These included ARIAS (UK) and the LMAA, which are not institutions but associations of arbitrators. The LMAA's SCP is for use in ad hoc arbitral proceedings, but ICCA's memorandum does not mention this critical factor. ICCA and WGII appear, on the evidence of their reports, to have proceeded on the mistaken assumption that UNCITRAL was the only body to have published rules for ad hoc arbitrations and that existing rules for expedited arbitration were all institutional.

As recited in the introductory paragraph of the memorandum, the UNCITRAL Secretariat asked ICCA to identify provisions dealing with the following five issues:

(1) applicability of expedited arbitration rules;
(2) appointment of arbitral tribunal;
(3) challenge of an arbitrator;

26. LMAA arbitrators reported 1,807 new cases in 2022. The ICC reported 710 new arbitrations registered in the same year (*Global Arbitration News*, 2 October 2023: https://www.globalarbitrationnews.com/2023/10/02/arbitration-statistics-2022-the-number-of-arbitration-proceedings-continues-to-drop-but-the-amount-in-dispute-increases/). Cherine Foty & James Clanchy, *Conflicting Perceptions of Ethics in International Arbitration*, 85(2) Arbitration: The Int'l J. of Arb., Med. & Dispute Mgmt 185.
27. ICCA-Queen Mary Task Force Report on Third-Party Funding in International Arbitration, The ICCA Reports No. 4, The Hague, April 2018, 84.
28. Report of the Cross-Institutional Task Force on Gender Diversity in Arbitral Appointments and Proceedings, The ICCA Reports, No. 8, The Hague, 2020, 2022.
29. *Ibid.*, 61.
30. UNCITRAL, *Report of Working Group II (Dispute Settlement) on the work of its seventieth session* (Vienna, 23-27 September 2019), 3; https://uncitral.un.org/en/working_groups/2/arbitration.

(4) time limits and deadlines;
(5) award.[31]

Provisions on cost were omitted from ICCA's remit. WGII's questionnaire for institutions likewise did not contain any questions about costs or cost control.[32]

As for speed, ICCA was not apparently asked to review the setting in which the above provisions would operate. An ad hoc arbitration, without an administering institution, should normally be quicker. However, WGII reached the opposite conclusion. In the Explanatory Note to the UNCITRAL Expedited Arbitration Rules, the commentary on Article 3, paragraph 1 includes the following:[33]

> Paragraph 1 is a reminder to parties that when referring their dispute to arbitration under the Expedited Rules, they are agreeing to cooperate in ensuring the efficiency of the proceeding as well as for a swift resolution of the dispute, particularly in an ad hoc setting where there is no administering institution to further expedite the process.[34]

The notion that an arbitration will be accelerated if administered by an institution is counter-intuitive. The involvement of an intermediary, including the time required by it to be introduced to the parties and to learn about their dispute, to provide its administrative services, and to collect fees for those services, could be expected to protract, not to shorten, the process. There are, of course, ad hoc arbitrations in which a party is uncooperative, and the other party resorts to an appointing authority to resolve the problem(s). No doubt, it was experience of such outliers which led members of WGII to assume that all ad hoc arbitrations would benefit from institutional assistance. Other rules for expedited ad hoc arbitration, such as ARIAS (UK) and the LMAA's SCP, do not make, and have no need to make, such an appeal for the parties' cooperation to overcome the absence of an administering institution. Had WGII been more inclusive and thereby aware of existing and successful rules for ad hoc expedited arbitration, it might have reached different conclusions and formulated rules and commentary which could be even more conducive to promoting speed and cost-effectiveness.

[B] The LMAA's SCP in Context

WGII's remit to ICCA did not include any enquiries about the take-up of expedited arbitration procedures. Each of the 59 institutions was treated equally in ICCA's

31. Overview of Selected Expedited Arbitration Provisions by the International Council for Commercial Arbitration (ICCA), https://uncitral.un.org/sites/uncitral.un.org/files/media-documents/uncitral/en/overview_of_selected_expedited_arbitration_provisions.pdf, attached to report at n. 30.
32. Responses to UNCITRAL questionnaire on expedited arbitration, https://uncitral.un.org/sites/uncitral.un.org/files/media-documents/uncitral/en/responses_to_questionnaire_27_september.pdf, attached to report at n. 30.
33. 'The parties shall act expeditiously throughout the proceedings.'
34. UNCITRAL Arbitration Rules (2021) p. 51.

memorandum with no indication of the success of their respective rules. The ICC is rightly proud of the welcome given to its Expedited Procedure Provisions (EPP) introduced in 2017. As at the end of 2019, the third year of their operation, 146 cases had been or were being conducted under the EPP.[35] The LMAA's SCP was introduced in 1989. The association reported that 218 appointments of sole arbitrators were made under the SCP in 2019. Its recording of such appointments, as communicated to it by LMAA members, had begun in 1997. The total number of SCP appointments in the period 1997 to 2019 was 3,303.[36] With a trail of expedited arbitrations more than 20 times the size of the ICC's, the LMAA's experience and the reasons for the SCP's continuing success warranted investigation. The composition and perspectives of WGII were such that they were basically ignored.

LMAA ad hoc arbitration falls squarely into the definitions of international commercial arbitration in the UNCITRAL Model Law.[37] However, it is sometimes suggested that it is not international to the same extent as institutional arbitration, particularly ICC, and that it is somehow inferior to it.[38] Factors which attract thousands of international parties to LMAA arbitration, such as English shipping law (effectively an international commercial code), full-time expert arbitrators (who do not act simultaneously as counsel), and the availability of appeals on points of law (contributing to the development of the aforementioned international commercial code), are paradoxically perceived as problematic.[39]

LMAA arbitration does not fit into the alleged 'international arbitration culture' and cannot be described as 'comparative law in action'.[40] Remaining steadfastly ad hoc, it was unaffected by the 'Age of Institutionalization'.[41] It rarely features on the Kluwer Arbitration Blog or OGEMID forums, which the late Professor Emmanuel Gaillard said 'strongly contribute to the shaping of values underpinning international arbitration'.[42] The LMAA's Advice on Ethics prevents its arbitrator members from taking part in what Gaillard calls 'recognition tournaments'.[43]

As their biographies confirm, maritime arbitrators do not generally have numerous law degrees from 'the world's most prestigious universities', let alone professorships, which Professor Catherine A Rogers regards as characteristics of international

35. ICC Dispute Resolution 2019 Statistics, 16, ICC, 2020.
36. https://lmaa.london/statistics-of-appointments-awards/, accessed 25 March 2023.
37. UNCITRAL Model Law, Article 1(3) and n. 2 to Article 1, Article 2(a).
38. *See, e.g.*, Yves Dezalay & Bryant G. Garth, *Dealing in Virtue*, Chicago, University of Chicago Press, 1996, 129. *See also*, Clanchy, *supra* n. 18, 536, 542.
39. *Ibid.*
40. Joshua Karton, *The Culture of International Arbitration and the Evolution of Contract Law*, Oxford Univ. Press, 2013; Joshua Karton, *International Arbitration as Comparative Law in Action*, 2020 Journal of Dispute Resolution 293 (2020).
41. Schinazi, *supra* n. 2.
42. Emmanuel Gaillard, Freshfields Lecture 2014, *Sociology of International Arbitration*, Arbitration International, 2015, 31, 1,9.
43. *Ibid.*; https://lmaa.london/advice-on-ethics/, accessed 25 March 2023. LMAA members are forbidden from seeking to draw comparisons with other arbitrators, e.g., through awards or directory rankings.

arbitrators.[44] Some of the most highly regarded maritime arbitrators, appointed in thousands of arbitrations (large and small), do not have law degrees.[45] They include former shipbrokers, chartering managers, traders and master mariners, knowledgeable about the subject matter of a dispute and able to reach a quick determination when required.[46]

Being erroneously perceived as outside the international arbitration community may have done LMAA arbitration little harm, except during discussions and consultations in relation to the formulation of rules and guidance.[47] However, its exclusion deprives the wider community of opportunities to learn from the LMAA's success, notably in relation to speed and costs and its rules for smaller cases. It would have been especially appropriate for WGII to study the LMAA's SCP because it was seeking to formulate expedited arbitration rules to accompany the UNCITRAL Arbitration Rules, which had been designed for ad hoc arbitrations.

The White & Case Queen Mary 2021 International Arbitration Survey report, in a section headed 'Which ad hoc procedural rules are most used?', notes that the UNCITRAL Rules were chosen by 76% of its respondents and the LMAA Terms by 13%. The report speculates that this finding 'may be because the UNCITRAL Arbitration Rules are used across all sectors in both commercial and investment treaty arbitration'.[48] Bearing in mind that the United Nations Conference on Trade and Development (UNCTAD) identified only 10 investment treaty arbitrations commenced under the UNCITRAL Rules in 2021 while the LMAA saw more than 1,600 arbitrations commenced under its sets of rules in the same year, this comment may say more about the survey's pool of respondents, and the perspectives of its researchers, than it does about the actual use of the respective ad hoc rules.[49]

The LMAA's Terms and Procedures are used across a wide range of sectors. A commercial party that loads goods on a ship is likely to have a contract subject to LMAA arbitration. Likewise, parties in the energy and commodities sectors are accustomed to LMAA arbitration.[50] Shipping is an essential component of international commerce, so many different business sectors encounter it. If parties in the shipping industry choose ad hoc arbitration for the resolution of their disputes, then so do

44. *See* listings of arbitrating members on the LMAA's website: https://lmaa.london/arbitrators-full-members/; Catherine A. Rogers, *The Vocation of the International Arbitrator*, 2005 Am. U. Int'l L. Rev. 957, 958 (2005).
45. Eva Litina, *Sustainable diversity in international arbitration: the case of ad hoc, maritime and commodities trade arbitration* in *Diversity in International Arbitration* (Shahla F. Ali et al., eds, Edward Elgar, 2022) 83, 93.
46. For lists of LMAA arbitrators and details of their professional backgrounds, *see* https://lmaa.london/product/full-membership/.
47. Foty & Clanchy, *supra* n. 26, 201.
48. https://arbitration.qmul.ac.uk/research/2021-international-arbitration-survey/, accessed 26 March 2023, 9.
49. https://investmentpolicy.unctad.org/investment-dispute-settlement, accessed 26 March 2023.
50. *See* LMAA website page, 'Shipping, Trade, Offshore Energy', https://lmaa.london/about-lmaa/, accessed 26 March 2023.

parties from the industries with which they do business. The choice of ad hoc is not specific to the shipping industry, as scholars sometimes suggest.[51]

In terms of arbitrations which reach the desks of tribunals, in 2021, the LMAA saw some 2,777 appointments of arbitrators, more than the ICC's, London Court of International Arbitration (LCIA)'s, Singapore International Arbitration Centre (SIAC)'s, and Hong Kong International Arbitration Centre (HKIAC)'s numbers added together (2,651).[52] These statistics cast doubt on Gary Born's claim that 'Although there is room for debate, most experienced international practitioners fairly decisively prefer the more structured, predictable character of institutional arbitration, and the benefits of institutional rules and appointment mechanisms, at least in the absence of unusual circumstances arguing for an *ad hoc* approach.'[53] As will be discussed below, rules for expedited procedures in ad hoc arbitration can provide structure and certainty, saving time and costs, in ways which institutional arbitration rules do not.

§7.04 SPEED AND COSTS IN AD HOC ARBITRATION

[A] UNCITRAL Model Law and AA 1996

Rules for ad hoc arbitration rely on the law of the seat, and on its courts, to fill in gaps and to carry out various functions. Just as the UNCITRAL Expedited Arbitration Rules need to be considered against the background of the UNCITRAL Model Law, so the LMAA's SCP needs to be considered against the background of the AA 1996.

Some features of the AA 1996 risk making an arbitration slower than one under the Model Law. Notably, the availability of appeals on points of law allows an award to go through potentially three courts (Commercial, Court of Appeal and Supreme Court). In practice, appeals are rare and appeals from Commercial Court decisions on arbitral awards even rarer.[54]

---

51. *See, e.g.*, Gerbay, *supra* n. 5, 42; Thomas Dietz, *International Arbitration and Efficiency* in *International Arbitration & Global Governance* (Walter Mattli & Thomas Dietz, eds, Oxford Univ. Press, 2014), 192.
52. *See* J. Clanchy, *Arbitration statistics 2021: from sole arbitrators to sole arbitrations*, LexisNexis Arbitration Blog, 7 December 2022, https://www.lexisnexis.co.uk/blog/research-legal-analysis/arbitration-statistics-2021-from-sole-arbitrators-to-sole-arbitrations, accessed 22 March 2023. In 2021, 95% of appointments in LMAA arbitrations were made by parties, 5% by the president, mainly in SCP cases: https://lmaa.london/wp-content/uploads/2023/03/Statistics-up-to-2022-for-website.pdf, accessed 9 October 2023.
53. Born, *supra* n. 5 at 192. In support of this proposition, Born cites Coyle & Drahozal, *An Empirical Study of Dispute Resolution Clauses in International Supply Contracts*, 52 Vanderbilt Journal of Transnational Law 323 (2019). The authors of this article concluded that 90% of arbitration clauses in international supply contracts specified institutional arbitration. Their finding was based on a sample of 157 international supply contracts collected from filings with the US Securities and Exchange Commission (SEC) from 1 January 2011 to 31 December 2015. It is respectfully submitted that this evidence is neither representative of international commerce nor a reliable source for gauging the preferences of 'international practitioners'.
54. AA 1996, section 69. *See* Osborne Clarke report, *Arbitration in Court: Observations on over a decade of arbitration-related cases in the English courts*, 4: 143 section 69 appeals in the 11 years 2010 to 2020. *See also* Litina, *supra* n. 19, 123-126.

Unsurprisingly, in seeking to limit the time in which a small claim is to be resolved, the LMAA removed the right of appeal in its expedited rules, as AA 1996, section 69 allows it to do.[55] On the other hand, there are some aspects of the AA 1996 which can make parts of the arbitral process quicker than they would be under the Model Law. A significant example is the appointment of arbitrators. Under the Model Law, the default number of arbitrators is three.[56] A party is to appoint a second arbitrator within 30 days of receipt of a request from the other party. The two arbitrators thus appointed are then to appoint the third within 30 days of their appointment.[57] The same timescale applies in the UNCITRAL Arbitration Rules.[58] The AA 1996 has the opposite default rule for the number of arbitrators: the tribunal is to consist of a sole arbitrator.[59] The parties are to appoint the arbitrator jointly not later than 28 days after service of a request by either party to do so.[60] The Departmental Advisory Committee on Arbitration Law (DAC), which advised on and drafted the AA 1996, noted: 'The employment of three arbitrators is likely to be three times the cost of employing one … . The provision for a sole arbitrator also accords with both common practice in this country, and the balance of responses the DAC received.'[61]

If the parties have agreed that there should be three arbitrators, then the AA 1996 provides that each party is to appoint one arbitrator not later than 14 days after service of a request by either party to do so and the two so appointed are to appoint the third 'forthwith'.[62] The normal timescale for the appointment of a three-member tribunal in an ad hoc arbitration under the AA 1996 is thus two weeks plus a few days. This contrasts markedly with the timescale of two months under the Model Law.

The tendency of institutions to follow the Model Law's more generous timescale may be one of the reasons why most international commercial arbitrations seated in London, governed by the AA 1996, take place outside the institutions, the ICC and LCIA.[63] Institutional rules build delay into the process of having a case put into the hands of a tribunal, which is absent from the default rules governing ad hoc arbitrations in London. This delay is exacerbated by the practice of institutions directing advances on costs before the appointment of the tribunal is confirmed. This

55. SCP, para. 4 ('Right of Appeal Excluded'). The provision does not apply to any ruling by an arbitrator on their own jurisdiction.
56. UNCITRAL Model Law, Article 10(2).
57. *Ibid.*, Article 11(3)(a).
58. UNCITRAL Arbitration Rules, Article 9.
59. AA 1996, section 15(3).
60. *Ibid.*, section 16(3).
61. DAC Report on the Arbitration Bill 1996, para. 79.
62. AA 1996, section 16(3).
63. *See* the statistics collated by TheCityUK for its report, *Legal excellence, internationally renowned: UK legal services 2022*, 40, https://www.thecityuk.com/our-work/legal-excellence-internationally-renowned-uk-legal-services-2022/, accessed 28 March 2023. *See also* statistics for London-seated awards enforced through Chinese courts during 2012-2022: half were made in ad hoc arbitrations, notably LMAA, only 3% were ICC and LCIA, the rest being administered by trade associations: Sam (Ronghui) Li et al., 'Recognition and Enforcement of Foreign Arbitral Awards in China Between 2012-2022: Review and Remarks (Part I)', Kluwer Arbitration Blog, 12 September 2023,, https://arbitrationblog.kluwerarbitration.com/2023/09/12/recognition-and-enforcement-of-foreign-arbitral-awards-in-china-between-2012-2022-review-and-remarks-part-i/.

is one of the reasons why numerous institutional arbitrations do not progress beyond the filing stage and do not reach arbitrators' desks.[64] First impressions are important. Parties may cease pursuing an arbitration, which they have commenced, if the length of time required to see a tribunal put in place and the advances on costs sought by an institution are not what they expected and are found to be prohibitive.

At the other end of the process, the Model Law does not contemplate the making of an early award on an issue which could dispose of the substance of the dispute. Article 31 speaks only of 'the award'. However, the UNCITRAL Arbitration Rules did introduce this possibility.[65] In contrast, the AA 1996 includes the possibility for a tribunal to make 'more than one award at different times on different aspects of the matters to be determined'.[66] The statute goes on to specify that the tribunal may, in particular, 'make an award relating – (a) to an issue affecting the whole claim, or (b) to a part only of the claims or cross-claims submitted to it for decision'.[67]

In its report on the draft bill, the DAC referred to a shipping case, *The 'Kostas Melas'*. In that case, the court held that where the owner of a time chartered ship sought a prompt interim award in respect of hire, it was open to the arbitrators, when awarding a minimum sum as due and owing to the owner, to reject a claim by the charterers to exercise a right of deduction or set-off, if the charterer could not satisfy them that it was seeking to exercise that right in good faith and on reasonable grounds.[68] The AA 1996 thus encourages tribunals in ad hoc arbitrations to take a flexible approach to the order in which they deal with substantive issues, thereby saving time and costs. As will be explained below, in the discussion of the LMAA Terms, arbitrations conducted in this way can become de facto expedited arbitrations.

Finally, having considered the speed of appointing tribunals and of making awards, the treatment of costs should be considered. The Model Law does not, in fact, deal with costs; it leaves this to the law of the seat and to the courts there.[69] Again, the UNCITRAL Arbitration Rules fill this gap with quite detailed provisions in relation to awards of costs and deposits of advances of arbitrators' fees.[70] These provisions also apply in the UNCITRAL Expedited Arbitration Rules, which do not have any provisions of their own in relation to costs.

The AA 1996 contains provisions relating to the parties' joint and several liability for arbitrators' fees,[71] challenges to arbitrators' invoices,[72] awards and assessments of

64. *See* James Clanchy, *Arbitrations without arbitrators: an institutional paradox,* Lexis Nexis Arbitration Blog, 8 April 2021, https://www.lexisnexis.co.uk/blog/dispute-resolution/arbitrations-without-arbitrators-an-institutional-paradox, accessed 28 March 2023.
65. UNCITRAL Arbitration Rules, Article 34.
66. AA 1996, section 47(1).
67. *Ibid.*, section 47(2).
68. DAC report, para. 231, *SL Sethia Liners Ltd. v. Naviagro Maritime Corporation (The 'Kostas Melas')* [1981] 1 Lloyd's Rep 18.
69. Explanatory Note by the UNCITRAL secretariat on the 1985 Model Law on International Commercial Arbitration as amended in 2006, para. 17.
70. UNCITRAL Arbitration Rules, Articles 40 to 43.
71. AA 1996, section 28(1).
72. *Ibid.*, section 28(2)(4).

legal costs,[73] and, importantly, in the context of expedited procedures, a power to direct that 'the recoverable costs of the arbitration, or of any part of the arbitral proceedings, shall be limited to a specified amount'.[74] The latter power is rarely invoked by tribunals, but limits on cost recoveries are written into rules for expedited procedures in ad hoc arbitration. For example, the Business Arbitration Scheme (BAS) of the Chartered Institute of Arbitrators (CIArb), intended for 'low to medium value' disputes (GBP 5,000-GBP 100,000), limits a party's cost recovery to the fixed arbitration fee (GBP 2,500) and GBP 1,000 towards legal costs.[75] The LMAA's SCP likewise limits a cost recovery to the SCP fee of GBP 4,000 (plus GBP 350 if the LMAA President made the appointment of the sole arbitrator) and a maximum of GBP 5,000 in respect of costs.[76] These rules for expedited arbitration contain detailed provisions for fixed costs upfront because there is no institution involved to which case-by-case decisions on costs could be referred.

This commentary on the statutory treatment of salient aspects of an arbitration demonstrates that the AA 1996 supports ad hoc arbitration, contributing to its speed and cost-effectiveness. The Model Law does not support ad hoc arbitration in the same ways. The UNCITRAL Arbitration Rules cover some of the missed ground, but they leave some critical gaps open.

[B] The LMAA Terms

The LMAA's introduction to its Terms begins; 'Arbitrations in London are conducted under the Arbitration Act 1996.'[77] The Terms, on which LMAA arbitrators accept appointments, must be read with the AA 1996. They are not stand-alone. However, they contain some detailed procedural rules, providing structure and certainty in various areas which institutional rules do not cover.

The Terms are accompanied by six schedules, which include a questionnaire in the Third Schedule and a checklist in the Fourth Schedule. The latter contains guidelines issued 'with a view to making the decision-making process as cost-effective and efficient as possible'. A failure to comply with the checklist may be taken into account when the tribunal exercises its discretion as to liability for costs and in assessing costs.[78] A tribunal may also take into account the cost estimates which the parties are obliged to provide in the questionnaire in the Third Schedule after the exchange of written submissions. The LMAA's 'mild form of costs budgeting', which should help to tackle the high level of costs in arbitration, was highlighted as innovative by Sir Rupert Jackson, who had reformed the cost regimes in court litigation

73. *Ibid.*, sections 61, 63.
74. *Ibid.*, section 65.
75. BAS Rules available at https://www.ciarb.org/disputes/schemes/business-arbitration-scheme/, accessed 28 March 2023.
76. SCP, para. 8 and LMAA's Fees and Costs as from 1 January 2019, https://lmaa.london/fees/, accessed 28 March 2023.
77. https://lmaa.london/the-lmaa-terms/, accessed 28 March 2023.
78. LMAA Terms, para. 19(b).

in England.[79] Neither the UNCITRAL Arbitration Rules nor any major institutional rules require parties to inform the tribunal of their estimated legal costs during an arbitration.

The Terms also contain departures from the default provisions of the AA 1996. For example, they provide that if the arbitration agreement is silent on the number of arbitrators, it shall be deemed to provide for a tribunal of three, not a sole arbitrator.[80] However, in practice, it is usual for the two arbitrators appointed by the parties to defer the appointment of a third until a hearing is in prospect or they disagree on any matter relating to the arbitration, as permitted by the Terms.[81] A functioning tribunal of two arbitrators can be composed quickly within 14 days of the commencement of the arbitration. The tribunal is immediately able to deal with, for example, an application for a partial final award on a '*Kostas Melas*' basis as described above, setting an appropriate expedited timetable for an exchange of submissions. A partial final award in such a case may turn out to be the only award required. The LMAA Terms make room for this sort of flexibility as well as providing, in the Second Schedule, a detailed procedure which could be applied in a full-scale arbitration. Most LMAA arbitrations proceed on a documents-only basis.[82] Nevertheless, in relation to smaller claims, concerns about the potential length and complexity of proceedings and the proportionality of costs led the LMAA to introduce its SCP in 1989.

§7.05 FEATURES OF THE LMAA'S SCP

[A] Informality

The original SCP was accompanied by a commentary which explained: 'The Small Claims Procedure has been introduced to provide a simplified, quick and inexpensive procedure for the resolution of small claims … .'[83] The commentary went on to draw attention to various features of the rules, including 'informal procedure':

> There will be no formal pleadings and no discovery as such. Each party will be informed of the case against him by a simple exchange of letters accompanied by copies of all relevant documents, including witness statements. A strict but reasonable timetable is imposed, and, to avoid the dragging of feet, extensions of time will be allowed only sparingly....[84]

Lord Mustill referred to the informality of London maritime arbitration as a quality which should be brought to the attention of UNCITRAL.[85] It is a feature which

79. As reported by the Association of Costs Lawyers: https://www.associationofcostslawyers.co.uk/News/news-in-brief-07062018, accessed 28 March 2023.
80. LMAA Terms, para. 8(a).
81. *Ibid.*, paragraph 8(b)(ii).
82. In 2022, 22% of reported awards were made following an oral hearing (93/420). *See* table of LMAA statistics, *supra* n. 15.
83. The 1989 version of the SCP is available on the LMAA's website at https://lmaa.london/wp-content/uploads/2020/08/LMAASmallClaims1989.pdf.
84. *Ibid.*, 4.
85. *See supra* §7.03.

has been noted by other commentators.[86] The LMAA's commentary does not explain how informality is introduced into the SCP other than by having the parties set their case out in a letter instead of a formal pleading. Informality may also be discerned in the reduction of the procedure to an exchange of letters with 'copies of all relevant documents, including witness statements'.[87] A memorial procedure of this kind results in fewer procedural steps but can be longer.[88] However, in a documents-only procedure with a strict timetable, it allows the parties to digest their opponents' cases in just one or two bites. The procedure is quicker, and the lack of revisiting or repeating pleadings or material makes it less formal too.

Informality can also be seen in the method of commencing an arbitration under the SCP. As with the Terms, the provisions for commencement are not set out under that heading or under 'notice'. Instead, they come under 'Appointment of Arbitrator'. This is consistent with the default provisions for the commencement of an arbitration under the AA 1996:

> Where the arbitrator or arbitrators are to be appointed by the parties, arbitral proceedings are commenced in respect of a matter when one party serves on the other party or parties notice in writing requiring him or them to appoint an arbitrator or to agree to the appointment of an arbitrator in respect of that matter.[89]

In an institutional arbitration, the appointment of the tribunal, or the confirmation of its appointment, takes place sometime after the commencement of the arbitration. The integration of the appointment of the tribunal into the commencement process is a fundamental feature of ad hoc arbitration under the AA 1996. It helps to ensure that the dispute will reach the hands of arbitrators quickly after a claimant has decided to embark on the arbitration.[90] A tribunal can therefore be put in place and be on hand to deal with expedited procedures or interim measures, a possibility which can render a separate 'emergency arbitrator' procedure unnecessary.

In contrast, the appointment of a tribunal is not put under way upon the commencement of arbitral proceedings under the Model Law. Article 21 provides: 'Unless otherwise agreed by the parties, the arbitral proceedings in respect of a particular dispute commence on the date on which a request for that dispute to be referred to arbitration is received by the respondent.'[91] The request contemplated in Article 21 is converted into a notice of arbitration in Article 3 of the UNCITRAL Arbitration Rules. The mandatory contents of the notice do not include proposals for

86. For example, Leng Sun Chan, SC in *Common Types of Shipping Arbitration* in *The Role of Arbitration in Shipping Law*, 205 (Miriam Goldby & Loukas Mistelis eds, Oxford Univ. Press, 2016): 'Whether as a matter of tradition or under the framework of the LMAA Terms, a LMAA arbitration tends to be much more informal in tone than institutional arbitrations.'
87. In the SCP 2021, this requirement is that the letters be 'accompanied by paginated supporting documentation relevant to the issues between the parties' (SCP, para. 5(a)).
88. *See* the procedural timetables proposed by Tom Webster in *Proposed basic timetables for expedited arbitration*, 38 Arbitration International 262, 272 (2022) DOI: 10.1093/arbint/aiac017.
89. AA 1996, section 14(2).
90. For a discussion of the contrast with the commencement of an institutional arbitration, *see supra* n. 64.
91. UNCITRAL Model Law, Article 21.

the appointment of an arbitrator. These are expressly optional.[92] The UNCITRAL Expedited Arbitration Rules, however, do provide that a notice of arbitration is to include proposals for the designation of an appointing authority (if not already agreed) and for the appointment of an arbitrator.[93]

The remaining requirements for the contents of the notice are set out in Article 3 of the main UNCITRAL rules. They resemble the requirements for a request for arbitration to be filed with an institution under its rules. The explanation may be that, as indicated at the beginning of this chapter, WGII did not consider ad hoc arbitrations held outside the institutions or the experience of members of the international arbitration community in ad hoc, not institutional, arbitration. In a disintermediated ad hoc arbitration, one in which no intermediaries, such as an institution's secretariat, are involved, it should not be necessary for a claimant to put into a notice to be sent only to the respondent the respondent's own contact details, the arbitration agreement in, or relating to, the claimant's contract with it, or a description of its relationship with the respondent.[94] These are all matters which will be known to the respondent. Of course, these details could be helpful to an appointing authority if resort is had to one but at the commencement of the arbitration they are otiose and bureaucratic.

Paragraph 2(a) of the SCP provides: 'If a dispute has arisen and the parties have agreed that it should be referred to arbitration under the Small Claims Procedure, then, unless a sole arbitrator has already been agreed on, either party may give notice to the other requiring it to join in appointing a sole arbitrator.'[95] Nothing else has to be included in the notice. It can be a short email of just a few lines, perhaps adding to an email chain in which the claim has been discussed between the parties. It will be a notice commencing arbitration, as set out in the AA 1996, s 14(2) quoted above. This informality contrasts with the UNCITRAL regime.

[B] Appointment of a Sole Arbitrator: Process and Identity

As discussed, two arbitrators, as permitted under the LMAA Terms, can conduct a documents-only arbitration efficiently without the need to appoint a third. However, the LMAA recognised that under the SCP, the appointment of a sole arbitrator would provide a saving in both time and expense.[96] The obvious issue from a time-saving point of view is that if the parties to the dispute do not reach a quick agreement on the arbitrator to be appointed, a third party must then be brought in to make the appointment. The SCP provides that if the parties have not agreed on a sole arbitrator within 14 days of the notice commencing the arbitration, then either party may ask the president of the LMAA to make the appointment.[97]

92. UNCITRAL Arbitration Rules, Article 4.
93. UNCITRAL Expedited Arbitration Rules, Article 4(1).
94. UNCITRAL Arbitration Rules, Article 3(b)-(d).
95. LMAA SCP 2021, para. 2(a).
96. Commentary on the LMAA SCP 1989, para. 1.
97. LMAA SCP 2021, para. 2.

In practice, the president usually makes more than half of the appointments under the SCP every year, often making more than a hundred of them.[98] The president appoints almost exclusively from the LMAA's membership, mainly from among the Full Members, who are full-time professional arbitrators, and Aspiring Full Members, most of whom are also full-time and others of whom may have part-time activities which do not conflict with acting as an arbitrator (e.g., they cannot be practising lawyers).

The appointment of an experienced arbitrator can help to expedite the procedure in a number of ways. The arbitrator should be familiar with the SCP and confident in applying its rules. Having the necessary knowledge and experience, they should also be able to reach a quick decision. Parties in LMAA arbitrations expect an arbitrator not to require time to be spent in explanations of basic aspects of their business or of their approach to arbitration.[99] The LMAA's Advice on Ethics includes the following requirements under the heading 'Competence':

> To be competent an arbitrator should have:
>
> (a) sufficient knowledge and experience of the matters in dispute to enable him or her to understand them without requiring unduly long explanations; and
> (b) sufficient knowledge of the relevant law, and of arbitration law and procedure, to enable him or her to conduct the proceedings efficiently and to write a clear and enforceable Award.[100]

Subject to their availability, the LMAA president is able to choose from lists comprising 50 to 60 Full and Aspiring Full Members who are known to fulfil these criteria. The appointment can therefore be made quickly, normally within one or two days, after an application is received together with the administrative fee, currently GBP 450. Both the president and the parties can be expected to have confidence in the arbitrator selected. This cannot always be said of institutional appointments.[101]

The president may occasionally have queries to raise in relation to the case or the application but will not usually invite any comments or input from the respondent. The applicant is not to suggest any names of potential arbitrators.[102] It should provide a list

98. In 2022, the total number of president's appointments was 99 (out of 3,193) and there were 149 appointments of sole arbitrators in SCP cases: https://lmaa.london/wp-content/uploads/2023/03/Statistics-up-to-2022-for-website.pdf, accessed 9 October 2023.
99. *See, e.g.*, Miquel Roca Lopez, *An Introduction to London Maritime Arbitration* (Thomson Reuters, 2021) 90: 'At the LCIA the appointment of the arbitrator is totally opaque … . The person chosen may not even have any experience as an arbitrator. The LCIA has even appointed practicing solicitors as arbitrators, which is probably the worse of news for any arbitration, as one of the greatest advantages offered by the LMAA is that arbitrators are professional arbitrators, fully dedicated to the resolution of maritime disputes.'
100. LMAA Advice on Ethics, para. 3, https://lmaa.london/advice-on-ethics/. The IBA's Rules of Ethics for International Arbitrators do not contain any requirements in relation to knowledge, experience or competence, https://www.ibanet.org/document?id=Rules-of-ethics-for-international-arbitrators#:~:text=International%20arbitrators%20should%20be%20impartial,may%20be%20assessed%20in%20practice.
101. *See, e.g.*, Webster, *supra* n. 88, 262, 266: 'the appointment of a sole arbitrator is usually left to the arbitration institution or appointing authority. The results can be surprising … .'
102. LMAA SCP, para. 2(b).

of names already proposed and rejected by the parties so that these may be avoided. This is usually done by providing the president with copies of the parties' exchanges since delivery of the notice of arbitration. The application should 'if appropriate give an indication whether any particular expertise on the part of the arbitrator is thought desirable'.[103] The president will appoint an arbitrator 'having considered the nature of the dispute' and will give notice to the parties.[104]

Taking no more than one or two days, this appointment process is considerably faster than that provided in the UNCITRAL Expedited Arbitration Rules. Even where an appointing authority has been identified in the parties' arbitration agreement, there may well be uncertainty and delay while that authority deals with what might be quite a rare application. Further delay is inevitable if a second layer of intermediaries is involved when the Permanent Court of Arbitration (PCA) designates the appointing authority first. The Explanatory Note stipulates that the Secretary General of the PCA, in exercising its functions under article 6(1), would be required to give the parties an opportunity to present their views, including any proposals on the appointing authority.[105] As various people provide their services during this process, charges will be incurred. These may not be fixed or advertised in advance.

There is no reason why the LMAA's ability to act swiftly should not be replicated in other appointing authorities, whether specialised in other sectors or generalist, once a sufficient caseload is attained. Unfortunately, the UNCITRAL Expedited Arbitration Rules, by allowing delays and additional costs as described, do not set the ground for such a development.

[C] Fixed Fee and Capped Costs Recovery

When parties complain about the costs of arbitration, it is often uncertainty about their ultimate exposure to costs which is their real concern, not necessarily the overall sum which they will be compelled to pay. If they know at the outset of an arbitration what the tribunal's fee will be and how much they could recover in respect of their legal costs if they win, they can more easily set a budget and assess fee rates and estimates provided by their external lawyers.

The LMAA's SCP requires that the claimant pay the 'Small Claims fee' to the arbitrator within 14 days of their appointment being agreed.[106] If no agreement is reached and an application is made to the LMAA president, the fee is to be paid to the LMAA, who will send it to the arbitrator as soon as they are appointed. Except for jurisdiction challenges (see §7.06[B] below), there should be no need for the arbitrator to revert to the parties for further payments before the arbitrator makes their award. In an arbitration supervised by an institution, the arbitrator's fee would normally be held by the institution until completion or some other stage.

103. *Ibid.*
104. *Ibid.*
105. Explanatory Note to the UNCITRAL Expedited Arbitration Rules, para. 43.
106. LMAA SCP, para. 2(a).

The fixed fee is relatively modest (currently GBP 5,000 or, if there is a counterclaim exceeding the amount of the claim, GBP 8,000), but senior LMAA arbitrators accept it. Being in independent practice, they do not have to compare the fee to remuneration they might receive for other kinds of work, such as acting as counsel. Nor do they have to justify it to any partners or other colleagues. The procedure should normally be short and take place within parameters known in advance. In particularly simple cases, the fee could be more than adequate. In more complex and fraught cases, it could be on the low side. Arbitrators are used to their remuneration not always corresponding precisely to the amount of time and effort devoted to a case.

Having paid the fee at the beginning of the proceedings, a claimant may be more inclined to let the arbitration run than it might be in a full-scale arbitration. The LMAA's statistics indicate that a relatively high proportion (around two-thirds) of SCP arbitrations go to an award.[107] However, if the parties do settle the case, the arbitrator may retain a sum 'sufficient to compensate the arbitrator for services thus far rendered' and repay the balance.[108] The arbitrator thus acts as their own fundholder, obviating the need to involve an appointing authority.

As regards the parties' legal fees, the cap on the recovery of costs has been mentioned above in connection with the AA 1996's provisions on limiting costs. The limitation currently stands at GBP 6,000 (or GBP 7,000 if there has been a counterclaim exceeding the amount of the claim). This may be quite a low recovery, leaving a successful party with a shortfall in the fees paid to their external lawyers. However, it may be adequate for parties who instruct local lawyers whose rates are lower than those of London solicitors. Other parties or their insurers may prefer to deal with such an arbitration in-house. Overall, the SCP's costs regime can be seen as effective and inclusive, allowing parties to become involved in an arbitration and to see their dispute dealt with relatively quickly while limiting their exposure.

[D] Strict Procedural Timetable

The SCP is a documents-only procedure comprising the exchange of submission letters, with supporting documents, described above. An arbitrator may, however, call a hearing 'in exceptional circumstances', but this is extremely rare.[109] The arbitrator is also permitted to vary the procedure 'in any case which, in the arbitrator's discretion, the arbitrator considers exceptional'.[110] Again, save for occasional tweaks allowing short extensions of time or additional evidence, departures from the standard procedure are extremely rare.

The letter of claim (limited to 2,500 words) does not have to be sent simultaneously with the notice of arbitration. A claimant can put the procedure under way, demonstrating its seriousness and/or protecting time for limitation purposes, without

107. The LMAA's statistics, complied from data provided annually by members, are available on its website: https://lmaa.london/statistics-of-appointments-awards/.
108. LMAA SCP, para. 3(b).
109. *Ibid.*, para. 5(k).
110. *Ibid.*, para. 9(b).

taking that substantial step. The deadline for the letter of claim is 14 days from the confirmation or notice of the appointment of the arbitrator.[111] Extensions of time may be agreed between the parties, but the arbitrator is empowered to fix a final deadline for an outstanding submission letter with a maximum of 14 days.[112] The exchange of submissions will normally be completed between two and four months from the appointment of the arbitrator. It is then for the arbitrator to 'make every effort to publish the award within one month'.[113] In practice, arbitrators usually manage to comply with this deadline. After all, the awards are relatively short and are based on limited submissions and documents.

The procedure under the UNCITRAL Expedited Arbitration Rules is less strict, but Article 16 imposes a deadline for the award of six months from the constitution of the arbitral tribunal. This could be difficult to meet, particularly in a case in which the parties do not cooperate and in which, for example, one party seeks to extend the procedure.[114] The rules leave room for 'guerilla tactics' as the parties are given opportunities to shape the procedure. According to the Explanatory Note, 'Consultation between the arbitral tribunal and the parties at an early stage of the proceedings is particularly key to an efficient and fair organization of expedited arbitration.'[115] This will not always hold true. The success of the SCP suggests that fixing a strict timetable in the rules and not giving the parties opportunities to alter it in any material respects makes for a streamlined and certain procedure, which is both efficient and fair.

§7.06 CHALLENGES AND DRAWBACKS OF THE LMAA'S SCP

[A] Claim Limits

The introduction to the LMAA's SCP confirms that it is to apply to 'any dispute which parties have agreed should be referred to arbitration under this Procedure'. In principle, therefore the parties could submit large claims to the SCP. In practice, they prefer to have such claims dealt with in a full procedure, even if on a documents-only basis. In the absence of an agreement on a monetary limit, the SCP 2021 provides that it is to apply 'where the total amount of the claimant's claims and the total amount of any counterclaims does not exceed US$100,000'.[116] The substantial take-up of the SCP suggests that this limit has been about right. However, market fluctuations can have an impact. For example, disputes about final hire accounts on completion of a time charter, a frequent subject of SCP arbitrations, can fall outside the SCP if daily hire rates are such that the limit is exceeded.

Such is the success of the SCP and its reputation for speed that parties are prepared to reduce a claim so that it comes below their contractual limit or the SCP's

111. *Ibid.*, para. 5(b).
112. *Ibid.*, para. 5(g).
113. *Ibid.*, para. 7.
114. *See* Webster, *supra* n. 88.
115. Explanatory Note to the UNCITRAL Expedited Arbitration Rules, para. 60.
116. LMAA SCP, para. 1(a).

default limit. What they lose in giving up part of their claim they gain in time and costs saved.

[B] Jurisdiction Challenges

The SCP is well suited to contractual claims under English law of the kind described above. It is not so well suited to complex issues of jurisdiction, particularly if they involve conflicts of laws. The basic procedure does not contemplate bifurcation, but the SCP does recognise that an arbitrator may be put to additional work and should be entitled to remuneration for it.[117]

An associated issue is the situation where a chain of contracts, typically charter-parties, gives rise to a series of arbitrations, some involving the same tribunal appointed to hear them concurrently. If one of the claims is subject to the SCP, and therefore to a quicker award, this could cause inconsistencies up the contractual line. The SCP does not specifically cater for this scenario.

§7.07 CONCLUSION

By its nature, no expedited arbitration procedure can be perfect. Without the involvement of a supervising and administrative body, but with strict procedural rules, ad hoc arbitration can be both faster and less expensive than institutional. It lends itself well to expedited arbitration, and institutions could learn from it. This is a message which deserves to be heard at a time when institutions have reported declining caseloads and when dissatisfaction with the UNCITRAL Expedited Arbitration Rules has led to calls for new 'highly expedited arbitration rules'.[118] The LMAA's SCP has a long track record of success and merited more analysis than it received from UNCITRAL WG II. As and when WG II reviews the UNCITRAL Expedited Arbitration Rules, it might have regard to the LMAA's SCP, and consider whether any variations to the rules, model clauses and explanatory notes might be appropriate. An inclusive approach, recognising the diversity of procedures in international commercial arbitration and ready to challenge assumptions, has the potential to widen the appeal of arbitration in different business sectors.

117. *Ibid.*, para. 3(a).
118. *See supra* n. 26 and n. 52, Note by the Secretariat for WGII's 78th session, Vienna, 18-22 September 2023 at https://uncitral.un.org/en/working_groups/2/arbitration.

CHAPTER 8

ICC Expedited Arbitration Proceedings: Review and Analysis

Juan Felipe Merizalde & Juan Pablo Gómez

This chapter explores the International Chamber of Commerce's (ICC) Expedited Procedure Provisions, examining its policy reasons and implementation. It provides a comprehensive analysis of the key features, stages, advantages, and challenges of expedited arbitration from the perspective of arbitrators, counsel, and parties. The chapter also discusses the potential future reform of expedited arbitration to overcome existing obstacles. While the ICC expedited arbitration provisions offer a cost-effective and efficient dispute resolution, parties should carefully consider its suitability for their situation and ensure it is specifically included in their arbitration clauses.

§8.01 INTRODUCTION

International arbitration has shifted in favor of expedited procedures to avoid costly and lengthy proceedings.[1] In recent years, some of the most important arbitral institutions have adopted rules providing for what has been called "fast-track" or expedited arbitration provisions.[2] Today, there are several initiatives in this direction, such as the United Nations Commission on International Trade Law (UNCITRAL) Expedited Arbitration Rules and the recent amendments to the International Centre for

1. Crina Baltag, *Chapter 6: Expedited Arbitration Rules for Investment Disputes: ICSID Amendment Process and UNCITRAL Working Group II*, in *Stockholm Arbitration Yearbook, Stockholm Arbitration Yearbook Series, Volume 2*, 83-98 (Axel Calissendorff and Patrick Schöldström eds., Kluwer Law International 2020).
2. Gary Born, *International Commercial Arbitration 1088*, 8 (Kluwer Law International BV 3d ed. 2021).

Settlement of Investment Disputes (ICSID) Rules. Following the general tendency of international arbitration centers, the International Chamber of Commerce (ICC) first issued its Expedited Procedure Provisions in 2017.[3] By 2020, the ICC had administered 261 cases under its expedited arbitration provisions. Despite this, academic research on expedited arbitration has been relatively modest, focusing on specific issues or alternative procedures like emergency arbitration.

Against this backdrop, this chapter reviews the policy reasons behind the implementation of expedited arbitration, as well as the lessons learned from their implementation in arbitral practice. It offers a comprehensive approach to expedited arbitration. The chapter considers the fundamentals of expedited arbitration, looking at matters such as the main stages of such proceedings, their key features, and some critical matters of procedure. It also incorporates and discusses the main findings of the latest ICC Dispute Resolution Statistics concerning expedited arbitration.[4] The chapter adds to these considerations a practical viewpoint, from the position of arbitrator and counsel, on the main advantages and challenges of applying expedited arbitration provisions. Additionally, the chapter discusses the interests of parties and in-house counsel, including the advantages and disadvantages of including expedited arbitration in arbitral clauses or opting for expedited arbitration once proceedings have started, as well as handling frequent and complex issues arising in these cases.

§8.02 POLICY REASONS BEHIND IMPLEMENTATION OF THE EXPEDITED ARBITRATION PROCEDURES

[A] The Need for Expedited Procedures and How the Arbitral Community Perceives Them

Some authors have considered that fast-track or expedited arbitration procedures tackle the problem of the "banalization of arbitration."[5] As arbitration has become more popular to resolve disputes, particularly in international commercial transactions, the disputes brought before arbitral tribunals have increased in complexity.[6] These complex disputes often involve intricate legal and technical issues as well as large damages claims. As a result, the cost of arbitrating these disputes has increased. Parties often need to engage expensive experts and sophisticated lawyers to present their cases effectively. The duration of arbitration proceedings also has increased, as

3. ICC Arbitration Rules, 2017.
4. *Expedited Procedures in International Arbitration* (Laurent Lévy & Michael Polkinghorne eds., Dossiers, ICC Institute of World Business Law 2017).
5. Michael Mustill, *Comments on Fast-Track Arbitration*, 10 J. Int'l Arb. 125 (1993) DOI: 10.54648/joia1993034.
6. Crina Baltag, *Chapter 6: Expedited Arbitration Rules for Investment Disputes: ICSID Amendment Process and UNCITRAL Working Group II*, in *Stockholm Arbitration Yearbook, Stockholm Arbitration Yearbook Series*, Volume 2, 83-98 (Axel Calissendorff & Patrick Schöldström eds., Kluwer Law International 2020).

tribunals need to take more time to consider the evidence and arguments presented to them and to issue a carefully reasoned decision.[7]

In 1993, the arbitration community started discussing the idea of "fast-track" arbitration procedures.[8] Lord Mustill's commentary highlights this evolution by discussing how law practitioners and arbitration participants perceived arbitration during its early years compared to how it is viewed today:

> May I illustrate this by going back to the time, nearly forty years ago, when I first became concerned with international arbitration? The procedure was, by definition, fast-track. That was why the parties chose it as their method of resolving disputes. What has changed in the last forty years is the creation of the new, slow-track arbitration which is the kind of arbitration that is the subject of almost everything written and spoken on the subject. For example, in the days when London was a great port, it was a large importer of timber from the Baltic. This valuable and variable cargo tended to be a source of controversy ... The proceedings are bound to be time-consuming and expensive-although nothing like as time-consuming and expensive as is nowadays so often the case. But it seems to be assumed that these proceedings form the rule, whereas I suggest that it is fast-track arbitration which should be the norm, with slow-track arbitration as a regrettable, if sometimes necessary, exception.[9]

Lord Mustill identified a shift in the perception of arbitration by legal practitioners and participants from its nascent years to its current state. He suggested changes to achieve expedited arbitration: "undoubtedly, in part, by devising new and more efficient procedures, to restore to arbitration the virtues of simplicity and economy of time and effort which it used to possess."[10]

Years after Lord Mustill's commentary, Queen Mary University conducted a 2012 survey under the name "Current and Preferred Practices in the Arbitral Process."[11] Among other issues, the survey asked, "How common are fast-track arbitrations and how do they usually arise?" The answers to this question revealed that fast-track procedures were still a *nouvelle* feature in international arbitration at the time of the survey. "Over half of respondents (54%) had no experience of fast-track arbitration over the past 5 years, 41% were involved in a small number of fast-track arbitrations (between 1-5), and only 5% were involved in a substantial number of fast-track arbitrations (6 or more)."[12] The overall perception of the participants in the survey regarding their experience with fast-track arbitration showed that the international

7. Crina Baltag, *Chapter 6: Expedited Arbitration Rules for Investment Disputes: ICSID Amendment Process and UNCITRAL Working Group II*, in *Stockholm Arbitration Yearbook, Stockholm Arbitration Yearbook Series, Volume 2*, 84 (Axel Calissendorff & Patrick Schöldström eds., Kluwer Law International 2020).
8. Michael Mustill, *Comments on Fast-Track Arbitration*, 10 J. Int'l Arb. 121, 122 (1993) DOI: 10.54648/joia1993034.
9. *Ibid.*, 122.
10. *Ibid.*, 125.
11. Queen Mary University of London & White & Case, *2012 International Arbitration Survey: Current and Preferred Practices in the Arbitral Process*, 14 (2012).
12. *Ibid.*, 14.

arbitration community received fast-track procedures well.[13] However, when interviewed, those with experience with fast-track arbitration explained that it was effective for resolving simple cases but not suitable for complex ones because the quality of the award could be at risk in such cases.[14] The survey also questioned whether fast-track arbitration results in significantly faster proceedings. The survey data suggested that most participants considered that the shortened time limits in fast-track arbitrations were adhered to, either generally or with occasional compliance.[15] This first survey showed a common awareness of the importance and advantages of fast-tracking arbitration among practitioners and users of arbitration as a dispute resolution mechanism.

In 2015, Queen Mary University and White and Case LLP conducted another survey under the name "Improvements and Innovations in International Arbitration."[16] The survey carried out a comprehensive inquiry into global arbitration patterns and methodologies. Its results shed light on the state of the art of international arbitration in practice. This survey contained a complete section on reducing time and costs in international arbitration. One of the main conclusions of the survey was that "92 % of respondents favor inclusion of simplified procedures in institutional rules for claims under a certain value: 33 % would have this as a mandatory feature and 59 % as an optional feature."[17] This conclusion encompassed one of the survey's most interesting findings: the cost and (lack of) speed of arbitrations were perceived as the worst characteristics of international arbitration.[18] Specifically, 68 % of the answers referred to the cost of arbitral proceedings, and 36% of them to the lack of speed of the proceedings.[19]

When addressing the questions regarding the time and costs of international arbitration proceedings, those who conducted the survey elaborated a list of potential time- and cost-saving procedural innovations. They then asked the interviewees to rate them in accordance with their perceived effectiveness in reducing time and costs in international arbitration procedures.[20] Participants were also asked whether they would favor including institutional rules of simplified procedures for certain claims. Again, 92 % of the interviewees said they would favor simplified procedures to be included in institutional rules, mandatory or not. The interviewees were asked about the value of claims that should be addressed under simplified procedures. Over 94 % of respondents believed disputes above USD 1 million should not be eligible for such procedures.[21] Some interviewees also expressed the view that the parties should agree upon the cutoff value rather than being determined by an institution.[22] Finally, the

13. *Ibid.*, 15.
14. *Ibid.*
15. *Ibid.*
16. Queen Mary University of London & White & Case, *International Arbitration Survey: Improvements and Innovations in International Arbitration* (2015).
17. *Ibid.*, 26.
18. *Ibid.*, 24.
19. *Ibid.*, 7.
20. *Ibid.*, 28.
21. *Ibid.*
22. *Ibid.*

survey asked about the factors that influenced the parties' preferences on the expedited procedures. The results showed that one of the most important factors was the concern about the enforceability of decisions issued under simplified arbitral procedures.[23]

[B] Rise of Expedited Arbitration Within ICC's Framework and Other Institutions

The first institutions to provide for expedited arbitration proceedings were the World Intellectual Property Organization (WIPO), followed by the China International Economic and Trade Arbitration Commission (CIETAC), and the Arbitration Institute of the Stockholm Chamber of Commerce (SCC). WIPO introduced its expedited arbitration rules in 1994, providing a more efficient resolution of intellectual property rights disputes.[24] CIETAC also introduced its expedited procedure rules in the same year, offering a faster and more streamlined arbitration process for disputes arising in the context of international economic and trade transactions.[25] The SCC followed in 1995, introducing its own expedited arbitration rules to allow parties to resolve disputes more quickly and cost-effectively.[26] The 2016 Arbitration Rules of the Singapore International Arbitration Centre (SIAC) have specific clauses regarding expedited arbitration. The 2018 Arbitration Rules of the Hong Kong International Arbitration Centre (HKIAC) included expedited arbitration. These expedited arbitration rules typically involve shorter time frames for submitting evidence and making submissions, as well as reduced fees and a streamlined hearing process.[27] In addition, most accelerated arbitration procedures permit the parties to participate voluntarily based on their agreement.

Against this backdrop, the ICC issued its Expedited Procedure Provisions in response to the general tendency initiated by other arbitration centers since the mid-1990s. In 2002, the ICC's International Court of Arbitration (the Court) formed a task force to improve efficiency in small claims arbitration. Their recommendations helped inform changes in the ICC's rules for small claims arbitration, which were implemented in 2012.[28] These changes made the process more efficient and accessible to parties involved in small claims disputes.[29]

The ICC Commission on Arbitration & ADR (the Commission) started reviewing the 1998 ICC Arbitration Rules (ICC Rules) and recognized the need for focusing on

23. *Ibid.*
24. Crina Baltag, *Chapter 6: Expedited Arbitration Rules for Investment Disputes: ICSID Amendment Process and UNCITRAL Working Group II*, in *Stockholm Arbitration Yearbook, Stockholm Arbitration Yearbook Series*, Volume 2, 85 (Axel Calissendorff & Patrick Schöldström eds., Kluwer Law International 2020).
25. *Ibid.*
26. *Ibid.*
27. Fatih Serbest, *Fast-Track Arbitration: Should It Be Encouraged in International Commercial Disputes?* Conference (2012), https://www.serbest.av.tr/dosyalar/dosya_12305_Fast_Track_Arbitration_Should_it_be_Enco.pdf.
28. International Chamber of Commerce (ICC), *ICC Commission Report, Controlling Time and Costs in Arbitration*, 4 (2018).
29. *Ibid.*

mechanisms that improved the time- and cost-efficiency of arbitration.[30] As a result, the amendments made in 2012 introduced significant procedural mechanisms to ensure effective case management.[31]

The Commission published its final Report on Controlling Time and Costs in Arbitration in 2018 under the title "Techniques for Controlling Time and Costs in Arbitration," almost a year after the ICC's expedited arbitration rules were first issued. The last report recognized that introducing expedited arbitration answered the need to reduce the costs incurred by the parties under ICC Rules.[32] Specifically, the Commission recognized the need to reduce the costs "caused by unnecessarily long and complicated proceedings with unfocused requests for disclosure of documents and unnecessary witness and expert evidence."[33] Also, the duration of the proceeding played an important role in the reasons behind the implementation of the expedited arbitration. The Commission acknowledged that "the longer the proceedings, the more expensive they will be."[34]

The Commission's recommendations to address concerns related to time and costs in arbitration included the use of "fast-track procedures," which would be implemented through an arbitration agreement:

> Consideration may be given to setting out fast-track procedures in the arbitration clause. Indeed, Article 39(1) of the Rules enables the parties to shorten the time limits provided for in the Rules, while Article 39(2) enables the Court to extend those shortened time limits when necessary. Fast-track procedures are designed to enable an arbitration to proceed quickly, given the specific nature of the contract and the disputes that are likely to arise. However, experience shows that in practice it is difficult at the time of drafting the clause to predict with a reasonable degree of certainty the nature of disputes and the procedures that will be suitable for those disputes. Also, disagreements can arise later over the interpretation or application of fast-track clauses. Careful thought should therefore be given before such provisions are included in an arbitration agreement. Once a dispute has arisen, the parties could at that time agree upon a fast-track procedure, if appropriate.[35]

The ICC expedited arbitration procedures are an example of a worldwide trend among leading arbitration centers to adopt streamlined and effective arbitration processes. This trend typically involves incorporating certain essential elements, such as outlining particular criteria for the expedited procedure regulations to apply, utilizing mechanisms that aim to minimize time and cost, such as appointing a single

30. International Chamber of Commerce (ICC), *ICC Commission Report, Controlling Time and Costs in Arbitration* (2018).
31. *Ibid.*, 6.
32. *Ibid.*
33. *Ibid.*
34. International Chamber of Commerce (ICC), *ICC Commission Report Controlling Time and Costs in Arbitration*, ICCWBO 6 (March 2018). https://iccwbo.org/content/uploads/sites/3/2018/03/icc-arbitration-commission-report-on-techniques-for-controlling-time-and-costs-in-arbitration-english-version.pdf.
35. *Ibid.*, 15.

arbitrator, accelerating case management, permitting non-reasoned awards, and dismissing claims through summary proceedings at an earlier stage.[36]

§8.03 UNDERSTANDING ICC EXPEDITED ARBITRATION

[A] Scope of the Rules

The ICC expedited arbitration procedure is regulated by Article 30 and Appendix VI of ICC's Arbitration Rules. Both Article 30 of the ICC's Arbitration Rules and the articles of Appendix VI constitute the ICC Expedited Procedure Provisions (EPP). Three subparts of Article 30 establish the nature, scope, and applicability of the EPP. Article 30(1) provides: "By agreeing to arbitration under the Rules, the parties agree that Article 30 and the Expedited Procedure Rules outlined in Appendix VI (collectively the 'Expedited Procedure Provisions') shall take precedence over any contrary terms of the arbitration agreement."[37] Article 30(1) states that the ICC Expedited Procedure Provisions are part of the Arbitration Rules. Therefore, a party cannot claim that it only consented to arbitration under ICC Rules but not the expedited arbitration rules, for example, because the arbitration agreement does not refer to expedited arbitration.[38]

Under this provision, the expedited arbitration rules become integral to any arbitration agreement executed after March 1, 2017, that references the ICC rules because Article 30 and the ICC Expedited Procedure Provisions take precedence over any contrary terms of the arbitration agreement. Hence, the expedited arbitration rules are compulsory because Article 30 allows automatic application when certain criteria are met. This approach opposes the opt-in and opt-out alternatives adopted by other institution's expedited arbitration procedures.

The expedited arbitration rules apply if either of the two alternatives are satisfied. The expedited arbitration rules will apply if: (a) the amount in dispute does not exceed the limit set in Article 1(2) of Appendix VI at the time of the communication referred to in Article 1(3) of that Appendix; or (b) the parties so agree.[39] Appendix VI sets the monetary threshold at USD 2 million (if the arbitration agreement was concluded on or after March 1, 2017, and before January 1, 2021), or USD 3 million (if the arbitration agreement was concluded on or after January 1, 2021). The monetary threshold introduced by Article 30(2) is a departure from other expedited arbitration rules such as UNCITRAL or SCC. Those expedited arbitration provisions require that the parties agree that the arbitration is to be conducted accordingly.[40]

36. Yas Banifatemi, *Expedited Proceedings in International Arbitration*, in *Expedited Procedures in International Arbitration*, 9-33 (Laurent Lévy & Michael Polkinghorne eds., Dossiers, ICC Institute of World Business Law 2017).
37. ICC Arbitration Rules, Article 30.1.
38. ICC, *Note to Parties and Arbitral Tribunals on the Conduct of the Arbitration under the ICC Rules of Arbitration*, 19 (International Chamber of Commerce, International Court of Arbitration 2021).
39. ICC Arbitration Rules, Article 30.2.
40. SCC Expedited Arbitration Rules (2023), 3; UNCITRAL Expedited Arbitration Rules (2021), Article 1.

Alternatively, the parties can agree to have an arbitration conducted under the expedited arbitration rules, even if their dispute exceeds the monetary thresholds. This provides the alternative to opt in for expedited arbitration as other rules of a similar nature do. In practice, the ICC Secretariat often encourages the parties to opt in after review of the Request for Arbitration if the case does not appear to be too complex.

Article 30(3) establishes three exceptional circumstances in which the expedited arbitration will not apply, even though the conditions in Article 30(2) and Article 1 of Appendix VI are met. The Expedited Procedure Provisions will not apply if:

a) the arbitration agreement under the Rules was concluded before the date on which the Expedited Procedure Provisions came into force;
b) the parties have agreed to opt out of the Expedited Procedure Provisions; or
c) the Court, upon the request of a party before the constitution of the arbitral tribunal or on its motion, determines that it is inappropriate in the circumstances to apply the Expedited Procedure Provisions.[41]

The first scenario precludes application of the expedited arbitration rules if the arbitration agreement was concluded before March 1, 2017, when the expedited arbitration provisions came into force. The second circumstance allows parties to agree that the arbitration will not be conducted under the expedited arbitration provisions. Interestingly, this provision strikes a balance between expedited arbitration's compulsory nature and the other rules' voluntary nature. This rule is important because "not all cases are suitable for an expedited process, especially large complex matters with voluminous documents and many witnesses."[42] Also, for some countries and companies, a USD 2 or USD 3 million case could be considered a "bet-the-company case," and these parties may wish to opt out of the expedited arbitration.

Finally, the expedited arbitration rules will not apply if the Court considers their application "inappropriate in the circumstances" of the case, by the request of the parties or on its motion, at any time before the constitution of the arbitral tribunal. Therefore, when concluding their arbitration agreement, parties should acknowledge the automatic application of the expedited arbitration.

Appendix VI contains all the rules applicable to expedited arbitration in five articles. These articles cover all the stages of the procedure from the application of the expedited procedure rules (Article 1) to the award (Article 5).[43] Article 1 restates the scope of application of the expedited arbitration procedure: the monetary threshold for their application and the power of the Court to determine, ex officio or upon the request of a party, that the expedited arbitration shall not apply.[44]

Article 1(3) requires the Secretariat to inform the parties that the expedited arbitration will apply in a case. For that purpose, the Secretariat will assess, in accordance with Article 30(3), whether the dispute's amount in controversy aligns

41. ICC Arbitration Rules, Article 30.3.
42. Pettibone Peter J. *Due Process Considerations in Expedited Arbitration*, 10(1) Indian Journal of Arbitration Law 183 (2021), http://www.ijal.in/wp-content/uploads/2022/02/10_Due-Process-Consideration-in-Expedited-Arbitrations_PP.pdf.
43. ICC Expedited Procedure Rules, Appendix VI.
44. ICC Expedited Procedure Rules, Article 1.3.

with the monetary threshold outlined in Article 1(3) of Appendix VI or if the parties have mutually agreed to conduct their arbitration under the expedited arbitration procedure.[45] Under Article 1(3), the determination of whether the arbitration will be conducted under the expedited arbitration rules is merely an administrative procedure. The Secretariat only has to decide if: (i) the amount in dispute fits in the monetary threshold or the parties have agreed to apply expedited arbitration and (ii) whether any of the conditions of Article 30(3) are met.

The amount in controversy encompasses all quantifiable allegations, counterclaims, crossclaims, and claims under Articles 7 and 8, without considering those related to interest and costs.[46] Under Articles 4(3), 5(5)(b), 7(2), 7(4), 8(2), and 8(3) of the ICC Rules, the parties are required to quantify their claims, including nonmonetary ones. These quantifications will be considered by the ICC Secretariat to determine whether the procedure is conducted under the Expedited Procedure Provisions.[47] Decisions by the Secretariat or the Court on the amount in dispute do not bind the arbitral tribunal's substantive decisions. Further, when assessing costs, the tribunal may consider if a party artificially inflated its claims, thereby preventing the application of the expedited provisions. Finally, the parties must always bear in mind that the ICC Expedited Procedure Provisions do not apply in cases with nonquantifiable declaratory or nonmonetary claims unless they support a monetary claim or do not complicate the dispute significantly.[48]

However, the Court may decide that the expedited arbitration rules shall no longer apply to the case at any time during the arbitral proceedings, on its motion or upon the request of a party, and after consultation with the arbitral tribunal and the parties pursuant to Article 1(4) of the expedited arbitration provisions.[49] The Court's ability to determine the application of the expedited arbitration rules under Article 1(4) may impair the principle of party autonomy. This principle enables the parties to agree on the specific rules that apply to the merits of the dispute and the procedural framework of the arbitration.[50] Even though parties had agreed to have an expedited arbitration, the Court may unilaterally determine that the expedited arbitration provisions no longer apply despite the arbitration having already commenced.[51]

Submissions on the applicability of the Expedited Procedure Provisions must be made in the request for arbitration and the answer or within any subsequent time limit provided by the ICC Secretariat. If an objection is raised regarding the expedited

45. *Ibid.*
46. ICC, *Note to Parties and Arbitral Tribunals on the Conduct of the Arbitration under the ICC Rules of Arbitration*, 20 (International Chamber of Commerce, International Court of Arbitration 2021).
47. *Ibid.*, 20.
48. *Ibid.*
49. ICC Expedited Procedure Rules, Article 1.4.
50. Mohamed S. Abdel Wahab, *Chapter 6: Expedited Institutional Arbitral Proceedings Between Autonomy and Regulation*, in *Expedited Procedures in International Arbitration*, Volume 16, 135 (Laurent Lévy & Michael Polkinghorne eds., Dossiers of the ICC Institute of World Business Law, Kluwer Law International; International Chamber of Commerce (ICC) 2017).
51. ICC Expedited Procedure Rules, Article 1.

arbitration provisions' applicability, the Court will decide the matter after affording the other party the opportunity to express their views.[52]

[B] Distinctive Features of ICC Expedited Arbitration

[1] Constitution of the Tribunal

Article 2 regulates the constitution of the tribunal. Under Article 2(1), the ICC Court may appoint a sole arbitrator, which is the general rule under the expedited provisions.[53] Article 2(2) tries to solve a common problem of a party who tries to delay the arbitration by not participating in the nomination of the sole arbitrator. Article 2(2) establishes the parties' duty to nominate a sole arbitrator within the time limit determined by the Secretariat if they want to avoid a nomination by the Court.[54]

This provision reaffirms the precedence of the expedited arbitration rules over any contrary provision of the arbitration agreement, especially regarding the constitution of the tribunal. Parties have tried to set aside an award because the arbitration agreement provided that the tribunal should consist of three arbitrators, while the expedited arbitration provisions of the administering institution provided that a sole arbitrator would decide the dispute.[55]

Again, under this provision, party autonomy is limited in order to expedite the arbitration, which is what the parties presumably sought by agreeing to the ICC Arbitration Rules.[56] Despite these rules, the Court has been diligent in upholding the parties' agreements. As of 2022, only in 35 cases—6.68% of the total cases conducted under the ICC Expedited Arbitration Provisions—the Court had decided that a single arbitrator would preside over the case, notwithstanding that the arbitration agreement specified a three-member arbitral tribunal.[57] Furthermore, of the 524 cases conducted under the ICC Expedited Arbitration Provisions through December 2022, only seven challenges to arbitrators have been raised. However, in each of these instances, the challenges were either declared inadmissible or rejected on substantive grounds.[58]

[2] Proceedings and Procedure

Article 3 develops the specific procedures under expedited arbitration. This Article regulates, among other things: (i) which provisions of the ICC Arbitration Rules do not apply to expedited arbitration; (ii) the general restriction of making new claims once the tribunal is constituted; (iii) the time frame for conferences; and (iv) the discretion

52. *Ibid.*
53. ICC Expedited Procedure Rules, Article 2(1). *See* Javier Tarjuelo, *Fast Track Procedures: A New Trend in Institutional Arbitration*, 11(2) Dispute Resolution International (2017).
54. ICC Expedited Procedure Rules, Article 2.2.
55. *See infra* §8.04[B][2][a].
56. *See supra* n. 41.
57. Elina Zlatanska & Romain Dupeyré, *Expedited Procedures: Practical and Comparative Considerations* (ICC Dispute Resolution Bulletin 2023 No. 1), 77.
58. *Ibid.*

of the Tribunal to limit the written submissions or witness evidence, or to decide the dispute without any hearings.

Article 23 of the standard ICC Arbitration Rules does not apply to an arbitration under the Expedited Procedure Rules.[59] The terms of reference prepared in a normal arbitration are disregarded in order to speed up the arbitration.[60] Preparing the Terms of Reference can usually consume 30 to 60 days of a regular ICC Arbitration. Because expedited arbitration aims to offer a streamlined arbitration with reduced scales of fees,[61] eliminating procedures like the terms of reference lead to a quicker final decision.

Article 3(2) promotes efficiency by preventing parties from introducing new claims that were not included in their initial submission and that could potentially prolong the proceedings or unfairly prejudice the other party.[62] This provision strikes a balance between the need for finality and efficiency and the parties' right to present their case. By requiring the tribunal to carefully consider the nature and circumstances of any new claims, the provision ensures that the arbitration remains fair and balanced while preserving the process' efficiency and finality.[63]

The case management conference convened under Article 24 of the Rules shall take place no later than 15 days from the date on which the file was transmitted to the arbitral tribunal. The Court may extend this time limit pursuant to a reasoned request from the arbitral tribunal or on its own initiative if it decides it is necessary to do so.[64] This provision introduces one of the key features of expedited arbitration procedures: reducing the duration of the arbitration proceeding. Article 24 of the ICC Rules provides that the case management conference shall be held when drawing up the Terms of Reference or as soon as possible thereafter. In contrast, Article 3 of the expedited arbitration rules states a strict time frame of 15 days from the date the file was transmitted to the arbitral tribunal. This makes the arbitration more expeditious.[65]

Under the ICC expedited arbitration procedures, the arbitral tribunal has the discretion to adopt such procedural measures as it considers appropriate. In particular, the arbitral tribunal may, after consultation with the parties, decide not to allow

59. ICC Expedited Procedure Rules, Article 3.1.
60. ICC Arbitration Rules, Article 23. The terms of reference include: (i) the names in full, description, address, and other contact details of each of the parties and any person(s) representing a party in the arbitration; (ii) the addresses to which notifications and communications may be made; (iii) a summary of the parties' respective claims and the relief sought by each party, together with the amounts of any quantified claims and, to the extent possible, an estimate of the monetary value of any other claims; (iv) unless the arbitral tribunal considers it inappropriate, a list of issues to be determined; (v) the names in full, address and other contact details of each of the arbitrators; (vi) the place of the arbitration; and (vii) particulars of the applicable procedural rules and, if such is the case, reference to the power conferred upon the arbitral tribunal to act as amiable composition or to decide *ex aquod et bono*.
61. International Chamber of Commerce (ICC), *Arbitration Rules 2021*, Article 30 & app. VI (2021), https://iccwbo.org/dispute-resolution-services/arbitration/rules-of-arbitration/.
62. ICC Expedited Procedure Rules, Article 3.2.
63. ICC Arbitration Rules, Article 30.2.
64. ICC Expedited Procedure Rules, Article 3.3.
65. *Conduct of the Proceedings* in *Conduct of the Proceedings, in Redfern and Hunter on International Arbitration*, 7th ed. (Nigel Blackaby, Constantine Partsides, et al. Kluwer Law International; Oxford University Press 2023).

requests for document production or to limit the number, length and scope of written submissions and written witness evidence (both fact witnesses and experts).[66]

The provisions related to the decision-making authority of an arbitral tribunal, specifically Article 3(4) and (5), have the potential to be highly contentious. This is because the tribunal's decision to restrict a party's written submissions within a particular time frame, to disallow requests for document production, or even to decide the dispute without holding a hearing, could lead to challenges against the resulting award on the grounds that the party was not given a fair opportunity to present its case, in contravention of Article V(1)(b) of the New York Convention. A party may contend that the limitations imposed prevented it from adequately presenting its case.[67]

However, as interpreted by national courts, this rule requires that the challenging party "has been prevented from presenting his case by matters outside his control."[68] Thus, if a party were given a chance to present all relevant facts, including evidence and motions, the mere denial of additional evidence would not establish a violation of the right to be heard.[69] Moreover, a party that voluntarily executed an agreement after March 1, 2017, invoking the ICC Rules without opting out of the expedited arbitration provisions should be aware of the arbitral tribunal's powers under Articles 3(4) and 3(5) of Appendix VI, and so should be precluded from arguing that such powers were inconsistent with its arbitral agreement.[70]

[3] The Award

Article 4 of the expedited arbitration provisions regulates the rendering of the award and the fixation of the tribunal's fees. Article 4(1) states that the award must be rendered within six months from the case management conference date. Article 4(2) refers to the scale of administrative expenses and arbitrator's fees for the expedited procedure.[71]

Despite the six-month time limit for issuing the award, Article 4(1) refers to Article 31(2) of the ICC Arbitration Rules. This enables the ICC Court to "extend the time limit pursuant to a reasoned request from the arbitral tribunal or on its own initiative if it decides it is necessary to do so."[72] Therefore, even when the expedited arbitration provisions are applicable, the ICC Court may grant an extension.

66. ICC Expedited Procedure Rules, Article 3.4 & ICC Expedited Procedure Rules, Article 3.3.
67. ICC, *Note to Parties and Arbitral Tribunals on the Conduct of the Arbitration under the ICC Rules of Arbitration*, 21 (International Chamber of Commerce, International Court of Arbitration 2021).
68. *Minmetals Germany GmbH v. Ferco Steel Ltd*, 1 All ER (Comm.) 315 [1999].
69. International Bar Association (IBA), *So You Want to Challenge? The Right to Be Heard as a Path to Challenging Arbitration Awards Through the Courts in Austria* (August 4, 2021), https://www.ibanet.org/right-to-be-heard-arbitration-awards-courts-austria.
70. ICC Expedited Procedure Rules, Article 3.5.
71. *Ibid.*, Article 4.1.
72. ICC Arbitration Rules, Article 31(2).

The allocation of costs in arbitration is one of the features that influences parties' choices regarding the arbitration procedures for their disputes. Although administrative costs are consistent in both expedited and standard arbitration, a key distinction arises concerning arbitration fees. Expedited arbitration has notably lower fees in contrast to regular arbitration.[73]

[4] Conversion to Expedited Arbitration after Commencement of Arbitration under the Regular Rules

If the proceedings have already started, the parties may still apply for application of the ICC expedited arbitration procedures, subject to the other party's agreement and the ICC Court's approval. To apply for the ICC expedited arbitration procedure after commencement of the arbitration, the parties must submit a joint request stating their agreement to the expedited procedure and why they believe it is appropriate. The joint request should also include a copy of the arbitration clause in the relevant contract or agreement, specifically providing for the ICC expedited arbitration procedure. The ICC Court will review the joint request and may request additional information or clarification from the parties before deciding whether to approve the application. If the ICC Court approves the application, it will appoint a sole arbitrator to conduct the expedited arbitration proceedings by the ICC Expedited Procedure Rules.[74]

[5] Catch-All General Rule

In all matters concerning expedited procedures not expressly provided for in the Appendix, the ICC Court and the arbitral tribunal shall act in the spirit of the Rules and this Appendix.[75] This provision is also in Article 42 of the Rules and Article 8 of the emergency arbitration rules (Appendix V).[76]

§8.04 LESSONS LEARNED FROM THEIR IMPLEMENTATION IN REAL-LIFE SITUATIONS

[A] Findings of the Latest ICC Dispute Resolution Statistics

The ICC Case Load Statistics for 2020 showed that 946 cases were registered with the Secretariat that year, 929 under the ICC Arbitration Rules and the remaining 17 under

73. International Chamber of Commerce (ICC), *Arbitration Rules* 2021, app. III Article 3 (2021), https://iccwbo.org/dispute-resolution-services/arbitration/rules-of-arbitration/. Article 3 of Appendix III of the ICC Rules.
74. ICC Expedited Procedure Rules, Article 2.
75. *Ibid.*, Article 5.
76. ICC Emergency Arbitration Rules, Article 24.

the ICC Appointing Authority Rules.[77] The latest ICC Case Load Statistics show the impact of expedited procedure arbitrations from 2017 to 2020. The ICC centered its analysis on three main subjects: the amounts in dispute, the number of cases conducted under the expedited arbitration provisions, and the percentage of awards issued under the expedited arbitration. "[O]ver 50% of the cases filed in 2020 and 50% of the pending cases at the end of 2020 had an amount in dispute between US$ 1 million and US$ 30 million."[78]

From the quantitative analysis made by the ICC, the average amount in dispute for cases filed during 2020 was USD 54 million, and the median was USD 6 million. The former can only mean that it is still unusual that arbitration before ICC will be conducted under the expedited arbitration, considering the financial threshold required for an arbitration to be conducted under the expedited provisions because disputes under USD 3 million and USD 2 million are less frequent.[79]

The ICC also offers specific figures regarding what they call lower-value disputes. Specifically, the statistics showed that in 2020, 38% of cases registered involved an amount in dispute not exceeding USD 3 million[80] which is the threshold amount for a dispute to be conducted under the expedited arbitration for arbitration agreements concluded on or after January 1, 2021. The ICC considered that this proportion of lower-value cases demonstrated the necessity of expedited arbitration procedures.[81]

From 2017, when the Expedited Procedure Provisions were adopted, to 2020, 261 cases have been or were being conducted.[82] Of those cases, the expedited arbitration procedure applied automatically in 178 cases.[83] Further, there have been 291 requests to opt in to the expedited arbitration process, to which the other party or parties agreed.[84] More recent data confirms the success of the ICC Expedited Arbitration Provisions. This data shows a significant increase in the number of cases conducted under the expedited provisions in only two years. From March 2017 to December 2022, 524 cases were conducted under the ICC Expedited Procedure Provisions.[85] Of these, 77% automatically met the monetary procedural threshold, while in the rest, the parties intentionally opted in at different stages of the arbitration, irrespective of the amount in dispute or the agreement date.[86] Notably, only 23 cases, representing just 4.39% of the total cases conducted under these rules as of 2022, showed parties opting out of the ICC Expedited Procedure Provisions.[87]

77. International Chamber of Commerce (ICC), *ICC Dispute Resolution 2020 Statistics*, ICC (August 3, 2021), https://nyiac.org/wp-content/uploads/2021/09/ICC-Dispute-Resolution-2020-Statistics.pdf.
78. *Ibid.*, 17.
79. *Ibid.*, 17-18.
80. *Ibid.*, 18.
81. *Ibid.*
82. *Ibid.*
83. *Ibid.*
84. *Ibid.*
85. Elina Zlatanska & Romain Dupeyré, *Expedited Procedures: Practical and Comparative Considerations* (ICC Dispute Resolution Bulletin 2023 No. 1), 75.
86. *Ibid.*
87. *Ibid.*, 76.

Since the adoption of the expedited arbitration procedure until 2020, tribunals have rendered 115 final awards.[88] Of those rendered under the expedited procedures up to 2020, 77 were issued within or around the six-month time limit of Article 4 of the expedited arbitration rules.[89] The ICC clarified that delays in rendering the award were minimal.[90] Specifically, in 38 cases, the delay was just one month and most of the time, the delay was due to justified circumstances.[91] In five cases, the parties agreed to a new procedural timetable, and in eight disputes, the delay resulted in a fee reduction for the sole arbitrator.[92]

Recent data, extending to December 2022, provides additional insights into the efficiency of ICC Expedited Arbitration Provisions. Between 2017 and 2022, there were 269 final awards in ICC expedited arbitrations, with 154 issued by 2020. Only 55% involved hearings. Document production was infrequent and occurred in only 17% of the cases. Post-hearing briefs were filed in only 31% of cases, underscoring the streamlined nature of ICC Expedited Procedure Provisions.[93] From the 269 awards issued during this period, 67% were issued within or very close to the specified six-month time limit following the case management conference.[94]

[B] Advantages and Disadvantages of ICC Expedited Arbitration

[1] Advantages

In general, the advantages of the ICC Expedited Arbitration Provisions are: (i) streamlined arbitration; (ii) reduced fee scales; (iii) faster dispute settlements; (iv) the parties' freedom to opt out of the expedited proceeding; and (v) addressing the need for expeditious resolution of disputes that international trade demands.[95] Expedited arbitration's main advantages are: (i) speed; (ii) cost-effectiveness; (iii) use of a simplified procedure; (iv) flexibility; and (v) finality.

Expedited arbitration is designed to resolve disputes quickly, with a maximum time limit of six months from the case management conference date (held within 15 days of the date on which the file is transmitted to the arbitral tribunal) until the final decision is issued.[96] This benefits parties who want a faster resolution to their dispute.

88. International Chamber of Commerce (ICC), *ICC Dispute Resolution 2020 Statistics*, ICC (August 3, 2021), https://nyiac.org/wp-content/uploads/2021/09/ICC-Dispute-Resolution-2020-Statistics.pdf, 19.
89. *Ibid.*
90. *Ibid.*
91. *Ibid.*
92. *Ibid.*
93. Elina Zlatanska & Romain Dupeyré, *Expedited Procedures: Practical and Comparative Considerations* (ICC Dispute Resolution Bulletin 2023 No. 1), 78.
94. *Ibid.*
95. Queen Mary University of London & White & Case, *International Arbitration Survey: Improvements and Innovations in International Arbitration Improvements and Innovations in International Arbitration*, 24 (2015), https://arbitration.qmul.ac.uk/media/arbitration/docs/2015_International_Arbitration_Survey.pdf.
96. ICC Expedited Procedure Provisions, Article 3.3.

Expedited arbitration procedures can be less expensive than traditional arbitration because they involve fewer procedural steps and less time is spent on the case. Appendix III of the ICC Rules outlines a different fee structure for arbitrators in expedited proceedings, offering a cost-effective alternative to the fees applicable in standard-speed arbitration. The fees for expedited arbitrators begin with a minimum of USD 2,400, which is USD 600 less than the minimum fee for regular procedures when the dispute amount exceeds USD 50,000. For cases involving over USD 500,000,000, expedited arbitration fees range from a minimum of 0.0080% to a maximum of 0.0320% of the disputed amount. The reduced fees are intended to enhance efficiency and affordability for smaller or less complex disputes. In contrast, the fee structure for regular arbitrators typically involves higher percentages of the disputed amount. Under the expedited arbitration provisions, the fees are set at a 20% reduction compared to the general scale.[97]

Expedited arbitration involves fewer written submissions and a shorter hearing. The arbitral tribunal may decide that a hearing is not necessary in light of the circumstances. This can be advantageous for parties who prefer a more streamlined process. In particular, the ICC Expedited Procedure Provisions empower the tribunal to reach an agreement with the parties to either refrain from permitting requests for document production or impose restrictions on the quantity, length, and extent of written submissions and written witness evidence.[98] Moreover, the tribunal has the authority to resolve the dispute solely by considering the documents provided by the parties, without conducting a hearing or examining witnesses or experts.[99] Such rules not only shorten the length of the arbitration process but also reduce the parties' expenses because they will not be charged for the hearing and the other fees linked to it by their counsels.

A sole arbitrator conducting the arbitration also reduces the costs the parties would otherwise incur in a regular procedure. Parties can still choose their arbitrator and agree on the procedural rules to apply in their case. This provides flexibility and autonomy for parties to customize the process to their specific needs. This is especially relevant given the tribunal's power under Article 3(4) of Appendix VI to "decide not to allow requests for document production or to limit the number."[100] In international arbitration, the production of documents has emerged as a major factor increasing the duration and costs of the proceedings, requiring a substantial period of four to eight weeks exclusively dedicated to this process before advancing further in the arbitration.[101] Consequently, document production often results in the dismissal of numerous

97. ICC, Note to Parties and Arbitral Tribunals on the Conduct of the Arbitration under the ICC Rules of Arbitration, 20 (International Chamber of Commerce, International Court of Arbitration 2021).
98. ICC Expedited Procedure Provisions, Article 3.3.
99. *Ibid.*
100. ICC Expedited Procedure Rules, Article 3(4).
101. Michael W. Bühler & Pierre Heitzmann, *The 2017 ICC Expedited Rules: From Softball to Hardball?*, 34(2) Journal of International Arbitration 131 DOI: 10.54648/joia2017009.

document disclosure requests due to their overly expansive or irrelevant scope and leaves parties with evidence that may not significantly support their cases.[102]

Finally, the parties must bear in mind that expedited arbitration's awards are final and binding, with limited grounds for challenge. This can provide parties with certainty and finality in the resolution of their dispute.

[2] Disadvantages

The first potential disadvantage is related to expedited arbitration's application scope. Once the claimant has presented a clear valuation of their claim, the other party may want to avoid expedited arbitration by devising counterclaims to increase the total claims above the threshold stated in Article 30 of the ICC Arbitration Rules. The monetary threshold applicable for the application of the expedited arbitration provisions may not be coherent with the complexity of the dispute. The monetary threshold of USD 3 million stated in Article 1 of Appendix VI may not reflect the true nature and complexity of a specific arbitration. The parties may, nevertheless, opt in to the expedited procedure for disputes above the threshold.

The question of which disputes should be subject to fast-track arbitration has led some to conclude that fast-track arbitration may not be suitable when intricate legal issues or the interpretation of legal documents are involved.[103] Further, the parties and their counsel tend to be less inclined to endorse procedures that could enhance efficiency because they are mainly focused on ensuring that their right to due process remains unaffected.[104] The issue lies in the appropriateness of using a fixed threshold of USD 3 million—or any fixed monetary threshold—for the application of expedited arbitration procedures. This threshold does not necessarily answer to the complexity of cases. Cases with amounts in issue less than USD 3 million can be highly intricate, while cases exceeding USD 3 million may not. Determining whether a case falls above or below this threshold can be subjective because the parties' perspectives and assessments may differ. Additionally, the issue of converting amounts stated in currencies other than US dollars further complicates matters, raising questions about the appropriate timing and method of currency conversion. Some authors have argued that the ICC established a "rather high threshold amount to capture a large group of cases under its Expedited Rules."[105] While categorizing cases falling within this threshold as small and medium-sized, they overlook the fact that, as noted by Bühler and Heitzmann, this threshold amount could be considered significant for small businesses.[106]

102. *Ibid.*
103. Fatih Serbest, *Fast-Track Arbitration: Should It Be Encouraged in International Commercial Disputes?*, 238 (2006), https://www.researchgate.net/publication/259822761_FastTrack_Arbitration_Should_it_be_Encouraged_in_International_Commercial_Dispute.
104. Pierre Heitzmann, *The 2017 ICC Expedited Rules: From Softball to Hardball?* (2017), 34(2) Journal of International Arbitration 130, DOI: 10.54648/joia2017009.
105. *Ibid.*, 129.
106. *Ibid.*

Additionally, an award could be set aside or its enforcement rejected based on due process considerations under Article V of the New York Convention and UNCITRAL Model Law in International Commercial Arbitration. Arguments before State courts regarding the annulment of arbitration awards issued through accelerated procedures may give rise to legal challenges stemming from due process considerations. A party may assert it was deprived of the opportunity to adequately present its case because the tribunal precluded requests for document production; constrained the quantity, length, and extent of written submissions and witness evidence; or resolved the controversy exclusively based on the documents proffered by the parties, without any hearing or cross-examination of witnesses or experts. Hence, when opting for expedited arbitration, one must find a middle ground between the parties' rights regarding due process and the need for a quick and efficient resolution process.[107]

The primary factors that increase the likelihood of an award being invalidated in expedited arbitration procedures are related to due process issues. Specifically, the main concerns relate to the constitution of the arbitral tribunal (Article 2 of Appendix VI); not allowing a party to present its whole case (Article 3.2 of Appendix VI); limiting or refusing hearings (Article 3.4 of Appendix VI); limiting written submissions and written witness evidence (Article 3.4 of Appendix VI); and limiting the request for document production (Article 3.4 of Appendix VI).

[a] Constitution of the Tribunal

Article 2 of the ICC Expedited Arbitration Provisions provides that notwithstanding any contrary provision in the arbitration agreement, the ICC Court may appoint a sole arbitrator. Parties that have been dissatisfied with the decision have challenged the award, alleging that the constitution of the arbitration tribunal was not in accordance with the agreement of the parties. Article 34(2)(a)(iv) of the UNCITRAL Model Law and Article V(d) of the New York Convention provide this as a basis for annulment and refusal of the recognition and enforcement of an award.[108]

Specifically, national courts have analyzed cases where a party alleged that the tribunal's composition breached the arbitration agreement because the arbitration agreement provided that the tribunal had to be composed of three arbitrators and a sole arbitrator was appointed. In *AQZ v. ARA*, the Singapore High Court set aside an award issued in an expedited arbitration conducted under the expedited procedures pursuant to rule 5 of the Arbitration Rules of SIAC.[109] Although the parties had initially agreed to a three-arbitrator tribunal, the President of SIAC granted one party's request for the

107. Pettibone Peter J. *Due Process Considerations in Expedited Arbitration*, 10(1) Indian Journal of Arbitration Law 181 (2021), http://www.ijal.in/wp-content/uploads/2022/02/10_Due-Process-Consideration-in-Expedited-Arbitrations_PP.pdf.
108. Convention on the Recognition and Enforcement of Foreign Arbitral Awards, Article V(d); Model Law on International Commercial Arbitration 1985 (United Nations Commission on International Trade Law [UNCITRAL]) UN Doc A/40/17, Annex I, Article 34(2)(a)(iv).
109. *AQZ v. ARA*, SGHC 49 (2015).

arbitration to follow the institution's expedited procedures. As a result, the case was ultimately determined by a single arbitrator.

Dissatisfied with the sole arbitrator's ruling, the other party challenged the award based on Article 34(2)(a)(iv) of the UNCITRAL Model Law. However, the Singapore High Court found that the arbitral proceedings were conducted in accordance with the parties' agreement. It held that by submitting their dispute to the SIAC Rules, the parties had implicitly consented to give the SIAC President the power to refer the case to a sole arbitrator, regardless of the agreement to have the dispute decided by three arbitrators. The court found that while prejudice was not a legal requirement for an award to be set aside under Article 34(2)(a)(iv) of the Model Law, it is a relevant factor that the supervisory court considers in deciding whether the breach in question is serious:

> The SIAC Rules have been incorporated into the parties' contract and therefore the rules together with the rest of the contract must be interpreted purposively. A commercially sensible approach to interpreting the parties' arbitration agreement would be to recognize that the SIAC President does have the discretion to appoint a sole arbitrator.[110]

The Singapore High Court concluded that the SIAC Expedited Procedure provisions could override the parties' agreement for the arbitration even when the contract was entered into before the Expedited Procedure provision came into force.[111]

In *Noble Resources International Pte. Ltd. v. Shanghai Good Credit International Trade Co., Ltd*, the Shanghai No. 1 Intermediate People's Court refused to recognize and enforce an arbitral award issued under the SIAC expedited arbitration rules. The court found that the constitution of the arbitral tribunal did not follow the agreement reached by the parties:

> Article 5.2(b) of the SIAC Rules stating "the case shall be referred to a sole arbitrator, unless the President determines otherwise" should not be interpreted that the President of SIAC having absolute discretion on the composition of the tribunal; on the contrary, when exercising its discretion, the President must give full consideration to the parties' agreement with respect to the composition of the tribunal in order to preserve party autonomy.[112]

The Shanghai Court refused to recognize and enforce an award. It held that the composition of the Tribunal was not in accordance with the parties' arbitration agreement (Article V(1)(d) of the New York Convention). Specifically, the court found that the appointment by SIAC's President of a sole arbitrator was contrary to the parties' express agreement to have a three-member tribunal.[113]

Some authors have underscored the contrast between these two judgments by contending that both the *AQZ* and Noble Resources rulings seem to uphold the

110. *Ibid.*
111. *Ibid.*, §§133-135.
112. *Shanghai Intermediate Court: Noble Resources International Pte. Ltd. v. Shanghai Good Credit International Trade Co., Ltd.*, Hu 01 Xie Wai Ren No. 1 (2017).
113. *Ibid.*

principle of party autonomy in international arbitration.[114] The differentiation arises from the Singapore High Court's decision that adopts a commercially liberal construction and interpretation of the arbitration rules.[115]

[b] *Refusal to Allow Presentation of Witness Evidence*

Article 3(4) of the ICC Expedited Arbitration Provisions states that the arbitration tribunal may decide to limit the number, length and scope of written submissions, including written witness evidence. Therefore, a party dissatisfied with the award may seek its annulment or oppose its recognition and enforcement, alleging that the limitation to present evidence, such as witness evidence, did not allow that party to present its case. In *CBS v. CBP*, the Singapore Court of Appeal analyzed whether the decision of the arbitration tribunal to deny the entirety of the witness evidence constituted a breach of due process such that the award should be set aside:

> We are therefore satisfied that the arbitrator's denial of the *entirety* of the witness evidence from the Buyer constitutes a breach of natural justice. Whilst it is correct that the courts would generally accord a margin of deference to the tribunal's decisions, especially on procedural matters, this is a clear case of a serious breach of the rules of natural justice and to decide otherwise would be to reduce the content of those rules to a vanishing point (emphasis in original).[116]

The case involved an arbitration under the Rules of the Singapore Chamber of Maritime Arbitration (SCMA Rules). The Court upheld the Singapore High Court's earlier decision, setting aside the resulting arbitral award because the denial of witness evidence by the arbitral tribunal was, in fact, a breach of natural justice. When addressing the tribunal's powers under the SCMA Rules, the Singapore Court of Appeal said that "the broad procedural powers of an arbitral tribunal are subject to the fundamental rules of natural justice."[117]

This raises several questions about whether an arbitration conducted under the ICC Expedited Arbitration Proceedings might be seen by the courts as contrary to natural justice because it entitles the tribunal to suppress certain procedural steps. However, as the Singapore Court of Appeal said, even in arbitration conducted under ICC Expedited Arbitration Provisions, "the tribunal must weigh the laudable desire for efficient and effectual arbitral proceedings against the necessity of affording parties their right to be heard."[118]

---

114. Sacchit Joshi & Brijesh Chhatrola, *Expedited Procedure Vis-à-Vis Party Autonomy, Enforceable?* (Kluwer Arbitration Blog 2018).
115. Gary B. Born & Jonathan W. Lim, *AQZ v. ARA: Singapore High Court Upholds Award Made under SIAC Expedited Procedure* (Kluwer Arbitration Blog 2015).
116. Singapore Court of Appeal: *CBS v. CBP* [2021] SGCA 4, Originating Summons No. 215 of 2019 (2021).
117. *Ibid.*, 62.
118. *Ibid.*, 68.

[c] Lack of Reasoned Award

Several expedited arbitration rules, such as those of UNCITRAL, SCC or SIAC, permit rendering unreasoned awards. However, some countries' public policy requires that legal dispute decisions must be properly reasoned.[119] Such a failure may subject an expedited arbitration award to challenge. This should not be a concern under the ICC Expedited Arbitration Provisions because Article 32 explicitly mandates that awards must include the reasons for the decision.

National Courts from different legal systems have adopted different approaches when analyzing the lack of reasoning of an award as a ground for annulment or denial of recognition. In countries like Austria or Spain, the lack of reasoning for an award constitutes a breach of procedural public policy or fundamental principles of their legal systems.[120] In contrast, in Germany, the lack of reasoning for an award has not been considered sufficient to refuse the recognition and enforcement of an award.[121] For example, the High Court of Justice of Galicia, in its judgment of May 2, 2012, underscored the requirement of reasoned arbitral awards under Article 37(4) of the Spanish Arbitration Act. This requirement is considered a fundamental principle within the Spanish legal system, and failure to comply with it would constitute a breach of public policy.[122] In contrast, the OLG Schleswig, in its decision dated March 30, 2000, suggested that failure to provide a reasoned award may not be a sufficient ground to refuse recognition and enforcement.[123] This is particularly true in cases where the law of the State seeking enforcement does not explicitly mandate the provision of a reasoned award.

§8.05 BRIEF COMPARISON OF THE ICC AND UNCITRAL EXPEDITED ARBITRATION RULES

Although the ICC Expedited Procedure Provisions and UNCITRAL Expedited Arbitration Rules each seek to reach a final resolution of disputes in a cost- and time-effective manner by providing for streamlined arbitration with a reduced scale of fees,[124] they have several differences. The ICC Expedited Arbitration Provisions apply automatically once parties reach an agreement for arbitration under the ICC Rules and fulfill the

119. Tarjuelo, Javier, *Fast Track Procedures: A New Trend in Institutional Arbitration*, 11(2) Dispute Resolution International 115 (2017).
120. Spanish Arbitration Act (Ley 60/2003 de 23 de diciembre, de Arbitraje), Article 37.4; Lukic Sebastian and Grill Anne-Karina (Kluwer Arbitration Blog, 2015).
121. OLG Schleswig, March 30, 2000, Docket No. 16 SchH 5/99, in 46 RIW 709 (2000).
122. High Court of Justice of Galicia: Parties' name under confidentiality, RJ 2012, 6364 (May 2, 2012).
123. Germany, Oberlandesgericht Schleswig: Parties' name under confidentiality, Docket No. 16 SchH 5/99, in 46 RIW 709 (2000).
124. *See* Explanatory Note to the UNCITRAL Expedited Arbitration Rules (2021), https://uncitral.un.org/sites/uncitral.un.org/files/mediadocuments/uncitral/en/explanatory_note_to_the_expedited_rules_advance_copy.pdf; International Chamber of Commerce (ICC), *Expedited Procedure Provisions*, ICCWBO, Expedited Procedure Provisions—ICC—International Chamber of Commerce (iccwbo.org).

criteria outlined in Article 30, particularly the monetary threshold.[125] These provisions seamlessly integrate into the broader framework of the ICC Rules. In contrast, the UNCITRAL Expedited Rules stand as a distinct procedure, separate from the UNCITRAL Model Arbitration Rules, which are tailored for ad hoc proceedings. The parties must have agreed that the UNCITRAL Expedited Rules apply.[126] Thus, the ICC's expedited rules apply automatically, while UNCITRAL's model expedited rules apply optionally.[127] This contrast underscores the institutional nature of the ICC expedited procedure.

A second difference is the constitution of the arbitral tribunal. Under the ICC expedited arbitration provisions, the Court may appoint a sole arbitrator, even if the arbitration agreement provides otherwise.[128] Under UNCITRAL's Expedited Rules, the parties' agreement determines the constitution of the Tribunal.[129] Additionally, under the UNCITRAL Expedited Rules, the Permanent Court of Arbitration acts as an appointing authority when parties have not agreed on an appointing authority.[130]

Another difference is the powers that the ICC Court have on arbitration proceedings. For example, under the ICC expedited arbitration rules, the Court may: (i) decide that the expedited arbitration provisions shall no longer apply to the case[131] and (ii) extend the time limit when the arbitral tribunal must render its final award.[132] Under UNCITRAL's Expedited Arbitration Rules, these determinations are left to the arbitral tribunal. Thus, under the ICC Expedited Arbitration Provisions, the Court may make decisions contrary to the parties' wishes, while the UNCITRAL Expedited Rules prefer the parties' agreement over the Tribunal's discretion.

Finally, under UNCITRAL's Expedited Rules, a hearing must be held if the parties request one.[133] In contrast, under Article 3 of the ICC Expedited Arbitration Provisions, the arbitral tribunal has the discretion to decide the dispute solely based on documents.[134]

§8.06 CONCLUSION

The ICC expedited arbitration rules provide a procedure for resolving disputes in a faster and more streamlined manner than regular arbitration. The ICC expedited arbitration procedure is designed for disputes that involve smaller amounts of money

125. ICC Rules, Article 30(2).
126. UNCITRAL Expedited Arbitration Rules, Article 1.
127. Tarjuelo J. Fast Track Procedures: *A New Trend in Institutional Arbitration*, 11(2) Dispute Resolution International (2017), https://www.perezllorca.com/wp content/uploads/es/actualidadPublicaciones/ArticuloJuridico/Documents/javier-tarjuelo-article.pdf.
128. ICC Expedited Procedure Provisions, Article 2(1).
129. UNCITRAL Expedited Arbitration Rules, Article 7 ("*Unless otherwise agreed by the parties, there shall be one arbitrator.*").
130. UNCITRAL Expedited Arbitration Rules, Article 6(1).
131. ICC Expedited Procedure Provisions, Article. 1(4).
132. *Ibid.*, Article. 4.
133. UNCITRAL Expedited Arbitration Rules, Article 11.
134. ICC Expedited Procedure Provisions, Article. 4.

or less complex issues. Both the ICC Expedited Procedure Provisions and the UNCITRAL Expedited Arbitration Rules aim for cost-effective and efficient dispute resolution through streamlined arbitration with reduced fees. However, they differ significantly. The ICC Expedited Arbitration Provisions apply automatically when monetary thresholds are met and are integrated into the ICC Rules. In contrast, the UNCITRAL Expedited Rules require the parties' explicit agreement, making it an optional choice. This means the UNCITRAL Expedited Rules are more respectful of the parties' agreement to arbitrate and the principle of party autonomy.

Under the ICC expedited arbitration procedure, the parties effectively agree to limit the time for the proceedings and to waive certain procedural steps, such as the hearing of witnesses and the production of documents. The ICC expedited procedure also provides for a sole arbitrator, who the ICC Court appoints. Under specific conditions, clauses stipulating a single arbitrator or the omission of certain procedural phases may be perceived by judicial authorities as conflicting with the parties' agreement or infringing upon the due process principles inherent in the public order of the arbitration's seat.

The objective of the ICC's expedited arbitration procedure—to deliver a more efficient and cost-effective approach to dispute resolution while upholding fairness and impartiality—proves especially beneficial for parties seeking swift resolutions while circumventing the time and costs associated with comprehensive arbitration. Notably, the ICC Expedited Arbitration Procedure provisions impose a strict six-month time frame for the tribunal to issue an award. In contrast, the UNCITRAL Expedited Rules allow for a potential extension of three additional months beyond the initial six-month period.

Nevertheless, the ICC Expedited Arbitration Procedure is inappropriate for all disputes. Parties should carefully consider whether it is the right choice for their situation. If it is, the arbitration clause in the relevant contract or agreement should specifically provide for the application of the ICC expedited arbitration procedure. Otherwise, this procedure may not be automatically applicable.

CHAPTER 9

The Australian Approach to Expedited Arbitration: Exploring the 2021 ACICA Rules

Guillermo García-Perrote, Ella Wisniewski & Daniel O'Neil

This chapter explores the expedited arbitration rules introduced by the Australian Centre for International Commercial Arbitration in 2021 (ACICA Expedited Rules). It provides an overview of the key strategies that the ACICA Expedited Rules deploy in order to minimise delay and reduce expense in the conduct of arbitral proceedings. It then considers the efficacy of those strategies, including by comparison to those adopted by other leading arbitral institutions in the Asia-Pacific region. The chapter also reflects on the balancing act at play in all systems of expedited arbitration and considers what may be sacrificed in the quest for speed. The chapter takes a broadly optimistic view of the ACICA Expedited Rules, concluding that the rules are well placed to provide a mode of commercial dispute resolution that is efficient, cost-effective, and credible.

§9.01 INTRODUCTION

On 1 April 2021, the Australian Centre for International Commercial Arbitration (ACICA) published a revised set of arbitration rules (2021 ACICA Rules), which incorporated new rules for the conduct of arbitrations on an expedited basis (ACICA Expedited Rules). This chapter explores the ACICA Expedited Rules in several stages. First, it summarises the key devices that the ACICA Expedited Rules adopt to enable a quicker and more cost-effective arbitral procedure. Second, it considers the likely efficacy of each of these devices. Third, it examines how the ACICA Expedited Rules measure up against the expedited rules adopted by other leading arbitral institutions in the Asia-Pacific region (Singapore, Hong Kong, Malaysia and China). Finally, it reflects on the balancing act involved in any attempt to craft an expedited system for resolving disputes.

Overall, the ACICA Expedited Rules impose a welcome regime of discipline, which will go a considerable way towards reducing the most serious drags on efficiency in international arbitration, the effects of which are particularly felt in the context of lower-value claims. The ACICA Expedited Rules measure up well against other comparable expedited rules in the Asia-Pacific region, mirroring the best features of other institutions' rules in many respects and innovating in others. They provide a form of dispute resolution that is speedy and cost-effective but which does not, in achieving that speed and cost-effectiveness, unduly sacrifice procedural integrity or the quality of arbitral decision-making.

§9.02 THE ACICA EXPEDITED RULES IN CONTEXT

Litigation of commercial disputes in the courts has many merits. Speed, however, is not traditionally one of them. Indeed, lamentations on courts' interminable delays - and the resulting expense - can be found at least as far back as the Roman Principate.[1] Arbitration has historically been trumpeted as a solution to these woes, as a means by which commercial people could achieve a brisk and reasonably priced resolution of disagreements into which they may fall. Arbitration, it was said, enabled parties to secure a speedy hearing, to reduce the costs of litigation and to have a sensible and experienced person look at a problem in a more informal way than courts typically do in order to determine the dispute with greater speed than typically the court system can offer.[2] No longer would businesspeople be required to trudge through the tedious and costly mire of the courts to have their agreements enforced and wrongs against them righted.

Around the world, statutes passed in the name of facilitating the resolution of disputes by arbitration contain statements of purpose expounding the purported benefits of this non-curial method of resolving disputes. The Australian states' respective *Commercial Arbitration Acts* are typical in this regard, announcing that their 'paramount object ... is to facilitate the fair and final resolution of commercial disputes by impartial arbitral tribunals without unnecessary delay or expense'.[3] Similar statements of purpose may be found in the equivalent Acts of, *inter alia*, England and Wales[4] and Hong Kong.[5]

However, the practical reality of arbitration has not always realised this intent. In recent years, an increasingly loud chorus of academics, practitioners and users have voiced concerns that international arbitration is too slow and expensive.[6] As the Chief

1. *See generally Hodgson v. Amcor Ltd.* (2011) 32 V.R. 495, 500; [2011] V.S.C. 63 [11] (Vickery J.).
2. *Ferris v. Plaister* (1994) 34 N.S.W.L.R. 474, 490 (Kirby P.).
3. *Commercial Arbitration Act 2010* (NSW) section 1C(1); *Commercial Arbitration Act 2013* (Qld) section 1AC(1); *Commercial Arbitration Act 2011* (SA) section 1C(1); *Commercial Arbitration Act 2011* (Tas) section 1C(1); *Commercial Arbitration Act 2011* (Vic) section 1AC(1); *Commercial Arbitration Act 2012* (WA) section 1C(1).
4. *Arbitration Act 1996* (England and Wales and Northern Ireland) section 1.
5. *Arbitration Ordinance* (Hong Kong) cap. 609, section 3(1).
6. *See, e.g.*, Jan Paulsson, *Fast-Track Arbitration in Europe (With Special Reference to the WIPO Expedited Arbitration Rules)*, 18 Hastings Int'l & Compar. L. Rev 713, 713 (1995); David Hacking

Justice of Singapore succinctly declared, 'The myth that international arbitration is to be preferred over litigation because it is a simpler and more cost-effective method of dispute resolution has long been shattered.'[7] Consideration of the precise reasons for this apparent gap between promise and reality - an assessment, for example, of allegations that arbitration has become pathologically 'judicialized'[8] - is beyond the scope of this chapter. For present purposes, it suffices to say that it is at least partly in response to such criticisms that expedited arbitration procedures such as those embodied in the ACICA Expedited Rules were created, and it is therefore relevant to consider them against this backdrop.

§9.03 KEY FEATURES OF THE ACICA EXPEDITED RULES

[A] Criteria for Application

The 2021 ACICA Rules provide that prior to an arbitral tribunal being constituted in a given matter, a party may make an application to ACICA for the proceedings to be conducted in accordance with the ACICA Expedited Rules. This option is available where the amount in dispute is less than AUD 5,000,000;[9] where the parties agree (in writing) to the application of the ACICA Expedited Rules;[10] or where 'it is a case of exceptional urgency'.[11] The 'exceptional urgency' criterion appears to suggest that the ACICA Expedited Rules may apply in circumstances where at least one party has not consented to the arbitration being so conducted.

---

and Michael E Schneider, *Towards More Cost-Effective Arbitration*, 3 Int'l Bar Ass'n Newsl. (Arb. and ADR) 26, 26 (1998); Klaus Peter Berger, *The Need for Speed in International Arbitration: Supplementary Rules for Expedited Proceedings of the German Institution of Arbitration (DIS)*, 25 J. Int'l Arb. 595, 595-596 (2008) DOI: 10.54648/joia2008046; Peter Morton, *Can a World Exist Where International Arbitration Becomes the Default Procedure?*, 26 Arb. Int'l 103, 104 (2010) DOI: 10.1093/arbitration/26.1.103; Constantine Partasides and Ben Prewett, *Rediscovering the Lost Promise of International Arbitration* in *Expedited Procedures in International Arbitration* 110, 110 (Laurent Lévy & Michael Polkinghorne eds, Kluwer Law International 2017); Haflidi Kristjan Larusson, *Expedited Arbitration – Meeting the Needs of SMEs*, 63 Scandinavian Stud. L. 169, 179 (2017).

7. Sundaresh Menon, *Some Cautionary Notes for an Age of Opportunity*, 79 Arb. 393, 397 (2013).
8. *See, e.g.*, Günther J. Horvath, *The Judicialization of International Arbitration: Does the Increasing Introduction of Litigation-Style Practices, Regulations, Norms and Structures into International Arbitration Risk a Denial of Justice in International Business Disputes?* in *International Arbitration and International Commercial Law: Synergy, Convergence and Evolution* (Stefan M Kröll et al., eds, Kluwer Law International, 2011); Leon Trakman & Hugh Montgomery, *The 'Judicialization' of International Commercial Arbitration: Pitfall or Virtue?*, 30 Leiden J. Int'l L. 405 (2017) DOI: 10.1017/s0922156517000024.
9. Approximately USD 3,172,000 or EUR 3,030,000 as at 3 October 2023. *Ibid.*, Appendix A cl. 2.2 provides that the amount in dispute is to be calculated by adding claims, counterclaims and any set-off defences. Claims for interest are not to be included in this calculation unless the interest claimed exceeds the principal claimed, in which case only the claim for interest is included.
10. ACICA Expedited Rules Article 2.1.
11. 2021 ACICA Rules Article 8.

[B] Constitution of the Tribunal

The ACICA Expedited Rules provide that a tribunal must consist of a single arbitrator,[12] who is to be appointed by ACICA within 14 days of the arbitration commencing.[13] Challenges to ACICA's choice of arbitrator are permitted within seven days of the tribunal's appointment.[14]

[C] Conduct of the Proceedings

The ACICA Expedited Rules adopt a flexible, tribunal-driven approach to determining how proceedings will be conducted. Subject to the ACICA Expedited Rules themselves, the arbitrator may conduct the proceedings 'in such manner as he or she considers appropriate', so long as 'the parties are treated equally and … each party is given a reasonable opportunity of presenting their case'.[15] However, the arbitrator is only permitted to proceed *ex aequo et bono* or as an *amiable compositeur* if, first, the parties have expressly authorised them to do so, and, second, such an approach is permissible under the applicable law.[16] Arbitrators are also obliged to 'adopt suitable procedures for the conduct of the arbitration in order to avoid unnecessary delay and expense'.[17] To facilitate the achievement of this objective, the arbitrator is expressly permitted to harness videoconferencing and other virtual technologies to hold procedural conferences or hear witnesses.[18]

[D] Restrictions on Submissions

The compression of the timeline for the service of the parties' submissions or pleadings is another means by which the ACICA Expedited Rules seek to minimise delay. A claimant's statement of claim must be contained within (and filed simultaneously with) their notice of arbitration.[19] This rule naturally expedites the close of submissions in a given set of proceedings. Amendments to statements of claim and defence are strictly controlled. Such amendments may only be made with leave of the tribunal, having 'regard to the delay in making it or prejudice to the other party or any other circumstances it considers relevant, including the overriding objective' set out in the broader 2021 ACICA Rules.[20] That is, 'to provide arbitration that is timely, cost effective and fair, considering especially the amounts in dispute and complexity of issues or facts involved'.[21]

12. *Ibid.*, Article 9.1.
13. *Ibid.*, Article 9.2.
14. *Ibid.*, Articles 10-11.
15. *Ibid.*, Article 14.1.
16. *Ibid.*, Article 30.2. This element of the ACICA Expedited Rules is explored in further detail below.
17. *Ibid.*, Article 14.2.
18. *Ibid.*, Article 14.3.
19. *Ibid.*, Article 18.1.
20. *Ibid.*, Article 20.
21. 2021 ACICA Rules Article 3.

[E] Restrictions on Document Production

The ACICA Expedited Rules state that '[t]here shall be no discovery'.[22] The term 'discovery' is not defined (nor does that term appear in the 2021 ACICA Rules). The drafters of the ACICA Expedited Rules presumably intended 'discovery' to be read in the general sense that an Australian legal practitioner would understand it, that is, to refer to the practice peculiar to common law systems, whereby parties to litigation can be compelled to produce to one another, for inspection and copying, all the documents in their possession or control which contain information that may assist another party to advance its own case or to damage the case of the disclosing party.[23]

Despite this apparently wholesale rejection of discovery, the ACICA Expedited Rules do provide that the tribunal may compel parties 'to produce such particular documents as he or she may believe to be relevant'.[24] There is no express mechanism by which a party may request that the tribunal require another party to produce documents in its possession. However, ACICA Expedited Rules Article 5 contemplates communications by parties with the arbitrator outside the context of formal pleadings. In combination with the broad discretion granted to the tribunal by ACICA Expedited Rules Article 14.2, this could allow a party to make a request to the tribunal that another party disclose particular documents in their possession. Ultimately, the tribunal must decide whether that party in fact ought to be compelled to produce those documents.

[F] Presumption Against Oral Hearings

The default position under the ACICA Expedited Rules is that no oral hearings will be held unless two conditions are met.[25] First, the arbitrator must determine that 'exceptional circumstances' exist, such as to justify an oral hearing, and, second, either the arbitrator or the parties must 'require a hearing to take place'. Where these conditions are met and an oral hearing is held, the hearing cannot, absent special provision by the tribunal, exceed one working day in length.[26] The ACICA Expedited Rules stipulate that the tribunal 'may decide where the proceedings shall be conducted', including whether they ought to be held 'in person or virtually'.[27] Therefore, where oral hearings are held, they need not be conducted in person. It is relevant to note that, given Australia's distance from many of its regional neighbours (e.g., it is more than an eight-hour flight from Singapore to Sydney, almost a 10-hour flight from Tokyo, and more than 10 hours from Seoul), the time and cost expended in travelling to a single physical venue is often significant.

22. ACICA Expedited Rules Article 24.4.
23. *Expense Reduction Analysts Group Pty. Ltd. v. Armstrong Strategic Management & Marketing Pty. Ltd.* (2013) 250 C.L.R. 303, 319; [2013] H.C.A. 46 [44] (French C.J., Kiefel, Bell, Gageler and Keane JJ.).
24. ACICA Expedited Rules Article 24.5.
25. *Ibid.*, Article 24.6.
26. *Ibid.*, Article 24.7.
27. *Ibid.*, Article 14.3.

[G] Tribunal May Proceed Notwithstanding Parties' Failure to File Documents or Appear at Hearings

Finally, the ACICA Expedited Rules aim to reduce delays by permitting tribunals to take a hard-line approach where parties fail to meet deadlines for pleadings, appear at hearings (if they are held) or produce documents (if such production is ordered). In each case, the tribunal is expressly empowered to forge ahead and make determinations, regardless of the party's default.[28] Parties will be quite readily taken to have waived their right to object to procedural non-compliance by other parties or the tribunal.[29] Both provisions are likely to reduce the scope for trivial interlocutory squabbles or allegations that a party has been denied procedural fairness.

[H] Ethical Obligations on Parties and Practitioners

The ACICA Expedited Rules require that parties apply their 'best endeavours' to ensure that their legal representatives comply with the International Bar Association Guidelines on Party Representation in International Arbitration (the IBA Guidelines).[30] The IBA Guidelines set standards for parties' conduct in relation to, *inter alia*, dealings with lay and expert witnesses, document production, and communications with the tribunal.

[I] Deadlines for Handing Down the Award

The ACICA Expedited Rules provide for awards to be handed down relatively rapidly. The tribunal must render an award within four months of its appointment if the proceedings do not involve any counterclaim (or any claim for set-off) or five months of its appointment if the proceedings do involve any counterclaim (or any claim for set-off).[31] To help facilitate the achievement of these deadlines, the ACICA Expedited Rules provide that the tribunal must state the reasons for its decision in summary form, unless the parties have agreed that no reasons are required.[32] Thus, it is arguably not open to the arbitrator to provide detailed reasons in the award, even where the parties may desire these.

§9.04 COMPARISON WITH ACICA'S 2016 EXPEDITED RULES

The current ACICA Expedited Rules are not the first to have been published by ACICA. Its first expedited rules appeared in 2008, and revised forms of expedited procedure accompanied ACICA's 2011 and 2016 rules. In substance, the rules have remained

28. *Ibid.*, Articles 26.1, 26.2 and 26.3.
29. *Ibid.*, Article 27.
30. *Ibid.*, Article 7.2.
31. *Ibid.*, Article 28.
32. *Ibid.*, Article 29.3.

broadly consistent from 2008 to 2021. That said, the 2021 ACICA Expedited Rules introduce welcome new features. These include express stipulations about how parties are to communicate with the arbitrator and with each other, an express power to tribunals to grant early dismissal of a claim, and the express imposition of a *Harman* obligation on parties.[33] Most significantly, the 2021 ACICA Expedited Rules incorporate, for the first time, a number of innovations that expressly recognise and implement recent advances in communications technology. These innovations commendably remove any lingering doubt about such technology's permissibility and thereby any reluctance by tribunals to use that technology to ensure that proceedings are conducted as efficiently as possible.

For example, under the 2021 ACICA Expedited Rules, tribunals are expressly authorised to use videoconferencing or 'other communications technology' to conduct preliminary procedural conferences.[34] The 2016 rules had stated, somewhat more ambiguously, that such conferences could be arranged 'by telephone or other means'.[35] Because this did not make plain that a conference could permissibly be held over, say, Microsoft® Teams, the ambiguity may well have encouraged tribunals to abjure such technology out of an abundance of caution. More broadly, the 2021 ACICA Expedited Rules empower tribunals to hear witnesses and undertake proceedings 'virtually' where the tribunal deems this appropriate.[36] In this regard, the 2021 ACICA Expedited Rules also make clear that where hearings are held virtually, they are 'deemed to be held at the seat' (barring party agreement or the tribunal's stipulation to the contrary).[37] They also provide that tribunals may sign and issue awards electronically.[38]

§9.05 ANALYSIS OF THE ACICA EXPEDITED RULES

[A] Overview

What is the likely efficacy of the key features of the ACICA Expedited Rules? Considering some of the chief vectors of excessive delay and cost in arbitration, are the ACICA Expedited Rules likely to address those issues?

[B] Fewer Arbitrators

A tribunal of three (or indeed more) arbitrators has its advantages. The scrutiny of a dispute by three esteemed minds rather than one is likely, all other things being equal, to enhance the quality of the resulting award. Moreover, parties may place consider

33. *Ibid.*, Articles 6, 14.5 and 15.3. The *Harman* obligation (also referred to as the *Harman* undertaking) is a rule derived from the common law. In substance, it prevents parties from using or disclosing information obtained in a litigation for a collateral or ulterior purpose outside of the proceedings: *see Harman v. Secretary of State for the Home Department* [1983] 1 A.C. 280.
34. *Ibid.*, Article 14.2.
35. 2016 ACICA Expedited Rules Article 13.2.
36. ACICA Expedited Rules Article 14.3.
37. *Ibid.*, Article 16.2.
38. *Ibid.*, Articles 29.4 and 29.5.

able value on the right to nominate one of the arbitrators and have input on the chair of the tribunal. However, such tribunals may also bring certain inefficiencies, particularly in the context of expedited arbitration proceedings. Where there is more than one arbitrator, the preparation of an award will involve a process of conferral, including exchanges of draft awards between the arbitrators. This process will likely be more time-consuming than a single arbitrator preparing his or her draft in solitude.[39] Multiple arbitrators also means multiple calendars that must be managed. In most cases, finding a free slot for a hearing or a procedural conference that accommodates the availabilities of three arbitrators will be more difficult than accommodating the availability of a single arbitrator.[40] By mandatorily stipulating that tribunals will be constituted of single arbitrators, the ACICA Expedited Rules avoid these pitfalls, and so, to that extent, should provide for a more efficient arbitral process.

[C] Curtailing Document Production Limits Scope for Procedural Snarl-Ups

A judge of the Supreme Court of Queensland once opined, 'In most substantial civil cases, too many documents are collected, copied, scanned, reviewed, discovered and put into a 'trial bundle'. This comes at a great cost, and it impedes access to justice.'[41] Decades of scholarship suggest that document production is 'the procedure most open to abuse, the most costly and the most in need of court supervision and control'.[42] Procedural abuses arise both in how requests for document disclosure are crafted and how parties respond to such requests.[43]

For example, parties may pursue oppressively broad demands for documents with the intention of harassing or vexing opponents.[44] In responding to requests, parties may adopt a deliberately obstructive posture by 'refusing to provide or destroy[ing] or conceal[ing] relevant documentation which might have assisted the other side'.[45] Alternatively, they may produce an avalanche of documents, either to force the recipient to expend as much time and money as possible in sifting the relevant from the irrelevant or to conceal the proverbially damaging needle within a haystack of irrelevant documents.[46] It is little wonder that the 2021 International Arbitration

39. International Bar Association, *Consistency, Efficiency and Transparency in Investment Treaty Arbitration* (Report, November 2018) 39.
40. *Ibid.*
41. Peter Applegarth, *The Rise of Documents and the Disappearance of Witnesses*, speech at Australian Lawyers' Alliance National Conference, Yeppoon, 20 October 2011, 1, https://archive.sclqld.org.au/judgepub/2011/applegarth201011.pdf.
42. Australian Law Reform Commission, *Managing Justice: A Review of the Civil Justice System*, Report 89 (2000) 431 [6.67].
43. *Ibid.*, 431-432 [6.67]-[6.68]. *See also* Peter Vickery, *Managing the Paper: Taming the Leviathan*, 22 J. Jud. Admin. 51, 62-63 (2012).
44. Australian Law Reform Commission, *supra* n. 42, 431-432 [6.68].
45. *Ibid.*
46. *Ibid. See also* Edna Sussman & Solomon Ebere, *All's Fair in Love and War – Or Is It? Reflections on Ethical Standards for Counsel in International Arbitration*, 22 Am. Rev. Int'l Arb. 611, 613 (2011).

Survey conducted by Queen Mary University identified document production as one of the features of the arbitral process that users would be most open to forgo for the sake of efficiency.[47]

Viewed in this context, the near-total abandonment of discovery (in the common law litigation sense) is one of the most meaningful steps the ACICA Expedited Rules take towards remedying the causes of excess delay and expense in arbitral proceedings. By restricting the compulsory production of documents to those that the tribunal itself regards as relevant, the ACICA Expedited Rules remove the process from the hands of the parties and place it squarely within the tribunal's control. In so doing, the ACICA Expedited Rules necessarily limit the freedom of the parties to conduct the proceedings as they choose. This limitation may seem striking in the context of arbitration, a forum where party autonomy is treated with near-sacred reverence.[48] However, as cardinal a principle as party autonomy may be in arbitration, it must be recognised that untrammelled autonomy comes with its own costs.

[D] Appropriateness of Monetary Thresholds

Some commentators have queried whether a simple currency-value threshold for the application of expedited arbitration rules is appropriate.[49] In one view, the monetary value of a given claim cannot reliably be used as a proxy for that claim's complexity or for the time and effort it will take to be resolved before an arbitral tribunal. A claim for a relatively small sum of money may raise fiendishly complex issues of law and fact that could prove totally inappropriate for expedited arbitration. Equally, parties may have doctrinally and evidentially straightforward issues in connection with very large sums of money. Thus, an element of arbitrariness exists in the choice of a particular currency-value threshold.

The ACICA Expedited Rules do not explain why a threshold of AUD 5,000,000 was chosen as opposed, for example, a threshold of AUD 1,000,000. There is also no apparent mechanism to account for inflation, which will necessarily cause a greater number of disputes to fall within the AUD 5,000,000 threshold as time passes. Nor is there any officially sanctioned means by which foreign exchange conversions are to be calculated for the purposes of satisfying the AUD 5,000,000 threshold. Fluctuations in the value of a given currency against the Australian dollar could well cause a given dispute to reach the AUD 5,000,000 threshold on one day, but fall below it on the next.

Nevertheless, the simple fact remains that the impact of procedural inefficiencies is more keenly felt where the monetary value of a claim is lower. And although

47. Queen Mary University of London and White & Case, *2021 International Arbitration Survey: Adapting Arbitration to a Changing World* (Report, 2021) 5.
48. *See, e.g.*, *Rinehart v. Welker* (2011) 93 N.S.W.L.R. 311, 323-324; [2011] N.S.W.C.A. 403 [42] (Bathurst C.J. and McColl J.A.); *Indian Farmers Fertiliser Cooperative Ltd. v. Gutnick* (2015) 304 F.L.R. 199, 208; [2015] V.S.C. 724 [22] (Croft J.).
49. *See, e.g.*, Chan Leng Sun & Tan Weiyi, *Making Arbitration Effective: Expedited Procedures, Emergency Arbitrators and Interim Relief*, 6 Contemp. Asia Arb. J. 349, 358 (2013); Hamish Lal & Brendan Casey, *Ten Years Later: Why the 'Renaissance of Expedited Arbitration' Should Be the 'Emergency Arbitration' of 2020*, 37 J. Int'l Arb. 325, 336-337 (2020) DOI: 10.54648/joia2020015.

monetary thresholds are not a simple proxy for the complexity of a matter, they do provide at least one means by which a matter's *likely* complexity may be assessed by an observer (at a glance). For these reasons, despite its inherent arbitrariness, a monetary threshold makes sense simply as a pragmatic measure. Importantly, the rigidity of this monetary threshold is mitigated by the fact that it is not the only metric by which the appropriateness of the rules' application is assessed. Rather, the AUD 5,000,000 ceiling is just one of three possible ways that the ACICA Expedited Rules may be applied in a given dispute (along with party consent and the existence of 'exceptional urgency').[50]

[E] Delay Caused by Arbitrators and Parties' Lack of Availability

Another source of delay which the ACICA Expedited Rules seek to address is delay occasioned by the limited availability of arbitrators and counsel. In the world of international arbitration, experienced arbitrators typically find themselves highly sought after by parties,[51] and their diaries fill quickly as they take on appointments. Once such an individual is appointed in a given matter, the parties involved will often find themselves at the mercy of that diary. To a lesser extent, the same phenomenon is observable with respect to sought-after arbitration counsel.[52] In an effort to address this, the ACICA Expedited Rules require would-be arbitrators to 'sign a statement of availability' before they will be considered for appointment.[53]

There may well be more effective means of assessing arbitrators' availability. For example, the International Centre for Settlement of Investment Disputes (ICSID) frequently requires arbitrators to disclose their calendars to its Secretariat in order to give an indication of their likely availabilities if appointed. The need for such measures is arguably greater in an investor-State context, given the notoriously slow progress of investor-State proceedings[54] and the particularly small pool of practitioners who are repeatedly appointed. Bearing in mind that the ACICA Expedited Rules are intended to govern disputes of a significantly lower quantum, parties to such disputes will often be willing to brief or appoint from a much broader pool of practitioners.

Ultimately, even where preventative measures such as ICSID's 'open calendar' method are deployed, there are likely to be few (if any) consequences for arbitrators who have overcommitted and, as a result, defaulted on timetabled deadlines. Some jurisdictions have sought to address this via the threat of award annulment. As explored in a recent Privy Council decision, Mauritius' *Civil Procedure Code* provides that an arbitrator's mandate to determine a dispute expires six months from the date of their appointment, unless the arbitration agreement provides otherwise, or unless the parties agree to an extension. Any award delivered after that expiration will be open to

50. 2021 ACICA Rules Article 8.1.
51. Lucy Greenwood, *The Rise, Fall and Rise of International Arbitration: A View from 2030*, 77 Arb. 435, 436 (2011).
52. Morton, *supra* n. 6, 105.
53. ACICA Expedited Rules Article 9.3.
54. International Bar Association, *supra* n. 39, 41.

annulment.[55] This provides a compelling incentive for Mauritian arbitrators to comply with procedural deadlines. However, how such consequences benefit the parties who, having arrived at the end of a lengthy (and costly) process, would then face significant uncertainty as to the enforceability of the award is difficult to discern.

[F] Parties' Misbehaviour and Misfortune

There is a further stumbling block that not even the most carefully drafted arbitral rules are likely ever to fully overcome: skulduggery by the parties themselves and unavoidable contingencies in the lives of parties, lawyers and arbitrators. While participants in the world of arbitration may wish it were otherwise, tribunals ultimately cannot force participants to do (or refrain from doing) certain things. They can merely lay down incentives for compliance and consequences for non-compliance. As Lord Mustill once put it, 'the only way to get arbitration back on to the fast track' is for all involved to adopt 'a new psychology'.[56] In other words, no matter how carefully crafted a given set of expedited arbitral rules may be, they will remain 'an empty shell' unless its participants (including the arbitral tribunal) commit themselves seriously to conducting the proceedings with an appropriate degree of despatch.[57]

Legal practitioners in most jurisdictions are subject to stringent ethical and professional obligations.[58] However, lawyers perhaps inevitably will engage in various forms of sharp practice in the name of gaining some tactical advantage or other in the course of a dispute. For example, and avoiding scenarios of flagrant misconduct, they may seek to deliberately prolong proceedings through exaggerated or even meritless objections to evidence.[59] Such tactics frequently have delay either as their express object or as a collateral consequence. Policing tactics of this kind has proven particularly difficult in the context of international arbitration. Counsel may be admitted to practise in a range of jurisdictions with differing professional obligations. As a result, a course of conduct regarded as entirely unremarkable in one jurisdiction may be grounds for professional sanction in another.[60] Even where some breach of an obligation can be clearly identified, tribunals are often powerless to levy sanctions on rogue practitioners.[61]

The ACICA Expedited Rules attempt to mitigate this risk by stipulating that parties must use their best endeavours to ensure that their lawyers adhere to the IBA Guidelines.[62] The IBA Guidelines, in turn, arm tribunals with the ability to admonish

55. *Alphamix Ltd. v. District Council of Rivière du Rempart* [2023] U.K.P.C. 20 [1] (Lord Leggatt).
56. Michael Mustill, *Comments on Fast-Track Arbitration*, 10 J. Int'l Arb. 121, 125 (1993) DOI: 10.54648/joia1993034.
57. Berger, *supra* n. 6, 608.
58. *See, e.g.*, *Legal Profession Uniform Law Application Act 2014* (NSW); *Legal Profession Uniform Law Application Act 2014* (Vic); *Legal Profession Uniform Law Application Act 2022* (WA).
59. Sussman & Ebere, *supra* n. 46, 613-615.
60. *See ibid.*, 611.
61. *Ibid.*
62. ACICA Expedited Rules Article 7.2.

lawyers for their misconduct, draw adverse inferences against those lawyers' clients and factor misconduct into decisions to award costs.[63] Therefore, if a tribunal presiding over expedited proceedings takes the view that a party has not used their best endeavours to comply with the IBA Guidelines, this could factor into the tribunal's exercise of its discretion to apportion costs.[64]

Whether the threat of adverse cost orders is sufficient to deter misconduct is questionable, but it is equally open to question whether any arbitral tribunal could deploy strict disciplinary powers. This is especially so given that (among other reasons) the foundation of arbitration lies ultimately in the consent of all involved and because tribunals are not able to directly avail themselves of the coercive powers of the state in the way that courts are.[65] Moreover, the reality is that practitioners and client instructors alike are human and as such are vulnerable to the proverbial slings and arrows of outrageous fortune, including illness, accidents, and the like, that can either physically or psychologically prevent them from meeting an arbitral tribunal's procedural deadlines. Such matters are beyond the control of any institution, no matter how stringent its rules.

§9.06 THE ACICA EXPEDITED RULES IN COMPARATIVE PERSPECTIVE

[A] Overview and Assessment

Arbitral institutions in the Asia-Pacific region have adopted different approaches in seeking to achieve the promise of a speedy and efficient form of dispute resolution. The ACICA Expedited Rules have adopted a different approach relative to its peers.[66] Although each institution has adopted broadly similar measures to combat delay and other inefficiencies, there are important points of distinction between them. Key examples include whether there is a presumption against multi-arbitrator tribunals and whether it is possible for an expedited procedure to be imposed in the absence of the parties' agreement. In certain respects, the ACICA Expedited Rules adopt bolder measures than other institutions, for example, in fortifying the presumption against the holding of oral hearings. In so doing, the ACICA Expedited Rules have been able to draw from the best of other institutional rules in the Asia-Pacific region and, in some respects, go further in pursuing the effective and efficient conduct of expedited proceedings.

63. International Bar Association Guidelines on Party Representation in International Arbitration cl. 26.
64. ACICA Expedited Rules Article 38.
65. *See generally* Catherine A. Rogers, *Fit and Functional in Legal Ethics: Developing a Code of Conduct for International Arbitration*, 23 Mich. J. Int'l L. 341, 341 (2002).
66. Namely, the Singapore International Arbitration Centre (the SIAC Rules), the Hong Kong International Arbitration Centre (the HKIAC Rules), the Asian International Arbitration Centre (the AIAC Expedited Rules), and the China International Economic and Trade Arbitration Commission (the CIETAC Rules).

[B] Criteria for the Application of the Rules

Each of the ACICA Expedited Rules, SIAC Rules, HKIAC Rules and CIETAC Rules include a monetary threshold as one criterion (beyond express agreement by the parties) for their application in a given dispute. For the ACICA Expedited Rules, this threshold is AUD 5,000,000.[67] For the SIAC Rules, it is SGD 6,000,000 (or approximately AUD 6,773,000).[68] For the HKIAC Rules, it is HKD 25,000,000 (or approximately AUD 4,792,000) as of March 2023.[69] The HKIAC Rules have in-built flexibility in this respect, stipulating that the applicable monetary threshold is that published on HKIAC's website from time to time.[70] For the CIETAC Rules, the applicable threshold is RMB 5,000,000 (or approximately AUD 1,095,000).[71] By contrast, the AIAC Expedited Rules do not specify a monetary threshold; they will apply simply where there is an agreement by the parties to that effect.[72]

A key point of distinction between the various rules is whether they permit expedited arbitration to occur even where one party does not consent to that course. The ACICA Expedited Rules, SIAC Rules and HKIAC Rules each may apply 'in cases of exceptional urgency'.[73] The AIAC Expedited Rules and CIETAC Rules, however, cannot apply without the agreement of both parties.[74] In this respect, the ACICA, SIAC and HKIAC position is preferable. This is because some recipients of notices of arbitration (or counterclaims) have no interest in a speedy resolution of the claims. On the contrary, many respondents will regard delaying the matter for as long as possible as their primary strategic objective, even where their legal position is devoid of merit.[75] Requiring such respondents' consent as a precondition for the application of an expedited arbitral procedure simply arms those respondents with another weapon by which to prejudice claimants' interests.

[C] Constitution of the Tribunal

Generally, the various institutions' rules favour determination of expedited arbitrations by sole arbitrators, although they vary in the degree to which they compel parties to adopt this approach. The ACICA Expedited Rules are perhaps the most stringent in this regard. They stipulate that '[t]here shall be one arbitrator',[76] with no apparent scope for the addition of further arbitrators under any circumstances. The SIAC Rules similarly

67. Approximately USD 3,172,000 or EUR 3,030,000 as at 3 October 2023. ACICA Expedited Rules Article 8.1.
68. Approximately USD 4,365,548 or EUR 4,169,856 as at 3 October 2023. SIAC Rules R. 5.1.
69. Approximately USD 3,192,785 or EUR 3,049,847 as at 3 October 2023.
70. HKIAC Rules Article 42.1; Hong Kong International Arbitration Centre, '2018 Schedule of Fees' https://www.hkiac.org/content/2018-schedule-fees.
71. Approximately USD 688,259 or EUR 658,076 as at 3 October 2023. CIETAC Rules Article 56(1).
72. AIAC Expedited Rules Article 1.1.
73. ACICA Expedited Rules Article 8.1(c); SIAC Rules R. 5.1(c); HKIAC Rules Article 42.1(c).
74. AIAC Expedited Rules R. 1.1; CIETAC Rules Article 56.1.
75. Mustill, *supra* n. 56, 125.
76. ACICA Expedited Rules Article 9.1.

take this decision out of the parties' hands, but they do envision that the President of SIAC may determine that a larger tribunal is appropriate in a given case.[77]

By contrast, the HKIAC Rules, AIAC Expedited Rules and CIETAC Rules merely indicate that determination by a sole arbitrator is the default position, which may be overridden by the parties' agreement.[78] The HKIAC Rules do, however, evince a soft, non-mandatory preference for matters to be heard by a sole arbitrator. Where the arbitration agreement in a given matter provides for a tribunal of three, the parties must be invited – but cannot be compelled – to consider referring the matter to a single arbitrator.[79]

[D] Conduct of the Proceedings

The ACICA Expedited Rules' tribunal-driven approach to procedure corresponds to that of the SIAC Rules, HKIAC Rules and AIAC Expedited Rules. In this respect, the SIAC Rules provide that the tribunal is free to 'conduct the arbitration in such manner as it considers appropriate', which includes the freedom to apply or not apply the applicable law's rules of evidence.[80] Similarly, the AIAC Expedited Rules provide that the tribunal 'may conduct the arbitration in such manner as it deems appropriate', providing a non-exhaustive list of examples of permissible exercises of this power. This includes dispensing with the rules of evidence (or applying 'any rules of evidence') and adopting a civil law-style inquisitorial approach by which the tribunal 'shall itself take the initiative in identifying relevant issues', subject to the stipulation that the parties may agree to exclude each of these.[81] Likewise, the HKIAC Rules also provide generally that the tribunal 'shall adopt suitable procedures for the conduct of the arbitration in order to avoid unnecessary delay or expense', bearing in mind the complexity of the issues, the quantum in dispute, the available technology and considerations of procedural fairness.[82] This flexibility extends to allowing the tribunal to determine 'whether to apply strict rules of evidence'.[83] Finally, the CIETAC Rules provide that the tribunal 'may examine the case in the manner it considers appropriate'.[84]

The ACICA Expedited Rules expressly empower a tribunal to proceed with an arbitration notwithstanding a party's failure to file particular documents or appear at a hearing (if one is held). This device finds analogues in the SIAC Rules[85] and HKIAC Rules.[86] The AIAC Expedited Rules expressly permit arbitrators to adopt such an

77. SIAC Rules R. 5.2(b).
78. HKIAC Rules Article 42.2(a); AIAC Expedited Rules R. 4(2)-(3); CIETAC Rules Article 58.
79. HKIAC Rules Article 42.2(b).
80. SIAC Rules RR. 19.1, 19.2.
81. AIAC Expedited Rules R. 7(4).
82. HKIAC Rules Article 13.1.
83. HKIAC Rules Article 22.2.
84. CIETAC Rules Article 60.
85. SIAC Rules RR. 20.9, 24 and 27(l).
86. HKIAC Rules Article 26.3.

approach with respect to parties' failure to attend hearings only,[87] while the CIETAC Expedited Rules do so in circumstances where a party fails to attend a hearing or to file its evidence.[88] Comparable rules providing for the ready waiver of parties' objections for procedural non-compliance also exist in the SIAC Rules,[89] HKIAC Rules[90] and CIETAC Expedited Rules.[91]

[E] Document Production (or Lack Thereof)

The ACICA Expedited Rules contain the most emphatic rejection of the traditional common law approach to document production: 'There shall be no discovery.'[92] However, the relatively tight control of document production is a common thread across each of these rules. The ACICA Expedited Rules,[93] SIAC Rules,[94] HKIAC Rules[95] and AIAC Expedited Rules[96] all empower the tribunal to direct parties to produce documents relevant to particular issues in dispute in a given proceeding but grant the parties no right for broader discovery in the conventional sense. Document production is even more restricted under the CIETAC Rules, which apparently only contemplate the compulsory production of documents in relation to a process by which tribunals are permitted to 'consult experts or appoint appraisers for clarification on specific issues of the case'.[97]

Of these approaches, those adopted by the ACICA Expedited Rules, SIAC Rules, HKIAC Rules and AIAC Expedited Rules provide a sensible middle ground. Restrictions on document production are a welcome means of addressing one of the main generators of cost and delay in arbitral proceedings. However, some form of targeted document production will likely be necessary for the proper consideration and resolution of most disputes. This is especially so where the dispute hinges on a factual question, and where a document that would dispose of that factual question is in the possession of only one party (and damaging to that party's case). In such a case, the tribunal possessing a flexible power to compel production of certain documents would be a great aid to the efficient determination of the dispute. Restricting that power as the CIETAC Rules do – that is, permitting arbitrators to use the power only for the purpose of facilitating the preparation of expert evidence of various kinds – is likely to place many such documents beyond the scope of the power.

87. AIAC Expedited Rules R. 18(5).
88. CIETAC Rules Articles 39 and 41.
89. SIAC Rules R. 41.1.
90. HKIAC Rules Article 32.1.
91. CIETAC Rules Article 10.
92. ACICA Expedited Rules Article 24.4.
93. ACICA Expedited Rules Article 24.5.
94. SIAC Rules R. 27(f).
95. HKIAC Rules Article 22.3.
96. AIAC Expedited Rules R. 7(4)(e).
97. CIETAC Rules Article 44(2).

[F] Oral Hearings (or Lack Thereof)

There are broadly three different approaches to oral hearings in these various expedited rules: no oral hearing by default, oral hearing by discretion, or oral hearing by default. The ACICA Expedited Rules and HKIAC Rules stipulate that, by default, there will be no oral hearings. In this regard, the ACICA Expedited Rules make this presumption clearer by requiring 'exceptional circumstances [to] exist' before any oral hearings will be held.[98] In contrast, the HKIAC Rules merely require that the tribunal considers the holding of such hearings to be 'appropriate'.[99] The SIAC Rules and CIETAC Rules adopt the middle ground approach by conferring a discretion on the tribunal to determine, having consulted with the parties, whether an oral hearing would be appropriate. The AIAC Expedited Rules, by contrast, appear to adopt oral hearings as the default position, though they provide for two scenarios in which a 'documents-only arbitration' will be held. The first is where the parties so agree. The second is where the 'aggregate amount of dispute' is below USD 75,000 or equivalent (in the case of an international arbitration) or below RMY 150,000 (in the case of a domestic arbitration).[100]

Therefore, the ACICA Expedited Rules adopt a unique approach by combining a default position (i.e., no oral hearings) with specific parameters around when a departure from the default position is warranted (i.e., in 'exceptional circumstances' only). This diminishes the discretion of tribunals to conduct the hearings as they see fit. However, it also provides an additional layer of clarity, which allows parties (and their counsel) to adjust expectations accordingly. It may therefore result in fewer procedural disputes regarding the format of the hearing, which is often a hotly contested issue.

[G] Handing Down the Award

Each of these rules sets a deadline for the rendering of the tribunal's award by specifying that the award must be handed down within a certain number of months following a particular event. However, there is some variation in the point at which the clock begins to run for the tribunal and in the length of the window in which the tribunal must publish their award. The ACICA Expedited Rules, SIAC Rules, and HKIAC Rules all set the clock running at the constitution of the tribunal. The SIAC Rules and HKIAC Rules each give the tribunal six months from that moment to publish an award. The ACICA Expedited Rules only give them four.[101]

Concerning the content of the award, the ACICA Expedited Rules are again aligned with the SIAC Rules and HKIAC Rules in providing that arbitrators may (or must, in the case of the ACICA Expedited Rules) articulate their reasons in summary form. Additionally, the arbitrators may provide no reasons at all where the parties have

98. ACICA Expedited Rules Article 24.6.
99. HKIAC Rules Article 42.2(e).
100. AIAC Expedited Rules R. 16.
101. SIAC Rules R. 5.2(d); HKIAC Rules Article 42.2(f).

so agreed.[102] The AIAC Expedited Rules and CIETAC Rules, however, both require that arbitrators provide reasons in any award.[103]

Therefore, while the ACICA Expedited Rules are the most stringent in terms of the time frame imposed, they soften the impact on tribunals by stipulating the provision of short-form reasons only. Of course, it is impossible to accommodate the expectations and priorities of individual parties in every case. Some may care little for well-crafted written reasons and welcome the shorter time frame for receipt of a decision in summary form. Others may feel short-changed by the process, potentially opening the door to more requests for clarification or potentially a higher number of set-aside applications. This a clear example of the trade-off involved in crafting expedited rules, where formality is sacrificed for the sake of speed. The consequences will no doubt be carefully monitored in the years to come.

[H] Ethical Obligations on Parties and Practitioners

The ACICA Expedited Rules are alone in seeking to impose specific ethical and professional standards - the IBA Guidelines - on parties and practitioners. By contrast, neither the SIAC Rules, nor AIAC Expedited Rules, nor CIETAC Rules refer to rules of professional conduct. The HKIAC Rules oblige both tribunal and parties to 'do everything necessary to ensure the fair and efficient conduct of the arbitration' but make no express reference to any particular standard by which such fairness or efficiency ought to be measured.[104] Notwithstanding issues with the enforceability of such obligations, the inclusion of an express reference to some form of ethical and professional standard in the ACICA Expedited Rules is commendable. It signals to practitioners that their conduct in the course of an arbitration held under the ACICA Expedited Rules will be monitored by the tribunal and measured against a defined standard. However aspirational the imposition of such a standard may be, it is surely better than setting no standard at all.

§9.07 REFLECTIONS ON THE GOALS OF EXPEDITED PROCEDURE: SPEED AT ANY PRICE?

One of the fundamental premises of any expedited set of arbitral rules is that speed in the presentation and determination of claims ought to be a paramount goal. And, of course, speed has a great many benefits; it facilitates greater commercial certainty, reduces parties' expenditure on legal fees, and mitigates the strain on witnesses, client instructors and legal representatives.[105] But how can these benefits be obtained

102. SIAC Rules R. 5.2(e); HKIAC Rules Article 42.2(g).
103. AIAC Expedited Rules Article 19(2); CIETAC Rules Article 49.3 (applicable by virtue of CIETAC Rules Article 64).
104. HKIAC Rules Article 13.4.
105. *Aon Risk Services Australia Ltd. v. Australian National University* (2009) 239 C.L.R. 175, 214; [2009] H.C.A. 27 [100]-[101] (Gummow, Hayne, Crennan, Kiefel and Bell JJ.).

without sacrificing the features that have earned arbitration its reputation as a safe and credible form of dispute resolution?

For an arbitral process to be speedy, it must be relatively informal, and it must treat the cases before it in a relatively uniform way.[106] Insistence by tribunals on observing the formalities of traditional arbitral procedure – ensuring, for example, that each party has the opportunity to be heard on each point that may arise – takes time. The delivery of the award may be deferred by weeks or months as parties exchange evidence and submissions on some new issue that has surfaced during the course of the arbitration. Similarly, allowing parties extensive input into the manner in which a given arbitration is conducted is also likely to consume time, inasmuch as parties will ordinarily seek to maximise (and not minimise) their opportunities to put their case across to the tribunal.

If the delivery of an award as soon as possible is regarded as a given tribunal's paramount objective, formality and particularity must, beyond a certain point, be viewed as thieves of time. Weeks or months that go by as a tribunal fastidiously observes the formalities of procedural fairness are, on this view, weeks or months during which time the arbitration could have been brought to a close. Accordingly, one of the unspoken assumptions of expedited arbitral procedure is that there is an upper limit in formality and particularity that ought to be accepted in an arbitral process. Beyond that limit, formality and particularity are burdens that any expedited arbitral procedure worth the name will seek to shake off. For a mode of dispute resolution that is founded on participants' ability to decide the rules and procedures by which their disagreements will be resolved, that may be an unpalatable proposition.

This said, arbitration has always involved parties accepting a degree of trade-off. Indeed, in centuries past, businesspeople have often been willing to sacrifice a great many procedural safeguards in the name of resolving disputes swiftly and simply. Lord Mustill once recounted the historical arbitral practices of those involved in London's Baltic timber trade as follows:

> [the parties] would choose as an umpire a man respected for his knowledge of the trade. There would be no written submissions, nor need for any. Still less would there be any Terms of Reference. The arbitrator would already know what the dispute was about, and he would go down to the wharf and climb over the timber and look at it and publish an award which simply said: 'The buyers have no right of rejection. There will be an allowance of 5% against the price.'[107]

Such a procedure is certainly speedy. But however satisfactory that procedure may have once been to timber merchants, those involved in today's complex commercial transactions probably would not consider this to represent an adequate means of resolving disputes, however much such a procedure may save them in lawyers' fees. In fact, it may well be the very speed with which the timber merchants' method of arbitration was conducted that diminishes its attraction in the present day. A modern

---

106. Cf. Herbert L. Packer, *Two Models of the Criminal Process*, 113 U. Penn. L.R. 1, 10-11 (1964) DOI: 10.2307/3310562.
107. Mustill, *supra* n. 56, 122.

businessperson might well ask at least two questions of the timber merchants' arbitrator. First, how could the timber merchants be confident that the arbitrator had truly made an informed and well-reasoned assessment of their dispute in so short a space of time? And second, what if the timber merchants wanted their dispute to be dealt with slightly differently? If a method of arbitration dedicating itself to the achievement of speedy outcomes sacrifices procedural fairness and party autonomy along the way, what benefit remains?

If speed were the only consideration, rules of procedure could be envisaged that would allow a greater number of disputes to be dealt with very rapidly indeed. Decision-makers, for example, could be freed entirely from any requirement to apply contractual provisions and applicable laws, accord natural justice or justify their determinations by way of written reasons.[108] But would parties truly wish to have their disputes adjudicated through such a system, in which there would always be at least some doubt about whether the outcome was really fair, whether their case was really assessed with the appropriate diligence? To put the matter another way, it is true that justice delayed is justice denied '[b]ut justice can equally be denied if inappropriately accelerated'.[109]

There is also a further danger that comes with speed: the risk that, in the rush to deliver awards as soon as possible, tribunals may compromise the quality of their decision-making. In prioritising speed in arbitral (or judicial) decision-making above all else, a former judge of the High Court of Australia once reminded judicial officers to remain 'alert to the dangers to which Lord Brougham fell victim when pursuing his single-minded objective of despatch'.[110] The historical study cited recalled that while Lord Brougham was famous for the speed of his decision-making as Lord Chancellor, many contemporaries considered that speed could be achieved only by fairly radical departures from what would ordinarily be regarded as the core tasks of the judicial function. For example, he would often not bother to read much (or any) of the evidence or pleadings in a given case. Predictably, these practices brought about a decline in the perception of the quality of Lord Brougham's decision-making. Some observers wondered whether many of the matters before him 'might just as well be decided by tossing a halfpenny'.[111] Such a method of dispute resolution, speedy though it may have been, hardly seems calculated to have left litigants feeling as though their grievances had been resolved in a just fashion.

On the one hand, the more an expedited set of arbitral rules seeks to speed up the arbitral process, the greater the likelihood that parties may regard it as resulting in lower-quality decisions being made in a way that is restrictive and unfair. It is for this reason that, for all its virtues, speed is not the sole objective that any set of arbitral rules – even expedited arbitral rules – will ordinarily pursue. As a former Chief Justice of New South Wales once explained, up to a point, '*inefficiencies in the administration of*

108. *Ibid.*
109. *Re S-W* [2015] 1 W.L.R. 4099, 4109; [2015] E.W.C.A. Civ. 27 [54] (Munby P.).
110. *Byron v. Southern Star Group Pty. Ltd.* (1995) 123 F.L.R. 352, 354 (Kirby P.).
111. 1 J.B. Atlay, *The Victorian Chancellors* (Smith, Elder & Co 1906) 318.

justice ... are not unintentional'.[112] The degree to which it is acceptable to exchange more speed for less ironclad procedural fairness is a matter that plays on the mind of those responsible for designing or finessing the architecture of any such system.

On the other hand, pitfalls exist at the other end of the spectrum, where timeliness is disregarded in favour of punctilious observation of formal requirements. As has been said in connection with litigation in the courts, it is 'no longer the role of the court simply to provide a level playing field and to referee whatever game the parties choose to play upon it'.[113] Broader considerations are at play. Some reasons for curtailing party autonomy in the context of the courts relate to the fact that courts are public institutions. The wasting of judicial time through endless amendments to pleadings represents the squandering of a precious (and finite) public resource.[114] But many of those reasons are just as compelling in the arbitral context. When commercial disputes plod on, sitting as contingent liabilities on a company's books, that company's ability to plan financially may well be affected, and 'employees and officers who may be crucial witnesses, have to bear the strain of impending litigation and the disappointment when it is not brought to an end'.[115] Thus, the business community's faith in arbitration as a viable means of resolving disputes may well begin to fade if tribunals prove themselves incapable of resolving those disputes in a timely way.[116]

Thankfully, the choice for rule-makers is not between crippling procedural complexity on the one hand and manifestly unfair 'palm tree justice' on the other. Various middle paths are open, any of which could provide an acceptable framework for governing the conduct of arbitrations with expediency. Indeed, the ACICA Expedited Rules do not pull out all the proverbial stops in the name of increasing the speed of proceedings. A good example of this is found in the ACICA Expedited Rules' restrictive approach to arbitrations conducted *ex aequo et bono*.

The true spirit of *ex aequo et bono* involves a principled consideration of matters in accordance with flexible notions of justice and fairness.[117] However, the very flexibility of the process means that litigants will typically have limited visibility over, and therefore limited understanding of, the norms by reference to which their dispute is being determined. It may well seem to the parties that the tribunal is simply 'mak[ing] up the rules as they go along'.[118] In turn, this opacity (or perceived opacity)

---

112. J.J. Spigelman, *Judicial Accountability and Performance Indicators*, 21 Civ. Just. Q. 18, 24 (2002) (emphasis added).
113. *Jameel v. Dow Jones & Co. Inc.* [2005] Q.B. 946, 965; [2005] E.W.C.A. Civ. 75 [54] (Lord Phillips M.R.), quoted in *Expense Reduction Analysts Group Pty. Ltd.*, *supra* n. 23, 318; [39] (French C.J., Kiefel, Bell, Gageler and Keane JJ.).
114. *See, e.g.*, *Macquarie Bank Ltd. v. National Mutual Life Association of Australia Ltd.* (1996) 40 N.S.W.L.R. 543, 553 (Clarke J.A.); *U.B.S. A.G. v. Tyne* (2018) 265 C.L.R. 77, 100; [2018] H.C.A. 45 [59] (Kiefel C.J., Bell and Keane JJ.).
115. *Aon Risk Services Australia Ltd.*, *supra* n. 105, 214, [101] (Gummow, Hayne, Crennan, Kiefel and Bell JJ).
116. Cf *Byron*, *supra* n. 110, 354 (Kirby P.).
117. Leon Trakman, *Ex Aequo et Bono: Demystifying an Ancient Concept*, 8 Chi. J. Int'l L. 621 (2008).
118. William W. Park, *The 2002 Freshfields Lecture – Arbitration's Protean Nature: The Value of Rules and the Risks of Discretion* (2002) 19 Arb. Int'l 279, 286. *See also* William W. Park, *Arbitration's Discontents: Of Elephants and Pornography* (2001) 17 Arb. Int'l 263, 265.

magnifies the risk that an unsuccessful party will regard their loss not merely as a disappointment but as an injustice.[119] Parties experiencing such a sense of injustice may be more inclined to resist enforcement of the award by calling into question the legitimacy of the process by which it was rendered, thereby delaying the final resolution of the dispute.[120] Indeed, under various jurisdictions' laws, it is at least open to doubt that awards handed down pursuant to an arbitration conducted truly *ex aequo et bono* are enforceable.[121]

Accordingly, if arbitrators were empowered to impose a mandatory *ex aequo et bono* procedure, far from expediting the final resolution of the parties' disagreements, such a procedure could simply generate additional uncertainty in the form of enforcement risk. Additionally, it may exacerbate parties' perception that the outcome of a given dispute 'all depends on whom we get as an arbitrator'.[122] Such a perception may cause parties to think twice about incorporating arbitration clauses in their agreements.[123] Moreover, if parties perceive that outcomes in arbitration under the ACICA Expedited Rules involve an element of chance, they will likely find it harder to make a rational assessment of their prospects and to that extent will be less likely to consider a negotiated settlement with their opponents. Thus, in the case of *ex aequo et bono* decision-making, the ACICA Expedited Rules sacrifice speed in the name of achieving an equally worthy goal: certainty and credibility.

§9.08 CONCLUSION

This chapter has assessed the efficacy of the ACIA Expedited Rules by examining them in light of their context, both the context of comparable rules published by other arbitral institutions in the Asia-Pacific region and the broader context of the perceptions and dilemmas that arbitration faces as a global method for resolving disputes. It has also reflected on the balancing act that the drafters of expedited arbitral rules grapple with when seeking to diminish the formality and particularity of arbitral proceedings in order to maximise their speed. If tribunals were unshackled from procedural restrictions beyond their own sense of fairness and broader mercantile practice, this would almost certainly enable them to resolve disputes more quickly than they would pursuant to a formalised set of rules. However, a hallmark of any dispute-resolution system worth its salt is that it is able to attract the confidence of those subject to it by ensuring that its mechanisms for arriving at determinations are transparent and predictable.[124] The ACICA Expedited Rules have bravely grasped the

119. Park, *2002 Freshfields Lecture*, *supra* n. 118, 288, 293.
120. Park, *Arbitration's Discontents*, *supra* n. 118, 272.
121. *See, e.g.*, *Woodbud Pty. Ltd. v. Warea Pty. Ltd.* (1995) 125 F.L.R. 346, 355-356 (Young J.), quoting *Rowland v. Cassidy* (1888) 13 App. Cas. 770, 772 (Lord Selborne); *Yesodei Hatorah College Inc. v. Trustees of the Elwood Talmud Torah Congregation* (2011) 38 V.R. 394, 422-425; [2011] V.S.C. 622 [48]-[49] (Croft J.).
122. Park, *2002 Freshfields Lecture*, *supra* n. 118, 297.
123. *Ibid.*, 297.
124. *See generally* John Finnis, *Natural Law and Natural Rights* (Clarendon Press 1980) 270-271, 287; John Rawls, *A Theory of Justice* (Oxford University Press rev. ed. 1999) 208-210; P.S.

nettle of seeking to provide the commercial world with a mode of dispute resolution that is at once speedy, cost-effective, and credible. They strike the right balance between maximising efficiency and safeguarding the procedural integrity of arbitral proceedings conducted under them, and to this extent they are likely to elevate Australia's stature as a leading jurisdiction for international arbitration.

Atiyah, *Justice and Predictability in the Common Law: The 7th Wallace Wurth Memorial Lecture*, 15 U. N.S.W. L. J. 448, 449-451 (1992) DOI: 10.1057/9780230226203.2234.

CHAPTER 10

Expedited Arbitration under ICSID Institution Rules 2022 and What It Means for Investors

Venetia Argyropoulou

This chapter analyzes the shortcomings in International Center for Settlement of Investment Disputes (ICSID) arbitration rules that have led to their reform, and especially to the introduction of the option for expedited arbitration set forth in Chapter XII of the Arbitration Rules. It presents the evolution of the rules from when they were proposed until their adoption on March 21, 2022, reviewing both the tribunals' case law and the Working Papers published by ICSID. It examines the reasoning behind the choices made and evaluates them. The chapter further presents the rules on expedited arbitration and critically assesses them from an investors' point of view. This assessment considers both their procedural efficiency and whether they maintain due process and a balance between investors and States, focusing, among others, on the concept of express consent.

§10.01 INTRODUCTION

The International Center for Settlement of Investment Disputes (ICSID) arbitration has recently reformed its Arbitration Rules in response to the criticisms the rules have faced in recent years. Among others, the reformed rules now provide for the establishment of expedited arbitration as set out in Chapter XII of the Arbitration Rules. These new rules were finally adopted on March 21, 2022. This chapter examines in depth both the relevant case law and the working papers that were published by the ICSID. This examination will unveil the reasoning behind the final draft of the rules. Additionally, the expedited Arbitration Rules will be critically assessed through an evaluation of their procedural efficiency as well as whether they do, in fact, maintain due process and a balance between investors and States. This critical review will be developed by focusing on the concept of express consent from the point of view of investors.

§10.02 THE REASONS FOR REFORM

The amendment of the Arbitration Rules of ICSID (new Rules) was the product of a six-year-long process, which was not without any complications or impediments. The amendment process was initially launched by ICSID in October 2016 with an open call to ICSID Member States, and later to the public, to suggest topics that could be taken into account for changes.[1] It took more than half a decade and the publication of six Working Papers before the final amended rules were approved by ICSID's Administrative Council on March 21, 2022.[2] The new Rules came into force on July 1, 2022.

The amendment of the ICSID rules was triggered amidst the heavy criticism of International Investment Agreements (IIAs) in general[3] and the investor-State dispute settlement mechanisms (ISDS) in particular.[4] It was within this background that the European Court of Justice criticized ISDS as found in intra-EU bilateral investment treaties (BITs) as incompatible with EU law.[5] This decision started the idea of the creation of a Multilateral Investment Court.[6] Similarly, it was in this context that UNCITRAL issued a broad mandate to its Working Group III to identify concerns relating to ISDS, examine the need for possible reform of ISDS, and make recommendations for any reforms.[7]

ICSID rules had also been criticized by scholars, nongovernmental institutions and governments for several years ahead of the reform.[8] Among other complaints, the ICSID regime had been heavily criticized for its inconsistent decisions and inefficient time- and cost-consuming procedures that have contributed to a prolonged legitimacy

1. ICSID Working Paper 2, Proposals for Amendment of the ICSID Rules (2019).
2. ICSID Administrative Council approves amendment of ICSID rules, ICSID (2022), https://icsid.worldbank.org/news-and-events/communiques/icsid-administrative-council-approves-amendment-icsid-rules (last visited April 1, 2023).
3. *See, e.g.*, Muthucumaraswamy Sornarajah, Resistance and change in the International Law on Foreign Investment (2015) and José E. Alvarez, ISDS Reform: The Long View, 36 ICSID Review—Foreign Investment Law Journal 253-277 (2021) DOI: 10.1093/icsidreview/siab036 for an analysis.
4. *See indicatively* Malcolm Langford, Daniel Behn & Runar Hilleren Lie, The Revolving Door in International Investment Arbitration, 20 Journal of International Economic Law 301-332 (2017), as well as Relatório 'Profiting from Injustice: How Law Firms, Arbitrators and Financiers Are Fueling an Investment Arbitration Boom', 10 Revista Brasileira de Arbitragem 189-193 (2013) DOI: 10.1093/jiel/jgx018.
5. Case C-284/16 *Slovak Republic v. Achmea BV* [2018], ECLI:EU:C:2018:158 ('Case C-284/16 *Slovak Republic v. Achmea BV*').
6. For an analysis, *see* Venetia Argyropoulou, 'ISDS Reform in the EU: Are We There Yet?', in Alan M. Anderson & Ben Beaumont (eds.), *The Investor-State Dispute Settlement System: Reform, Replace or Status Quo?* (Kluwer Law International, 2021), 33-53.
7. UNCITRAL, Report of Working Group III (Investor-State Dispute Settlement Reform) on the Work of Its Thirty-Fourth Session, UN Doc. A/CN.9/930/Rev.1, December 19, 2017, 2-3, para. 6.
8. For a detailed analysis of the criticism by developing countries, *see* Katia Fach Gómez, Latin America and ICSID: David Versus Goliath?, SSRN Electronic Journal (2010) coupled with the withdrawals from accession to ICSID submitted by Bolivia and Venezuela, while for a wider criticism of ICSID as a time- and cost-consuming regime that was impractical and inefficient, *see* Diana Marie Wick, The Counter-Productivity of ICSID Denunciation and Proposals for Change, 11 The Journal of International Business & the Law (2012).

crisis of nearly 20 years, with almost all aspects of the system being challenged.[9] As several scholars asserted:

> the costs to litigate an ISDS case are unsustainable, ad hoc tribunals with no appellate mechanism would produce inconsistent and incoherent awards across time, ISDS tribunals do not sufficiently balance investor rights with other areas of international law such as human rights or environmental protection, there are significant challenges regarding compliance with arbitral awards; and the ISDS protects foreign investors' rights with no corresponding responsibilities.[10]

As part of the reform process, ICSID reviewed the duration of 63 cases which concluded with an award between January 1, 2015 and June 30, 2017.[11] The review demonstrated that the average duration was 1,336 days, i.e., 3 years and 7 months, while in the case of joint proceedings, the average duration was 1,382 days, i.e., 3 years and 7 months. For bifurcated proceedings, the average duration was 1,301 days, i.e., 3 years and 5 months, while proceedings on merits only took 829 days.[12] These findings aligned with the data in PluriCourt's Investment Treaty Arbitration Database that shows an average time of three years and seven months for decided proceedings.[13] However, duration can be affected by the amount in dispute, with higher amounts being adjudicated in longer periods of time. The 2021 empirical study conducted by the British Institute of International and Comparative Law found that claims in excess of USD 1 billion on average took almost eight years to resolve.[14] The same study noted that recent proceedings lasted roughly five and a half years, i.e., one year and six months longer than those decisions were published before June 2017.[15]

The duration of proceedings has a significant impact on costs, with costs ranging on average between USD 4 and 6 million, depending on duration.[16] The first ICSID working paper issued as part of the amendment process in early 2018 raised this issue, and it was also raised in the 34th Session of UNCITRAL Working Group III. This Session

9. Daniel Behn, Ole Kristian Fauchal & Malcolm Langford, Introduction: The Legitimacy Crisis and the Empirical Turn, in Daniel Behn, Ole Kristian Fauchal & Malcolm Langford (eds.), The Legitimacy of Investment Arbitration: Empirical Perspectives (Cambridge University Press 2022) 4-5.
10. Malcolm Langford & Daniel Behn, Managing backlash: The Evolving Investment Treaty Arbitrator?, 29 European Journal of International Law 551-580 (2018) DOI: 10.1093/ejil/chy030.
11. ICSID rules and Regulations Amendment, ICSID (2020), https://icsid.worldbank.org/resources/rules-amendments (last visited April 2, 2023).
12. ISDS Academic Forum Working Group 2, Duration of ISDS Proceedings (2019), https://www.cids.ch/images/Documents/Academic-Forum/2_Duration_-_WG2.pdf (last visited April 2, 2023).
13. PITAD, https://pitad.org/index#static/illustrations (last visited April 2, 2023).
14. Matthew Hodgson, Yarik Kryvoi & Daniel Hrcka, Empirical Study: Costs, Damages and Duration in Investor-State Arbitration, British Institute of International and Comparative Law (2021), https://www.biicl.org/publications/empirical-study-costs-damages-and-duration-in-investor-state-arbitration (last visited April 2, 2023).
15. *Ibid.*, 32.
16. Jeffery P. Commission, Gábor Kökényesi & Mushegh Manukyan, How Much Does an ICSID Arbitration Cost? A Snapshot of the Last Five Years, Kluwer Arbitration Blog (2016), https://arbitrationblog.kluwerarbitration.com/2016/02/29/how-much-does-an-icsid-arbitration-cost-a-snapshot-of-the-last-five-years/ (last visited April 2, 2023).

identified, *inter alia*, the causes for the delay as the growing complexity of investor-State dispute cases; the fragmented nature of investor protection provisions found in IIAs; and the multiplication of interlocutory proceedings.[17]

In this context, the need for ICSID, the dominant venue for investor-State dispute resolution, to review its rules became imperative. The goals of the amendments that took 16 years to finalize were to improve cost- and time-efficiency as well as transparency, "with the ultimate goal of facilitating foreign investment for economic growth."[18] The previous rules were amended widely to address these key objectives.

§10.03 EXPEDITED ARBITRATION

When ICSID issued Working Paper 1 (WP1) on August 3, 2018, the three main goals of the new arbitration rules were increasing transparency, efficiency, and time and cost economy.[19] ICSID commissioned its own review of the length of its proceedings. This review focused, however, not only on the overall length of the process but also on the time required for certain segments, namely the length of the tribunal constitution process, the written process, and tribunal deliberation.

WP1 found on the basis of available data that it takes much longer to constitute tribunals than the intended 60 days after the date of registration of a case, with the average time for cases where parties agreed on a method being 222 days. In contrast, the average for cases where the default method applied was 294 days.[20] Among the causes for the delay are: (i) settlement negotiations between the parties; (ii) no initial participation by the respondent due to delay in organizing its defense; (iii) methods that provide for a long appointment process; (iv) no immediate request by a party for the Chairman of the Administrative Council to appoint a missing arbitrator after the expiry of the 90-day period provided in Article 38 of the Convention; and (v) agreed methods that eventually lead to default.[21] These reasons for the delay relate to the parties as well as to the process of the tribunal.

Similarly, significant delays were reported regarding both the determination of jurisdiction and the determination of the merits. Indicatively, in proceedings dealing jointly with the merits and jurisdiction, the average duration of the written process was 581 days (308 days for first-round submissions and 273 days for second-round submissions). Bifurcated cases took significantly longer.[22] WP1 identified as the reasons for the delay, among others: the (i) suspension of the proceedings; (ii) longer

17. Justine Touzet et al., The Investor-State Dispute Settlement System: The Road to Overcoming Criticism, Kluwer Arbitration Blog (2018), https://arbitrationblog.kluwerarbitration.com/2018/08/06/the-investor-state-dispute-settlement-system-the-road-to-overcoming-criticism/ (last visited April 2, 2023).
18. ICSID Administrative Council approves amendment of ICSID rules, ICSID (2022), https://icsid.worldbank.org/news-and-events/communiques/icsid-administrative-council-approves-amendment-icsid-rules (last visited April 1, 2023).
19. ICSID Working Paper 1, Proposals for Amendment of the ICSID Rules, ICSID Secrétariat (2018).
20. *Ibid.*, 309.
21. *Ibid.*, 903.
22. *Ibid.*

than expected preparation times; (iii) requests for production of documents that led to an extension of time limits; (iv) requests for bifurcation; and (v) consecutive written schedules on an objection that a claim manifestly lacks legal merit, followed by a bifurcated proceeding on jurisdiction, followed by a proceeding on the merits.[23] The majority of these reasons relate directly to the parties and not so much to the tribunal.

Lastly, the report examined the length of tribunal's deliberation, which ranged between 200 days and over 600 days in bifurcated proceedings.[24] The length is attributable to the tribunal alone.

Based on these findings, new rules for the reduction of the time required in each segment of the proceeding were necessary. WP1 therefore made a series of suggestions, including shorter default timelines unless the parties expressly decided otherwise.[25] The proposals were heavily discussed as part of the next working papers with several commentators formulating the final output of the rules.

The new rules on expedited arbitration are not the only measures to address the length and cost of proceedings before ICSID tribunals. Several other measures were introduced to reduce time and costs, including streamlining various processes, reducing time limits, and requiring tribunals and parties to "conduct the proceeding in good faith and in an expeditious and cost-effective manner."[26] In this context, Rule 69 introduces a modification of the award rendition, which should be rendered "as soon as possible."[27] More specifically, the new Rules introduced strict time frames consisting of:

> 60 days after the later of the Tribunal Constitution or the last submission, if the award is rendered pursuant to Rule 41(3), 180 days after the last submission if the award is rendered pursuant to Rule 44 (3)(c) or 240 days after the last submission in all other cases.[28]

The process for expedited arbitration aims at a certain type of claimant and specific type of claims, for which ICSID adjudication was not appealing. The expedited rules are ICSID's response to various commercial arbitral institutions, including the Singapore International Arbitration Centre (SIAC), Hong Kong International Arbitration Centre (HKIAC), International Chamber Commerce (ICC), and Stockholm Chamber of Commerce (SCC), whose expedited arbitration rules have been in place for some time.[29] As noted in Working Paper 6, expedited arbitration can be used for "low value claims,"[30] although notably no threshold is set. Similarly, the Secretary General of

23. *Ibid.*
24. *Ibid.*, 904.
25. *Ibid.*, 911.
26. ICSID Additional Facility Arbitration Rules, 2022, Rule 3(1). For a review of these measures, *see* Nick Lawn & Helin Laufer, The 2022 ICSID Arbitration Rules, 16 Rom. Arb. J. 37 (2022).
27. ICSID Additional Facility Arbitration Rules, 2022, Rule 69.
28. *Ibid.*
29. Charalampos Giannakopoulos, The 2022 amendments to the ICSID Arbitration Rules: Incremental Improvements Against the Backdrop of ISDS Reform CIL.NUS.EDU.SG, https://cil.nus.edu.sg/blogs/the-2022-amendments-to-the-icsid-arbitration-rules-incremental-improvements-against-the-backdrop-of-isds-reform-by-charalampos-giannakopoulos/ (last visited April 3, 2023).
30. ICSID Working Paper 6, Proposals for Amendment of the ICSID Rules, ICSID Secrétariat (2021).

ICSID underlined that expedited arbitration is more suited for investment contract disputes involving small- and medium-sized enterprises (SMEs).[31] Finally, expedited arbitration was also introduced as a tool toward the time and cost reduction objective in the framework of a "general duty to act expeditiously."[32]

The process for expedited arbitration is set forth in Rules 79 to 88 of the new Rules. Expedited arbitration is not a completely new process but is based on the rules applicable for other proceedings to the extent not explicitly excluded or amended by Rules 79 to 88.[33] The procedure starts with the mutual and express consent of the parties pursuant to Rule 79(1), which "must be jointly communicated to the Secretary General in writing."[34] Expedited Arbitration under the new Rules is envisioned as a simpler process with only one arbitrator being appointed, although there is the possibility for a three-member tribunal.[35] The parties must decide on the formation of the tribunal within 30 days after the date of the notice of consent is given to the Secretary General.[36] Following the formation of the tribunal, the parties have 20 days to appoint a single arbitrator[37] or 40 days to appoint the president and co-arbitrators in case of a three-member tribunal.[38] Importantly, if the time limits are not respected, the Secretary General can proceed to appoint the arbitrator(s).[39] The arbitrator must accept their appointment within 10 days.[40] Thus, the overall time for appointment of the tribunal is 60 days in the case of a single arbitrator or 80 days in the case of a three-member tribunal. In non-expedited arbitration, the time frame is double.

Rule 84 requires that the first session be held within 30 days from the constitution of the tribunal,[41] as opposed to 60 days in the cases of non-expedited arbitration.[42] Pursuant to Rule 85(a), the period for submitting the memorials is reduced to 60 days,[43] and the same time is allowed for submission of a counter-memorial. From the date of expiry of the deadline for filing the counter-memorial, the claimant has 40 days to file a reply. Rule 85(g) requires that the hearing takes place within 60 days after the last written submission.[44] Finally, Rule 85(i) limits the time for rendering the award to 120 days after the hearing, as opposed to 240 days under the ordinary, non-expedited, rules.[45] Thus, the overall time required for resolution of a case under the expedited arbitration rules is 430 days, i.e., a little over a year. Aside from the time restraints set,

31. ICSID Rules and Regulations Amendment, ICSID, https://icsid.worldbank.org/resources/rules-amendments (last visited April 3, 2023).
32. ICSID Working Paper 1, *supra* n. 19.
33. ICSID Additional Facility Arbitration Rules, 2022, Rule 34(2).
34. *Ibid.*, Rule 79(1).
35. *Ibid.*, Rule 80.
36. *Ibid.*
37. *Ibid.*, Rule 81.
38. *Ibid.*, Rule 82.
39. *Ibid.*
40. *Ibid.*, Rule 83.
41. *Ibid.*, Rule 84.
42. *Ibid.*, Rule 29.
43. *Ibid.*, Rule 85(a).
44. *Ibid.*, Rule 85(g).
45. *Ibid.*, Rule 85(i).

the new Rules on Expedited Arbitration allow for remote sessions and limits to the number of pages for written submissions to ensure an efficient process timewise.[46]

§10.04 EXPEDITED ARBITRATION FROM THE INVESTORS' POINT OF VIEW

The rules on expedited arbitration appear to promise an efficient process in terms of time and cost. However, is expedited arbitration as effective as it promises to be, especially for investors?

ICSID introduced expedited arbitration as a way of remaining competitive against other arbitration regimes that had introduced similar rules.[47] Despite the seemingly universal adoption of expedited arbitration in institutional rules of investment arbitration venues, there is very little data evidencing that such rules have been applied in an investment treaty setting. Although expedited arbitration rules have existed in the ICC and SCC since 2017,[48] they have not been applied to any investment treaty disputes to date.[49] What are the reasons that expedited arbitration rules have not been as widely used as one would expect?

§10.05 PARTICULARITIES OF INVESTMENT ARBITRATION

Expedited arbitration is a theme borrowed from commercial arbitration. Evidence indicates that in commercial arbitration, expedited arbitration processes have been a very successful way of resolving disputes. According to the ICC's statistics, expedited arbitration has been used in 261 cases up to 2020.[50] Similarly, expedited proceedings amounted roughly to 25%-30% of the total number of cases administrated by the SCC.[51] However, in both institutions, the experience of using expedited arbitration is linked with cases that are simpler in nature or of a lower monetary value. Indeed, in the ICC, the expedited rules are triggered automatically when the disputed amount does not exceed a set monetary threshold, currently set at USD 3 million. Although there is an opt-in option also available, the majority of the cases where expedited arbitration

46. *Ibid.*, Rule 85.
47. *For a comparative review of these rules, see* Arbitrating small value claims in investment arbitration, Ibanet, https://www.ibanet.org/document?id=Arbitrating-Small-Value-Claims-in-Investment-Arbitration-2022 (last accessed April 6, 2023), p. 62.
48. The SCC rules were originally enacted in 1995, but they have most recently been amended in 2017 and again in 2023.
49. Joel Dahlquist, The Use of Commercial Arbitration Rules in Investment Treaty Disputes: Domestic Courts, Commercial Arbitration Institutions and Tribunal Jurisdiction 204 (2021) DOI: 10.1163/9789004413689_005.
50. ICC Dispute Resolution 2020 Statistics, International Chamber of Commerce (2019), https://nyiac.org/wp-content/uploads/2021/09/ICC-Dispute-Resolution-2020-Statistics.pdf (last visited April 9, 2023).
51. Markus Manninen, Pontus Ewerlöf & Minja Jantunen, Expedited Arbitration Clause – Use Responsibly Hannes Snellman (2021), https://www.hannessnellman.com/news-views/blog/expedited-arbitration-clause-use-responsibly/ (last visited April 9, 2023).

was used were cases where the expedited rules applied automatically.[52] Similarly, in the SCC, where expedited arbitration is only available via a joint opt-in by the parties, the majority of the expedited arbitrations cases in 2018 related to commercial agreements between small- and medium-sized companies in Sweden or within the EU.[53] In subsequent years, the majority of disputes often relate to limited, straightforward business transactions where full-fledged arbitration appeared unnecessary or where the value of the transaction would make regular arbitration less cost-inefficient.[54]

However, investment arbitration is different from commercial arbitration. Investment arbitration is inherently more complex, given States' involvement as respondents. State-party involvement often necessitates complex internal organization, approvals and authorizations before any decision can be reached, translating to longer periods needed before the submission of memorials and evidence.[55] Additionally, a State party's involvement may also raise other concerns, such as public interest considerations, that may have a bearing on the case and may also result in the participation of amici curiae by third parties.[56] These additional considerations are in addition to the individual perplexities, such as the intricacy of the factual background and bifurcation of proceedings.[57]

Does expedited arbitration also guarantee the quality of the arbitration outcome for cases of intrinsic complexity, such as investor-State dispute resolution? The complexity of each case will matter significantly in the selection of expedited arbitration. For example, skepticism has been voiced about whether expedited arbitration is suitable for energy-related investor claims, which are particularly fact intensive.[58] Expedited arbitration also may not be suitable for disputes that arise in the context of sovereign default, especially in multiparty arbitration, due to the complexity of those cases, the high public policy concerns, and the complex set of facts that surround such cases.

Working Paper 5 underlined that expedited arbitration is suitable for investment contract disputes involving SMEs because it can greatly reduce the time and costs.[59]

52. ICC Dispute Resolution 2020 Statistics, *supra* n. 50, where it is indicated that as of the 261 cases of expedited arbitration, 178 were cases where the rules applied automatically as the monetary threshold was not met.
53. Anja Ipp, Anna Howard & Wairimu Karanja, Expedited Arbitration at the SCC: One Year with the 2017 Rules, Kluwer Arbitration Blog (2018), https://arbitrationblog.kluwerarbitration.com/2018/04/02/expedited-arbitration-scc-one-year-2017-rules-2/ (last visited April 9, 2023).
54. *Ibid.*
55. Crina Baltag (Managing Editor), Patricia Shaughnessy & Mihaela Maravela, UNCITRAL Working Group II: Investment Disputes and Expedited Arbitration: A Probable Symbiosis?, Kluwer Arbitration Blog (2020), https://arbitrationblog.kluwerarbitration.com/2020/09/15/uncitral-working-group-ii-investment-disputes-and-expedited-arbitration-a-probable-symbiosis/ (last visited Apr 6, 2023).
56. *Ibid.*
57. *Ibid.*
58. Lucy McKenzie, Emma Johnson & Tom Cummins, New ICSID Arbitration Rules: Implications for Energy and Resources Sectors Ashurst, https://www.ashurst.com/en/news-and-insights/legal-updates/new-icsid-arbitration-rules-implications-for-energy-and-resources-sectors/ (last visited April 10, 2023).
59. ICSID Working Paper 5, Proposals for Amendment of the ICSID Rules, ICSID Secrétariat, 268 (2021).

Working Paper 5 provided no definition of what claimants can be considered SMEs. No universal definition exists. However, the International Finance Corporation defined SMEs as companies with: (1) fewer than 250 employees; (2) less than USD 50-USD 70 million turnover; and/or (3) USD 50-USD 62 million in assets,[60] a definition that seems to be followed by arbitral tribunals.[61] Available data suggests that SMEs constitute a large number of claimants before ICSD tribunals.[62] The Center for Strategic & International Studies (CSIS) conducted a study in 2015 of 105 ISDS proceedings initiated by American investors before ICSID and found that two-thirds of the claimants were SMEs or individuals.[63] SMEs and individuals thus tend to be the claimants in small-value claims.[64] Irrespective of the significant involvement of SMEs in ISDS, costs and duration of ICSID proceedings can and do inhibit SMEs from instigating proceedings before ICSID.[65] The growing demands for third-party funding[66] attest to the inability of SMEs to fund litigation before ICSID and to the disparity in financial means among claimants and respondents. In this context, expedited arbitration appears to be a solution for SMEs to address their concerns regarding time and costs. However, claims brought by SMEs are not necessarily simpler or smaller or less complex[67], and thus the same caveat that applies to multinational corporations applies to SMEs. Expedited arbitration may not be suitable for certain disputes. For some cases, it could be extremely challenging for the parties to present their case fully under the expedited procedures, especially for complicated and intense fact-finding cases. If the arbitrator must make their decision in a single procedure, the parties may be deprived of the opportunity to test the accuracy of evidence through cross-examination of witnesses. Moreover, the 200-page limit for the memorial and counter-memorial may not be appropriate in disputes with major factual disputes.[68] Thus, before resorting to expedited arbitration, the claimants must carefully determine whether the benefits of expedition outweigh the obstacles that can be posed by these limitations.

Finally, in Working Paper 6, one State proposed that the Secretariat draw the parties' attention to the possibility of expedited arbitration for "low value claims." The

60. MSME Country Indicators 2014, Towards a Better Understanding of Micro, Small, and Medium Enterprises (International Finance Corporation, December 2014), available at www.smefinanceforum.org/sites/default/files/analysis per cent20note.pdf (last visited April 10, 2023).
61. *Supra* n. 48, p. 13.
62. Thilo Rensmann & Joachim Karl, The Treatment of Small and Medium-Sized Enterprises in International Investment Law, in Thilo Rensmann (ed.) Small and Medium-Sized Enterprises in International Economic Law (Oxford University Press 2017) 291-308.
63. Scott Miller & Gregory N. Hicks, Investor-State Dispute Settlement: A Reality Check Center for Strategic and International Studies, A Report of the CSIS Scholl Chair in International Business 2015 (2015), http://csis.org/files/publication/150116_Miller_investorStateDispute_web.pdf.
64. *Supra* n. 48, p. 13.
65. Lee M. Caplan, "Making Investor-State Arbitration More Accessible to Small and Medium-Sized Enterprises" in Catherine A. Rogers and Roger P. Alford (eds.), The Future of Investment Arbitration (Oxford University Press 2009) 29, 300.
66. Florence Dafe & Zoe Williams, Banking on Courts: Financialization and the Rise of Third-Party Funding in Investment Arbitration, 28 Review of International Political Economy 1362-1384 (2020) DOI: 10.1080/09692290.2020.1764378.
67. *Supra* n. 48, p. 5.
68. Guglielmo Verdirame, Revised ICSID Arbitration Rules: Key Changes, Conference hosted by BIICL on September 15, 2022.

Secretariat stated that it would adopt this suggestion as a matter of administrative practice.[69] Although smaller claims are not necessarily simpler in nature, the benefits of reduced time for the completion of the case and lower costs of arbitral proceedings may be particularly useful to parties with limited resources.[70] But again, the same caveats should apply. Parties should assess the risk that the increased speed and procedural simplicity can result in awards that may be legally and/or factually incorrect if granted by a single arbitrator.[71] Thus, expedited arbitration is not "a one-size-fits-all" solution, even for low-value claims or SMEs. There are limits to its practicality.

§10.06 EXPRESS MUTUAL CONSENT

The starting point for expedited arbitration is the express consent of both parties. In addition to the agreement to arbitrate, the parties must also agree to expedited arbitration. The need for the express consent of both parties was set as a prerequisite in WP1. WP1 underlined that expedited arbitration does not apply absent the mutual consent of both parties.[72] This approach is contrary to other arbitral institutions, for example, the ICC, where expedited arbitration is automatically triggered if the dispute amount is below a certain threshold.[73]

Automatic application of the expedited arbitration rules was also explored as part of the formulation of the new Rules. Indeed, Working Paper 4 mentioned that one State suggested that the ICSID Secretariat explore the automatic application of expedited arbitration for smaller claim cases using an ad valorem system.[74] The Secretariat indicated it would explore an ad valorem system for ICSID arbitrations and how this could be used with expedited arbitration to address efficiency and access to justice,[75] noting, however, that the majority of states supported the optional application of expedited arbitration rules. This proposal was not approved, and expedited arbitration is only available subject to both parties' written consent.

That said, in their agreement for expedited arbitration, the parties are free to agree on various qualifiers, including a maximum threshold above which expedited arbitration rules would not apply.[76] Reference to expedited arbitration can be included in the arbitration agreement, or be in an IIA, or in the domestic legislation of the host

69. ICSID Working Paper 6, Proposals for the Amendment of the ICSID Rules, ICSID Secretariat (2022) 31.
70. *Supra* n. 48, p. 7.
71. Haflidi Kristjan Larusson, Expedited Arbitration – Meeting the Needs of SMEs, 63 Scandinavian Studies in Law (2017).
72. *Supra* n. 13, p. 668.
73. Article 30(2) and Article 1(2) of Appendix VI of the 2021 ICC Arbitration Rules, *see also* HKIAC Rules, Article 42.1(a); Swiss Rules, Article 6(4); SIAC Rules, Rule 5; UNCITRAL EAR, Article 1.
74. ICSID Working Paper 4, Proposals for Amendment of the ICSID Rules, ICSID Secrétariat (2020) 167.
75. *Ibid.*, 168.
76. Arbitrating small value claims in investment arbitration, Ibanet (2022), *supra* n. 47.

State, or be agreed ad hoc after the dispute has arisen.[77] Working Paper 2 suggested a format for such consent as follows:[78]

> The [Government]/[name of constituent subdivision or agency] of [name of Contracting State] and [name of investor] hereby consent to submit to the International Centre for Settlement of Investment Disputes (hereinafter the "Centre") any dispute arising out of this agreement for settlement by arbitration pursuant to the Convention on the Settlement of Investment Disputes between States and Nationals of Other States (hereinafter the "Convention"). The Parties agree to apply Chapter XII of the [2019] Arbitration Rules of the Centre (Expedited Arbitration) to the arbitration proceeding.[79]

Consent to arbitrate is in most cases inferred from the investor's submission of a claim to arbitration under the terms of the relevant IIA, which contains the State's approval to resolve matters stemming from the IIA through arbitration.[80] Hence, there is no interaction between investors, especially smaller ones, and States, meaning that unless States are willing to amend their IIAs or their national law, an ad hoc agreement after the fact seems unlikely.

Because submission to the rules of expedited arbitration is a matter of mutual consent of the parties, if consent is later retracted, the new rules provide for an opt-out mechanism. In particular, Rule 88(1) provides that the parties "may opt out of an expedited arbitration at any time by jointly notifying the Tribunal and Secretary-General in writing."[81] But even absent the mutual agreement of both parties to opt out, if one party desired to opt out, that party can request from the Tribunal for the arbitration to no longer be expedited.[82] The Tribunal will assess this request on the basis of "the complexity of the issues, the stage of the proceeding and all other relevant circumstances."[83] The opt-out mechanism described by WP2 as an "exit ramp"[84] was requested by various States that felt that the possibility to opt out of expedited arbitration should not depend solely on party agreement.[85] One State noted that in case a State is faced with a change of circumstances (such as an emergency or financial crisis) that could impact its ability to comply with the expedited arbitration procedure, a tribunal should be empowered to assess the circumstances and determine whether opting out would be permissible.[86] Similar concerns were also voiced by the International Institute for Sustainable Development, which indicated that the shorter time frames envisaged by the expedited arbitration rules could place significant constraints

77. Crina Baltag (Managing Editor), Patricia Shaughnessy & Mihaela Maravela, *supra* n. 55.
78. *Supra* n. 1, p. 668.
79. *Ibid.*
80. Baltag (Managing Editor), Shaughnessy & Maravela, *supra* n. 55.
81. ICSID Additional Facility Arbitration Rules, 2022, Rule 88(1).
82. *Ibid.*, Rule 88(2).
83. *Ibid.*
84. *Supra*, p. 497, note 1.
85. ICSID Working Paper 3, Proposals for Amendment of the ICSID Rules, ICSID Secrétariat (2019) 185.
86. Daniel Amado &Jackson Shaw Kern Martin Doe Jose, Rule Amendment Project – Member State and Public Comments on Working Paper # 2 ICSID (2019), https://icsid.worldbank.org/sites/default/files/amendments/State_Public_Comments_WP2.pdf (last visited April 7, 2023).

on developing States that are struggling to finance arbitration.[87] ICSID decided not to address State comments regarding the automatic extension of the expedited arbitration procedures to post-award remedies because, as stated in WP4, it assumed that "parties wish to expedite the full case when they consent to expedited arbitration."[88] The opt-out mechanism provides the parties with the possibility of returning to the regular procedure at any point when they deem it necessary.

With the possibility of unilateral retraction from expedited arbitration, it is questionable which States and under which conditions would ever likely agree to expedited arbitration. Aside from legal fees piling up, any delay in the process usually operates in the States' favor. But even for claimants, agreeing to expedited arbitration might not be as easy, especially at the beginning of the process. Given the limitations the new Rules set in terms of both time and the length of the memorial and the counter-memorial, a party to the dispute may want to better evaluate the case before agreeing to such constraints. This aligns with findings Guglielmo Verdirame shared during the event held by the British Institute of International and Comparative Law on September 15, 2022. Verdirame noted that respondents would likely hesitate to agree to expedite from the beginning and would prefer to wait to receive the claimant's memorial before committing to expedited arbitration. This would permit the respondent to assess the claimant's evidence, the number of witnesses and experts, etc. He further noted that considering time and resource management, respondents would probably wait until after their counter-memorial to opt for expedited procedures to avoid being constrained by a 60-day time limit.[89]

Indeed, despite the fact that WP1 initially provided that the consent of the parties was to be notified "within 20 days after the date of registration of the Request for arbitration,"[90] Working Paper 2 removed the requirement of the 20-day notification, thus allowing the parties to consent to expedited arbitration at any time.[91] Therefore, the popularity and applicability of expedited arbitration rules and whether parties will eventually opt in remains to be seen. UNCITRAL launched a questionnaire on this topic soliciting answers from arbitral institutions already administering expedited arbitration.[92] Answering to the question of how well expedited arbitration is perceived by the parties, the Vienna International Arbitration Center answered:

> Our rules for expedited proceedings exist since 2013. Due to the fact that they are opt-in and there is no automatic monetary threshold, we only have a handful cases, as parties do not agree on these rules in their arbitration agreement although

87. *Ibid.*
88. WP5, para. 139.
89. Elodie Fortin, 2022 ICSID Arbitration Rules-Views on Key Changes: LexisNexis Blogs LexisNexis (2022), https://www.lexisnexis.co.uk/blog/research-legal-analysis/2022-icsid-arbitration-rules-views-on-key-changes (last visited April 8, 2023).
90. *Supra*, Rule 69, note 10.
91. *Supra*, p. 497, note 1.
92. Responses to the UNCITRAL questionnaire on expedited arbitration, UNCITRAL (2020), https://uncitral.un.org/sites/uncitral.un.org/files/media-documents/uncitral/en/responses_to_questionnaire_30_january_2020.pdf (last visited April 9, 2023).

we have a wording for it in our suggested model clause. We have no explanation for this.[93]

In the case of the ICC, the expedited arbitration procedure applies if the monetary threshold is met. Rule 30(1) of the ICC Rules provides that the expedited arbitration procedure applies to all disputes which do not exceed the amount of USD 2,000,000, if the agreement was concluded between March 1, 2017, and January 1, 2021. If the agreement was concluded after January 1, 2022, and the amount in dispute does not exceed USD 3,000,000, then the rules on expedited arbitration apply.[94] In disputes that exceed these amounts, the expedited arbitration rules may also apply with the consent of the parties.[95] In other words, the monetary threshold is lifted if the consent threshold is met. However, the automatic application of the expedited arbitration procedure renders the procedure before the ICC more efficient than that envisaged in the ICSID Rules.

§10.07 THE ANNULMENT PROCESS

The new Rules on expedited arbitration cannot be examined in vacuum. Rather, they need to be assessed within the context of other ICSID rules and especially those on annulment because these rules will depict the overall risk for investors when entering into ICSID arbitration. Upon the issuance of an award by an ICSID tribunal, there is very limited recourse available to challenge the award. In fact, the only recourse envisioned under the ICSID rules is the annulment process.[96] Unlike an appeal process, which does not exist in ICSID, the annulment process does not examine the merits, either the facts or law. It only reviews the limited grounds listed in Article 52(1) of the ICSID Convention.[97] The limited scope of the annulment process evidences how the drafters of the ICSID Convention viewed annulment as an exceptional remedy.[98] The grounds in Article 52(1) ICSID Convention are to be interpreted reasonably, neither extensively nor restrictively.[99] The review of the ad hoc committee envisioned in Article 52(1) is one that aims to "safeguard the integrity, not the outcome, of ICSID arbitral proceedings."[100] Furthermore, in deciding whether to annul an award, the ad

93. *Ibid.*
94. Article 30(1), ICC Rules.
95. *Ibid.*
96. Article 53(1) of the ICSID Convention.
97. *See* Christoph Schreuer & Loretta Malintoppi, The ICSID Convention: A Commentary: A Commentary on the Convention on the Settlement of Investment Disputes Between States and Nationals of Other States 881 (Cambridge University Press 2013).
98. Yarik Kryvoi, Johannes Koepp & Jack Biggs, Empirical Study: Annulment in ICSID Arbitration British Institute of International and Comparative Law (2021), https://www.biicl.org/publications/empirical-study-annulment-in-icsid-arbitration (last visited April 13, 2023).
99. Decision on annulment, January 28, 2002, *Wena Hotels Ltd. v. Arab Republic of Egypt*, 41 ILM 933 (2002), # 18 (referred to as *Wena*); Decision on Annulment, July 3, 2002, *Companía de Aguas del Aconquija S.A. and Vivendi Universal v. Argentine Republic*, 41 ILM 1135 (2002), # 62 (referred to as *Vivendi*).
100. Lucy Reed, Nigel Blackaby & Jan Paulsson, The ICSID Review Regime, in Guide to ICSID Arbitration 162-163 (Kluwer Law International 2010).

hoc committee enjoys some discretion because it may examine the materiality of any violation.[101] In other words, there are cases where even though the conditions of Article 52(1) are met, the ad hoc committee need not annul an award unless the violation is material.[102]

Despite the exceptional nature of the annulment process, applications for annulment are increasingly common.[103] This has not led to more annulments being granted. Instead, as the study carried out by the British Institute of International and Comparative Law in 2021 shows, the number of successful annulment applications is low. The study examined approximately 355 ICSID awards as of January 31, 2021 and found that while almost half were subject to annulment proceedings, only 19 (around 5%) were annulled in full or in part.[104]

As part of the work carried out by Working Group III of UNCITRAL in reviewing possible reform of the ISDS, the formation of an appellate court has been examined as a response to the concerns for procedural and substantive correctness of ISDS tribunals' decisions.[105] Working Group III has noted that the creation of an appellate body would align ISDS tribunals with adjudicatory bodies. It would assist in the ISDS process becoming more accountable by allowing for the creation of a body of "legally authoritative general principles and interpretations" that would improve "the coherence and predictability of the investment regime."[106]

However, not all investors share the same desire for the creation of an appellate body. The 2020 Queen Mary University of London, Corporate Counsel International Arbitration Group Survey on Investors' Perceptions of ISDS reveals this. In the survey, the percentage of respondents in favor of the creation of the appellate body (35%) was the same as the respondents that were against it (35%).[107] What is interesting is the reason behind investors' opposition to the creation of an appellate body. The survey suggests that this is directly linked to the fact that an appellate mechanism would add additional costs and time to the dispute settlement process. The survey notes, "An appeal mechanism would impact costs, factual and legal findings and efficiency negatively, as it would open the door to an endless process which would drive up costs and would have a detrimental effect on the efficiency of the ISDS process."[108]

This leaves investors unprotected, especially in the context of expedited arbitration. Due to the procedural limitations and strict time frames in expedited arbitration,

101. Gabrielle Kaufmann-Kohler, Annulment of ICSID Awards in Contract and Treaty Arbitrations: Are There Differences?, Juris Arbitration Law (2004).
102. *Ibid.*
103. Kryvoi, Koepp & Biggs, *supra* n. 98.
104. *Ibid.*
105. Possible reform of investor-State dispute settlement (ISDS) Appellate and multilateral court mechanisms, Note by the Secretariat, A/CN.9/WG.III/WP.185 (2019), https://documents-dds-ny.un.org/doc/UNDOC/LTD/V19/113/57/PDF/V1911357.pdf?OpenElement (last visited April 13, 2023).
106. *Ibid.*
107. School of International Arbitration, 2021 International Arbitration Survey: Adapting Arbitration to a Changing World – School of International Arbitration (2020), https://arbitration.qmul.ac.uk/research/2021-international-arbitration-survey/ (last visited April 14, 2023).
108. *Ibid.*

there can be a real concern whether arbitrators might pursue simplicity by, *inter alia*, lowering the required level of proof.[109] This raises due process concerns that could be addressed by an appellate body, but the only solution would be an annulment process under ICSID. Even more, expedited arbitration is not suitable for all cases, with complex and intense fact-finding procedures being unsuitable for expedited arbitration. In such cases, investors are faced with the long delays and high costs described without any available remedy.

§10.08 CONCLUSION

The new ICSID Rules addressed several of the concerns previously raised against ICSID arbitration. But are the new Expedited Arbitration Rules nuanced enough to cover most of the essential shortcomings of the regular rules, and, if so, will this lead to new challenges? Will the regime of expedited arbitration as established by the new Rules, in an effort to address numerous shortcomings, lead to new challenges? And, more specifically, will provisions of the new Rules, such as the lack of automatic application in specific cases or an opt-out mechanism, render them vague provisions with little practical application? In other words, are the new Rules an efficient mechanism, or rather a set of rules superficially tackling the issue of time- and cost-efficiency?

Three main characteristics of the expedited arbitration rules raise questions regarding its efficiency. The first is the strict time frame, which raises concerns regarding the in-depth examination of the issues brought before ICSID. The second is that they seem to address mostly cases which are not very complex, and thus mostly "lower value claims cases."[110] Indeed, the greater the factual complexity, the less attractive expedited arbitration becomes. Where the tipping point lies is difficult to say, and this very much depends on the parties in each case and the likely overall cost of arbitration compared to the amount in dispute.[111] The third characteristic is the fact that because application requires the consent of both parties, expedition can prove to be inefficient in practice compared to similar mechanisms of other arbitration institutions. For expedited arbitration to prove successful, it must demonstrate that it is a cost- and time-efficient method for the resolution of less-complex disputes.

109. Using fast track arbitration for resolving commercial disputes, Global law firm | Norton Rose Fulbright (2018), https://www.nortonrosefulbright.com/en/knowledge/publications/981af4b9/using-fast-track-arbitration-for-resolving-commercial-disputes (last visited April 14, 2023).
110. https://www.hfw.com/What-do-the-new-2022-ICSID-Arbitration-Rules-mean-for-the-parties.
111. Haflidi Kristjan Larusson, Expedited Arbitration – Meeting the Needs of SMEs, 63 Scandinavian Studies in Law (2017).

CHAPTER 11

A Comparative Analysis of Expedited Arbitration Rules in ICSID and UNCITRAL for Investor-State Disputes

Carlos Eduardo Torres Giraldez

Investor-State arbitration often encounters procedural hurdles that lead to extended and cumbersome proceedings. To alleviate this issue, institutions have introduced expedited arbitration rules. The International Centre for Settlement of Investment Disputes (ICSID) and the United Nations Commission on International Trade Law (UNCITRAL) have recently revised their arbitration rules to incorporate expedited procedures, impacting various facets of the arbitration process. Other significant arbitral bodies, such as the Permanent Court of Arbitration (PCA) and the Arbitration Institute of the Stockholm Chamber of Commerce (SCC), have adopted UNCITRAL's expedited arbitration rules. This chapter offers a comprehensive comparison of the expedited arbitration rules of ICSID and UNCITRAL, shedding light on their distinctive features and implications.

§11.01 INTRODUCTION

Investor-State arbitration, distinct from commercial or State-State arbitration, plays a pivotal role as a mechanism for resolving disputes between foreign investors and host States, offering an alternative to traditional judicial systems. Historically, these disputes were often litigated in the host State's courts, leading to concerns about bias, impartiality, and the inefficiency of lengthy court proceedings. To remedy these issues, alternative dispute resolution (ADR) methods, such as investor-State arbitration, gained prominence.

Notwithstanding its advantages, investor-State arbitration has come under scrutiny, particularly for its perceived sluggishness in resolving disputes.[1] The absence of one of arbitration's core attributes – expeditiousness – has garnered significant attention. Consequently, two prominent sets of rules governing investor-State arbitration have been recently amended to accommodate 'expedited arbitration rules' or 'fast-track' arbitration. Expedited arbitration rules aim to streamline the arbitration process, imposing strict time frames and simplified procedural regulations. While these rules aspire to expedite proceedings, in this context, they remain a subject of debate, given the complexity inherent to most investor-state disputes.

This chapter provides a concise overview of the context in which investment arbitration operates, setting the stage for an examination of its compatibility with expedited arbitration. Subsequently, it conducts a comparative analysis of the expedited arbitration rules introduced by UNCITRAL in 2021 and ICSID in 2022. While both sets of rules share a common overarching objective, they exhibit similarities and distinctions when applied to investment arbitration cases.

§11.02 BRIEF VIEW TO THE 'STATE CONTEXT' OF INVESTMENT ARBITRATION

'Investment disputes are defined as controversies that arise out of an "investment" and are between a Contracting State (or "host State") or a designated state-related entity from that state and a national of another Contracting State (or "investor").'[2] The backdrop for resolving such disputes is often bilateral investment treaties (BITs), which 'are treaties negotiated between two states which frequently provide mechanisms for the resolution of international investment disputes '.[3]

The international legal system has witnessed the growth of a vast network of over 2,800 BITs currently in force.[4] These treaties stand as the primary mechanisms for resolving disputes in the realm of modern investor-state relations. For example, the Venezuela-Canada BIT meticulously delineates the precise conditions under which

1. Peter Morton, Can a World Exist Where Expedited Arbitration Becomes the Default Procedure. *Arbitration International*, Volume 26, Issue 1, pp. 103, 114 n. 103 (2010), available at: DOI: 10.1093/arbitration/26.1.103:

> The reputation of arbitration as the quick and informal alternative to court proceedings is, for many, now consigned to history. Complaints are rife of the increased 'judicialization' of arbitration, whereby counsel and arbitrators (who may be former judges) are all too ready to import the court procedures which they know and love into the arbitration process, with little more than a moment's thought as to whether there may be a quicker and cheaper means of concluding that particular dispute.

2. Gary B. Born, International Commercial Arbitration 119 (Holanda Wolters Kluwer Arbitration 2d ed. 2014).
3. Gary Born, BITS, BATS and Buts, Reflections on International Dispute Resolution, available at: www.wilmerhale.com/uploadedFiles/Shared_Content/Editorial/News/ Documents/BITs-BATs-and-Buts.pdf.
4. Investment Policy Hub: International Investment Agreements Navigator (20 October 2023), available at: https://investmentpolicy.unctad.org/international-investment-agreements/countries/228/venezuela-bolivarian-republic-of.

investments made by Venezuelan entities within Canadian territory are safeguarded, as well as the procedures to follow in the event of disputes. In a symmetrical fashion, the BIT offers a reciprocal protection framework for investments made by Canadian entities in Venezuela.[5] These treaties serve not only as shields for foreign investments but also as guideposts for the dispute resolution process, underpinning the stability and confidence necessary for cross-border investments.

'International investment arbitration was adopted because it was seen to be the most neutral, most efficient, most objective, most expert and most fair means of international dispute resolution.'[6] In fact, 'over the past twenty years, more than 500 publicly-reported disputes',[7] 'involving amounts ranging in value from a few hundred thousand to over a hundred billion US dollars have been resolved under BITs'.[8] International investment disputes are between foreign investors and states in which they have made investments. Therefore, they operate within a distinctive 'State context' characterized by complex legal and geopolitical dynamics. To gain a comprehensive understanding of this unique field, it is vital to consider the following features:

- Open offer to arbitrate: One of the main characteristics of BITs is the open offer to arbitrate to foreign nationals of the other party of the treaty. In this sense, 'the state makes an open offer to arbitrate against any foreign investor that falls within a defined category in the BIT'.[9] This open offer forms the foundation for investor-state arbitration.
- Asymmetric power dynamics: 'Investment arbitration is mixed in the sense that it involves a sovereign State (the host State), on one side, and a private foreign investor, on the other.'[10] This creates a distinctive power dynamic and regulatory framework that differs from other forms of arbitration such as commercial arbitration or State-State arbitration. Investor-State arbitration inherently involves an imbalance of power. In this context, States wield significant authority and resources, giving them a dominant position in the proceedings. 'Most of the investors are corporations, but at times, individuals also appear as claimants in investment arbitration.'[11] This power asymmetry can manifest in various ways, affecting elements like the choice of legal representation.
- Public Interest: Public interest significantly impacts investment arbitration by influencing the delicate balance between the rights of foreign investors and the

5. Agreement between the Government of Canada and the Government of The Bolivarian Republic of Venezuela for the Promotion and Protection of Investments, 1.7.1996, available at: https://investmentpolicy.unctad.org/international-investment-agreements/treaty-files/644/download.
6. Born, BITS, BATS and Buts, *supra* n. 3.
7. United Nations Conference on Trade and Development, Latest developments in investor-State dispute Settlement, IIA MONITOR No. 1 (2008), available on: https://unctad.org/system/files/official-document/iteiia20083_en.pdf.
8. Born, BITS, BATS and Buts, *supra* n. 3.
9. *Ibid.*
10. Rudolf Dolzer & Christoph Schreuer, Principles of International Investment Law 214 (Oxford University Press 2d ed. 2012).
11. *Ibid.*, 235.

legitimate policy objectives of host States. Balancing public interest and investor rights is a unique challenge in expedited investment arbitration. The accelerated nature of expedited arbitration requires a heightened level of efficiency and strict adherence to timelines. However, it is equally important to ensure that the rights of both the State and the investor are considered and protected.

- Enforcement challenges: Enforcing arbitral awards against States can be a complex process due to sovereign immunity issues and the need for diplomatic solutions. The issue of State immunity from execution 'has come to the fore in light of a number of attempts by award-creditors to attach their awards against the assets of a foreign State located in jurisdictions considered to be "pro-enforcement", such as France and Belgium'.[12]
- Transparency and Public Interests: The participation of States in disputes often engages broader public interests, underscoring the need for transparency in the arbitration process to address these interests and maintain public confidence. Therefore, expedited rules should incorporate measures for transparency, such as granting the public access to certain documents or summaries of proceedings and implementing robust safeguards to safeguard sensitive information, including proprietary business secrets.

In the realm of expedited arbitration within investment arbitration, the challenge lies in the need to tailor the rules to account for these specificities. These arbitration rules should consider the distinctive elements of investor-State disputes. Adapting expedited arbitration rules to investment arbitration involves recognizing and accommodating the unique characteristics and challenges introduced when States are parties to disputes with investors. A tailored approach is essential to strike a balance between the need for efficiency and the complexities associated with investor-State disputes. The development and implementation of such adapted rules are crucial for ensuring that the expedited arbitration process remains fair, transparent, and enforceable in this distinct context.

In evaluating the suitability of expedited arbitration for international investment disputes, several factors come into play, significantly influencing the appropriateness of this approach. The nature of the investment dispute, the parties' preferences, the balance between speed and fairness, the public interest element inherent in investment disputes, and the availability of necessary resources all collectively shape the feasibility of expedited arbitration in the 'State context'.

The nature of international investment disputes holds a pivotal role in this determination. Expedited arbitration is inherently designed to expedite dispute resolution and reduce costs, making it better suited for straightforward disputes characterized by clarity and simplicity. In such cases, the expeditious nature of the process aligns well with the parties' objectives, promoting efficiency and cost-effectiveness.

12. Phoebe D. Winch, State Immunity and the Execution of Investment Arbitration Awards. In: C. Titi (eds) Public Actors in International Investment Law. European Yearbook of International Economic Law. Springer. 57-77 n. 55 (2021), available at: DOI: 10.1007/978-3-030-58916-5_4.

However, complex cases that demand intricate legal analysis, expert examination, and extensive procedural steps may not be well suited for expedited arbitration.

Balancing speed and fairness is a fundamental consideration. While expedited arbitration seeks to expedite the resolution process, it should not compromise the fundamental principles of due process, fairness, and the right to a full and fair hearing. Achieving this equilibrium is essential, especially in investment arbitration, where the public interest often plays a prominent role.

Nonetheless, there are investment cases that, while not overly complex, could benefit from the efficiency of expedited arbitration. Such cases are characterized by their relative simplicity and suitability for a streamlined resolution process, provided that certain conditions are met. These conditions include the presence of appropriate rules specifically designed for investment disputes, the engagement of high-calibre arbitrators with the necessary expertise, the availability of well-equipped arbitration centres, and the utilization of advanced technology to facilitate remote proceedings and document submissions.

However, the suitability of expedited arbitration may differ from one case to another. Some investment disputes may readily align with expedited procedures, particularly those that are relatively straightforward and where both parties embrace the concept. However, other cases may involve intricate legal, financial, or technical issues that warrant a more traditional approach to ensure a comprehensive and equitable resolution, preserving the public interest and safeguarding the rights of all stakeholders.

§11.03 COMPARISON BETWEEN ICSID AND UNCITRAL EXPEDITED ARBITRATION RULES

The International Centre for Settlement of Investment Disputes (ICSID) is a renowned institution focused on resolving international investment disputes and is part of the World Bank Group. It implemented new arbitration rules on 1 July 2022, featuring a dedicated chapter on expedited arbitration. Similarly, the United Nations Commission on International Trade Law (UNCITRAL), a United Nations (UN) entity dedicated to harmonizing and unifying international trade law, introduced its new arbitration rules on 19 September 2021, which include an appendix on expedited arbitration. As one commentator stated:

> Arbitrations can be put on a 'fast track' by adopting simplified procedures and avoiding some of the procedural excesses of modern arbitral practice. Several arbitral institutions have developed rules for the faster resolution of disputes by means of a simplified procedure. As might be expected, the rules differ from one institution to another.[13]

By dissecting the differences between the approaches of ICSID and UNCITRAL, a deeper understanding of how these rules function and how they might best serve the

13. Dolzer & Schreuer, Principles of International, *supra* n. 10, at 33.

needs of parties involved in expedited arbitration will be gained. This exploration will encompass areas such as the imposition of time limits, the methodology for arbitrator selection, consent requirements, and other crucial elements. In doing so, the paths available for parties seeking swift and efficient dispute resolution in the international arena will be illuminated.

[A] Party Consent in Expedited Investment Arbitration

The principle of party autonomy is a fundamental concept that underpins arbitration proceedings. To uphold this principle, 'leading international arbitration conventions and national arbitration laws accord parties broad autonomy to agree upon the substantive laws and procedures applicable to their arbitrations'.[14] This principle empowers parties to tailor the arbitration process to their unique requirements and preferences while still adhering to essential standards of due process and fairness. This flexibility ensures that the arbitration remains efficient, effective, and equitable. Parties can exercise this autonomy to make various critical decisions, including the selection of arbitrators, the choice of the arbitration's location and language, and even the decision to opt for either expedited or standard proceedings.

In ICSID Expedited Arbitration, the parties may agree to expedite the arbitration by jointly submitting written consent to the Secretary-General at any point in the proceedings.[15] Parties must voluntarily agree to expedite the arbitration, and their consent must be officially conveyed through written communication to the Secretary-General. This provision ensures that the parties actively opt for the expedited procedure and permits this consent to be given at any time, either before the initiation of the arbitration in the relevant instrument of consent or during its course.[16] While deciding to opt for an expedited process before a dispute arises might seem somewhat premature, waiting until a dispute emerges also poses challenges as reaching an agreement may become more complex. Therefore, if parties intend to decide this matter before a dispute arises, including such a provision in the arbitration agreement is a prudent decision.

Consistent with the party autonomy principle, the ICSID Expedited Rules empower the parties to opt out of expedited arbitration at any time by jointly informing the Tribunal and Secretary-General in writing of their decision.[17] Here again, the emphasis is on the parties' agreement because they are the ultimate decision-makers in the proceedings, with the ability to determine what serves their dispute resolution needs best. This agreement must be clear and unequivocal. This provision grants parties the flexibility and control to adapt the arbitration process to their specific requirements.

14. Born, International Commercial Arbitration, *supra* n. 2, at 84.
15. International Centre for Settlement of Investment Disputes, ICSID Arbitration Rules, Chapter XII: Expedited Arbitration, Rule 75(1) (2022), available at: https://icsid.worldbank.org/rules-regulations/convention/arbitration-rules/chapter-xii-expedited-arbitration.
16. *Ibid.*
17. ICSID Arbitration Rules, Chapter XII, *supra* n. 15, at Rule 86 (1).

However, the ICSID Rules establish that the parties may opt out of expedited arbitration without mutual consent.[18] 'If only one party requests that the arbitration no longer be expedited, the Tribunal will decide, taking into account the complexity of the issues, the stage of the proceeding and all other circumstances.'[19] The Tribunal must assess whether continuing with the expedited process would negatively impact the arbitration or infringe upon the parties' rights. The suitability of expedited arbitration can vary on a case-by-case basis, and there is no one-size-fits-all solution. Opting out of expedited arbitration is particularly relevant in cases where an arbitration agreement initially stipulates expedited arbitration, but as the dispute unfolds, the parties recognize that the nature of the dispute is not conducive to expedited proceedings. In such instances, the Tribunal should remain vigilant to prevent any attempts at dilatory tactics by either party.

However, the UNCITRAL Arbitration Rules (UARs) specify that the Expedited Arbitration Rules apply when the parties mutually agree to their application.[20] In alignment with the party autonomy principle, the express consent of the parties holds paramount importance, underscoring their ability to decide on the use of expedited rules. Furthermore, the UNCITRAL Expedited Rules reinforce that the parties' explicit consent is a prerequisite for adoption and that parties can reach this agreement at any point, even after a dispute has emerged.[21]

The explanatory notes accompanying the UNCITRAL Expedited Rules highlight that parties should be mindful of the consequences when changing from non-expedited to expedited arbitration. For example, they note that a notice of arbitration filed in accordance with the non-expedited UNCITRAL Arbitration Procedure might not fulfil the requirements outlined in Article 4 of the Expedited Rules, which requires the claimant to propose the appointment of a sole arbitrator and an appointing authority.[22]

Situations may arise where the parties have initially established a three-member arbitral tribunal under the UARs but subsequently opt to modify their agreement by changing to a sole arbitrator under the Expedited Rules. While this may appear to be a means to expedite the decision-making process, such a change in the tribunal's composition could result in an extended procedure. Altering the composition of the arbitral tribunal might necessitate the parties to revisit statements and evidence they had previously submitted. Consequently, this possibility has the potential to introduce delays in the proceedings, which runs contrary to the intended expeditious nature of the expedited procedure. Therefore, parties transitioning to expedited arbitration

18. *Ibid.*, at Rule 86 (2).
19. ICSID: Procedures, Expedited Arbitration Rules (5 October 2023), https://icsid.worldbank.org/procedures/arbitration/convention/expedited-arbitration/2022.
20. United Nations Commission on International Trade Law, UNCITRAL Arbitration Rules, Appendix: UNCITRAL Expedited Arbitration Rules, Article 1 (2021), available at: https://uncitral.un.org/sites/uncitral.un.org/files/media-documents/uncitral/en/21-07996_expedited-arbitration-e-ebook.pdf.
21. *Ibid.*
22. United Nations Commission on International Trade Law, Explanatory Note to the UNCITRAL Expedited Arbitration Rules, para. 6 (2021), available at: https://uncitral.un.org/sites/uncitral.un.org/files/media-documents/uncitral/en/explanatory_note_to_the_expedited_rules_advance_copy.pdf.

should be aware of the distinctions between the UARs and the Expedited Rules. Beyond this example, they should thoughtfully consider whether the Expedited Rules are suited to their dispute.

Additionally, the UNCITRAL Expedited Rules provide parties the option to jointly agree to terminate their application at any point during the proceedings.[23] The Rules also allow the arbitral tribunal, at the request of a party and in exceptional circumstances, to decide that the Expedited Rules should no longer apply, after inviting the parties to express their views.[24] The tribunal must provide reasons for its decision, signifying that mutual agreement is not required. Instead, the tribunal makes the determination. In this regard, the circumstances for such a change are subject to specific criteria.

The phrase 'in exceptional circumstances' implies that a party requesting withdrawal must present compelling and well-justified reasons. The arbitral tribunal should grant such requests only in specific situations, maintaining a high threshold for unilateral withdrawal from expedited arbitration.[25] Moreover, when making such a determination, the tribunal should evaluate the appropriateness of the Expedited Rules for resolving the dispute.[26] Factors to consider include:

- the urgency of resolving the dispute;
- the stage of the proceeding at which the request is made;
- the complexity of the dispute (e.g., the anticipated volume of documentary evidence and the number of witnesses);
- the anticipated amount in dispute (the sum of claims made in the notice of arbitration, any counterclaim made in the response thereto as well as any amendment or supplement);
- the terms of the parties' agreement to expedited arbitration and whether the current circumstances could have been foreseeable at the time of the agreement; and
- the consequences of the determination on the proceedings.[27]

When making this determination, in accordance with Article 17(1) of the UARs, the arbitral tribunal can decide that specific articles or the entire Expedited Rules no longer apply to the arbitration.[28] The tribunal must clarify how the arbitration will proceed and which rules will govern the process. For example, the tribunal may decide that specific procedural requirements from the Expedited Rules will continue to apply if they benefit the arbitration's conduct, even if the entirety of the Expedited Arbitration Rules no longer applies. This flexibility aligns with the core principle of adapting

23. UNCITRAL, Expedited Arbitration Rules, *supra* n. 20, at Article 2.1.
24. *Ibid.*
25. UNCITRAL, Explanatory Note, *supra* n. 22, at para. 12.
26. *Ibid.*, at para. 13.
27. *Ibid.*
28. *Ibid.*, at para. 15.

arbitration procedures to individual case needs while retaining the efficiency advantages of the Expedited Rules. When the Expedited Rules no longer apply, the arbitral tribunal conducts the arbitration following the UARs as the default governing rules.[29]

Both the ICSID and UNCITRAL expedited arbitration rules primarily align when it comes to the aspect of parties' consent in expedited arbitration. A pivotal consideration here is the autonomy and preference of the parties involved. In both sets of rules, parties have the option to choose expedited arbitration either before or after the arbitration dispute emerges. Furthermore, both rules provide the parties with the flexibility to opt out of the expedited process at any point, subject to mutual consent. However, in cases where unilateral withdrawal is sought, as in the absence of mutual agreement, the tribunal steps in to make the final determination, taking into account the specific circumstances of the case.

In both cases, the expedited arbitration rules apply where parties agree, in contrast with other institutions' expedited rules, 'since there is no automatic application based on specific criteria such as the amount in dispute'.[30] Given this common ground in the ICSID and UNCITRAL rules, the introduction of a predefined monetary threshold for cases that would, by default, be subject to expedited arbitration in the absence of specific agreement by the parties may be worth consideration.

[B] Selection of Arbitrators in Expedited Arbitration

In investment arbitration, the majority of cases have a tribunal composed of three arbitrators. In most cases, the investor and the host State each appoint an arbitrator. 'The third arbitrator, also called the presiding arbitrator, is appointed either by the parties jointly, or by agreement of the two party-appointed arbitrators or by the arbitral institution involved.'[31] However, the ICSID expedited arbitration rules deviate from this standard.

ICSID expedited arbitration gives the parties the autonomy to choose between two tribunal structures: a sole arbitrator or a three-member tribunal.[32] This initial choice is a critical decision in the arbitration process. Pursuant to the ICSID Rules, the parties are required to jointly notify the Secretary-General in writing of their selection within 30 days of their consent to expedited arbitration.[33] If the parties fail to communicate their choice within this time frame, the default outcome will be a Sole

29. UNCITRAL, Expedited Arbitration Rules, *supra* n. 20, at Article 2.3.
30. Mayer Brown: Legal Update, 'UNCITRAL's Expedited Arbitration Rules: 15 Q&A's to get you up to speed' (2021), at 1, available at: https://www.mayerbrown.com/-/media/files/perspectives-events/publications/2021/08/uncitrals-expedited-arbitration-rules.pdf.
31. Albert Jan Van den Berg, Qualified Investment Arbitrators? A Comment on Arbitrators in Investment Arbitrations, The Practice of Arbitration: Essays in Honour of Hans van Houtte, Hart Publishing, Oxford, 53, 60 n. 54 (2012), available at https://www.hvdb.com/wp-content/uploads/Qualified-Investment-Arbitrators.pdf.
32. ICSID Arbitration Rules, Chapter XII, *supra* n. 15, at Rule 76(1).
33. *Ibid.*, at Rule 76(2).

Arbitrator, which is in line with the expedited nature of these proceedings.[34] This mechanism ensures that the arbitration process remains prompt and efficient.

There are two pathways for the appointment of a sole arbitrator:[35] one involving the parties and the other the Secretary-General. In the first scenario, the parties must jointly appoint the sole arbitrator within 20 days of notifying their preference for either a sole arbitrator or a three-member tribunal.[36] In contrast, there are other scenarios in which the Secretary-General is tasked with the appointment of a sole arbitrator. These situations include instances where the parties fail to reach an agreement within the designated time frame, they declare their inability to agree on an arbitrator, or when an appointee declines the appointment.[37]

There is a structured procedure for the appointment of a sole arbitrator by the Secretary-General.[38] The Secretary-General will make the appointment using a list-ranking procedure.[39] First, the parties will receive a list of five candidates within 10 days after the expiry of the 20 days for appointment. The parties then rank the candidates in the order of preference, giving the highest number to the most preferred candidate. They then return the list to the Secretary-General within 10 days of its receipt. The Secretary-General notifies the parties of the results of the list-ranking procedure on the next business day after receiving both parties' lists. The highest-ranked candidate is appointed, or, if there is a tie, the Secretary-General selects one of the tied candidates. As soon as the appointee is selected, the Secretary-General seeks his or her acceptance.

In the case of a three-member tribunal, the key feature continues to be party autonomy. In this scenario, each party is required to appoint an arbitrator, often referred to as a 'co-arbitrator', within 20 days of the notification established in Rule 76(2).[40] Furthermore, the parties must jointly select the president of the tribunal within 20 days of both co-arbitrators accepting their roles.[41]

However, there are occasions where the Secretary-General might need to intervene in the appointment process.[42] These scenarios include instances where an appointment is not made within the defined time limit, the parties declare their inability to agree on the tribunal president, or an appointee declines or fails to comply with Rule 79(1).[43]

Rule 78(3) of the ICSID Rules outlines a consultative procedure by the Secretary-General when appointing arbitrators. The Secretary-General initially appoints any co-arbitrators not yet designated. Following this, the Secretary-General presents a list of five potential tribunal presidents to the parties. Each party has the authority to strike

34. *Ibid.*
35. *Ibid.*, at Rule 77.
36. *Ibid.*, at Rule 77(1).
37. *Ibid.*, at Rule 77(2).
38. *Ibid.*, at Rule 77(3).
39. ICSID: Procedures, Expedited Arbitration Rules, supra n. 19.
40. ICSID Arbitration Rules, Chapter XII, *supra* n. 15, at Rule 78(1)a.
41. *Ibid.*, at Rule 78(1)b.
42. *Ibid.*, at Rule 78(2).
43. *Ibid.*, at Rule 78(1)a, b and c.

one name from the list and rank the remaining candidates by preference, with this ranking transmitted to the Secretary-General. The Secretary-General then informs the parties of the final selection, favouring the candidate with the best ranking. In cases of tied rankings, the Secretary-General exercises discretion to make the final choice while ensuring fairness. If the selected candidate declines or does not comply with Rule 79(1), the Secretary-General proceeds to appoint the next highest-ranked candidate.

In summary, the ICSID Expedited Arbitration Rules provide parties with options and structured procedures for selecting arbitrators. These rules strike a balance between party involvement and a prompt and fair arbitration process. Although the Secretary-General plays a role in certain situations, these provisions are designed to minimize potential delays, ensuring a fair and impartial arbitration process.

The UNCITRAL Expedited Arbitration Rules set out a fundamental principle regarding the number of arbitrators.[44] 'It establishes that unless otherwise agreed, there shall be one arbitrator.'[45] This provision simplifies the arbitration process, promoting efficiency and cost-effectiveness, which is especially crucial in expedited cases. Parties retain the flexibility to agree on multiple arbitrators. However, opting for an arbitral tribunal composed of more than one arbitrator might lead to less expeditious proceedings because the coordination and decision-making processes can naturally take more time.

The UNCITRAL Expedited Rules outline the procedure for appointing the sole arbitrator.[46] It underscores the significance of party autonomy in the appointment process, stating that the sole arbitrator should be appointed jointly. Nevertheless, in cases where the parties cannot reach an agreement on the appointment of a sole arbitrator within 15 days after receiving a proposal, the rules provide a mechanism for resolving the impasse. At the request of a party, the appointing authority will step in and appoint the sole arbitrator.[47] This safeguard ensures that the arbitration process can proceed even if the parties are unable to reach a consensus.

When parties opt for multiple arbitrators, Articles 9 and 10 of the UNCITRAL Expedited Arbitration Rules apply. Article 9 prescribes the process where each party appoints one arbitrator, with those two arbitrators selecting the third, who serves as the presiding arbitrator. However, if a party fails to notify its choice within 30 days, or if the two arbitrators cannot agree on the presiding arbitrator within the same time frame, the appointing authority steps in, functioning similarly to the appointment of a sole arbitrator under Article 8.[48]

Notably, the role of the appointing authority, as outlined in the UNCITRAL Expedited Arbitration Rules, is pivotal in expediting proceedings, particularly concerning the constitution of the arbitral tribunal. The explanatory note to the rules further emphasizes this role. In cases where parties have not agreed on an appointing authority, Article 6 of the UNCITRAL Expedited Rules provides a mechanism for the

44. UNCITRAL Expedited Arbitration Rules, *supra* n. 20, at Article 7.
45. Mayer Brown, Legal Update, *supra* n. 30, at 3.
46. UNCITRAL Expedited Arbitration Rules, *supra* n. 20, at Article 8.
47. *Ibid.*, at Article 8(2).
48. *Ibid.*, at Articles 9 and 10.

Secretary-General of the Permanent Court of Arbitration (PCA) to designate an appointing authority or to serve as one, thereby streamlining the process and leading to an earlier engagement of the appointing authority.[49]

The selectivity of the appointing authority extends to ensuring the independence and impartiality of the arbitrator. The authority ensures that the appointed arbitrator upholds these essential principles. Furthermore, when parties have initiated arbitration under the UNCITRAL Expedited Rules without a separate agreement on the number of arbitrators, the appointing authority is specifically instructed to appoint a sole arbitrator. This allocation of responsibilities and procedures within the UNCITRAL Expedited Arbitration Rules ensures that the process is well structured, adaptable, and efficient. It also preserves the fundamental principles of independence and impartiality within the arbitration process.

The ICSID and UNCITRAL expedited arbitration rules exhibit both similarities and differences in the appointment of arbitrators. In ICSID arbitrations, parties are presented with an initial choice between a three-member tribunal or a single arbitrator. In the event that an agreement cannot be reached between the parties, the default configuration will be that of a single arbitrator. Under the UNCITRAL Rules, the default is a sole arbitrator unless the parties mutually agree otherwise. The UNCITRAL approach better conforms to the essence of expedited arbitration. Given its inherent focus on expediency and cost-efficiency, the provision designating the sole arbitrator as the default rule aligns more closely with the objectives of this form of arbitration.

This single arbitrator typically incurs lower fees and expenses compared to a three-member tribunal, in harmony with the core objectives of efficiently and economically resolving disputes. However, there may be drawbacks to a sole arbitrator. While it may expedite the process, a single arbitrator may have limited perspectives because the entire decision hinges on one individual. Furthermore, they may lack the specialized expertise required for complex cases. In contrast, a three-member tribunal introduces a diversity of viewpoints and can bring valuable specialized knowledge to complex disputes. Nonetheless, this approach may result in higher costs or extended deliberation times. Such factors can run counter to the primary goals of expedited arbitration, where swift resolution and cost-effectiveness are pivotal.

The choice between an internal or an external appointing authority offers distinct advantages. Internal appointing authorities leverage their deep familiarity with the arbitration centre's rules, fostering efficient communication and a smoother process. External appointing authorities bring a perceived neutrality and specialized expertise in impartial appointments. This may be particularly beneficial in handling complex cases and may thereby enhance trust in the appointment process. However, opting for a predefined appointing authority such as the Secretary-General of ICSID can significantly streamline proceedings, eliminating potential delays associated with the authority's selection.

49. *Ibid.*, at Article 6.

[C] Procedural Schedules

ICSID '[e]xpedited arbitration aims to expedite the overall proceeding by reducing the time taken for the main steps in the process: selection and appointment of Tribunal members; the first session; the procedural schedule; the Tribunal's Award'.[50] The procedural journey of the ICSID expedited arbitration begins with the first session within 30 days after the constitution of the Tribunal.[51] This inaugural meeting shall be conducted remotely, unless all involved parties - claimant, respondent, and the Tribunal - unanimously opt for an in-person session.[52] This provision recognizes the global nature of investment arbitrations, typically involving stakeholders from diverse jurisdictions. The implementation of remote hearings aligns with the overarching goal of expedition, and its significance is not to be underestimated. By allowing parties and arbitrators to engage in the process from their individual locations, this method reduces the need for travel, maximizes the efficient use of time, and expedites the scheduling of hearings. As a result, the arbitration process becomes more streamlined and cost-effective, which often motivates parties to readily embrace the proceedings.

For example, consider a hypothetical scenario involving a dispute between an Australian investor and Germany. In this hypothetical case, the Australian investor is backed by a legal team headquartered in Sydney, while Germany is represented by its own legal team. The adoption of remote first sessions is invaluable in this context, enabling both parties and their respective legal counsel to actively participate in the initial session without the burdensome requirement of extensive and expensive travel to the venue of the arbitration. This not only simplifies the procedural aspects but also reduces costs and facilitates accessibility for all involved, making the arbitration process notably more efficient.

The ICSID Rules outline a detailed procedural schedule in expedited arbitration, which plays a critical role in promoting both efficiency and fairness in the arbitration process.[53] 'The schedule anticipates two rounds of written submissions with page limits, a hearing, and an Award within 120 days after the hearing.'[54] Also, expedited arbitration joins all matters before the tribunal into one proceeding. A party may raise preliminary objections but cannot request bifurcation of the objections. The tribunal deals with all questions in its award. The timetable established after the tribunal's first session is as follows:

- The claimant files a memorial within 60 days after the first session, to which the respondent responds with a counter-memorial within the same time frame.
- This is followed by the claimant's reply and the respondent's rejoinder, each submitted within 40 days of the respective preceding document.

50. ICSID: Procedures, Expedited Arbitration Rules, *supra* n. 19.
51. ICSID Arbitration Rules, Chapter XII, *supra* n. 15, at Rule 80(1).
52. *Ibid.*, at Rule 80(2).
53. *Ibid.*, at Rule 81.
54. ICSID: Procedures, Expedited Arbitration Rules, *supra* n. 19.

- A hearing is then scheduled within 60 days after the last written submission, and the parties must file statements on costs within 10 days after the hearing's conclusion.
- The tribunal is mandated to render an award as soon as possible, but no later than 120 days after the hearing, encouraging the swift resolution of the dispute.[55]

The key features of this schedule are the precise timelines set for the submission of memorials, counter-memorials, replies, and rejoinders, all of which contribute to expediting the proceedings. Notably, these documents are subject to strict page limits, with memorials and counter-memorials capped at 200 pages each and replies and rejoinders limited to 100 pages. The allowance of 300 pages could be seen as potentially counterproductive to the fundamental goal of expedited arbitration - to resolve disputes swiftly and economically. Allowing documents of this length might not only undermine the expeditious nature of the procedure but also increase the burden on both parties, arbitrators, and the overall administration of the case. 'Under ICSID expedited arbitration rules, the proceeding would conclude within 470-530 days after the date of registration.'[56]

However, the UNCITRAL Expedited Arbitration Rules involve a series of steps that aim to expedite the resolution of disputes while maintaining procedural integrity. The expedited procedure begins with the claimant serving a 'notice of arbitration' and a statement of claim.[57] This notice not merely is a formal requirement but also serves a critical function. It allows the claimant to propose the designation of an appointing authority and suggest an arbitrator if these appointments have not been agreed in advance. This early stage is vital for promptly identifying key figures in the arbitration process, ensuring a smooth and efficient journey. Within 15 days of receiving the notice of arbitration, the respondent is obligated to provide a response. Notably, this response also includes the respondent's statement of defence. This prompt response requirement ensures that both parties initiate their positions without undue delay, setting the stage for the arbitration proceedings to follow. Once the arbitral tribunal is constituted, a 'case management conference' is conducted.[58] During this conference, all parties engage in discussions with the tribunal to establish a clear procedure for the arbitration. Details such as the choice of language for proceedings, the venue for hearings, timetables and other procedural matters are addressed, with the ultimate goal of aligning the process with the parties' needs. This early engagement fosters efficiency.

The UAR set a clear time frame for delivering the final award. The standard time frame for an award is six months from the constitution of the arbitral tribunal. However, this period can be extended up to nine months in exceptional circumstances, provided the parties unanimously agree to the extension. If unanimity is not reached,

55. ICSID Arbitration Rules, Chapter XII, *supra* n. 15, at Rule 81.
56. ICSID: Procedures, Expedited Arbitration Rules, *supra* n. 19.
57. UNCITRAL Expedited Arbitration Rules, *supra* n. 20, at Article 8.
58. *Ibid.*, at Article 9.

any party involved may request that the expedited rules no longer apply, thereby allowing the arbitration to continue under the standard UNCITRAL rules.[59]

Regarding evidence and hearings, the arbitral tribunal has the authority to decide, after consulting with the parties, whether in-person hearings are necessary.[60] This discretion is vital for efficiency because hearings are resource-intensive. The tribunal must specify which documents and witnesses are relevant to the case, streamlining the process and focusing on the key aspects of the dispute.[61]

Both the ICSID and UNCITRAL expedited arbitration procedures share the advantage of promoting efficiency in the resolution of investment disputes. They achieve this through early engagement, setting precise procedural timelines, and offering flexibility, all of which facilitate prompt decision-making. Both procedures acknowledge the benefits of remote hearings, reducing travel-related burdens and enhancing accessibility for parties involved in cross-border disputes. While implementing strict page limits on documents can help manage excessive document volumes, both ICSID and UNCITRAL procedures should explore a balanced approach. This flexibility can be achieved by establishing reasonable page limits while also affording parties the opportunity to request extensions when required. Given the increasing relevance of remote hearings in enhancing efficiency, both ICSID and UNCITRAL offer comprehensive guidelines and standards for conducting remote hearings, capitalizing on the available technological tools. This may encompass best practices for leveraging technology, ensuring security, and addressing potential challenges related to differing time zones, connectivity and systems.

To further expedite the dispute resolution process, both sets of rules could contemplate the introduction of mechanisms that encourage parties to explore settlement options. This may involve the inclusion of optional mediation or early neutral evaluation stages aimed at resolving disputes prior to their escalation into full-blown arbitration proceedings. In this context, the mediator should not serve as the arbitrator.

§11.04 CONCLUSION

The appropriateness of expedited arbitration in international investment disputes within the 'State context' hinges on a careful and case-specific evaluation. While it can be a valuable tool for expediting certain investment cases, its suitability depends on the complexity of the dispute, party consent, the delicate balance between speed and fairness, and the availability of necessary resources and expertise. Careful consideration of these factors is essential to determine whether expedited arbitration is the right approach for a particular investment dispute. Parties' preferences are a critical element in this equation. When both parties willingly consent to expedited procedures or agree to their application, expedited arbitration can be a viable and efficient option. However, it may face challenges in situations where one party objects or when the

59. *Ibid.*, at Article 16(4).
60. *Ibid.*, at Article 11.
61. *Ibid.*, at Article 15.

dispute involves a State, which may have specific procedural requirements based on its public interest considerations.

When expedited arbitration applies to investment disputes, there are available rules provided by prominent entities such as ICSID and UNCITRAL to govern the proceedings. While these rules may differ in some aspects, their overall objective and goal remain consistent - to expedite the resolution of investment disputes while upholding the principles of fairness and due process. Use of such expedited rules should help the parties and interested parties overcome the hurdles that often lead to extended and cumbersome proceedings in investor-State disputes. Parties should be encouraged to consider and use expedited rules in appropriate disputes. The expedited rules should continue to evolve to improve the attainment of their primary goal.

CHAPTER 12

Balancing Efficiency and Party Autonomy in Expedited Procedures: Assessing Reforms under the ICC and Swiss Rules

Yassine Sangaré

In recent years, France has experienced a notable upswing in expedited dispute resolution, driven by the escalating demand for efficient conflict resolution mechanisms. Responding to this need, the International Chamber of Commerce (ICC) has implemented an expedited arbitration process that streamlines proceedings and cuts costs for disputes under USD 3 million. This positions France as an attractive jurisdiction for those seeking swift dispute resolution. Despite simplifying the process, concerns have emerged about potential challenges to arbitral awards by the losing party. Critics contend that these expedited procedures may compromise the fundamental principle of party autonomy in arbitration. This chapter critically assesses the preservation of party autonomy under ICC Rules, comparing them to the Swiss Rules, with a specific focus on expedited procedures in France and Switzerland. It scrutinizes how the delicate balance between party autonomy and efficiency is maintained in the context of expedited procedures.

§12.01 INTRODUCTION

In today's globalized business world, disputes between parties from different jurisdictions are increasingly common. Traditional litigation can be a slow and expensive process, leading businesses to turn to alternative dispute resolution mechanisms such as arbitration, which offers numerous advantages. Arbitration is an excellent tool for permanent dispute resolution. Nonetheless, this theoretical advantage diverges from practical reality. Over the years, concerns have been expressed by users regarding escalating costs, excessive formalities, and delays that have made arbitration burdensome and similar to court proceedings.[1] Medium-sized companies with disputes generally not exceeding USD 1,000,000 or straightforward disputes have been prejudiced by the implementation of regular arbitration procedures.[2]

France has a long-standing tradition of supporting arbitration, with the first modern arbitration law – the French Arbitration Law of 1980. Arbitration in France has a well-established status regulated by the French Code of Civil Procedure (CCP), which contains provisions governing both domestic and international arbitration from Articles 1442 to 1527.

The French arbitration landscape underwent a significant transformation in 2011 with the enactment of Decree No. 2011-48. This legislative update brought about substantial changes to the CCP governing arbitration in France. These changes aimed to improve the transparency and reliability of French arbitration law. In conjunction with the proactive adjustments made by arbitration institutions to align with the evolving demands of arbitration, these reforms have played a pivotal role in maintaining Paris as a leading and preferred destination for arbitration proceedings.

Paris is home to several arbitral institutions, including the International Chamber of Commerce (ICC), a globally renowned arbitral institution that has administered over 28,000 cases since its establishment in 1923.[3] Recognizing the imperative need to address the issues of time- and cost-efficiency, the ICC undertook a thorough revision of its rules, leading to the expedited procedure provisions (EPP) in 2017.[4] These provisions aim to expedite the arbitral process. However, their implementation may inadvertently impact the enforceability of arbitral awards. Balancing efficiency with the fundamental principle of party autonomy presents a key issue for expedited arbitration. While such proceedings are desirable, they must not infringe upon the parties' autonomy to shape their dispute resolution process. Indeed, efficiency in arbitration proceedings is a paramount consideration for leading arbitral institutions worldwide, such as the Swiss Arbitration Centre (formerly Swiss Chambers' Arbitration Institution (SCAI)).[5]

The introduction of expedited procedures in institutional arbitration rules has become increasingly common since the Swiss Rules included such provisions in 2004. Switzerland has been a preferred venue for hosting international arbitrations for over a century, consistently ranking among the top three venues for ICC arbitration proceedings worldwide.[6] Nevertheless, expediting arbitration proceedings while maintaining

1. 2018 International Arbitration Survey: The Evolution of International Arbitration, https://arbitration.qmul.ac.uk/research/2018/.
2. *Ibid.*
3. 'ICC reaches arbitration milestone with case 28,000', https://iccwbo.org/news-publications/news/icc-reaches-arbitration-milestone-with-case-28000/.
4. Christophe Seraglini & Patrick Baeten, 'Expedited Rules and the Possibility of Immediate Measures once a Tribunal is Constituted', in *Expedited Procedures in International Arbitration*, Laurent Lévy & Michael Polkinghorne, eds (Kluwer Law Int'l, 2018), 37.
5. Philipp Habegger, 'Revised Swiss Rules of International Arbitration – An Overview of the Major Changes', 30 *ASA Bull.* 269 (2012) DOI: 10.54648/asab2012027.
6. 2021 International Arbitration Survey: Adapting arbitration to a changing world, https://www.whitecase.com/publications/insight/2021-international-arbitration-survey.

the fundamental principles of party autonomy and due process has been an ongoing challenge for leading arbitral institutions.

This chapter delves into the realm of expedited arbitration procedures, focusing on the ICC's EPP and the Swiss rules. It addresses the question of whether the arbitral institutions have succeeded in preserving the delicate and complex balance between efficiency and the principle of autonomy in the arbitration context. This chapter provides a comprehensive analysis of expedited arbitration procedures offered by two prominent arbitration institutions: the ICC and the Swiss Arbitration Centre. This chapter examines the current developments and challenges of expedited arbitration procedures in France and Switzerland, exploring the intricate balance between efficiency and party autonomy in their respective legal frameworks.

§12.02 HARNESSING SWITZERLAND'S LONG-STANDING EXPEDITED ARBITRATION PROCEDURES

Switzerland has a long-standing and distinguished tradition in the field of arbitration. The Swiss Arbitration Centre and its rules play a prominent role. The 2021 Queen Mary International Arbitration Survey revealed that Switzerland is highly regarded as a major hub.[7] Geneva is among the most preferred seats of arbitration, alongside London and Paris.[8] This reputation can be attributed to several factors, including its political neutrality, which establishes it as a reliable and impartial hub for resolving even the most sensitive disputes.[9] Switzerland has become a preferred choice for international commercial arbitrations with approximately two-thirds of such arbitrations involving non-Swiss parties.[10] This is because Switzerland is situated in the heart of Europe but not bound by EU law as a non-EU member. It therefore benefits from a well-established legal framework and efficient institutional support.[11] This preference is also due to the advantageous nature of Swiss arbitration law, which is frequently utilized in international contracts and disputes. Indeed, with its robust legal framework governed by the Federal Act on Private International Law,[12] Switzerland has established a reputation for its liberal and flexible approach to international arbitration.[13] This framework, which was updated in 2021, serves as a strong foundation for facilitating the efficient and effective resolution of international disputes. Additionally, domestic arbitration in Switzerland is regulated by Part 3 of the Civil Procedure Code (CPC),[14] providing a more structured framework for domestic arbitration proceedings.

---

7. *Ibid.*
8. *Ibid.*
9. *Ibid.*
10. Statistical data released by the Swiss Chamber in 2009 reveals that 48% of the involved parties originated from Western Europe, while 24% were from Switzerland, 6% from Eastern Europe and Russia, 12% from Asia/Middle East, and 5% from Northern America.
11. *Ibid.*
12. Chapter 12 of Federal Act on Private International Law (PILA), https://www.swissarbitration.org/wp-content/uploads/2021/05/20210129-Chapter-12-PILA_Translation_English.pdf.
13. De Philippe Bärtsch & Dorothee Schramm, *Arbitration Law of Switzerland: Practice & Procedure* (JurisNet LLC, 2014).
14. Swiss Civil Procedure Code, https://www.fedlex.admin.ch/eli/cc/2010/262/en.

Arbitral institutions play a significant role in the country's arbitration landscape. Switzerland has two primary arbitral institutions. First, following the revision of the 2021 Swiss Rules, the SCAI was renamed the Swiss Arbitration Centre, reflecting its continued commitment to advancing arbitration practice and its pivotal role as a leading institution in Switzerland.[15] The second arbitral institution is the ICC, a renowned global arbitration institute headquartered in Paris "with a Swiss National Committee in Zurich."

The Swiss legal landscape has a rich history of embracing and implementing expedited arbitration. It was an early proponent of these time-sensitive dispute resolution mechanisms. The introduction of the expedited procedures in the 2004 Swiss Rules was met with enthusiasm within the arbitration community.[16] These came into effect on 1 January 2004, replacing the rules on international arbitration previously followed by participating Chambers of Commerce.[17] Based on the UNCITRAL Arbitration Rules of 1976, the Swiss Rules of International Arbitration (Swiss Rules) have been expanded to suit institutional arbitrations with a view to reflect contemporary practices in international arbitration. This procedural mechanism allows for a more streamlined and efficient resolution of disputes and aims to render an arbitral award within a significantly shorter time frame.[18]

The Swiss Rules attempt to address the demands of modern arbitration practice and offer parties the option to obtain a prompt and enforceable arbitral award within a relatively condensed time frame. Article 42(e) provides that the final award shall be made within six months from the date on which the arbitral tribunal received the file from the Secretariat.[19] In exceptional circumstances, the competent Court may extend this time limit.[20] This was illustrated in *Swiss Pharma Contract Ltd. v. Manhattan Pharmaceuticals Inc.*,[21] where the Chamber granted an extension for issuing the final award despite the initial time limit. The arbitral award was rendered within a period of nine months. The case provides empirical support for the assertion that the Swiss Rules establish an effective framework for arbitration. The Chamber's decision to grant an extension further illustrates the operational flexibility within the Swiss Rules, allowing the competent Court to exercise discretion in extending the time limit under exceptional circumstances. This practical manifestation reinforces the argument that the Swiss Rules attempt to facilitate timely and efficient resolution in arbitration proceedings.

Since their adoption in 2004, the Swiss Rules have accounted for 24% of the Swiss Chambers' cases in 2008 and have consistently represented 32% of cases.[22] The

15. https://www.swissarbitration.org/new-swiss-arbitration-centre-and-revised-swiss-rules/.
16. Caroline dos Santos, 'Arbitration Law Reform in Switzerland: William Tell's Apple-Shot Revista Brasileira de Arbitragem', 16 *Rev. Bras. Arb.* 61, 204 (2019) DOI: 10.54648/rba2019010.
17. Matthias Scherer, 'New Rules of International Arbitration in Switzerland', 7 *Intl Arb. L. Rev.* (2004).
18. Philipp Habegger, 'Revised Swiss Rules of International Arbitration – An Overview of the Major Changes', 30 *ASA Bull.* 269 (2012).
19. Article 42(e) of the Swiss Rules.
20. *Ibid.*
21. Case No. 600103-2007, https://jusmundi.com/fr/document/decision/en-swiss-pharma-contract-ltd-v-manhatthan-pharmaceuticals-inc-final-award-friday-5th-september-2008.
22. Swiss International Arbitration law reports (2008) vol. 2, no. 1.

Federal Supreme Court of Switzerland had its first opportunity in 2008[23] to rule on an application to set aside an award rendered under the Expedited Procedures of the Swiss Rules.[24] The case involved a dispute arising from a sales contract for petrochemical products between a Swiss and a Canadian company, with the amount in dispute falling below CHF 1 million. As required by the automatic application of the Expedited Procedures, the award was rendered within six months by a sole arbitrator.

The application to challenge the award claimed a violation of the respondent's right to be heard based on the conduct of the proceedings and the alleged lack of 'real reasons' in the award.[25] The Supreme Court dismissed the application.[26] Importantly, the Court did not specifically refer to the parties' agreement to arbitrate under the Swiss Rules, which included the acceptance of an accelerated procedure and an award providing reasons 'in summary form' only. This suggests that the Supreme Court applied its approach to challenges against arbitral awards generally. It thereby confirmed the validity and enforceability of arbitral awards rendered under the Expedited Procedures compared to those in regular proceedings. The Court thereby affirmed the effectiveness and credibility of the Swiss Chambers' Expedited Procedures as a dispute resolution mechanism.

In 2010, a working group was established to revise the 2004 Swiss Rules, incorporating the experience gained and recent developments in arbitral practice.[27] The objectives of the revision included enhancing flexibility for multiparty and multi-contract arbitrations, introducing emergency interim relief for urgent cases, and improving the efficiency of proceedings in terms of time and cost while striving to respect the autonomy of the parties and the arbitral tribunal.[28] The revised Swiss Rules, which largely retained the structure and content of the 2004 Swiss Rules, became effective on 1 June 2012.[29]

To enhance the efficiency in terms of time and cost, several new provisions were introduced. Article 15(7) plays a crucial role, requiring all participants in the arbitration to act in good faith and make efforts to contribute to the efficient conduct of the proceedings while avoiding unnecessary costs and delays.[30] Violations of this obligation may impact on the apportionment of costs. Additionally, Article 42 outlines the features of the expedited procedure. These features include the transmission of the case file to the arbitral tribunal following payment of a provisional deposit; generally allowing for only one exchange of submissions; a single hearing, if applicable, for

23. 4A_294/2008, Swiss Federal Supreme Court, 28 October 2008.
24. Article 42 of the Swiss Rules.
25. 4A_294/2008, Swiss Federal Supreme Court, 28 October 2008.
26. *Ibid.*
27. Philipp Habegger, 'Revised Swiss Rules of International Arbitration – An Overview of the Major Changes', 30 *ASA Bull.* 269 (2012).
28. *Ibid.*
29. Xavier Favre-Bulle, 'Swiss Rules of International Arbitration (Swiss Rules): From 2004 to the (Light) 2012 Revision', 50 *Intl Bus. L.J.* 21 (2013).
30. 2012 Swiss Rules, https://www.swissarbitration.org/wp-content/uploads/2021/05/SwissRules2012_German_2019.pdf.

witnesses and oral arguments; issuance of the award within six months and a concise statement of the award's reasons.[31]

In 2012, 40% of all Swiss Chambers' arbitral proceedings were conducted under the Expedited Procedure,[32] indicating its widespread acceptance and effectiveness. Acknowledging the favourable reception and notable achievements of the Expedited Procedures, the drafters of the 2012 Swiss Rules made a judicious decision to leverage the existing framework rather than make substantial revisions to Article 42. This approach reflects their recognition of the procedure's effectiveness and underscores the importance of continuity and stability in promoting efficient dispute resolution.

Building upon the success of the 2012 Swiss Rules, the Swiss Arbitration Centre introduced the revised Swiss Rules in 2021, representing a significant step forward in the evolution of arbitration in Switzerland.[33] These revised rules reflect the continuous efforts to enhance and modernize the Swiss arbitration framework, addressing emerging needs and aligning with international best practices. With a focus on efficiency, transparency, and party autonomy, the 2021 revision reaffirms Switzerland's commitment to providing a cutting-edge platform for effective and fair dispute resolution in the global arbitration community. The 2021 Swiss Rules offer various features, including the use of paperless submissions, virtual hearings, a revised cost provision, and an online cost calculator for cases administered under these rules.[34]

Because Switzerland is recognized for its efficiency in handling small- and medium-sized disputes, the 2021 Swiss Rules provide for an expedited procedure that can be invoked either upon the agreement of the parties or when the disputed amount does not exceed CHF 1,000,000, unless the competent Court decides otherwise.[35] The aim is to ensure expeditious resolution of disputes, with the expectation that the arbitral award will be rendered within six months from the receipt of the case file, and extensions will only be granted in exceptional circumstances.[36] Furthermore, the rules default to a sole arbitrator and streamline the number of written submissions required.[37] Some of these provisions were already in the previous versions of the Swiss Rules but have been restructured for clarity.[38] Notably, the possibility for parties to agree that no reasons need to be given by the arbitral tribunal in the award, as provided in the 2012 Swiss Rules,[39] has been removed. Nevertheless, the tribunal is permitted to provide a summary of the reasoning for the award.[40] How tribunals will exercise this

31. *Ibid.*
32. https://www.swissarbitration.org/wp-content/uploads/2021/05/SCAI_flyer_englisch_A5_27-05-2016_web.pdf.
33. https://www.swissarbitration.org/centre/arbitration/arbitration-rules/.
34. This is included in the 2021 Swiss Rules' cost schedules. https://www.swissarbitration.org/centre/arbitration/cost-calculator-2021/; https://www.swissarbitration.org/wp-content/uploads/2023/08/Swiss-Rules-2021-EN.pdf.
35. Article 42.1 of the Swiss Rules.
36. Article 42 of the Swiss Rules.
37. Article 42(2) of the Swiss Rules.
38. Former Article 42.1 of the Swiss Rules.
39. *Ibid.*
40. Article 42.2(f) of the Swiss Rules.

right remains to be seen because they may be cautious due to the potential for judicial challenges to their awards.[41]

Second, Article 27(2) of the 2021 Swiss Rules clarifies that hearings can be conducted remotely via videoconference or other suitable means.[42] The 2012 Swiss Rules already referred to videoconference use for witness examination in Article 25(4), providing tribunals with flexibility in ordering remote hearings.[43] The updated provision in the 2021 Swiss Rules reinforces the acceptance and utilization of remote hearing methods, which have become more prevalent during the COVID-19 pandemic.

Finally, the Swiss Rules now explicitly require parties and the tribunal to discuss cybersecurity issues at an early stage of the proceedings.[44] This provision acknowledges the increased importance of addressing cybersecurity concerns in the context of remote hearings and the digital exchange of information. It highlights the need for parties and the tribunal to assess and implement appropriate measures to safeguard the security and integrity of the arbitration process in the digital era. Approximately 32% of newly filed cases were administered under this procedure.[45]

§12.03 ADVANCING EFFICIENCY: A SIX-YEAR REVIEW OF EXPEDITED ARBITRATION PROCEDURES IN FRANCE UNDER THE ICC'S PROVISIONS

France's reputation as an arbitration-friendly jurisdiction can be traced to its progressive legal system, which is deeply rooted in the principles of party autonomy and procedural flexibility. The reform of 2011 played a pivotal role in modernizing France's arbitration laws, aligning them with international standards and cementing the country's position as an attractive seat for arbitration.[46] France has solidified its position as a leading hub for international arbitration owing to its arbitration-friendly legal framework and the presence of the ICC headquartered in Paris.

The ICC has also played a significant role in shaping the landscape of international arbitration in France. It is one of the latest institutions to introduce expedited arbitration procedures, joining other arbitral institutions, including the Swiss Arbitration Centre (formerly SCAI),[47] Hong Kong International Arbitration Centre (HKIAC),[48]

41. In the same vein, the 2021 Swiss Rules introduced new provisions aimed at facilitating the online management of arbitration proceedings. These provisions address various aspects of arbitration, including filing requirements, remote hearings, and cybersecurity considerations. The reform introduces paperless filings as the default standard, with hard copies being required only under specific circumstances. This shift towards electronic filings reflects the growing trend in arbitration to embrace digital technology and reduce reliance on physical documents.
42. Article 27(2) of the 2021 Swiss Rules.
43. Article 25(4) of the 2012 Swiss Rules.
44. *See* Article 19(2) of the Swiss Rules.
45. https://www.swissarbitration.org/update-from-the-swiss-arbitration-centre/.
46. Yassine Sangare & Margaret Liu, '10 Years on with French Arbitration Law Reform: Does the Judicial Control Frustrate or Facilitate the Enforcement of Arbitral Awards?', 1 *Intl Arb. L.R.* (2023).
47. 2021 Swiss Rules, https://www.swissarbitration.org/resources/swiss-rules-2021.

and the Singapore International Arbitration Centre (SIAC).[49] These institutions have successfully adopted mechanisms for expedited arbitration with the aim to provide prompt, swift and cost-efficient arbitration proceedings.

The evolution of expedited dispute resolution within the ICC can be traced to the early 1990s.[50] At that time, there was an absence of explicit references to expedited dispute resolution in the Arbitration Rules.[51] However, even during this period, the ICC did oversee expedited arbitration proceedings, albeit on a case-by-case basis.[52]

Two well-known cases illustrate the ICC's supervision of expedited arbitration proceedings in the 1990s – *United States v. Panhandle Eastern Corp.*[53] and *Walkinshaw and others v. Diniz.*[54] *Panhandle Eastern Corp.* involved a long-term gas supply contract between Canada and the United States, which allowed for the resolution of a price determination dispute within two months.[55] With a one-week extension, the final award was issued within nine weeks of the arbitration request.[56] This efficiency was achieved due to two factors. First, the arbitral tribunal restricted its attention to price determination issues that fell within the scope of the expedited procedure, effectively excluding other matters such as contract validity that were not encompassed by the arbitration clause. Second, the parties demonstrated commendable adherence to prescribed deadlines, thereby mitigating the necessity for time extensions. Both the tribunal and the parties recognized the importance of adhering to the procedural requirements and limitations associated with the expedited procedure, ultimately leading to a more streamlined and efficient resolution of the dispute.

Similarly, *Walkinshaw and others v. Diniz*[57] exemplified remarkable arbitration speed, lasting approximately one month. The dispute, centred around the paint of Formula One racing cars, witnessed the exchange of submissions within seven-day intervals. The tribunal finalized the draft award within 48 hours after the hearing, and an emergency session of the ICC Court promptly approved it on the same day. Strikingly, a three-member tribunal was constituted within seven days of the arbitration request during the Christmas holidays. These two cases underscore the potential for achieving utmost efficiency in arbitration, even without exhaustive rules on expedited procedures. They demonstrate the effectiveness of efficient arbitration practices despite the absence of specific rules on expedited procedures.

---

48. 2018 HKIAC Rules, https://www.hkiac.org/arbitration/rules-practice-notes/hkiac-administered-2018.
49. 2016 SIAC, https://siac.org.sg/siac-rules-2016.
50. Benjamin G. Davis, Odette Lagacé & Michael Volkovitsch, 'When Doctrines Meet – Fast-Track Arbitration and the ICC Experience', 10 *J. Intl Arb.* 4 (1993).
51. International Chamber of Commerce: Rules for the ICC Court of Arbitration (1975 Revision), 15 Intl Legal Materials 395 (1976).
52. *Ibid.*
53. Case 7385/7402 (1992) ICC International Court of Arbitration Bulletin vol. 8, no. 1, https://jusmundi.com/en/document/publication/en-award-in-case-7385-7402-extract.
54. [2002] 2 Lloyd's Rep. 165.
55. *United States v. Panhandle Eastern Corp.*, 681 F. Supp. 229 (D. Del. 1988); Case 7385/7402 (1988).
56. Case 7385/7402 (1992) ICC International Court of Arbitration Bulletin vol. 8, no. 1, https://jusmundi.com/en/document/publication/en-award-in-case-7385-7402-extract.
57. *Walkinshaw and others v. Diniz*, [2002] 2 Lloyd's Rep. 165.

In 2001, the ICC formed a Task Force to address and define what constitutes a 'small claim', with suggestions varying from USD 5,000 to USD 5 million. The Task Force resulted in the publication of Guidelines for Arbitrating Small Claims in 2003.[58] The ICC also encouraged parties to consider accelerated procedures through the issuance of a practical note, 'Note on Expedited ICC Arbitration Procedure' in 2002.[59] It also published a report on time and cost management entitled 'Techniques for Controlling Time and Costs in Arbitration' in 2007.[60] This latter report marked a shift in focus, transitioning from a mere reminder to actively promoting the inclusion of fast-track procedures in arbitration clauses. It emphasized the importance of encouraging parties to consider and incorporate such procedures as a means of enhancing efficiency and managing time and costs in arbitration proceedings.[61] Although the idea of simplified procedures for small claims was considered prior to the 2012 ICC Arbitration Rules, it was not implemented due to uncertainties and concerns surrounding the potential impact on due process, the quality of awards, and the fundamental principle of party autonomy.[62] Nonetheless, user demand led to the inclusion of simplified procedures in the 2012 rules that predicted further ICC developments in this respect.[63] Because the 2012 ICC Rules failed to meet the expectations of ensuring the efficiency of the proceedings while providing flexibility to the parties using case management techniques, the ICC created predetermined procedural rules applicable to certain categories of disputes. This released the parties from tailor-making the proceedings. The expedited procedure under the ICC Arbitration Rules aims to maintain the quality of awards, protect party autonomy and ensure the enforceability of arbitral awards by preventing due process and the right to a fair trial.[64]

The next phase marked a significant change in approach, as the ICC introduced predetermined procedural rules specifically for expedited procedures in the 2017 amendments to the Arbitration Rules. This departure from the previous approach aimed to address time and cost concerns more effectively and enhance efficiency.

The 2017 ICC reform arguably represents the most important restructuring of the ICC Arbitration Rules. It enshrines expedited arbitration procedures and aims to make

58. Louise Barrington, 'ICC's New Guidelines for Arbitrating 'Small' Claims: A View from Behind the Scenes in a Global Task Force', 11 *LAWASIA* (2003).
59. ICC International Court of Arbitration Bulletin vol. 13, no. 1 (2002).
60. ICC Arbitration Commission Report on Techniques for Controlling Time and Costs in Arbitration, https://iccwbo.org/news-publications/arbitration-adr-rules-and-tools/icc-arbitration-commission-report-on-techniques-for-controlling-time-and-costs-in-arbitration/.
61. Michael Bühler & Pierre Heitzmann, 'The 2017 ICC Expedited Rules: From Softball to Hardball?', 34(2) *J. Intl Arb.* (2017) DOI: 10.54648/joia2017009.
62. *Ibid.*
63. According to the 2015 International Arbitration Survey: Improvements and Innovations in International Arbitration conducted by Queen Mary University of London and White & Case, 92% of respondents expressed a preference for simplified procedures to be included in institutional rules for claims below a certain value. These procedures were favoured either as a mandatory feature by 33% or as an optional feature by 59% of the participants. http://www.arbitration.qmul.ac.uk/research/2015/.
64. Christophe Seraglini & Patrick Baeten, 'Expedited Rules and the Possibility of Immediate Measures once a Tribunal is Constituted', in *Expedited Procedures in International Arbitration*, Laurent Lévy & Michael Polkinghorne, eds (Kluwer Law Int'l, 2017), 37.

arbitration more accessible to users of arbitration worldwide. Other arbitral institutions have also adopted expedited procedures, either through separate rules or by incorporating provisions into their existing arbitration rules.[65] The ICC chose the latter approach, defining the fundamental principles of the expedited procedure in Article 30 and providing detailed rules in Appendix VI, collectively known as the 'Expedited Procedure Provisions' (EPP).[66] Annex VI provides a set of procedural rules for the expedited procedure, which deviates from those of the 'classical' procedure at all stages of the proceedings, from the constitution of the arbitral tribunal to the arbitral award.

The expedited procedure under the ICC Arbitration Rules strives to improve efficiency while maintaining the quality of awards, preserving parties' autonomy, ensuring enforceability, and upholding due process and the right to a fair trial. The expedited procedure has been widely used and successful. The ICC's published statistics for 2019 reveal that out of the 869 registered cases, 146 were conducted under the EPP, constituting around 17% of ICC arbitration proceedings.[67] This percentage surged in the wake of the COVID-19 health crisis, with the 2020 ICC statistics indicating that 261 cases had been conducted under the EPP since March 2017. Furthermore, a comparison of the length of proceedings under the expedited rules versus those under the standard ICC Rules demonstrates a clear time benefit.[68] The ICC's statistics for 2020 reported that 67% of final awards rendered under the EPP were delivered on or around the six-month time limit.[69] No clear trend appeared, however, regarding the number of applications for expedited proceedings and the number of arbitrator challenges in such proceedings.[70]

Amidst the unprecedented challenges posed by the COVID-19 pandemic, the ICC has responded to its record caseload by unveiling a visionary outlook for the future of dispute resolution through the introduction of updated arbitration rules. The 2021 ICC Arbitration Rules, which became effective as of 1 January 2021, signify a significant milestone in the evolution of international arbitration practice.[71] These revised rules epitomize the ICC's commitment to providing a robust and forward-looking framework for the resolution of commercial disputes, further cementing its position as a leading institution in the field of international arbitration.

65. Stockholm Chamber of Commerce (SCC) Expedited Arbitration https://www.acerislaw.com/wp-content/uploads/2023/01/2023-SCC-Expedited-Arbitration-Rules.pdf; London Court of International Arbitration (LCIA) Expedited Arbitration https://www.acerislaw.com/wp-content/uploads/2023/09/LCIA-Arbitration-Rules-Effective-1-October-2020-DL.pdf; International Centre for Settlement of Investment Disputes (ICSID) Expedited Arbitration, https://www.acerislaw.com/wp-content/uploads/2023/02/The-ICSID-Arbitration-Rules.pdf.
66. ICC Expedited Procedure Provisions, https://www.acerislaw.com/wp-content/uploads/2023/09/2021-ICC-Arbitration-Rules.pdf.
67. ICC, 'ICC Releases 2019 Dispute Resolution Statistics' (15 July 2020), https://iccwbo.org/news-publications/news/icc-releases-2019-dispute-resolution-statistics/#:~:text=The%20ICC%20Court%20registered%20a,was%20acting%20as%20appointing%20authority.
68. *Ibid.*
69. ICC Case No. 24926/GR; ICC Case No. 24437/GR, https://jusmundi.com/en/document/decision/en-claimant-v-respondent-final-award-monday-17th-february-2020-1.
70. *Ibid.*
71. *Ibid.*

The general framework for the expedited arbitration procedure is delineated in Article 30(1) and Appendix VI of the ICC Rules.[72] The EPP shall apply if the amount in dispute does not exceed USD 2,000,000 for the arbitration agreements concluded between 1 March 2017 and 1 January 2021.[73] Alternatively, if the arbitration agreement was concluded on or after 1 January 2021, the EPP are triggered if the amount in dispute does not exceed USD 3,000,000.[74] Additionally, regardless of the arbitration agreement's conclusion date or the amount in dispute, the EPP apply if the parties opt in. This flexibility allows for the EPP's application to higher-value disputes when mutually agreed by the parties. In the latter case, the parties may add the following to their arbitration agreement: 'The parties agree, pursuant to Art. 30(2)(b) of the Rules of Arbitration of the International Chamber of Commerce, that the Expedited Procedure Rules shall apply irrespective of the amount in dispute.'[75]

Thus, parties possess the autonomy to incorporate the EPP, thereby guaranteeing their application to their arbitration proceedings. This autonomy is irrespective of the dispute's monetary value or the temporal context of the agreement. Parties may mutually consent to the utilization of the EPP, even where the dispute surpasses the customary threshold for such proceedings. Parties may also mutually agree to exclude themselves from the purview of the EPP, either in the arbitration agreement or at any subsequent point in the arbitration process.[76] By incorporating precise language into their arbitration agreement, parties can exercise this flexibility, affirming the ICC's commitment to accommodating their preferences. This strategic approach empowers them to harness the streamlined and cost-effective features inherent in the expedited procedure, even when confronted with disputes of elevated monetary value. In situations where the parties do not explicitly manifest their agreement for expedited procedures, the EPP will apply if the amount in controversy level is satisfied, thereby superseding party autonomy. This approach reflects the ICC's dedication to offering a wide range of arbitration options that align with the diverse needs and circumstances of the parties. Nonetheless, it presents a trade-off between expeditious resolution and the parties' freedom to shape the arbitral process according to their unique circumstances and preferences.

The success of the expedited rules has led the ICC to widen the scope of their automatic application from disputes valued at USD 2,000,000 to USD 3,000,000 for arbitration agreements entered into on or after 1 January 2021.[77] By elevating the threshold, the ICC seeks to encompass a wider spectrum of disputes within the purview of the expedited rules. This change is fully in line with the desire to make the ICC arbitration procedure more efficient and cost-effective for small claims.[78] Nevertheless, this change raises questions regarding its responsiveness to the continuing effects of

72. Article 30(1) and Appendix VI of the ICC Rules.
73. *Ibid.*
74. https://iccwbo.org/dispute-resolution/dispute-resolution-services/arbitration/rules-procedure/arbitration-clause/.
75. Article 30(2)(b) of the ICC Rules.
76. Article 30(3)[5] of the ICC Rules.
77. *See* Article 30.2 of the ICC Rules.
78. *See* Article 30.3 of the ICC Rules.

inflation, as the value of disputes and the associated costs may evolve over time. While the rationale behind this amendment is to encompass a broader spectrum of disputes within the expedited rules, the fixed nature of the threshold may raise concerns about its adaptability to economic conditions and the diminishing real value of currency due to inflation.

However, Article 30(3) of the ICC Rules dictates that the EPP are inapplicable: (i) if the arbitration agreement predates 1 March 2017; (ii) if the parties expressly agreed to opt out of the EPP in the arbitration agreement or subsequently; or (iii) if the Court, either at the request of a party before the constitution of the arbitral tribunal or on its own, determines application of the EPP would be inappropriate under the particular facts of the matter.[79] This article not only may limit the ability of parties to benefit from the advantages of the expedited procedure but also ensures that the expedited procedure is used only when appropriate and necessary, which may be beneficial in some cases where the complexity or value of the dispute warrants a more traditional arbitration process.

Certain institutional rules, such as the ICC, the Swiss Arbitration Centre, and the HKIAC, offer an opt-out system, allowing parties to access expedited procedures for claims under a specific threshold.[80] Under this system, parties must explicitly exclude themselves from the expedited procedure rules if they do not wish to be subject to them. Conversely, an alternative approach is an opt-in mechanism, where parties must expressly refer to expedited procedure rules to ensure their application. For example, the DIS Supplementary Rules for Expedited Proceedings will only apply if parties refer to them in their arbitration agreement or agree to their application before filing a statement of claim.[81]

Thus, the possibility to opt out of the expedited procedure represents a key aspect of the EPP in that the ICC Court has the authority to exclude them upon a party's request or its own initiative. Nonetheless, even if the proceedings transfer from expedited to regular arbitration, it is rare for the ICC Court of Arbitration to replace the sole arbitrator with a tribunal of three arbitrators.[82] Such a replacement would require a new constitution of the tribunal, leading to inevitable delays. Therefore, when parties include an ICC arbitration clause in their contract, they should thoroughly evaluate whether their potential disputes are best resolved by a single arbitrator or if opting out of the EPP would be more appropriate in order to avoid any unforeseen consequences or compromises, particularly in exceptional circumstances. For instance, the COVID-19 pandemic catalysed substantial changes and adaptations within arbitral institutions,

79. ICC Rules, Article 30(3).
80. Article 30(b) and Appendix VI of the 2021 ICC Rules; Article 42.3 of the 2021 Swiss Rules; Article 42.3 of the 2018 HKIAC Administered Arbitration Rules.
81. Article 1.1 of the DIS-Supplementary Rules for Expedited Proceedings, http://www.disarb.org/de/16/regeln/dis-supplementary-rules-for-expedited-proceedings-08-srep-id4.
82. Christophe Seraglini & Patrick Baeten, 'Expedited Rules and the Possibility of Immediate Measures once a Tribunal is Constituted', in *Expedited Procedures in International Arbitration*, Laurent Lévy & Michael Polkinghorne, eds (Kluwer Law Int'l, 2017), 37.

leading to a greater reliance on technology.[83] As a result, the expedited procedure has become even more feasible and efficient, benefiting from enhanced technological tools and platforms.[84]

§12.04 NAVIGATING THE PANDEMIC: HOW THE ICC AND SWISS RULES HAVE SIMPLIFIED THE PROCESS IN THE WAKE OF COVID-19

The COVID-19 pandemic significantly impacted dispute resolution, as courts worldwide face unprecedented challenges in maintaining operations and ensuring access to justice. Consequently, parties are increasingly resorting to alternative methods, including arbitration, to address their disputes. Expedited arbitration procedures gained renewed attention during this time, offering a faster and more efficient resolution for smaller claims or urgent matters.[85] These procedures provide distinct advantages, including swift and cost-effective dispute resolution compared to traditional arbitration, which were particularly relevant during the pandemic, when parties faced financial difficulties and required expedited resolution to address urgent financial or operational concerns. Additionally, expedited arbitration procedures offer flexibility, accommodating the unique legal and commercial challenges arising from the health crisis. This adaptability allows tailoring the process to meet specific needs, such as remote hearings and electronic filings, enabling accessibility and efficiency in light of lockdowns and social distancing measures implemented in many countries.

Various arbitral institutions undertook revisions to their regulations in response to the COVID-19 pandemic, specifically incorporating or enhancing provisions for expedited procedures. For example, SIAC modified its rules to afford parties the option of an expedited procedure under defined circumstances.[86] This resulted in a surge in its use during 2020.[87] The ICC, anticipating the need for expeditious resolutions, introduced Emergency Arbitrator Rules back in 2012, positioning itself well in advance of the pandemic's onset.[88] Additionally, the ICC's operational transition to a paperless

83. Domenico Piers de Martino & Katharina Plavec, 'Has COVID-19 Unlocked Digital Justice? Answers from the World of International Arbitration', 6 *Cambridge L. Rev.* 45 (2021); Stephan Wilske 'The Impact of COVID-19 on International Arbitration – Hiccup or Turning Point?', 13 *Contemp. Asia Arb. J.* 7 (2020).
84. Indeed, as the world grappled with the unprecedented challenges posed by the COVID-19 pandemic, international arbitration experienced significant disruptions. The implementation of restrictions including court closures led to a surge in the demand for alternative dispute resolution mechanisms. In this context, expedited arbitration procedures emerged as a vital tool for parties seeking efficient and timely resolution of their disputes.
85. Amy J. Schmitz, 'Arbitration in the Age of COVID: Examining Arbitration's Move Online', 22 *Cardozo J. Conflict Resol.* 245 (2020-2021); Maxi Scherer, Niuscha Bassiri & Mohamed S. Abdel Wahab, *International Arbitration and the Covid-19 Revolution* (Wolters Kluwer, 2020).
86. SIAC Rules 2016, https://siac.org.sg/siac-rules-2016.
87. SIAC received a total of 88 requests for expedited procedures in 2020 compared to 61 in 2019. Out of these 88 requests, SIAC accepted 37, resulting in a cumulative total of 361 requests in 2021.
88. Article 29 of the Rules and Appendix V.

environment underscores its commitment to facilitating electronic exchanges and videoconferencing in arbitration proceedings.

New provisions in the 2021 Swiss Rules also reflect the evolving landscape of arbitration practice, taking into account advancements in technology and the increased use of remote proceedings. The revised rules embrace paperless filings, allow for remote hearings, and emphasize cybersecurity discussions.[89] The new Swiss Rules thereby align with the evolving landscape of arbitration practice in the digital age and post-COVID-19.

A report by the International Centre for Dispute Resolution (ICDR) found that the use of expedited procedures had increased in 2020,[90] with many parties seeking to resolve disputes at a swifter pace due to the pandemic. The use of virtual hearings had also increased as parties looked for ways to conduct hearings safely and efficiently.[91] For example, in *Enercon GmbH v. Enercon (India) Ltd.*,[92] the parties agreed to an expedited arbitration procedure due to the COVID-19 pandemic. The arbitration was conducted remotely, with the parties and the arbitrator participating via videoconference. The expedited procedure allowed for a final award to be issued just 55 days after the filing of the notice of arbitration.[93]

Although expedited procedures may not be universally applicable, it remains difficult to predetermine their suitability for disputes arising post-contract formation. Nonetheless, rules governing expedited arbitration should not be restricted solely to certain industries or cases involving minimal amounts. Various factors warrant consideration in this regard.

First, the increasing complexity of the business world calls for more efficient dispute resolution mechanisms. Lengthy proceedings can be time-consuming and costly, hindering the parties' ability to resolve their disputes promptly. Expedited procedures offer a way to address this challenge by providing a streamlined process focused on the key issues at hand.

Second, the prevalence of lengthy proceedings may be attributed to the tendency of practitioners to become accustomed to such processes. A shorter decision-making process can lead to lower legal costs. By compelling all parties, including counsel, to concentrate on the essential aspects of the dispute, expedited procedures encourage efficiency and reduce unnecessary expenses. Parties can incorporate tailored procedural schedules or specific rules for expedited arbitration in their arbitration clauses. By doing so, they proactively establish clear expectations and procedures from the outset, ensuring that the arbitration process is streamlined and expeditious. This proactive approach empowers the parties to manage their disputes efficiently and achieve a swift resolution.

89. Articles 3 and 27 of the 2021 Swiss Rules.
90. ICDR 2020 Caseload Statistics, https://www.adr.org/sites/default/files/document_repository/AAA-2020-B2B-Caseload-Press-Release-11Feb2021_1.pdf.
91. *Ibid.*
92. Civil appeal no. 2086 (2014), https://main.sci.gov.in/pdf/SupremeCourtReport/2014_v2_piv.pdf.
93. *Ibid.*

However, the ICC revised Rules have sparked discussions among practitioners.[94] Indeed, Article 30 of the ICC Arbitration Rules establishes that the EPP take precedence over any contrary terms in the parties' arbitration agreement. Furthermore, the dispute is resolved by a sole arbitrator, regardless of the parties' original agreement. This aspect of the EPP has generated further debate, as some may argue that such provisions infringe upon the parties' consent.

§12.05 MAXIMIZING EFFICIENCY AND COST SAVINGS: APPOINTMENT OF A SOLE ARBITRATOR AND CHALLENGES TO THE PRINCIPLE OF AUTONOMY

The appointment of a sole arbitrator is among the issues that are within the realm of debate under expedited procedures. Under Article 2(1) of the EPP, a sole arbitrator may be appointed by the ICC Court notwithstanding any contrary provision of the arbitration agreement.[95] Accordingly, the parties' autonomy may be superseded by this provision. This is illustrated in the ICC Note to Parties and Arbitral Tribunals on the Conduct of the Arbitration.[96] It reflects the parties' agreement that in the context of expedited arbitration procedures, any reference made to three arbitrators in their arbitration agreement is subject to the Court's discretion to appoint a sole arbitrator.[97] Other institutional arbitration rules have adopted a different approach to the issue. For example, the Swiss Rules do not mandate the automatic appointment of a sole arbitrator.[98] The Swiss Rules provide that the Secretariat shall invite the parties to agree to refer the case to a sole arbitrator if the arbitration agreement provides for an arbitral tribunal composed of more than one arbitrator.[99]

This illustrates a notable difference regarding party autonomy between the ICC Rules and the Swiss Rules. The EPP grant authority to the ICC Court to appoint a sole arbitrator regardless of any conflicting provisions in the parties' arbitration agreement. Thus, the party autonomy which typically encompasses the determination of the number of arbitrators may be overridden by the EPP, provided the parties have consented to such procedures. This discretion bestowed upon the Court delineates a curtailment of party autonomy concerning the composition of the arbitral tribunal.

The Swiss Rules adopt a different approach. While they do not automatically mandate the appointment of a sole arbitrator in expedited procedures, they confer upon the Secretariat the power to invite the parties to consider agreeing to a sole

94. Christophe Seraglini & Patrick Baeten, 'Expedited Rules and the Possibility of Immediate Measures once a Tribunal is Constituted,' in *Expedited Procedures in International Arbitration*, Laurent Lévy & Michael Polkinghorne, eds (Kluwer Law Int'l, 2017), 37.
95. Article 2(1) of Appendix VI of the ICC Rules, https://iccwbo.org/dispute-resolution-services/arbitration/rules-of-arbitration/.
96. ICC Note to Parties and Arbitral Tribunals on de conduct of the Arbitration, https://cdn.iccwbo.org/content/uploads/sites/3/2017/03/icc-note-to-parties-and-arbitral-tribunals-on-the-conduct-of-arbitration.pdf.
97. *Ibid.*
98. Article 42(2)(c) of the SCAI Rules.
99. *Ibid.*

arbitrator when their arbitration agreement specifies a multi-member tribunal. For example, in *UIT v. Prolific Umwelt- und Ingenieurtechnik GmbH v. Prolific Mining Corp.*,[100] the Secretariat notified the parties that because the amount in dispute fell below CHF 1 million, the arbitral proceedings would be conducted in accordance with the expedited procedure rules. The arbitral award was rendered within six months.

This approach preserves a higher degree of party autonomy because it affords the parties the opportunity to deliberate and consent or dissent to the suggestion. Statistics released by the Swiss Chamber in 2009 revealed that 43% were resolved by a panel of three arbitrators, while 53% were handled by a sole arbitrator.[101] This demonstrates the Swiss Rules' emphasis on party autonomy, providing greater freedom to parties compared to the ICC rules. In essence, the ICC Rules facilitate the potential abrogation of the parties' mutual agreement regarding the number of arbitrators in expedited procedures, while the Swiss Rules maintain a more pronounced adherence to party autonomy by allowing the parties to decide whether to accept or reject the proposal to appoint a sole arbitrator.

A sole arbitrator may serve as an effective means of reducing time and costs in arbitration, a practice adopted by many arbitral institutions. Under the 2018 SCC Rules, expedited arbitral proceedings are typically conducted by a sole arbitrator unless the parties have agreed otherwise.[102] In such cases, the parties' agreement prevails. In a slightly different approach, the HKIAC invites parties to consider referring the case to a sole arbitrator if the arbitration agreement stipulates three arbitrators.[103] Nonetheless, if no agreement is reached, the case proceeds with three arbitrators.

Notably, the SIAC Rules state that in expedited procedures, the case is generally referred to a sole arbitrator, unless the President determines otherwise.[104] Similar to the ICC Arbitration, the SIAC Rules' provisions on expedited procedures override any contrary terms in the arbitration agreement, resulting in the mandatory appointment of a sole arbitrator regardless of the parties' choice. Although this approach resembles that of the ICC, it is not identical. The EPP empower the ICC Court to appoint a sole arbitrator notwithstanding any contrary provision in the arbitration agreement. This implies that the ICC's appointing authority actively engages in the process, while the SIAC Rules facilitate an automatic switch to a sole arbitrator without requiring the president's endorsement in each specific case. Furthermore, unlike the ICC Arbitration Rules, SIAC follows an opt-in mechanism for the application of expedited procedures,[105] making its approach to the mandatory appointment of a sole arbitrator less restrictive.

---

100. SAC Case No. 600634-2021, https://jusmundi.com/en/document/other/en-umwelt-und-ingenieurtechnik-gmbh-v-prolific-mining-corp-motion-for-default-against-prolific-mining-corp-monday-11th-july-2022.
101. Federal Statistical Office 'Statistical Data on Switzerland 2009', https://www.bfs.admin.ch/bfs/en/home/statistics/catalogues-databases/publications.assetdetail.347152.html; https://internationalbusinesslawadvisor.com/international-arbitration-swiss-arbitrations-increase-with-success-of-expedited-arbitration-procedures/.
102. Article 17 of the 2018 SCC Rules.
103. HKIAC Rules, https://www.hkiac.org/arbitration/rules-practice-notes/hkiac-administered-2018; Article 41.2(b).
104. *See* Article 10 of the SIAC Rules.
105. Article 10.1 of the 2016 SIAC Rules.

When examining arbitral institutions that endorse the opt-out system, nuances exist. Under the Swiss Rules' expedited procedure, the matter is referred to a sole arbitrator unless the arbitration agreement explicitly states otherwise. However, akin to the HKIAC, the Swiss Rules stipulate that if the arbitration agreement specifies a tribunal comprising multiple arbitrators, the parties are invited to mutually agree to refer the case to a sole arbitrator.[106] In the absence of a consensus, the case proceeds with three arbitrators, albeit with reduced arbitrator fees. In *A. Nattermann & Cie. GmbH and May & Baker Limited v. R&D Ferrlecit Capital Resources, Inc.*,[107] the claimants proposed a panel comprising three arbitrators. In its answer, the respondent agreed to the appointment of three arbitrators. Consequently, the panel of three arbitrators was duly constituted, and the arbitral award was rendered within a relatively expeditious period of five months.[108]

Notably, no consensus exists among different arbitral institutions regarding the mechanism for referring a dispute to a sole arbitrator when the expedited procedure is applicable. The approach adopted by the ICC, which mandates the appointment of a sole arbitrator even when the expedited procedure automatically applies, is widely perceived as imposing greater restrictions on party autonomy.[109] This provision has generated considerable controversy among commentators.[110] Appointing a sole arbitrator contrary to the parties' agreement gives rise to concerns regarding the potential impact on the enforceability of awards issued under the expedited procedure.[111]

The appointment of a sole arbitrator could appear problematic, considering party autonomy and consent represent the backbone of this dispute mechanism. Accordingly, the parties should be able to tailor the proceedings to their needs. The appointment of a sole arbitrator, irrespective of the fact that the parties may have decided otherwise, could contradict the general principles of arbitration. For example, in *AQZ v. ARA*,[112] one of the parties challenged the award based on the fact that the other party requested the application of expedited procedures under the SIAC Rules,

106. Article 42(2)(b).
107. SCAI Case No. 600140-2008, https://jusmundi.com/fr/document/decision/en-a-nattermann-cie-gmbh-and-may-baker-limited-uk-v-r-d-ferrlecit-capital-resources-inc-u-s-a-final-award-monday-18th-may-2009.
108. *Ibid.*
109. Christophe Seraglini & Patrick Baeten, 'Expedited Rules and the Possibility of Immediate Measures once a Tribunal Is Constituted', in *Expedited Procedures in International Arbitration*, Laurent Lévy & Michael Polkinghorne, eds (Kluwer Law Int'l, 2017), 37.
110. Lucja Nowak & Nata Ghibradze, 'The ICC Expedited Procedure Rules – Strengthening the Court's Powers', Kluwer Arbitration Blog, http://arbitrationblog.kluwerarbitration.com/2016/12/13/reserved-for13-december-the-icc-expeditedprocedure-rules-strengthening-the-courts-powers/; Tarjuelo Javier, 'Fast Track Procedures: A New Trend in Institutional Arbitration', 11 *Dispute Resolution Int'l* 2, 110 (2017).
111. According to Article V(1)(d) of the New York Convention, the recognition and enforcement of an award may be refused if the composition of the arbitral authority is not in accordance with the parties' agreement. Therefore, whether an award rendered by a sole arbitrator in an expedited procedure, appointed contrary to the parties' agreement, can be set aside or enforcement can be refused based on Article V(1)(d) of the New York Convention indicates that in order to avoid the adverse effect of Article 2(1), the ICC 'has prudently ring-fenced the enforceability of the arbitral awards rendered under its EPP."
112. *AQZ v. ARA*, [2015] SHGC 49.

resulting in the appointment of a sole arbitrator instead of three as stated in the arbitration agreement. This therefore constituted grounds to set aside because the proceedings had not been conducted in accordance with the parties' agreement.[113] In its decision, the Court denied the challenge and enshrined the SIAC Court President's discretion to appoint a sole arbitrator under the SIAC Rules. The Supreme Court of Singapore made several key observations. First, the Court ruled that because the parties had expressly chosen a version of the SIAC Rules that included expedited procedures, it was consistent with party autonomy for the EPP to supersede their agreement for arbitration before three arbitrators.[114]

Second, the court emphasized that 'express assent' in the traditional sense was not necessary for the EPP to prevail over the parties' agreement.[115] It further highlighted the need to interpret the arbitration agreement in a purposive manner, with a commercially sensible approach, taking into account the incorporation of the SIAC Rules 2010 and their allowance for a sole arbitrator in cases of expedited procedure.[116] Based on these considerations, the court concluded that the arbitral tribunal had been formed in accordance with the parties' agreement and upheld the award rendered by the sole arbitrator.[117] This approach treats institutional rules as a binding contract rather than a mere template.

This decision suggests that incorporating institutional rules implies consent to the overriding effect of EPP over any contrary terms in the arbitration agreement. It also underscores the importance of interpreting the parties' arbitration agreement with a commercially sensible approach and recognizing the role of the appointing authority under institutional rules. Furthermore, it provides support for the provisions of Article 30(1) and Article 2(1) of Appendix VI to the ICC Arbitration Rules, which can serve as persuasive authority to domestic courts, indicating that the mandatory appointment of a sole arbitrator in expedited procedures aligns with the parties' agreement. Such an interpretation preserves the enforceability of arbitral awards under Article V(1)(d) of the New York Convention. Nonetheless, certain jurisdictions may prioritize specific agreements between the parties over general provisions of institutional rules. To mitigate the risk and protect party autonomy, parties who prefer a three-member tribunal should expressly opt out of Article 2(1) of the EPP.

In *Noble Resources International Pte Ltd v. Shanghai Good Credit International Trade Co, Ltd,*[118] the Shanghai No. 1 Intermediate Court reached a different decision. It

113. For further analysis of the decision, *see* Gary Born & Jonathan W. Lim, 'AQZ v. ARA: Singapore High Court Upholds Award Made under SIAC Expedited Procedure', http://arbitrationblog.kluwerarbitration.com/2015/03/09/aqz-v-ara-singapore-high-court-upholds-award-made-under-siac-expedited-procedure/.
114. *AQZ v. ARA*, [2015] SHGC 49.
115. *Ibid.*
116. *Ibid.*
117. *Ibid.*
118. *Noble Resources International Pte Ltd v. Shanghai Good Credit International Trade Co.*, Ltd., [2016] Shanghai No.1 Intermediate People's Court (Hu 01 Xie Wai Ren No. 1), https://content.next.westlaw.com/practical-law/document/Idf529f688dc711e79bef99c0ee06c731/Noble-Resources-International-Pte-Ltd-v-Shanghai-Good-Credit-International-Trade-Co-Ltd-2016-Shanghai-No-1-Intermediate-People-s-Court-Hu-01-Xie-Wai-Ren-No-1?viewType=FullText&

denied enforcement of an arbitral award from an expedited SIAC arbitration under Article V(1)(d) of the New York Convention. The relevant arbitration agreement provided for SIAC arbitration seated in Singapore before a three-member tribunal and for application of the SIAC Rules in force at the time. Noble Resources International commenced an arbitration procedure and invoked the application of the expedited procedure, which would entail the appointment of a sole arbitrator despite the parties' agreement to a three-member tribunal. Good Credit International Trade opposed this application and insisted on the appointment of three arbitrators as originally agreed. The Vice Chairman of the SIAC granted the application for the expedited procedure and has appointed a sole arbitrator.[119]

However, the Shanghai Court refused to recognize and enforce the resulting arbitral award because the composition of the arbitral tribunal did not align with the parties' explicit arbitration agreement. The court held that the appointment of a sole arbitrator by SIAC contradicted the parties' explicit agreement for a three-member tribunal.[120] Thus, courts may arrive at divergent conclusions regarding the enforceability of awards in expedited arbitrations, particularly in light of Article V(1)(d) of the New York Convention. To reinforce the parties' consent to the expedited procedure, Article 5(3) of the 2016 SIAC Rules has been amended to incorporate specific language with the aim of enhancing clarity and legal effectiveness.[121]

This decision may indeed prompt arbitral institutions to revise their expedited procedure rules in order to bring clarity to the issue of appointing a sole arbitrator when the parties' agreement indicates a three-member tribunal. This case may also lead arbitral institutions to be more cautious when exercising their discretion in such situations, particularly if one party objects to the appointment of a sole arbitrator. Some scholars have criticized this attempt to uphold party autonomy, arguing that party autonomy could have been recognized by interpreting the parties' agreement to a three-member tribunal as subject to the arbitral rules they had chosen, which allowed for a sole arbitrator when adopting an expedited procedure.[122]

Article 30 of the ICC Rules strikes a balance between party autonomy and regulation within the expedited procedure. It establishes that the EPP take precedence over any conflicting terms in the arbitration agreement.[123] Furthermore, the EPP do not apply to arbitration agreements made prior to the implementation of the ICC expedited procedure,[124] thereby confirming that parties are considered to have given their consent to its application. While parties have the right to exclude the application of

---

originationContext = document&transitionType = DocumentItem&ppcid = a506a8229179489fbb565f9500398058&contextData = (sc.Default).

119. *Ibid.*
120. *Ibid.*
121. SIAC Rules, https://siac.org.sg/siac-rules-2016.
122. Mohamad S. Abdel Wahab, 'Expedited Institutional Arbitral Proceedings Between Autonomy and Regulation', in *Expedited Procedures in International Arbitration*, Laurent Lévy & Michael Polkinghorne, eds (Kluwer Law Int'l, 2017), 140.
123. Article 30.1 of the ICC Rules.
124. Christophe Seraglini & Patrick Baeten, 'Expedited Rules and the Possibility of Immediate Measures once a Tribunal Is Constituted', in *Expedited Procedures in International Arbitration*, Laurent Lévy & Michael Polkinghorne, eds (Kluwer Law Int'l, 2018).

expedited procedure,[125] they cannot contractually deviate from the EPP when they are applicable to the dispute. Therefore, if the terms of the arbitration agreement contradict Article 30 of Appendix VI of the ICC Arbitration Rules, the EPP will supersede the parties' express choices in the arbitration agreement.

The significance of Article 30 is twofold. First, it ensures the efficiency of the proceedings, particularly by enforcing the six-month time limit for rendering an award which is considered crucial in expedited procedures. This implies that when parties resort to ICC Arbitration, they have consented to the ICC Court's power to appoint a sole arbitrator regardless of their initial choice in the arbitration agreement. This interpretation allows domestic courts to uphold awards rendered in an expedited procedure by a sole arbitrator. Nonetheless, in some jurisdictions, implied consent to the restriction of rights may be considered invalid. Some jurisdictions prioritize the parties' express choice over the provisions of institutional rules based on the principle *generalia specialibus non derogant*. In both cases, there is an increased likelihood of challenges to enforcement of arbitral awards or setting aside such awards.

Second, Article 30 emphasizes that by agreeing to arbitration under the ICC Arbitration Rules, parties have consented to the primacy of the EPP over the provisions of the arbitration agreement. In other words, parties have willingly accepted limitations on their autonomy by selecting institutional rules to govern the procedure.[126] This interpretation ensures the enforceability of arbitral awards rendered in expedited procedure and reduces the risk of successful challenges. It also safeguards the integrity of the proceedings and avoids protracted debates between the parties regarding the content of applicable procedural rules. Nevertheless, the wording of Article 30(1) may not offer a straightforward solution to all potential issues that parties and arbitrators may encounter when determining the priority of institutional rules or provisions in the arbitration agreement.[127] In this regard, explicit derogations made by the parties in the arbitration agreement should prevail over the provisions of institutional rules notwithstanding Article 30(1). The ICC Court should carefully consider the enforceability of the award when deciding on the appointment of a sole arbitrator, both at the seat of arbitration and in jurisdictions where enforcement may be sought.

§12.06 CONCLUSION

The adoption of expedited procedure rules in international arbitration has significantly enhanced the speedy resolution of disputes. These rules are designed to provide a time- and cost-effective mechanism for dispute resolution. They concurrently aim to preserve the parties' agreement, a foundational element of arbitration proceedings, and

125. Article 3(4) of Appendix VI to the ICC Rules.
126. Under the ICC Arbitration Rules, as stated in Appendix IV on Case Management Techniques, hearings can be conducted via telephone or videoconferencing if physical attendance is not essential, but only when ordinary procedure applies. In contrast, the EPP do not impose such limitations.
127. Michael Bühler & Pierre Heitzmann, 'The 2017 ICC Expedited Rules: From Softball to Hardball?', 34 *J. Int'l Arb.* 2, 131-132 (2017).

uphold their fundamental procedural rights during the expedited process. The use of expedited procedures has increased in France and Switzerland in recent years, reflecting the growing demand for efficient dispute resolution. Additionally, the availability of such procedures makes France and Switzerland appealing jurisdictions for parties seeking streamlined dispute resolution.

Nevertheless, certain features of the expedited procedure raise issues regarding potential conflicts with the principle of party autonomy, presenting challenges to the enforceability of awards rendered through such mechanisms. In balancing party autonomy and efficiency, the EPP under the ICC Rules prioritize the latter. To effectively address the challenges posed by the use of expedited procedures, arbitral tribunals must diligently balance party autonomy and efficiency when making procedural decisions. The objective is to ensure the enforceability of awards without compromising the efficiency of the process. It serves as a crucial and timely reminder that parties who regularly engage in arbitration should carefully assess the institutional rules they select in their arbitration agreements. While some parties may have a strong preference for resorting to three arbitrators in all cases, case law underscores the importance of considering the specific provisions of institutional rules to ensure that they align with the parties' preferences and expectations. Under the ICC and Swiss Rules expedited procedures, the arbitral tribunal retains discretionary powers to implement appropriate procedural measures. Both the ICC rules and the Swiss rules strive to strike a balance between party autonomy and enforceability in expedited procedure cases. The ICC Court, in its commitment to ensure the enforceability of arbitral awards, may seek the parties' input regarding the appointment of a sole arbitrator before the appointment, thereby safeguarding enforceability. By considering the parties' comments and aligning the composition of the arbitral tribunal with their agreement, the ICC Court could enhance the prospects of upholding awards rendered through expedited procedures.

Expedited arbitration presents a valuable tool for parties seeking a faster and more efficient resolution of their disputes. Nevertheless, parties should carefully weigh the advantages and disadvantages of expedited arbitration procedures in each jurisdiction and select the system that best suits their needs.

CHAPTER 13

Expedited Arbitration as a Competitive Factor of Arbitration Institutions: A Comparative Analysis of ISTAC, DIS and ICC

Esra Yildiz Üstün

Expedited proceedings have gained in popularity because they are time- and cost-effective. Drawing inspiration from traditional arbitration, institutions have prepared different rules for expedited proceedings. Such institutions include the International Chamber of Commerce (ICC), the German Arbitration Institute (DIS) and the Istanbul Arbitration Centre (ISTAC). There are differences and similarities between the rules of these institutions. In some cases, the rules are advantageous. While in others, they are disadvantageous. The ISTAC is international in scope and is therefore advanced in certain aspects, but it also has shortcomings. In comparison, however, and despite its shortcomings, the ISTAC is a preferred option for expedited arbitration.

§13.01 INTRODUCTION

Arbitration is the most popular dispute resolution mechanism for cross-border commercial disputes. Legal practitioners have cited enforceability, avoidance of national courts and law, flexibility, and the ability of parties to appoint their arbitrators as their fundamental advantages. However, these advantages have turned into disadvantages such as high costs and long-time requirements over time.[1] In the last few years, practitioners have voiced concerns, in particular about costs and the extension of

1. Queen Mary University of London and White & Case LLP, 2018 International Arbitration Survey: The Evolution of International Arbitration, White & Case LLP (2018); 2015 International Arbitration Survey: Improvements and Innovations in International Arbitration (Queen Mary University of London and White & Case).

procedural deadlines. As a result, arbitration has become less appealing and increasingly equated with the justice handed down by national courts. Small- and medium-sized companies are the most affected because they lack the chance to access this form of justice, are unaware of it, or are deterred by its high procedural costs.[2] In addressing these various challenges and obstacles, legal reformers have (re)engaged arbitration as a 'new litigation venue'[3] and have sought to re-establish its previous reputation by introducing a series of reforms to speed up the arbitral procedure and reduce costs. They have drafted expedited arbitration rules that will, *inter alia*, reduce the number of disputes, the time required and the number of arbitrators. They have done this with the intention of expediting issuance of a final decision, in the expectation that this will help expedited arbitration rules emerge as an established alternative to both state court litigation and an arbitration 'trial'.[4]

The well-known arbitration institutions have sought to promote the swifter resolution of disputes by introducing expedited procedures. The expedited arbitration rules have a dual purpose: first, to increase the speed of arbitral proceedings and, second, to uphold the disputing parties' entitlement to due process and fair treatment. However, a comparison of the expedited arbitration rules of the International Chamber of Commerce (ICC) and the more regional but moving towards international Istanbul Arbitration Centre (ISTAC) (which was inspired by the German Arbitration Institute (DIS)) highlights some fundamental differences that could impede the improvement of ISTAC in the international arena. Although the ICC's expedited arbitration rules are by no means perfect, ISTAC lags behind both it and the DIS in a number of respects.

This chapter reviews and compares the expedited arbitration rules of ISTAC, DIS and ICC. It demonstrates their respective advantages and disadvantages. It does not simply compare them but also considers how ISTAC's expedited rules could be revised to make them more attractive to disputing parties in international commercial disputes.

§13.02 AN ALTERNATIVE TO LITIGATION AND ARBITRATION: EXPEDITED ARBITRATION

Expedited arbitration rules emerged in response to growing concerns about the trend in arbitral procedures. When considered as a means of extrajudicial resolution, expedited arbitration is not different from traditional arbitration. It is an alternative method for

---

2. Ylli Dautaj, *Fragmentation and Judicialization of International Commercial Arbitration: Expedited Arbitration and the 'Arbitral Trial'*, 13 Arbitration L. Rev. 1, 4 (2021). Maria João Mimoso, *Accelerated Arbitration: An Expedited Method of Resolving Disputes* § 55.66 (B. Jin, & C.E.P. Tache eds, Adjuris 2022). Irina Tymczyszyn, *Using Fast Track Arbitration for Resolving Commercial Dispute*, 6 Corp. and Com. Disp. Rev. 1, 25 (2018).
3. Thomas J. Stipanowich, *Arbitration: The 'New Litigation'*, 1 U. Ill. L. Rev. 1, 4 (2010). Tymczyszyn, *supra* n. 2.
4. QMUL 2015 Survey, *supra* n. 1. Jan Paulsson, *Fast-Track Arbitration in Europe (With Special Reference to the WIPO Expedited Arbitration Rules)*, 18 Hastings Int'l & Comp. L. Rev. 713, 713 (1995).

resolving private disputes between two or more parties that have previously consented, which could speed up and simplify arbitration's procedural component.[5]

Party autonomy may produce two questions. First, why do the parties not draft time limits to resolve their cases? Second, why do arbitration institutions need to have such rules? The ICC arbitration rules have already shown that cases were resolved in a short period of time. Although the ICC only introduced rules that specifically address expedited arbitration in 2017, Article 39 of its Arbitration Rules already provided for the opportunity to accelerate ordinary proceedings, subject to the agreement of the parties and the arbitral tribunal confirming it is appropriate.[6] The new 'Expedited Procedure Provisions', set out in Article 30 and Appendix VI of the ICC Arbitration Rules, establish new, comprehensive and detailed expedited arbitration procedures.[7]

Several examples illustrate the efficacy of agreeing to expedited arbitration. In the *Panhandle* case, a long-term gas supply contract between Canada and the United States, the parties had agreed that any disputes would be settled by an ICC arbitral tribunal within two months of an arbitration request being submitted to disputing parties. The parties ultimately agreed to extend the deadline by one week, meaning that a final award would be made nine weeks after the initial request for arbitration was submitted to ICC.[8] In the *Formula One* case, the claimant submitted the ICC arbitration request between Christmas and New Year's Eve. On 1 January, a three-person arbitral tribunal was established. Within seven days, the parties exchanged submissions, and 48 hours after the hearing, the arbitral tribunal delivered its draft award to the ICC's Court for review. On the very last day of January, the parties received notice of the final award. It took about a month to complete the arbitration process.[9]

However, while ICC arbitration theoretically offers the opportunity for a quick resolution, this does not always apply in practice. Accordingly, several arbitration institutions have developed expedited arbitration rules that automatically apply to disputes.[10] They cannot lead the parties if one or both are not willing to settle the dispute.

Speed, however, may come at the expense of certain procedural guarantee standards. Expedited arbitration is not an urgent procedure to be supported by temporary and injunctive relief from a state court or conducted by an urgent or emergency arbitrator.[11] In general, expedited arbitration does restrict the use of

---

5. Irene Welser & Christian Klausegger, *The Arbitration and the Arbitration Procedure – Fast Track Arbitration: Just Fast or Something Different?*, § 259, 267-269 (Klausegger, Klein, Kremslehner, et al. eds, Austrian Arbitration Yearbook 2009).
6. Javier Tarjuelo, *Fast Track Procedures: A New Trend in Institutional Arbitration*, 11 Disp. Resol. Int'l 105 (2017).
7. *Ibid.*, 106.
8. *Ibid.*, 107.
9. ICC No. 1021/AER in Nigel Blackaby et al., *Redfern and Hunter on International Arbitration* 6-26 (6th ed., Kluwer Law International 2015).
10. Tarjuelo, *supra* n. 6, at 108-110.
11. Article 29 of the ICC Arbitration Rules establishes that '[a] party that needs urgent interim or conservatory measures that cannot await the constitution of an arbitral tribunal ("Emergency Measures") may make an application for such measures pursuant to the Emergency Arbitrator Rules'.

documents, hearings and electronic communications, which will reduce the workload of the sole arbitrator and other intervening parties, and produce other benefits, including faster processing and lower expenses.[12]

Can the requirement to uphold fair and quality arbitration be met when an arbitrator decides an international commercial or investment dispute in a limited period of time? Concerns could legitimately be raised about aspects that might have been overlooked or neglected. Aside from anything else, this could also hinder the enforcement of the award. Parties should not be required to choose between a speedy resolution and justice.[13] In other words, parties should not suffer from 'due process paranoia'.

Expedited dispute resolution evenly serves small- and medium-sized companies in commercial cases. But arbitration institutions tend to extend expedition to multi-party cases and attach particular importance to party autonomy. Although arbitration institutions impose certain conditions on the application of expedited arbitration, an agreement between the parties to settle their disputes within the framework of the expedited rules will suffice for the expedited rules to apply. In terms of the ICC's application criteria, if the parties have agreed to opt in, the Expedited Procedure Provisions will apply regardless of the date of the arbitration agreement or the amount in dispute. Such opt-in agreements may be entered into at any time.[14] The Court may, at any moment, also decide that the Expedited Procedure Provisions no longer apply (Article 1(4) of Appendix VI), either at the request of a party or on its own initiative after consulting the arbitral panel and the parties.

In the pandemic period,[15] e-arbitration, which means a method to settle disputes through online platforms providing arbitration services,[16] emerged as a trend in the settlement of cross-border disputes. E-arbitration contributed to efforts to achieve an expedited arbitration procedure. E-arbitration decreases time and other costs because participants do not have to travel to the seat of arbitration and can instead attend virtual hearings.[17] The online platforms have time limits, but they can be extended. These limitations can help shorten (in comparison to proceeding on a face-to-face basis) the arbitration process. And, if digital expedited arbitration is the default

---

12. Yasemin Aydoğmuş, *Fast-Track Arbitration and its Current Practices*, 41 Public and Private International Law Bulletin 287-327 (2021). Welser & Klausegger *supra* n. 5, at 277: As an opposing approach 'The question of whether a sole arbitrator or a tribunal can better serve this purpose cannot generally be answered, because, even though a sole arbitrator can decide all questions by himself, he must be prepared to work on the case "full time" and is not able to divide the workload.'
13. Wolfgang Hahnkamper stated 'justice delayed is justice denied' in his abstract of the Vienna Arbitration Days (2008) in Welser & Klausegger, *supra* n. 5, at 276.
14. *ICC official website*, https://iccwbo.org/dispute-resolution/dispute-resolution-services/arbitration/rules-procedure/expedited-procedure/#anchor-scope-of-the-rules.
15. It is difficult to speak in terms of a 'start' and 'end' date generally, as the pandemic is still ongoing in some parts of the world (e.g., China).
16. Mira Fayad & Habib Kazzi, *Electronic Arbitration in Lebanon – Overview and Trends*, European Scientific Journal 11.7 (2015).
17. Esra Yıldız Üstün, *The Practice of E-Arbitration in the Legal Concept* § 11, 117-139 (Prof. Alexander J. Bělohlávek, Prof. Naděžda Rozehnalová eds, CYArb – Czech and Central European Yearbook of Arbitration 2021).

method, this will help to address expectations of cost-reduction and improved speed that have been seen as the drawbacks of traditional arbitration.[18] But, the suitability of an arbitral procedure for a particular dispute should be carefully assessed. Particular attention should be simultaneously given to its theoretical and practical dimensions, as it may not be possible to balance cost, speed and quality.[19]

Both arbitral institutions and parties can choose ad hoc arbitration for expedited arbitration by deciding the rules.[20] Arbitration institutions have emerged as the most frequent users of expedited procedures in the last decade. Institutions that have expedited rules that are separate from their arbitration rules make expedited arbitration an alternative not only to state courts but also to traditional arbitration procedures. Almost all arbitration institutions have expedited arbitration rules, which is in large part due to parties being repeatedly alerted to the availability of this option. But while some automatically apply expedited rules, others adopt totally different approaches to expedited arbitration in practice.

ISTAC has very specific and detailed regulations for expedited procedures. It does not allow time to be lost in expedited arbitration proceedings. Parties can access clear information before applying the mechanism, and they do not have to be experienced in its application. The institution clearly states what should be included in party statements.[21] The ICC also sets out specific provisions for expedited arbitration that do not resemble the ISTAC counterpart.[22] DIS adopts a more general approach to expedited arbitration and broadly applies party autonomy. While the ICC and ISTAC are suited to small- and medium-sized disputes, DIS' flexible arbitration rules mean that they can be applied to disputes of any size.[23]

Finally, speed and cost-effectiveness are the two primary factors that need to be considered when deciding to use arbitration as a dispute resolution method. Some international arbitration surveys demonstrate that respondents listed cost and lack of timeliness as two of the worst aspects of international arbitration.[24] Other considerations may also recommend it as an effective substitute for state jurisdiction, including, *inter alia*, party autonomy, equal treatment, arbitrator neutrality and the enforceability of arbitral awards. These 'fundamental principles of arbitration' may also apply to fast-track arbitration, although not necessarily to all of its aspects. Fast-track arbitration is not a different arbitration system but rather a broad description of a quicker arbitral procedure.[25]

18. Dautaj, *supra* n. 2, at 6.
19. Jennifer Kirby, *Efficiency in International Arbitration: Whose Duty Is It?*, 32(6) J. of Int. Arb. 689 (2015) DOI: 10.54648/joia2015032.
20. Herman Verbist, *Contribution of Benjamin Davis to Expedited Arbitration*, 52 U. Tol. L. Rev. 463 (2021). On 9 July 2021, the United Nations Commission on International Trade Law, commonly known as UNCITRAL, adopted the UNCITRAL Expedited Arbitration Rules, which came into force on 19 September 2021 (the '(UNCITRAL) Expedited Rules').
21. Article 2 of ISTAC Fast-Track Arbitration Rules.
22. ICC Expedited Arbitration Rules, *supra* n. 14.
23. German Arbitration Institute (DIS), https://www.disarb.org/en/tools-for-dis-proceedings/dis-rules#c344.
24. 2015 International Arbitration Survey, *supra* n. 1, at 25.
25. Alan Redfern, *Law and Practice of International Commercial Arbitration* 6-43 (2004).

[A] The *Modus Operandi* of Expedited Arbitration

The scope of application of the expedited procedure rules provided by many arbitral institutions can be classified into the automatic and elective option groups.[26] ICC, ISTAC and DIS use the same systems but with variations that apply in some circumstances. While this may provide an opportunity to choose the best-suited institution, it may also cause disputing parties to select international and well-known institutions, such as the ICC, which best exemplifies the automatic applicability of expedited arbitration. In any agreement to arbitrate under the ICC Rules, the Expedited Procedure Provisions will apply over any of the arbitration agreement's contrary terms in two circumstances:

(1) if the amount in dispute is less than USD 2,000,000, and the arbitration agreement was concluded on or after 1 March 2017 and before 1 January 2021;
(2) if the amount in dispute does not exceed USD 3,000,000, and the arbitration agreement was concluded on or after 1 January 2021.[27]

This cost-limit change should be evaluated in the post-pandemic setting when countries' purchasing power has lowered. As a result, the ICC must raise its limit. The amount in dispute must be considered when deciding whether the Expedited Procedure Provisions apply, including all quantified claims, counterclaims, cross-claims, and Articles 7 and 8 claims (but not interest and expense claims). Expedited procedure requirements should not apply in cases involving declaratory or non-monetary claims whose worth cannot be ascertained unless it appears that they only support a monetary claim or do not considerably increase the complexity of the dispute. If an objection is raised against the applicability of the expedited procedure requirements, the ICC Court will evaluate the matter. However, this should only be done after the other parties have been given an opportunity to voice their views.[28]

The key point is that if neither party explicitly 'opted out' of the ICC Expedited Procedure Rules in their arbitration agreement and did not do so later, the ICC Expedited Procedure Provisions apply irrespective of the arbitration agreement's

26. Tarjuelo, *supra* n. 6. Rudolf Fiebinger & Christian Gregorich, *Arbitration on Acid*, Austrian Arbitration Yearbook 237-254 (2008). 'To find out how these issues might be dealt with, the Queen Mary Survey scrutinised the predisposition of the users towards simplified procedures as a way of addressing time and cost issues. In particular, respondents were asked whether they would favour including simplified procedures for claims under a certain value in institutional rules. Some 92% of respondents wanted simplified procedures to be included in institutional rules: 33 per cent opted for it to be included as a mandatory feature and 59 per cent preferred it to be an optional feature.' 2015 International Arbitration Survey, *supra* n. 1. Rute Alves, *Fast-Track Arbitration: Back to Basics?* § 40. 5 (Carlos González-Bueno ed., International Arbitration 2018).
27. Article 30 of the ICC Arbitration Rules and Appendix VI ('Expedited Procedure Provisions'), https://iccwbo.org/dispute-resolution-services/arbitration/expedited-procedure-provisions/.
28. Note to Parties and Arbitral Tribunals on the Conduct of the Arbitration. *See* https://iccwbo.org/wp-content/uploads/sites/3/2020/12/icc-note-to-parties-and-arbitral-tribunals-on-the-conduct-of-arbitration-english-2021.pdf.

finalisation date or the dispute's value. 'Opt-in' agreements of this kind can be put in place at any time, which emphasises the importance of the parties' autonomy. They can utilise the expedited procedure by using a standard clause offered by the ICC.[29]

The DIS has been providing dispute resolution services in both domestic and international arbitrations since 1992. It is a private and independent non-profit organisation not related to any chamber of commerce or governmental bodies. It maintains seats in Berlin and Bonn and a satellite office in Munich.[30] Although less heavily administered than other institutions, it still manages to answer the questions of disputing parties, arbitrators and academics. This is one of its most attractive features. Its 1,500 members, both in Germany and further afield, include practitioners and academics whose work focuses on domestic and international arbitration.[31]

The DIS adopts a different approach to the ICC when 'opting in' to expedited arbitration provisions because it does not require a certain amount in controversy. In DIS, the parties have two options when deciding on the expedited arbitration agreement. The first, which is the institution's preference, is more flexible and gives the disputing parties discretion to agree on DIS expedited rules in their arbitration agreement. The second, which is applied in the absence of the first, involves the arbitral tribunal engaging with the parties at the case management conference to discuss the application of the DIS expedited rules on terms established by the DIS Arbitration Rules to promote procedural efficiency.[32]

Deciding on the application of the DIS expedited rules before the dispute arises avoids complications that will arise from the parties being unable to agree on anything. They also contain foreseeable dispute resolution procedures that will enable the parties to manage their case accordingly. The respondent disputing party should be careful in this circumstance because while the claimant has months (the DIS expedited rules allow for a maximum time limit)[33] to prepare for the arbitration by collecting documents and recruiting experts, they may have insufficient time to defend themselves.[34] The DIS also provides several model clauses that can be written in arbitration agreements like ICC. Parties should only consider the type of dispute that will be settled by the DIS expedited rules and which will be resolved by 'opting out'.

By 'opting in' at the case management conference, the parties have a chance to postpone the decision to apply to expedited arbitration rules when a dispute arises in

---

29. Note on Expedited ICC Arbitration Procedure ICC International Court of Arbitration Bulletin Vol. 13 (2022), 1.
30. DIS Arb., *supra* n. 23.
31. Korinna Von Trotha, *German Arbitration Institute (Deutsche Institution Für Schiedsgerichtsbarkeit) (DIS)* § 2 (Loukas Mistelis & Laurence Shore eds, 2nd ed., 2021).
32. *Ibid.*
33. Article 7.3 of the DIS Arbitration Rule. 'If the Respondent maintains that due to exceptional circumstances a total of 75 days is insufficient for filing the Answer, the arbitral tribunal may grant a longer time limit. If the arbitral tribunal is not yet constituted, the DIS shall grant a preliminary extension of the time limit that shall be valid until the arbitral tribunal decides upon the request for an extension.'
34. Trotha, *supra* n. 31.

DIS. The parties are encouraged to consult with the arbitral tribunal and then make this decision during the case management conference.[35]

Predicting the nature of the dispute, along with various factors, including arbitrator costs and identity, is difficult. Some parties may justifiably want to postpone a decision on the application of the expedited arbitration rules. DIS gives the disputing parties a substantial amount of time to decide, which may help to clarify if the dispute is suited to the expedited arbitration procedure or not. Even if the party is a respondent, they will not be disadvantaged in the case. This also applies to agreeing to use the expedited arbitration rules in the arbitration agreement. However, one drawback is that when a dispute arises, the parties will often not agree on anything, which will confound the application of the DIS expedited arbitration procedure in practice with a further obstacle. For example, in all DIS expedited proceedings that began in 2019, fast-track arbitration proceedings were part of the arbitration agreement.[36]

ISTAC is the most recently formed institution that has shown the greatest ability to develop in the field, as improvements in its rules and reforms clearly demonstrate. It refers to expedited rules as 'fast-track arbitration rules'. Turkish law is generally inspired by its German counterpart, meaning that while ISTAC differs from the DIS in some respects, it resembles ICC expedited rules in the area of expedited arbitration procedures. One reason for this may be because ICC parties apply from across the world, and not just Turkey.[37]

The ISTAC's Fast-Track Arbitration Rules apply in three instances. First, if at the initiation of arbitration, the total amount of claims and any counterclaims do not exceed TRY 5,000,000. The only exception is if the parties agree to different rules. Second, if the parties agree on Fast-Track Arbitration Rules where the contested amount exceeds this limit. When this applies to both the claims and any counterclaims, Fast-Track Arbitration Rules will still apply, unless a party agreement stipulates otherwise. Finally, the Fast-Track Arbitration Rules will apply if the sum of the claims does not exceed TRY 5,000,000. However, the ISTAC Board may, after receiving a request from one of the parties, and considering the facts and circumstances, decide not to apply the Fast-Track Arbitration Rules.[38]

When considering the scope of ISTAC's fast-track arbitration procedures, some obstacles exist, including the amount of the case. Unlike DIS (but like ICC), ISTAC established the amount in dispute as a limit for the expedited rules and as an automatic application. But the amount can also be a hindrance. The Turkish lira depreciated considerably against foreign currency during the pandemic, meaning that even if ISTAC increased the amount from TRY 300,000 to TRY 5,000,000, it would be akin to

35. Article 27.4(ii) of the DIS Arbitration Rules.
36. As of 19 June 2019, DIS has registered 150 new claims since the entry into force of the updated DIS Rules. However, only in 13 of these cases did the parties agree to expedite the proceedings. Elena V. Sitkareva & Andrei A. Konstantinov, *Expedited Arbitration as a Competitive Element of Arbitration Centers,* 12 Talent Development and Excellence 2, 699-705 (2020). Flecke-Giammarco, Gustav et al., *The DIS Arbitration Rules: An Article-by-Article Commentary* (2020).
37. Orçun Çetinkaya, *The Rise of Arbitration in Turkey*, Chambers and Partners (29 November 2016), https://chambers.com/articles/the-rise-of-arbitration-in-turkey.
38. ISTAC Fast-Track Arb. Rules, *supra* n. 21.

a drop in the ocean.[39] While this amount is insignificant for international disputes, it is more likely to be significant at the national level.[40] In this regard, parties can also apply for fast-track arbitration even if their case amount exceeds TRY 5,000,000. Party autonomy is still active but not to the same extent as in DIS. This 'opt-out' system has been criticised for limiting party autonomy, particularly because the court may choose a single arbitrator even when the parties' agreement envisages multiple arbitrators. The 'opt-in' approach of Article 24(7) of the 2018 DIS Arbitration Rules establishes that the rules that govern expedited processes must be explored during the case management meeting. This approach appears particularly advantageous from this perspective. The requirement for discussion reduces the possibility that the 'default effect' will occur.[41]

[B] Appointment of a Sole Arbitrator

Party autonomy has long been regarded as one of the main principles of the international arbitration process,[42] and many arbitral institutions adhere to it when drafting their arbitration provisions and expedited arbitration rules. The main difference of expedited arbitration is that it imposes time limits that parties and arbitrators must obey. In particular, it obliges disputing parties to promptly appoint the arbitrator and submit their statements, documents and evidence within certain deadlines. It also obliges the sole arbitrator to render the decision on time. The failure of the tribunal to render a timely decision is a defect of traditional arbitration that expedited rules seek to cure.

A sole arbitrator is selected on the basis of their ability to provide quick and low-cost arbitration. Arbitrator expenses, discovery fees, trial costs and long-term outsourced legal services arbitration are the basis of costs.[43] In a simplified procedure with fewer arbitrators, the proceedings will play an important role in reducing party

39. ISTAC just announced that as of 21 April 2024, the limit for application of fast-track arbitration rules has been changed to TRY 5,000,000. When converted to US dollars, it is nearly USD 153,000 (USD 1 = TRY 32.56).
40. According to the ICC Statistics, the sum at issue in 36% of commercial disputes is USD 5,000,000 or less below the US dollar. In 23% of the conflicts, the settlement amount is USD 100,000 or less than USD 100,000. *2017 ICC Dispute Resolution Statistics*, ICC Dispute Resolution Bulletin, 2.61 (2018). As for the dispute-value threshold at which expedited procedures would be suitable, at least 94% of respondents believe that disputes exceeding USD 1 million should fall outside the provision, and a significant number feel that the threshold value should be even lower (32% set the threshold value at USD 500,000 and 22% at USD 100,000). 2015 International Arbitration Survey, *supra* n. 1.
41. Renate Dendorfer-Ditges & Philipp Wilhelm, *DIS Arbitration Rules 2018 in a Nutshell: Revision for Efficiency, Transparency and Modernization*, 6 Y.B. on Int'l Arb. 73 (2019). This refers to the phenomenon that parties do not select expedited procedure, because it is not the default choice under the institutional rules, e.g., because they have not been fully aware of this option. Still, in contrast to the ICC Arbitration Rules, under the DIS Arbitration Rules 2018, the parties remain flexible on making their decision on a case-to-case basis.
42. Klaus Peter Berger, *Institutional Arbitration: Harmony, Disharmony and the 'Party Autonomy Paradox'*, Arbitration International, 473-93 (2018) DOI: 10.1093/arbint/aiy028.
43. Aydoğmuş, *supra* n. 12, at 296.

costs and common expenses over a short period of time.[44] Using a single arbitrator shortens the selection time; makes it easier for them to accept the tasks offered to them; streamlines the decision-making process; and reduces travel and accommodation expenses and the arbitrator's fee in particular.[45] This is why arbitration institutions generally support sole arbitrators, in the expectation that this will expedite arbitration procedures. But this is not a mandatory rule. ISTAC Expedited Arbitration Article 3 gives the parties discretion to select more than one arbitrator. The ISTAC Board will appoint a sole arbitrator under Article 3(2) only if the parties fail to do so within 15 days of the Secretariat notifying the claimant that their statement has been submitted to the respondent.

The ICC adopts a similar approach. Article 2 of Appendix VI of the expedited arbitration provisions authorises the ICC to appoint a sole arbitrator, even though the arbitration agreement stipulates otherwise. In agreeing to arbitration under the Rules, the parties agree that their right to an arbitration agreement that refers disputes to three arbitrators is, if the Expedited Procedure Provisions apply, subject to the ICC's authority to appoint a sole arbitrator. In upholding its responsibilities, the ICC will invite the disputing parties to comment in writing before taking any decision and will take every effort to ensure the award is enforceable in all cases. The ICC's orientation towards a sole arbitrator under its expedited arbitration rules is intended to ensure the arbitration is expeditious and cost-effective. Despite the party autonomy aspect of arbitration, the ICC is ultimately the final authority. Thus, the ICC does not attach particular importance to party autonomy. If the ICC forces a dispute into the arbitration rules based on the amount in controversy, one party cannot successfully refuse it. While parties agree to the application of the expedited procedures by agreeing to the ICC Rules, the ICC Court cannot impose an expedited procedure on parties who do not meet the standards set out in the Rules. When a party objects to the application of the expedited arbitration rules, the case is sent to the ICC Court. The Court will decide whether or not to apply the expedited procedure on a case-by-case basis.[46]

In contrast, ISTAC has proven reluctant to assume exclusive responsibility for nominating arbitrators.[47] The qualification of arbitrators chosen for cases will inevitably impact the institution's success, and so it is essential that arbitration institutions exert jurisdiction on this matter. This is why renowned arbitral institutions like the ICC so strongly insist on tight exclusivity and final power.

ISTAC could have sought to assuage concerns about arbitrators by giving the parties as much freedom as possible when selecting them. However, in the long term, this could compromise its institutionalism, effectiveness and reputation,[48] which could then impact its perceived impartiality and independence and in turn undermine the

44. Begüm Hande Ertürk, *International Arbitration Recent Developments: Reducing the Duration of and the Costs in Arbitration Proceedings*, 19.2 Marmara Üniversitesi Hukuk Fakültesi Hukuk Araştırmaları Dergisi 1596-1597 (2013).
45. Aydoğmuş, *supra* n. 12.
46. Romain Dupeyré & Elina Zlatanska, *Expedited Procedures – Practical and Comparative Considerations*, ICC Dispute Resolution Bulletin 1 (2023).
47. Çetinkaya, *supra* n. 37.
48. *Ibid.*

enforcement of arbitral awards. The German style is more flexible than ICC and ISTAC because the institution is strongly managed by the parties. In contrast to other accelerated arbitration rules, the DIS rules do not require the dispute to be handled by a single arbitrator and instead leave this to the disputing parties to decide.[49] However, in many cases, this question does not arise because parties usually opt for a sole arbitrator.[50]

Although arbitration is conducted by the parties, the fast-track procedure establishes that institutions should influence the number of arbitrators. If this is not the case, there is a danger that the parties could manipulate the procedure with the deliberate aim of drawing out arbitration proceedings.

Some institutions, such as the ICC and ISTAC, still refer to the arbitrator's traditional 'terms of reference', which involves framing the scope of arbitrators' duties and powers in the proceedings. However, this does not apply to expedited arbitration, as the ISTAC, DIS, and ICC demonstrate. The preparation of 'terms of reference' takes additional time.[51]

[C] Hearings

Expedited arbitration rules usually contain provisions that allow the tribunal to restrict the number, length and scope of proceedings.[52] A formal hearing would take more time. This could be skipped if an expedited arbitration procedure was applied to the dispute. A formal hearing would only be held if requested by a disputing party. However, even then, a sole arbitrator should be entitled to disregard this as unnecessary and render an award on the basis of documents alone.[53]

This reiterates the need to balance equality between the disputing parties against compliance with due process. A problem arises when the claimant has sufficient time to prepare their case in depth before initiating arbitration while the respondent is obstructed by stringent time limits.[54] This could well impede the arbitral award's enforcement because the failure to uphold the equality of parties has previously been cited as a consideration in this regard. The award was simply a piece of paper, which

---

49. Christine Russ, Anke C. Sessler & Max. D. Stein, *Need for Speed – Revised DIS Rules for Expedited Proceedings*, Lexology (5 March 2020), https://www.lexology.com/commentary/arbitration-adr/germany/skadden-arps-slate-meagher-flom-llp/need-for-speed-revised-dis-rules-for-expedited-proceedings.
50. *Ibid.*
51. Leyla Keser Berber, *Uluslararası Ticaret Odası (ICC) Tahkim Tüzüğü ve Uygulaması* (Seçkin 1999). Ali Yeşilırmak, *Türkiye'de Ticari Hayatın ve Yatırım Ortamının İyileştirilmesi İçin Uyuşmazlıkların Etkin Çözümünde Doğrudan Görüşme, Arabuluculuk, Hakem Bilirkişilik ve Tahkim: Sorunlar ve Çözüm Önerileri* (On İki Levha 2011).
52. ICC, *supra* n. 14. Choonwon Lee, *Introduction and Prospects of UNCITRAL Expedited Arbitration*, J. Arb. Stud. 32 (2022). Explanatory Note to the UNCITRAL Expedited Arbitration Rules, https://uncitral.un.org/en/content/expedited-arbitration-rules.
53. Article 5 of ISTAC Fast-Track Arbitration Rules, Article 3(5) of ICC Expedited Arbitration Rules, Article 4 of DIS Expedited Arbitration Rules.
54. *Ibid.*, 6.

again reiterates that 'speed kills'.[55] If the parties were not treated equally due to speed alone, this could be grounds for annulment of an arbitration award. Of course, no arbitration decision has ever been annulled solely due to speed.

In using hearings during the expedited procedure, institutions have sought to limit the time taken while ensuring that the tribunal acts fairly and impartially. They have done this in various ways, including by giving each party an opportunity to present their case. Under the ICC expedited arbitration rules, the tribunal has the discretion to adopt procedural measures of this kind. It can, for example, decide the case only on the basis of documents; omit hearings and witness examinations; reject requests to produce documents; and/or limit the number, scope and length of submissions.[56]

Appendix IV of the ICC Arbitration Rules ('Case Management Techniques') permits meetings and hearings to be conducted through media like tele/videoconferences.[57] Past ISTAC experience establishes that if the sole arbitrator decides to hold a hearing, they should, after consulting with the disputing parties, determine the date of the hearing and summon them to appear on the day, time and location of the hearing while giving at least 15 days' notice. The sole arbitrator is completely in charge of the conduct of the hearing. In the ICC, the sole arbitrator may, after consulting with the parties, make a decision purely on a documentary basis and will not be required to hold a hearing, like the ISTAC fast-track arbitration.[58]

In the DIS expedited arbitration procedure, the number of parties in the hearing can surprisingly be limited, subject to their agreement. Similarly, an oral hearing can be skipped or only held once by a tribunal, including the taking of evidence.[59] Although DIS has more flexibility than other institutions, the rules used in its oral hearings resemble those in both ICC and ISTAC. This could be cited as evidence that it privileges procedural proceedings, including hearings, exchanges of documents and the taking of evidence. All institutions should seek to balance the disputing parties' needs and requirements, including by giving them equal hearing rights and time. In doing so they should acknowledge that national courts have frequently cited the violation of the right of defence when refusing to enforce arbitral awards.[60] The right to an equal hearing is also covered by public policy.[61]

55. Pelin Baysal & Bilge Kagan Cevik, *Is Good, Fast, and Cheap Arbitration a Dream?*, Gun Partners (24 October 2018), https://gun. av.tr/media/5sca43to/ln-europe-is-good-fast-and-cheap-arbitration-a-dream-24-10-2018.pdf.
56. Note to Parties and Arbitral Tribunals on the Conduct of the Arbitration, *supra* n. 28.
57. *Ibid.*
58. Article 5 of ISTAC Fast-Track Arbitration Rules.
59. Article 3 of Annex IV of DIS Arbitration Rules.
60. Andrew Tweeaddle & Keren Tweeaddle, *Arbitration of Commercial Disputes, International and English Law and Practice* (Oxford, 1st ed., 2005), §13.43-13.55, 425-429; Christoph Müller, *International Arbitration A Guide to the Complete Swiss Case Law Unreported and Reported* (Schulthess, 1st ed., 2004), 257-262; Vesselina Shaleva, *The Public Policy Exception to the Recognition and Enforcement of Arbitral Awards in the Theory and Jurisprudence of the Central and East European States and Russia*, 19(1) Arbitration International (2003), 67, 72-73 DOI: 10.1093/arbitration/19.1.67. Mehmet Akif Gül, *New York Sözleşmesi Bağlamında Hukukî Dinlenilme Hakkının İhlâli*, 7(29) Türkiye Adalet Akademisi Dergisi (2017). Pascal Hollander, *Report on the Public Policy Exception in the New York Convention*, 10(1) Dispute Resolution

[D] Rendering an Arbitral Award

Rendering an award is the last, but not least, of expedited arbitration proceedings. The arbitrator must be quick to render a decision within a time limit. It may be more difficult than a traditional arbitration proceeding due to the fact that the sole arbitrator has more workload in a short time. The various institutions have more or less similar rules which give three or six months to issue a final award.[62]

Article 7 of the ISTAC fast-track arbitration rules establishes that a decision must be made on the merits of the dispute within three months of the sole arbitrator receiving the file. The award's time limit can be extended if the disputing parties agree or if the Board, in responding to an application by one of the parties or the sole arbitrator, considers it necessary. The sole arbitrator must make the award no later than one month after the submission of the last statement or the last hearing date, whichever comes later. The ISTAC expedited arbitration rules are silent on reasoned awards. The traditional arbitration rules of ISTAC require that the final award must be reasoned. Similarly, Article 14(2) of the Turkish International Arbitration Code states that the final decision must be reasoned. As a result, even though the ISTAC expedited arbitration rules are silent on the matter, final arbitral awards should be reasoned to avoid challenges to enforcement. Otherwise, the awards may face public policy obstacles in enforcing states regarding the right to a fair trial.[63]

The ICC allows more time to complete the expedited arbitration procedure. An expedited arbitration under the ICC rules should be completed within six months of the case management conference. The ICC anticipates that arbitral tribunals, in implementing the expedited arbitration provisions, will enable the deadline to be met without any extensions. If an extension is still required, the arbitral tribunal must submit a reasoned application to the ICC Court, and any award made under the Rules must be justified.[64] Here, it is especially desirable to limit the factual and/or procedural sections of the award to what the tribunal deems to be necessary for understanding it and also to communicate the reasons for the award as briefly and concisely as possible.

The ICC has also encouraged the timely completion of the procedure. An arbitral tribunal that operates in accordance with the Expedited Procedure Provisions is required to produce its draft award no later than six months after the case management conference.[65] In cases where the arbitral tribunal has promptly handled the arbitration, the ICC Court may increase the arbitrators' fee above what it would normally consider appropriate. Conversely, when the draft award is submitted after the deadline, it can

---

International (2016), 35-43. Reinmar Wolff, *New York Convention, Convention on Recognition and Enforcement of Foreign Arbitral Awards of 10 June 1958 Article by Article Commentary* (Hart Beck Nomos, 2nd ed., 2019), 416.

61. Yargıtay 2. HD., 4.10.2005 T., 2005/10735 E., 2005/13428 K. 'Violation of the right to defense constitutes a clear violation of Turkish public policy'.
62. Article 7(1) of ISTAC Expedited Arbitration Rules. Article 1 of Annex IV of DIS Expedited Arbitration Rules. Article 4 of Annex VI of ICC Expedited Arbitration Rules.
63. Article 35 of ISTAC Arbitration Rules. Article 14(2) of Turkish International Arbitration Code. Aydoğmuş, *supra* n 12, at 312.
64. Article 4 of Appendix VI to the ICC.
65. *Ibid.*

reduce the fees without limiting any other actions, including replacing one or more of the arbitrators. If the ICC Court is satisfied that the delay can be attributed to factors outside the control of the arbitrators or exceptional circumstances, it is not required to impose any adverse measures.[66] However, while the ICC exerts power over the arbitrators and can therefore assure the parties it will provide expedited arbitration on time, ISTAC has no sanctions that can be applied to laggard arbitrators.

Under DIS, the arbitral tribunal must hold a case management meeting as soon as practicable after its establishment, which is generally within 21 days. The final award should then be issued no more than six months after the case management conference. If it is not possible for the arbitral tribunal to issue an award within this timeframe as set in Article 1 of Annex 4 of the DIS Arbitration Rules, it must write to the parties and the DIS.[67] Rather uniquely, the arbitral tribunal retains jurisdiction even if the deadline is passed and will then need to issue the final award as soon as possible.[68] ICC and DIS allow similar time for the completion of awards, albeit from different starting points. They are therefore able to resolve awards quickly, are more internationally oriented, and are able to provide decisions in more complex and larger-scale disputes. ISTAC instead is more regionally focused. Taking into account its time limits and the number of disputes managed, it is better suited to smaller disputes.

[E] Enforceability of Arbitral Award

Although the expeditious treatment of a dispute benefits the parties in a number of ways, enforceability is ultimately the key consideration in any assessment of the value of any decision.[69] Arbitrators in expedited arbitration proceedings must acknowledge that key principles, including party autonomy, equality between parties during the process and independency and impartiality of arbitrators, are key considerations in this regard. A failure to do so may result in an arbitral award being set aside under the applicable national law or a separate justification for non-enforcement. Expedited arbitration awards will be examined in particular under Article V, section 1(b), which relates to the violation of due process rights, and section 2(b), which relates to public policy issues, of the Convention on the Recognition and Enforcement of Foreign Arbitral Awards (1958 New York Convention).

[1] Article V, Section 1(b) of the New York Convention

Article V, section 1(b) of the New York Convention covers the failure to treat disputing parties equally in arbitration proceedings. It would also apply to expedited arbitration

66. Benjamin Davis, *The Case Viewed by a Counsel at the ICC Court's Secretariat, Fast-Track-Arbitration: Different Perspectives*, 3 ICC Bulletin 8 (1992).
67. Article 1 of Annex IV to the DIS.
68. *Ibid.*
69. *Ibid.*

awards. International case law establishes that some national courts such as Turkey, Korea and Russia tend to cite claimed violations of due process when rejecting the recognition and enforcement of arbitral awards.[70] Under Article V, section 1(b) of the New York Convention, it is generally insufficient to demonstrate that the parties' procedural rights have been violated. Rather, it is necessary to show that the violation has directly influenced the proceeding's outcome.[71]

Turkish courts have defined the following procedural defects as a denial of a party's right to due process: (1) failing to inform a party of the opposing party's arguments; (2) failing to provide a party with a substantial document submitted to the arbitrator and denying them the opportunity to comment thereon; and (3) failing to provide a party with the opportunity to comment on experts' written reports or oral statements.[72] However, Turkish courts did not deem basing an award on only a few select arguments rather than all of the arguments made by a party during a denial of due process. In that case, the arbitrator implicitly limited the deadline for submissions by announcing a decision would be made by a specific date on the basis of the documents made available up until that date.[73] These decisions clearly establish that the utmost care and attention should be given to ensuring that all submissions by one party in a proceeding are submitted to the other party. Imposing time restrictions will not be deemed to jeopardise the enforcement of an arbitral ruling.[74]

In summary, expedited arbitration may not be risky for enforcing states if only time limits are enforced. Otherwise, there appear to be no issues, as long as the parties agreed to the expedited procedure and were fully aware of the time limits for submitting documents. However, if the disputing parties are forced into fast track by the institution against their will, they can opt out from the expedited arbitration procedure at various stages of the proceeding. If they do not, they cannot claim that they were forced by the institution to use expedited procedures against their will.[75] Expedited arbitration proceedings will address the only conceivable issues if they follow the rules and acknowledge the main principles that could hinder future enforcement problems. Accordingly, the arbitrator should uphold due process and protect the rights of both parties.

70. George A. Bermann, *Recognition and Enforcement of Foreign Arbitral Awards: The Interpretation and Application of the New York Convention by National Courts*, Recognition and Enforcement of Foreign Arbitral Awards. Ius Comparatum – Global Studies in Comparative Law § 23, 42-44 (George A. Bermann ed., Springer 2017).
71. Welser & Klausegger, *supra* n. 5, at 270.
72. Yargıtay 11. H.D. (7.1.2019) 2018/5474E. and 2019/99K (Turkish Supreme Court).
73. *Ibid.*
74. According to the author, even though the notification has not been made, if the relevant person is aware of the concerns to be communicated sufficiently to make a counter-declaration, then the irregularity is a violation of the rule of good faith. Ziya Akıncı, *Milletlerarası Tahkim* (Vedat, 5th ed., 2020) 352. Yargıtay 11 HD 631/5860, 27.04.2015 (Turkish Supreme Court).
75. Only 23 parties had opted out of the procedure (either in the arbitration agreement following the ICC standard clause or at various stages of the proceedings) as of the end of 2022. Dupeyré & Zlatanska, *supra* n. 46.

[2] *Public Policy Objections*

State courts frequently cite public policy as a reason when rejecting the enforcement of an arbitral award, including in expedited arbitration.[76] This is in part because there is no universally recognised definition of the term, meaning that it covers a wide range of objections.[77] The New York Convention Article V, section 2(b) establishes that an international arbitral award may be ex officio refused recognition and execution 'if the competent authority in the country where recognition and enforcement are sought finds that the recognition or enforcement of the award would be contrary to the public policy of that country'.[78] Thus, national courts may refuse to enforce the award if it contradicts the state's economic or public order or its fundamental laws.

For example, a Swiss tribunal determined that parties not being permitted to remark on an expert report during arbitration proceedings violated public order.[79] The same decision has been cited to uphold the claim that in instances where the law of the 'enforcing' state does not require a reasoned award, a failure to render a reasoned award is not sufficient to refuse recognition and enforcement.[80] As a result, when agreeing to arbitration rules that do not compel the arbitrator to deliver a reasoned decision, parties should remember that state courts may require a reasoned award as a prerequisite for enforcement.[81] In these state courts, DIS expedited rules come with higher risks. Under section 7 of the DIS Rules of Expedited Arbitration Procedure, unless the parties agree otherwise, the tribunal can render an award without giving

76. Nuray Ekşi, *Yargıtay Kararları Işığında Yabancı Hakem Kararlarının Tenfizinde Kamu Düzeni*, Public and Private International Law Bulletin 40.1 (2020) 143-201. Nuray Ekşi, *Yargıtay Kararlarında Yabancı Hakem Kararlarının New York Konvansiyonuna Göre Tenfizine İlişkin Bazı Sorunlar* § 1, 116-149 (Nuray Ekşi, Turgut Kalpsüz & Müslüm Yılmaz eds, Beta 2008). 'Violation of public policy has always been used as a weapon to prevent the enforcement of foreign arbitral awards and will continue to be used. In Turkish doctrine and foreign doctrine, the Supreme Court's old Considering the decisions of the Turkish courts, it was determined that this weapon was used for purposes other than its intended purpose expressed. The Supreme Court, especially in its decisions until the 2000s, public order as a cover for preventing the recognition or enforcement of arbitral awards has been criticized for using.'
77. *Ibid.*
78. UNCITRAL, https://uncitral.un.org/sites/uncitral.un.org/files/media-documents/uncitral/en/new-york-convention-e.pdf.
79. *See supra* n. 4, 271. Tribunal Fédéral (Bundesgericht), Feb 8, 1978, *Chrome Resources S.A. v. Léopold Lazarus Ltd.*, in XI Yearbook Commercial Arbitration 541 (1986) (Switzerland), *Guide on the Convention on the Recognition and Enforcement of Foreign Arbitral Awards* ch 11 (E. Gaillard & G.A. Bermann, eds, 2017).
80. *Ibid.*
81. According to Article 37.4 of the Spanish Arbitration Act, arbitral awards shall always be reasoned. In this regard, courts held that the requirement of reasoning is a main principle of the Spanish legal system, and so if an arbitrator fails to comply with this it will constitute a violation of public policy. Judgment by the High Court of Justice of Galicia, of 2 May 2012, [RJ 2012, 6364]. Similarly, the Austrian Supreme Court concluded that lack of reasoning constitutes a breach of procedural public policy and justifies an annulment of the award. Judgment by the Austrian Supreme Court, 8 September 2016, Docket 18 OCg 3/16i. Commented on by Anne-Karin Grill & Sebastian Lukic, *Austrian Supreme Court Establishes New Standards as Regards the Decisive Underlying Reasoning of Arbitral Awards* (Kluwer Arbitration Blog 24 December 2016): http://kluwerarbitrationblog.com/2016/12/24/ austrian-supreme-court-establishes-new-standards-as-regards-the-decisive-underlyingreasoning-of-arbitral-awards/.

reasoning.[82] This option has been offered to arbitrators to guarantee a prompt trial. German law also establishes that the arbitral award can only be annulled if the violation can be proven to have affected the merits of the award.[83]

The Bremen Court of Appeal, in providing further insight into another public policy issue, reached a decision about the lack of reasoning for an Istanbul Chamber of Commerce award.[84] It observed that although German courts may refuse to enforce lack of a reasoned award under German domestic arbitration, it is not a reason to reject enforcement of an international arbitral award under German international procedural public policy.[85] While ISTAC underlines that an arbitral award should have clear grounds, a lack of reasoning is not sufficient for it to be annulled under Article 15 of the Turkish International Arbitration Law.[86] Turkish legal doctrine argues the opposite and maintains that if arbitral awards are unreasoned, arbitral tribunals should be given broad discretion.[87] Parties should be entitled to waive their right to appeal the fast-track arbitration award. In German and Turkish law, the only condition of waiver is clear and written consent, which is consistent with the aim of the procedure because attempts at annulment are more often used to postpone compliance with the award.[88] Thus, if national courts cannot examine the merits of the case, they are instead authorised to check procedural claims.

§13.03 CONCLUSION

Expedited arbitration procedures will fail if they are not welcomed by all parties, the arbitral tribunal and the 'framing' institution. If they are administered professionally by all concerned parties, fast-track arbitration should be considered to be efficient.[89] Expedited arbitration procedures are necessary because parties to international commercial disputes, who have fled litigation for high-cost and slow-motion arbitration, have exacerbated their situation and made it worse. However, expedited arbitration procedures cannot apply to all types of disputes because time limits hinder the sole arbitrator's best efforts to decide complex disputes. If the case needs to be decided by consideration of an expert report and witness documents, the additional time required may result in expedited arbitration being limited to small- or medium-sized cases. Although the ICC, DIS and ISTAC limit the application of expedited rules based on the amount of money in dispute, the complexity of the dispute may not be defined accordingly. And the disputed amount varies in accordance with the positions of

82. German Civil Procedure Act § 1059 Abs. No. 2 1 (d).
83. *Ibid.*
84. Parties are not indicated, Yearbook Commercial Arbitration, Ch. 31 (A.J. Van den Berg ed., 2006), 640-651.
85. Andrey Ryabinin, *Procedural Public Policy in regard to the Enforcement and Recognition of Foreign Arbitral Awards* (Lambert 2018).
86. Turkish International Arbitration Code, Article 15.
87. Gizem Ersen Perçin, *An Evaluation of Setting Aside of Arbitral Awards on Turkish International Arbitration Code*, 40.2 Public and Private International Law Bulletin 1053-1087 (2020).
88. *Ibid.*, 1080.
89. Welser & Klausegger, *supra* n. 5.

disputing parties. In these circumstances, it may be better to find additional conditions for the application of expedited procedures, as this will produce greater benefits.

When assessed as a comparative factor, ISTAC fast-track arbitration seems the more attractive option to the ICC and DIS for only small disputes. As an impartial and independent institution, ISTAC is used to administer both domestic and international arbitration disputes. The use of the Turkish lira and the affordability of its registration and arbitrator fees and administrative costs has enabled it to emerge as a relatively (compared to other arbitration institutions) cost-effective arbitration centre. In addition, ISTAC's status as a desirable alternative dispute resolution process for parties in numerous different jurisdictions favours its use. Istanbul's unique position as the hub of Europe, Asia, the Middle East and Africa, and Turkey's prioritisation of the development of arbitration are also significant factors. Turkish travel is generally visa-free.[90] ISTAC procedures more clearly relate to fast-track arbitration proceedings and cover petition details, which reduces the time that the parties and arbitrator need to commit.[91]

These lower-value cases automatically began to be tried by the ISTAC on the basis of expedited criteria. Many arbitral institutions still include exceptions to expedition that call for party initiation. ISTAC's pragmatism should be acknowledged and it should receive due credit. The ISTAC rules require the arbitral tribunal to create a procedural timetable that establishes, *inter alia*, hearing dates, submission deadlines and other procedural activities like the ICC and DIS. Dialogue with the parties creates the schedule, and the process appears to have been devised on the basis of ICC regulations. However, ISTAC lacks a 'Case Management Conference' that would enable parties to express their views on the arbitration process and reach an agreement on procedural issues. ISTAC has never been as flexible as DIS and has never possessed a strict fast-track arbitration procedure that is comparable to the ICC counterpart.

Apart from these benefits, ISTAC has not been in a well-deserved place in practice. The reason is that it is a newer arbitration institution than the DIS and the ICC. Some expedited arbitration rules might be revised, such as the application dispute value limit because the Turkish lira has been losing its value against foreign currency. While the DIS and ICC have been stable on the amount in dispute limitation, ISTAC has not, and so the application of the ISTAC fast-track rules has been narrowing. This might be an obstacle to applying the institution in the parties' agreement for international commercial disputes. Therefore, ISTAC may stay more national in scope.

The reputation of institutions is vital to choosing the arbitration institution in practice. During the execution of an arbitration award, the enforcing country often considers which arbitration institution rendered it. The rate of enforcement of ICC decisions is not the same as the rate of enforcement of the other institutions' decisions.

90. Republic of Türkiye Ministry of Interior Presidency of Migration Management official website, https://www.goc.gov.tr/turkiyenin-vize-uygulamadigi-ulkeler. Nearly 90 country citizens can travel without visa requirement.

91. Candan Yasan Tepetas, *Key Features of the Istanbul Arbitration Centre Arbitration Rules*, 4 Turk. Com. L. Rev. 69 (2018). *Istanbul Arbitration Center (ISTAC) Fast-Track Arbitration Rules* (25 October 2022), https://www.ongurpartners.com.

Also, if the parties have not had arbitration experience before, ISTAC and DIS fast-track procedures might be difficult to follow because the institutions give importance to party autonomy. However, the seat of arbitration is important because trust of jurisdiction may also be a factor in choosing the institution.

In sum, parties should consider ISTAC and the other two institutions from different angles based on the specific facts and factors of their cases. This will conceivably enable and assist the development of quicker, more high-quality, and perhaps most importantly, cheaper dispute resolution solutions.

Chapter 14

ICSID's Mediation Rules and Procedures: An Initiative Towards an Expedited and Equitable Resolution of Investor-State Disputes

Srilal M. Perera

The enactment of the International Centre for the Settlement of Investment Disputes (ICSID) Mediation Rules in March 2022 promises to be an effective alternative dispute resolution (ADR) mechanism to resolve investor-State disputes. Its timely introduction is a clear response to the run-away costs and inordinately lengthy judicial and arbitral proceedings to resolve investor-State disputes. The key characteristic of mediation is that apart from its informality, it is a process that is less costly and, if utilized effectively, can produce expedient outcomes for dispute resolution when compared to alternative forms. Mediation can also supplement and complement arbitration, including expedited arbitration. Mediation, however, is not without its draw-backs. Mediation may not be the most optimum vehicle to resolve complex multi-issue disputes that have matured into intensely adversarial relations between the disputing parties. However, the introduction of the well-designed and flexible ICSID Mediation Rules (ICSID-MR) bodes well for the resolution of investor-State disputes in a timely, effective and fair manner.

§14.01 INTRODUCTION

Following United Nations Commission on International Trade Law's (UNCITRAL) adoption of new Expedited Arbitration Rules in 2021, and consonant with UNCITRAL's Model Mediation Rules of 2018, the International Centre for the Settlement of Investment Disputes (ICSID), in March 2022, also adopted, in addition to its standard rules,

ICSID's Expedited Arbitration Rules.[1] At the same time, as the world's primary international organization dedicated exclusively to the resolution of investor-State disputes, ICSID took the bold initiative of adopting its own Mediation Rules.[2] With their enactment, the ICSID Mediation Rules (ICSID-MR) were the 'first institutional mediation rules designed specifically for investment disputes'.[3] In adopting the mediation rules, ICSID was heavily influenced and furthermore coordinated its efforts with the work of UNCITRAL's Working Group III (WGIII) that first initiated the work on drafting its mediation rules. More recently, UNCITRAL WGIII, at its 56th Session, proposed draft provisions on mediation specifically designed for Investor-State Dispute Settlement (ISDS)[4] and provided a further 'Draft UNCITRAL Guidelines on Investment Mediation'.[5]

Mediation as a method of settling disputes is not a new phenomenon. The concept has been included in many domestic legal systems as an alternative dispute resolution (ADR) mechanism to arbitration. Some examples include the 2013 Commercial Arbitration Rules and Mediation Procedures of the American Arbitration Association (AAA) and provisions in numerous bilateral investment treaties (BITs) which include the obligation to resort to mediation or similar actions. Similarly, on a multilateral level, the 1966 Washington Convention creating ICSID, in addition to providing for arbitration, also established an alternative set of rules for conciliation of disputes between investors and States. Equally, the 1985 Convention establishing the Multilateral Investment Guarantee Agency (MIGA) enables MIGA to settle disputes between investors and States. The 2014 Mediation Rules adopted by the International Chamber of Commerce (ICC) also included mediation as a method to resolve commercial disputes.[6]

Despite the lack of information about the success of mediation as a method of dispute resolution between States and investors, the demand for it is present and timely. This demand has evolved out of the frustration encountered by both investors and States that have experienced protracted legal proceedings in arbitral or judicial fora

1. ICSID Expedited Arbitration Rules, adopted by ICSID's Administrative Council on 21 March 2022 and in effect on 1 July 2022 available at https://icsid.worldbank.org/procedures/arbitration/convention/expedited-arbitration/2022.
2. ICSID Mediation Rules, adopted by ICSID's Administrative Council on 21 March 2022 and in effect on 1 July 2022, available at https://icsid.worldbank.org/sites/default/files/ICSID_Mediation_Rules.pdf.
3. ICSID Mediation Rules. A Preview, available at https://mediationblog.kluwerarbitration.com/2020/01/10/a-preview-of-icsids-new-investor-state-mediation-rules/.
4. UNCITRAL Draft provisions on mediation, Fifty-sixth session Vienna, 3-21 July 2023. [There is also the date of 25 April 2023 on the same document] available at: https://documents-dds-ny.un.org/doc/UNDOC/GEN/V23/027/46/PDF/V2302746.pdf?OpenElement.]
5. Draft UNCITRAL guidelines on investment mediation, Note by the Secretariat Fifty-sixth session Vienna, 3-21 July 2023 [There is also the date of 25 April 2023 on the same document] available at: https://documents-dds-ny.un.org/doc/UNDOC/GEN/V23/027/58/PDF/V2302758.pdf?OpenElement].
6. The Energy Charter Treaty also has a set of mediation rules, available at https://www.energycharter.org/process/energy-charter-treaty-1994/energy-charter-treaty/. *See* in particular, Energy Charter, Guide on Investment Mediation (2016), available at: https://www.energycharter.org/media/news/article/the-use-of-mediation-in-investor-state-disputes.

with concurrent and heavy costs. Mediation, because of its informality and consideration of facts and circumstances beyond rigid adherence to legal technicalities, has the potential to resolve disputes early and expediently. Importantly, because of the requirement *ab initio* of agreement of the parties about the nature of the dispute and their amenability to resolve the dispute based on factors such as fairness and equity, mediation can play an effective role in the ultimate resolution of a dispute. In this regard, MIGA's experience as a singular multilateral organization designed to also engage in settling investor-State disputes through mediation, rather than only commercial disputes, is convincing.

With this foundation, ICSID's adoption of the more formal Expedited Arbitration Rules and ICSID-MR is clearly a step in the right direction, adding to the global effort to reform dispute resolution between investors and States. This chapter explains the justification for mediation, its potential, and provides an analysis of ICSID-MR from the perspective of expediency and reduction of costs associated with dispute resolution between investors and States. Importantly, it will show that mediation can supplement and complement ongoing investor-State arbitration proceedings, including expedited arbitration proceedings, thereby having the potential to achieve the twin objectives of cost-efficiency and timeliness of resolution also sought by expedited arbitration procedures.

§14.02 THE CASE FOR MEDIATION

The justification for mediation as an effective alternative, supplementary or complimentary dispute resolution mechanism has been assumed by many national jurisdictions opting to adopt mediation rules. Additionally, State parties are increasingly agreeing to include requirements to mediate in bilateral investment/trade agreements. Indeed, the provision for conciliation had already been included in the 1966 ICSID Convention and thereafter inclusion of formal mediation in multilateral entities such as the ICC and under multilateral conventions such as in the 2016 Energy Charter Treaty, and importantly, settlement of investment disputes under the 1985 MIGA Convention. Much of the momentum for adoption of the ICSID-MR came from the regular availability, success and application of these rules in commercial disputes at all three levels. Undoubtedly, the flexible, expedient and cost-effective nature of mediation as an ADR method may have contributed heavily to its formalization under the ICSID 2022 rules.

[A] National Mediation Rules

The acceptance of mediation in national jurisdictions was mostly aimed at resolving commercial disputes rather than investor-State disputes. There is good reason for this. Simple contractual disputes or trading transactions are more amenable to be mediated and satisfactorily resolved than complex investment claims against States. The fundamental principles on which settlement can be reached through mediation, however, remain consistent and applicable to investor-State disputes. The AAA Arbitration Rules and Mediation Procedures[7] is a key example, among many, that reflects the informality and flexibility associated with mediation. Under its Commercial Mediation Procedures (AAAMP), the only precondition for mediation is that the parties must have stipulated or have included in a contract or agreement that in the event of a dispute, resort could be had to mediation or conciliation under Mediation Procedures.[8] Given that this is the only requirement, an investor-State dispute can also be resolved under the aegis of the AAAMP.

The AAAMP clearly articulates the applicable requirements which need to be conformed with by parties once mediation is initiated. The initiating party is required, *inter alia*, to submit: '(i) a copy of the mediation provision of the parties' stipulation to mediate' and '(ii) a brief statement of the nature of the dispute and the relief requested'.[9] Mediation of a dispute under the AAAMP is conducted by a single mediator, who can be agreed upon by the parties, failing which a mediator is appointed by AAA.[10] The importance of the mediator's impartiality is clearly very important and it is crucial to any outcome.[11] The duties and responsibilities of the mediator are succinctly outlined as well, and, importantly, the mediator is required to facilitate but not coerce' a decision by parties, leaving the outcome entirely to the 'self-determination' of the parties.[12] The mediator is entitled to conduct separate ex parte meetings, permit the exchange of memoranda on issues and help the parties to 'reach a satisfactory resolution of their dispute'.[13]

One other important requirement of AAAMP concerns the maintenance of confidentiality. The mediator cannot be compelled to divulge any records of mediation proceedings or to testify in any adversary proceedings before any judicial forum. Importantly, the parties to the mediation are obligated to maintain confidentiality and 'cannot rely on, or introduce as evidence in any arbitral, judicial or other proceedings' (unless agreed to by parties or required by applicable law), any '(i) views expressed or suggestions made by a party or other participant with respect to possible settlement of the dispute; (ii) admissions made by a party or other participant in the course of the mediation proceedings; (iii) proposals made or views expressed by a mediator; or (iv) the fact that a party had or had not indicated willingness to accept a proposal for settlement made by the mediator'.[14]

These elements of confidentiality are vital to the success or failure of mediation. Failure or success of mediation, in whole or in part, can have serious impacts on parallel arbitration proceedings. In complex multiple-issue disputes, the effectiveness

7. American Arbitration Association, Commercial Arbitration Rules and Mediation Procedures, available at https://www.adr.org/sites/default/files/Mediation%20Procedures%20of%20the%20American%20Arbitration%20Association%20Oct%2001%2C%202009.pdf.
8. *Ibid.*, section M-1. The parties by mutual agreement may vary any part of the procedures 'including, but not limited to, agreeing to conduct the mediation via, telephone or other electronic or technical means'.
9. *Ibid.*, section M-2.
10. *Ibid.*, section M-4.
11. *Ibid.*, section M-5.
12. *Ibid.*, section M-7.
13. *Ibid.*
14. *Ibid.*, section M-10.

of mediation can be inhibited if parties are not permitted to use evidence in parallel arbitration or judicial proceedings on issues that the parties had clearly agreed on during mediation proceedings because of the strict application of confidentiality provisions. Such an eventuality will only lead to re-litigating those issues, thereby protracting arbitral or judicial proceedings. As a result, it will defeat the very purpose of mediation as a supplementary or complimentary mode of dispute settlement.

The termination of mediation occurs with the parties concluding a settlement agreement.[15] Several alternative criteria, such as a written agreement by both parties to the effect that further pursuit of mediation will not resolve the disputes between them or a written or verbal agreement of both parties that the mediation conference has been concluded, will also result in a termination.[16] Termination can also result from non-communication between the mediator and any party or representative of a party for 21 days following the conclusion of the mediation conference.[17]

As with many mediation rules in national jurisdictions, one clear omission was the absence of reference to an enforcement mechanism for settlement agreements.[18] However, with the adoption of the Singapore Convention for Enforcement of Settlement Agreements, this concern has been significantly abated[19] (at present, 56 States are signatories to the Convention, with a few States entering reservations). Complex multi-issue investor-State disputes can be challenging for resolution by mediation alone. In general, however, adoption of mediation rules in national jurisdictions has served very practical needs and contributed to lessening the need for time-consuming judicial or arbitral proceedings. Another element that may have contributed to the increasing reliance on mediation in national jurisdictions is that the mediation procedures do not require submission of detailed evidence or application of discovery rules to procure evidence. Indeed, if timely used, mediation can resolve issues where both parties can agree on fundamental issues quite expeditiously and leave the remaining unresolved complex issues to be litigated in parallel or subsequent arbitration proceedings. The significant informality of mediation and its movement away from the rigid application of legal technicalities and towards taking into account fairness, equity, and confidentiality are additional positive factors, which may have served as the impetus for many States to adopt mediation as an effective ADR mechanism.[20] Clearly, the most important incentives for mediation are expediency and cost-efficiency.

15. *Ibid.*, section M-12.
16. *Ibid.*
17. *Ibid.*
18. A large number of countries have now adopted mediation rules as an alternate or complimentary method of dispute resolution to arbitration. The AAAMP is one such example. They all, however, do not refer to the final and binding nature of such an agreement and do not refer to enforcement. For the most part, this anomaly has been resolved through the adoption in 2018 of the United Nations Convention on International Settlement Agreements Resulting from Mediation.
19. *See*, United Nations Convention on International Settlement Agreements Resulting from Mediation (2018) (the 'Singapore Convention'), available at: https://uncitral.un.org/en/texts/mediation/conventions/international_settlement_agreements.
20. *See* relevantly, Claire Mulder, *Commercial Mediation, The United States and Europe*, Dispute Resolution Magazine, Fall 2017.

[B] Bilateral Agreements/Free Trade Agreements

Recognition of the utility of mediation as a practical, preliminary, complimentary or alternative means for resolving investor-State investment disputes is evident in many BITs and increasingly in the new generation of free-trade agreements (FTAs) and international investment agreements. In a useful study undertaken by Kessedjian, van Aaken, Lie, Mistelis and Reis, of 2,577 International Investment Agreements, nearly 627 of them included provisions for conciliation or mediation.[21] The authors postulate, however, that mediation and conciliation are mechanisms that can be implicitly employed also within the 'cooling-off' periods included in the dispute resolution provisions of these agreements where there is no explicit reference to mediation.[22]

In a preparatory study undertaken by ICSID of nearly 900 BITs and FTAs on dispute resolution, nearly 350 such clauses provided for mediation as a mandatory requirement prior to arbitration or as a non-obligatory amicable mode for resolution of a dispute.[23] This study indicates that a significant number of investment agreements have considered mediation and amicable settlement of disputes to be a precursor to arbitration or as an alternate method of dispute resolution.

A typical reference to conciliation and mediation can be found in Article 10.15 of the US-Panama Trade Promotion Agreement of 2012, which states: 'In the event of an investment dispute, the claimant and the respondent should initially seek to resolve the dispute through consultation and negotiation, which may include the use of non-binding, third party procedures such as conciliation and mediation.'[24] This provision requires that the parties to a dispute must seek to resolve such dispute through consultation and negotiation which may be facilitated by utilizing non-binding, third-party procedures such as conciliation and mediation. It is obligatory for parties to consult and negotiate, but it is optional for the parties to engage third-party procedures to do so. The other important factor is that any outcomes resulting from such consultations are not binding. This latter premise significantly weakens any incentive for parties to engage.

Article 31.5 of the United States, Mexico, Canada Free Trade Agreement[25] (USMCA) also carries an optional method of ADR by referring disputes among parties to conciliation and mediation. Article 31.5 states:

21. Catherine Kessedjian et al., *Mediation in Future Investor – State Dispute Settlement,* Journal of International Dispute Settlement, 2022, 1-24, available at DOI: 10.1093/jnlids/idac015. For the purposes of the article, the authors consider conciliation and mediation to be the same.
22. *Ibid.*, 4. The authors, however, state 'Since it is impossible to have data on how exactly cooling-off periods are used, we thus describe only the possibility of using them in potentially different ways, not describing how these periods are *actually* used' (emphasis added).
23. International Centre for Settlement of Investment Disputes, *Overview of Investment Treaty Clauses on Mediation,* July 2021, available at https://icsid.worldbank.org/resources/publications/overview-investment-treaty-clauses-mediation.
24. United States-Panama Trade Promotion Agreement ('US-Panama TPA') of 2012, available at https://ustr.gov/trade-agreements/free-trade-agreements/panama-tpa/final-text.
25. The United States, Mexico, Canada, Free Trade Agreement (USMCA) [1 July 2020] available at https://ustr.gov/trade-agreements/free-trade-agreements/united-states-mexico-canada-agreement/agreement-between.

1. Parties may decide at any time to voluntarily undertake an alternative method of dispute resolution, such as good offices, conciliation or mediation.
2. Proceedings that involve good offices, conciliation or mediation shall be confidential and without prejudice to the rights of the Parties in another proceeding.
3. Parties participating in proceedings under this Article may suspend or terminate those proceedings.
4. If the disputing Parties decide, good offices, conciliation, or mediation may continue while a dispute proceeds for resolution before a panel established under Article 31.6 (Establishment of a Panel).[26]

There are several key factors here. Unlike the previous example included in the Panama-US TPA, where referring a matter to conciliation or mediation is mandatory, referral here is optional. Proceedings are confidential and without prejudice, meaning that any and all information cannot be used in other proceedings. While mediation or conciliation is continuing, parties can suspend or terminate other proceedings. The article also provides that parallel dispute resolution proceedings can continue.[27] No reference is made to whether parties can refer the dispute to institutional mediation or conciliation proceedings.

One other important element in many of the provisions that include mediation proceedings is that it could be undertaken by the parties at any time. However, many such provisions also require parties to stay other proceedings if the parties agree to mediate. The presumption here is that parallel proceedings on the same issues may undermine one or the other proceeding.[28] But to the extent that in parallel proceedings both parties agree not to litigate the same issues, parallel proceedings can be constructively used to resolve disputes expediently. Thus, despite what could be deemed several shortcomings, the very inclusion of references to mediation and/or conciliation in an increasing number of BITs and FTAs lends credence and recognition to the potential of mediation and conciliation as an expeditious ADR mechanism.

[C] Multilateral Agreements Supporting Mediation

Ultimately, the impetus for ICSID to adopt separate institutional mediation rules may have come from other multilateral instruments that have been in place or have had success in mediation or conciliation.[29] The requirements for mediation at the multilateral level were overwhelmingly focused on commercial disputes rather than investor-State disputes. However, the fundamental principles that guide mediation or conciliation in commercial disputes could easily be replicable to investor-State disputes in achieving rapid and less costly alternatives to judicial or arbitration recourse.

26. *Ibid.*, the reference to Article 31.6 here is to the institution of formal dispute resolution proceedings under USMCA.
27. *Ibid.*
28. *Ibid.*, USMCA n. 2 at 9.
29. While some have posited that there are very minor differences between conciliation and mediation and have used the two terms interchangeably, there are significant differences in, at least, how ICSID's conciliation rules differ from mediation.

[1] *International Chamber of Commerce Mediation Rules*

The ICC-MR adopted in 2014 are one of the earliest multilateral efforts to adopt mediation as an alternative institutional dispute resolution method.[30] The ICC-MR is administered by the ICC's International Centre for ADR.[31] For the most part, the ICC-MR are similar to the AAAMP. As with AAAMP, the formal precondition to initiate mediation requires a written agreement between the disputing parties requesting mediation.[32] Mediation can be commenced in parallel or concurrent with other dispute resolution procedures.[33] The ICC-MR only provides for a single mediator to be appointed with the joint approval of the disputing parties.[34]

As with most mediation rules, provision for strict confidentiality reflects both the strength and weakness of mediation. Article 9 of the ICC-MR contains the applicable confidentiality provisions. Unless agreed to by the parties, confidentiality has to be strictly maintained.[35] The exception is where confidentiality is prohibited by 'applicable law'.[36] Confidentiality must be maintained, and unless the parties have prior agreement, they are precluded from producing 'as evidence in any judicial, arbitral or similar proceedings', *inter alia*, 'any documents, statements or communications which are submitted by another party or by the Mediator in or for the Proceedings'[37] or 'any admissions made by another party within the Proceedings'.[38] Whether a settlement agreement itself is subject to the confidentiality provisions is unclear.

Resort to mediation has been quite successful under ICC-MR, although many of the disputes referred to mediation were commercial in nature and not necessarily investor-State disputes arising out of investment agreements or BITs. In any event, ICC dispute resolution statistics for 2020 indicate a very significant move towards using mediation/conciliation as a mode of dispute resolution.[39] The ICC's International Centre for ADR received a total of 77 new cases under its rules, 45 of which were filed under its Mediation Rules.[40] Nine parties were State entities from the Republic of China, the Dominican Republic, France, the US and Qatar.[41] The statistics indicate a diverse range of business sectors, mostly related to construction and engineering contracts (24%) and 'disputes relating to energy and telecommunications'.[42] The remedies sought in each dispute ranged from as low as 'few thousand dollars' to 'over

30. International Chamber of Commerce 2014 Mediation Rules, available at https://www.iccwbo.org.
31. *Ibid.*, Article 1(1).
32. *Ibid.*, Article 2(1).
33. *Ibid.*, Article 2(1)(d).
34. *Ibid.*, Article 5(1-5). However, under Article 5(6), the Parties may nominate more than one mediator or the Centre may propose to the parties that 'there be more than one mediator'.
35. *Ibid.*, Article 9(1).
36. *Ibid.*
37. *Ibid.*, Article 9(2)(a).
38. *Ibid.*, Article 9(2)(c).
39. ICC Dispute Resolution, 2020 Statistics, available at https://nyiac.org/wp-content/uploads/2021/09/ICC-Dispute-Resolution-2020-Statistics.pdf.
40. *Ibid.*
41. *Ibid.*
42. *Ibid.*

US$ 800 million (with an average amount in dispute of US$ 66 million)'.[43] The report concludes, therefore, that mediation can be considered suitable both for 'low and high value disputes'.[44] More importantly, the statistics indicate that the average cost of proceedings with mediators was USD 25,900.[45] This is an overwhelmingly lower cost than what a full-scale arbitration proceeding would have cost. What would have been helpful, however, would have been indicators with reference to the time span taken on average for the mediated dispute and some information about their success or failure.

[2] ICSID Convention: Conciliation Rules

The question can be legitimately raised as to why ICSID adopted Mediation Rules in 2022, when it already had Conciliation Rules in place since the effective date of the ICSID Convention in 1966.[46] Importantly, ICSID's Conciliation Rules were the earliest known set of formal rules to provide conciliation exclusively for resolution of investor-State disputes. The ICSID Conciliation Rules have been utilized to resolve investor-State disputes, but only sporadically.[47] One study reports that since the first reported request for conciliation under the Conciliation Rules in 1982, 12 other requests have been registered. Of the 13 requests, proceedings have been concluded in 9 and in 4 (the first registered in 2012 and the last in 2020), conclusions are still pending.[48] It would appear, therefore, that conciliation proceedings under ICSID have taken an inordinate amount of time. In that regard, conciliation is very similar to arbitration proceedings. This factor perhaps may have contributed largely to the need for expedited arbitration and mediation rules now enacted by ICSID.

A distinction between ICSID's Conciliation Rules and ICSID's newly adopted Mediation Rules exists to avoid the often-assumed conclusion that mediation and

43. *Ibid.*
44. *Ibid.*
45. *Ibid.*
46. Convention on the Settlement of Investment Disputes between States and Nationals of Other States (opened for signature 18 March 1965, entered into force 14 October 1966) ('ICSID Convention') (2022) Article 25(1), available at https://icsid.worldbank.org/sites/default/files/ICSID_Convention_EN.pdf, Chapter III. Conciliation.
47. There is still a blurring of the differences between 'conciliation' and 'mediation'. While the end objective is the same in a neutral third-party's intercession to enable two disputing parties to reach 'settlement' of a dispute, procedurally the two modes can be very different which should be noted. *See*, particularly, Mulder, *supra*, n. 20, 8, who states:

    > Whereas many in the United States may see conciliation as an equivalent to mediation (and often use the phrase to describe mediation, if in slightly more evaluative form), in many European countries people see conciliation as a distinct concept, with deep roots in their civil-law countries' legal systems. Switzerland's Code of Civil Procedure, for example, considers conciliation procedurally distinct from mediation: conciliation is a magistrate-led form of non-binding adjudication, whereas mediation is a non-evaluative process that involves not magistrates but accredited professionals from a wider range of disciplines.

48. *See* Kessedjian et al., *supra* n. 21, Table 1.

conciliation are one and the same or are duplicative.[49] Several factors illustrate the differences among them. The ICSID Conciliation rules broadly follow conditions applicable to arbitration rules. First, as with arbitration, the disputing parties must have the proper nationality of the signatory State.[50] Second, much like ICSID arbitration, the ICSID Conciliation Rules accommodate the appointment of a single conciliator or an uneven number of them as the parties agree. The appointment of a conciliation commission mirrors the same structure as with arbitration.[51] Third, the procedural requirements largely follow arbitration procedures. Jurisdiction and merits can and often follow legal formalities in conciliation proceedings as it is with requirements for discovery. The ICSID Background Paper on Investment Mediation further provides that 'the role of the conciliation commission is to clarify the issues in dispute, whereas the role of the mediator is solely to assist the parties with reaching a mutually agreeable solution'.[52] Clearly, the sporadic use of conciliation with the same formalities that constrain arbitration, attendant high costs and time-consuming procedures have all rendered conciliation to be a less effective ADR mechanism over time.

[3] The Convention Establishing MIGA[53]

From the very inception of its operations, MIGA was designed to provide political risk insurance to investors investing in the Agency's developing member countries. Both in its guarantee operations and in providing technical assistance for investment promotion in its developing member countries, MIGA's Convention and its operational documents provided for avoidance of and settlement of investment disputes.

To achieve these objectives, MIGA's Convention facilitates the deployment of two methods. One involves intervention under Article 23(b)(i) of the MIGA Convention where it requires the Agency to 'encourage the amicable settlement of disputes between investors and host countries'.[54] Although rarely used, wherever investors and Member States have requested MIGA's intercession under this article, there have been extremely positive outcomes. Parties seeking mediation need not be Member States of MIGA. The outcomes benefited both the investors and States.[55]

---

49. *See* for an explanatory summary of the differences between the two sets of ICSID Rules, International Centre for Settlement of Investment Disputes, *Background Paper on Investment Mediation,* July 2021, available at https://icsid.worldbank.org/resources/publications/background-paper-investment-mediation.
50. *Ibid. See also supra* n. 46, ICSID Convention, Article 28(1).
51. *Ibid.*, ICSID Convention, Articles 29 and 37.
52. *Supra* n. 49, ICSID Background Paper, *see* particularly section 5.
53. Convention establishing the Multilateral Investment Guarantee Agency, 11 October 1985, 1508 U.N.T.S. 99 (I-26012) (entered into force 12 April 1988). The MIGA Convention has been signed and ratified by 182 member countries.
54. *Ibid.*, Article 23(b)(i).
55. Because of confidentiality, details of outcomes and consequent settlement agreements are not available. Some of the examples cited in this section can only be anecdotal taking also into account the author's personal awareness of the circumstances and issues at the time.

One of the most significant achievements in this regard was the settlement of over 40 outstanding investment disputes between investors and the Government of Ethiopia. In accordance with Article 23(b)(i) of the MIGA Convention, in 2001, the Government of Ethiopia appointed MIGA 'as a mediator for the resolution of the disputes between the Ethiopian government and foreign investors for projects not guaranteed by MIGA'.[56] No special rules were developed for the conduct of mediation, but investors were advised by MIGA that claims for compensation should be filed before a specified date.[57] Nearly 42 claims were filed for review by MIGA and consideration for compensation by the Government of Ethiopia.[58] In these claims, it was not disputed that the properties were expropriated by the Government of Ethiopia. The central issue related to the quantum of compensation. At the time, the severe economic crisis faced by the Government also had to be considered. In any event, in the vast majority of the filed claims, an agreement was reached as to the amounts of compensation offered by the Government. In a comparatively short time, the Government of Ethiopia, with the assistance of MIGA, satisfactorily resolved, with a very few exceptions, all the claims against it.[59] The settlement of disputes in Ethiopia, with MIGA's intervention, had extremely positive ramifications for all parties. Ethiopia's determination to settle outstanding investment disputes, which had remained unsettled for decades, immediately revived confidence in investors internationally. Soon after the settlement of the disputes, Ethiopia was able to enter into several key bilateral investment agreements with other States. Second, those investors who agreed to settlement were immediately paid the agreed-upon compensation, and some were given incentives to reinvest in the country. Third, MIGA satisfactorily fulfilled one of the main mandates in its Convention of 'settling disputes' between investors and developing countries with the objective of promoting foreign investments into developing countries. Finally, and most importantly, the whole process was streamlined, time-bound and informal, giving ample opportunities for the disputing parties to engage amicably and settle the matter of compensation expeditiously.[60] All of these factors are quintessential for any successful mediation efforts.

The second method of settlement of disputes between investors and Member States of MIGA concerns investments guaranteed by the Agency. Here, the objective of the Agency is to pre-empt a claim under a contract of guarantee issued to the guarantee holder because of possible actions taken or anticipated to be taken by a host

56. Multilateral Investment Guarantee Agency, available at https://www.miga.org/history.
57. Claims filed after such date were rejected.
58. The claims all related to expropriation by the Mengistu Government in the 1970s of foreign investments.
59. *See* in general, Investment Dispute Mediation in Ethiopia, Press release 18 December 2002, available at https://www.miga.org/press-release/investment-dispute-mediation-services-ethiopia.
60. There was no appointment of a mediator; MIGA's General Counsel at the time was the assumed 'mediator'. Costs were minimal and each party bore its own costs. Other than Ethiopia, there were several other settlements concluded with MIGA's intervention involving investors and States.

government. For this purpose, MIGA requires a guarantee holder of the Agency to notify it of any circumstances or factors that might engender a possible claim under the contract of guarantee.[61] MIGA's Investment Guarantee Guide clearly expresses what the Agency seeks to achieve through this early intervention before events mature into a formal claim that MIGA will consider for a possible payout. By providing an opportunity for MIGA's early intervention, this ultimate eventuality is forestalled. MIGA:

> derives its unique strength from being a member of the World Bank Group and as a treaty based international organization whose shareholders include most countries in the world. This enables MIGA to provide an umbrella of deterrence against government actions that could disrupt projects and assist in resolving disputes between investors and governments.[62]

Consequently, where guarantee holders have notified MIGA of circumstances that might result in a claim being filed, the Agency has formally considered such circumstances to be pre-claim situations. In such circumstances, the Agency is able to engage the governments concerned fully and has been extremely successful in not only heading off formal claims being filed in many instances but also enabling investors to continue with their investments in the host country.[63]

MIGA's dispute resolution and pre-claim experience point to some very important factors that will be invaluable for ICSID's future resolution of investor-State disputes through the application of its mediation rules. First, an international organization, because of its leverage, impartiality and apolitical nature, is likely to be more successful in resolving disputes. Second, the success rate of resolution is higher, where the circumstances of a potential dispute are brought to the attention of an international organization's mediation process early rather than when such circumstances develop into a full-scale adversarial dispute. Third, in such circumstances, the areas of conflict can be discerned on factual/technical basis rather than an entirely legal basis, lending further to fairness and equity being considered as bases for settlement. Fourth, procedural flexibility without encumbering rules creates a non-formal environment conducive to establishing trust between parties. Fifth, a speedy resolution can enable development projects that have contributed to the host State's development to be restored and continue to benefit both parties. Finally, resolutions through settlement have been mostly expeditious and undoubtedly carried out at a fraction of the cost that would have been expended had the dispute ended up in arbitration.

61. *See* in this regard, the Multilateral Investment Guarantee Agency, Operational Regulations (1985, as amended by the Board of Directors through 1 October 2007). *See* in particular, section IV, Warranties and Undertakings of the Guarantee Holder, para. 2.14 (iv) that requires the Guarantee Holder 'to notify the Agency of any event that might give rise to a covered loss, or significantly increase the likelihood of such a loss promptly upon learning of such an event'.
62. MIGA/Investment Guarantee Guide, available at: https://www.miga.org/sites/default/files/2022.
63. Because of strict confidentiality, it is not possible to include any information about the Agency's track record of settling pre-claim situations.

[4] UNCITRAL Model Law on International Commercial Mediation (2018)

The single most influential recent development that may have precipitated the adoption of ICSID-MR is the 2018 UNCITRAL's Model Law on International Commercial Mediation and the International Settlement Agreements Resulting from Mediation.[64] The Model International Commercial Mediation Law (MICML) streamlines domestically or multilaterally consistent rules/binding laws applicable to international commercial transactions. MICML clearly addresses cross-border commercial transactions that implicate foreign and domestic parties.[65] Second, the disputes amenable for mediation must be 'commercial'. While not explicit, the broad description of 'commercial' may be conducive also for investor-state settlement of investment disputes.[66] Third, there is no bar that one of the parties cannot be a State party. Fourth, as with many previous mediation rules, the MICML is exhaustive about the appointment of mediators, where the preference, unless otherwise agreed by parties, is for a single mediator to be appointed.[67] Fifth, the MICML's emphasis on expediency is reflected in Article 5(2), which requires the party seeking settlement to 'invite' the other party to respond within 30 days (or as such other time as specified) after which if there is no response, the party seeking mediation can assume that 'this is a rejection of the invitation to mediate'.[68] In addition, in the conduct of mediation, the mediator is required to take into account 'any wishes that the parties may express and the need for a speedy settlement of disputes'.[69] Article 11 of MICML contains all the restrictions applicable to admissibility as evidence in other proceedings any and all information submitted during settlement proceedings, except where such information is required under law for the sole purpose of enforcement of a settlement agreement.[70]

Article 15 of MICML refers to one of the critical elements in mediation. It states that 'if the parties conclude an agreement settling a dispute, that settlement agreement is binding and enforceable'.[71] The lack of a binding nature of a settlement agreement was a huge lacuna in previous mediation and conciliation rules, and Article 15 squarely addresses that omission. Also, MICML Section 3 addresses the scope and application of International Settlement Agreements.[72]

---

64. UNCITRAL Model Law on International Commercial Mediation and International Settlement Agreements Resulting from Mediation (2018), available at https://uncitral.un.org/en/texts/mediation/modellaw/commercial_conciliation.
65. *Ibid.*, Article 3(2) MICML.
66. *Ibid.*, *see* note 1 of MICML which states that 'the term commercial should be given the widest interpretation so as to cover matters arising from all relationships of a commercial nature, whether contractual or not'.
67. *Ibid.*, Article 6.
68. *Ibid.*, Article 5(2).
69. *Ibid.*, Article 7(2).
70. *Ibid.*, Article 11.
71. *Ibid.*, Article 15.
72. *Ibid.*, section 3. Articles 16-20.

[5] *The United Nations Convention on Settlement Agreements Resulting from Mediation*

One of the most important and constructive developments in mainstreaming mediations as a viable ADR mechanism is the adoption of the United Nations Convention on International Settlement Agreements Resulting from Mediation (2018 Singapore Convention).[73] Its adoption resolves one of the key problems associated with mediation that settlement agreements concluded between parties had no binding effect or were not enforceable. The 2018 Singapore Convention resolves this anomaly and brings settlement agreements concluded between parties to be on par with arbitral awards. Settlement agreements are fully binding and enforceable in all signatory countries of the 2018 Singapore Convention, just as arbitral awards are fully enforceable and binding under the 1958 New York Convention on the Recognition and Enforcement of Foreign Arbitral Awards.[74]

The language of the 2018 Singapore Convention follows verbatim UNCITRAL's MICML's section 3. Fundamentally, settlement agreements must be between two parties from two different States, just as they must arise out of a cross-border 'commercial' dispute.[75] As with the 1958 New York Convention, the 2018 Singapore Convention includes in Article 5 various grounds on which relief could be refused by the authority before which enforcement is sought.[76] Furthermore, Article 8 permits signatory States to enter reservations to exclude acts of States and State agencies from application of the Singapore Convention, although such reservations are not mandatory.[77] This, of course, weakens significantly the efficacy of mediation for countries that make reservations.

[D] ICSID-MR 2022

With such a strong foundation now in place at every level (nationally, bilaterally and multilaterally) recognizing the importance of mediation as an ADR mechanism, the adoption by ICSID of mediation rules in 2022 is an invaluable addition, exclusively dedicated to resolving investor-State disputes. The ICSID-MR follow closely all the provisions of MICML and are also consistent with the recent UNCITRAL draft provisions for mediation for investor-state dispute resolution.[78] Whether ICSID-MR will be utilized, and moreover, its success in resolving investor-State disputes through mediation, will depend on a number of key factors. These include the nature of the dispute and its accessibility and availability to disputing parties, consent and timing, cost-efficiency, confidentiality, expediency of the procedures, mediator appointments and

73. *Supra* n. 19. The United Nations Convention on Settlement Agreements Resulting from Mediation (2018).
74. The 1958 New York Convention on the Recognition and Enforcement of Foreign Arbitral Awards, available at https://www.newyorkconvention.org/english.
75. *Supra* n. 19, Article 1.
76. *Ibid.*, Article 5.
77. *Ibid.*, Article 8.
78. *Supra* n. 4.

their role, termination and enforcement. Broadly, ICSID-MR appears to facilitate expedient resolution of investment disputes through mediation in a cost-efficient manner.

[1] Nature of Disputes, Broad Accessibility/Availability

Rule 2(1) extends the scope of ICSID-MR to 'mediations that relate to an investment' and involve a State or a Regional Economic Integration Organization (REIO), 'and which the parties' consent in writing to submit to the Centre'.[79] A key precondition is that the dispute must 'relate' to an 'investment'. Also, the dispute does not necessarily have to be a 'legal dispute', nor does it have to arise 'directly out of an investment', unlike disputes brought under Article 25 of the ICSID Convention.[80]

ICSID-MR require that a State[81] or a REIO must be involved in a mediation, and such States do not have to be Contracting States to the ICSID Convention as compared with disputes brought under Article 25 of the ICSID Convention. Similarly, the Rules do not require that the other party to the mediation be 'a national of another Contracting State'.[82] Under ICSID-MR, the 'parties' are not defined. The mediation must only 'involve a State or an REIO' on one side or the other.[83] There is possibility for interpretation about which party can institute mediation, the only qualifying criteria being that the dispute be related to an investment.[84] Such flexibility may, at least theoretically, lead to requests for mediations between two different States, a State and an REIO, an REIO and one of its constituent Member States, or even between a State and its own nationals. While the flexibility is very convenient, discerning who the right parties are can get mired in protracted deliberations. This could weaken the application of ICSID-MR.

[2] Consent

Similar to disputes instituted under the ICSID Arbitration Rules, mediation under the ICSID-MR can only be administered by ICSID upon written consent of the parties.[85] Consent is not only needed in order to institute the mediation[86] but is also required

79. *Supra* n. 2, ICSID-MR, Rule 2(1).
80. *Supra* n. 46, ICSID Convention, Article 25(1).
81. *Supra* n. 2, ICSID-MR 2(2) makes clear that a State also 'includes a constituent subdivision of the State, or an agency of the State or the REIO' with the requirement that the consent of such constituent subdivision or agency be approved by the State or the REIO or the State or the REIO notifies ICSID 'that no such approval is required'.
82. *Supra* n. 46, ICSID Convention Article 25(1). *Ibid.*, Rule 2(1).
83. *Supra* n. 2. ICSID-MR, Rule 2(1).
84. *Ibid.* The term 'investment' is also not defined. Nor is it defined in the ICSID Convention, although it could generally be understood from ICSID jurisprudence that 'investment' in the context of the ICSID Convention generally refers to long-term foreign direct investments or cross-border investments.
85. *Ibid.*, n. 2 ICSID-MR 2(1).
86. *Ibid.*, ICSID-MR (2)(1) and ICSID-MR (5)(1).

throughout the mediation process because the ICSID-MR contemplate that any party to a mediation can unilaterally withdraw from the process at any time.[87] The consent to mediate may be in a contract, a specific agreement between parties providing for ICSID mediation, or in a bilateral or multilateral investment instrument, an example of which was earlier referred to in the United States-Panama TPA.[88] Evidence of prior consent to ICSID mediation must be provided by the party instituting a mediation.[89] Where prior consent has been obtained and a party instituting mediation has satisfied the procedural requirements[90], the ICSID Secretary-General is required to 'promptly' acknowledge receipt of the request and transmit the request to the other party.[91]

A further advance in the ICSID-MR is that parties who do not have prior written consent can also seek ICSID's intervention to mediate a dispute.[92] In such a case, the request for a mediation should comply with the same form and content requirements as a mediation requested with agreement of the parties.[93] However, instead of attaching an agreement to mediate, the requesting party must include 'an offer to the other party to mediate' and a request that the ICSID Secretary-General 'invite the other party to advise whether it accepts the offer to mediate'.[94] The Rules provide that the Secretary-General will then invite the other party to accept or reject the offer to mediate within 60 days.[95] If the other party accepts the offer, ICSID initiates a screening process. If the other party rejects the offer, the Secretary-General will inform the parties that there will be no further action taken in the matter.[96]

[3] Streamlined and Time-Bound Procedures

The objective of concluding mediations between investors and States expeditiously and within a set time period has been extensively addressed in the ICSID-MR. Appointment of a mediator (or mediators) by agreement of the parties sets a 60-day period. If the parties are unable to agree on a mediator during that period, they can request the Secretary-General of ICSID to appoint a mediator within a period of 30 days.[97] If for a period of 120 consecutive days, a mediator has not been appointed, the request for mediation is terminated.[98] Once appointed, a mediator has a 20-day period to accept an appointment.[99] Within a 15-day period 'after the date of the transmittal of the Request

87. *Ibid.*, ICSID-MR 22(1)(c).
88. *Supra* n. 24. US-Panama PTA.
89. *Supra* n. 2, ICSID-MR 5(3)(i).
90. *Ibid.*, ICSID-MR 5(3).
91. *Ibid.*, ICSID-MR 5(5).
92. *Ibid.*, ICSID-MR 6.
93. *Ibid.*, ICSID-MR 5.
94. *Ibid.*, ICSID-MR 6(2)(b) and (c).
95. *Ibid.*, ICSID-MR 6(3)(c).
96. *Ibid.*, ICSID-MR 6(5).
97. *Ibid.*, ICSID-MR 13(4).
98. *Ibid.*, ICSID-MR 13(5).
99. *Ibid.*, ICSID-MR 14(3).

pursuant to Rule 15', each party is required to file an initial statement about the substance of the request.[100] The mediator(s) is required to convene the first session within 30 days after the date of the transmittal of the request pursuant to Rule 15.[101]

ICSID-MR are clear in their aim of an effective conclusion of a mediation process with a settlement, by requiring the parties to consider what such a settlement process might look like. Each party is to file with the Secretary-General an initial statement that describes: (i) the issues in dispute, (ii) the views of the party on such issues, and (iii) the party's views on the mediation procedure.[102] These initial written statements must be filed within 15 days of the transmittal of the Request to the mediator(s), unless the parties agree to another time period.[103] As early as the first session, each party will have to consider which person or entity is authorized to negotiate and settle the issues on the party's behalf and how each party will describe the process of concluding and implementing a settlement.[104] The first session is to take place within 30 days of the transmittal of the Request to the mediator(s) unless the parties agree to a different time period.[105] One of the outcomes of the first session is a Protocol for the conduct of mediation, setting out the procedure, administration and any agreements reached and to be followed throughout the mediation process.[106] ICSID-MR specify which procedural and administrative matters must be addressed in the Protocol, as well as the matters on which parties are to seek agreement.[107] If not at the first session, each party is required to identify who is authorized to settle the dispute and to describe the settlement process within a specified time period as determined by the mediator.[108]

[4] Cost-Efficiency

With expediency, the obvious result is cost reduction and efficiency. Under the ICSID-MR, the cost of each mediation will differ depending on the complexity of the issues, its time duration, and each party's expenses such as costs of legal representation or experts, if necessary, as well as the fees and expenses of mediators and administrative charges and expenses of ICSID.[109] Generally, however, a mediation may be significantly less costly than an arbitration or conciliation proceeding brought under the ICSID Convention or ICSID Additional Facility Rules. Costs will also be reduced when conducted efficiently within preset time periods.

100. *Ibid.*, ICSID-MR 19(1).
101. *Ibid.*, ICSID-MR 20(1).
102. *Ibid.*, ICSID-MR 19(1).
103. *Ibid.*
104. *Ibid.*, ICSID-MR 20(4).
105. *Ibid.*, ICSID-MR 20(1).
106. *Ibid.*, ICSID-MR 20(3).
107. *Ibid.*, ICSID-MR 20(3)(a)-(i).
108. *Ibid.*, ICSID-MR 20(4).
109. *Ibid.*, ICSID-MR Rule 9.

A party wishing to institute a mediation is required to pay a lodging fee[110] which is USD 1,000, pursuant to the ICSID Schedule of Fees currently in effect.[111] Unlike for arbitration, conciliation or post-award proceedings, there is no administrative fee charged upon the registration of a mediation or annually thereafter.[112] Instead, a charge of USD 200 per hour is levied for each hour of the Centre's staff services that will be spent.[113] For each mediation, the Secretary-General will appoint a secretary to represent the Secretary-General to ensure that the procedural steps required under the ICSID-MR are observed and to assist with the mediation.[114]

Additionally, the administrative charges and expenses as well as the fees and expenses of mediators will be paid by ICSID from advance payments[115] deposited by the parties.[116] ICSID will request the first advance payment upon registration of a request from the party requesting mediation to 'defray the estimated costs of the mediation through the first session'.[117] A subsequent advance payment will be requested from both parties upon the transmittal of the case file to the mediator(s) to 'defray the estimated costs of the subsequent phase of the mediation'.[118] Supplemental advance payments may be requested as needed throughout the mediation.[119] Such advance payments are not based on the amount in dispute. Rather, they are based on estimated costs to be incurred at the various stages of the mediation.[120] The fees and expenses of mediator(s) will be deducted from the advance payments. The hourly fees, reimbursement of expenses, travel and per diem allowances for mediator(s) follow the fees and expenses for members of tribunals, commissions and committees iterated in ICSID's Memorandum on the Fees and Expenses.[121]

Finally, the ICSID-MR provide that the costs of the mediation, including the fees and expenses of the mediator, administrative costs and costs of ICSID, are to be shared equally between the parties unless otherwise agreed, and each party shall bear any other costs they incur in conducting the mediation.[122] Unlike ICSID Convention arbitration proceedings, it is not envisioned that a mediator or a mediation panel, other

110. *Ibid.*, ICSID-MR Rule 5(1); ICSID Mediation Administrative and Financial Regulations (adopted on 21 March 2022 and in effect on 1 July 2022), Regulation 10.
111. ICSID Schedule of Fees (2022), available at https://icsid.worldbank.org/services/cost-of-proceedings/schedule-fees/2022.
112. *Ibid.*
113. *Ibid.*
114. *Supra* n. 110, ICSID Mediation Administrative and Financial Regulations, Regulation 2.
115. ICSID Cost of Proceedings, available at https://icsid.worldbank.org/services/cost-of-proceedings#:~:text=ICSID's%20Administrative%20Charges%20and%20Expenses,divided%20equally%20between%20the%20parties.
116. *Supra* n. 111, Regulation 6.
117. *Ibid.*, Regulation 7(1)(a). Such payment by the initiating party is considered as its partial payment on the advance payment to be subsequently requested upon the transmittal of the case file to the mediator(s).
118. *Ibid.*, Regulation 7(1)(b).
119. *Ibid.*, Regulation 7(1)(c).
120. *Ibid.*, Regulations 6 and 7.
121. ICSID Memorandum on the Fees and Expenses (2022), available at https://icsid.worldbank.org/services/cost-of-proceedings/memorandum-fees-expenses/2022.
122. *Supra* n. 2 ICSID-MR 9; *see also, supra* n. 110, ICSID Administrative and Financial Regulations, Regulation 7(2).

than the parties themselves, assess the parties' expenses or decide how fees and expenses are to be paid.[123] The parties to the dispute bear their own costs regardless of the outcome.

[5] *Confidentiality*

Provisions on confidentiality under ICSID-MR for the most part follow established rules in mediation. However, unlike ICSID arbitration and conciliation proceedings, the occurrence of which must be published as part of its registry functions,[124] ICSID will only 'maintain a Register for each mediation',[125] and the information therein regarding the institution, conduct or final disposition of a mediation 'shall not be published, unless the parties agree otherwise'.[126] Additionally, the ICSID-MR provide that 'the fact that [the parties] are mediating or have mediated shall be confidential' unless agreed otherwise by the parties.[127] While maintaining confidentiality may be beneficial for parties, given that the outcome may adversely affect one party or the other, it makes the study of mediation trends and effectiveness impossible to gauge, as is evident from every attempt to review the results of past mediations. However, ICSID-MR provide for a high degree of transparency if the parties mutually agree that all relevant information can be disclosed or where disclosure of all such information is mandated by law.[128]

[6] *Prohibition on Use of Information in Other Proceedings*

As with standard practice in mediation proceedings, the parties are prohibited from using any positions, admissions, offers of settlement or views expressed by the other party during the mediation in any other judicial, arbitration or similar proceeding, except upon agreement.[129] This gives the parties greater freedom and flexibility in endeavouring to reach positions of mutual understanding on issues without legally compromising themselves on positions they have taken during mediation proceedings. The positions taken and views expressed may not be used against them in any other proceedings. The ICSID Convention provides a similar 'without prejudice' principle with regard to conciliation proceedings.[130] There is, however, a negative aspect to this restriction. Most mediation rules are premised on an assumption of a 'single-issue' dispute. This may not, however, be the case. Disputes can have multiple issues. It is particularly so in investor-State investment disputes. Contested issues can arise regarding the proper parties to the dispute and substantive material issues.

123. *Supra* n. 46, Article 61(2).
124. ICSID Administrative and Financial Regulations (2022) (adopted on 21 March 2022 and in effect on 1 July 2022), Regulation 26; ICSID Additional Facility Administrative and Financial Regulations (2022) (adopted on 21 March 2022 and in effect on 1 July 2022), Regulation 3.
125. *Supra* n. 110, ICSID Mediation Administrative and Financial Regulations, Regulation 3.
126. *Ibid.*
127. *Supra* n. 2, ICSID-MR 10(2).
128. *Ibid.*, ICSID-MR 10(1).
129. *Ibid.*, ICSID-MR 11.
130. *Supra* n. 46, ICSID Convention, Article 35.

For example, in mediation proceedings, parties may agree and settle on who the parties to the dispute are but fail to reach agreement on substantive issues. In such circumstances, to prohibit parties from introducing evidence of agreement about the standing of parties in a parallel proceeding not only results in protracted alternate proceedings but also leads to re-litigating a fundamental issue on which the parties had previously agreed. Hence, in drafting and concluding the initial agreement for mediation, the parties should signify that issues the parties intend to and conclusively settle during mediation proceedings be admitted into ongoing arbitration proceedings and entered into such parallel proceedings as a partial settlement agreement.

[7] Appointment of a Mediator(s) and Their Roles

The only qualifications provided by the Rules are that a mediator be impartial and independent of the parties.[131] No further qualifications are required, unless parties agree that he or she should possess specific qualifications or expertise.[132] Notably absent are any nationality restrictions that apply in ICSID arbitration proceedings.[133] Like in most mediation rules, ICSID-MR provide for a single mediator and at most two by agreement of the parties.[134] Once appointed, the mediator(s) must also provide a signed declaration of 'independence, impartiality, availability and commitment to maintain the confidentiality of the mediation'[135] and undertake an ongoing obligation to disclose any changes of circumstances relevant to such declaration.[136]

Unlike in ICSID arbitration and conciliation proceedings where the qualifications, nationality and impartiality of mediators or conciliators can be challenged and thereby stall, delay and impede the proceedings,[137] ICSID-MR allow a mediator to resign at any time, without providing reasons for such resignation or requesting consent from parties (or co-mediator) for such resignation.[138] At the same time, the Rules require a mediator to resign if both parties make a request for resignation or if the mediator 'becomes incapacitated or fails to perform the duties required of a mediator'.[139] Unlike arbitration proceedings, a vacancy created by a mediator's resignation does not suspend the mediation, rather it is filled by either the same method as the original appointment or by the Secretary-General if a vacancy is not filled within 45 days.[140] Moreover, where two mediators are appointed and there is one vacancy, the parties have the flexibility to agree on continuing with the 'remaining co-mediator acting as a sole mediator'.[141]

131. *Supra* n. 2, ICSID-MR 12(1).
132. *Ibid.*, ICSID-MR 12(2).
133. *Supra*, n. 46, ICSID Convention, Articles 38 and 39; ICSID Convention, ICSID Arbitration Rules 13(2) and (3) (2022).
134. *Supra*, n. 2, ICSID-MR 13.
135. *Ibid.*, ICSID-MR 14(3)(b).
136. *Ibid.*, ICSID-MR 14(6).
137. *Supra* n. 46, ICSID Convention; ICSID Arbitration Rule 26(2) provides that the 'proceeding shall be suspended from the date of notice of the vacancy until the vacancy is filled'.
138. *Supra* n. 2, ICSID-MR 16(1).
139. *Ibid.*, ICSID-MR 16 (2).
140. *Ibid.*, ICSID-MR 16(3)(a).
141. *Ibid.*, ICSID-MR 16(3)(b).

The process of appointing a second mediator then is eliminated. In this way, ICSID-MR seek the continuation of proceedings in as seamless a manner as possible without interruption.

Ultimately, the success of mediation will depend on the efficiency with which a mediator manages the proceedings. In this regard, the consummate understanding of and by a mediator that they are not an arbitrator or judge but a facilitator - not a commander but a conductor - will be key to the ultimate success of mediation. In this regard, the role of a mediator is clearly stated in the ICSID-MR by limiting their role to assisting 'the parties in reaching a mutually acceptable resolution of all or part of the issues in dispute', and stating the mediator 'has no authority to impose a resolution of the dispute on the parties'.[142] A mediator's mandate is not to decide the dispute and issue binding orders or decisions,[143] nor is it to clarify the issues in dispute or recommend terms of settlement, unlike in the case of ICSID Arbitrators or Conciliators.[144] A mediator, however, may make recommendations for the resolution of mediated issues only if requested to do so by all parties.[145] Additionally, a mediator, under ICSID-MR, unlike a member of an ICSID arbitral tribunal or a conciliation commission, does not make a jurisdictional determination or determination as to the mediator's own competence.[146]

Finally, a mediator's duties are clearly stated and principally include conducting a mediation in good faith, expeditiously, cost-effectively, and treating the parties equally.[147] At the same time, a mediator may communicate with the parties separately. However, in such circumstances, they are under an obligation not to disclose information received from one party to the other without authorization from the disclosing party.[148]

[8] Expedient Termination

One of the key elements under any mediation rules is the requirement for expedient termination. Parties will be able to proceed with enforcing a settlement agreement as soon as convenient or if there is no settlement, parties will be able to proceed with parallel judicial and arbitral proceedings without any further delay. ICSID-MR are, however, silent on the binding nature of a settlement agreement. Grounds for termination are clearly stated in ICSID-MR 22.[149] In addition to parties' agreeing either to settle or to terminate the mediation, or dispense with mediation due to a delay in appointing a mediator for a period of more than 120 days,[150] ICSID-MR provide an additional two grounds to accomplish an expedient termination of a mediation. One is

142. *Ibid.*, ICSID-MR 17(1).
143. *See, supra* n. 46, ICSID Convention, Article 53.
144. *Ibid.*, ICSID Convention. Article 34(1).
145. *Ibid.*, ICSID-MR 21(4).
146. *See, supra* n. 64. ICSID Convention, Articles 32(1) and 41(1).
147. *Supra* n. 2, ICSID-MR 17(2) and (3).
148. *Ibid.*, ICSID-MR 17(4).
149. *Ibid.*, ICSID-MR 22.
150. *Ibid.*, ICSID-MR 22(1)(a), (b) and (e).

the unilateral withdrawal by one party from a mediation, at any time, which will trigger the termination of the proceedings regardless of the other party's or the mediator's views on it.[151] Second, a mediator may terminate a mediation without the consent of the parties upon a mediator's determination that 'there is no likelihood of resolution through the mediation'.[152]

[9] Mediation and Other Proceedings

Unlike the case of BITs where the texts often state that mediation, conciliation and similar ADR efforts should precede arbitration proceedings and even that parallel proceedings must be stayed, there is no bar for parties to request settlement proceedings under ICSID-MR at any time.[153] There is also no requirement under the rules to stay parallel arbitration or expedited arbitration proceedings. The fact that both the ICSID Expedited Arbitration Rules and ICSID-MR were adopted at the same time leads inevitably to a presumption that ICSID-MR can and should be a complement to expedited dispute resolution or even as an entirely independent dispute resolution mechanism.

§14.03 CONCLUSION

Despite the paucity of information regarding the success of utilizing mediation proceedings in investor-State disputes, there is indeed a case and a demand for mediation as an ADR mechanism in commercial disputes and increasingly in ISDS. At the core of this need is the understanding that mediation could be the least costly and most expedient form of dispute resolution when compared to judicial, arbitration or conciliation proceedings.

Apart from expediency and cost-effectiveness, several practical advantages to mediation exist. Mediation is most conducive where the dispute has not matured into a full-fledged adversarial dispute between an investor and the State or State entity. ICSID-MR certainly recognizes this advantage of enabling an early and constructive dialogue between disputing parties. The objective is to convince both parties to resolve any issues and head off protracted and costly litigation. Rather than being constrained by issues, from the standpoint of early intervention and settlement, existing investments and in particular development projects which are clearly beneficial to all parties can continue to operate. It ultimately helps to achieve a 'win-win' situation.

Additionally, no bar exists for parties who have opted for arbitration on an expedited basis or otherwise to agree to mediation at any time during such proceedings. The parties can clearly agree about the discrete issues to be settled by mediation and those to be litigated in arbitration. This way duplication in consideration of issues can be avoided and they can be expeditiously resolved. ICSID-MR and the ICSID

151. *Ibid.*, ICSID-MR 22(1)(c).
152. *Ibid.*, ICSID-MR 22(1)(d).
153. *Ibid.*, ICSID-MR 3.

Expedited Arbitration Rules can certainly be utilized in this complimentary and supplementary manner and achieve the objectives for which they were formalized.

Another clear advantage is that mediation, by its nature, is not entirely trammelled by formal legal applications as with judicial or arbitral proceedings. Mediation proceedings are, rather, fact-based and often technical in nature. To the extent there is, *ab initio,* agreement between parties to mediate and settle, fairness and equity or the principle of *ex aequo et bono* can play a much more functional and practical role in reaching final settlements. Settlement pursuant to mediation can also result in restitution, whereby continuation of an investment project can be facilitated. Finally, a high degree of success in mediated settlements together with expedited resolution of disputes can be envisaged with the adoption of mediation rules by an international organization such as ICSID. Given its international nature, disputes can and will be reviewed in an apolitical, unbiased and on entirely technical terms.

Mediation, however, is not without its own inherent problems. The entire process is based on building trust and consensus between disputing parties, without which it is bound to fail. In this regard, a single-issue dispute is more likely to succeed than a multiple-issue dispute. ICSID-MR do not address the consequences where parties have incontrovertibly agreed on some issues and not others. In other words, can there be a partial settlement agreement (similar to a partial award) that can be fully enforceable? Relatedly, should parties not be permitted to introduce as evidence those issues on which there is agreement in parallel judicial or arbitral proceedings to avoid re-litigation on those issues where there is agreement? If, therefore, mediation fails, it defeats the very purpose for which it was used in the first place and would be counterproductive to expedient and cost-efficient dispute resolution. Therefore, a clear agreement by the parties, *ab initio*, on issues that are to be settled and those that will be resolved in expedited arbitration is absolutely crucial.

ICSID-MR are well designed to achieve all the positive objectives of mediation. With the provisions for international enforcement of settlement agreements resulting from mediation contained in the 2018 Singapore Convention,[154] the one pivotal piece to complete the loop has been accomplished. This bodes well for the ultimate success of mediation under ICSID-MR, and it will no doubt supplement and complement ICSID's 2022 adoption of the Expedited Arbitration Rules as well. Moreover, and in the final analysis, its operational and practical functionality will be proof that mediation can be an extremely practical ADR mechanism to resolve investor-State or commercial international arbitration disputes in an expeditious and cost-effective manner, perhaps even more so than expedited arbitration alone.

154. *Supra* n. 19.

CHAPTER 15

Expedited Arbitration and Arb-Med in the Far East (Macau)

Hugo Luz dos Santos

As arbitration-mediation (Arb-Med) gains traction and becomes increasingly institutionalised, concerns about both the neutrality and impartiality of the arbitrator-mediator have been mounting. Pundits often aver that Arb-Med disfigures core values, and fundamental tenets, of arbitration. While scholars have not been neither coy nor bashful in overtly decrying Arb-Med, there is a perceived paucity of research on the role that disputants' principle of self-determination plays in the purview of Arb-Med. Put differently, the principle of self-determination must be parsed in conjunction with the disputants' cultural background. This stands as one central contention of this chapter. Against this background, this chapter demonstrates that a fine-grained attention must be paid to disputants' cultural background in both the Arb-Med process and expedited arbitration settings when they blend together. The foundational principle of self-determination – a linchpin of the Arb-Med process – accordingly ought to be painted in a glaringly different light.

§15.01 INTRODUCTION

The primary duty of an arbitrator is to decide quarrels and produce a binding and enforceable arbitral award. On the opposite pole, the primary responsibility of a mediator is to iron out areas of disagreement while paving the way to settle the dispute in both a brisk and fuss-free manner. Whatever the underlying rationale of these dispute resolution mechanisms, both the arbitrator and the mediator are vested with the obligation to put an end to the dispute. In this vein, the central thrust of both arbitration and mediation is to provide avenues through which parties can solve their dispute swiftly. Most importantly, and more in tune with the overriding goal to hammer out the dispute from which it was borne, both arbitration and mediation are premised on the seminal concept of self-determination. To that end – simmer down the sweltering temperature of the dispute while ushering in a new relationship dynamic between the estranged disputants – arbitration and mediation are often bundled into one single category.

Put differently, these dispute resolution mechanisms are often weaved together to lay the foundations upon which a sought-after resolution will stand. In a colloquial tone, parties to a dispute are ascribed the unmissable opportunity to gain access to the multitudinous benefits of arbitration-mediation (Arb-Med) – the acronym that comprises and summarises both arbitration and mediation – in the remit of expedited arbitration in international settings. In that regard, the arbitrator that temporarily wears the hat of a mediator is allotted the task of a stellar steward of both procedural fairness[1] and procedural justice.[2] This nugatory statement, albeit seemingly trivial, poses sizable challenges for Macau. Macau[3] lies at the crossroads between East[4] and West.[5] The relationship[6] between Macau (East) and Portugal (West) dates to the 16th century and spans centuries[7] accordingly.[8]

1. On procedural fairness in international arbitration: Fabricio Fortese and Lotta Hemmi, 'Procedural Fairness and Efficiency in International Arbitration', Groningen Journal of International Law, 3(1) (2015): 110-124; John Fellas, 'A Fair and Efficient International Arbitration Process', PLI Course Handbook, International Arbitration, no. 10796 (2007): passim; Cristina Florescu, 'The Arbitration Agreement and Arbitrability – Towards Achieving Efficiency in International Arbitration', Austrian Yearbook of International Arbitration (2015): 51-71.
2. Rebecca Hollander-Blumoff and Tom R. Tyler, 'Procedural Justice and the Rule of Law: Fostering Legitimacy in Alternative Dispute Resolution', Journal of Dispute Resolution 1 (2011): 1 (noting that procedural justice is closely linked to perceptions of legitimacy).
3. *See*: B.V. Pires, 'Origins and Early History of Macau', 2nd ed., R.D. Cremer (ed.), Macau: City of Commerce and Change, Hong Kong, API Press (1991): 1-7.
4. Historical accounts state that Portuguese establishment in Macau emerged from an informal agreement between the Portuguese Captain Chief of Maritime Journey to China and Japan (*Capitão-Mor da Viagem da China e do Japão*) and Chinese ruling authorities of Canton (Macau's closest neighbour which exerted power over Macau back then). The foregoing informal agreement was unbeknownst to both the Portuguese king and the Chinese emperor. *See* in the Macanese doctrine: João Vieira Guedes, 'Contributo para uma História do Direito Penal e Processual Penal e das Instituições de Administração de Justiça de Macau', Estudos Comemorativos XX Anos do Código Penal e Código de Processo Penal de Macau, Pedro Pereira de Sena e José Miguel Figueiredo (Coordenação Científica), Macau, Fundação Rui Cunha (2016): 62.
5. Beatrice Leung, 'The Portuguese Appeasement Policy in Macau's Church and State Relations', Journal of Contemporary China, 19 (64) (2010): 181-200 DOI: 10.1080/10670560903444306 ('In the Middle Ages, Europe was not able to contact Asia due to the Muslim occupation in between. The Portuguese Prince, Henry the Navigator (1394-1460), launched exploratory voyages along the western coast of Africa and eventually Vasco da Gama reached India (1460-1524)').
6. When it comes to describing the relationship between Chinese and the Portuguese, tolerance is a word that one should bear very firmly in mind. Although the early Portuguese (sailors, settlers, and business men) began to exercise trade with local Chinese authorities from 1557 onwards, there are a few historical accounts that signal an early tolerance towards the Portuguese dating as far back as 1535. From this date onwards, the Portuguese business men and sailors were given a 'sort-of' free pass to anchor their ships and perform some business activities provided they did not stay onshore. *See* G.L. Zhao and G.L. Liu, A New Conspectus of Macau Law, Macau, Macau Foundation (2005): 2 and passim.
7. Trust and trustworthiness, which are fuelled by a prior creation of a harmonious and healthy relationship (a hallmark of Confucian-beliefs-based Chinese culture), might help explain the long-standing relationship between the Portuguese and the Chinese. First establish rapport and trust, then (and only then) do business. Back then, like now, Chinese millenary culture would not fall far behind from its founding tree (Confucianism). Back then, like now, culture nurtured business and trade relationships. On Trust and Trustworthiness in contract law and public policy, *see* Matthew Harding, 'Trust and Fiduciary Law', Oxford Journal of Legal Studies, 33 (2013): 81;

On the one hand, Macao's legal system builds on a western legal framework outlined by the Portuguese at the twilight of 20th century (1999), which affords primacy to court adjudication[9] as opposed to conciliatory means to solve disputes (arbitration, conciliation, and mediation). On the other hand, Macao's underlying legal culture and legal tradition[10] draws on Confucianism traits,[11] which awards preference to solving disputes through amicable means.

Mark A. Hall, 'Law, Medicine, and Trust', Stanford Law Review, 55 (2002): 463; Matthew Harding, 'Responding to Trust', Ratio Juris, 24 (2011): 75; Mark A. Hall, 'The Importance of Trust for Ethics, Law, and Public Policy', Cambridge Quarterly of Healthcare Ethics 14 (2005): 156.

8. Religion – especially Christianity brought along to Macau by Portuguese Jesuits – played a pivotal role in Macau both before and after 1573. Before the construction (in 1573) of the China-Macau border gate (*Portas do Cerco*), there were no Chinese unconverted to Christianity living in Macau. An exception was made to the Chinese that were converted to Christianity. From the construction of *Portas do Cerco* onwards, Chinese unconverted to Christianity were allowed to work in Macau provided they did not stay overnight. They were forced to go across *Portas do Cerco* towards China before sunset in a daily basis. Chinese unconverted to Christianity were not allowed to live or possess any kind of property in Macau, unless special authorisation was issued by the Procurator (Procurador). Those unconverted Chinese who got caught both living and working illegally in Macau were chastised with merciless corporal punishments. *See*, C.A. Montalto de Jesus, Macau Histórico, tradução do inglês por Maria Alice Morais Jorge, 1a edição, Macau, Livros do Oriente (1990): 58. *See also* João Vieira Guedes, 'Contributo para uma História do Direito Penal e Processual Penal e das Instituições de Administração de Justiça de Macau', *supra*: 62 and passim, whose research I will follow closely in this regard.

9. Acclaimed doctrine is championing for a paradigm shift in the realm of justice, in which alternative dispute resolution (ADR; especially Mediation) plays a pivotal role. In Italian doctrine, *see* Michelle Taruffo, 'Un'alternativa alle alternative: modeli di risoluzione dei confliti', Revista de Processo, 152 (2007): 319-331. On Portuguese doctrine, *see* Paula Costa e Silva, 'De minimis non curat praetor. O acesso ao sistema judicial e os meios alternativos de resolução de controvérsias', O Direito, 140 (2008): 735. On German doctrine, *see* Peter Gottwald, 'Mediation und gerichtlicher Vergleich: Unterschiede und Gemeinsamkeiten', Festschrift fur Akira Ishikawa zum 70 (2001): 137-155. *See also* Jacqueline N. Font-Guzmán, 'Programa de Derivación en Puerto Rico desde la Perspectiva de la Mediación', Contemporary Tendencies in Mediation, Humberto Dalla Bernardina de Pinho and Juliana Loss de Andrade (eds), Madrid, Editorial Dykinson (2015): 31-32 (in a similar vein, Porto Rican doctrine (Spanish language) has lavished praise on the multidisciplinary approach in the realm of mediation as follows: 'Mis experiencias a través de los años me han convencido de la necesidad de adoptar modelos interdisciplinarios en el desarrollo y la implementación de programas de métodos alternos de resolución de conflictos').

10. Peter Chi Hin Chan, 'The Enigma of Civil Justice in Imperial China: A Legal Historical Enquiry', Maastricht Journal of European and Comparative Law, 19 (2012): 317-337 (China sits on a deep-seated legal tradition of compromising in the remit of dispute resolution. However, 'contrary to the view that the magistrate was unrestrained by the law and only by the law and only played the role of a mediator, state law had profound influence over magisterial adjudication. Yet the magistrate did not apply the law in a positivistic sense. The adjudicative discourse involved searching for a balanced solution that took into account the statutory law and non-statutory norms (local customs and Confucian moral values). *However, civil justice in imperial China lacked fundamental attributes of a modern civil justice system, such as judicial specialization, an autonomous (and sophisticated) civil procedural regime and a systemic enforcement of civil law based on the jurisprudential understanding of individual rights*') (italics added). On legal tradition, *see* Thomas E. Carbonneau, 'Book Review, Patrick Glenn, Legal Traditions of the World, Sustainable Diversity in Law', The American Journal of Comparative Law, 48 (2000): 729. Harold J. Berman, Law and Revolution: The Formation of the Western Legal Tradition, Cambridge, Massachusetts, Harvard University Press (1983).

11. Tong Io Cheng and Wu Yanni, 'Legal Transplants and the On-Going Formation of Macau Legal Culture', Saidat Law Review, Legal Culture and Legal Transplants, 1 (Special Issue 2) (2012): 644-645 (as asserted by local doctrine: 'it is quite obvious that both the Ming Dynasty and Qing

The mismatch between the fundamental tenets of Macau's legal system – which is essentially Portuguese – and its underlying legal culture and legal tradition – which is essentially Chinese – begets a plethora of legal irritants.[12] Among them stands the perceived difficulty of being an umpire – e.g., an arbitrator/mediator in expedited arbitration settings – a dispute in which both disputants have different cultural backgrounds, which is not a rarity in Macau, given its multicultural nature.

A great deal of ink has been spilled, pondering whether and to what extent arb-med is feasible in western jurisdictions.[13] Yet the impact of markedly different

Dynasty had jurisdiction over Macau for a long time. Chinese residents in the area *followed their own customs* and were ruled by the Guangdong government under the Imperial law. *The written laws of the Ming and Qing dynasties are of course a part of the Macau legal history* (...) as a process of cognition, the interpretation of law is of course influenced by a number of internal and external factors. *The Chinese way of thinking, influenced by Confucianism, still has its impact on the whole of East Asia in general, and Macau in particular*') (italics added).

12. Gunther Teubner, 'Legal Irritants', The Modern Law Review, 61 (1998): 10-14 (pouring in trenchant criticism on the stance according to which rules, legal institutions are amenable to be transplanted from one legal system to another).
13. One of the most eloquent examples of the impact of cultural backgrounds in dispute resolution is the way disputants behave in hybrid dispute resolution mechanisms (such as Med-Arb and Arb-Med). The principle of self-determination, when seen through cultural lenses, impacts the way disputants tend to consider – and hold dear – the latter. In cultures of dignity, disputants tend to consider that the principle of self-determination and mediator's neutrality and independence is put in jeopardy whenever the same person presides the mediation sessions and the subsequent arbitration tribunal. In cultures of face the exact opposite happens. Disputants from cultures of face and collectivist countries not only do not consider that the principle of self-determination is violated but also approve such a 'dance and change of hats' whose protagonist is the mediator-arbitrator. *See* about the reluctance to accept Med-Arb in cultures of dignity on the grounds of violation of neutrality, impartiality of mediator-arbitration: Brian A. Pappas, 'Med-Arb and the Legalization of Alternative Dispute Resolution', Harvard Negotiation Law Review, 20 (2015): 157 (arguing that 'as both mediation and arbitration become increasingly formalized, Med-Arb is perceived as one way to correct the adversarial disadvantages of each by providing for both "finality" and "flexibility". However, the key principles of both mediation and arbitration are compromised by Med-Arb. The core values of mediator neutrality, party self-determination, and confidentiality cannot be satisfied by Med-Arb. In arbitration, the promise of arbitrator impartiality, the due process right to equal treatment and confrontation, and the enforceability of the arbitral award are weakened'); the Texas Ethical Guidelines for Mediators provides that such thing (a neutral serving as a mediator and subsequently serving as arbitrator) is not allowed. In this vein, *see* Approval of Ethical Guidelines for Mediators, Misc. Docket No. 05-9107 (Tex. Ct. App 13 June 2005), available at: http://www.supreme.courts.state.tx.us (access: 9.6.2019); Ontario Arbitration Act, R.S.O., 1991, available at: http://www.e-laws.gov.on.ca/html/statutes/english/elaws_statutes_91a17_ehtm (access: 10.3.2023) (which expressly prohibits any process that 'might compromise or appear to compromise the arbitral tribunal's ability to decide the dispute impartially'). Some commentators argued that Med-Arb disfigures core values of arbitration such as the opportunity that is conferred to the disputants to presenting their case and be treated both fairly and even-handedly in arbitration. *See*, Klaus Peter Berger, 'Integration of Mediation Elements into Arbitration: "Hybrid" Procedures and "Intuitive" Mediation by International Arbitrators', Arbitration International, 19 (2003): 387-391 DOI: 10.1093/arbitration/19.3.387; the UNCITRAL Model Law on International Commercial Arbitration, available at: http://www.uncitral/en/uncitral_texts/arbitration/1985 Model_Arbitration_status.html (access: 10.3.2023) provides (regarding arbitration) that 'the parties shall be treated with equality and each party given a full opportunity of presenting his case'. *See*: Paul E. Mason, 'The Arbitrator as Mediator, and Mediator as Arbitrator', Journal of International Arbitration, 28 (2008): 479-482 (noting that the role of arbitrators and mediators are radically different); David J. Mclean and Sean-Patrick Wilson, 'Compelling Mediation in the Context of Med-Arb Agreements', Dispute Resolution Journal (2008): 28 (showing some enthusiasm

towards this hybrid dispute resolution mechanism); Peter Lankta, 'The Use of Alternative Dispute Resolution in the Federal Magistrate Judge's Office: A Glimmering Light Amidst the Haze of Federal Litigation', University of West Los Angeles Law Review, 36 (2005): 71-80 ('arguing that the benefits of Med-Arb are usually tempered by the fact that litigants are tempted to hold back information during mediation for fear that it will be used against them at a later date'); Gerald F. Philips, 'Back to Med-Arb: Survey Indicates Process Concerns Are Decreasing', Alternatives to High Cost Litigation, 26 (2008): 73-78; Thomas J. Stipanovich and J. Ryan Lamare, 'Evolving Perceptions and Use of Mediation, Arbitration, and Conflict Management in Fortune 1000 Corporations', Harvard Negotiation Law Review, 19(1) (2014): 3 (noting that lawyers in the US are adhering to hybrid dispute resolution mechanisms); Ellen E. Deason, 'Combinations of Mediation and Arbitration with the Same Neutral: A Framework for Judicial Review', Yearbook of Arbitration and Mediation, 5 (2013): 219 (parsing the doctrinal positions in this regard); American Arbitration Association, Drafting Dispute Resolution Clauses, 38 (2004): 1 (available at: http://www.adr.org/si.asp?id4125 (access: 10.3.2023)) (noting that 'except in unusual circumstances, a procedure whereby the same individual who has been serving as a mediator becomes an arbitrator when the mediation fails is not recommended, because it could inhibit the candour which should be characterize the mediation process and/or it could convey evidence, legal points or settlement positions ex parte, improperly influencing the arbitrator'). *See* on the acceptance of Med-Arb in cultures of face and collectivist countries like China (and CIETAC's China): Carlos de Vera, 'Arbitrating Harmony: "Med-Arb" and the Confluence of Culture and Rule of Law in the Resolution of International Commercial Disputes in China', Columbia Journal of Asian Law, 18 (2004): 149-169; Gabrielle Kaufmann-Kohler and Kun Fan, 'Integrating Mediation into Arbitration: Why It Works in China', Journal of International Arbitration, 25 (2008): 479-480; Sally A. Harpole, 'The Combination of Conciliation with Arbitration in the People's Republic of China', Journal of International Arbitration, 24 (2007): 623-624 DOI: 10.54648/joia2007046; Fuyong Chen, 'Striving for Independence, Competence, and Fairness: A Case Study of the Beijing Arbitration Commission', American Review of International Arbitration, 18 (2007): 313; Russell Thirgood, 'A Critique of Foreign Arbitration in China', Journal of International Arbitration, 24 (2007): 623-626; Tai-Heng Cheng, 'Reflections on Culture in Med-Arb', New York Law School, Research Paper Series No. 34 (2010): 427 (averring that culture plays a pivotal role in this regard). Arb-Med awards – deemed as consent awards – are raising concerns over its enforceability, since New York Convention only covers the enforceability of awards, not Arb-Med agreements. In Hong Kong, the question of enforceability has been raised in 2008. The lower courts have decided to reject the award. The High Court has decided to affirm the award thus conferring enforceability to the award. *See*: Herbert Smith Freehills, 'ADR Notes, Hong Kong High Court Consider the Med-Arb Procedure', available at: http://hsf-adrnotes.com/2011/06-2008/hong-kong-courts-consider-the meditation-arbitration-procedure (access: 16.3.2023) (averring the high court's decision to affirm an Arb-Med award pursuant the lower court's decision not to enforce the award); *see also* Mun Yeow and Morgana Brady, 'Hong Kong Enforces PRC "Med-Arb" Award', available at: http:www.allens.com.au/pubs/asia/foasia10jan12.htm (access: 16.3.2023) (noting that 'this decision confirms Hong Kong's pro-enforcement approach to arbitral awards, and reminds parties ... that, whe(n) they believe some irregularity has occurred in the arbitral or med-arb process, they must raise issue promptly'); Chuyang (Alexis) Liu, 'Navigating Med-Arb in China', University of Pennsylvania Journal of Business Law, 17(4) (2015): 1310 ('alerting for the issue of lack of enforceability of Med-Arb, as the New York Convention only recognizes the enforceability of arbitral awards, not mediation agreements. Parties are more likely to comply with a voluntary settlement agreement (reached through mediation) than an award or judgment') though. *See* on the issue of apparent bias: *Gao Haiyan v. Keeneye Holdings Lts* (HCCT 41/2010) (12 April 2011) (arbitral award likely to be set aside should allegations of apparent bias are proved). Further remarks on the Mediation in China (especially China's Grand Mediation Strategy) fall conspicuously outside the scope of this chapter. For further developments, *see* Peter C.H. Chan, 'China's Grand Mediation Strategy for Social Stability: A Study on Out-of-Court Mediation Procedures', Revista de Processo, 6(3) (2017): 81-111; Yulin Fu and Xing Meng, 'Civil Justice in China', Brics Law Journal, III(4) (2016): 95 (on the absolute superiority of conciliation on civil disputes for cultural reasons). In the realm of cultures of dignity (*see infra* §15.02 and §15.03), I agree with the assertion according to which that with the use of Arb-Med (arbitrating cultural backgrounds in arb-med in expedited arbitration settings has been somewhat forsaken. The central contention of this chapter is one in which the principle of self-determination – one of the bedrocks of arbitration – must take into account the disputants' cultural background. This is crucially important in expedited arbitration settings in Macau.

Section 15.02 briefly fleshes out the overriding importance of the principle of self-determination in the remit of dispute resolution. Section 15.03 pores over the dichotomy between cultures of dignity and of face and its impact in dispute resolution in a broad sense. Section 15.04 outlines a bevy of remarks on the impact of the dyad between cultures of dignity and cultures of face on the foundational principle of self-determination in the remit of expedited arbitration settings in Macau. The upshot is that disputants' cultural background and underlying legal culture play a pivotal role in expedited arbitration settings whenever Mediation and Arbitration are brought together.

§15.02 THE FUNDAMENTAL – AND UNIVERSAL – PRINCIPLE OF SELF-DETERMINATION

Self-determination, from which party autonomy derives, plays a starring role in dispute resolution,[14] especially in cultures of dignity.[15] Cultures of dignity consist of cultures that are underpinned by individualism. Unsurprisingly, cultures of dignity award primacy to both the principle of self-determination and the sacrosanct principle of party autonomy, which, as hinted above, are tightly interlocked. The mediator, at least a stellar mediator, should be well acquainted with this taxonomy.

Mediators and relevant stakeholders have long embraced self-determination as a fundamental principle in dispute resolution. Not surprisingly, the *Model Standards of Conduct for Mediators* has been expressly adopted by the American Bar Association (ABA) Section of Dispute Resolution, the American Arbitration Association, and the Association for Conflict Resolution (formerly known as the Society of Professionals in Dispute Resolution). Its importance is equally valid in expedited arbitration settings.

first, and mediating later) comes along the bevy of qualms. In this vein, the Arbitrator would hold the arbitration hearings prior to any mediation sessions. Further, in the arbitration hearings, the arbitrator would issue an arbitral award and would put it in a sealed envelope. Then parties would be steered to mediation. Should they resolve their dispute in mediation, the arbitral award would be destroyed. If mediation does not resolve the dispute, the arbitrator would reveal the arbitral award. Converging: Kristen M. Blankley, 'Keeping a Secret from Yourself? Confidentiality When the Same Neutral Serves Both as Mediator and as Arbitrator in the Same Case', Baylor Law Review, 63(2) (2011): 334; Arnold M. Zack, 'The Quest for Finality in Airline Disputes: A Case for Arb-Med', Dispute Resolution Journal (2003-2004): 34-35 ('arguing that if agreement is reached, the neutral tears up the envelope and the decision is never revealed'). In the same vein: *Soc'y of Lloyd's v. Moore,* No. 1:06-CV-286, 2006 WL 3167735 (S.D. Ohio 1 November 2006).

14. Nancy A. Welsh, 'Do You Believe in Magic? Self-Determination and Procedural Justice Meet Inequality in Court-Connected Mediation', SMU Law Review, 70 (2017): 723-761 (advocating the paramount role that self-determination plays in the realm of dispute resolution).
15. *See infra*, §15.03.

The foregoing standards of quality have placed self-determination[16] at their higher echelons. The 1994 *Model Standards* has set forth a definition of self-determination according to which, 'self-determination is a fundamental principle of mediation'.[17] However, the Model Standards of Conduct for Mediators Standard I is adamant in averring that: 'A mediator shall conduct a mediation based on the principle of party self-determination. Self-determination is the act of coming to a voluntary, uncoerced decision in which each party makes free and informed choices as to process and outcome.'[18] Self-determination[19] ranks first among the quality standards of mediation for one good reason:[20] it gives room to disputants to solve[21] their disputes the way they see[22] fit,[23] which is entirely consistent with the high levels of individualism[24] and low levels of power distance[25] of most of the cultures of dignity.[26]

16. Nancy A. Welsh, 'The Current Transitional State of Court-Connected ADR', Marquette Law Review, 95 (2012): 875-883 (880) (asserting the principle of self-determination is all about giving to the disputant's tools to 'enabling them *to take responsibility for making serious decisions in a deliberative, thoughtful manner*') (italics added).
17. American Arbitration Association, 'Model Standards of Conduct for Mediators', Journal of National Association of Administration of Law Judiciary, 17 (1997): 323-326 (on the model standards of conduct for mediators).
18. Model Standards of Conduct for Mediators Standard I (American Arbitration Association, American Bar Association of Dispute Resolution Section & Association for Conflict Resolution) (2005): passim (on the model standards of conduct for mediators).
19. Daniel Thürer *and Thomas Burri, 'Self-Determination', Max Planck Encyclopaedia of Public International Law,*http://opil.ouplaw.com/search?sfam=&q=Self-determination&prd=EPIL&searchBtn=Search *(access: 16.03.2023) (noting that 'the political origins of the modern concept of self-determination can be traced back to the Declaration of Independence of the United States of America of 4 July 1776, which proclaimed that governments derived "their just powers from the consent of the governed" and that "whenever any Form of Government becomes destructive of these ends, it is the Right of the People to alter or to abolish it". The principle of self-determination was further shaped by the leaders of the French Revolution, whose doctrine of popular sovereignty').*
20. Nancy A. Welsh, 'The Current Transitional State of Court-Connected ADR', *supra*: 875-883 (passim) (arguing that self-determination is a structural principle of mediation).
21. In German doctrine, L. Oliver Michaelis, 'Mediation im Strafrecht – der *Täter – Ausgleich', Juristische Arbeitsblätter, 37 (11) (2005): 832 (emphasising that the quests for a consensual solution to the dispute are (is) a wichtige resozialisierende Momente (important resocialising moments) in victim-offender mediation).*
22. Kimberlee K. Kovach, 'Mediation', Handbook of Dispute Resolution, Michael Moffitt and Robert Bordone (eds), San Francisco, Jossey-Bass (2005): 304 ff. (notes that this principle allows disputants to craft their own outcomes in mediation settings).
23. Be that in arbitration, mediation, conciliation, or negotiation. *See*: S.I. Strong, 'Clash of Cultures: Epistemic Communities, Negotiation Theory, and International Law-Making', Akron Law Review, 50 (2016): passim (on the uppermost value of the principle of self-determination in dispute resolution); Nancy A. Welsh, 'Introduction', Yearbook on Arbitration and Mediation, V, Texas, University of Texas (2013): passim (echoing the same views).
24. Nancy A. Welsh, 'The Current Transitional State of Court-Connected ADR', *supra*: 875-883 (880) (asserting that disputants possess 'a certain sort of faith, grounded in the principle of self-determination (and) ... believe in providing people with the opportunity and tools to be their best'). *See*: §15.03 and §15.04.
25. *See*: §15.03 and §15.04.
26. *See*: §15.03 and §15.04.

Unsurprisingly, one of the fundamental tenets of dispute resolution in cultures of dignity is the principle of self-determination,[27] which means that *coercion in mediation*[28] and informed dispute resolution choices[29] in cultures of dignity are an oxymoron. Even in cultures of face, the tonality of the principle of self-determination differs greatly from cultures of dignity.[30] But let us take a step back to pore over the notions of cultures of dignity and cultures of face (§15.03) while emphasising its importance in expedited arbitration settings (§15.04).

§15.03 APPLIED PSYCHOLOGY IN DISPUTE RESOLUTION: TAXONOMIES OF CULTURAL LOGICS OF DIGNITY AND CULTURAL LOGICS OF FACE

[A] Cultural Logics of Dignity or Cultures of Dignity

A cohort of cross-cultural applied psychology researchers[31] have laid down an academic approach according to which culture is to be portrayed in a new light[32] in dispute resolution settings. The pinpointed cultural backgrounds range from cultural logics of honour to cultures[33,34] of dignity.[35] This distinction plays a pivotal role in the remit of

27. Nancy A. Welsh, 'Do You Believe in Magic? Self-Determination and Procedural Justice Meet Inequality in Court-Connected Mediation', SMU Law Review, 70 (2017): 723-761 (noting that 'resolution of disputes in mediation shall occur only if the people involved in the dispute choose resolution on their own and without anyone forcing their hands').
28. Frank E. Sander et al., 'Judicial (Mis)Use of ADR? A Debate', University of Toledo Law Review, 27 (1996): 885-887 (drawing the seminal distinction between coercion *into* mediation and coercion *in* mediation).
29. Jacqueline Nolan-Haley, 'Does ADR's Access to Justice Come at the Expense of Meaningful Consent', Ohio State Journal of Dispute Resolution, 33 (2018): 374 (arguing that 'legal scholars and policymakers are rightly concerned with access to justice, asking whether potential litigants from all economic backgrounds have meaningful access to the legal system').
30. *See infra* §15.03 and §15.04.
31. Angela K.-Y. Leung and Dov Cohen, 'Within-and Between- Culture Variation: Individual Differences and the Cultural Logics of Honor, Face and Dignity Cultures', Journal of Personality and Social Psychology, 100(3) (2011): 507-526 (passim) (set forth the fundamental tenets of cultural logics of honour, face, and dignity cultures). I will follow this exciting piece of research very closely.
32. *See*: R. Benedict, The Chrysanthemum and the Sword, Boston, MA: Mariner Books (2006 a): passim; *see* R. Benedict, Patterns of Culture, Boston, MA: Mariner Books (2006 b): passim; P. Berger, B. Berger and H. Kellner, The Homeless Mind, New York: NY, Random House (1973): passim; V. Benet Ramirez, J. Leu, F. Lee and M. Morris, 'Negotiating Biculturalism: Cultural Frame Switching in Bicultural with Oppositional vs. Compatible Cultural Identities, Journal of Cross-Cultural Psychology, 33 (2002): 492-516; V. Benet Ramirez and Z. Aygun Karakitapoglu, 'The Interplay of Cultural Syndromes and Personality in Predicting Life Satisfaction', Journal of Cross-Cultural Psychology, 34 (2003): 38-60; M. Bond et al., 'The Present and Future State of Cultural Research and Theory: A Dialogue', R.S. Wyer, C-Y Chiu and Y.Y. Hong (eds), Understanding Culture: Theory, Research, and Application, New York, NY: Psychology Press (2009): 469-505 (on cultural identities and cultural syndromes).
33. On the cultural logics of honour: J.A. Vandello and D. Cohen, 'When Believing Is Seeing: Sustaining Norms of Violence in Cultures of Honor', M. Schaller and C.S. Crandall (eds), The Psychological Foundations of Culture, Mahwah, NJ, Erlbaum (2004): 281-304.
34. On the cultural logics of face: N. Zane and M. Yeh, 'The Use of Culturally-Based Variables in Assessment: Studies on Loss Face', K. Kurasaki, S. Okasaki and S. Sue (eds), Asian American

expedited arbitration as there is a perceived paucity of research in this regard. Section 15.04 sketches out the impact of this dichotomy (cultural logics of dignity and cultural logics of face), according to which the arbitrator must conduct cross-cultural arb-med in expedited arbitration settings.

Dignity is viewed as the primal logic of modern North American and Western culture.[36] 'Moral consciousness'[37] is the expression coined in this regard. Dignity has been commonly defined as 'the conviction that each individual at birth possessed an intrinsic value at least theoretically equal to that of every other person'.[38] The keystone in dignity cultures is that 'each individual has inherent worth, and this worth does not

Mental Health, Norwell, MA, Kluwer (2002): 123-138; M.J. Gelfand et al., 'Cultural Influences on Cognitive Representations of Conflict: Interpretations of Conflict Episodes in the United States and Japan', Journal of Applied Psychology, 86 (2001): 1059-1074 DOI: 10.1037//0021-9010.86.6.1059. See also: Peter Chi Hin Chan, "Hong Kong. Selective Adoption of the English Woolf Reforms", Civil Litigation in China and Europe: Essays on the Role of the Judge and the Parties, Springer Netherlands, (2013), pp. 71-125; Peter Chi Hin Chan, "China's Grand Mediation Strategy for Social Stability: A study on Out-of Court Mediation Procedures", Revista de Processo Comparado, 6 (3), julho-dezembro de 2017, São Paulo, Editora Revista dos Tribunais, (2017): 81-111; Peter Chi Hin Chan, "Framing the structure of the court system in the perspective of case management", Peking University Law Journal, Volume 6, Issue 1, Routledge, London, (2018), pp. 55-79; Peter Chi Hin Chan, The Position of Mediation in Contemporary Chinese Civil Justice: A Procedural Perspective, Dissertation to obtain the degree of Doctor at Maastricht University, Maastricht, Netherlands, (2016): 1-298.

35. On the cultural logics of dignity: See: Hugo Luz dos Santos, Towards a Four-Tiered Model of Mediation, Singapore/Beijing/New York, Springer, (2023) (Part III, Chapter IV, point 4.1.3. on the seminal taxonomies of cultures of honour, cultures of face and cultures of dignity drawing upon Leung/Cohen's Grid). On the interplay between cultural logics of honour and cultural logics of dignity: Hugo Luz dos Santos, Multidisciplinary Dynamics of Mediation, Singapore/Berlin/New York/Beijing, Springer, (2024), pp. 1-850 (Part II, Chapter II, point 2.4. a point 2.4.2.3.3.6.). See also: C. Y. Cheng, F. Lee and V. Benet Ramirez, 'Assimilation and Contrast Effects in Cultural Frame Switching (CFS): Bicultural Identity Integration (BII) and Valence of Cultural Cues', Journal of Cross-Cultural Psychology, 37 (2006): 742-760; J.Y. Chiao and K.D. Blizinsky, 'Culture-Gene Coevolution of Individualism-Collectivism and the Serotonin Transporter Gene', Proceedings of the Royal Society of London, Series B: Biological Sciences (2010): 529-537; D. Cohen, 'Methods of Cultural Psychology', S. Kitayma and D. Cohen (eds), Handbook of Cultural Psychology, New York, NY: Guildford Press (2007): 196-236; D. Cohen, E. Hoshino-Browne and A.K.-Y Leung, 'Culture and Structure of Personal Experience: Insider and Outsider Phenomenology of the Self and Social World', M. Zanna (ed.), Advances in Experimental Social Psychology, Volume 39, San Diego, CA: Academic Press (2007): 1-67; D. Cohen and A.K.-Y. Leung, 'The Hard Embodiment of Culture', European Journal of Social Psychology, 39 (2009): 1278-1289; D. Cohen and R.E. Nisbett, 'Self-Protection and the Culture of Honor: Explaining Southern Homicide', Personality and Social Psychology Bulletin, 20 (1994): 551-567; D. Cohen et al., 'Insult, Aggression, and the Southern Culture of Honor. An "Experimental Ethnography"', Journal of Personality and Social Psychology, 70 (1996): 945-960 DOI: 10.1037//0022-3514.70.5.945; S.J. Heine, 'Self as a Cultural Product', Journal of Personality, 69 (2001): 881-905; S.J. Heine et al., 'Is There a Universal Need for Positive Self-Regard', Psychological Review, 106 (1999): 766-794 DOI: 10.1037//0033-295x.106.4.766 (on the influence that culture plays in shaping the way people think and behave in the outer world); Adam Smith, The Theory of Moral Sentiments, Oxford, England, Clarendon Press (Original work published 1759): passim.

36. P. Berger, B. Berger and H. Kellner, The Homeless Mind, New York: NY, Random House (1973): 88 (giving nuanced accounts about modern and Western cultures).

37. P. Berger, B. Berger and H. Kellner, The Homeless Mind, *supra*: 88.

38. E. Ayers, Vengeance and Justice, New York, NY, Oxford University Press (1985): 18-20 (providing an overview about dignity cultures and their effects on the way that people think and behave).

depend on the esteem of other people. This worth is neither conferred by others nor it can be taken away by them. As such, it is inalienable'.[39]

With this backdrop in mind,[40] 'dignity is relatively impervious to insults[41] and threats from others'.[42] The focal point of dignity is lodged on the individual. The individual stands at the heart of dignity cultures or cultures of dignity. Hence the expression 'glorification of the individual'.[43] In dignity cultures, there is a perceived gap between the individual and the *others*. To keep his dignity unscathed, the individual is not to be vilified or corrupted by the noxious influence of *others*. The individual is supposed to uphold his own moral integrity without being swayed by *others*. The un-permeability (or lack thereof) to insults accounts as one of the linchpins of dignity cultures. No matter what *others* say, do, or think, the individual's dignity is not to be marred.

As well asserted by Ayers 'sticks and stones may break my bones, but names will never hurt me'.[44] The dignity resonates with a simple motto, 'Dignity might be likened to an internal skeleton, to a hard structure at the centre of the self.'[45] As reminiscent of Roman Catholic Church-inspired commandments, guilt, rather than shame, is a cornerstone of both honour cultures[46] and face-saving cultures[47] and is an important device of self-control.[48]

39. A.K.-Y. Leung and D. Cohen, 'Within-and Between- Culture Variation: Individual Differences and the Cultural Logics of Honor, Face and Dignity Cultures', Journal of Personality and Social Psychology, 100(3) (2011): 507-526 (passim).
40. D. Oyserman and S.W.S. Lee, 'Does Culture Influence What and How We Think?', Psychological Bulletin, 134 (2008a): 311-342 (noting the impact that culture has in shaping our thoughts, mindsets, acts, behaviours).
41. D. Cohen et al., 'Insult, Aggression, and the Southern Culture of Honor: An "Experimental Ethnography"', Journal of Personality and Social Psychology, 70 (1996): 945-960 (noting the high rates of both verbal and physical aggression in South American cultures of honour).
42. A.K.-Y. Leung and D. Cohen, 'Within-and Between- Culture Variation: Individual Differences and the Cultural Logics of Honor, Face and Dignity Cultures', Journal of Personality and Social Psychology, 100(3) (2011): 507-526 (passim).
43. James M. Buchanan, The Collected Works of James M. Buchanan, Vol. 3. The Calculus of Consent: Logical Foundations of Constitutional Democracy, with a Foreword by Robert D. Tollison, Indianapolis, Liberty Fund (1999): passim (canvassing the foundations of the glorification of the individual).
44. E. Ayers, Vengeance and Justice, *supra*: 20.
45. *Ibid.*
46. J.A. Vandello, D. Cohen and S. Ransom, 'U.S. Southern and Northern Differences in Perceptions of Norms about Aggression: Mechanisms for the Perpetuation of a Culture of Honor', Journal of Cross-Cultural Psychology, 39 (2008): 162-177 (highlighting the cultural differences between U.S. Southern and Northern differences and the so-called perpetuation of a culture of honour); D. Cohen and R.E. Nisbett, 'Self-Protection and the Culture of Honor: Explaining Southern Homicide, Personality and Social Psychology Bulletin, 20 (1994): 551-567 (explaining Southern hemisphere homicide from a culture of honour point of view).
47. N. Zane and M. Yeh, 'The Use of Culturally-Based Variables in Assessment: Studies on Loss Face', K. Kurasaki, S. Okasaki and S. Sue (eds), Asian American Mental Health, Norwell, MA, Kluwer (2002): 123-138 (outlining the contours of loss-face shame in Eastern cultures).
48. A.K.-Y. Leung and Dov Cohen, 'Within-and Between- Culture Variation: Individual Differences and the Cultural Logics of Honor, Face and Dignity Cultures', Journal of Personality and Social Psychology, 100(3) (2011): 507-526 (passim).

The primary source of self-worth[49] and dignity lies in the individual alone.[50] Dignity is not given by *others*. Let alone endorsed by *others*. The individual is praiseworthy of dignity for (inherently) who he/she is instead, chiefly when they socially interact with others. In cultures of dignity, there is no such thing as pariah/outcast.

Systems of exchange in dignity cultures[51] 'are most compatible with those of a market economy'.[52] Market economy and the idea of dignity are a perfect match. Both amount to mainsprings, and are the encapsulation, of the 'glorification of the individual'. Market economy and the idea of dignity are thus interlocking concepts. Unsurprisingly, egalitarian ideas stand at the heart of both.

Egalitarian ideas, so voguish in modern-Western cultures, account for the benchmark of both market economy and dignity cultures. Only the fittest will be able to climb their way up to the economic system ladder and reach the pinnacle of social, and thus economical, glorification. Theoretically, everyone can do it.

Not surprisingly, moral integrity, trust, and trustworthiness play a pivotal role in dignity cultures. Positive reciprocity and negative reciprocity are the yardsticks in this regard. *Positive reciprocity* relates to the morally correct (a clear sign of moral integrity, trust,[53] and trustworthiness[54]). Whereas positive reciprocity does not have the same

49. Adam Smith, The Theory of Moral Sentiments, Oxford, England, Clarendon Press (Original work published 1759): passim (referring to the indelible stain of moral sentiments).
50. Thomas Hobbes, Leviathan, New York, NY, Penguin (1982) (Original work published in 1651): passim (stating that the Leviathan state does not hinders individuality).
51. A.K.-Y. Leung and D. Cohen, 'Within-and Between- Culture Variation: Individual Differences and the Cultural Logics of Honor, Face and Dignity Cultures', Journal of Personality and Social Psychology, 100(3) (2011): 507-526 (passim).
52. E. Ayers, Vengeance and Justice, *supra*: passim.
53. Tom R. Tyler, 'Trust and Law Abidingness: A Proactive Model of Social Regulation', Boston University Law Review, 81 (2001): 361; Jack Barbalet, 'A Characterization of Trust, and Its Consequences', Theory and Society, 38 (2009): 367-372; Henry Farrell, 'Institutions and Midlevel Explanations of Trust', Karen S. Cook, Margaret Levi and Russell Hardin (eds), Whom Can We Trust? How Groups, Networks, and Institutions Make Trust Possible, Manhattan, New York City, Russell Sage Publication (2009): 128-129; Bernard Barber, The Logics and Limits of Trust, New Brunswick, New Jersey, Rutgers University Press (1983): 15-21; Frank B. Cross, 'Law and Trust', Georgetown Law Journal, 93 (2005): 1457 ff. (parsing the relationship between the concept of trust in the realm of groups and trust networks in Western cultures). *See* Mathew Harding, 'Trust and Fiduciary Law', Oxford Journal of Legal Studies, 33 (2013): 81 ff.; Anthony J. Bellia Jr, 'Promises, Trust, and Contract Law', American Journal of Jurisprudence, 47 (2002): 47 ff.; Roger Cotterell, 'Trusting in Law: Legal and Moral Concepts of Trust', Current Legal Problems, 46 (2/1) (1993): 75 ff.; James Coleman, Foundations of Social Theory, Cambridge, Massachusetts, Harvard University Press (1994): passim; Mathew Harding, 'Responding to Trust', Ratio Juris, 24 (2011): 75 ff. David Vitale, 'Trust Network Model for Social Rights Fulfilment', Oxford Journal of Legal Studies, 38(4) (2018): 706-732 (noting that there is a well-established and strong relationship between trust and cooperation in Western cultures, primarily the United States of America).
54. Mark A. Hall, 'The Importance of Trust for Ethics, Law, and Public Policy, Cambridge Quarterly of Healthcare Ethics, 14 (2005): 156 ff.; Niklas Luhmann, 'Familiarity, Confidence, Trust: Problems and Alternatives', Diego Gambetta (ed.), Trust: Making and Breaking Cooperative Relations, Oxford, Basil Blackwell (1988): 97; Karen S. Cook and Alexandra Gerbasi, 'Trust', Peter Hedstrom and Peter Bearman (eds), The Oxford Handbook of Analytical Sociology, Oxford, Oxford University Press (2009): passim (depicting trust and trustworthiness as the cornerstones of cooperative relationships and trust networks in Western cultures). *See* A.

social weight and importance as in cultures of honour and face-saving cultures,[55] it also plays a moderate role in cultures of dignity.[56] Negative reciprocity amounts to the willingness to punish those who have either hurt you or crossed you.[57] Self-defence is a key feature of negative reciprocity.[58] Countries like the United States, France, Belgium, Switzerland, the Netherlands, Portugal, United Kingdom stand as paradigmatic examples of cultures of dignity.

[B] Cultural Logics of Face or Cultures of Face and Cultures of Honour

Things pan out differently in cultures of face.[59] While cultures of dignity are premised on, and revolve around, the mighty individual, cultures of face award primacy to the behemoth collective instead. Cultures of honour – mostly located in Africa and Latin America – afford primacy to honour itself. Yet, to some extent, cultures of face and cultures of honour overlap.

Like honour, face is interwoven with the way other people see the individual.[60] In this vein, face and honour are interlocking concepts. Face and honour are thus intertwined. Sentiments (the *others*' eyes and hearts) play a starring role in both cultures of honour and cultures of face. To a certain extent, face and honour meld seamlessly into the other. 'Face is like honour in that the sentiments of other people are extremely important. Like honour, face also can involve a claim to virtue or to prestige.'[61]

The similarities between cultures of honour and cultures of face do not dilute, much less dispel, the sizable differences between them nonetheless. The *role of expectations* is radically different for cultures of honour and cultures of face. Cultures of face are underpinned by rigid, obdurate, unbending, and unmovable hierarchies in

---

Tocqueville, Democracy in America, H. Mansfield (ed.), Chicago, IL; University of Chicago Press (Original work published 1840) (2010): (dissecting the virtue of self-interest and of 'being rightly understood' in Western cultures).

55. M. Mauss, The Gift, New York, NY, Norton (2000): (alluding to the gift exchange so voguish in face cultures).
56. A.K.-Y. Leung and D. Cohen, 'Within-and Between- Culture Variation: Individual Differences and the Cultural Logics of Honor, Face and Dignity Cultures', *supra*: 507-526.
57. *Ibid.*
58. *Ibid.*
59. M.J. Gelfand et al., 'Cultural Influences on Cognitive Representations of Conflict: Interpretations of Conflict Episodes in the United States and Japan', Journal of Applied Psychology, 86 (2001): 1059-1074 DOI: 10.1037//0021-9010.86.6.1059; M.J. Gelfand, L.H. Nishii and J. Raver, 'On the Nature and Importance of Cultural Tightness-Looseness', Journal of Applied Psychology, 91 (2006): 1225-1244 (comparing the cultural influences on cognitive representations of conflict on cultures of face and cultures of dignity).
60. T. Hamamura and S. Heine, 'The Role of Self-Criticism in Self-Improvement and Face Maintenance among Japanese', E.C. Chang (ed.), Self-Criticism and self-Enhancement: Theory, Research, and Clinical Implications (2008): 105-122; T. Hamamura et al., 'Approach-Avoidance Motivation and Information Processing: A Cross-Cultural Analysis', Personality and Social Psychology Bulletin, 35 (2009): 454-462 (providing an overview of cultures of face and cultures of dignity).
61. A.K.-Y. Leung and D. Cohen, 'Within-and Between- Culture Variation: Individual Differences and the Cultural Logics of Honor, Face and Dignity Cultures', Journal of Personality and Social Psychology, 100(3) (2011): 507-526 (passim).

which *social cooperation* is not only expected but warmly welcomed. This is a detail that makes all the difference in expedited arbitration settings where the arbitrator has considerably less time to prepare the arbitration hearings. Preparation ushers in a successful outcome in dispute resolution.

Cultures of face are prone, and thus displaying a clear proclivity, to settling disputes through conciliatory means.[62] This proclivity is nothing but formulaic. Cultures of face are also collectivist societies in which the collective is far more important than the individual. Both social harmony and social stability stand as overriding goals.

Abiding by the social role ascribed to the individual is paramount in cultures of face. It promotes social harmony and eschews social strife altogether. No wonder face[63] is described as 'the respectability and/or deference which a person can claim ... by virtue of (his and her) relative position'[64] in an unyielding hierarchy.[65] The proper fulfilment of the individual's social role in cultures of face is a cardinal part of being (or not) socially fit. Due to unbending hierarchic positions, face is unequally distributed among individuals. Everyone can have face. But some are entitled to have more than others. Social imbalance is placidly accepted, even expected, by all individuals within a culture of face. The higher the social role assigned to an individual, the more they are entitled to have face.[66] 'Everyone in the hierarchy can have some face, though some may have more than others due to their position. Implicitly, people have face – unless they lose it. A person can gain face, and one can "give face" to another, but the major

62. *See*: Hugo Luz dos Santos, Towards a Four-Tiered Model of Mediation – Against the Background of a Narrative of Social Sub-system in Everlasting Cross-Fertilization, Singapore/Berlin, Beijing/New York, Springer, 2023, passim.
63. S.J. Heine, 'Self as Cultural Product', Journal of Personality, 69 (2001): 881-905 (highlighting the foundations of cultures of face and its impact on social behaviour); X. Zou, M. Morris and V. Benet-Martinez, 'Identity Motives and Cultural Priming: Cultural (Dis)identification in Assimilative and Contrastive Responses', Journal of Experimental Social Psychology, 44 (2008): 1151-1159. *See*: A.K.-Y. Leung and D. Cohen, 'Within-and Between- Culture Variation: Individual Differences and the Cultural Logics of Honor, Face and Dignity Cultures', Journal of Personality and Social Psychology, 100(3) (2011): 507-526 (passim).
64. D.Y.-F. Ho, 'On the Concept of Face', American Journal of Sociology, 81 (1976): 867-884 (emphasising the contours of face cultures and the extent to which the individual blends in the collective). *See*: A.K.-Y. Leung and D. Cohen, 'Within-and Between- Culture Variation: Individual Differences and the Cultural Logics of Honor, Face and Dignity Cultures', *supra*: 507-526, whose research serves as an intellectual lodestar.
65. D. Oyserman and S.W.S. Lee, 'Does Culture Influence What and How We Think?', Psychological Bulletin, 134 (2008 a): 311-342; D. Oyserman and S.W.S. Lee, 'A Situated Cognition Perspective on Culture: Effects of Priming Cultural Syndromes on Cognition and Motivation', R. Sorentino and S. Yamaguchi (eds), Handbook of Motivation and Cognition Across Cultures (2008 b): 237-265 (stating that cultural programmes do impact the way people think and act in face cultures and dignity cultures). *See*: A.K.-Y. Leung an D. Cohen, 'Within-and Between- Culture Variation: Individual Differences and the Cultural Logics of Honor, Face and Dignity Cultures', *supra*: 507-526.
66. N. Zane and M. Yeh, 'The Use of Culturally-Based Variables in Assessment: Studies on Loss Face', K. Kurasaki, S. Okasaki and S. Sue (eds), Asian American Mental Health, Norwell, MA, Kluwer (2002): 123-138 (focusing on the contours – and perils – of losing face on cultures of face).

focus is primarily on not losing face. This is reflected in the expression "saving face", a saying that came into the English from British expatriates living in China.'[67]

A culture of face and an unbending social hierarchy are interlocking concepts. Unlike in cultures of honour,[68] face is not to be considered in a competitive manner.[69] Rather, in face cultures, people tend to cooperate[70] with each other[71] to preserve each other's face[72] with a view to bolstering harmony within their social circle.[73] Furthermore, 'because it is bad form to cause another to lose face, formalities are carefully observed'.[74] Conflict is to be avoided at any cost.[75] Open and direct conflict disrupts the social harmony in which a culture of face sits. Conflict tarnishes social cooperation. Conflict evinces disrespect for the social hierarchy, which is not by all means to be disregarded. Conflict undermines - often derails - a future relationship between the parties thus creating *social irritants* in cultures of face. The hallmark of a culture of face is its *cultural tightness* (as opposed to *cultural looseness*, a keystone of cultures of dignity).[76]

In cultures of face, there is a holy trinity not to be glossed over: the deemed 3 H's. The 3 H's stand for hierarchy, humility, and harmony.[77] The gist of a culture of face is not amenable to be grasped devoid of, and decoupled from, a nuanced attention to such

67. A.K.-Y. Leung and D. Cohen, 'Within-and Between- Culture Variation: Individual Differences and the Cultural Logics of Honor, Face and Dignity Cultures', *supra*: 507-526.
68. *Ibid.* (noting that 'in an honour culture, one person may take another's honour and appropriate it as his or her own; however, one cannot increase one's face by taking another's').
69. As 'unlike in honour cultures, it is not incumbent on the victim to directly redress the grievance him - or herself. Direct retaliation would be undesirable because it would further upset the harmony of the system'. *See*: A.K.-Y. Leung and D. Cohen, 'Within-and Between- Culture Variation: Individual Differences and the Cultural Logics of Honor, Face and Dignity Cultures', *supra*: 507-526.
70. M.J. Gelfand et al., 'Cultural Influences on Cognitive Representations of Conflict: Interpretations of Conflict Episodes in the United States and Japan', Journal of Applied Psychology, 86 (2001): 1059-1074 (congregating and comparing the main characteristics of both cultures of face and cultures of dignity and how such a tandem impacts the unfolding of a conflict in United States of America and Japan, respectively).
71. T. Hamamura et al., 'Approach-Avoidance Motivation and Information Processing: A Cross-Cultural Analysis', Personality and Social Psychology Bulletin, 35 (2009): 454-462 (providing an overview of cultures of face and cultures of dignity).
72. A.K.-Y. Leung and D. Cohen, 'Within-and Between- Culture Variation: Individual Differences and the Cultural Logics of Honor, Face and Dignity Cultures', *supra*: 507-526.
73. T. Hamamura and S. Heine, 'The Role of Self-Criticism in Self-Improvement and Face Maintenance among Japanese', E.C. Chang (ed.), Self-Criticism and Self-Enhancement: Theory, Research, and Clinical Implications (2008): 105-122 (noting the pivotal role of self-criticism and self-improvement in Asian cultures, especially Japanese).
74. A.K.-Y. Leung and D. Cohen, 'Within-and Between- Culture Variation: Individual Differences and the Cultural Logics of Honor, Face and Dignity Cultures', *supra*: 507-526.
75. J.H.-Y. Fu et al., 'Epistemic Motives and Cultural Conformity: Need for Closure, Culture, and Context as Determinants of Conflict Judgments', Journal of Personality and Social Psychology (2007): 191-207.
76. M.J. Gelfand, L.H. Nishii and J. Raver, 'On the Nature and Importance of Cultural Tightness-Looseness', Journal of Applied Psychology, 91 (2006): 1225-1244 (on the difference between cultural tightness and cultural looseness).
77. A.K.-Y. Leung and D. Cohen, 'Within-and Between- Culture Variation: Individual Differences and the Cultural Logics of Honor, Face and Dignity Cultures', *supra*: 507-526.

pillars. No culture of face can be fully functional without the mightiness and immovability of such foundational pillars. If one mars the equilibrium in which such pillars sit, its social harmony is to be sapped in the process.

The hierarchy, humility, and harmony pillars resonate with the assertion according to which individuals, narrowed down to their tiniest expression, are supposed to show unquenchable respect to social hierarchy. 'They are supposed to display humility and not overreach on status claims (lest they learn a painful and humiliating lesson about how much status others are willing to accord them).'[78] Harmony is to be pursued 'relentlessly'. Henceforth (from the very minute they get accepted in a given social circle), 'they are to pursue, or at least not disturb, the harmony of the system'.[79] If the fundamental tenets of this culture of face are besmirched (or disrupted), a draconian punishment is to be (must be) inflicted upon the wrongdoer: shame. 'Shame is the punishment for bad behaviour in a system of face. Those who do not have enough concern for their face and the good opinion of others will behave selfishly or inappropriately.'[80]

It gets worse and worse for cultures of face's wrongdoers: 'They may also be boorish and not sensitive enough to fulfil their particularistic obligations to peers, subordinates, superiors, or others to whom they owe loyalty. Someone not concerned with face will be insensitive to its loss.'[81] In a nutshell, the wrongdoers may become social pariahs over time. And 'such people cannot be shamed or are shameless'.[82]

Countries like China, Japan, South Korea, Singapore,[83] Malaysia, Indonesia, and regions like Hong Kong SAR, Macau SAR and Taiwan stand among cultures of face. This ground-breaking finding has a direct and significant impact on the unfolding of dispute resolution.

§15.04 THE EXTENT TO WHICH THE TAXONOMIES OF CULTURAL LOGICS OF DIGNITY AND CULTURAL LOGICS OF FACE IMPACT EXPEDITED ARBITRATION IN MACAU

[A] What Do Disputants from Different Cultural Backgrounds Expect from the Arbitrator/Mediator in Expedited Arbitration Settings in Macau?

Against this background, the principle of self-determination – a cornerstone of arb-med – must be painted in a glaringly different light. This finding is crucially important in

78. *Ibid.*
79. *Ibid.*
80. *Ibid.*
81. *Ibid.*
82. *Ibid.*
83. D. Quek Anderson, E. Chua and N. Tra My, 'How Should the Courts Know Whether a Dispute Is Ready and Suitable for Mediation? An Empirical Analysis of the Singapore Courts "Referral of Civil Disputes to Mediation"', Harvard Negotiation Law Review, 23 (2018): 265-317 (277 ff.) (on dispute resolution in Singapore).

expedited arbitration in Macau where conflicts between members with different cultural backgrounds abound. To the extent that Macau Arbitration Law does not govern this issue, a myriad of guidelines is utterly needed for the sake of legal security in this regard.

In the future, should an arbitrator be asked to perform as a mediator in the context of arb-med in expedited arbitration settings in Macau, they will most likely be met with seemingly insurmountable obstacles. Among which stands the difficulty to meet both the requirements and the expectations of members of cultures of dignity (who reckon that the principle of self-determination allots them the privilege to craft the best solution for the case at hand by themselves) and of members of face (who reckon that the principle of self-determination's perimeter should be ebbed and the role of the arbitrator/mediator should be augmented accordingly).

To put it bluntly, members of cultures of dignity attach greater importance to the principle of self-determination than do members of cultures of face. This means that members of cultures of dignity are not fond of an evaluative style of mediation.[84] Rather, members of cultures of dignity yearn for a facilitative style of mediation,[85] which is squarely aligned with the exceedingly high levels of individualism that underpins Western cultures of which its members are so keenly fond.

In a diametrically opposed plan, members of cultures of face crave for a directive style of mediation[86] in the remit of which the arbitrator/mediator offers their own views on the strengths and weaknesses of the case while bringing a concrete solution to iron out areas of disagreement and hash out the dispute ('put the dispute to bed'). This finding is hardly flummoxing as Macau is lodged at the heart of a Chinese

84. Leonard L. Riskin, 'Understanding Mediator Orientations, Strategies and Techniques: A Grid for the Perplexed', Harvard Negotiation Law Review, 1 (1996): 7-49 (defining evaluative mediation in light of which the mediator assesses the weaknesses and strengths of the case or legal position, thereby predicting the likelihood of success – or lack thereof – of the latter and directing 'some or all of the outcomes of the mediation').

85. Leonard L. Riskin, 'Understanding Mediator Orientations, Strategies and Techniques: A Grid for the Perplexed', *supra* 7-49 (24) (notes that the mediator who happens to facilitate 'assume that the parties are intelligent, able to work their counterparts, and capable understanding their situations better than the mediator which means that the disputants can develop better solutions than any the mediator might create. It falls to the facilitative mediator to clarify and enhance communication between the parties in order to help them decide what to do').

86. Leonard L. Riskin, 'Decision-Making in Mediation: The New Old Grid and the New Grid System, Notre Dame Law Review (2003): 18 ff. (amidst harsh criticism, Riskin has outlined a new grid in which the author replaced the taxonomy 'evaluative' by 'directive'. Upon reviewing the batch of harsh criticism to his old grid, Riskin noted that by evaluative he bore in mind that the mediator can, in some situations, guide (direct) disputants towards a certain outcome). *See also*: D. Quek, 'Facilitative Versus Evaluative Mediation: Is There Necessarily a Dichotomy?', Asian Journal on Mediation (2013): 69. The directive style of mediation seems to have caught on. *See*, among many other examples, Nancy A. Welsh, 'The Current Transitional State of Court-Connected ADR', Marquette Law Review 95 (2012): 873-884 (noting that court-connected mediator elicits a directive approach to mediation). Nancy A. Welsh, 'Do You Believe in Magic? Self-Determination and Procedural Justice Meet Inequality in Court-Connected Mediation', SMU L. Review 70 (2017): 721 (adducing that a directive approach to mediation is usually preferred in the West, the cradle of cultures of dignity).

Confucian[87] zone.[88] This finding is also consistent with the high levels of collectivism[89] that undergirds cultures of face.

No surprise stems from the fact that Chinese mediation, and in an overarching sense, Asian mediation, differs greatly from Western mediation.[90] This assertion stands

87. *See* Guy Olivier Faure, 'Practice Note: Informal Mediation in China', Conflict Resolution Quarterly, 29(1) (2011): 85-99 (this renowned Sociologist, who has spent several years studying China's exquisite dispute resolution system, has contended that the Confucian moral values do play a pivotal role in mediation in China. Consistent with this assertion '*guidance is provided by a set of social values, here mostly Confucian,* expressing a moderate and compassionate approach. This very specific combination assures the effectiveness of the overall process') (italics added).
88. *See also* Shiga asserted that civil justice in imperial China, which was soaked in Confucianism traits, was a distinct form of 'Kadi' justice in which magistrates would arbitrarily decide cases relying upon a bevy of Confucian moral principles rather than statutory law: S. Shiga, 'A Study of Chinese Legal Culture Focusing on the Litigation Landscape', Journal of Comparative Law, 3 (1988): 18-26. *See also* Peter Chi Hin Chan, 'The Enigma of Civil Justice in Imperial China: A Legal Historical Enquiry', Maastricht Journal of European and Comparative Law, 19 (2012): 317-337. Converging: Peter Chi Hin Chan, 'Civil Mediation in Imperial, Republican and Modern-Day China Historical and Cultural Norms under the Traditional Chinese Legal Order', The Legal History Review, 85 (2017), 577-602 (578 ff.); Peter Chi Hin Chan, Mediation in Contemporary Chinese Civil Justice: A Proceduralist Diachronic Perspective, Amsterdam, Martinus Niijhoff Publishers (2017), passim; Peter Chi Hin Chan, Efficiency and Truth in Civil Fact-Finding: The Evolving Role of the Judge in Mainland China and Hong Kong and the Effect of the Policy Preference for Court Mediation on Fact-Finding in the People's Courts, in C.H. van Rhee and A. Uzelac (eds), Truth and Efficiency in Civil Litigation: Fundamental Aspects of Fact-Finding and Evidence-Taking in a Comparative Context, Antwerp: Intersentia (2012), 231-260; Peter Chi Hin Chan, David Chan and Chen Lei, 'China: Hong Kong – Selective Adoption of the English Woolf Reforms', Civil Litigation in China and Europe, Part of the Ius Gentium: Comparative Perspectives on Law and Justice book series (IUSGENT, volume 31) (2013), 71-125; Peter Chi Hin Chan, Do the 'Haves' Come Out Ahead in Chinese Grassroots Courts? – Rural Land Disputes Between Married-Out Women and Village Collectives, Hastings Law Journal, 71(1) (2019) DOI: 10.2139/ssrn.3352346; Peter Chi Hin Chan and KH Ng, '"What Gets Measured Gets Done": Metric Fixation and China's Experiment in Quantified Judging', Asian Journal of Law and Society, 8(2) (2021): 255-281; Peter Chi Hin Chan, 'China's Grand Mediation Strategy for Social Stability: A Study on Out-of-Court Mediation Procedures', Revista de Processo Comparado, 6(3) (2017): 81-111.
89. Harry C. Triandis et al., 'Simpatía as a Cultural Script of Hispanics', Journal of Personality and Social Psychology, 47 (1984): 1363-1375; Triandis, Harry C., 'Cross-Cultural Studies of Individualism and Collectivism', Nebraska Symposium on Motivation, Lincoln, University of Nebraska Press (1989 a): 41-133; Harry C. Triandis, 'The Self and Social Behaviour in Differing Cultural Contexts', Psychological Review, 96 (1989 b): 506-520; Harry C. Triandis, M. Kim, C. Kagitcibasi, C.S. Choi and G. Yoon (eds), Individualism and Collectivism: Theory, Method and Application, Thousand Oaks, CA: Sage (1994 a): 137-156; Harry C. Triandis, Culture and Social Behavior, New York, NY: McGraw-Hill (1994 b): 3 ff.; Harry C. Triandis, Individualism and Collectivism: New Directions in Social Psychology, Boulder, CO, Westview (1995); Harry C. Triandis, 'Generic Individualism and Collectivism', The Blackwell Handbook of Cross-Cultural Management, Gannon J. Martin and L.K. Newman (eds), John Wiley and Sons, Inc, Hoboken, New Jersey (2002): 1-509 (15 ff.) (on the dichotomy between individualism and collectivism).
90. *See*: Guy Olivier Faure, 'Practice Note: Informal Mediation in China', *supra*, 85-99 (98) (arguing that 'the Chinese practice of mediation does not exactly coincide with a Western definition of mediation'). Converging: Dorcas Quek Anderson, 'The Evolving Concept of Access to Justice in Singapore's Mediation Movement', International Journal of Law in Context, Cambridge University Press (2020): 1-18 (7) (arguing presciently that '*many of the cultural assumptions underlying the facilitative mediation model are therefore incompatible with Asian preferences. For instance, expectations about individual autonomy stand in stark contrast to the primacy of social hierarchy*') (italics added).

at the heart of the newly crafted concept of *cultural differentiation of voice*.[91] On that account, mediation bears a faint resemblance to arbitration.[92]

Cultural differentiation of voice amounts to the axiom according to which disputants' voice has starkly different tonalities.[93] Put otherwise, voice – mirrored on an undeterred yearning to speak and to be heard while doing so – hinges upon the disputants' cultural background and underlying legal culture. Members of cultures of face talk less than do members of cultures of dignity, who are kittenish, garrulous and loquacious. Voice is a befitted tool to convey both their stance on the case and their *individuality* of which they are so fond of. Silence, for members of cultures of dignity, is an unshattering sign of weakness. Tellingly, winning a given dispute[94] is far more important than keeping a shapeless social harmony in which members of cultures of dignity are both insouciant and nonchalant. The befitted style of mediation for these disputants is the facilitative one.

On the opposite pole, members of cultures of face are less talkative – even lukewarm – while entertaining a dispute. Voice stands as a bespoke tool to – parsimoniously – exude the *group's* views on the case. Voice thereby consists of a tool to express the deep-rooted interests of the interlaced thread of relationships around which a given individual – a tiny part of the humongous collective – revolves. Silence, for members of cultures of face, is gold. Maintaining both social harmony and social stability within a given thread of interlaced relationships outweighs winning a given dispute. A piece of empirical evidence is poised to give credence to this central contention. The bespoke style of mediation for these disputants is the directive or evaluative one. The mediator – the stellar mediator partaking in Med-Arb in expedited arbitration settings – should not only be cognisant of *cultural differentiation of voice* but, foremost, also must shrewdly and deftly master it.

Against this background, the directive style[95] of mediation[96] is best suited to cultures of face due to the exceedingly high values of power distance.[97] According to

---

91. *See*: Hugo Luz dos Santos, Towards a Four-Tiered Model of Mediation – Against the Background of a Narrative of Social Sub-system in Everlasting Cross-Fertilization, Singapore/Berlin, Beijing/New York, Springer, 2023, passim.
92. Guy Olivier Faure, 'Practice Note: Informal Mediation in China', *supra*: 85-99 (98) (contending that Chinese mediation is 'somehow closer to arbitration').
93. *See*: Hugo Luz dos Santos, Towards a Four-Tiered Model of Mediation – Against the Background of a Narrative of Social Sub-system in Everlasting Cross-Fertilization Singapore/Berlin, Beijing/New York, Springer, 2023, passim.
94. This is consistent with the findings arising out of a survey undertaken in the remit of psychology and neurobiology whose participants were members of cultures of dignity. *See*: Elisabeth E. Bader, 'The Psychology and Neurobiology of Mediation', Cardozo Journal of Conflict Resolution, 17 (2015): 363-364; *see also* Elizabeth E. Bader, 'The Psychology of Mediation: Issues of Self and Identity and the IDR Cycle', Pepperdine Dispute Resolution Law Journal, 10 (2010): 183; Elizabeth E. Bader, 'Self, Identity and the IDR Cycle: Understanding the Deeper Meaning of "Face" in Mediation', *International Journal of Applied Psychoanalytic Studies*, 8 (2011): 301 (this renowned author states that 'at the outset of a mediation, parties often had unrealistically optimistic hopes for resolution in their own favor, and on their own terms. This was also coupled with an attitude of "*I am a winner, and I can do this*!"') (italics added).
95. Converging: Dorcas Quek Anderson, Eunice Chua and Ngo Tra My, 'How Should the Courts Know Whether a Dispute Is Ready and Suitable for Mediation? An Empirical Analysis of the

this style, an arbitrator/mediator sits atop the social hierarchy. Its use in hybrid procedures like Arb-Med or Med-Arb seems to raise less eyebrows in Asia. This is something that an arbitrator/mediator in expedited arbitration settings should bear very firmly in mind while entertaining disputes between members of cultures of dignity and members of cultures of face in Macau, which is set to play a starring role on the purview of administration of justice[98] in this tiny territory.

[B] Empirical Research on CIETAC's and Beijing Arbitration Commission's Arbitrators Which Lends Weight to the Appropriateness of Arb-Med or Med-Arb in Macau

Empirical research supports the appropriateness of hybrid dispute resolution mechanisms, such as Arb-Med or Med-Arb, within the purview of Expedited Arbitration in a Chinese Confucian zone[99] like Macau.[100] This research portrays Arb-Med or Med-Arb in a positive light.

Singapore Courts' Referral of Civil Disputes to Mediation', Harvard Negotiation Law Review, 23 (2018): 265-317 (277 ff. and passim).

96. Dorcas Quek Anderson, 'The Evolving Concept of Access to Justice in Singapore's Mediation Movement', International Journal of Law in Context, Cambridge University Press (2020 a): 1-18 1-18 (7) (which means that '*a more Asian-oriented approach requires the mediator, and not the parties, to be at the heart of the mediation. The mediator is thus expected to lead and guide the parties as well as express opinions and give input*') (italics added).

97. Geert Hofstede, Culture's Consequences: International Differences in Work-Related Values, London, United Kingdom, Sage (1980); Geert Hofstede, 'The Cultural Relativity of Organizational Practices and Theories', Journal of International Business Studies, 14 (1983): 75-89 DOI: 10.1057/palgrave.jibs.8490867; Geert Hofstede, Cultures and Organizations: Software of the Mind, London, McGraw-Hill (1991); L.K.F. Hsu, Under the Ancestor's Shadow: Chinese Culture and Personality, New York, Columbia University Press (1984); H.G. Hofstede, Culture's Consequences: International Differences in Work-Related Attitudes, Beverly Hills, CA: Sage (1986); Geert Hofstede and Michael Bond, 'The Confucius Connection: From Cultural Roots to Economic Growth', Organizational Dynamics, 16 (1988): 5-20 (16-19) DOI: 10.1016/0090-2616 (88)90009-5; H.G. Hofstede, Culture's Consequences: International Differences in Work-Related Attitudes, Beverly Hills, CA: Sage (1989); Geert Hofstede, Software of the Mind, Berskshire, United Kingdom, McGraw-Hill (1991 a) (on the concept of power distance which is linked with the concept of collectivism in Asian countries). *See* Harry C. Triandis, Individualism and Collectivism, New Directions in Social Psychology, Boulder, CO, Westview (1995): 1-288 (passim) (noting the high power distance between legal officials and citizens and the propensity that the former have to respect and accept its clout gracefully) ('a thorough examination of the differences between collectivists (those who view themselves primarily as part of a whole, and who are motivated by the norms and duties imposed by the collective entity) and individualists (those who are motivated by their own preferences and needs)').

98. *See generally* E. Severin, 'Comment l'esprit du management est venu à l'administration de la justice', La Nouveau Management de la Justice et l'indépendance des juges, Paris, Dalloz (2011).

99. *See* on Huntington's taxonomy of 'eight major cultural zones', which includes, among a set of other religion-laden cultural zones, China, which is a 'Chinese Confucian Zone'. *See*: Samuel Huntington, The Clash of Civilizations and the Remaking of World Order, New York, Simon & Schuster (2011): 18-48 (this scholar argued that the world we all live in is engulfed in staggering cultural differences. Huntington further asserted that religion has played a key role in shaping the foregoing eight 'major cultural zones').

100. Kun Fan, 'An Empirical Study of Arbitrators Acting as Mediators in China', Cardozo Journal of Conflict Resolution, 15 (2014): 789 ('the data generated by the survey will be verified against

The findings of this empirical evidence can be broken down as follows: (i) the extent to which the arbitrators-mediators considered it appropriate to hash out an agreement in expedited arbitration and arbitration proceedings; (ii) who came up with the idea to resort to mediation during expedited arbitration and arbitration proceedings; (iii) and an appraisal on the success rate (or lack thereof) of mediation during arbitral proceedings. This boils down to the simple question of whether the disputants were comfortable to resort to mediation. The Confucian-based cultural differentiation of voice strikes again.

[1] The Extent to Which the Arbitrators-Mediators Have Considered It Appropriate to Hash Out an Agreement in Expedited Arbitration and Arbitration Proceedings

Standing in sharp alignment with China's underlying fondness for mediation, all the Chinese arbitrators interviewed have shown a great proclivity to use mediation during expedited arbitration and arbitration proceedings.[101] The reason for such a heightened proneness to use mediation is consistent with the concept of *cultures of face*[102] *and cultural differentiation of voice*[103] against the backdrop of which maintaining *social harmony*[104] is of paramount importance. The Chinese arbitrators believed that mediation is an apposite way to grasp a win-win solution acceptable – and profitable – to both disputants in expedited arbitration and arbitration proceedings. This finding chimes in with China International Economic and Trade Arbitration Commission (CIETAC) arbitrators' penchant for awarding partial wins[105] in an earnest attempt to ensure both social harmony and social stability within circumscribed geographic boundaries (China). In this vein, 88.9% of the respondents keenly believed that using mediation during expedited arbitration and arbitration proceedings was both advisable and fruit-bearing on the heels of the following reasons: (i) cost-effectiveness and efficiency;[106] (ii) it is far easier to enforce a mediated settlement agreement than an arbitral award.[107]

---

the qualitative information obtained through in-depth personal interviews with arbitrators who have repeated experience, data provided by the arbitration institutions, as well as direct discussions with case managers at the CIETAC and the BAC, who oversee arbitration proceedings taking place in China on a day-to-day basis. A number of respondents of the survey have also made specific comments, and this offers additional qualitative resource for our assessment').

101. *Ibid.*
102. *See* §15.03.
103. *Ibid.*
104. *See* §15.03 of this book chapter.
105. *See*: Pat K. Chew, 'Opening the Red Door to Chinese Arbitrations: An Empirical Analysis of CIETAC Cases 1990-2000', Harvard Negotiation Law Review, 22 (2017): 242-274.
106. Fan Kun, 'An Empirical Study of Arbitrators Acting as Mediators in China', *supra*: 790.
107. Converging: Peter Chi Hin Chan, The Position of Mediation in Contemporary Chinese Civil Justice: A Procedural Perspective, Dissertation to obtain the degree of Doctor at Maastricht University, Maastricht, Netherlands (2016): 1-298 (151-152) (averring that is much easier (for cultural reasons?) to enforce a settlement agreement than an award or a judgment in China. 'Apart from saving costs, time and business relationships, mediation has a unique advantage

[2] Who Came up with the Idea to Resort to Mediation During the Expedited Arbitration and Arbitration Proceedings?

Against the backdrop of Leung-Cohen's concept of cultures of face[108] and Hofstede's concept of collectivism[109] and cultural differentiation of voice,[110] it was the Chinese arbitrators who themselves came up with the idea to resort to mediation during the expedited arbitration and arbitration proceedings.[111] According to this body of empirical research, 50% of the respondents held that they had proposed mediation to disputants in over 90% of the cases first referred to arbitration.[112]

These findings are consistent with newly crafted concepts of a Confucian-based *cultural differentiation of voice* (a willingness to compromise for cultural reasons), *long-term harmony-equilibrium* (solving the case while restoring disputants' relationship to induce a future voluntary compliance with the outcome of a mediated settlement agreement) and *wealth procedural maximisation* (in voluntarily complying with the outcome of the mediated settlement agreement, the disputants would crowd out the spectre of enforcement while easing the strains inflicted upon a given system of administration of justice).[113]

[C] Appraisal on the Success Rate (or Lack Thereof) of Mediation During Expedited Arbitration and Arbitral Proceedings

Both the interviews and the body of empirical research have shown that the Chinese disputants have portrayed the Med-Arb, during both expedited arbitration and arbitration proceedings, in a rather positive light.[114] In stark contrast, foreign disputants (members from cultures of dignity[115]) have shown a hardly unforeseen[116] resistance to resort to mediation during the expedited arbitration and arbitration proceedings.[117] Such findings add further academic plausibility to the concept of *cultural differentiation of voice*.

These findings adroitly support, and give credence to, the concept of *cultural differentiation of voice*.[118] According to which members of cultures of dignity, who display exceedingly high levels of individualism, tend to nurture the idea that one must

in China. Enforcement of arbitral awards and court judgements is particularly difficult in China. *Parties are more likely to comply with a voluntary settlement agreement (reached through mediation) than an award or judgment*') (italics added).

108. *See* §15.03.
109. *Ibid.*
110. *Ibid.*
111. Fan Kun, 'An Empirical Study of Arbitrators Acting as Mediators in China', *cit.*: 791.
112. *Ibid.*
113. *See*: Hugo Luz dos Santos, Towards a Four-Tiered Model of Mediation – Against the Background of a Narrative of Social Sub-system in Everlasting Cross-Fertilization Singapore/Berlin, Beijing/New York, Springer, 2023, passim.
114. *Ibid.*, at 792.
115. *See* §15.03.
116. *Ibid.*
117. *Ibid.*
118. *Ibid.*

fight for their own rights while downplaying the importance of compromising. The latter – compromising – is thus viewed as a sign of weakness. Against this background, *voice* – which is deeply steeped at the heart of both the principle of self-determination and the principle of party autonomy – varies greatly across cultural backgrounds and legal cultures.

[D] What Should the Mediator-Arbitrator Do to Overcome the Perceived Cultural Differences with Which He Will Most Likely Be Met During Future Expedited Arbitration Proceedings in Macau?

Macau lacks a legal framework solely devoted to expedited arbitration.[119] Rather, it boasts a legal framework devoted to emergency arbitration, Article 2., ¶6 of Law No. 19/2019 ('Macau Arbitration La'), whereby disputants are entitled to seek a myriad of interim reliefs from a temporary sole arbitrator pending the formation of the arbitral tribunal.[120]

De iure condendo, the mediator-arbitrator, whenever mediation and arbitration are blended or weaved together within the remit of a forthcoming expedited arbitration legal framework in Macau, should never lose sight of the cultural differences between *cultures of dignity* and *cultures of face* against the backdrop of which *cultural differentiation of voice*[121] unfolds. The mediator-arbitrator should use an *adaptive style of mediation*[122] whereby the cultural differences displayed by members of cultures of dignity and members of cultures of face can be both accounted for and dwindled. The mediator-arbitrator should use a *facilitative style of mediation*, which is suitably tailored to members from *cultures of dignity*. The mediator-arbitrator should refrain from offering their own views on the strengths and weaknesses of the case, which would most likely upset members from cultures of dignity that attach great importance to both the principle of self-determination and party autonomy.

Conversely, the mediator-arbitrator should use an *evaluative style of mediation*, which is suitably tailored to members from *cultures of face*. The mediator-arbitrator should neither be coy nor bashful in offering their insights on the strengths and

119. 'Expedited arbitration is a streamlined and simplified procedure with a shortened time frame, which makes it possible for the parties to reach a final resolution of the dispute in a cost- and time-effective manner. The UNCITRAL Expedited Arbitration Rules provide a set of rules which parties may agree for expedited arbitration. The Expedited Rules balance on the one hand, the efficiency of the arbitral proceedings and on the other, the rights of the parties to due process and fair treatment. Article 1(5) of the UNCITRAL Arbitration Rules incorporates the Expedited Rules, which are presented as an appendix to the UNCITRAL Arbitration Rules. The phrase "where the parties so agree" in that paragraph emphasizes the need for the parties' express consent for the Expedited Rules to apply to the arbitration.' *See* https://uncitral.un.org/en/content/expedited-arbitration-rules (access: 4.10.2023).
120. Articles 16-18 of Macau Arbitration Law. *See* Aditya Singh Chauban, 'Pushing Arbitral Boundaries to Pave Way for Emergency Arbitration', Indian Journal of Arbitration Law, 11(1) (2023): 9-16 (9).
121. *See* §15.03.
122. *See* Hugo Luz dos Santos, Towards a Four-Tiered Model of Mediation – Against the Background of a Narrative of Social Sub-System in Everlasting Cross-Fertilization Singapore/Berlin, Beijing/New York, Springer, 2023, passim.

weaknesses of the case, which would be praised by Asian disputants. To the extent that the mediator-arbitrator eschews any claims of ethnocentrism[123] during expedited arbitration proceedings, the former should hold fewer joint sessions. Failure to do so would greatly enhance the perceived difficulties arising out of sheer cultural differences between Western disputants and Asian disputants to expedited arbitration while augmenting the caucuses,[124] whereby each disputant would freely[125] exude his own views on the case devoid of any cultural hindrances whatsoever.

Time is money for members of cultures of dignity, who are very eager to iron out outstanding issues while swiftly paving the way to hammering out the dispute sooner rather than later. However, time is time and money is money for members of cultures of face, who are very fond of both slow-paced and fuss-free joint mediation sessions and peace-fraught caucuses which, taken together, can usher in a reshuffled business relationship amenable to bearing sapid fruits somewhere along the line. This reality should not be unbeknownst to the stellar mediator-arbitrator to expedited arbitration proceedings. Avoidable cultural misunderstandings may otherwise occur.

§15.05 CONCLUSION

Culture plays a key role in the purview of Expedited Arbitration, especially, yet not exclusively, when mediation and arbitration dovetail seamlessly within the realm of Expedited Arbitration. More often than not, cultural reasons underpin disputants' choice for an approach to mediation within the remit of expedited arbitration. A bevy of empirical research has shown that culture is of paramount importance when it comes to shaping dispute resolution mindsets, which is not by all means baffling.

According to Hofstede, culture stands as both a mental programme and a software of the mind against the backdrop in which disputants make their dispute resolution choices. As a result, each culture portrays the foundational principles of self-determination and party autonomy (and within which core, *voice*) in a glaringly different light. This adds plausibility to newly crafted concepts of cultural differentiation of voice, adaptive mediation, long-term harmony-equilibrium and wealth procedural maximisation.

123. Günther Frankenberg, Comparative Constitutional Studies: Between Magic and Deceit, Elgar Monographs in Constitutional and Administrative Law, Cheltenham, Edward Elgar (2018): passim (discusses the hazard of falling prey to a stance fraught with ethnocentrism).
124. Thomas J. Stipanowich, 'Insights on Mediator Practices and Perceptions', Dispute Resolution Magazine, Winter 2016 (2016): 7 ff.; Lynne S. Bassis, 'Face-to-Face Sessions Fade Away: Why Is Mediation's Joint Session Disappearing?', Dispute Resolution Magazine, Fall 2014 (2014): 33 ff.; Jay Folberg, 'The Shrinking Joint Session: Survey Results', Dispute Resolution Magazine, Winter 2016 (2016): 19 ff.; Eric Galton and Tracy Allen, 'Don't Torch the Joint Session', Dispute Resolution Magazine, Fall 2014 (2014): 25-27 (stressing the burgeoning importance of private or caucuses sessions in mediation settings).
125. Lorig Charkoudian, Deborah Thompson Eisenberg and Jamie L. Walker, 'What Difference Does ADR Make? Comparison of ADR and Trial Outcomes in Small Claims Court', Conflict Resolution Quarterly, 35 (2017): 7 ff. (parses the importance and effectiveness of caucuses in mediation settings).

Cultural differentiation of voice means that *voice* (one of the cornerstones of dispute resolution) has different levels and tonalities against the backdrop of different cultural backgrounds. The stellar mediator-arbitrator, in entertaining disputes in the remit of expedited arbitration, must not lose sight of cultural differentiation of voice, or avoidable cultural misapprehensions will otherwise occur. Cultural differentiation of voice is consistent with the fact that members of cultures of face display a heightened proneness to compromise for cultural reasons (the hallmark of long-term harmony-equilibrium), a lesson that members of cultures of dignity must bear very firmly in mind.

The mediator-arbitrator should use an *adaptive style of mediation* whereby the cultural differences displayed by members of cultures of dignity and members of cultures of face can be both accounted for and dwindled. To cater for that, the mediator-arbitrator should use a facilitative style of mediation, which is suitably tailored to members from cultures of dignity. The mediator-arbitrator should refrain himself from offering their own views on the strengths and weaknesses of the case, which would most likely upset members from cultures of dignity that attach utmost importance to both the principle of self-determination and party autonomy. Conversely, the mediator-arbitrator should use an evaluative style of mediation, which is suitably tailored to members from cultures of face. The mediator-arbitrator should neither be coy nor bashful in offering his insights on the strengths and weaknesses of the case, which would be praised by Asian disputants.

CHAPTER 16

Examining the Practice of Expedited Arbitration in China: Strengths, Difficulties, and Prospects

Yuan Fang[*]

The criticism that international arbitration is deviating from its foundation of expeditiously and efficiently resolving international disputes has drawn the attention of practitioners, scholars and stakeholder representatives. As one of the intellectual efforts to address this issue, this chapter examines expedited international arbitration distinctively from a Chinese angle. Through a careful investigation of the expedited rules and procedures of representative Chinese arbitral institutions, this chapter underscores the strengths and weaknesses of the existing mechanism of expedited arbitration in China. Comparing the expedited arbitration rules and procedures of Chinese institutions with those of the leading institutions across the globe, this chapter advises on the best practice for Chinese arbitration institutions by responding to the question of which global institution's approach to expedited arbitration is most appropriate for China. This chapter concludes with a call for reform of the expedited arbitration mechanisms in China at both the institutional level and legislative level.

§16.01 INTRODUCTION

Arbitration has traditionally been seen as the cheaper and faster method of dispute resolution, particularly in comparison with litigation.[1] However, practitioners, scholars and stakeholders have raised the criticism that international arbitration is departing

* The author acknowledges and thanks Mr. Yan Wang, who currently serves as a case manager at the BAC/BIAC for his generous support for this chapter, especially the invaluable information provided under the subtitle of "BAC/BIAC in Review: Expedited Arbitration in 2022."

1. Chan Leng Sun & Tan Weiyi, *Making Arbitration Effective: Expedited Procedures, Emergency Arbitrators and Interim Relief*, 6 Contemp. Asia Arb. J. 349, 351 (2013).

from its foundation of expeditiously and inexpensively resolving international disputes in recent years. Indeed, two primary concerns regarding traditional arbitration include the extended duration of the process and the increasing cost associated with arbitrations.[2] As a response to the increasingly emergent demand for less time-consuming procedures, expedited arbitration has been introduced to the international arbitration community.

While procedures similar to the modern expedited procedures were already used in Venice between the 12th and 16th centuries,[3] expedited arbitration is still a relatively new concept in contemporary commercial arbitration.[4] The earliest modern institutional rules for expedited procedures were introduced as a fast-track procedure under the Rules of Arbitration of the International Court of Arbitration of the International Chamber of Commerce.[5] Subsequently, a number of other arbitration institutions adopted expedited rules and procedures in various forms, making the expedition of arbitration a trending feature on a global scale.[6]

Compared to the literature studying expedited arbitration in the past, this chapter aims to respond to the challenges facing the expedited arbitration uniquely from a Chinese perspective. Specifically, this chapter is divided into five primary sections. Section 16.02 examines the practice of expedited arbitration of a representative Chinese arbitral institution, the Beijing Arbitration Commission/Beijing International Arbitration Center (BAC/BIAC). The next section expands the investigation to all the major Chinese arbitration institutions, outlining their limitations in common pertaining to expedited arbitration. Section 16.04 paves the path forward for the best practice of Chinese arbitration institutions through a comparative study, where the expedited arbitration rules and procedures of Chinese institutions are compared to those of the leading arbitral institutions across the world. This chapter concludes with expectations of the prospective expedited arbitration.

§16.02 AN EMPIRICAL STUDY ON BAC/BIAC PRACTICE OF EXPEDITED ARBITRATION

Since its establishment in 1995, BAC/BIAC has rapidly developed into an arbitration body with an extensive reputation in China.[7] The number of cases accepted by BAC/BIAC has climbed to 8,421 in 2022, while the amount in dispute incurred has

---

2. Shannon Webb & Terry Wagar, *Expedited Arbitration: The View from Canadian Lawyers*, 35 Ohio St. J. Disp. Resol. 133, 135 (2019) DOI: 10.7202/1044430ar.
3. Mirèze Philippe, *Are Specific Fast-Track Arbitration Rules Necessary?*, in 3 *Arbitration in Air, Space and Telecommunications Law: Enforcing Regulatory Measures* 255 (International Bureau of The Permanent Court of Arbitration ed., 2002).
4. Peter J. Pettibone, *Due Process Considerations in Expedited Arbitrations*, 10 Indian J. Arb. L. 175, 175 (2021).
5. Chan & Tan, *supra* n. 1, at 352.
6. *Ibid.*, 352-355.
7. *Beijing Arbitration Commission*, the BAC/BIAC (unknown), http://www.bjac.org.cn/english/page/gybh/introduce_index.html.

reached CNY 97.04 billion.[8] Given its important role in Chinese arbitration practice, BAC/BIAC is representative among all the Chinese arbitral institutions for analysis.[9] Empirical statistics regarding BAC/BIAC's performance in terms of expedited arbitration in 2022 will first be reviewed. Thereafter, a comprehensive analysis of the data to identify the strengths and weaknesses of the expedited arbitration rules and procedures of the BAC/BIAC will be examined.

[A] BAC/BIAC in Review: Expedited Arbitration in 2022

The Expedited Procedure was first introduced to BAC/BIAC Arbitration Rules in 1996, only a year after BAC/BIAC was established. With multiple updates in the past years, the present Expedited Procedure has been exclusively covered by Chapter VII of the BAC/BIAC Arbitration Rules. Specifically, Chapter VII governs the scope of the application of Expedited Procedure, the composition of the arbitral tribunal, the time limit for defense and counterclaim, the notice of hearing, the conversion from Expedited Procedure to Ordinary Procedure, the time limit for rendering the award, and the reference to other provisions.[10]

According to the BAC/BIAC 2022 Annual Report released recently, among the 8,421 cases accepted by BAC/BIAC in 2022, 6,734 cases have adopted the Expedited Procedure. By contrast, the Ordinary Procedure has been applied to only 1,466 cases.[11] In other words, roughly 80% of the cases brought to the BAC/BIAC in 2022 have been subject to expedited arbitration.

The sum in dispute does not exceed CNY 5,000,000 in most cases where the Expedited Procedure is applied. In the meantime, there are approximately 12 cases adopting the Expedited Procedure where the sum in dispute exceeds CNY 5,000,000. In these cases, the parties have agreed to apply the Expedited Procedure regardless of the dispute amount in their arbitration agreement in pursuit of efficiency. In addition, the parties in several cases agreed to adopt the Ordinary Procedure rather than the Expedited Procedure even if the sum in dispute does not exceed CNY 5,000,000. This usually happens where there is a series of disputes between the parties, and the result of one case might affect the results of other cases. If the first rendered award is negative to the respondent, the respondent may strategically request a procedural conversion despite the fact that the sum in dispute does not exceed CNY 5,000,000.[12]

8. *BAC/BIAC 2022 Annual Report*, the BAC/BIAC (20 March 2023), http://www.bjac.org.cn/english/news/view?id=4481. For comparison, CNY 97.04 billion is roughly equivalent to USD 13.27 billion or EUR 12.53 billion (according to the exchange rates as of 25 September 2023).
9. In 2022, the BAC/BIAC remained one of the top three arbitration institutions in Mainland China in terms of the amount in dispute. The other two institutions, the CIETAC and the SCIA, respectively with a dispute amount of CNY 126.9 billion and CNY 127.3 billion.
10. *BAC/BIAC Arbitration Rules*, the BAC/BIAC (unknown), https://www.bjac.org.cn/english/page/zc/guize_en2022.html#7a.
11. *See supra* n. 8.
12. CNY 5,000,000 is roughly equivalent to USD 684,000 or EUR 646,000 (according to the exchange rates as of 25 September 2023).

The average time from filing the case to rendering the award for cases applying the Expedited Procedure at BAC/BIAC in 2022 varies, depending on whether the cases fall within the domestic or cross-border type. For domestic expedited arbitration, the average time required to complete the entire expedited procedure was 174 days. For international expedited arbitration, the time required for the whole process was 202 days on average. As a comparison, the average days needed to complete the Ordinary Procedure for domestic and cross-border cases were respectively 222 days and 276 days. Lastly, the average length of time for all the case types with different procedures was 181 days.[13] The length of time required for expedited arbitration at BAC/BIAC in 2022 does not necessarily reflect normal situations, given that the routine operation of BAC/BIAC, along with the rest of the Chinese arbitral institutions, was significantly impacted by the outbreak of the COVID-19 pandemic since 2020.[14] Prior to 2020, the median duration from registration to conclusion at BAC/BIAC was 147.82 days for 2019[15] and 136.73 days for 2018 (expedited and ordinary procedure cases combined).[16]

According to the long-standing practice at BAC/BIAC, applications to convert arbitral proceedings between the Expedited Procedure and the Ordinary Procedure are extremely rare. Few of them are eventually approved.[17]

The primary issue for post-award proceedings that most concerns BAC/BIAC as well as other arbitral institutions in China is the lack of enforceability of the arbitration awards. The enforcement of awards represents the conversion of a favorable award into concrete relief for the claimant. In practice, certain factors may prevent the claimant from successfully doing so. One of the factors is the court sets aside an arbitral award. In terms of the rate of setting aside, only a very limited number of awards rendered by BAC/BIAC were set aside by the courts in 2022, taking up only a small portion of all the awards rendered. Specific to the awards made through the proceedings of the Expedited Procedure, the rate of setting aside is not evidently higher than the awards made through the proceedings of the Ordinary Procedure, if not lower. Furthermore, there was no reported BAC/BIAC case in 2022 where the setting aside of the rendered award was caused by the application of the Expedited Procedure itself. In no cases was an award rendered under the Expedited Procedure not enforced because of the losing party arguing it did not have a full and fair opportunity to present its evidence. As a comparison, the number of cases where the awards rendered are eventually unenforceable due to other reasons, such as the lack of recognition of the

13. This information is publicly unavailable. The author acquired the information through personal communication with the current staff at BAC/BIAC. The disclosure of the information is with their permission.
14. *See generally* Yuan Fang & Yan Wang, *Online Dispute Resolution during COVID-19: The Practice of Major Arbitral Institutions in China, in Covid-19 and International Business and Economic Law: China and a Changing World* (Kun Fan & Charlie Xiao-chuan Weng eds, 2023).
15. *2019 Annual Report*, the BAC/BIAC (20 May 2020), https://www.bjac.org.cn/english/news/view?id=3718.
16. *2018 Annual Report*, the BAC/BIAC (10 April 2019), https://www.bjac.org.cn/english/news/view?id=3408.
17. This information is publicly unavailable. The author acquired this information through the personal communication with the current staff at BAC/BIAC. The disclosure of this information is based upon their permission.

legal effects of delivering the awards via notarization, is dramatically higher than the number of cases where the awards rendered are set aside. There are usually several dozen awards made by the BAC/BIAC proven to be unenforceable each year, a number which is normally seven times higher than the number of the awards set aside every year.[18]

[B] Analysis of the BAC/BIAC Practice of Expedited Arbitration

A detailed analysis of BAC/BIAC expedited arbitration practice in combination with specific BAC/BIAC expedited rules and procedures shows the strengths that BAC/BIAC expedited arbitration practices possess. It also reveals the weaknesses it has in exercising the rules and procedures of expedited arbitration.

[1] The Strengths of BAC/BIAC Expedited Rules and Procedures

Evaluating the overall degree of satisfaction with BAC/BIAC expedited arbitration, BAC/BIAC's performance is generally satisfactory. This is especially true when looking at the factors for assessment such as whether the expedited rules have been circumvented by the parties or the tribunal and how these rules have been received by the reviewing courts.

[a] Circumvention of Expedited Proceedings

The practice at BAC/BIAC in 2022 has confirmed that the parties and the tribunal are more willing to embrace the expedited rules and procedures instead of circumventing them in any manner. As mentioned above, the percentage of cases to which the expedited arbitration procedure applied rocketed to nearly 80% in 2022, signaling that the expedited proceeding is preferable to an increasing number of stakeholders in arbitration. The reason why expedited arbitration at BAC/BIAC is gaining popularity simply lies in the fact that the threshold for the application of expedited procedures has been loosened since the BAC/BIAC revised its Arbitration Rules in 2019. Prior to 2019, expedited proceedings could apply if the sum in dispute did not exceed CNY 1,000,000.[19] In 2019, the sum in dispute was sharply increased to not exceeding CNY 5,000,000.[20] This adjustment has prompted the development of expedited arbitration at BAC/BIAC by significantly broadening the scope of its application. The other criteria for assessing whether the expedited arbitration rules have been circumvented is how well these rules are followed by the parties and the tribunal. Except for very occasional circumstances where the parties apply for the conversion from the expedited procedure

18. The information provided in this paragraph is not publicly available. The author acquired the information through the personal communication with the current staff at BAC/BIAC. The disclosure of the information is based upon their permission.
19. Article 53 of the BAC/BIAC Arbitration Rules (effective as of 1 April 2015).
20. Article 54 of the BAC/BIAC Arbitration Rules (effective as of 1 September 2019).

to the ordinary procedure, the long-lasting practice has shown consistent obedience by the parties and the tribunal to the BAC/BIAC expedited rules.[21]

[b] Review of Arbitration Awards by Courts

In considering whether the BAC/BIAC expedited rules and procedures have been well received by the courts, both the rate of setting aside and the enforceability issue should be considered. The extremely low probability that awards rendered via expedited proceedings might be set aside can be seen as evidence that the BAC/BIAC expedited rules and procedures are in good standing. Meanwhile, the relatively low likelihood that the awards made through expedited proceedings are held unenforceable by the court also highlights the generally satisfactory quality of the BAC/BIAC expedited rules and procedures.[22]

[2] The Weaknesses of the BAC/BIAC Expedited Rules and Procedures

Aside from their strengths, the BAC/BIAC expedited rules and procedures are simultaneously faced with challenges, especially within the areas of the scope of application, the time limits, and the procedure conversion.

[a] Scope of Application of Expedited Procedure

The BAC/BIAC expedited procedure applies where: (1) the amount in dispute does not exceed CNY 5,000,000 (unless otherwise agreed by the parties);[23] (2) the parties have agreed that the arbitration concerned shall be heard by a sole arbitrator (unless otherwise agreed by the parties);[24] (3) the parties have agreed to apply the expedited procedure even though the amount in dispute has exceeded CNY 5,000,000.[25] Although the current BAC/BIAC rules governing the scope of the application of expedited procedure have offered the flexibility for the parties to choose the types of procedures they expect to apply, the de facto threshold in relation to the amount in dispute plays an opposite role in this process. While the maximum amount in dispute has been increased from CNY 1,000,000 to CNY 5,000,000 to include more potential cases, the fact that only a very limited number of cases adopting the expedited proceedings have the amount in dispute over CNY 5,000,000 in 2022 indicates that the amount in dispute itself already constitutes a barrier to the further extension of the scope of the application of the expedited proceedings at the BAC/BIAC.

21. *See supra* n. 17.
22. *See supra* n. 18.
23. Article 54(1) of the BAC/BIAC Arbitration Rules (effective as of 1 February 2022).
24. Article 54(2) of the BAC/BIAC Arbitration Rules (effective as of 1 February 2022).
25. Article 54(3)(4) of the BAC/BIAC Arbitration Rules (effective as of 1 February 2022).

[b] *Time Limits for Expedited Procedure*

BAC/BIAC explicitly formulates the time limits for expedited proceedings within its rules governing the expedited procedure. For example, BAC/BIAC requires the parties to jointly nominate a sole arbitrator or jointly request the chairperson to appoint a sole arbitrator within 10 days of receipt of the notice of arbitration.[26] The respondent is required to submit its statement of defense and counterclaim (if any) to BAC/BIAC within 10 days of receipt of the request for submission of defense.[27] Finally, the arbitral tribunal shall render its award within 75 days from the date of its constitution.[28] As previously mentioned, the average time for BAC/BIAC expedited proceedings from the case filing to the award rendered is 174 days for domestic cases and 202 days for cross-border cases, both of which excessively go beyond the 75 days originally anticipated.[29] Even taking into account the influence of the COVID-19 pandemic and the length of time between the case filing and the constitution of the tribunal, the time actually spent for BAC/BIAC expedited proceedings is still disproportionately lengthy.

[c] *Change of Procedure*

BAC/BIAC stipulates that the expedited procedure is to be converted to the ordinary procedure primarily under two circumstances: (1) upon the joint request of the parties or upon the request of one party with the approval of the other parties;[30] (2) upon the request of the party which argues that the proceedings under the expedited procedure may be affected when the amendment to the claim, the submission of a counterclaim or any amendment have caused the amount in dispute to exceed CNY 5,000,000.[31] A certain degree of consistency concerning amount in dispute does exist among the different stages of the expedited proceedings. For example, since the BAC/BIAC expedited rules set the maximum amount in dispute for automatically applying the expedited proceedings as CNY 5,000,000, the minimum amount in dispute for quitting the expedited proceedings without joint agreement is CNY 5,000,000 as well. However, the existing BAC/BIAC rules pertaining to the change of procedure lack internal consistency because they distinguish two tremendously different premises for procedure conversion solely based on the amount in dispute. This distinction is unreasonable because it neglects the fact that it is essentially the difficulty of the case instead of the amount in dispute that determines the necessity of procedure conversion. Because the "CNY 5,000,000" requirement for the application of the expedited proceedings can be harmful to the expansion of the territory of expedited arbitration, the "CNY 5,000,000"-related requirement for the procedural conversion is an impediment to the prospective evolution of the expedited arbitration at the BAC/BIAC.

---

26. Article 55 of the BAC/BIAC Arbitration Rules (effective as of 1 February 2022).
27. Article 56 of the BAC/BIAC Arbitration Rules (effective as of 1 February 2022).
28. Article 59 of the BAC/BIAC Arbitration Rules (effective as of 1 February 2022).
29. *See supra* n. 13.
30. Article 58(1) of the BAC/BIAC Arbitration Rules (effective as of 1 February 2022).
31. Article 58(2) of the BAC/BIAC Arbitration Rules (effective as of 1 February 2022).

§16.03 THE EXAMINATION OF OTHER CHINESE ARBITRATION INSTITUTIONS

With a comprehensive understanding of the pros and cons of the BAC/BIAC expedited rules and procedures, what modifications or reforms should be sought to the expedited rules and procedures that have been adopted by the BAC/BIAC? Are the difficulties facing the BAC/BIAC expedited rules ubiquitous, or are they a reflection of the problems that are commonly seen in Chinese arbitral institutions? This section examines other Chinese arbitration institutions, specifically the China International Economic and Trade Arbitration Commission (hereinafter "CIETAC"), the China Maritime Arbitration Commission (hereinafter "CMAC"), the Shenzhen Court of International Arbitration (hereinafter "SCIA"), and the Shanghai International Arbitration Center (hereinafter "SHIAC"). While there are both convergence and divergence of the approaches to expedited arbitration that have been implemented by the various arbitral institutions, the following discussion will emphasize three aspects of each arbitral institution's expedited arbitration rules and procedures, namely the scope of application, the time limits, and the change of procedure.

[A] CIETAC Expedited Rules and Procedures

The CIETAC summary procedure applies to any case where: (1) the amount in dispute does not exceed CNY 5,000,000, unless otherwise agreed by the parties; (2) the amount in dispute exceeds CNY 5,000,000, yet one party applies for arbitration under the summary procedure and the other party agrees in writing; (3) both parties have agreed.[32]

With regard to the time limits for the expedited proceedings, CIETAC requires the respondent to submit its statement of defense, evidence and other supporting documents within 20 days of its receipt of the notice of arbitration. A counterclaim (if any) shall also be filed with evidence and supporting documents within the same time period. The claimant shall file its statement of defense to the respondent's counterclaim within 20 days of its receipt of the notice of acceptance of the counterclaim.[33] Additionally, the arbitral tribunal shall render an arbitral award within three months from the date on which the arbitral tribunal is formed.[34]

Regarding the change of procedure, CIETAC supports the continuation of the summary procedure despite the amendment of the claim or the filing of a counterclaim in excess of the claim limitation. Nevertheless, where the amount in dispute of the amended claim or that of the counterclaim exceeds CNY 5,000,000, the summary procedure is likely to be converted to the general procedure if the parties agree or the arbitral tribunal decides that a change to the general procedure is necessary.[35]

32. Article 59(1) of the CIETAC Arbitration Rules (effective as of 1 January 2024).
33. Article 62(1)(2) of the CIETAC Arbitration Rules (effective as of 1 January 2024).
34. Article 65(1) of the CIETAC Arbitration Rules (effective as of 1 January 2024).
35. Article 66 of the CIETAC Arbitration Rules (effective as of 1 January 2024).

[B] CMAC Expedited Rules and Procedures

The CMAC expedited rules and procedures shall apply to any case where: (1) the amount in dispute does not exceed CNY 5,000,000; (2) the amount in dispute exceeds CNY 5,000,000 but one party applies for arbitration under the expedited procedure and the other party consents in writing; or (3) both parties have agreed to adopt the expedited procedure.[36]

Concerning time limits, CMAC requires the respondent to submit its statement of defense, evidence and other supporting documents within 20 days of its receipt of the notice of arbitration. A counterclaim, if any, shall also be filed with evidence and supporting documents within the same time period.[37] The claimant is required to file its statement of defense to the respondent's counterclaim within 20 days after receipt.[38] The arbitral tribunal is required to render an arbitral award within three months from the date on which the arbitral tribunal is constituted.[39]

In terms of procedure conversion, the CMAC's position is that regardless of the amendment to the claim or the filing of a counterclaim, the expedited procedure shall continue. However, where the quantum of the dispute in the amended claim or counterclaim exceeds CNY 5,000,000, the expedited procedure may cease to apply upon the parties' agreement or the arbitral tribunal's decision that a change to the ordinary procedure is necessary.[40]

[C] SCIA Expedited Rules and Procedures

The SCIA expedited procedure shall apply to any case where: (1) the amount in dispute does not exceed CNY 3,000,000; (2) the amount in dispute exceeds CNY 3,000,000, but the parties agree in writing that the expedited procedure shall apply; or (3) the parties agree to apply the expedited proceedings.[41]

Concerning the time limits for the expedited proceedings, the SCIA expedited arbitration rules require the respondent to submit its statement of defense and evidentiary materials within 10 days after receipt of the notice of arbitration. The respondent must submit its counterclaim (if any) within 10 days after receipt of the notice of arbitration, and the claimant has to submit its statement of defense to the respondent's counterclaim within 10 days after receipt of the notice of acceptance of counterclaim.[42] Finally, SCIA requires the arbitral tribunal to render an arbitral award within two months from the date on which the arbitral tribunal is formed.[43]

With regard to the procedure conversion, the expedited procedure may be changed to the general procedure by SCIA upon one of the parties' request or the

36. Article 66(1) of the Rules of Arbitration of the CMAC (effective as of 1 October 2021).
37. Article 69(1) of the Rules of Arbitration of the CMAC (effective as of 1 October 2021).
38. Article 69(2) of the Rules of Arbitration of the CMAC (effective as of 1 October 2021).
39. Article 72(1) of the Rules of Arbitration of the CMAC (effective as of 1 October 2021).
40. Article 73 of the Rules of Arbitration of the CMAC (effective as of 1 October 2021).
41. Article 56(1) of the SCIA Arbitration Rules (effective as of 21 February 2019).
42. Article 57 of the SCIA Arbitration Rules (effective as of 21 February 2019).
43. Article 50(3) of the SCIA Arbitration Rules (effective as of 21 February 2019).

suggestion of the arbitral tribunal, and SCIA considers it necessary, where the amount in dispute of the amended claim or that of the counterclaim exceeds CNY 3,000,000.[44]

[D] SHIAC Expedited Rules and Procedures

The expedited procedures of SHIAC apply to any case where: (1) the amount in dispute does not exceed CNY 5,000,000; (2) the amount in dispute exceeds CNY 5,000,000, but with the written consent of the parties or the arbitration agreement stipulates that summary or expedited proceedings or other similar expressions are applicable.[45]

In terms of the time limits for the expedited procedures, SHIAC requires the respondent to submit its defense, relevant evidence, documents certifying the party's identity, and other supporting documents within 15 days upon the receipt of the notice of arbitration. If the respondent has counterclaims, the counterclaims should be submitted in writing within the same period of time. In addition, within 15 days upon the receipt of the notice of acceptance of counterclaim, the claimant shall submit its statement of defense to the respondent's counterclaim.[46] Apart from that, the arbitral tribunal is required by SHIAC to render the award within three months of the date the tribunal is constituted.[47]

Regarding the change of procedures, the application of the summary procedures should not be affected by any amendment to the claim or by the filing of or any amendment to a counterclaim.[48] However, the procedures of the case shall be changed from the summary procedures to the ordinary procedures where the amount in dispute of the amended claim or filing of or amendment of a counterclaim exceeds CNY 5,000,000.[49]

The expedited rules and procedures of CIETAC, CMAC, SCIA, and SHIAC reveal that the weaknesses of the BAC/BIAC expedited rules and procedures are also the difficulties facing the other primary Chinese arbitral institutions. While the maximum amount in dispute to be automatically considered for expedited arbitration varies from CNY 3,000,000 to CNY 5,000,000 among the institutions, the fact that all the institutions require a certain amount in dispute will inevitably impair their capabilities of further expanding the application of the expedited proceedings. Further, although all the representative Chinese arbitration institutions have set a relatively short period of time for the expedited procedures, ranging from two to three months between the constitution of the arbitral tribunal and the award rendered, the core inquiry here is essentially how well the arbitration participants can strictly adhere to the time limitations. Similarly, the parties will keep struggling with converting from expedited to ordinary procedures so long as the amount in dispute still plays a vital role in determining the permissibility of the change of procedure. These three problems that

44. Article 61(2) of the SCIA Arbitration Rules (effective as of 21 February 2019).
45. Article 69 of the SHIAC Arbitration Rules (effective as of 1 January 2024).
46. Article 71(1)(2) of the SHIAC Arbitration Rules (effective as of 1 January 2024).
47. Article 74(1) of the SHIAC Arbitration Rules (effective as of 1 January 2024).
48. Article 75(1) of the SHIAC Arbitration Rules (effective as of 1 January 2024).
49. Article 75(2) of the SHIAC Arbitration Rules (effective as of 1 January 2024).

the major Chinese arbitral institutions have encountered are urgently awaiting to be tackled.

§16.04 BRIDGING THE GAPS THROUGH A COMPARATIVE APPROACH

This section considers the aforementioned barriers to the development of expedited arbitration facing the Chinese arbitral institutions from a comparative perspective. The expedited arbitration rules of the representative Chinese institutions will be compared with the rules of the leading institutions across the globe, including the Singapore International Arbitration Centre (SIAC), the London Court of International Arbitration (LCIA), the International Centre for Dispute Resolution (ICDR), and the International Chamber of Commerce (ICC) International Court of Arbitration. The model rules of the United Nations Commission on International Trade Law (UNCITRAL) also are considered. Conclusions will be reached concerning which institution's approach to expedited arbitration is most appropriate for China under certain circumstances.

[A] Scope of Application of Expedited Procedure

Taking a deeper look at the practices of the global institutions pertaining to the scope of the application of expedited procedures, there are generally two different approaches. One approach is similar to those adopted by the Chinese arbitration institutions, where the amount in dispute matters in the determination of the application of the expedited proceedings. The other approach has nothing to do with the amount in dispute. Instead, it pays more attention to the parties' will.

[1] The Expedited Rules and Procedures Beyond China

Arbitral institutions like SIAC, ICDR and ICC adopt the first approach. According to the SIAC Arbitration Rules, one of the criteria for the application of the expedited procedure is that the amount in dispute does not exceed the equivalent of SGD 6,000,000.[50] Resembling SIAC, the ICDR stipulates that the expedited procedures shall apply in any case where no disclosed claim or counterclaim exceeds USD 500,000 (unless the parties agree or the administrator determines otherwise).[51] The ICC stipulates that the expedited proceedings shall apply if the amount in dispute does not exceed USD 2,000,000 or USD 3,000,000, depending on when the arbitration agreement was concluded.[52]

50. Article 5.1 of the SIAC Arbitration Rules (entered into force on 1 August, 2016). SGD 6,000,000 is roughly equivalent to USD 4,387,000 or EUR 4,143,700 (according to the exchange rates as of 25 September 2023).
51. Article 1(4) of the ICDR International Arbitration Rules (effective as of 1 March 2021).
52. Article 1(2) of the ICC Expedited Procedure Rules (entered into force on 1 January 2021); Article 30(2) of the ICC Arbitration Rules (entered into force on 1 January 2021).

On the contrary, the UNCITRAL model rules choose the second approach. Under the UNCITRAL Expedited Arbitration Rules that entered into force in 2021, the expedited procedures apply where parties have agreed that disputes between them in respect of a defined legal relationship, whether contractual or not, shall be referred to arbitration under the UNCITRAL Expedited Arbitration Rules.[53]

The LCIA is different from the other institutions examined and the UNCITRAL Expedited Arbitration Rules. The LCIA does not have expedited rules governing the entire process of arbitration and therefore does not raise any requirements in terms of the amount in dispute.[54]

[2] The Comparison of Different Expedited Arbitration Rules

The second approach adopted by the UNCITRAL Expedited Arbitration Rules is a better model for the reforms and revisions of the expedited rules and procedures of the Chinese arbitral institutions. Compared to the approach adopted by SIAC, the ICDR, and the ICC, removing the amount in dispute requirement from the existing rules provides more incentives for the parties to get involved in the expedited procedures, which will therefore facilitate the development of expedited arbitration. Indeed, the removal of the requirement of amount in dispute may not incentivize parties that always seek delay, but it provides a signal to the parties who seek to resolve disputes efficiently by encouraging them to use expedited proceedings without interference from the dispute amount.

[B] Time Limits for Expedited Procedure

A comparison of the variety of the time limits set for expedited arbitration by the various international arbitration institutions provides a useful framework for considering changes to the time limits set by Chinese arbitral institutions. The period of time for rendering the final award in particular is the subject of comparison to ensure a certain degree of uniformity among arbitral institutions.

[1] The Expedited Rules and Procedures Beyond China

The method used by the UNCITRAL model rules and SIAC for setting time limits for rendering the final award, which calculates the time between the arbitral tribunal's constitution and the award being rendered, is identical to the approach of the primary Chinese arbitration institutions. The UNCITRAL model expedited rules require the

53. Article 1 of the UNCITRAL Expedited Arbitration Rules (entered into force on 19 September 2021).
54. Article 9 of the LCIA Arbitration Rules (effective as of 1 October 2020).

arbitral award to be made within six months from the date of the constitution of the arbitral tribunal, unless otherwise agreed by the parties.[55] The related rules of SIAC are basically the same as UNCITRAL's.[56] The ICDR, however, sets the starting point of the time limit for rendering the final award as the date of the closing of the hearing or the time established for final written submissions. The award shall be made not later than 30 days from the closing date or deadline for final submissions.[57] The ICC utilizes another method for the calculation of the time for rendering the award. It requires the arbitral tribunal to render its final award within six months from the date of the case management conference.[58] The LCIA does not set any time limit for making the final award, given the lack of expedited rules and procedures.[59]

[2] The Comparison of Different Expedited Arbitration Rules

On the surface, the time limits set by the major international arbitration institutions for the expedited procedures are not stricter than those set by the Chinese arbitral institutions. Nonetheless, the key issue is how well the arbitral proceedings will be able to conform to these requirements. Some of the Chinese arbitration institutions do not perform very well regarding adherence to the time limits for expedited procedures. Therefore, further measures should be taken by Chinese arbitral institutions to urge the obedience of the arbitration participants to the time limits for expedited proceedings. The arbitration participants here include the parties, the arbitral tribunal and arbitrators as well as the participants involved in the arbitration proceedings in other ways. In essence, the time limit for expedited procedures can be followed only if the arbitration participants jointly engage in the efforts of expeditiously and efficiently advancing the proceedings.

[C] Change of Procedure

There are two distinguishable approaches for changing the procedure from expedited to ordinary procedures. The first approach, which is adopted by the UNCITRAL model expedited rules, SIAC, and the ICC, gives priority to the parties' will in determining the permissibility of change of procedure. The second approach, adopted by the ICDR, recognizes the importance of the amount in dispute in the determination of procedure conversion.

55. Article 16(1) of the UNCITRAL Expedited Arbitration Rules (entered into force on 19 September 2021).
56. Article 5.2 of the SIAC Arbitration Rules (entered into force on 1 August 2016).
57. Article E-10 of the ICDR International Expedited Procedures (effective as of 1 March 2021).
58. Article 4(1) of the ICC Expedited Procedure Rules (entered into force on 1 January 2021).
59. Article 26 of the LCIA Arbitration Rules (effective as of 1 October 2020).

[1] The Expedited Rules and Procedures Beyond China

The UNCITRAL model expedited arbitration rules provide one of the lowest thresholds for change of procedure. The UNCITRAL model rules allow the parties to change the procedure at any time during the proceedings as long as they agree that the expedited rules shall no longer apply to the arbitration. In addition, the arbitral tribunal may determine that the expedited rules shall no longer apply at the request of a party, with the precondition that the parties have been invited to express their views.[60] SIAC offers the tribunal freedom to order that the arbitral proceedings shall no longer be conducted in accordance with the expedited procedure upon application by a party after giving all the parties the opportunity to be heard.[61] The ICC, similarly, allows for its International Court of Arbitration to decide at any time that the expedited procedures shall no longer apply to the case, on its own motion or upon the request of a party, and after consulting with the arbitral tribunal and the parties.[62]

The second approach adopted by the ICDR gives less weight to the parties' will in determining the conversion of procedure. Within its rules regarding the objection to the applicability of the expedited procedures, the ICDR has made clear that the arbitrator should primarily look to the amount in dispute to make a final determination. The parties' autonomy, in contrast, will be taken into account merely as one of the "other relevant circumstances."[63]

[2] The Comparison of Different Expedited Arbitration Rules

The second approach, where more weight is given to the amount in dispute in the decision of change of procedure, is closer to the approach presently adopted by Chinese arbitral institutions. However, Chinese arbitration institutions should shift from the second approach to the first approach. To maintain the integrity of expedited arbitration, providing the parties the opportunities to "opt out" from the expedited proceedings is equally important to allowing them to "opt in." As the freedom to choose whether expedited proceedings will apply to any dispute incentivizes the parties' participation in expedited arbitration, the freedom to decide when the expedited proceedings shall cease to apply can also become an attraction for the parties to proceed with expedited arbitration. As a result, any requirement in relation to the amount in dispute should be removed from the existing expedited rules and procedures of Chinese arbitral institutions regarding the determination of change of procedure.

---

60. Article 2(1) of the UNCITRAL Expedited Arbitration Rules (entered into force on 19 September 2021).
61. Article 5.4 of the SIAC Arbitration Rules (entered into force on 1 August 2016).
62. Article 1(4) of the ICC Expedited Procedure Rules (entered into force on 1 January 2021).
63. Article E-4 of the ICDR International Expedited Procedures (effective as of 1 March 2021).

§16.05 CONCLUSION

International arbitration has been criticized as deviating from its foundation of expeditiously and efficiently resolving international disputes from a Chinese perspective. Taking BAC/BIAC as an example of the arbitral institutions in China for analysis, both the strengths and weaknesses of the BAC/BIAC practice of expedited arbitration have been examined. Deepening the exploration into some of the other Chinese arbitral institutions, the shortcomings in terms of scope of application of expedited proceedings, time limits for expedited procedure, and change of procedure are in common. A comparison of the expedited rules and procedures of Chinese arbitral institutions with those of the leading institutions in the world suggests the best practices for China under certain circumstances.

Chinese arbitral institutions should remove their "amount in dispute"-related requirements from the existing expedited rules and procedures so that the parties are more incentivized to participate in expedited proceedings. Specific measures should be sought by the Chinese arbitration institutions to guarantee the arbitration participants' adherence to the time limits set for expedited proceedings. Concerning the conversion of procedure, the requirements of Chinese arbitral institutions relating to the amount in dispute should be removed from the current expedited rules and procedures. The parties' freedom of conveniently leaving the expedited proceedings based upon consensus or the decision of the arbitral tribunal if only one party requests should be paramount.

Efforts should be made not only at the institutional level but more vitally at the legislative level to highlight the significant role expedited arbitration plays in advancing arbitral efficiency. Contrary to the reality that the practice of expedited proceedings in China can be dated to as early as 1994 by CIETAC, the mechanism of expedited arbitration has continuously been absent from Chinese legislation concerning arbitration.[64] It is also not reflected in the latest efforts to amend the existing laws governing arbitration.[65] The absence of expedited arbitration from Chinese legislation has constituted a legal barrier to the emergence of expedited procedures in China. Therefore, the mechanism of expedited arbitration should be incorporated into prospective amendments to the relevant laws. The affirmation of the legal status of expedited procedure will be beneficial to the enhancement of expedited arbitration in China, which in the end is likely to fuel the public's confidence in arbitration's promise of expeditiously and efficiently resolving disputes.

64. *See generally* The Arbitration Law of the People's Republic of China (amended on 1 September 2017, effective since 1 January 2018).
65. *See* The Arbitration Law of the People's Republic of China (Amendment) (Public Consultation), Ministry of Justice of the People's Republic of China (30 July 2021), https://npcobserver.com/wp-content/uploads/2020/11/Arbitration-Law-2021-Draft-Revision.pdf (in Chinese).

CHAPTER 17

The Development of Expedited Arbitration in the Offshore Space: An Examination of Expedited Arbitration in the British Virgin Islands, Bermuda and the Cayman Islands

Peter Ferrer, Marcia McFarlane & James Petkovic

This chapter explores the development of expedited arbitration procedures in the Overseas Territories of the United Kingdom, specifically the British Virgin Islands (BVI), Bermuda and the Cayman Islands. All three jurisdictions have adopted, with varying modifications, the UNCITRAL Model Law on International Commercial Arbitration, 1985. Nevertheless, the progress made in each jurisdiction to facilitate expedited arbitration varies. This chapter compares the procedures applicable in the BVI, Bermuda and the Cayman Islands to facilitate expedited arbitral proceedings. The chapter's thesis is that the more detailed procedure adopted in the BVI, and to a lesser extent Bermuda, is preferable to the higher-level and less detailed approach adopted in the Cayman Islands with respect to expedited arbitrations.

§17.01 INTRODUCTION

Cognisant of the need to enable urgent disputes to be resolved swiftly and cost-effectively, a number of major arbitral institutions have instituted rules to facilitate expedited proceedings. For instance, the UNCITRAL Expedited Arbitration Rules 2021 contain a detailed regime with the objective of 'settling disputes that arise in the context of international commercial relations ... in a cost- and time-effective manner'.[1] Similarly, the SIAC Rules 2016 (SIAC Rules) provide in Article 5 for an expedited procedure in cases of 'exceptional urgency'. The SIAC Rules provide for a sole arbitrator unless the president determines otherwise and for a final award to be made

1. UNCITRAL Expedited Arbitration Rules 2021 (26 September 2023), p. 1.

within six months from the date when the tribunal is constituted.[2] Where the rules of major arbitral institutions do not contain a detailed expedited arbitration regime, they may nonetheless provide for the expedited formation of a tribunal with powers to bridge periods of time which would otherwise apply. The London Court of International Arbitration (LCIA) rules adopt this approach.[3]

Not to be left behind by these developments in major arbitral centres such as Singapore and London, the British Virgin Islands (BVI), Bermuda and the Cayman Islands have also instituted procedures for expedited arbitrations in varying degrees. This chapter compares those expedition regimes. The chapter focuses particularly on the measures available for selecting a tribunal, the powers given to them, and the procedural rules available for conducting an arbitration, including the grant of preliminary relief and interim measures as well as the provisions available to achieve cost-efficiency.

The progress made in the development of expedited arbitration regimes in the BVI, Bermuda and the Cayman Islands varies. The BVI's regime is particularly advanced, with a detailed regime in place. Bermuda similarly has detailed rules, albeit these are less developed than the BVI's regime. The approach adopted in the Cayman Islands is a more basic one with less detail given by the relevant rules regarding the available expedited arbitration procedures. The better approach is that adopted by the BVI, and to a lesser extent Bermuda, where detailed expedited arbitration rules enable arbitral parties to know in advance the measures available on expedition. The more high-level and basic approach adopted by the Cayman Islands carries with it more uncertainty for the parties in an expedited arbitration.

§17.02 EXPEDITED ARBITRATION IN THE BVI

The BVI is a United Kingdom Overseas Territory located in the Caribbean to the east of Puerto Rico. It is a self-governing territory with its own parliament that is empowered to enact legislation as necessary. There are certain reserved powers such as defence and foreign policy that are retained by the United Kingdom government. In addition, the BVI is domicile to over 367,000 companies.[4] It is a holding company jurisdiction with assets held worldwide by BVI entities. The BVI legislature has ensured that public policy weighs heavily in favour of arbitration. Accordingly, the BVI courts are likely to grant stays in favour of arbitration and will grant orders in aid of the enforcement of final arbitral awards.[5]

2. SIAC Rules 2016 (26 September 2023), https://siac.org.sg/siac-rules-2016, Article 5.2.
3. For example, LCIA Arbitration Rules 2020 (26 September 2023), https://www.lcia.org/Dispute_Resolution_Services/lcia-arbitration-rules-2020.aspx#Article%209, Article 9A.
4. BVI Financial Services Commission (5 April 2023), https://www.bvifsc.vg/sites/default/files/q4_2022_statistical_bulletin_draft_final_version.pdf.
5. Eastern Caribbean Supreme Court, Territory of the Virgin Islands, BVIHCM2021/0192: *AB Limited, CD Limited, EF Limited v. GH Limited*, 27 January 2023.

[A] The Legislative Framework for Arbitration in the BVI

The Arbitration Act 2013 (BVI 2013 Act) repealed and replaced the 1976 Arbitration Ordinance. The BVI 2013 Act adopts, with some modifications, the provisions of the UNCITRAL Model Law on International Commercial Arbitration 1985 (the 'UNCITRAL Model Law') and applies to both domestic and international arbitrations.

The BVI has its own International Arbitration Centre (BVI IAC), established by the BVI 2013 Act and benefitting from the financial and political support of the Government of the Virgin Islands. The BVI IAC is comprised of a Secretariat and is governed by the British Virgin Islands International Arbitration Centre Board (BVI IAC Board), led by the chief executive officer.[6] The BVI IAC Board initially passed the BVI IAC Arbitration Rules dated 16 November 2016 (BVI 2016 Rules). However, to keep abreast of the evolving needs of arbitration, the BVI IAC comprehensively reviewed its BVI 2016 Rules and passed new arbitration rules on 16 November 2021 (2021 BVI IAC Rules). The revised 2021 BVI IAC Rules are intended to be responsive to the needs of its users and tribunals so they can remain on par with the demands of technological developments. The 2021 BVI IAC Rules therefore encourage the adoption of environment-friendly measures in arbitration which include the use of remote hearings and electronic filing platforms.

Parties are not required to adopt the 2021 BVI IAC Rules when arbitrating in the BVI.[7] However, the rules dovetail neatly with the governing BVI 2013 Act in providing detailed provisions in respect of expedited arbitral proceedings, which can save time and expense in the resolution of disputes. This provides an incentive for the adoption of the 2021 BVI IAC Rules by potential parties.

[B] Expedited Arbitration Proceedings in the BVI

The availability of expedited proceedings to resolve urgent disputes in a timely and cost-effective manner accords with a key stated objective of arbitration in the BVI, stated in section 44 of the BVI 2013 Act. Section 44 provides that the parties and tribunals are to use procedures that are appropriate to the particular case, avoiding unnecessary delay or expense so as to provide a fair means for resolving the dispute to which the arbitral proceedings relate.[8]

Appendix 2 of the 2021 BVI IAC Rules neatly dovetails with the objective set down in section 44 of the BVI 2013 Act and provides for an expedited procedure which can override any contrary terms of the parties' arbitration agreement.[9] The overriding objective of the expedited regime in Appendix 2 is to provide a procedure that is timely,

6. BVI International Arbitration Centre (31 March 2023), https://bviiac.org/Media-News/Press-Releases/Article/ID/153/British-Virgin-Islands-International-Arbitration-Centre-Announces-New-CEO-Shan-M-Greer-an-international-arbitrator-from-Arbitra-International#: ~ :text = January% 2027% 2C% 202023,Greer% 20as% 20CEO.
7. Article 1 of the 2021 BVI IAC Rules expressly provides that the rules apply where the parties have agreed that disputes between them shall be governed by the rules.
8. BVI Arbitration Act 2013, section 44.
9. 2021 BVI IAC Rules, 2021, Appendix 2, Article 1.

cost-effective and fair, considering especially the amount in dispute and the complexity of the issues and facts involved.[10]

The 2021 BVI IAC Rules provide when the expedited procedure is to apply, giving the parties a high degree of certainty in this regard. The procedure applies if any one of three factors is met, specifically: (1) the amount in dispute does not exceed USD 4,000,000, representing the aggregate of the claim, counterclaim and any defence or set-off or cross-claim; (2) the parties agree; or (3) the arbitration committee determines this is appropriate, in circumstances where, prior to the constitution of the arbitral tribunal, a party applies to the Secretariat for the arbitration to be conducted in accordance with the expedited procedure. The arbitration committee will determine the application by considering: (a) the views of the parties and (b) the circumstances of the case, specifically whether it is a case of exceptional urgency warranting the expedited procedure.[11]

The 2021 BVI IAC Rules also set out three circumstances in which the expedited procedures will not apply. They are: (1) if the arbitration agreement was concluded before the date on which the expedited procedure came into force, that is, 16 November 2021; (2) the parties agree to opt out of the expedited procedure; or (3) on the application of a party before an arbitral tribunal is formed, if the arbitration committee determines that it is inappropriate in the circumstances to apply the expedited procedure.[12]

In addition to providing the parties with a high degree of certainty when the expedited procedures will apply, a key strength of the 2021 BVI IAC Rules is that they specify when an award is to be rendered. The rules stipulate that an award is to be rendered within six months from the date the Secretariat transmitted the case file to the tribunal. The Secretariat may extend the time beyond six months for rendering an award only in exceptional circumstances.[13] The six-month time limit is facilitated by Article 5(2) of Appendix 2, which permits the arbitral tribunal in an expedited proceeding to deliver the reasons on which the final award is based in summary form. This thereby enables the faster issuance of awards by arbitral tribunals than if they had to formulate more detailed reasons.

The selection of the tribunal under the expedited procedure is also designed to facilitate the swift issuance of an award. Article 3 of Appendix 2 provides that the case shall be referred to a sole arbitrator unless the arbitration committee determines otherwise. The parties are to agree on this sole arbitrator in a time limit set down by the Secretariat, failing which the arbitrator shall be appointed by the CEO of the BVI IAC within as short a time as possible.[14] The default provision for a sole arbitrator enables an award to be rendered more rapidly than might otherwise be the case if a larger panel of arbitrators had to conclave in order to come to a decision.

10. *Ibid.*, Article 1(2).
11. *Ibid.*, Article 2(1).
12. *Ibid.*, Article 2(3).
13. *Ibid.*, Article 5.
14. *Ibid.*, Article 3.

The expedited procedure in the 2021 BVI IAC Rules also provides detailed case management provisions designed to ensure the swift resolution of disputes. The Secretariat may abbreviate time limits otherwise stipulated by the rules. After consulting the parties, the arbitral tribunal may dispense with a hearing, the examination of witnesses and experts, and determine that the dispute shall be decided on the basis of documentary evidence only.[15] This is in contrast to the non-expedited procedure, where a tribunal is required to hold a hearing for the presentation of evidence, witnesses and experts or for oral argument if at an appropriate stage of the proceedings any party so requests.[16]

In addition, the arbitral tribunal has, under Article 4 of Appendix 2, a discretion to adopt the procedural measures it considers appropriate. In consultation with the parties, the arbitral tribunal may decide not to allow requests for document production and limit the number, length and scope of written submissions and written evidence submitted by witnesses and experts. The first procedural conference stipulated by Article 4 should be convened no later than 10 days from the date on which the case was transmitted to the arbitral tribunal. The Secretariat has the power to extend this time if this is deemed necessary or the arbitral tribunal requests it.[17] These expedited measures are in contrast to the statelier procedure adopted in non-expedited proceedings. For instance, Article 26 of the 2021 BVI IAC Rules in a non-expedited context permits a period not generally exceeding 45 days for the communication of written statements of case with the potential to extend that time limit if the tribunal considers it justified.[18]

A further measure to encourage expedition is the requirement in Article 4(2) of Appendix 2 that once the tribunal is constituted, no party shall make new claims or counterclaims unless it is authorised by the arbitral tribunal. In deciding whether to permit new claims, the tribunal shall consider the nature of such claims, the stage of the arbitration, any delay and cost implications, and any prejudice to other parties. Article 4(2) of Appendix 2 accordingly prevents a party from derailing the expedited process by seeking to introduce new claims leading to the ballooning of the dispute.

The expedited regime in Appendix 2 of the 2021 BVI IAC Rules does not contain provisions specifically targeted to interim measures. However, Article 27 of the rules grants wide powers to the tribunal to institute interim measures 'at any time prior to the issuance of the final award by which the dispute is finally decided'.[19] There is, therefore, no reason why an arbitral tribunal could not grant interim measures under the wide powers contained in Article 27 even when undertaking an expedited procedure.

A particular strength of the 2021 BVI IAC Rules is the clarity it affords with regard to costs. The expedited regime states that the fees of the arbitral tribunal shall be fixed

15. *Ibid.*, Article 4.
16. 2021 BVI IAC Rules, 2021, Article 19(4).
17. 2021 BVI IAC Rules, 2021, Appendix 2, Article 4.
18. 2021 BVI IAC Rules, 2021, Article 26.
19. *Ibid.*, Article 27.

according to the schedule set out in Annex C to the rules.[20] Annex C provides a detailed schedule, including the maximum amount that can be paid to one arbitrator depending on the sums in dispute. Annex C, which also applies in a non-expedited context,[21] accordingly provides parties entering into arbitration governed by the 2021 BVI IAC Rules with further certainty, in particular regarding the fees which arbitrators can incur for their services. A cap on fees should also encourage arbitrators to attempt to resolve disputes in a timely manner.

The BVI thus has a detailed regime which allows for expedited arbitration and which provides the parties with certainty and clarity as to the applicable procedure, should proceedings be expedited. The rules are carefully designed to ensure that the arbitration is conducted in a timely and cost-effective manner.

§17.03 EXPEDITED ARBITRATION IN BERMUDA

Bermuda is Britain's oldest and smallest Overseas Territory. It is internally self-governed (except for external affairs and defence). It is located 600 miles east of the nearest mainland of the USA's North Carolina and 900 miles north of the Caribbean.[22] According to the World Bank,[23] Bermuda ranks as one of the top four jurisdictions in the world in gross national income per capita. Bermuda is an important strategic offshore business jurisdiction, providing domicile to thousands of multinational companies and corporations largely from the USA, Canada, Europe, Russia and Hong Kong. These companies provide services in aviation, computers, investment, insurance and reinsurance, pharmaceuticals, oil, property (real estate), shipping, software, unit trust and other companies. Bermuda's total land area is 21 square miles, that is, 56 kilometres, comprising a cluster of small islands (6 main islands and 120 others) in the North West Atlantic Ocean. At the end of 2019, there were 63,908 resident adults and children.[24]

The insurance and reinsurance industries are the major source of international arbitration activity in Bermuda. However, arbitration clauses in these types of contracts do not usually provide for any arbitral institution to administer arbitrations with a Bermuda seat. In the authors' experience, the Appointments Committee of the Bermuda Branch of the Chartered Institute of Arbitrators is used as an appointing body. Also, in the authors' experience, London is often preferred as the seat of the arbitration in liability insurance policies written in 'Bermuda Form'.

Bermuda does not have a dedicated centre for holding arbitrations. Therefore, there is an increased administrative cost incurred in renting a location. In addition, there are few resident arbitrators who are suitably qualified in Bermuda arbitrations. Most arbitration clauses in Bermudan law agreements require that the arbitrator holds an executive position in the insurance/reinsurance industry. This results in few

20. 2021 BVI IAC Rules, 2021, Appendix 2, Article 5(3).
21. 2021 BVI IAC Rules, 2021, Article 47.
22. Bermuda Online (28 March 2023), https://bermuda-online.org/.
23. *Ibid.*, http://data.worldbank.org/country/bermuda.
24. *Ibid.*, http://www.bermuda-online.org/population.htm.

arbitrations being held in Bermuda. Indeed, even where Bermuda is the designated seat of the arbitration, the hearings are often held in London. Practically and logistically, it is generally more convenient for parties involved to attend arbitrations in London.

[A] The Legislative Framework for Arbitration in Bermuda

The Government of Bermuda has passed two statutes to cater to the jurisdiction's arbitration needs: (1) the Arbitration Act 1986 (Bermuda Act 1986), which applies to domestic disputes and (2) the Bermuda International Conciliation and Arbitration Act 1993 (BICA 1993), which applies to international commercial arbitrations. The BICA 1993 adopts, without significant modifications, the UNCITRAL Model Law.

Parties to an international commercial arbitration may expressly agree that the Bermuda Act 1986 will apply. The Bermuda Act 1986 is based on the UK Arbitration Acts 1950 to 1979 and remains in force. It applies, absent party agreement to the contrary, to any arbitration which names Bermuda as its seat and is not governed by BICA 1993.[25]

There are no mandatory rules for the conduct of arbitrations under BICA 1993. Pursuant to Article 18 of the UNCITRAL Model Law, the prevailing position is that parties are to be treated equally and given a fair opportunity to present their respective case. The Bermuda Act 1986 provides that unless a contrary intention is expressed in an arbitration agreement, where an arbitration is held in Bermuda, the proceedings shall be governed by the procedural law of Bermuda.[26] There are no stated objectives in the Bermuda Act 1986. However, the aim of BICA 1993 is to provide for the conduct of international commercial conciliations and arbitrations and the recognition and enforcement of foreign arbitral awards in Bermuda and for connected matters.[27]

[B] Expedited Arbitration Proceedings in Bermuda

Neither the BICA 1993 nor the Bermuda Act 1986 provides regimes by which arbitrators can conduct expedited arbitration. Notably, however, the key CIArb Arbitration Rules (Bermuda) 2019 (2019 CIArb Rules) are supplemented by an expedited arbitration regime contained in the CIArb Cost-Controlled Expedited Arbitration Rules (Bermuda) (May 2019) (CCEA Rules). In disputes governed by the 2019 CIArb Rules, arbitrators can choose to apply the CCEA Rules when, among other things, a dispute is over USD 250,000 and the parties have not opted out of the rules applying.[28] Accordingly, the

25. Section 29 of the BICA 1993 provides: 'Where the parties to an arbitration agreement have, whether in the agreement or in any other document in writing, agreed that any dispute that has arisen or may arise between them is not to be settled in accordance with the Model Law, the Model Law does not apply in relation to the settlement of that dispute and in such a case unless otherwise agreed in writing by the parties the Arbitration Act 1986 shall apply.'
26. Bermuda Act, 1986, section 19.
27. BICA 1993, recital.
28. CIArb Bermuda Chapter (31 March 2023), https://www.ciarb.org/media/4854/ciarb-cost-controlled-expedited-arbitration-rules-bermuda-final.pdf, Article 1.

2019 CIArb Rules in effect have an expedition regime, albeit one contained in a separate document, specifically the CCEA Rules.

The CCEA Rules are designed to apply to arbitrations of any value, including high-value arbitrations. The CCEA Rules have mandatory application if the parties agreed to arbitration under the 2019 CIArb Rules, the arbitration agreement was concluded after 1 June 2019 and (a) the value of the claim does not exceed USD 250,000 or (b) the parties have agreed that they will apply the CCEA Rules regardless of the amount in dispute.[29]

If the dispute is over USD 250,000 and, although this is not expressly stated in the rules, the parties have not reached agreement either way on whether the CCEA Rules should apply, the arbitrator can then determine whether to apply the CCEA Rules or the 2019 CIArb Rules. In making this decision, the arbitrator can take into account considerations such as whether it is in the interest of the fair and efficient resolution of the dispute to do so, the need to treat parties fairly, and the need to give each party a reasonable opportunity to present its case.[30] As with the 2021 BVI IAC Rules, the CCEA Rules give parties the opportunity to opt out of the expedited regime.[31]

Assuming the CCEA Rules apply, they then provide for useful steps in support of expedition. Under the CCEA Rules, a sole arbitrator shall conduct the arbitration.[32] Promptly after being appointed, the arbitrator shall consult with the parties and shall establish a timetable setting out the various steps to be followed in the arbitration.[33] The arbitration shall proceed on a documents-only basis, unless the arbitrator determines that a hearing is appropriate, in which case the arbitration shall not exceed one day unless the arbitrator determines otherwise.[34]

The arbitrators and parties are to act in the spirit of the CCEA Rules to make every effort to expedite the arbitration process.[35] The arbitrators and parties may use electronic means to communicate and serve documents.[36] Within 28 days of the arbitrator's appointment, the claimant is to provide the respondent with its written statement of claim and provide the arbitrator with all documents, witness statements and expert reports on which it relies.[37] The defendant has 28 days from service of the claim to file its defence or counterclaim. The claimant is given 28 days from the service of the defence to file a reply.[38] The arbitrator will then consider the appropriate directions to be given, including which witnesses and experts should be heard and how the examination should take place.

In respect of interim measures, Article 26 of the 2019 CIArb Rules contains extensive provision in this regard, including measures for the preservation of assets

29. CIArb Bermuda Chapter (31 March 2023), https://www.ciarb.org/media/4854/ciarb-cost-controlled-expedited-arbitration-rules-bermuda-final.pdf, Article 1.1 and 1.2.
30. *Ibid.*, Article 1.2.
31. *Ibid.*, Articles 1.1 and 1.2; cf. 2021 BVI IAC Rules, Appendix 2, rule 3(b).
32. *Ibid.*, Article 2.
33. *Ibid.*
34. *Ibid.*, Article 5.1.
35. *Ibid.*, Article 2.
36. *Ibid.*
37. *Ibid.*, Article 3.
38. *Ibid.*

and evidence.[39] These can be applied when following an expedited procedure under the CCEA Rules. Article 1.1 of the CCEA Rules provides that the 'provisions of the [2019 CIArb Rules] shall apply except to the extent that these [CCEA Rules] provide otherwise'.[40]

Article 6 of the CCEA Rules provides that the final award is to be delivered within 180 days from the date on which the arbitrator was appointed. The arbitrator may, in exceptional circumstances, extend that time by a further 30 days. If more time is required, the extension request must be escalated to the Chair of the Bermuda Branch of the CIArb.[41] As will be readily apparent, the 180-day default deadline provided by the CCEA Rules is broadly comparable to the default six-month deadline provided in Appendix 2, Article 5 of the 2021 BVI IAC Rules. Both the BVI and Bermudan regimes sensibly provide for the potential of an extension should 180 days (Bermuda) or six months (BVI) prove insufficient.

Regarding costs, the CCEA Rules ensure that there is clarity in expedited arbitrations. The general position is set out in Article 4, which provides that legal fees recoverable by parties are capped at 15% of the total amount in dispute. The arbitrator's fees are capped at 10% of the total amount in dispute. A party may recover other incurred costs if the arbitrator determines that those costs are reasonable.[42]

Overall, the CCEA Rules share many of the commendable features of the BVI expedition regime. They provide for the swift resolution of disputes in an approximately six-month time frame and contain provisions for the control of costs which will no doubt be welcomed by parties. While the 2019 CIArb Rules do not explicitly provide for an expedited procedure, they are supplemented by the CCEA Rules which potentially apply where the parties have agreed to arbitration under the 2019 CIArb Rules and the requirements in Articles 1.1 and 1.2 of the CCEA Rules are satisfied. While the 2021 BVI IAC Rules are preferable to the Bermudan regime, the two expedition regimes share many features which parties are likely to welcome in facilitating the cost-efficient and timely resolution of disputes.

The CIArb Expedited Arbitration Rules (Bermuda) (May 2019) (EA Rules) should also be mentioned. These rules target disputes of a relatively low value, where the amount claimed is less than USD 50,000.[43] They are, accordingly, of limited relevance to international commercial arbitration, and the main provisions will only be briefly summarised.

The EA Rules provide for short statements of the case and witness statements not exceeding 5,000 words, with a sole arbitrator issuing an award in less than 90 days after their appointment.[44] Costs are also carefully controlled. The initial fee on the commencement of the arbitration is USD 1,500 each for the applicant and respondent.[45]

39. CIArb Bermuda Chapter (31 March 2023), CIArb Rules, Article 26.
40. *Ibid.*, https://www.ciarb.org/media/4854/ciarb-cost-controlled-expedited-arbitration-rules-bermuda-final.pdf,Article 1.1.
41. *Ibid.*, Article 6.2.
42. *Ibid.*, Article 4.
43. *Ibid.*
44. *Ibid.*, p. 1.
45. *Ibid.*, Articles 4 and 5.

Article 12 of the EA Rules provides that 'it is for the arbitrator to decide if one side can recover from the other any costs of the arbitration, which includes the arbitral fees and reasonable legal fees. Unless the parties agree otherwise, one side shall not however recover more than the arbitral fees plus a further $3,000 towards their legal costs'.[46] On the authors' reading of the rules, they accordingly provide for a default maximum of USD 4,500 to be recovered from the opposing party, unless the parties have agreed otherwise (i.e., adding the figures of USD 1,500 and USD 3,000 referred to in this paragraph).

The EA Rules therefore also provide for a timely and efficient expedition procedure. Nonetheless, the EA Rules are designed to apply to low-value claims and so are of limited relevance to international commercial arbitration.

§17.04 EXPEDITED ARBITRATION IN THE CAYMAN ISLANDS

The Cayman Islands is the fifth-largest banking centre in the world and one of the world's leading international financial centres. The Cayman Islands has over 28,000[47] investment funds and is home to many of the world's biggest funds, both hedge and private equity. As a consequence, the disputes commonly adjudicated in the Cayman Islands arise out of fraud and mismanagement of funds, contentious valuations of underlying assets, and disputes arising from the entitlement to and/or the quantum of management or carry fees, breaches of partnership agreements and winding-up of funds. However, the Cayman courts see a variety of litigation beyond funds disputes, including shareholder and director disputes, insolvency, contentious probate, and trust litigation.

The Cayman courts have developed an increasingly pro-arbitration stance and will, therefore, stay proceedings that are commenced in breach of an arbitration agreement.[48] For example, in *FamilyMart China Holding Co Ltd v. Ting Chuan (Cayman Islands) Holding Corporation* [2023] UKPC 33, the Privy Council granted a stay in favour of arbitration despite the fact that remedy of winding up of a company could only be granted by a Court. In essence, the Privy Council held that the Court could be bound by the arbitral tribunal's decision in respect of matters susceptible to arbitration (such as whether a loss of trust and confidence and an irretrievable breakdown in the relationship had occurred). Similarly, *In R*e Grand State Investments Limited,[49] the court dismissed an application to liquidate a company and appoint provisional liquidators on the basis of its failure to pay a debt. The company's defence was that the debt was disputed, and in any event, the parties had agreed, through a shareholders' agreement, to resolve their disputes by arbitration. The court dismissed the application, being satisfied that there was a substantial dispute that the debt was payable, and confirmed that, in any event, it would have stayed the claim in favour of

46. *Ibid.*, Article 12.
47. Cayman Islands Monetary Authority, December 2022 Fact Sheet (30 March 2023), https://www.cima.ky/upimages/publicationdoc/CIMAFACTSHEET-De_1679336692.pdf.
48. Cayman Islands Arbitration Act, 2012, section 9.
49. Cayman Islands Grand Court, Unreported, FSD 11 of 2021, 28 April 2021.

arbitration. Further, in the recent case of *In Re Civ Nebula (Cayman) Limited,*[50] the court stayed proceedings brought in the Cayman Islands in breach of agreements to arbitrate in Hong Kong. The decision reaffirmed commercial parties' freedom to contract and the willingness of the Cayman courts to hold parties to their contractual bargains. It also demonstrated that the Cayman Islands' liberal and broad approach to interpreting the construction and enforcement of arbitration agreements is consistent with other common law jurisdictions.

Despite a history of favouring arbitration in the Cayman courts, the arbitration industry in the Cayman Islands is still in its infancy. The long-awaited Cayman International Mediation and Arbitration Centre (CI-MAC) finally opened its doors in January 2023. Its mission statement is 'to help develop the Cayman Islands into a well-recognized seat and venue for international and domestic arbitration and mediation in the Caribbean, the Americas, and beyond'.[51] CI-MAC published its Arbitration Rules (CI-MAC Rules) very recently, in March 2023. The CI-MAC Rules seek to incorporate and build on the best elements of the rules of more established arbitration institutions, including creating a mechanism for parties to apply for expedited arbitration where there is an agreement between the parties or in exceptional circumstances.[52]

The Cayman Islands' court system has operated effectively and efficiently, producing sound and timely decisions. In some respects, therefore, that has slowed the development of arbitration in the jurisdiction. There has always been a flow of Cayman-seated or Cayman law-governed arbitrations, but the recent opening of CI-MAC is indicative of a steady increase in the number of arbitrations touching the jurisdiction. Anecdotal reports from local practitioners suggest there is increasing interest from clients in using arbitration as their agreed dispute resolution mechanism, and the number of arbitrations seems likely only to increase.

[A] The Legislative Framework for Arbitration in the Cayman Islands

Arbitration in the Cayman Islands is governed by the Arbitration Act 2012 (Cayman Act). The Cayman Act is supplemented by the Grand Court Rules which contain procedural rules specifically governing the court's practice in relation to arbitration.[53] The Cayman Act closely follows the UNCITRAL Model Law and the English Arbitration Act 1996 and incorporates some aspects of the arbitration legislation from Hong Kong and Singapore. The Cayman Islands is also a party to the New York Convention on the Recognition and Enforcement of Foreign Arbitral Awards, which has been localised by the Foreign Arbitral Awards Enforcement Law (1997 Revision) (FAAEL).[54] Applications in aid of

50. Cayman Islands Grand Court, Unreported, FSD 210 of 2022 (16 February 2023).
51. Cayman International Mediation & Arbitration Centre Ltd (30 March 2023), https://www.caymanarbitration.com/about-us.
52. *Ibid.*, the CI-MAC Rules (rule 5).
53. Official Cayman Gazette (31 March 2023), Grand Court Rules – Vol. 1 – Orders (2023 Revision), http://gazettes.gov.ky/portal/pls/portal/docs/1/13242597.PDF, order 73.
54. Conyers Dill & Pearman, *Cayman Islands Company & Commercial Law,* Sweet & Maxwell HK, 2nd ed., 2019, 17.150.

arbitration or to enforce an arbitration award pursuant to the Cayman Act must be commenced in the Financial Services Division of the Grand Court.[55]

The Cayman Act is founded on three principles set out in section 3 and which accord with allowing for an expedited approach to encourage the timely and cost-effective resolution of disputes. These principles are summarised below:

(1) impartiality and the fair resolution of a dispute by a neutral tribunal without any undue delay or expense;
(2) party autonomy subject only to public policy restrictions;[56] and
(3) limited court intervention.[57]

[B] Expedited Arbitration under the CI-MAC Rules in the Cayman Islands

Unlike the BVI and Cayman Islands which provide detailed expedition regimes, the CI-MAC Rules are far sparser in their provision for expedited proceedings. As the authors read the CI-MAC Rules, the expedited procedure is confined to one article, Article 5, of the CI-MAC Rules. In the authors' view, Article 5 is far more of high level than the extensive regimes provided for in the BVI and Cayman Islands.

Parties may apply to CI-MAC to invoke the expedited procedure for their arbitration.[58] The expedited procedure may be engaged by agreement of both parties or in exceptional circumstances, by CI-MAC on the application of only one party.[59] CI-MAC cannot decide to conduct an arbitration by the expedited procedure of its own accord; this must be initiated at least by one party.[60]

Under the CI-MAC Rules, a party requesting expedited arbitration must notify the other party and outline the grounds for the exceptional urgency requiring the expedited formation of the tribunal.[61] CI-MAC will review the application as soon as possible and modify any time limits specified in the rules or agreed between the parties in order to expedite the arbitration. The CI-MAC Rules do not provide any details as to what constitutes 'exceptional urgency' or what other criteria it may apply to determine whether an expedited arbitration should be permitted.[62] This is in contrast to the

55. Official Cayman Gazette (31 March 2023), Grand Court Rules Vol. 1 – Orders (2023 Revision), O.72 r.1 (2)(m), http://gazettes.gov.ky/portal/pls/portal/docs/1/13242597.PDF rule 2(n).
56. Cayman Islands Law Report, *Re Cybernaut Growth Fund, LP*, [2014] 2 CILR 413.
57. Cayman Islands Arbitration Act 2012, section 3(3) and *Appalachian Reinsurance (Bermuda) Ltd v. Greenlight Reinsurance Ltd* [2014] 1 CILR 152.
58. Cayman International Mediation & Arbitration Centre Ltd (30 March 2023), the CI-MAC Rules, https://www.caymanarbitration.com/arbitrationrules2023, Article 5.
59. *Ibid.*
60. Article 1 of the UNCITRAL Arbitral Rules homepage website draws particular attention to the fact that the express consent of the parties is required to engage the expedited procedure under the model law. *See*: https://uncitral.un.org/en/texts/arbitration/contractualtexts/arbitration.
61. Cayman International Mediation & Arbitration Centre Ltd (30 March 2023), the CI-MAC Rules, https://www.caymanarbitration.com/arbitrationrules2023, Article 5.
62. *Ibid.*, Article 5.2.

detailed provisions available in the BVI and Bermuda which clearly state when the expedited procedures will be available.

The CI-MAC Rules provide no guidance regarding the procedure which should be adopted once CI-MAC has decided the matter is one appropriate for expedition. The parties, therefore, face an uncertainty as to what procedure CI-MAC will decide to institute in the event it determines expedition is appropriate. Curiously, the CI-MAC rules state that if the application for expedition is granted, 'CI-MAC may modify any time limits specified in the Rules or in any prior agreement between the Parties in order to expedite the formation of the Tribunal' but do not state what other steps the Tribunal is permitted to take on an expedited procedure.[63] For instance, the CI-MAC Rules do not state, in contrast to the BVI[64] and Bermudan regimes,[65] that oral hearings can be abandoned in an expedited procedure. Indeed, Article 19.1 of the CI-MAC Rules states that a hearing 'shall' take place on the merits of the dispute, including jurisdictional issues 'unless the parties agree otherwise or as otherwise provided in these rules'.[66] The lack of specificity in the CI-MAC Rules regarding what steps are permitted on the expedited procedure may give rise to disputes between the parties as to what the Tribunal is permitted to order. However, this risk is to some extent ameliorated by the wide discretion given to the Tribunal in the conduct of the arbitration in the CI-MAC Rules, and in particular Article 12.1, which provides, 'Subject to these Rules, the Tribunal will conduct the arbitration in a manner it deems appropriate … .'[67] Article 12.4 also states that 'the Tribunal may, subject to these Rules, make any procedural order it considers appropriate with regard to the fair, efficient and expeditious conduct of the arbitration'.[68]

As for interim measures, Articles 23 and 26 of the CI-MAC Rules give the Tribunal a wide degree of powers, including for the preservation of assets and the delivery of evidence.[69] These provisions are similar to those which exist in the BVI and Bermuda. No reason exists why they could not be used in the expedited procedure.

There is no time frame specified for when a tribunal should render a decision in an expedited context under the CI-MAC Rules.[70] However, rule 5.3 provides that CI-MAC may modify any time limits specified in the Rules or any prior agreement between the parties in order to expedite the formation of the tribunal. It can therefore be inferred from CI-MAC rule 28 that a tribunal conducting expedited arbitration should render its award in a shorter time frame than is stipulated for ordinary circumstances.[71] In ordinary circumstances, a tribunal is required to communicate an

63. *Ibid.*, Article 5.
64. 2021 BVI IAC Rules, 2021, Appendix 2, Article 4.
65. CIArb Bermuda Chapter (31 March 2023), https://www.ciarb.org/media/4854/ciarb-cost-controlled-expedited-arbitration-rules-bermuda-final.pdf, Article 5.1.
66. Cayman International Mediation & Arbitration Centre Ltd (30 March 2023), the CI-MAC Rules, https://www.caymanarbitration.com/arbitrationrules2023, Article 19.1.
67. *Ibid.*, Article 12.1.
68. *Ibid.*, Article 12.4.
69. *Ibid.*, Articles 23 and 26.
70. *Ibid.*, Article 5.
71. *Ibid.*, Article 28.

award within six months from the closure of proceedings.[72] The lack of an express time limit for rendering an expedited award is in marked contrast to the 2021 BVI IAC Rules, which provide for an award to be rendered within six months from the date the Secretariat submitted the case file to the Tribunal[73] and the 180 days from the date the Tribunal was appointed as set down in relevant provisions of the Bermudan CCEA Rules.[74]

Regarding costs, the tribunal's fees will be determined either according to an hourly rate or a schedule of fees based on the sum in dispute.[75] The parties must agree in writing on the method of determining the Tribunal's fees and expenses and inform CI-MAC of their choice within 30 days of the date on which the Respondent receives the Notice of Arbitration. If parties fail to agree on the method, the default position is for the tribunal's fees to be incurred on an hourly basis.[76] Again, this provides the parties with less certainty than the carefully crafted schedule of fees in Annex C to the 2021 BVI IAC Rules.

Finally, one strength of the CI-MAC Rules is that it permits the early determination of points of law or fact which are without merit or outside the Tribunal's jurisdiction.[77] This provides a further basis for expediting the conduct of the arbitration, albeit it is short of a fully fledged expedited procedure leading to the earlier issuance of a final award. This is because the early determination procedure is designed to determine points of law and fact as opposed to finally determining issues between the parties.

Overall, then, the CI-MAC Rules are far less detailed than either 2021 BVI IAC Rules or the CCEA Rules in Bermuda. Significant lacunae exist in the CI-MAC Rules, such as the time limit for a tribunal to render its award. This in turn provides arbitral parties with less certainty as to what they can expect when attempting to invoke the expedition procedure set down in the CI-MAC Rules.

§17.05 CONCLUSION

This chapter has explored the various arbitral regimes of the BVI, Bermuda and Cayman Islands with a particular focus on their arrangements for expedited arbitration. Overall, the BVI provides the most detailed and comprehensive expedition regime, followed by Bermuda. The expedition procedure in the Cayman Islands is the least developed of the three jurisdictions.

72. *Ibid.*, Article 28.2.
73. 2021 BVI IAC Rules, 2021, Appendix 2, Article 5.
74. CIArb Bermuda Chapter (31 March 2023), https://www.ciarb.org/media/4854/ciarb-cost-controlled-expedited-arbitration-rules-bermuda-final.pdf, Article 6.2.
75. Cayman International Mediation & Arbitration Centre Ltd (30 March 2023), the CI-MAC Rules, https://www.caymanarbitration.com/arbitrationrules2023, Article 35.
76. *Ibid.*
77. *Ibid.*, Article 25.

While both the BVI and Bermudan regimes clearly indicate when the expedition procedure is available,[78] the cost implications of such a procedure being adopted,[79] and contain many similarly commendable provisions, the 2021 BVI IAC Rules are more detailed than Bermuda's. By way of example, the 2021 BVI IAC Rules provide in cases of expedition that the first procedural conference stipulated by the rules should be convened no later than 10 days after the case file was transmitted to the arbitral tribunal.[80] In contrast, the CCEA Rules of Bermuda merely provide that 'promptly' after appointment the arbitrator shall establish a timetable setting out the various steps in the arbitration.[81] The 2021 BVI IAC Rules therefore offer arbitral parties with a particularly high level of certainty and clarity as to the procedure on expedited arbitration over and above that of Bermuda.

The most basic of the three regimes is that of the Cayman Islands. The passing of the CI-MAC rules with effect from 9 March 2023 is an important development for the Cayman Islands' arbitration regime. However, the current expedited arbitration framework is in its infancy with details on the process and powers available to an arbitrator left to be developed over time. The CI-MAC rules for expedited arbitration are contained in essentially one article (Article 5) as opposed to the far more developed and detailed regimes provided for in the BVI and Bermudan regimes. The CI-MAC rules are of more high level than both the BVI and Bermudan regimes, which in turn means it is uncertain what parties are to expect when the CI-MAC procedure is adopted. For example, the CI-MAC Rules do not provide a time limit for rendering an award when expedited arbitration is adopted.

The BVI should be commended for developing a clear and comprehensive expedited arbitration regime. With such a regime in place, parties can benefit from the prospect of a fast and efficient way to resolve arbitral disputes and are given a high degree of certainty in respect of the expedition regime. The BVI's regime, accordingly, provides a model which other offshore jurisdictions would do well to emulate, particularly Bermuda and the Cayman Islands.

78. *See, e.g.*, 2021 BVI IAC Rules, 2021, Appendix 2, Article 2(1); cf. CIArb Bermuda Chapter (31 March 2023), https://www.ciarb.org/media/4854/ciarb-cost-controlled-expedited-arbitration-rules-bermuda-final.pdf, Articles 1.1 and 1.2.
79. *See, e.g.*, 2021 BVI IAC Rules, Annex C and CIArb Bermuda Chapter (31 March 2023), https://www.ciarb.org/media/4854/ciarb-cost-controlled-expedited-arbitration-rules-bermuda-final.pdf, Article 4.
80. 2021 BVI IAC Rules, Appendix 2, Article 4.
81. CIArb Bermuda Chapter (31 March 2023), https://www.ciarb.org/media/4854/ciarb-cost-controlled-expedited-arbitration-rules-bermuda-final.pdf, Article 2.2.

CHAPTER 18

Expedited Arbitration Rules: When Are They Applied?

Rose Maria Sebi, Rahul Kr. Kanoujia & Parnika Rai

Arbitration has become the preferred method for resolving commercial disputes due to its efficiency and speed. However, there are cases that require even faster resolution without sacrificing fairness and due process. Expedited arbitration (EA) procedures have emerged as a solution, offering a streamlined process for resolving disputes in a cost-effective and efficient manner. This chapter examines the features of EA rules and how they are applied in various institutional settings such as the International Chamber of Commerce (ICC), Singapore International Arbitration Centre (SIAC), Hong Kong International Arbitration Centre (HKIAC), and emerging arbitration institutions of India such as the Mumbai Centre of International Arbitration (MCIA) and Delhi International Arbitration Centre (DIAC). Additionally, the chapter explores ad hoc arbitration under the UNCITRAL Arbitration Rules. It also explores the conditions for applying expedited rules and possible grounds for challenging an award made under ICC, SIAC, HKIAC, MCIA, and DIAC expedited rules. Ultimately, this chapter offers insights into the EA process, providing guidance for parties seeking swift and fair dispute resolution.

§18.01 INTRODUCTION

Arbitration has emerged as the most popular and common mode of dispute resolution between commercial entities due to its cost-efficiency and speed. It now has become even more paramount to have an alternative procedure available for cases which need adjudication in an even shorter time frame without compromising due process of law and fair treatment of the parties. This is where expedited procedure steps in with a simplified and streamlined process of arriving at a final resolution of disputes in a cost-effective manner.[1]

This chapter initially discusses the principal features of various expedited arbitration rules (EA rules) to examine the manner in which they are applied. Thereafter, the chapter considers the manner in which expedited rules are introduced in the different arbitration rules and the conditions under which they are applied. Finally, the possible grounds for challenge of an award issued under expedited rules are discussed.

§18.02 INSTITUTIONAL EA RULES: A COMPARATIVE ANALYSIS

The circumstances under which expedited procedures would apply are not identical across different institutional and ad hoc arbitration rules. The principal features of EA rules are first examined, including the manner in which they are applied and how they are effective in achieving the goal of a simplified and streamlined process. The ad hoc arbitration rules for EA under the United Nations Commission on International Trade Law Model (UNCITRAL), which were adopted on 21 July 2021 and became effective on 19 September 2021, are first considered. Thereafter, the International Chamber of Commerce (ICC), Singapore International Arbitration Centre (SIAC), and Hong Kong International Arbitration Centre (HKIAC) rules are examined. Finally, the rules of emerging institutions in India – the Mumbai Centre of International Arbitration (MCIA) and Delhi International Arbitration Centre (DIAC) – are reviewed.

[A] UNCITRAL EA Rules

The UNCITRAL Law model encompasses an international legal framework providing for a harmonized platform that could strengthen and unite the arbitration laws of different legal systems. Article 1(5) of the UNCITRAL Arbitration Rules incorporates the Expedited Rules, which are an appendix to the UNCITRAL Arbitration Rules. Parties are free to agree to the expedited procedures. After the arbitration has begun, they still can opt out of EA. In such circumstances, the tribunal will not cease to exist. Instead, it will operate in accordance with the usual UNCITRAL Arbitration Rules.[2]

Given the object behind the formulation of expedited procedure, the parties and the tribunal are obliged to act expeditiously and abide by the timeline. The tribunal has the discretion to decide on the technological mode for the conduct of the proceedings.[3] A notice for arbitration must include a proposal for the designation of an appointing authority unless one has been decided beforehand, and for the appointment of an arbitrator.[4] The claimant must send the respondent a copy of their statement of claim

1. *See, e.g.*, Explanatory Note to the UNCITRAL Expedited Arbitration Rules, UNCITRAL Arbitration Rules, Expedited Arbitration Rules, Rules on Transparency in Treaty-based Investor-State Arbitration (2021), para. 1.
2. 2021 UNCITRAL Expedited Arbitration Rules, Article 1(5).
3. *Ibid.*, Article 3(3).
4. *Ibid.*, Article 4(1).

together with their notice of arbitration.[5] As soon as the arbitral panel is constituted, the claimant must give it the notice of arbitration and the statement of claim.[6]

In accordance with Article 4(1)(a) and (b) of the Expedited Rules, the respondent must send the claimant a response to the notice of arbitration within fifteen days of receiving it. This response must address all of the information provided in the notice of arbitration. Within fifteen days of the arbitral tribunal's formation, the respondent must provide the claimant and the tribunal with its statement of defence.

If the parties disagree regarding the designation of an appointing authority for the arbitrator, any party may approach the Secretary-General of the Permanent Court of Arbitration to designate the appointing authority or to serve as appointing authority. The Permanent Court of Arbitration must decide if, in a particular case, they are fit to be the appointing authority. If they decide to the contrary, an appointing authority shall be designated by them. Unless otherwise agreed by the parties, there shall be only a sole arbitrator. The appointing authority shall appoint a sole arbitrator at the request of a party in accordance with Article 8(2) of the UNCITRAL Arbitration Rules if the parties have not agreed on the appointment of a sole arbitrator within fifteen days after a proposal has been received by all other parties.

The arbitral tribunal may at any time, after allowing the parties to express their opinions, extend or shorten any time period specified under the UNCITRAL Arbitration Rules and the Expedited Rules or agreed by the parties, subject to Article 16 of the Expedited Rules. Hearings are optional and the tribunal decides whether to hold a hearing and the nature of the submissions made by the parties.[7] If the arbitral tribunal has jurisdiction over the dispute, a counterclaim or a claim for the purpose of a set-off must be made no later than in the statement of defence.[8] Unless the arbitral tribunal deems it appropriate to allow such a claim, taking into account the delay in making it or prejudice to other parties or any other circumstances, the respondent is not permitted to make a counterclaim or rely on a claim for the purpose of a set-off at a later stage in the arbitration proceedings.[9]

The award must be rendered within six months.[10] However, if exceptional circumstances exist and more time is needed, the timeline may be extended to a maximum of six months.[11] If the arbitral tribunal determines that it runs the risk of failing to render an award within nine months of the date it was established, it must propose a final extended time limit, justify the proposal, and invite the parties to respond within a predetermined window of time.[12] The final extension will be accepted only if all the parties consent within the designated time period.[13]

5. *Ibid.*, Article 4(2).
6. *Ibid.*, Article 4(3).
7. *Ibid.*, Article 11.
8. *Ibid.*, Article 12(1).
9. *Ibid.*, Article 12(2).
10. *Ibid.*, Article 16(1).
11. *Ibid.*, Article 16(2).
12. *Ibid.*, Article 16(3).
13. *Ibid.*

[B] International Chamber of Commerce

In 2017, the ICC amended the ICC Rules of Arbitration (ICC Rules). As part of its main innovation, the ICC introduced the guidelines for EA. Article 30 of the Rules combined with Appendix VI regulate the EAs under the ICC Rules. Article 30 of the ICC Rules provides that by agreeing to arbitration under the ICC Rules, the parties agree that the Expedited Procedure Rules will take precedence over any contrary terms in the parties' arbitration agreement, unless the arbitration agreement was not concluded prior to the entry into force of the EA provisions. Article 30 of the ICC Rules and Appendix 6 of the Expedited Procedure Rules overhaul the expedited procedure rules under the ICC.

[1] Article 30 of the ICC Rules

Article 30 is divided into three subclauses. Article 30(1) generally provides for the precedence of Appendix VI and Article 30 over any other contrary terms present in the arbitration agreement. Article 30(2) describes when the expedited procedures are applicable. There are two conditions for their application. First, if the amount in dispute does not exceed the limit provided for in Article 1(2) of Appendix 6 at the time of communication of the request for arbitration in accordance with Article 1(3). Second, the expedited rules will apply if the parties have agreed.[14]

Article 30(3) states three conditions under which the expedited rules shall not be applicable. First, if the agreement was entered into before the expedited procedure was set out. Second, if the parties choose to opt out of expedited procedure. Finally, if the court decides, under specific circumstances that entering into or opting for expedited procedure will not be appropriate.[15]

[2] Appendix VI of the ICC Rules, 2021

Appendix VI consists of six articles. Article 1 discusses application of the expedited procedure rules. Article 1(2) describes the valuation of dispute under which the provisions shall be applicable. The valuations are: (i) USD 2,000,000 if the arbitration agreement under the Rules was concluded on or after 1 March 2017 and before 1 January 2021; or (ii) USD 3,000,000 if the arbitration agreement was concluded on or after 1 January 2021.[16]

If the expedited rules apply, the tribunal shall be composed of a sole arbitrator. The parties must agree on the arbitrator nominated. If the parties do not agree, then the ICC court shall appoint the sole arbitrator in discretion.[17] In addition, the Terms of Reference, described in Article 23 of the ICC Rules, do not apply to EA.[18] Further, after

14. 2021 ICC Rules, Article 30.
15. *Ibid.*, Article 30(3).
16. *Ibid.*, Article 1(2) of Appendix VI.
17. *Ibid.*, Article 2 and Appendix 6.
18. *Ibid.*, Article 3(1) of Appendix VI.

the constitution of the tribunal, no new claims may be added unless approved by the tribunal, considering cost implications or any other relevant circumstances.[19]

The intent behind these procedures is to facilitate speedy disposition of cases with minimal intervention, greater party autonomy and more efficiency. Therefore, the manner for conduction the arbitration is solely decided by the arbitral tribunal in consultation with the parties. The tribunal may choose to conduct the arbitration without any oral hearing or to limit the number, length and scope of written submissions and written witness evidence, both fact witnesses and experts.[20] The award should be rendered within six months, which is extendable pursuant to Article 31(2) of the ICC Rules.[21]

[C] Singapore International Arbitration Centre

Rule 5 of the SIAC elucidates the expedited procedures. The rule stresses the importance of filing an application with the Registrar for adopting the EA rules for a dispute. The following conditions exist for application of the EA procedures: (i) the amount in the dispute should not exceed SGD 6,000,000, aggregating the claim, counterclaim and set-off, if any; (ii) if the parties agree to application of the expedited rules; or (iii) if there is an exceptional urgency.[22]

When an application is sent to the Registrar opting for EA, a copy must be sent to the other party and the Registrar must be notified.[23] If such an application is approved by the SIAC President, considering all the considerations and the factual matrix of the case in question, the procedures stated in Rule 5 of the SIAC Rules shall be followed. Under Rule 5, the timelines may be abbreviated at the discretion of the Registrar. A sole arbitrator will constitute the tribunal. The hearing may be held based on documentary evidence only, unless a hearing is required for examination of any witness or for oral argument. Because time is of the utmost importance in a fast-track procedure, the award must be rendered within six months, unless extended by the Registrar in exceptional circumstances. Finally, the tribunal may provide reasons for the award only in summary fashion, unless the parties have agreed otherwise.[24]

[D] Hong Kong International Arbitration Centre

Article 42 of the HKIAC Rules discusses the Expedited Procedure Rules. Before the arbitral tribunal is constituted, a party must apply to HKIAC for the arbitration to be conducted in an expedited manner. The following criteria must be met: (i) the amount in dispute does not exceed HKD 25,000,000 (over USD 3 million); (ii) the parties have

19. *Ibid.*, Article 3.
20. *Ibid.*, Article 3(4) and (5).
21. *Ibid.*, Article 31.
22. *Ibid.*, Article 5.1.
23. 2016 SIAC Rules, Article 5.1.
24. *Ibid.*, Article 5.2.

agreed to the application of the expedited rules; or (iii) in cases of exceptional urgency.[25]

After due consideration of all factors and the views of both the parties, the HKIAC may grant the application for EA. If this occurs then the manner in which the arbitration is conducted changes. The tribunal shall be comprised of a sole arbitrator unless the arbitration agreement provides otherwise. If the agreement calls for a panel of arbitrators, HKIAC attempts to persuade the parties to agree to a sole arbitrator. However, if the parties do not agree, the tribunal will consist of a panel of three arbitrators. Second, the timelines for the arbitration may be modified and shortened, deviating from the standard rules. In general, the parties are entitled to submit one statement of claim, one counterclaim and, if appropriate and justified, one statement of defence in response to the counterclaim after the submission of the answer to the notice of arbitration. The final award will be based on documentary evidence only, unless an oral hearing is mandated or is necessary. The final award should be rendered within six months unless there is an exceptional urgency. The tribunal must provide the rationale behind the award unless the parties have agreed to the contrary.

Any party may request that the expedited procedures under Article 42 no longer apply. The HKIAC may agree after discussion with the parties and any confirmed or appointed arbitrators and taking into account any new information that has come to light. The arbitral tribunal continues to function unless HKIAC determines it is appropriate to rescind the confirmation or appointment of any arbitrator.[26]

[E] Mumbai Centre of International Arbitration

Rules 12 and 13 of the Arbitration Rules of the MCIA Rules provide for expedited procedure. In accordance with the rules, before the tribunal is constituted, the parties must submit that they both consent to expedited procedures if: (i) the anticipated amount in dispute at the time of the application does not exceed INR 100,000,000, representing the aggregate of the claim, counterclaim and any set-off defence; or (ii) the parties agree in writing to EA.[27]

When a party submits an application to the Registrar in accordance with MCIA Rule 12.1, and the Chairman of MCIA decides, after taking into account the opinions of the parties, that the arbitral proceedings should be conducted using the Expedited Procedure, then the Registrar is required to promptly notify the parties that the Expedited Procedure will be used.[28] The Chairman's decision regarding the use of the expedited procedure will be final and enforceable.[29]

25. 2018 HKIAC Rules, Article 41.1. The monetary threshold recently was raised from the equivalent of USD 250,000.
26. 2018 HKIAC Rules, Article 42.
27. 2016 MCIA Rules, Rule 12.1.
28. *Ibid.*, Rule 12.2.
29. *Ibid.*

The procedures for EA are stated in Rule 12.3 of the MCIA Rules. The Registrar is vested with the power of shortening the timelines as they deem appropriate.[30] The tribunal is a single arbitrator under all circumstances unless the chairman of MCIA decides the contrary.[31] Similar to the ICC rules, the tribunal must hold a hearing for the examination of all witnesses and expert witnesses as well as for any argument, and the dispute shall be resolved solely on the basis of recorded evidence.[32] The final award must be a reasoned decision unless the parties have agreed otherwise.[33] The decision must be issued within a strict timeline of six months.[34]

MCIA Rule 13 concerns the expedited formation of the tribunal. Any party may request the Council to hasten the tribunal's establishment in cases of extreme urgency.[35] A copy of the request for arbitration (if made by a claimant) or the answer (if made by a respondent) and a copy of the application must be submitted to the Registrar in writing, preferably electronically, and delivered to all other participants in the arbitration.[36] The application must detail the precise reasons for the extraordinary urgency necessitating the tribunal's rapid creation.[37] The application will be decided by the Council as quickly as possible under the circumstances.[38] If the application is approved, the Council may shorten any deadline stipulated in the arbitration agreement or for the purpose of establishing the tribunal.[39]

[F] The Delhi International Arbitration Centre

Rules 12 and 13 of the Delhi International Arbitration Centre Arbitration Proceedings Rules (DIAC Rules) provide for a fast-track procedure. The parties may opt for a fast-track procedure not later than one month after the formation of the arbitral tribunal. If the parties agree to an expedited procedure, they must sign an undertaking that they will dispense with oral evidence. The guidelines call for the claimant to submit its documents in accordance with Rule 4 of the DIAC Rules.[40]

After the receipt of the documents by the other party, it must submit its reply within thirty days along with any supporting documents.[41] Thereafter, the parties shall appoint a sole arbitrator in accordance with the provisions in the rules. If they fail to do so, the Chairperson of DICA or the Sub-Committee appointed by the Chairperson shall make the appointment within one week after the expiry of the thirty-day period. The confirmation of the appointment of an arbitrator shall be duly communicated to the

30. *Ibid.*, Rule 12.3(a).
31. *Ibid.*, Rule 12.3(b).
32. *Ibid.*, Rule 12.3(c).
33. *Ibid.*, Rule 12.3(e).
34. *Ibid.*, Rule 12.3(d).
35. *Ibid.*, Rule 13.1.
36. *Ibid.*, Rule 13.2.
37. *Ibid.*
38. *Ibid.*, Rule 13.3.
39. *Ibid.*
40. 2023 DIAC Rules, Rules 12 and 13.
41. *Ibid.*, Rule 12.4.

parties.[42] Furthermore, Rule 13 sets forth the procedure to be followed by the arbitral tribunal in adjudicating the dispute by way of a fast-track procedure. The fast-track procedure under the DIAC Rules is largely akin to that in other jurisdictions. The tribunal is to make the award based on documents, written pleadings and submissions filed by the parties.[43] However, it is also vested with the authority to call for any further information or clarification as may be needed.[44] An oral hearing is held only if: (i) the parties agree for pleadings to take place and for the award to be based on pleadings; and (ii) the tribunal decides it is necessary to have an oral hearing for clarification of a specific issue.[45] The award must be rendered within six months, which is extendable by the court under section 29A of the Arbitration and Conciliation Act only under exceptional circumstances.[46]

§18.03 CONDITIONS FOR THE APPLICATION OF EXPEDITED RULES

In order to simplify and speed up the resolution of relatively less complicated disputes, some institutions have implemented EA rules. Individual institutions have adopted these rules through separate, incorporated, or supplementary rules. Institutions may also decide whether the rules should apply automatically or if parties need to opt in to access them. Additionally, there may be provisions for a fallback position to switch to standard arbitration rules if the case is more complicated than expected. Each of these points will be briefly examined in turn.

[A] A Separate, Incorporated or Supplementary Rules

The decision to apply expedited procedure rules may be made by individual institutions through separate, incorporated, or supplementary rules. The World Intellectual Property Organisation (WIPO) has been at the forefront of implementing expedited procedures. It has created a distinct set of rules for this purpose – the WIPO Expedited Arbitration Rules, effective since 2021.[47] Thus, WIPO has opted for separate rules to introduce expedited proceedings. In contrast, other institutions, such as the ICC, have included expedited rules in their general arbitration rules by way of incorporation. This approach has also been adopted by several Asian arbitration institutions such as SIAC,[48] HKIAC,[49] MCIA[50] and DIAC.[51]

42. *Ibid.*, Rule 12.5.
43. *Ibid.*, Rule 13.1(a).
44. *Ibid.*, Rule 13.1(b).
45. *Ibid.*, Rule 13.1(c).
46. *Ibid.*, Rule 13.2 and Rule 13.3.
47. WIPO Expedited Arbitration Rules (effective from 1 July 2021), accessible at: https://www.wipo.int/amc/en/arbitration/expedited-rules/.
48. 2016, Singapore International Arbitration Centre Rules.
49. 2018 HKIAC, Rules.
50. 2016 MCIA Rules.
51. 2023 DIAC Rules.

The German Institution of Arbitration (DIS) unveiled its Supplementary Rules for Expedited Proceedings in 2008. These rules complement the DIS Arbitration Rules and allow for speedy arbitration within six to nine months. A key contrast between these rules and the standard DIS Arbitration Rules is the shorter deadlines for the nomination of arbitrators and submission of written pleadings. Moreover, the Supplementary Rules require the arbitral tribunal to consider the parties' desire to expedite the proceedings when determining the procedure.[52]

Apart from adopting EA rules through separate, incorporated, or supplementary rules, some institutions have opted for other mechanisms to hasten the dispute resolution process. For example, the London Court of International Arbitration (LCIA) has not implemented an expedited procedure but has included a fast-track option in its rules. This allows parties to request the swift formation of the tribunal, and the tribunal may, at the request of any party or on its own initiative, shorten or extend any time limits set out in the arbitration agreement, any other agreement between the parties, or any order issued by the tribunal.[53] Similarly, in 2006, the International Centre for Settlement of Investment Disputes (ICSID) added Rule 41(5) to its Arbitration Rules to specifically address unmeritorious claims.[54] In 2022, ICSID added expedited rules to which the parties must specifically consent.[55]

[B] Opt-In or Automatic Application

EA rules often include an automatic application for disputes falling below a certain pecuniary threshold. For disputes exceeding this threshold, institutions may still encourage expedited proceedings through an opt-in mechanism. For example, the ICC's latest expedited procedure rules automatically apply to disputes involving a value below USD 3 million,[56] while the Swiss Chamber's Arbitration Institution (SCAI) applies a threshold of CHF 1 million,[57] and the ICDR refers to disputes with an amount

52. 2018 German Institution of Arbitration (DIS) Supplementary Rules for Expedited Proceedings, section 1.4.
53. 2020 LCIA Arbitration Rules, Article 9A.
54. Inna Uchkunova and Oleg Temnikov, 'Rule 41(5) of the ICSID Arbitration Rules: The Sleeping Beauty of the ICSID System', *Kluwer Arbitration Blog*, 27 June 2014, accessible at: https://arbitrationblog.kluwerarbitration.com/2014/06/27/rule-415-of-the-icsid-arbitration-rules-the-sleeping beauty-of-the-icsid-system/.
55. ICSID Arbitration Rule, Chapter XII (2022).
56. 2021 ICC Arbitration Rules, Article 30(2) ('The Expedited Procedure Rules set forth in Appendix VI *shall apply* if: a) the amount in dispute does not exceed the limit set out in Art. 1(2) of Appendix VI at the time of the communication referred to in Art. 1(3) of that Appendix' (emphasis added)) and Appendix VI, Article 1(2) ('The amount referred to in Art. 30(2), subparagraph a), of the Rules is US$3 million').
57. 2012 Swiss Rules of International Arbitration, Article 42(2): 'The following provisions shall apply to all cases in which the amount in dispute, representing the aggregate of the claim and the counterclaim (or any set-off defence), does not exceed CHF 1,000,000 (one million Swiss francs), unless the Court decides otherwise, taking into account all relevant circumstances: ...'.

of USD 250,000 or less.[58] The Japan Commercial Arbitration Association (JCAA) applies a claim value limit of JPY 20 million,[59] and China International Economic and Trade Arbitration Commission (CIETAC) refers to disputes where the amount in question does not exceed RMB 5 million.[60]

However, some institutions do not apply EA rules on a default basis. They have implemented an opt-in system where parties must choose to participate. These rules are also often based on a specific monetary threshold, such as SGD 6,000,000 for SIAC[61] or HKD 25,000,000 (approx. USD 3,200,000) for HKIAC.[62] In the case of institutions like the SCC, the decision regarding participation is typically at the discretion of the parties or the institution, depending on the circumstances.[63]

---

58. 2014 ICDR Arbitration Rules, Article 1(4): 'Unless the parties agree or the Administrator determines otherwise, the International Expedited Procedures shall apply in any case in which no disclosed claim or counterclaim exceeds US$250,000 exclusive of interest and the costs of arbitration.'
59. 2015 JCAA Arbitration Rules, Rule 75.2: 'Expedited procedures shall be conducted where the amount or economic value of the claimant's claim(s) is not more than ¥20,000,000; unless, within two weeks from the respondent's receipt of the notice of the Request for Arbitration: ...'. Rule 75.3 provides that 'The amount of any interest, rent, damage, penalty, expense, or cost that is incidental to the principal claim shall be excluded when calculating the amount or the economic value of the claim, counterclaim, or set-off defense under Rule 75.2.' Where it is difficult to calculate the amount or economic value of claim(s), the economic value is deemed to exceed JPY 20,000,000 (Rule 75.4).
60. 2015 CIETAC Arbitration Rules, Article 56(1): 'The Summary Procedure shall apply to any case where the amount in dispute does not exceed RMB 5,000,000 unless otherwise agreed by the parties; or where the amount in dispute exceeds RMB 5,000,000, yet one party applies for arbitration under the Summary Procedure and the other party agrees in writing; or where both parties have agreed to apply the Summary Procedure.' Article 63 provides that 'The Summary Procedure shall not be affected by any amendment to the claim or by the filing of a counterclaim. Where the amount in dispute of the amended claim or that of the counterclaim exceeds RMB 5,000,000, the Summary Procedure shall continue to apply unless the parties agree or the arbitral tribunal decides that a change to the general procedure is necessary.' It should be noted that the pecuniary threshold has been increased; as in the 2012 Arbitration Rules, the amount was RMB 2 million.
61. 2016 SIAC Arbitration Rules, Rule 5.4: 'Upon application by a party, and after giving the parties the opportunity to be heard, the Tribunal may, having regard to any further information as may subsequently become available, and in consultation with the Registrar, order that the arbitral proceedings shall no longer be conducted in accordance with the Expedited Procedure. Where the Tribunal decides to grant an application under this Rule 5.4, the arbitration shall continue to be conducted by the same Tribunal that was constituted to conduct the arbitration in accordance with the Expedited Procedure.'
62. 2018 HKIAC, Administered Arbitration Rules, Article 42.1(a).
63. *See* 2023 SCC Rules for Expedited Arbitrations, Article 11: 'After receiving the Answer, and prior to the appointment of the Arbitrator, the SCC may invite the parties to agree to apply the Arbitration Rules with either a sole arbitrator or three arbitrator(s), having regard to the complexity of the case, the amount in dispute and any other relevant circumstances.' It is important to note that, to the extent the application of the expedited procedure rules, under this provision, depends on an agreement between the parties ('the SCC may invite the parties to agree to apply the Arbitration Rules with either a sole arbitrator or three arbitrator(s)'), absent such an agreement, the SCC is not in a position to force expedited procedure rules: *see, e.g., Yuri Bogdanov and Yulia Bogdanova v. Republic of Moldova*, SCC Case No. V 091/2012, Final Award, 16 April 2013, *Juris Arbitration Law*, where the SCC informed the parties that there had been no agreement regarding the applicability of the Expedited Arbitration Rules after the Republic of Moldova left unanswered the claimants' request for an expedited proceeding.

[C] Fallback Provision

The flexibility of international arbitration is essential, and it is important that the parties, tribunals, or institutions have the option to switch to standard procedures if the dispute is more intricate than anticipated or if a party's request for an expedited process is unsuitable. The 2016 SIAC Arbitration Rules allow for a switch to standard procedures if the expedited procedure is no longer appropriate.[64] Similarly, the 2023 SCC Rules for Expedited Arbitrations enable a standard arbitration if the complexity of the case, amount in dispute, or other relevant circumstances justify it.[65] The ICC also considers the case's circumstances and may determine whether the expedited procedure is suitable[66] or should be discontinued and replaced with standard arbitration rules upon a party's request or its own motion.[67]

Article 2(1) of the UNCITRAL Expedited Arbitration Rules allows discontinuance from EA rules.[68] Additionally, Article 2(2) allows a party to ask the tribunal to no longer apply the expedited rules.[69] If the EA rules are no longer applicable, Article 2(3) requires the tribunal to continue working on the case and to conduct the arbitration according to the standard UNCITRAL arbitration rules.[70]

When a party requests the tribunal to discontinue the EA process, they must demonstrate the presence of 'exceptional circumstances' by convincing and justified reasons. Tribunals should grant the request only in limited circumstances.[71] To make a decision on whether EA rules are to be applied, tribunals should consider various factors, including the urgency of the dispute, the stage of the proceedings when the request was made, the complexity of the dispute, the anticipated amount in dispute, the terms of the parties' agreement to EA, and the potential consequences of the

64. 2016 SIAC Arbitration Rules, Rule 5.1(a): 'Prior to the constitution of the Tribunal, a party may file an application with the Registrar for the arbitral proceedings to be conducted in accordance with the Expedited Procedure under this Rule, provided that any of the following criteria is satisfied: a. the amount in dispute does not exceed the equivalent amount of US$6 million, representing the aggregate of the claim, counterclaim and any defence of set-off; ...'.
65. 2023 SCC Rules for Expedited Arbitrations, Article 11: 'After receiving the Answer, and prior to the appointment of the Arbitrator, the SCC may invite the parties to agree to apply the Arbitration Rules with either a sole or three arbitrator(s), having regard to the complexity of the case, the amount in dispute and any other relevant circumstances.'
66. 2021 ICC Arbitration Rules, Article 30.3(c): '3. The Expedited Procedure Provisions shall not apply if: ... (c) the Court, upon the request of a party before the constitution of the arbitral tribunal or on its own motion, determines that it is inappropriate in the circumstances to apply the Expedited Procedure Provisions.'
67. 2021 ICC Arbitration Rules, Appendix VI (Expedited Procedure Rules), Article 1.4: 'The Court may, at any time during the arbitral proceedings, on its own motion or upon the request of a party, and after consultation with the arbitral tribunal and the parties, decide that the Expedited Procedure Provisions shall no longer apply to the case. In such case, unless the Court considers that it is appropriate to replace and/or reconstitute the arbitral tribunal, the arbitral tribunal shall remain in place.'
68. 2021 UNCITRAL Expedited Arbitration Rules, Article 2(1).
69. *Ibid.*, Article 2(2).
70. *Ibid.*, Article 2(3).
71. Draft Explanatory Note to the UNCITRAL Expedited Arbitration Rules (A/CN.9/WG/II/WP/219) 28 July 2021, paras 12-13, available at https://undocs.org/A/CN.9/WG.II/WP.219 (last accessed 24 October 2023).

determination on the proceedings.[72] These factors are not an exhaustive compilation. Consequently, in situations where an expedited procedure may not be appropriate for resolving a dispute, the EA rules offer fallback provisions that enable parties to transition to the standard arbitration rules.

§18.04 ENFORCEMENT OF AWARDS UNDER EA RULES

The ultimate test of an arbitration procedure's effectiveness in dispute resolution hinges on the enforceability of the resulting award. While expedited proceedings excel in efficiency, promptness, and providing a swifter resolution, the award must remain unchallenged and enforceable, thereby safeguarding the integrity and finality of the resolution process.

[A] Setting Aside Awards on Grounds of Composition of Tribunal

EA procedures commonly provide for the appointment of a sole arbitrator.[73] Almost all institutional rules prioritize time- and cost-efficiency by appointing a single arbitrator instead of a panel of three members. Some of these rules also include provisions that appointment of a sole arbitrator may override contrary provisions of the parties' arbitration agreement.[74] For example, the ICC requires a sole arbitrator, even if the arbitration agreement specifies otherwise.[75] This rule aligns with the ICC's general philosophy of promoting efficiency through the adoption of expedited procedure rules in 2017. The parties agree to prioritize the Expedited Procedure Provisions and Article 30 in Appendix VI over any conflicting terms in the arbitration agreement by agreeing to arbitrate under the Rules.[76]

However, when there is no such overriding provision in the EA rules, the appointment of a sole arbitrator regardless of contrary terms in the arbitration agreement can cause tension between the requirement for arbitral institutions to uphold party autonomy and to ensure efficiency in proceedings. Parties may challenge enforcement of awards in such cases.

For example, in *Noble Resources International Pte Ltd v. Shanghai Good Credit International Trade Co, Ltd (Noble Resources)*,[77] the issue arose as to whether the award could be enforced because a sole arbitrator was appointed under the institution's rules despite contrary terms in the arbitration agreement. In *Noble Resources*, the

72. 2021, Explanatory Note to the UNCITRAL Expedited Arbitration Rules, para. 13.
73. 2023 SCC Rules for Expedited Arbitrations, Article 17; 2016 ACICA Expedited Arbitration Rules, Article 8.1; 2014 WIPO Expedited Arbitration Rules, Article 14(a); 2015 JCAA Arbitration Rules, Rule 79.1; 2014 ICDR International Expedited Procedures, Article E-6.
74. 2021 ICC Arbitration Rules, Appendix VI (Expedited Procedure Rules), Article 2.1.
75. *Ibid.*
76. 2021 ICC Arbitration Rules, Article 30.1. *See also* ICC Note, para. 76: 'By submitting to arbitration under the Rules, the parties agree that any reference of disputes to three arbitrators in their arbitration agreement is subject to the Court's discretion to appoint a sole arbitrator if the Expedited Procedure Provisions apply.'
77. *[2016] Shanghai No. 1 Intermediate People's Court (Hu 01 Xie Wai Ren No. 1).*

parties were the seller and buyer of iron ore. The claimant in the dispute had entered into an iron ore purchase and sale agreement with the respondent. The contract incorporated a standard iron ore trading agreement. Article 16 of the standard agreement contained the arbitration clause. Article 16.1.1 of the standard agreement provided for three arbitrators.[78]

When a dispute arose between the parties, the claimant commenced arbitration under the SIAC Rules and applied for the expedited procedure under the 2013 SIAC Rules. Under Article 5.1 of the 2013 SIAC Rules,[79] SIAC appointed a sole arbitrator under the expedited procedures. However, the respondent opposed the application of the expedited rules and insisted that three arbitrators be appointed pursuant to the arbitration agreement. The respondent refused to participate in the arbitration, and an award was rendered in favour of the claimant.[80]

The claimant sought to enforce the award in the Shanghai courts. However, the respondent challenged enforcement under the New York Convention on the Recognition and Enforcement of Foreign Arbitral Awards 1958 (New York Convention) and the Civil Procedure Law of the People's Republic of China on various grounds. One of the key arguments raised by the respondent in resisting enforcement was that SIAC's appointment of a sole arbitrator was contrary to the parties' agreement for a three-member tribunal.[81]

The Shanghai Court upheld the respondent's argument and refused to enforce the SIAC award on the grounds that the composition of the arbitral tribunal was not in accordance with the agreement of the parties. The court found that the expedited procedures under the 2013 SIAC Rules did not exclude other means of composing a tribunal nor empower the chairman of SIAC to compel parties to accept a sole arbitrator despite their agreement to a three-member tribunal. The court held that Article 5.2 should not be interpreted to mean that the President of SIAC had absolute discretion on the composition of the tribunal. Instead, when exercising its discretion, the president must consider the parties' agreement with respect to the composition of the tribunal in order to preserve party autonomy. Thus, the court held that the appointment of the sole arbitrator violated the parties' arbitration agreement. It also emphasized that party autonomy is the foundation of arbitration proceedings.[82]

In 2015, a very similar issue was also considered by the Singapore High Court in *AQZ v. ARA*.[83] In that case, a sole arbitrator was appointed under the expedited procedures in the 2010 SIAC Rules. The applicant argued that the award should be set

78. Douglas Thomson, 'Shanghai Court Refuses to Enforce SIAC Sole Arbitrator's Award', *Global Arbitration Review*, 30 August 2017; Mohammed Salahudine Abdel Wahab, 'Expedited Institutional Arbitral Proceedings Between Autonomy and Regulation', Laurent Lévy and Michael Polkinghorne (eds), *Expedited Procedures in International Arbitration, Dossiers of the ICC Institute of World Business Law*, vol. 16, Kluwer Law International (2017), at 142-144.
79. 2016 SIAC Rules, Article 5.2(b): '[T]he case shall be referred to a sole arbitrator, unless the President determines otherwise.'
80. *Ibid.*, 78.
81. *Ibid.*
82. *Ibid.*
83. *AQZ v. ARA* [2015] SGHC 49.

aside because the parties had expressly agreed to arbitration before three arbitrators.[84] Contrary to the decision in *Noble Resources*, the Singapore High Court upheld SIAC's appointment of a sole arbitrator. It rejected the argument that the arbitration should not have been conducted before a sole arbitrator. The court adopted a 'commercially sensible' construction of the arbitration agreement. It decided that by adopting the 2010 SIAC Rules into their contract, the parties had recognized the SIAC President's power and discretion to appoint a sole arbitrator where the expedited procedure applied.[85]

In 2016, SIAC published an updated version of its rules to bring clarity to the composition of tribunal. Article 5.3 of the SIAC rules now states that 'by agreeing to arbitration under these Rules, the parties agree that, where arbitral proceedings are conducted in accordance with the Expedited Procedure under this Rule 5, the rules and procedures set forth in Rule 5.2 shall apply even in cases where the arbitration agreement contains contrary terms'.[86] The court, in *Noble Resources*, would have come to a different conclusion under the revised 2016 SIAC Rules.

[B] Challenge Based on Due Process Considerations and Role of the Tribunal

The requirement to follow due process in arbitration may be illustrated in several jurisdictions. For example, the 1996 Arbitration Act of the United Kingdom imposes a duty on the arbitral tribunal to 'act fairly and impartially as between the parties giving each party a reasonable opportunity of putting his case and dealing with that of his opponent'.[87] It also requires the tribunal to avoid 'unnecessary delay or expense, so as to provide a fair means for the resolution'. Similarly, the 1996 Arbitration and Conciliation Act of India provides that 'the parties shall be treated with equality and each party shall be given a full opportunity to present his case'.[88] This requirement is also reflected in institutional rules. The 2021 ICC Rules provide that the arbitral tribunal shall 'make every effort to conduct the arbitration in an expeditious and cost-effective manner having regard to the complexity and value of the dispute' and 'shall act fairly and impartially and ensure that each party has a reasonable opportunity to present its case'.[89]

Striking a balance between due process and efficiency in arbitral proceedings is of primary importance. While it is important to adhere to timelines, the parties should be allowed to present their case fully and effectively. The way in which arbitrators conduct arbitral proceedings may impose constraints on the parties' presentation of their case. Such restrictions include whether to allow parties to make oral submissions of their arguments; whether to allow examination of witnesses; and whether to allow

84. *Ibid.*, 83 at para. 123.
85. *Ibid.*, 83 at paras 130-132.
86. 2016 SIAC Arbitration Rules, Rule 5.3.
87. 1996 Arbitration Act, section 33(1)(a).
88. 1996 Arbitration and Conciliation Act, section 18.
89. 2021 ICC Rules, Articles 22.1 and 22.4.

parties to opt out of expedited procedures. These restrictions may become grounds for the losing party to seek to set aside the award based on a lack of due process.

Hearings including procedural hearings, examination and cross-examination of witnesses, and submission of final arguments take a significant amount of time and add to the cost of arbitration. Generally, under international arbitration rules, parties are entitled to request a hearing.[90] However, hearings often are optional in EA. A dispute may be decided based on documentary evidence alone in an expedited procedure. Alternatively, the tribunal and the parties may decide to allow hearings. Article 5.2(c) of the 2016 SIAC Rules provides that the tribunal may, in consultation with the parties, decide whether the dispute is to be decided on the basis of documentary evidence only or if a hearing will be held. The tribunal also may decide if a hearing is required for the examination of any witness and expert witness.[91]

Similarly, the UNCITRAL and ICC Rules provide for a hearing to be held only when a party requests one.[92] Some rules go further by allowing hearings only when a party requests them and the tribunal finds it necessary.[93] The tribunal must exercise this discretion cautiously because it could lead to an award being set aside on the ground that the party was unable to present its case and due process was not followed.

If the tribunal does not allow the parties to examine or cross-examine witnesses, the award may be challenged. In 2021, the Singapore Court of Appeal in *CBS v. CBP*[94] held that an arbitrator's decision to not allow the parties to present any witness evidence amounted to a breach of natural justice.[95] It upheld the Singapore High Court's earlier decision,[96] setting aside the arbitral award on that basis. In this case, the arbitration was conducted under the Singapore Chamber of Maritime Arbitration Rules (SCMA Rules). The respondent had not filed any witness statements, but had requested a hearing to present oral witness evidence. Article 28.1 of the SCMA Rules on hearings provided that 'Unless the parties have agreed on a documents-only arbitration or that no hearing should be held, the Tribunal shall hold a hearing for the presentation of evidence by witnesses, including expert witnesses, or for oral submissions.'[97]

After the respondent asked to present oral witness evidence, the sole arbitrator ruled that he would determine if such evidence was necessary only after the respondent had submitted witness statements so that he could evaluate if there was 'substantive value' in having those witnesses present evidence at the hearing. The respondent refused to submit witness statements. The arbitrator held a hearing only for oral submissions and issued an award in favour of the claimants.[98] While setting aside the award, the Singapore Court of Appeal clarified that under Rule 28.1, the tribunal

90. 2013 UNCITRAL Rules 2013, Article 17.3; 2021 ICC Rules, Article 26.
91. 2016 SIAC Rules, Article 5.2(c).
92. UNCITRAL Expedited Arbitration Rules, Article 11; 2021 ICC Rules, Article 5 of Appendix VI.
93. Stockholm Chamber of Commerce (SCC) Expedited Rules, Article 33.1.
94. [2021] SGCA 4.
95. *Ibid.*, 94 at para. 79.
96. *CBP v. CBS* [2020] SGHC 23.
97. 2015 Singapore Chamber of Maritime Arbitration (3rd ed.), Article 28.1.
98. *Ibid.*, 94 at para. 63.

must hold a hearing for oral witness evidence if requested by a party.[99] Further, the court ruled that the tribunal could not require the parties to first show that its evidence had 'substantive value' before deciding whether to hold an oral hearing.[100]

In contrast, some EA rules provide greater discretionary powers to the tribunal. The 2018 Rules on the Efficient Conduct of Proceedings in International Arbitration 2018 (Prague Rules) increase the efficiency of arbitral proceedings by adopting a more inquisitorial style. As is common in most civil law countries, the tribunal takes a more active role in managing the proceedings. Under the Prague Rules, the tribunal decides whether a witness who has submitted a witness statement should be called for examination at the hearing.[101] However, if the tribunal finds that the witness need not be examined, but the opposite side insists on calling the witness, as a general rule, the arbitral tribunal should allow the witness to testify at the hearing, unless there are good reasons not to do so.[102]

Finally, another way the tribunal exercises discretion is in opt-out rules. The timelines in EA rules can be rigid. A party may argue it cannot present its case fully within the restricted timeline. In such cases, several EA rules allow parties to mutually opt out by requesting the tribunal to remove the case from the expedited procedures.[103] However, where one party wants to opt out, while the other does not, and the tribunal decides to continue with the expedited procedure, a potential due process issue may arise. The party whose opt-out request was denied could challenge the tribunal's decision and argue that it was unable to fully present its case and that its due process rights were violated.

[C] Non-reasoned Awards and Their Impact on Setting Aside Awards

Generally, different arbitral institutions' rules have different requirements on whether an award has to be reasoned. Some arbitration rules, such as the ICC International Arbitration Rules, require a reasoned award.[104] Some rules state that the award has to be reasoned unless the parties have agreed otherwise.[105] Other rules, such as the 2016 SIAC Arbitration Rules[106] and Australian Centre for International Commercial Arbitration (ACICA) Expedited Arbitration Rules,[107] provide that the reasons for the award may be stated in summary form only. Under the 2023 SCC Expedited Arbitration Rules, a reasoned decision is optional, unless a party requests a reasoned award no later than at the closing statement.[108] Thus, these rules have reversed the usual assumption that

99. *Ibid.*, 94 at para. 79.
100. *Ibid.*, 94 at para. 71.
101. 2018 International Arbitration ('Prague Rules'), Article 5.6.
102. *Ibid.*, Article 5.7.
103. ICC Expedited Rules, CPR Fast Track Rules, UNCITRAL Expedited Rules.
104. 2021 ICC International Arbitration Rules, Article 32.2.
105. 2015 CIETAC Arbitration Rules, Article 49.3; 2014 ICDR International Arbitration Rules, Article 30; 2021 WIPO Expedited Arbitration Rules, Article 57(c).
106. 2016 SIAC Rules, Rule 5.2(e).
107. 2021 ACICA Rules, Article 28.3.
108. 2023 SCC Expedited Arbitration rules 2023, Article 42.

awards should be reasoned unless parties agree otherwise and have introduced non-reasoned awards as a default.

An agreement to not require a reasoned award or allow an award with reasons stated in summary form should reduce the time to complete the arbitral procedure. However, the absence of reasoning could impact the enforcement or setting aside of the arbitral award. If the parties have agreed that the award need not be reasoned, issues of enforcement are unlikely to arise. For example, the Bombay High Court rejected a challenge to an unreasoned arbitral award because the parties had agreed that the award did not have to be reasoned.[109] The Gujarat High Court dismissed a challenge to an unreasoned arbitral award because the arbitration agreement allowed the tribunal to issue an award without stating reasons.[110] Further, the Supreme Court of India, in *Rajasthan State Mines and Minerals Ltd. v. Eastern Engineering Enterprises*,[111] ruled that in case of an unreasoned award, the court's jurisdiction is limited. The award could only be set aside if the arbitrator had exceeded his jurisdiction. In situations where no reasons are given by the arbitrator, the court cannot speculate on the factors that influenced the arbitrator's conclusion and cannot interfere by setting aside the award.[112]

While parties have the option to forgo a reasoned award, there are strong incentives for them to refrain from doing so. First, a reasoned award enhances transparency and justifiability by offering an account of the arbitrator's thought process in arriving at a decision. Second, a reasoned award holds significant importance for potential appellate and judicial review. It enables the reviewing court to evaluate the accuracy of the arbitrator's legal analysis and rationale. In the absence of reasoning, the extent and effectiveness of any potential review may be constrained. Thus, parties should be cautious if they waive their right to a reasoned award because it significantly affects their right to challenge an award.

§18.05 CONCLUSION

Ideally, if the parties apply for an EA, they will deal with fewer procedural steps and have shorter time limits and lower costs and expenses. The option to apply expedited procedures initially depends on whether the rules selected by parties provide expedited rules and if the dispute comes within the monetary threshold set under such rules. The decisive factor depends on the agreement between the parties, and in some cases whether the arbitration institution has accepted the request by parties to follow expedited procedures. Important factors considered to ascertain the suitability of expedited procedures include the complexity and nature of a dispute; whether written submissions alone would be sufficient or if oral hearings would be necessary; the volume of documents and evidences to be brought on record; and overall, whether it is possible to deliver an award within the shortened time period.

109. *Mutta International v. Nandnandan Silk Mills Pvt. Ltd.* (2007) 4 Mah LJ 503.
110. *Gujarat Industrial Devp. Corpn. v. S.R. Parmar & Co.* (1996) 1 Arb LR 394.
111. (1999) 9 SCC 285.
112. *Ibid.*, 112 at paras 8 and 18.

This promise of a faster and less expensive method of dispute resolution has contributed to the growing popularity and acceptance of EA procedures. This popularity is evident from the caseload of arbitrations registered under expedited procedures in different arbitral institutions. For example, in 2022, SIAC received 87 requests for expedited procedures, of which 48 were accepted.[113] SIAC has received a total of 802 Expedited Procedure applications (and accepted 465 requests) since the introduction of these provisions in 2010.[114] In 2021, there were 15 applications for expedited formation of the tribunal pursuant to Article 9A of the LCIA Rules, 2 more than in 2020.[115]

The widespread adoption of expedited procedure rules by arbitration institutions demonstrates a clear desire by users for simplified and streamlined proceedings that can be resolved within a short time frame. These rules have been successful in achieving their intended purpose, and the similarity of the rules among different institutions indicates a trend towards homogenization and standardization of international arbitration procedures. As the demand for efficient dispute resolution mechanisms continues to increase, these expedited procedures likely will continue to play a significant role in the evolution of international arbitration.

113. SIAC Annual Report 2021-2022.
114. *Ibid.*
115. LCIA 2021 Annual Casework Report.

CHAPTER 19

Expedited International Arbitration in the MENA Region

Can Eken & Tariq Mahmood

As international developers and contractors continue to invest in construction projects, there has been an increasing trend in the use of arbitration in the Middle East and North Africa (MENA) region. Expedited arbitration has emerged as an important and convenient process to maintain the status quo, preserve evidence or assets, prevent the irreparable loss or harm, obtain other urgent interim measures even before the formation of an arbitral tribunal or to complete arbitration in an expedited manner. In recent years, numerous arbitral institutions have adopted 'expedited arbitration' procedures. The chapter provides a comprehensive analysis of expedited arbitration rules of major arbitral institutions in the MENA region, namely Bahrain (BCDR), Saudi Arabia (SCCA), the United Arab Emirates (DIAC), Turkey (ISTAC), Qatar (QICCA), Egypt (CRCICA), Morocco (CIMAC) and Lebanon (LIAC).

§19.01 INTRODUCTION

Expedited arbitration has developed and gained traction over the last couple of years in the Middle East and North Africa region (MENA). A number of factors such as urgency, the amount in dispute and party agreement have resulted in its greater use. In certain circumstances, a need exists to conduct arbitration proceedings through a more expeditious method than the normal arbitration process. Traditionally, international arbitration is considered to be a faster method of resolving a dispute than the elongated litigation process. The need to resolve commercial disputes in a short period gave rise to expedited arbitration. This need resulted from a number of reasons. The most common were the urgency of the proceeding, the need for legal certainty in trade, and budget control. Naturally, the longer the process takes, the more expensive it becomes.

Expedited arbitration is a unique process where the time limits are shortened, and the entire dispute resolution process can be completed much faster than a normal arbitration proceeding. The history of expedited arbitration rules goes back to the 1990s. As an example, the 1998 International Chamber of Commerce (ICC) rules included rules on expedited arbitration.[1] These rules have been improved over time. In 2017, the ICC introduced the mechanism of 'expedited arbitration' with the objective of having final awards rendered by sole arbitrators within six months after the case management conference.[2] Recently, UNCITRAL Working Group II has developed model expedited arbitration rules.[3]

§19.02 EXPEDITED PROCEDURES IN THE REST OF THE WORLD

According to the United Nations Commission on International Trade Law, 'Expedited arbitration is a streamlined and simplified procedure with a shortened time frame, which makes it possible for the parties to reach a final resolution of the dispute in a cost-effective manner.'[4] Arbitration centres around the world have realised that a significant proportion of arbitration matters involve claims that involve some combination of relatively low quantum and that are non-complex in terms of substantive issues. This is true for the traditional and established arbitration centres, such as in London, Geneva, and Paris, as well as the recently established arbitration centres. Expedited arbitration rules have become popular. Notably, arbitration centres in the MENA region adopted expedited arbitration rules in the last decade, following a growing trend in the world. The 2014 LCIA Rules[5] and 2016 DIFC-LCIA Rules[6] are notable exceptions to both groups of arbitration centres because they do not have expedited arbitration rules per se.

Expedited rules can be categorised into two types: (i) automatic application or (ii) opt-in. Under the automatic application, a dispute involving claims under a certain threshold is automatically diverted to an expedited procedure. Under the opt-in approach, the parties typically must agree on adopting the expedited procedure. If they do not agree, the procedure defaults to the standard rules of that institution.[7] The opt-in 2016 SIAC Rules require one party to file an application in order to proceed under the expedited procedure but does not require agreement from the opposing party.

---

1. Herman Verbist, *Contribution of Benjamin Davis to Expedited Arbitration*, 52(3) U. Toledo L. Rev. 463, 464 (2021).
2. *Ibid.*
3. *See* UNCITRAL Working Group II's work at https://uncitral.un.org/en/working_groups/2/arbitration. The UNCITRAL Expedited Arbitration Rules were finalised in 2021 and are available at https://uncitral.un.org/en/content/expedited-arbitration-rules.
4. United Nations Commission on International Trade Law, Expedited Arbitration Rules (2021), https://uncitral.un.org/sites/uncitral.un.org/files/media-documents/uncitral/en/21-07996_expedited-arbitration-e-ebook.pdf.
5. LCIA Arbitration Rules (2014), https://www.lcia.org/Dispute_Resolution_Services/lcia-arbitration-rules-2014.aspx.
6. DIFC-LCIA Arbitration Rules (adopted to take effect for arbitrations commencing on or after 1 October 2016), https://www.lcia.org/News/update-difc-lcia.aspx.
7. Practical Law Arbitration, Which institution and why: a comparison of major international arbitration institutions (2023), https://uk.practicallaw.thomsonreuters.com/9-204-3989?contextData=(sc.Default)&transitionType=Default&firstPage=true.

Some of the key features of expedited procedure based on the 2021 ICC Rules are the following:

- Appointment of a sole arbitrator unless stated otherwise in the arbitration agreement.[8]
- A case management conference within a short period of time from the case being filed.[9]
- The tribunal may decide the case on the documents only.[10]
- The tribunal may limit the number, length, and scope of the written submissions and written witness evidence.[11]
- A final award issued within six months of the case management conference.[12]

Table 19.1 indicates how certain major centres approach the quantum threshold and the automatic application/opt-in question.

Table 19.1 Expedited Arbitration Rules in Different Institutions

Arbitration Institutional Rules	*Threshold Amount for Value of Dispute*	*Automatic Application or Opt-In*
ICC Rules 2021	USD 3 million (Article 30(2))[13]	Automatic application. Opt-in available for higher-value disputes.
2015 CIETAC	RMB 5 million (Article 56.1, Chapter IV)	Automatic application. Opt-in available for higher-value disputes.
SIAC Rules 2016	SGD 6 million (Rule 5.1)	Opt-in.
HKIAC Rules 2018	HKD 25 million (Article 42)	Opt-in.
SCC Rules 2023	No threshold amount	Opt-in.
2021 Swiss Chambers' (SCAI) Rules	CHF 1 million (Article 42(2))	Automatic application. Opt-in available for other disputes.

Expedited arbitration, also referred to as fast-track arbitration, has garnered increasing prominence in recent years as a direct response to the protracted duration and escalated costs associated with conventional international arbitration. The Chamber of Commerce and Industry of Geneva (CCIG) was the first institution that

8. 2021 ICC Arbitration Rules, Appendix VI-Expedited Arbitration Rules, Article 2/1.
9. *Ibid.*, Article 3/3.
10. *Ibid.*, Article 3/5.
11. *Ibid.*, Article 3/4.
12. *Ibid.*, Article 4.
13. *Ibid.*, Article 1/2 states that 'USD 2,000,000 if the arbitration agreement under the Rules was concluded on or after 1 March 2017 and before 1 January 2021'.

introduced expedited arbitration procedures in 1992.[14] Over the last two decades, numerous institutions have implemented particular provisions with the sole aim of expediting the progression of arbitral proceedings. For example, the ICC, as a world-wide institution with a global reach, first introduced expedited arbitration rules in the ICC Arbitration Rules in 1998, which were amended in 2017.[15]

Thus, expedited arbitration has been an important topic over the last three decades. As is evident from Table 19.1, arbitration centres around the world have grappled with the problem of small or non-complex claims that would traditionally be dealt with under conventional arbitration procedures. Similar to the trends around the world, the MENA region has also embraced expedited arbitration to not fall behind in the competition among international arbitration fora. However, so far, arbitration centres in the Middle East have resisted changing their rules.

§19.03 HISTORICAL PERSPECTIVE TO EXPEDITED ARBITRATION IN THE MENA REGION

The swift pace at which infrastructure projects are advancing in the MENA region has resulted in construction disputes taking the top position among the types that undergo arbitration. Qatar's 2022 World Cup, Dubai's World Expo 2020 and Egypt's Rod al-Farag Axis Bridge (ranked as the world's widest cable-stayed bridge) are just a few examples of the recent mega-infrastructure projects. The advancement of such projects has raised questions as to the use of expedited arbitration in the MENA region.

In the MENA region, arbitration institutions such as the Bahrain Chamber for Dispute Resolution (BCDR), Saudi Center for Commercial Arbitration (SCCA), Dubai International Arbitration Centre (DIAC), Casablanca International Mediation and Arbitration Centre (CIMAC) and Istanbul Arbitration Centre (ISTAC) have adopted specific provisions for expedited arbitration in response to the growing demand for more efficient dispute resolution. Notably, in the Middle East, not every jurisdiction offers fast-track court proceedings. And even if they offer fast-track court proceedings, these State courts generally consist of several tiers, and the appeal process can result in decisions not being handed down for a number of years. However, exceptions exist, such as the small court tribunal of the Emirate of Ras Al Khaimah. Resolution No. 38 established a fast-track small claims court for civil and commercial claims under AED 20,000.[16]

In general, commercial litigants in the region do not have access to a reliable fast-track court that can bring a debtor to justice expeditiously. It is not uncommon for a creditor to write off a debt of several hundred thousand dollars. Therefore, a need exists for efficient and proportionate litigation options which are not available for

14. Christophe Imhoos, *The 1992 Geneva Chamber of Commerce and Industry Arbitration Rules under Scrutiny*, 9(4) J. Intl. Arb. 121, 134-135 (1992) DOI: 10.54648/joia1992038.
15. *See supra* n. 2.
16. Ammar Haykal, Small Claims Court in Ras Al Khaimah, https://www.tamimi.com/law-update-articles/small-claims-court-in-ras-al-khaimah/. AED 20,000 equates to roughly USD 5,500 dependent on the exchange rate.

certain commercial claims. This need is a further reason to implement options for fast-track arbitration.

§19.04 COMPARISON OF EXPEDITED ARBITRATION RULES IN THE MENA REGION

[A] Bahrain Chamber for Dispute Resolution

In Bahrain, the Bahrain Chamber for Dispute Resolution (BCDR) has established specific rules for expedited arbitration proceedings, as outlined in Article 6.[17] The BCDR's rules for expedited arbitration proceedings aim to provide a more efficient and timely resolution for disputes. The rules set monetary thresholds, address counterclaims, determine the composition of the arbitral tribunal, and establish strict timelines for issuing the final award and seeking interpretations or corrections. By streamlining the arbitration process, Bahrain seeks to promote fair and expeditious dispute resolution in the MENA region.

According to paragraph 6.1(a), the monetary value of the claim should not exceed USD 1 million, unless the parties have agreed in writing to proceed regardless of the claim's value.[18] This provision ensures that smaller-scale disputes receive swift attention. It also aligns with the view of one commentator that expedited procedures can significantly reduce time and costs in dispute resolution.[19] Paragraph 6.6 clarifies the situation when a respondent presents a counterclaim that would increase the total amount in dispute to an amount greater than USD 1 million. In such cases, if the parties have not agreed in writing for the expedited procedure to apply regardless of the claim or counterclaim's value, Articles 6.4 and 6.7 to 6.13 will not be applicable, and the respondent must file their response in accordance with the provisions of Article 4.[20]

The BCDR's rules also consider situations where a party amends their claim or counterclaim after the initial filing, resulting in the total amount in dispute exceeding USD 1 million. Paragraph 6.7 states that unless the parties agree otherwise or the Chamber or arbitral tribunal determines otherwise, the case will continue to be administered under the expedited procedure.[21] Moreover, paragraph 6.8 specifies that irrespective of any contrary agreement, the arbitral tribunal in expedited proceedings will consist of a sole arbitrator chosen by the Chamber, as outlined in paragraph 6.9.[22]

Furthermore, the BCDR's rules address counterclaims and adapt to changing circumstances. Paragraph 6.7 states that if a respondent presents a counterclaim that

17. 2022 Rules of Arbitration, Bahrain Chamber for Dispute Resolution (BCDR), https://bcdr.org/2022-rules-of-arbitration/.
18. Bahrain Chambers for Dispute Resolution (BCDR), 2022 Rules of Arbitration, Article 6/1(a), https://bcdr.org/2022-rules-of-arbitration/#a6.
19. Mark W. Friedman, *Expedited Procedure*, 4(2) BCDR International Arbitration Review, 261 (2017).
20. Bahrain Chambers for Dispute Resolution (BCDR), 2022 Rules of Arbitration, Article 6/6, https://bcdr.org/2022-rules-of-arbitration/#a6.
21. *Ibid.*, Article 6/7.
22. *Ibid.*, Article 6/9.

would surpass the USD 1 million threshold, the case can still continue under the expedited procedure.[23] This provision allows for flexibility, accommodating situations where amendments to claims or counterclaims occur, without sacrificing the efficiency of the process. Such adaptability is vital for ensuring fairness and maintaining the expeditious nature of proceedings.

In terms of timing, unless the parties or the Chamber agree otherwise, under paragraph 6.12, the arbitral tribunal must issue the final award within 30 days from the close of proceedings.[24] This provision emphasises the expeditious nature of the process, promoting a swift resolution to the dispute. Additionally, paragraph 6.13 shortens the deadlines for interpreting or correcting an award issued under the expedited procedure to 15 days, compared to the usual 30-day time frame specified in Article 37.[25]

However, the BCDR's expedited arbitration rules should be critically evaluated to illuminate potential drawbacks. One concern lies in the limitation of a sole arbitrator, as outlined in paragraph 6.8 of the BCDR's rules.[26] While this approach streamlines the decision-making process, it raises questions about the diversity of perspectives and expertise that a panel of arbitrators can offer. The consolidation of decision-making power in the hands of a single arbitrator may undermine the comprehensive evaluation of complex disputes. Additionally, the strict 30-day timeline for issuing the final award, as stipulated in paragraph 6.12, may pose challenges in cases requiring thorough examination. While the objective of efficiency is commendable, the expedited nature of the process places pressure on the arbitrator(s) to make hasty decisions, potentially compromising the quality or comprehensiveness of the final award.

Arbitration plays a crucial role in resolving disputes efficiently and effectively, and the BCDR has taken commendable steps to streamline the process through its rules for expedited arbitration proceedings. The BCDR's rules for expedited arbitration proceedings in Bahrain offer advantages such as accessibility, timeliness, and flexibility. However, concerns exist regarding the sole arbitrator limitation and the compressed timelines for issuing the final award.

[B] Saudi Center for Commercial Arbitration

Appendix II of the 2023 SCCA Arbitration Rules set out the rules for the expedited procedures.[27] The SCCA Expedited Procedure Rules come into effect either by mutual agreement of the parties or when the amount in dispute, excluding arbitration costs, does not exceed SAR 4,000,000 or its equivalent.[28] Should a party make amendments

23. *Ibid.*, Article 6/7.
24. *Ibid.*, Article 6/12.
25. *Ibid.*, Article 6/13.
26. *Ibid.*, Article 6/8.
27. Saudi Center for Commercial Arbitration (SCCA) Arbitration Rules, Appendix II – Expedited Procedure Rules (available at: https://sadr.org/ADRServices-arbitration-arbitration-rules?lang=en).
28. *Ibid.*, Article 1. SAR 4,000,000 equates to roughly USD 1,066,666.67 dependent on the exchange rate.

to its claim subsequent to the initial filing, resulting in it exceeding SAR 4,000,000 (excluding arbitration costs), the case will continue to be governed by the Expedited Procedure Rules, unless otherwise agreed by the parties or determined by the Administrator or the arbitral tribunal.[29] After the constitution of the arbitral tribunal, no new claims or alterations to the amount in dispute can be submitted without the approval of the tribunal.[30]

Concurrently with the submission of the request for arbitration, the claimant must send a copy of the request, along with all accompanying documents, to the respondent.[31] Furthermore, the claimant must notify the Administrator of this action, specifying the method and date of service.[32] Both parties are obligated to provide comprehensive submissions in the request for arbitration and the answer, including factual details, claims, defences, and all available evidence on which they intend to rely.[33]

Upon receipt of the request for arbitration, the Administrator may arrange an administrative conference involving the parties and their representatives.[34] The purpose of this conference is to discuss matters such as the implementation of procedures, the selection of arbitrators, potential mediation efforts, and other administrative considerations.[35] If any party raises an objection regarding the applicability of the Expedited Procedure Rules, the Administrator will render a final decision on the matter.[36]

The parties have the option to nominate a sole arbitrator within a specified time frame determined by the Administrator.[37] If no timely nomination is made, the Administrator will provide each party with an identical list of five potential arbitrators. The parties may mutually agree upon an arbitrator from this list and must inform the Administrator accordingly.[38] If an agreement cannot be reached, each party has the right to strike two names from the list, rank the remaining names in order of preference, and return the list to the Administrator within 10 days. The Administrator will invite an arbitrator from the approved names based on the designated order of mutual preference. If, for any reason, an appointment cannot be made from the submitted lists, the SCCA Court reserves the authority to appoint an arbitrator without circulating additional lists. In such a situation, the parties will be notified by the Administrator regarding the arbitrator's appointment, along with any relevant disclosures. At that point, each party will be considered to have waived their right to nominate an arbitrator.[39]

29. *Ibid.*, Article 5.
30. *Ibid.*
31. *Ibid.*, Article 2/1.
32. *Ibid.*
33. *Ibid.*, Article 2/2.
34. *Ibid.*, Article 3.
35. *Ibid.*
36. *Ibid.*, Article 4.
37. *Ibid.*, Article 6/1.
38. *Ibid.*, Article 6/2.
39. *Ibid.*

Once the arbitral tribunal is constituted, it may arrange a procedural conference in conjunction with the parties, their representatives, and the Administrator. The purpose of this conference is to discuss case management details, including the procedural steps and timetable. Within 14 days of its constitution, the arbitral tribunal will issue a procedural order. The Administrator may extend this time frame upon a reasoned request from the arbitral tribunal or if it deems such an extension necessary. The tribunal, after consulting with the parties, will determine whether the dispute will be resolved solely based on written submissions or if a hearing is required for witness examination, expert testimony, and oral arguments.[40]

In collaboration with the parties, the arbitral tribunal will establish a procedural timetable as outlined in the procedural order mentioned in Article 7. All written submissions are generally due within 30 days of the procedural order, unless the tribunal determines otherwise. Requests for document production should be limited to materials directly relevant to the dispute and reasonably restricted in terms of time frame, subject matter, and relevant individuals or entities.[41]

If an oral hearing is scheduled, the arbitral tribunal will determine the date, time, and location of the hearing. The hearing may be conducted in person or through alternative means like video conferencing, telephone, or other suitable methods, as decided by the tribunal. Unless otherwise agreed upon, a transcript or stenographic record is not mandatory. The oral hearing is expected to take place within 60 days of the procedural order, unless the tribunal deems it necessary to extend this period. Generally, the oral hearing should not exceed one day, unless the tribunal determines otherwise. The Administrator will provide advance notice of the hearing date to the parties.[42]

The tribunal must render its award in writing. The award is considered final and binding on the parties involved. Unless otherwise agreed upon by the parties, required by applicable law, or determined by the Administrator, the award should be issued within 30 days from the closure of the proceedings as stipulated in Article 33 of the Rules.[43] However, in any event the final award must be delivered within 180 days from the date of the arbitral tribunal's constitution, unless exceptional circumstances warrant an extension as determined by the Administrator.[44]

The administrative fees of the SCCA and the fees of the arbitral tribunal are determined by the SCCA Court in accordance with the prevailing SCCA Fee Schedule applicable under the Expedited Procedure Rules at the commencement of the arbitration.[45] The Expedited Procedure Rules are construed in addition to the regular arbitration rules and prevail over the regular arbitration rules where a conflict arises.[46]

40. *Ibid.*, Article 7.
41. *Ibid.*, Article 8.
42. *Ibid.*, Article 9.
43. *Ibid.*, Article 33.
44. *Ibid.*, Article 10.
45. *Ibid.*, Article 11.
46. *Ibid.* Expedited Procedure Rules (Appendix II).

The Administrator reserves the right to shorten the prescribed time limits set forth in Appendix II, as well as any other time limits it has imposed.[47]

The SCCA's new expedited arbitration rules are a positive step to make dispute resolution in Saudi Arabia more efficient and accessible. They allow parties to choose a faster process if they meet certain conditions or if both agree, simplifying arbitration and potentially reducing costs. These rules also stress that parties must provide all the necessary information from the beginning (Article 2). This ensures a sharp and efficient focus on the main issues, making it easier for the arbitral tribunal to make well-informed decisions. Article 3 even suggests having an early meeting to discuss procedures and possibly resolve the dispute through mediation.[48] This hands-on approach to case management promotes effective dispute resolution by encouraging cooperation between the parties and ensuring a smooth progression of the arbitration process.

However, potential downsides linked to these regulations exist. The constraints on modifying claims, as detailed in Article 5, might limit the capacity of parties to introduce fresh evidence or adapt their arguments in response to changing circumstances. While these restrictions aim to uphold procedural efficiency, they have the potential to obstruct parties from fully presenting their arguments. In addition, concerns may arise regarding the Administrator's role in appointing an arbitrator, as elucidated in Article 6, specifically regarding impartiality and independence. Despite the SCCA Court's authority to resolve appointment disputes or non-nominations, a transparent and just selection process is essential to uphold trust and confidence in the arbitration proceedings. Moreover, the stringent time frames stipulated in Article 10 for delivering the award could exert pressure on the arbitral tribunal. While the rules do allow for extensions under extraordinary circumstances, it is vital to strike a balance between efficiency and the arbitral tribunal's obligation to meticulously examine the evidence and deliver a well-founded decision.

[C] Dubai International Arbitration Centre

The provisions for expedited proceedings were a result of the DIAC's new arbitration rules which came into effect on 21 March 2022. Similar to other leading arbitral institutions, the new rules offer a mechanism for hearing the dispute on an expedited basis, with a time limit of three months, within which the tribunal must issue the final award. The provisions seek to save both time and costs under the expedited process. Article 32 of the 2022 DIAC Arbitration Rules sets out the rules for the expedited procedures.[49] Pursuant to Article 32.1, expedited proceedings shall take place:

(a) unless the parties agree otherwise in writing if the total of the sum(s) claimed and counterclaimed is below or equals AED 1,000,000 (exclusive of interest

47. *Ibid.*, Article 12.
48. *Ibid.*, Article 3.
49. Dubai International Arbitration Centre (DIAC), DIAC Arbitration Rules 2022, https://www.diac.com/wp-content/uploads/2023/05/DIAC-2022-Rules-EN.pdf.

and legal representation costs) or any other threshold amount as may be determined by the Board of Directors of DIAC from time to time; or
(b) if the parties agree in writing; or
(c) in cases of exceptional urgency as determined by the Arbitration Court upon an application by a party;
(d) and in all cases if considered appropriate by the Arbitration Court, based on the relevant circumstances.[50]

Disputes that exceed the quantum limit can also be heard on an expedited basis subject to the provisions set out under Article 32.[51]

According to Article 32.2, before the arbitration tribunal is constituted or before an answer is submitted, 'a party may submit an application for the arbitration to be conducted on an expedited basis'.[52] The mode of such application is indicated in the same article. The Centre then notifies all other parties accordingly. The other parties have seven days to comment on such application. If no comments are made after seven days, 'the application shall be deemed to be unopposed'.[53]

Under Article 32.4, the tribunal decides on the expedited arbitration procedure after consultation with the parties.[54] The scope of evidence can be limited by the arbitration tribunal due to the time limits in the expedited procedure.[55] The time limit for the final award in expedited arbitration is three months.[56] The tribunal may ask the Arbitration Court to switch from expedited arbitration to a non-expedited arbitration procedure.[57] The Arbitration Court will decide on such application as well as whether the same tribunal or a different one shall continue the arbitration.[58]

While the new expedited arbitration rules ensure the effective and efficient conduct of the proceedings, the system within DIAC is not without its imperfections. The main shortcoming in the expedited proceedings framework lies in the AED 1,000,000 claim threshold. This threshold is notably low, particularly because it includes the value of counterclaims.[59] In comparison, the ICC Rules and the SIAC Rules allow for expedited arbitration in cases with values of up to USD 3,000,000 and SGD 6,000,000, respectively. These higher thresholds seem more appropriate, considering the typical amounts in dispute in international arbitration. The ICC 2022 Preliminary Report states that the median dispute figure for cases filed with the ICC between January and October 2021 was USD 5,700,000. This serves as a striking illustration that the threshold criterion within DIAC is too low and highlights the need for a comprehensive review in due course.

---

50. *Ibid.*, Article 32/1.
51. *Ibid.*, Article 32.
52. *Ibid.*, Article 32/2.
53. *Ibid.*
54. *Ibid.*, Article 32/4.
55. *Ibid.*
56. *Ibid.*, Article 32/5.
57. *Ibid.*, Article 32/6.
58. *Ibid.*
59. *Ibid.*, Article 32/1(a). AED 1,000,000 equates to USD 272,293.336 dependent on the exchange rate.

[D] Casablanca International Mediation and Arbitration Centre

In Morocco, Article 43 of the 2018 CIMAC Arbitration Rules provides for an expedited procedure.[60] According to Article 43, the CIMAC Court may choose a quicker procedure, namely, the 'Expedited Procedure'.[61] The monetary limited is EUR 200,000 or equivalent. The Articles between 7 and 35 of the CIMAC Arbitration Rules are modified by the expedited procedure.[62] The respondent has 21 days to respond under the expedited procedures.[63] The default number of arbitrators is one.[64] After the arbitration tribunal is constituted, the tribunal has 15 days to prepare the timetable.[65] There will be only one round of submissions unless parties agreed otherwise, and there will be no post-hearing briefs.[66] Again, unless the parties agree otherwise, there will be no hearing.[67] As a rule, the proceedings must be completed within six months after the constitution of the arbitration tribunal.[68] Unless otherwise agreed by the parties, the tribunal must write an award with a brief reasoning.[69]

Additionally, the CIMAC Rules do not mandate the execution of terms of reference. This marks a significant contrast with the ICC Rules, which necessitate a restatement of the parties' agreement to resolve their dispute through arbitration and other requirements in the terms of reference. The CIMAC Rules do not impose terms of reference in order to facilitate expediency.[70]

CIMAC has positioned itself to emerge as a prominent arbitration centre with a strong approach towards expedited arbitration, particularly in the region of Africa. However, the low threshold value of the claim permitted is a problem. CIMAC allows parties to opt in to the expedited procedure if the amount in dispute does not exceed the equivalent of merely EUR 200,000. Considering that most international arbitration disputes involve disputes in excess of EUR 200,000, the threshold set by CIMAC establishes a notably constrictive framework.

[E] Istanbul Arbitration Centre

The ISTAC in Turkey introduced its Fast Track Arbitration Rules in 2017.[71] According to these rules, 'unless otherwise agreed by the parties, the Istanbul Arbitration Centre

60. Casablanca International Mediation and Arbitration Centre Arbitration Rules, Article 43, http://cimac.ma/wp-content/uploads/2019/03/CIMAC_Reglement_GB_04052018.pdf.
61. *Ibid.*, Article 43/1.
62. *Ibid.*, Article 43/2.
63. *Ibid.*, Article 43/3.
64. *Ibid.*, Article 43/4.
65. *Ibid.*, Article 43/5.
66. *Ibid.*, Article 43/6.
67. *Ibid.*, Article 43/7.
68. *Ibid.*, Article 43/8.
69. *Ibid.*, Article 43/9.
70. Séréna Salem, *Introduction to the Arbitration Rules of the Casablanca International Mediation and Arbitration Centre, the CIMAC*, DLA Piper (14 December 2017) https://www.dlapiper.com/en/insights/publications/2017/12/le-reglement-darbitrage-de-centre.
71. Istanbul Arbitration Centre, Fast Track Arbitration Rules, https://istac.org.tr/en/dispute-resolution/fast-track-arbitration/fast-track-arbitration-rules/.

Fast Track Arbitration Rules (Fast Track Arbitration Rules) shall apply to disputes where, as at the date of commencement of the arbitration, the total sum of the claims, and any counterclaims, do not exceed TRY 3,000,000'.[72] Moreover, 'the parties may also agree that the Fast Track Arbitration Rules shall apply where the amount in dispute exceeds this sum'.[73] Thus, an expedited procedure is available in Turkey for small-amount disputes. Parties may also mutually agree to opt in to the Fast Track Rules if the amount in dispute exceeds TRY 3,000,000.[74]

The Fast Track Rules have a number of differences that tend to shorten and simplify the procedure. For example, under the Fast Track Rules, the time limit for filing responses is 15 days (Article 2) as opposed to 30 days under the normal rules.[75] Additionally, the ISTAC Fast Track Rules provide for an arbitral tribunal of a single arbitrator.[76]

This initiative is commendable and inherently comprehensible for Turkish users, who have traditionally harboured scepticism towards arbitration. The Fast Track Rules could serve as the decisive factor in attracting parties to opt for ISTAC.[77] However, out of all the institutions in the MENA region that have provisions for expedited arbitration, ISTAC has the lowest claim value threshold. The TRY 3,000,000 threshold is remarkably low, especially considering that it includes the value of counterclaims.

[F] Institutions in the MENA Region with No Expedited Arbitration Rules

Despite the booming growth of industries in the MENA region and the concomitant need for expedited arbitration, the Qatar International Centre for Conciliation & Arbitration (QICCA),[78] the Cairo Regional Centre for International Commercial Arbitration (CRCICA)[79] and the Lebanese and International Arbitration Center of the Beirut Bar Association (LIAC-BBA)[80] have no provisions for expedited proceedings. However, on 24 June 2023, the CRCICA released a draft of updated Arbitration Rules ("2023 Draft Rules").[81] Annex 3 of the 2023 Draft Rules provides for an expedited procedure for claims where the value of the claim is less than USD 2,000,000.[82] The parties may opt

72. ISTAC Fast Track Arbitration Rules, Article 1. Three million Turkish Liras is equivalent to USD 108,000 as of 15 October 2023.
73. *Ibid.*, Article 1.
74. *Ibid.*
75. *Ibid.*, Article 2.
76. *Ibid.*, Article 3.
77. Nilüfer Hotan, *A Complete Guide to the Rules of the Istanbul Arbitration Centre,* Morogluarseven (15 February 2016), https://www.morogluarseven.com/news-and-publications/complete-guide-rules-istanbul-arbitration-centre/.
78. https://qicca.org/wp-content/uploads/2016/08/QICCA_Rules_Eng.pdf.
79. https://crcica.org/arbitration/crcica-arbitration-rules/.
80. https://www.bba.org.lb/en/Syndicat/Details/207/LIAC-BBA_Arbitration_Rules.
81. The Cairo Regional Centre for International Commercial Arbitration (CRCICA), Draft New CRCICA Arbitration Rules 2023, https://crcica.org/rules/arbitration/text/draft_cr_Arb_Rules_2023_EN.pdf.
82. *Ibid.*, Annex 3.

in to an expedited procedure, in which case they follow a separate set of rules provided in Annex 3.[83]

The CRCICA 2023 Draft Arbitration Rules present a remarkable update to the 2011 CRCICA Rules, which incorporated no provisions for expedited proceedings. The CRCICA has requested and received comments on the 2023 Draft Rules, and their final form will be established soon.[84] IF CRCICA implements Annex 3, it will introduce an innovative provision aimed at enhancing expeditious proceedings. The implementation of the new rules will encourage expedient, efficient and cost-effective dispute resolution. The draft rules will also position CRCICA as the institution with the highest claim value threshold in the MENA region. A threshold of USD 2,000,000 would undeniably encompass a broader spectrum of international arbitration disputes.

§19.05 POLICIES UNDERLYING EXPEDITED ARBITRATION

Currently, only ISTAC, DIAC and BCDR offer expedited procedures. Other prominent centres, such as CRCICA and the QICCA, do not offer expedited procedures.[85] The MENA regional arbitration centres have failed to capitalise on this gap. They seem to understand their mandate as a forum for resolving only high-value disputes.

A claimant with a small claim should not feel it has no recourse. Similarly, a would-be respondent should not consider itself immune to a meritorious claim simply because the fixed costs of arbitration far outweigh the prospect of a favourable award. The upfront arbitration costs associated with the centres and the tribunal discourage claimants from commencing proceedings where the value of the claim is low. The option to have an expedited process enables parties to bring small claims to arbitration. Arbitration is no longer an exceptional alternative but rather a default mechanism for cross-border transactions. Expedited arbitration rules help arbitration spread even further by increasing the scope and type of the disputes that can be arbitrated. With expedited arbitration, arbitration becomes accessible even for small disputes.

There is a genuine desire and hope that with public awareness the regional arbitration centres will wake up to an entirely untapped market and revise their rules and adopt expedited arbitration. A change in rules, particularly an automatic application of expedited procedures, would lead to an increase in cases filed before regional centres where the relevant (underlying) arbitration clauses already refer to such centres. This would then result in regional parties updating arbitration clauses specifically to include a regional centre in situations where previously a reference would have been made to a centre outside of the region.

Introducing a new set of rules would pose new challenges. According to one commentator, 'there is the common riposte that guerrilla tactics are all too common in the region and expedited procedures would worsen due process paranoia and imperil

83. *Ibid.*
84. CRCICA unveils its draft New Arbitration Rules 2023, https://crcica.org/arbitration/arbitration 2023/.
85. Qatar International Center for Conciliation and Arbitration, Rules of Conciliation and Arbitration, https://qicca.org/wp-content/uploads/2016/08/QICCA_Rules_Eng.pdf.

awards'.[86] Evidence from other regions suggests that the fear that awards under a fast-track procedure would be set aside is largely unfounded. With everything new, comes challenges but the 'Middle East needs expedited procedures.'[87]

§19.06 CRITICAL ANALYSIS OF THE EXPEDITED RULES IN THE MENA REGION

Expedited arbitration has advantages as well as disadvantages. The obvious advantage is to complete the process in a shorter time. The disadvantage is that the parties have less time for their submissions and preparations. However, as a result of the party autonomy, this is the choice of the parties to determine. Nevertheless, some provisions can help parties and tribunals to be flexible to extend these time limits if they need more time for submissions or to analyse complex issues, provided such requests are found reasonable by the tribunals and/or courts. Expedited rules may thereby provide faster and cheaper dispute resolution without risking the due diligence of the process as long as requests of the parties are considered diligently.

The expedited arbitration rules of arbitral institutions in the MENA region do not significantly differ from expedited arbitration rules of major arbitration institutions. However, some of the expedited rules in the MENA region allow arbitrators to render their awards without legal reasoning.[88] This can raise challenges against such awards in the enforcement stages. Apart from this major concern, the only remarkable difference is the amount set for the expedited rules to apply in the MENA region. The monetary threshold set for the expedited arbitration rules is significantly lower than the monetary threshold set by leading arbitration institutions. This is understandable, however, because the amount of the disputes in the MENA region can be lower than major arbitration centres. Nevertheless, this can be remedied with a rule allowing parties to submit their disputes under the expedited procedures even if their claims exceed the stated sum.

Overall, the advantages and disadvantages of expedited arbitration in the MENA region do not go far from the pros and cons of expedited arbitration in general. The question is how to ensure that the parties will have enough opportunity to present their cases and the arbitrators have sufficient time to reach a fair decision. If the parties are not given enough opportunity to present their cases, this can be another ground to challenge the arbitration awards at the enforcement stage.[89]

86. Khurram Khan, *Centres in the Middle East Need to Catch Up when It Comes to Expedited Procedures,* Practical Law Arbitration Blog (3 January 2019), http://arbitrationblog.practicallaw.com/centres-in-the-middle-east-need-to-catch-up-when-it-comes-to-expedited-procedures/. *See also China Machine New Energy Corp v. Jaguar Energy Guatemala LLC and another* [2018] SGHC 101.
87. Khan, *supra* n. 86.
88. *Ibid.*
89. United Nations Convention on the Recognition and Enforcement of Foreign Arbitral Awards (New York, 10 June 1958), https://www.newyorkconvention.org/english, Art. V/I-b; UNCITRAL Model Law on International Commercial Arbitration 1985 With amendments as adopted in 2006,

According to a survey,[90] the most preferred arbitral institutions chosen by parties from the Middle Eastern region are the International Chamber of Commerce (ICC), London Chamber of International Arbitration (LCIA), Singapore International Arbitration Centre (SIAC), International Centre for Settle of Investment Disputes (ICSID) and Hong Kong International Arbitration Centre (HKIAC). Thus, the expedited rules of these five institutions are also important because awards rendered by those institutions will likely be enforced in the MENA region. MENA region arbitral institutions should consider the expedited arbitration rules of these leading arbitration institutions when adopting expedited procedures, as well as the concerns previously stated.

§19.07 MENA REGION EXPEDITED ARBITRATION AND ENFORCEMENT CLAIMS BROUGHT IN NATIONAL COURTS

No available case law on expedited arbitration has been found in the MENA region. However, some of the arbitration law in the MENA region states that an arbitral award can be issued without reasoning.[91] This has two negative and one positive results. First, it prevents the development of case law on the subject. Second, it could lead to challenges in the enforcement stage. As a positive result, it allows arbitrators to render an award without delay. Faster and shorter awards might also mean an award with less consideration by the tribunal. However, awards without legal reasoning may be against public policy and may not be enforceable in some jurisdictions because public policy is one of the grounds to challenge an award under the New York Convention as well as many arbitration laws around the world.[92] This important point can have a significant effect on enforcement of expedited arbitration awards rendered in the MENA region. However, because there is no case law related to the enforcement of expedited awards in the MENA region, this issue will be a principal development in the region and worldwide to see how the courts react.

§19.08 CONCLUSION

Expedited arbitration is important to keep the international arbitration process a quick method of resolving disputes. The MENA region follows the developments in international arbitration around the world closely. MENA region arbitral institutions attempt

https://uncitral.un.org/en/texts/arbitration/modellaw/commercial_arbitration, Articles 34/2-a(ii) and 36/1-a(ii); English Arbitration Act 1996, https://www.legislation.gov.uk/ukpga/1996/23/contents, s. 103/2-c.

90. White and Case, *Current Choices and Future Adaptations* (6 May 2021) https://www.whitecase.com/insight-our-thinking/current-choices-and-future-adaptations.
91. For example, *see* Egyptian Arbitration Law, Article 43.
92. United Nations Convention on the Recognition and Enforcement of Foreign Arbitral Awards (New York, 10 June 1958), https://www.newyorkconvention.org/english, Article V/II-b; UNCITRAL Model Law on International Commercial Arbitration 1985 With amendments as adopted in 2006, https://uncitral.un.org/en/texts/arbitration/modellaw/commercial_arbitration, Articles 34/2-b(ii) and 36/1-b(ii); English Arbitration Act 1996, https://www.legislation.gov.uk/ukpga/1996/23/contents, section 103/3.

to stay abreast of, and equal to, any other arbitration institutions in the world. However, more institutions in the MENA region should adopt expedited arbitration rules. The current work and draft rules on expedited arbitration prepared by some institutions in the MENA region indicate the potential of some other institutions to offer expedited procedure.

Because not all arbitral institutions in the MENA region have expedited arbitration provisions, room still exists for further developments. Other arbitration institutions such as CRCICA in Cairo and QICCA in Doha should also have expedited arbitration rules. Because the number of small- and middle-value cases can be significantly higher in the MENA region, expedited arbitration has a great potential to offer a viable and efficient resolution platform for such disputes in the MENA region. Arbitration rules should also be improved. Provisions allowing arbitration awards to be rendered without reasoning can be an obstacle for developing case law because a proper legal analysis can be missing from awards. Courts would not have any legal reasoning to interpret. Requiring a reasoned opinion in expedited arbitration awards would improve enforcement of such awards worldwide.

Expedited arbitration rules are developing in the MENA region. The remaining arbitration institutions in the MENA regions that do not have expedited arbitration rules should add such provisions to compete with other major arbitration centres around the world. The existing expedited arbitration rules should be refined to ensure the smooth enforcement of awards rendered in the MENA region.

www.ingramcontent.com/pod-product-compliance
Lightning Source LLC
LaVergne TN
LVHW020646300926
849161LV00004B/829